Contemporary Plays by Women of Color

In the two decades since the first edition of *Contemporary Plays by Women of Color* was published, its significance to the theatrical landscape in the United States has grown exponentially.

Work by female writers and writers of color is more widely produced, published, and studied than ever before. Drawing from an exciting range of theaters, large and small, from across the country, Roberta Uno brings together an up-to-date selection of plays from renowned and emerging playwrights tackling a variety of topics. From the playful to the painful, this revised and updated edition presents a rich array of voices, aesthetics, and stories for a transforming America.

Roberta Uno is a theater director and Director of Arts in a Changing America based at the California Institute for the Arts.

"I wish I could be in the room when a reader experiences seeing themselves represented on a page, perhaps for the first time. It is a powerful, even life-changing, gift. Fierce, intelligent, flawed and funny, these voices are too often unheard."

Maha Chelahoui, *Co-founder, NOOR Theatre*

"If we want to claim America belongs to all of us, then we better make sure the theater is a place where all of us can speak. Roberta Uno's wonderful book provides stirring support for that inclusive vision."

Oskar Eustis, *Artistic Director, The Public Theater*

"Roberta Uno once again is forging a path a decade ahead. These inspired, complex, and brilliant playwrights are accelerating us towards the future of the American theater."

Kamilah Forbes, *Director*

"The first edition found its way to me freshman year of college. It was truth and permission—unapologetic, funny, furious, and as diverse as the world I had experienced. Local theaters were not producing these plays, high school teachers were not assigning these plays, but yet here they were—showing me these stories *do* exist, *do* matter."

Quiara Alegría Hudes, *Playwright, Pulitzer Prize for Drama*

"An invaluable collection of works from voices at the frontiers of our culture. I have always looked to Roberta Uno to find the bravest voices of writers who will ultimately define their generation's collective spirit."

Jim Nicola, *Artistic Director, New York Theatre Workshop*

"This book fills me with joy at seeing many of the contemporary plays I most admire, anticipation of meeting new writers whose work it is essential that I know, and hope that our field doesn't have to lag behind in fully reflecting who we are as a society. This is a must-have volume."

Bill Rauch, *Oregon Shakespeare Festival*

"This anthology is at the vanguard of theater that challenges and transforms … this anthology is not only about diversity and excellent theatre, it is essential to understanding ourselves."

Mia Yoo, *Artistic Director, La MaMa Theatre, NYC*

Contemporary Plays by Women of Color

An Anthology

Second Edition

Edited by
Roberta Uno

Assistant Editors:
Kristen Adele Calhoun,
Daniela Alvarez, and
Kassandra L. Khalil

Routledge
Taylor & Francis Group

LONDON AND NEW YORK

Second edition published 2018
by Routledge
2 Park Square, Milton Park, Abingdon, Oxon, OX14 4RN

and by Routledge
711 Third Avenue, New York, NY 10017

Routledge is an imprint of the Taylor & Francis Group, an informa business

First edition published by Routledge 1996

British Library Cataloguing-in-Publication Data
A catalogue record for this book is available from the British Library

Library of Congress Cataloging-in-Publication Data
Names: Uno, Roberta, 1956- editor.
Title: Contemporary plays by women of color / edited by
Roberta Uno; [and three others].
Description: Second edition. | Milton Park, Abingdon,
Oxon: New York: Routledge, 2017.
Identifiers: LCCN 2017011437 | ISBN 9781138189454 (hardback) |
ISBN 9781138189461 (pbk.) | ISBN 9781315641584 (ebook)
Subjects: LCSH: American drama—Minority authors. | American drama—
Women authors. | American drama—20th century. | American drama—
21st century. | Women—United States—Drama. | Minority women—
Drama. | Minorities—Drama.
Classification: LCC PS627.M5 C66 2017 | DDC 812/.60809287—dc23
LC record available at https://lccn.loc.gov/2017011437

ISBN: 978-1-138-18945-4 (hbk)
ISBN: 978-1-138-18946-1 (pbk)
ISBN: 978-1-315-64158-4 (ebk)

Typeset in Bembo
by codeMantra

In memory of my mother, Kiku Uno, and aunt, Fumiko Ide.
The sisters who taught me to love words and story.

Contents

Acknowledgments   ix

Introduction by Roberta Uno   xiii

1 *Cardboard Piano*   3
   Hansol Jung

2 *Clothes*   30
   Chitra Banerjee Divakaruni

3 *Daughter of a Cuban Revolutionary*   39
   Marissa Chibas

4 *Eclipsed*   53
   Danai Gurira

5 *Elliot, A Soldier's Fugue*   80
   Quiara Alegría Hudes

6 *Etchings in the Sand*   100
   Meena Natarajan and Ananya Chatterjea

7 *Food and Fadwa*   106
   Lameece Issaq and Jacob Kader

8 *Gunshot Medley*   138
   Dionna Michelle Daniel

9 *He Lei no Kākā'āko: Woven Memories*   150
   Tammy Haili'ōpua Baker

10 *Lines in the Dust*   164
   Nikkole Salter

11 *Mala Hierba*   200
   Tanya Saracho

12 *N★gg★*   229
   Lynn Nottage

13 *Our Lady of Kibeho*   237
    Katori Hall

14 *Our Voices Will Be Heard*   283
    Vera Starbard

15 *Scenes From 68* Years*   308
    Hannah Khalil

16 *Standoff at Hwy#37*   340
    Vickie Ramirez

17 *Sun Sisters*   367
    Vasanti Saxena

18 *The Adventures at Camp KaKeeKwaSha and the Magic Musky Casino!*   395
    Marcie R. Rendon

19 *The Wild Inside*   405
    Cusi Cram

20 *The Wong Street Journal*   427
    Kristina Wong

21 *What Would Crazy Horse Do?*   448
    Larissa FastHorse

22 *Zafira the Olive Oil Warrior*   472
    Kathryn Haddad

Appendix: Published plays by American women of color: selected works
after 1940   499

Acknowledgments

We extend our gracious thanks to the following individuals who connected us to many of the playwrights included in this collection: Keith Josef Adkins, Leonard Berkman, Maha Chehlaoui, Jorge Cortiñas, the Nathan Cummings Foundation, Tim Dang, Ty Defoe, Snehal Desai, Abby Dobson, Oskar Eustis, Kamilah Forbes, Jamil Khoury, Jenny Koons, Danielle Kovacs, Quiara Alegría Hudes, Maurine Knighton, Steven Lavine and the California Institute of the Arts, Eun Lee, Madison Lee, Jeff Liu, Sade Lythcott, Raphael Martin, Jonathan McCrory, Margaret Morton, Dipankar Mukherjee, Meena Natarajan, Jim Nicola, Evren Odcikin, Margaret Odette, Jorge Ortoll, Ralph Peña, Kathy Perkins, Corey Pond, Marlène Ramírez-Cancio, Bill Rauch, Emily Simoness and SPACE on Ryder Farm, Lloyd Suh, Diana Taylor and the New York University Hemispheric Institute for Performance and Politics, Mia Yoo, Darren Walker and the Ford Foundation, and Torange Yeghiazarian.

The editors are deeply appreciative of Elizabeth Webb for manuscript preparation as well as the work of Maia Paraginog, T. J. Keanu Tario, and Namiko Uno for their assistance with appendix research.

Introduction

Say her name

"Trayvon Martin…Oscar Grant…Eric Garner…" A list of names of people murdered at the hands of police is being read. A crowd of 800 is standing, listening intently as the names continue. "Michael Brown…Sean Bell… Philando Castile…" The audience has been asked to stand and remain standing until they hear a name they don't recognize. The room is heavy with collective grief and the swelling of suppressed rage as the names continue.

"Akai Gurley…Tamir Rice…Sandra Bland …" As the names change from male to female, a few people begin to sit. "Eleanor Bumpers… Aiyana Stanley Jones… Alberta Spruill…" More people sit down. Soon there are ripples, then waves of people sitting throughout the hall. "Alesia Thomas… Alexia Christian… Aura Rosser…" The trickle of names has widened to pour over a stunned audience until no one is standing. They are hearing the names and seeing projections of photos of cisgendered and transgendered women whose lives have been erased from the news cycle. Singer Abby Dobson's exquisite vocalized repetition of "Say her name…say her name…" lifts the names melodically higher into the rafters of the Cooper Union Great Hall, a space where presidents, suffragettes, poets, and organizers have found a platform of free speech for more than a century. The vast list of names is an act of historical restoration and resistance, part of a concert program by The Dream Unfinished Orchestra, programed July 13, 2016 on the one year anniversary of Sandra Bland's death. Dobson and Kimberlé Crenshaw are enacting #SAYHERNAME, inscribing women's narratives into the struggle for #BLACKLIVESMATTER. The participatory theatricality of their action radically undermines the pernicious marginalization of women's stories, perspectives, and agency.[1]

We are the narrative

Two decades have passed since Kathy Perkins and I coedited the original edition of *Contemporary Plays by Women of Color*. I'm writing the introduction to this new edition at a moment of national turmoil following the outcome of the 2016 U.S. presidential election and the enormity of the dawning ramifications. Much of the vitriol of the Republican campaign centered on the criminalization of immigrants, violence towards women, and the dehumanization of both. The campaign slogan "Make America Great Again" was thinly veiled code for "white again," exacerbating racism and harkening back to a pre-Civil Rights era of Jim Crow, voter disenfranchisement, immigrant exclusion, and second class citizenship for women. The new regime's agenda endangers national security and the public good—while bolstering the foundations of structural racism and misogyny. The need for the voices in this anthology—and the voices of the vast diversity of the people of this country—is critical. In another era, Martin Luther King said, "We are now faced with the fact that tomorrow is today. We are confronted with the fierce urgency of now."[2]

Women are answering that call on the streets in protest, on stages and screen, in social media and spiritually centered creative practices, in electoral politics, community organizing, and personal choices; they are boldly transforming the world they encounter. Women of color and our communities embody the transformational promise of a new America. The plays of this volume are evidence of this change—artistically brilliant, original, eclectic, and not simply relevant—they are written for a future that is already present in a demographically shifting America. The legislative gains of Civil Rights activism and the Immigration and Nationality Act of 1965 have made possible a truly pluralistic democracy. The U.S. Census Bureau has projected an unprecedented population shift: that by the year 2042, for the first time, people of color in aggregate will outnumber the historic Caucasian majority in a growing country of 439 million. That shift has already occurred in the birth rate of children of color, in the majority of metropolitan areas from New York City to Chicago to Dallas, and the states of California, Hawai'i, New Mexico, and Texas. As women of color in the theater, we are no longer the counternarrative. We are the narrative.

Yet, as this country transforms from the ground up—its institutions have lagged behind, remaining largely male and white. The #OscarsSoWhite social media protest about the failure of the 2016 Academy Awards to nominate any actors of color was symptomatic of larger inequities. Whatever the outcome had been of the 2016 presidential election, racial and economic inequality are deeply institutionalized. A *New York Times* photo-collage, "Faces of American Power," documented 500 of the most powerful people in American culture, business, education, and government and found only 44 people of color. The list included CEOs of the largest companies, the U.S. Senate and Congress, presidents of Ivy League universities, studio executives who decide which Hollywood movies and television shows get made, recording executives who determine what music is produced, publishers and critics who decide what books are read, and media executives who oversee what news is available.[3]

Risking a growing distance from the U.S. population, the leadership of the American theater largely conforms to this picture of the last century. In their analysis of the leadership of 74 American regional theaters, researchers Sumru Erkut and

Ineke Ceder found little progress from when they began their study in 2013–2014: "…there were no executive directors of color, female or male, and only 6 people of color had artistic director positions—5 men and 1 woman. Not much has shifted since then."[4] Arts philanthropy has furthered this inequity. In its landmark report, the National Committee on Responsive Philanthropy found that out of all the funding that goes to the arts, the majority goes to large organizations with budgets greater than $5 million, which are only 2% of the entire sector. These organizations focus primarily on Western European art forms, and their programs serve audiences that are predominantly white and upper income.[5] Strategies to redress this inequity are being supported by concerned philanthropies and progressive grantmakers. But many approach the work as emergent under titles such as "Future Audiences," "Future Collaborations," and "Future Leaders." While these are necessary and laudatory efforts, they implicitly postpone a truly 21st century American theater to the future and perpetuate the minoritization of work and leadership that exists now.[6]

Moving the legacy forward

Defying their characterization as a nascent phenomenon, theater makers of color are building cultural movements while giving insight into parallel and intersecting universes. On Broadway, Lin-Manuel Miranda's smash hit musical *Hamilton* asks in afterword, "Who lives, who dies, who tells your story?" Alexander Hamilton's widow, Eliza, replies, "I put myself back in the narrative," offering a brief glimpse of a woman who would go unrecognized, if not for a relationship to a founding father.[7] Meanwhile, elsewhere in New York City and across America, theater artists of color give the resounding reply—they have a long history of passionately telling their stories, against tremendous economic odds. *Catalyst: Moving the Black Theatre Legacy Forward* was organized in 2014 by Sade Lythcott and Jonathan McCrory, a new generation of artists leading the 49-year-old National Black Theatre in Harlem, NYC. They addressed systemic issues of sustainability, recognizing that for "over 300 years, Black Theatres from across the country have tirelessly documented, articulated, nurtured, and given breath to the often forgotten narratives of the nameless, voiceless, and underserved people in our communities. Despite this vital and important work, we find many of our institutions are perpetually on the brink of extinction."[8] The Consortium of Asian American Theaters and Artists (CAATA) began with six theater Asian-American theater companies in 2003 and in 2016 partnered with the Oregon Shakespeare Festival, one of the largest American theaters, to hold a third national convening "to respond to social injustice and inequality in American culture and what we, as theater practitioners, can do about it."[9] The Latino Theater Commons, began with a group of eight Latino/a theater makers in 2012 and has grown to a steering committee of over fifty from across the country working to transform the American theater through values based in service, radical inclusion, transparency, legacy and leadership cultivation, and advancement of the art form.[10]

Future-focused theaters know that to perpetuate outdated paradigms risks irrelevance and shrinking audiences. What was once a project of benevolent multicultural inclusion has now become a forecast of a new American cultural milieu, one that has been revitalized and can possibly be sustained by a wide array of voices, aesthetics, and stories. According to Oskar Eustis, Artistic Director of the Public Theater, "If the American theater is to fulfill its democratic promise, it has to embrace artists who represent the bracing diversity of our country, and our world."[11]

Fearless disruption

The playwrights of this book are fearless in the worlds they enter, disrupt, and conjure. They are of a particularly fertile era of intersectional artistic creativity and social response. More playwrights of color are breaking through the glass ceiling, emerging from marginalized and underresourced serial development programs, to garner full commissions and productions in large budget theaters. And theaters that have long held dedicated missions to produce their work are reinventing the play laboratory and other formats, like the short play, to be central, not ancillary, to artistic mission.[12]

For example, Noor Theatre, dedicated to artists of Middle Eastern descent, is an Obie award-winning company in New York City, cofounded by two women, Maha Chehlaoui and playwright Lameece Isaac. Like other artistically vital theaters, it develops theater, produces world premieres, and presents copartnered events. But it has shaken up the model of the short play festival not just to give exposure to a variety of unique voices, but also to redefine theater's role in society.

Chehlaoui, Noor's former executive director, described a board member's desire for a way the theater could respond to the onslaught of news in a post 9/11 America. Given that Noor's first production, like most new plays, took seven years from inception to production, the challenge was not just one of expediency, but of how to remain true to theater making and creativity. And Chehlaoui questioned, "Why is it all on us? Just because we are Middle Eastern, we have to answer all these questions that the entire world has participated in creating and that affect us all." Also implicit was the denial of Americans in recognizing our involvement in over a decade of being at war on several fronts. Noor's answer was to create *48 Hour Forum*, a program Chehlaoui playfully described as a "recipe." The project creatively speaks to a 48-hour news cycle by involving a culturally diverse group of theater makers.[13]

Recipe for 48-Hour Forum

Ingredients:

5 playwrights
5 directors
20 actors
News articles of interest
3 jars

Preparation Method:

In 3 jars, place:

1. 20 slips of paper, each with one actor name
2. 5 slips of paper, each with a different number, the total of which cannot exceed the number 20 (e.g. 5,3,2,6,4)
3. the news articles

Playwrights and directors are paired by the theater in advance, based on the potential to work together, but pairings are not announced until the clock starts on 48 hours when the playwright and director pairings are revealed. Each playwright/director pair draws a piece of paper from the number jar; that is the number of actors with which they have to work. Next, each playwright/director pair draws from the jar containing actor names; the number that will be their cast. Finally, from the last jar, each playwright/director pair draws a headline/article.

Total cooking time: 48 hours
Result: Theatrical op-eds at the rate of a news cycle

Staging 2042

Kristen Adele Calhoun, coassistant editor, and I selected the fourteen full-length plays, two dance-dramas, three solo performance pieces, two one-acts, and one radio play of this anthology leading with our instincts as theater makers. Kristen, an accomplished actor, hungered for roles for actors that would be substantive, thrilling, and exceptional. As a director, I sought revelatory plays that would captivate and challenge audiences. We both listened and looked for authors writing significant, meaningful works that would amplify the theatrical literary canon. And we looked for plays speaking in an urgent way about the multiplicity of perspectives and experience of women of color.

The Bechdel-Wallace Test has become the standard cultural meter of gender equality in the theater. It asks whether a play, film, or other work of fiction feature: 1) at least two women, who 2) talk to each other, about 3) something other than a man. In a demographically transformed America, challenged by a growing racial divide, might we similarly apply a 2042 Test as a cultural measure of racial equality? A 2042 Test might ask, particularly if the narrative takes place in a location that has already achieved the 2042 populations shift, does a play, film, or other work of fiction feature: 1) at least two people of color, who 2) are present not just to further the story line of white male or female characters and 3) who are central to the narrative. Applying this standard calls out the imperative for the production of a myriad of unheard narratives. It also challenges embedded cultural norms that exist within a society vexed with growing de facto segregation. Look, for example, at the genus of New York City-based popular TV series from *Friends*, to *Sex and the City*, to *Girls*—each located within the most racially cosmopolitan, multiethnic city in the world. We joke about how the prefix "White" could be added to each title to acknowledge the disconnect between the segregated world of the characters and their global environment.

Do the plays of this anthology pass both tests? Certainly, they are the embodiment and spirit of 2042. But as I write this, I can hear in my head a conversation I once had with my friend James Baldwin, "What about *Giovanni's Room*?" We were talking about why he chose to write the novel with white protagonists. And like *Giovanni's Room*, these plays defy expectation and limits. Is the Bechdel-Wallace Test even relevant to plays like *Elliot, A Soldier's Fugue*, by Quiara Alegría Hudes, or *Daughter of a Cuban Revolutionary*, by Marisa Chibas? When history, media, and curriculum converge to erase or distort the narratives of both women and men of color, the cultural measuring tape of western feminism falls short. Each of these works speak with their own fiercely independent voices; at the same time, these works are in fascinating conversation with each other. Hudes brings forward three generations of Puerto Rican men to poetically weave a genealogy of human experience through the crushing legacy of war, from WWII to Vietnam to Iraq. Eschewing categorization, she writes, "We are annihilators of reason and embracers of duality....We are the hackers of the status quo." Chibas also mines the collision of history and family. Passionately personal and keenly political, her one-woman play confronts the exclusion of her father and uncle from Cuban history. She equates surviving with remembering, "Telling these stories is both an act of defiance and reconciliation."

The major themes of the book include: the relationship of women to each other; their relationship to family/community; the impact of history and the remaking of history; violence and war, particularly as experienced through the bodies and spirits of women; identity and voice; boundaries of geography, love, and being. The contestation of borders, sovereignty, and identity is seen in two stylistically divergent plays: Hannah Khalil's *Scenes from 68★ Years* set in Palestine and Israel and Vickie Ramirez's *Standoff at Hwy#37*, which takes place at the border of a small town in upstate New York and the Haudenosaunee reservation. Khalil's point of departure is the 1948 founding of the state of Israel. A bricolage of skillfully linked scenes at the checkpoints of occupied Palestine, it reveals the human cost of ongoing conflict with poignant power and unexpected humor. In *Standoff at Hwy#37*, an elder deliberately places her chair on the border of the reservation, blocking the path of an encroaching highway construction project. Reversals of positions and shifting loyalties between different Native characters and multi-raced National Guardsmen unfold as the confrontation escalates beyond the daily grind of survival to the tipping point of resistance.

Two dramas, Hansol Jung's achingly beautiful *Cardboard Piano* and Katori Hall's transcendent *Our Lady of Kibeho*, probe war and trauma on the African continent, in Northern Uganda and Kibeho, Rwanda, respectively. Religion, more so than faith, is central to Hall's and Jung's works. In *Cardboard Piano*, a traumatized boy soldier stumbles into a church during the secret wedding of two girls who show him compassion, but in turn become the target of his homophobia. A chance reunion a decade later tests the limits of forgiveness and the fragility of repaired souls. Hall's *Our Lady of Kibeho*, based on an actual incident, is set in the innocent time "Before," ten years prior to the 1994 Rwandan genocide. A Tutsi convent school girl has a rhapsodic vision of the Virgin Mary that spreads to her disbelieving Hutu classmates. The mysteries of the heavens darken to a prophetic vision of hell on earth to come.

Contested space takes another form in Tammy Haili'opua Baker's *He Lei No Kākāʻāko*, which explores the shifting boundaries of ties to heritage and land in the rapidly gentrifying Kākāʻāko neighborhood in Honolulu. Hawai'i. In telling the stories of local people, Baker makes a critical distinction between being "house-less" for people for whom the land has historically been their home. *Lines in the Dust*, by Nikkole Salter, also explores neighborhood fault lines, but in the form of restrictive school district zoning. She unfolds the relationship between two African-American women who are determined to give their children opportunity through education. Commissioned to commemorate the sixtieth anniversary of the U.S. Supreme Court's decision in Brown v. Board of Education, the play underscores that while segregation has ended legally, de facto segregation persists. One of its most pernicious manifestations is inequality in the educational system.

The all-women cast of Tanya Saracho's kinetic *Mala Hierba*, set in a Texas border wracked with cartel executions, kidnappings and gang wars, has a parallel in the menacing women's world of Danai Gurira's *Eclipsed*, which takes place in civil war-torn Liberia. The women of *Eclipsed* endure a coerced kinship as "wives" defined by rape and war; they live confined by a brutal, unseen rebel commander. The women of *Mala Hierba* are also circumscribed to a world created by a violent, never seen man, but, in contrast, the boundaries of their lives are within a luxury narco compound. The abused trophy wife of a drug trafficker yearns to escape, hungers for the woman she loves, struggles with the seduction of an excessive material lifestyle, and is cognizant of the economic lifeline she plays for her extended family. These women are survivors of bodily horror who struggle to remember who they were, even as they grapple to remake their destinies.

Humor, even in the most chilling circumstances, is a tool of both Gurira and Saracho and many other playwrights of this volume, who deftly move their dramas forward with wit and irony. It's the aesthetic choice of Cuzi Cram, author of *The Wild Inside;* Kristina Wong, in her solo work, *Wong Street Journal*; Lameece Issaq and Jacob Kader in the touching comedy, *Food and Fadwa (Ecklit il Hob)*; and Marcie Rendon in *The Adventures at Camp KaKeeKwaSha and the Magic Musky Casino!* Cram, an actress who challenges stereotypical media depiction of Latinos in the media and on stage, muses on unrealizable love and desire. The play deploys magical realism to converge a tour guide, a talking 200-year-old tortoise, and a TV sit-com "family" on a trip to the Galapagos. Kristina Wong's hilarious *Wong Street Journal* is a self send-up that incisively comments on race and gender on the internet and the search for legacy based on her 2013 trip to Northern Uganda to volunteer for a women's micro-finance organization. In *Food and Fadwa,* Lameece Issaq's and Jacob Kader's protagonist is a resilient young Palestinian woman, Fadwa, who copes with humor by inventing an imaginary cooking show. Living under the volatility and indignities of the Israeli-occupied West Bank, the show she creates is as funny as it is revealing of her complicated family and absurd social context. Also influenced by the reach of media, *The Adventures at Camp KaKeeKwaSh* by Marcie Rendon was produced as a radio podcast by Raving Native Radio. It targets a youth audience, following the adventures of a zany crew of diverse Native adolescent campers.

Crossing transnational borders and the metamorphosis of women as immigrants and transplants is delicately, yet very differently revealed in two dance dramas from the South Asian diaspora: *Etchings in the Sand*, by Ananya Chatterjea and Meena Natarajan; and *Clothes*, by Chitra Banerjee Divakaruni. In *Etchings in the Sand*, memory blends with imagined moments – the fragments of memories that endure within and the unanswered questions of what might have been. The adaptation of Chitra Banerjee Divakaruni's exquisite short story, *Clothes*, allows women to embody both men and women characters, as it follows the evolution of a young village girl in India through a traditional arranged marriage and discovery of self far from her origins.

Like the aforementioned *Elliot, A Soldier's Fugue,* two other plays courageously confront deeply rooted U.S. trauma – and like *Elliot*, their settings are interstitial. In *Gunshot* Medley, set in "The Hereafter," Dionna Michelle Daniel channels her anguish about the 2015 Charleston, South Carolina church massacre of nine African Americans, the national epidemic of killings of black people by the police, and the keloid scar of slavery in America. The ancestral realm becomes a place to exorcise the deep spiritual and psychic wound of racism. Kathryn Haddad's post 9/11 *Zafira the Olive Oil Warrior* resonates as future-fiction, in a Minneapolis where Muslims have been rounded up in concentration camps, like the Japanese Americans of WWII. A cautionary tale for our times, *Zafira* lifts a curtain on where xenophobia and nativist hysteria can lead the country. Larissa FastHorse also turns to history, unspooling an inspired point of departure in *What Would Crazy Horse Do?* She was confounded by a 1926 flyer she found that advertised a pow wow sponsored by the Ku Klux Klan. She imagined contemporary characters seeking to adapt and thrive. Two Native American siblings of a tribe that is confronted with extinction find the first woman leader of the Ku Klux Klan at their door. She wants to spin the KKK as relevant to contemporary times. They consider a dangerous deal after discovering a mutual distrust of the U.S. government and a shared desire for racial preservation. Lynn Nottage, in her extended monologue *N*GG**, mines an American trauma deeply rooted in language, race, racism, history, and present. Her storyteller is baffled, stung, and affirmed by the blatant and nuanced uses of the N word in a continuous exploration.

Complex mother/daughter relationships, secrets, and the extent to which women go to protect each other are the intersection between the *Sun Sisters*, by Vasanti Saxena, and *Our Voices Will be Heard*, by Vera Starbard. Lesbian relationships and a gender spectrum of characters are embedded in plays throughout the collection; the *Sun Sisters*, by Vasanti Saxena, is an engrossing and fresh take on the coming out genre. Transformation cuts across gender, the generational divide, cultural norms, and love itself as a dying mother and daughter reconcile. In *Our Voices Will be Heard*, Vera Starbard weaves a contemporary story of child abuse, with a Tlingit myth of the Wolverine Woman, a shunned, lone brave survivor. The play asks, as it shatters silence, does the survival of the clan necessitate the denial of the individual?

These plays await your voice, embodiment, and production; they are the conversation that needs to happen and the performance to inspire the many voices that will surely follow. Dolores Huerta's rallying cry urges on new generations of women, "Walk the street with us into history. Get off the sidewalk."[14] These women playwrights—path makers and voyagers—assure our presence, as they call us undeniably to the future.

Roberta Uno

New York City

Notes

1. Lee, Eun, *The Dream Unfinished*. October 3, 2015. Accessed August 22, 2016. http://thedreamunfinished.org. Founded by Eun Lee in New York City, The Dream Unfinished is an activist orchestra which supports New York City-based civil rights and community organizations through concerts and presentations. Begun in 2015, it creates a platform for classical musicians to show solidarity with activists in the #BLACKLIVESMATTER movement. http://www.aapf.org/sayhername/ #SAYHERNAME is an initiative of the African American Policy Forum urging attention to police violence against Black women by offering a resource "to help ensure that Black women's stories are integrated into demands for justice, policy responses to police violence, and media representation of victims of police brutality." In addition to names cited, they listed: Danette Daniels, Duanna Johnson, Eleanor Bumpers, Frankie Ann Perkins, Gabriella Nevarez, India Kager, Janisha Fonville, Kathryn Johnston, Kayla Moore, Kendra James, Yam Livingston, LaTanya Taggerty, Malissa Williams, Margaret Laverne Mitchell, Meagan Hockaday, Michelle Cusseaux, Miriam Carey, Mya Hall, Natasha McKenna, Nizam Morris, Pearlie Golden, Rekia Boyd, Sandra Bland, Shantel Davis, Sharmel Edwards, Shelly Frey, Sheneque Proctor, Shereese Francis, Sonja Taylor, Tanisha Anderson, Tarkia Wilson, Tyisha Miller, and Yvette Smith.
2. King Jr, Martin Luther. "Beyond Vietnam: A Time to Break Silence." Speech, Riverside Church, New York, NY. April 4, 1967.
3. Park, Haeyoun, Josh Keller, and Josh Williams. "Faces of American Power, Nearly as White as the Oscar Nominees" *New York Times*. February 26, 2016. http://www.nytimes.com/interactive/2016/02/26/us/race-of-american-power.html
4. Erkut, Sumru and Ineke Ceder. "Women's Leadership: Research Results and Recommendations" Accessed on August 23, 2016, http://howlround.com/women-s-leadership-research-results-and-recommendations. This article's main thrust is a set of practical, thoughtful recommendations addressing gender-bias in hiring.
5. Sidford, Holly. *Fusing Arts, Culture and Social Change*. Washington DC: National Committee for Responsive Philanthropy, October 2011, http://www.ncrp.org/files/publications/Fusing Arts Culture Social Change.pdf.
6. The Grantmakers in the Arts Racial Equity group is advancing efforts towards an equitable and just arts field through research, identifying barriers and best practice, and forums for discussion and exchange. http://www.giarts.org

7. For cultural critiques of Lin-Manuel Miranda's Hamilton, see Monteiro, Lyra D. "Race-Conscious Casting and the Erasure of the BlackPast in Lin-Manuel Miranda's Hamilton." *The Public Historian* 38, no.1 (2016) and Thelwell, China A. "Hamilton Missed a Chance to Highlight the Haitian Revolution" *Miami Herald* August 6, 2016.

8. http://media.wix.com/ugd/25c546_a5d46080ad7749409df997b299677078.pdf "The National Black Theatre To Host Catalyst: Moving the Black Theatre Legacy Forward." Press release, July 24, 2014. For further information see http://www.nationalblacktheatre. org/catalyst--moving-the-legacy-forward Accessed August 23, 2016.

9. http://caata.net Accessed August 23, 2016. CAATA was spearheaded by: Pan Asian Repertory Theatre, East West Players, Ma-Yi Theater, the National Asian American Theatre Company (NAATCO), Second Generation and Mu Performing Arts.

10. http://howlround.com/latina/o-theatre-commons
    The Latina/o Theatre Commons, in partnership with HowlRound, is a national movement that uses a commons-based approach to transform the narrative of the American theater, to amplify the visibility of Latina/o performance making, and to champion equity through advocacy, art making, convening, and scholarship.

11. Oskar Eustis book jacket endorsement for *Monologues for Actors of Color*.
    Uno, Roberta. *Monologues for Actors of Color: Men*. Psychology Press, 2000.

12. Some examples are: http://www.thenewblackfest.org/, http://www.harlem9.org/48hours-in-harlem, http://www.firethistimefestival.com/, http://victorygardens.org/ignition/, https:// actorstheatre.org/humana-festival-of-new-american-plays/,http://www.culturaldc.org/performing-arts/source-festival/, http://www.fridakahlotheater.org/, http://www.townestreetla.org/# !10-minute-play-festival/c57j, https://www.bu.edu/bpt/our-programs/boston-theatre-marathon/, http://www.roundhousetheatre.org/performances/1mpf/, https://www. osfashland.org/experience-osf/upcoming/every-28-hours.aspx

13. Recorded interview Maha Chehlaoui, Founding Executive Director, Noor Theatre and the author June 2, 2016, New York City. I've taken the liberty to describe the program as a recipe.

14. Rallying cry of labor leader and civil rights activist Dolores Huerta during the United Farm Workers of America strikes.

Hansol Jung

Biography

Hansol Jung is a playwright and director from South Korea. Her plays include *Cardboard Piano* (Humana Festival at Actors Theatre of Louisville), *No More Sad Things* (co-world premiere at Sideshow Theatre Company and Boise Contemporary Theatre), *Among the Dead* (Ma-Yi Theater Company), *Wolf Play*, and *Wild Goose Dreams*. She has been commissioned by Playwrights Horizons, the Virginia B. Toulmin Foundation grant with Ma-Yi Theatre, and for a translation of *Romeo and Juliet* for Play On! at Oregon Shakespeare Festival. Her work has been developed at the Royal Court The-  atre, New York Theatre Workshop, Berkeley Rep's Ground Floor, O'Neill Conference, Sundance Theatre Lab, Lark Play Development Center, Salt Lake Acting Company, Boston Court Theatre, Bushwick Starr, Asia Society New York, and Seven Devils Playwright Conference. She is the recipient of the Rita Goldberg Playwrights' Workshop Fellowship at the Lark, 2050 Fellowship at New York Theater Workshop, MacDowell Colony Artist Residency, and International Playwrights Residency at Royal Court Theatre. She has translated over thirty English musicals into Korean, including *Evita*, *Dracula*, *Spamalot*, and *The 25th Annual Putnam County Spelling Bee*, while working on several award-winning musical theatre productions as director, lyricist, and translator in Seoul, South Korea. Jung holds a Playwriting MFA from Yale School of Drama and is a proud member of the Ma-Yi Theatre Writers Lab.

Artistic statement

A teacher once told me that tragedy—the story of sad things—is how humans process trauma. That WWII was the end of tragedy, and that's why we are so fucked up. We are made to hold the sad things in our bodies, without a communal ritual of processing them. Is this true? Are we all running around clutching on to our cancerous sad things because we lack the ritualistic stories to let them go?

I think about this a lot. About stories. What stories do, innocuously, effortlessly, not as bloodletting as a knife or as final as a bullet, but with as much staying power within a body. Dare I believe stories are the cultural currency of change in thought, that there are no 1% or 99% in the ownership of stories, that only through the exchange of stories do we weave through and stitch up the holes and gaps of the world?

Many of my stories begin with a trauma—traumas being held in bodies of people, nations, generations, and, a little bit, myself. I gravitate towards stories of personal and social trauma, in excited anticipation of solving the problem. I have never solved a problem. I understand trauma is not a problem to be solved. But the need is always there: the need to give an answer, give a nudge towards the "right" direction. My inner Pollyanna wants to hug everyone, lead them out into the sunlight, and start a conga line chanting everything's gonna be alright.

Play after play, I fail at creating the conga line. Play after play, I continue to try. Perhaps, the aspiration drives the creation of the play. The play itself will mostly just reveal how complex and difficult it is to rebuild what was broken and recover what was lost.

The act of breaking and the act of recovering are bridged and often obfuscated by time. I am very excited about how time can be made to work within the theatre. I love that our mode of storytelling requires all participants to give unbroken time, if not attention, to the story at hand. This unbroken time is given to me like playdough in a plastic jar, and I love experimenting with how a break in time is processed, how a past is registered, and how futures are projected. Time is the architectural playdough of plays.

All this is to find the right ritual—the conga line—to process the broken things in the story. What is the shape of the ritual that will, I don't know, *help*?

I love social rituals—weddings, funerals, births. I poach personal rituals—ice cream for breakups, *Star Wars* marathon for Christmas, gin martini and a pebble in hand for opening nights. To me, these rituals are stories told in repetition, creating a tiny float of stability we grasp on to while we try to process what the hell is going on—all the sadness, all the joy, all the incomprehensible.

Cardboard Piano poached many stories from various communities. Some are my own, some are not. I am grateful for all the people who graciously granted me their pains and stories for the creation of a made up one.

Production history

Cardboard Piano premiered at the Victor Jory Theatre as part of the 40th Humana Festival of New American Plays at Actors Theatre of Louisville in March 2016, directed by Leigh Silverman. The play was developed during a residency at the Eugene O'Neill Theater Center's National Playwrights Conference in 2015 alongside Wendy Goldberg as Artistic Director and Preston Whiteway as Executive Director.

1 *Cardboard Piano*
Hansol Jung

Characters

Part I

CHRIS a child in love, age 16
ADIEL a child in love, age 16
PIKA a child soldier, 13
SOLDIER a soldier

Part II

CHRIS a visitor, age 30
PAUL a pastor, Soldier from Part I, age 27
RUTH a pastor's wife, Adiel from Part I, age 29
FRANCIS a local ki, Pika from Part I, age 22

Time

Part I is New Year's Eve 1999
Part II is A Wedding Anniversary 2014

Setting

A township in Northern Uganda

Punctuation notes

-       a cut off either by self or other.
//   a point where another character might cut in.
[...]   Things that aren't spoken in words.

Luo translations

jal – le	I surrender
apwoyo matek	thank you very much
mzungu	(light-skinned) foreigner

PART I

Night.

A church—not one of stone and stained glass,
more a small town hall dressed up to be church
There's a hole in the roof of the church.
Two men, two women.
In separate spaces, they sing together, simple a capella
that might blow up into something bigger and scarier

ALL **Just as I am, without one plea,**[1]
But that Thy blood was shed for me,
And that Thou bidst me come to Thee,
O Lamb of God, I come, I come
Just as I am, though tossed about
With many a conflict, many a doubt,
Fightings and fears within, without,
O Lamb of God, I come, I come
Just as I am, Thy love unknown
Hath broken every barrier down;
Now, to be Thine, yea, Thine alone,
O Lamb of God, I come, I come
Just as I am, of that free love
The breadth, length, depth, and height to prove,
Here for a season, then above,
O Lamb of–

Rain. Loud. Pours through the hole in the roof.
Pews, chair, cushions arranged to create a hollow in the middle of church.
ADIEL, age 16, is asleep in the middle of the hollow, strewn with wild flower petals.
CHRIS, age 16, slips in, big suitcase in tow.
She hides the suitcase somewhere in the shadows
She tiptoes around the chairs, benches to lean into ADIEL's sleeping ear.
Whispers.

CHRIS The end of the world is near.

(ADIEL starts.)

ADIEL Hm!?
CHRIS Hi.
ADIEL Where am, what,
CHRIS It's me, just me.
ADIEL For heaven's sake Chris. You frightened me. What is the time. You are very late.
CHRIS Had to wait till the folks fell asleep.
ADIEL Your parents?

(CHRIS finds party blower.)

CHRIS Blowers!
ADIEL Why are they still here?

CHRIS Blue one's mine!
ADIEL What about the party? What happened?
CHRIS Nothing. They didn't wanna go, I guess.
ADIEL So your parents are still in the house?
CHRIS It's fine. They went to bed. Said they wanna be up in time to see the ball fall in New York. Miss me?
ADIEL I saw you just three hours ago.
CHRIS We didn't know if the world was gonna end, three hours ago.
ADIEL It did not.
CHRIS *(blows on blower)* yay!
ADIEL Shh!
CHRIS Happy New Year.

ADIEL Happy New Year. You'll wake them up.

(*Blow.*)

ADIEL (*cont.*) Chris it is not funny–

(*Blow.*)

ADIEL (*cont.*) Come now give it to me.

CHRIS Make me.

(*Blow.*)

ADIEL Haw this is a challenge now?

(*ADIEL jumps CHRIS, misses.*)

CHRIS Prepare for battle!

(*Battle trumpets blowblowblow.*)

CHRIS (*cont.*) Upon my honor I shall never surrender!

(*Blooooooooooooooooooooooooooo–
Blowing stops because ADIEL kisses her.*)

CHRIS (*cont.*) I surrender.

(*Kiss.*)

CHRIS (*cont.*) How do you say I surrender in Luo?

ADIEL *Jal – le.*

CHRIS *Jal – le.*

ADIEL I am very sexy when you speak my language.

CHRIS I am sexy.

ADIEL You too?

CHRIS No, I am sexy, to you. Sexy is a thing I am, that makes You want to get into My pants.

ADIEL Why are we turning this into English lesson?

CHRIS I am very sexy when you speak my language wrong.

ADIEL So both ways we are very sexy.

CHRIS Okay.

(*Hands in pants, hairs undone, shirts flung off, skirts riding up–
Thunder and lightning.*)

CHRIS (*cont.*) Woah.

(*CHRIS bolts upright like a meerkat.*)

ADIEL What is the matter?

CHRIS Think he's mad at us?

ADIEL Who?

CHRIS I'd be mad if people came to my house at night, mess it up, have sex all over my cushions in front of a picture of me hanging naked on a tree –

(*ADIEL kisses CHRIS.*)

ADIEL I think he is thrilled we included him.

CHRIS We didn't.

ADIEL Well I did and I think he is saying congratulations on your big day!

(*Thunder.*)
(*Meerkat.*)

ADIEL (*cont.*) He is happy for us! He is giving us extra fireworks. He is saying Happy happy wedding day!

CHRIS Fuck around in my house of worship and I'll throw a bolt in your head. Is what he's saying.

ADIEL Ag he did not bring us together to throw a bolt in our heads.

CHRIS Yeh. Well. We won't know till we know will we?

ADIEL Chris. What is the matter?

CHRIS Nothing. Just, thunderstorms. I don't like them.

(*re: church*) This, is beautiful. When did you have the time to set all this up?

ADIEL You were late.

CHRIS Candles… flowers… a, oreo?

ADIEL Ah that one is a gift. From Francis.

CHRIS Francis? The guy who's crushing on you?

ADIEL No, that is Philip. Francis is my cousin. The one who is crushing on You.

CHRIS You brought me a cookie from your competition.

ADIEL The competition is eight years old and he really wanted you to have this one. I am not worried. Very soon you belong only to me.

(*ADIEL holds out her palms.*)

CHRIS What?

ADIEL The rings?

CHRIS Oh. Um.

ADIEL What?

CHRIS –

ADIEL Ag Chris, that was the one thing you were in charge of.

CHRIS I'm sorry. My parents, found them and, took them

ADIEL Your parents? Why?

CHRIS Because. For safekeeping. They're paranoid, since the news up north. The whole town's so paranoid, it's contagious. Can't wait to get out of this place where we can live like normal people.

ADIEL This place is my home.

CHRIS It doesn't always have to be.

ADIEL Christina I do not want to argue about that right now.

CHRIS Don't call me Christina.

I wanted everything to be perfect too. I wanted rings. Champagne. Sunlight.

ADIEL We have candlelight. And here a ring. For now.

(The strip of aluminum from the bottle cap — ADIEL twists it into a pretty ring.)

CHRIS I knew this boy back home. He'd always play with wires, bend them into goats — sometimes other things but mostly goats, he loved goats — goat tribes, goat battle scenes, little goat armies lined up and at attention. He had no friends and was bullied a lot but then one of the teachers found his goats, and helped him apply to this arts school in Colorado, all for free, even the plane ticket. You know what I mean?

ADIEL No.

CHRIS I'm saying, you could probably do something like that.

ADIEL You want that I make armies of wire goats?

CHRIS No, I want that you apply to a school in America. You can make pretty things. You can go to school for free if you can make pretty things in my country, learn to make more pretty things, sell them, buy a car, buy a boat, a plane, an army of wire goats-

ADIEL Chris. If you are making stupid jokes because you do not want to do this, tell me right now.

CHRIS I do. I do want to. I'm sorry. Don't be angry.

ADIEL I am not angry. Just making sure.

CHRIS I am sure.

(ADIEL makes sure.)

ADIEL We have everything else, candle, cookie, tape recorder –

CHRIS Tape recorder?

ADIEL Because we do not have witnesses, we must record the vows, so when you are mine, you are mine forever.

CHRIS This isn't legal or anything, I can crush the records and run away whenever I like.

ADIEL But I will hunt you down to the ends of the earth. I will hunt you down forever. Forever forever I will say, "come back to meeeeeeeee come back to me my husbaaaaaaaaaand come back to meeeeeeeeeeeeeeeeeeeee I have this tape recordeerrrrrrrrrrrr"

CHRIS Okay let's do it.

(ADIEL pulls out a couple of neatly composed handwritten documents.)

ADIEL Number one, you must say this, with your name in there, and then I say the same, with My name not yours of course.

CHRIS Wow. You are not joking around.

ADIEL I never joke. Number two, You do the ring and say this part. Unless you want to be the bride, then I do the ring to you, and I say this part.

CHRIS Wait, where'd you get this stuff from?

ADIEL From our pastor.

(CHRIS takes a pen to ADIEL's vow papers.)

CHRIS Okay, strike "lawful," strike "according to God's holy ordinance," // and strike the second part of this whole section,

ADIEL AH! What are you doing, you are ruining the vow papers!

CHRIS – we are not endowing anything in the name of the Father the Son or the Holy Ghost. Because they don't care. Amen should go too.

ADIEL We must do the whole vow.

CHRIS No we don't. It's our wedding we can do whatever we want.

ADIEL Well that is not what I want.

(ADIEL clicks "rec" button on the tape recorder.)

ADIEL *(cont.)* This is the wedding of Christina Jennifer Englewood and Adiel Nakalinzi. January 1st, year 2000.

(She gestures to CHRIS: "go ahead, begin the vows.")

CHRIS What? Oh okay, me first. I, Chris Blank, take thee,

(ADIEL hits stop.)

ADIEL What are you doing.

CHRIS I'm gonna find another name. I've disowned my parents.

ADIEL What does that mean? Shoo, you are making this impossible, You have to have whole name, say I, Christina Jennifer Englewood. Start again.

(Rewind. Rec.)

ADIEL *(cont.)* This is the wedding of Christina Jennifer Englewood and Adiel Nakalinzi. January 1st, year 2000.

CHRIS I, Chris Blank, take thee, Adiel Nakalinzi, to be my wife, ugh, that's such dumb word.

(ADIEL hits stop.)

ADIEL Chris!

(CHRIS takes the recorder. Rec.)

CHRIS To be my wife, to have and to hold from this day forward, for better for worse for richer for poorer in sickness and in health to love and to cherish till death do us part, according to, I don't know, according to this dimly lit candle's holy ordinance, and thereto I give thee my troth. What's a troth? Sounds slimy.

ADIEL I, Adiel Nakalinzi, take thee, Christina Jennifer Englewood,

CHRIS Chris Blank

ADIEL Christina Jennifer Englewood, to be my lawful wedded husband, to have and –

(CHRIS hits stop.)

CHRIS Stop right there, I refuse to be a husband in this life or the next, do over.

ADIEL What, we have two wives then? That is a house of widows.

CHRIS I don't care, make it work, not gonna be a husband. Ew.

ADIEL A sad grieving house of sad sad widows.

(Sad face.)

CHRIS Ugh.

(ADIEL hits rec.)

ADIEL I, Adiel Nakalinzi, take thee, Christina Jennifer Englewood, to be my lawful wedded Husband,

(CHRIS leans into mic on recorder.)

CHRIS Ugh.

ADIEL – to have and to hold from this day, forward, for better for worse, for richer for poorer, in sickness and in health, to love and to cherish, till death us do part, according to God's holy ordinance; and thereto I plight thee my troth.

CHRIS With this ring I thee wed, with my body I thee worship, and with all my worldly goods I thee endow.

ADIEL In the name of.

CHRIS In the name of the Father, and of the Son, and of the Holy Ghost. Amen.

ADIEL Amen. Now I may kiss the husband.

(Kiss. With all the nerves and rituals of the Newly Weds' First Kiss.)

ADIEL *(cont.)* Now we must dance.

CHRIS No. We must not.

ADIEL **Oh my love, my darling**[2]

(CHRIS laughs out loud at the song choice, but soon surrenders to ADIEL's insistence.)

CHRIS Seriously?

ADIEL *(spoken)* Yes.

I've hungered for your touch
A long lonely time
And time goes by so slowly
And time can do so much,
Are you still mine?

(They dance together, like people in love, soaking in the cheese and tender, all of it.)

ADIEL/CHRIS **I need your love,**

I need your love
God speed your love to me
Lonely rivers flow to the sea, to the sea
To the open arms of the sea, yeah!
Lonely rivers sigh, "wait for me, wait for me"
I'll be coming home
Wait-

!!
(Scuffling of feet on dirt,
random shouts, coming from outside.)

CHRIS What's the time?

ADIEL After midnight at the very least.

CHRIS It must be people getting out from the party. Blow them out, the candles!

(Silence.
Then doors opening slamming, feet, shuffling on dirt, whispered sounds,)

ADIEL Did you lock the door?

CHRIS I'm getting it now

(BANG gun shots
CHRIS and ADIEL duck.)

CHRIS *(cont.)* Jesus!

ADIEL Chris!

CHRIS It's alright I'm fine are you? Are you okay?

ADIEL Get over here, get over here right now!

CHRIS I know, okay I'm [gonna lock the door first]

(Door opens, PIKA leaps in, grabs CHRIS, hand over mouth.)

PIKA Shh!

(Points bloody gun towards ADIEL, then to CHRIS's head.
Motions to CHRIS to lock the door. She does.
More footsteps, pad pad pad past the door, and away.
Wait wait.
Wait wait.
Wait wait.)

(PIKA leans against a wall, exhausted, out of breath,
faints.)
CHRIS leaps back away from him, ADIEL
leaps forward towards CHRIS.

ADIEL Are you okay.
CHRIS Mm. [yes]
ADIEL Did he hurt you? Any-
CHRIS Mm mm [no]
ADIEL Ok good ok. Hold on.

(Checks pulse. Breath.)

CHRIS Is he [dead]?
ADIEL He's okay.

(CHRIS looks for a rope type thing.)
(ADIEL pries gun from PIKA, wipes the blood
off the gun.)
(CHRIS has found a rope type thing, gives it to
ADIEL.)

ADIEL What?
CHRIS For [tying him up]

(ADIEL hands gun to CHRIS while she ties up
PIKA.)

ADIEL Ok.
CHRIS Ok.
ADIEL Sit there take a breath // and I will go
    bring your parents.
CHRIS Ok My –
ADIEL You said they were still here, right? They
    did not go to New Year Party.
CHRIS No.
ADIEL So I will bring them down.
CHRIS You can't. You can't bring them. You
    can't wake them up.
ADIEL Chris we must. That child is hurt.
CHRIS You can't.
ADIEL He cannot do anything to us now, I
    promise.
CHRIS No it's not that –
ADIEL What is it then?
CHRIS You can't call them.
ADIEL We need a grown up, Christina. That
    child needs help.
CHRIS That child tried to kill me.
ADIEL He was only asking for help. He –
CHRIS He tried to kill me.
ADIEL He is a rebel soldier, he is hurt. He
    needs bandage, doctor, do you understand
    Christina, if we do not wake up your parents
    that boy might die while we watch.
CHRIS We can't.

ADIEL I will not argue about this.
CHRIS No we seriously can't, they won't wake
    up. They won't wake up, Adiel, I—
    I drugged them.
ADIEL What?
CHRIS Sleeping pills. In the tea, not very much.
    Just two more than what they usually take.
ADIEL You did what?!
CHRIS I needed the car keys. He sleeps with
    them Velcro-ed in his pockets, I didn't
    know how else to—
ADIEL Every time? Every time we met, you
    were poisoning our pastor?
CHRIS It's not poison! And of course not every
    time, just tonight, I needed the keys, time
    to pack and—
    Look, I think there's a first aid kit in the office,
ADIEL Pack?
CHRIS We have to leave tonight. I have
    everything we need here, in this bag,
CHRIS *(cont.)* I meant to tell you as soon as-, but
    you were so cute and happy and the vows
    and song, I didn't want to ruin, I wanted to
    get through the-
ADIEL What are you saying?
CHRIS Escape.
ADIEL Escape.
CHRIS We have to escape. This this place, this
    prison of-
ADIEL We are in a church Chris.
CHRIS I mean metaphorically.
ADIEL So, escape metaphorically?
CHRIS No that part is real. The prison is meta-
    phor, the escape is real.
ADIEL - you are muddling my brain, there's a
    boy bleeding over here,
CHRIS We'll fix it. We can fix it, we'll find the
    first aid kit, fix the guy who tried to kill me,
    then we'll get in the car drive to the check
    point—
ADIEL Get in the car and drive to the- you can
    hardly find the way to the bus stop, how—
CHRIS We'll figure it out!
ADIEL Why?!
CHRIS They know. My parents. They know.
ADIEL About –
CHRIS Us.
ADIEL Ha.
CHRIS Yep.
ADIEL How?
CHRIS The rings. I had our names written on
    the inside, as a surprise for you,

She asked about – so I told.

ADIEL And?

CHRIS They didn't.

ADIEL Of course not! Why did you // do this, this this –

CHRIS It's not safe, not safe here anymore, I couldn't just // leave, didn't know if

ADIEL without even one word // to me, did you,

CHRIS I thought they might take you too, if I, for us, oh come // on, Adiel,

ADIEL My auntie is going to have me killed. Killed, Christina, did you even think about that what it means to me if the people here find out do you know what that means for me?

CHRIS It won't mean anything, because we are going to live in Tunisia.

ADIEL Tunisia?

CHRIS We'll patch up the kid, pack up the car, and drive past the checkpoint, you can hide in the trunk till we get to the border–

ADIEL You, are the missionary pastor's daughter! Missionary pastor's daughters do not do this way, poison their parents and then run away to–

CHRIS They're leaving. Moving boxes, plane tickets, Really Leaving Adiel. With me. I had to tell them, they are these people who are supposed to love me the most in the world

I thought maybe they would, understand, thought they'd–

But it went wrong, ok, it just went wrong and–

ADIEL So we must go to Tunisia?

CHRIS Adiel if we are gonna do this, each other is all we're gonna have left,

we have to put everything on the line. I mean EVERYTHING.

I have to put my God on the altar, you have to put your country on the altar,

and say, none of these things matter more to us than each other, each other is our everything, for each other we are willing to burn them destroy them // to to to give them up–

ADIEL Chris you are not making any sense,

CHRIS Whatever "them" is for either of us. You know that game, that game where they ask you, if you were stranded on an island, and you get to take just the one thing, what would you take? Except it's not a game, we Are stranded on an island, we are all

stranded on an island on our own, and we get to choose one thing just the one thing that we will carry with us always.

My parents chose God your parents chose country and look what happened to them!

Mine are forced to box up their house and dreams in a weekend, yours are dead.

I can't do that, I can't be stranded on an island on my own,

I Choose You. But it only works if you choose me too.

ADIEL So you poisoned them?

CHRIS Adiel!

ADIEL This is too much Chris.

CHRIS They were making me leave you.

ADIEL We had a plan, we were getting married

CHRIS That's not a real plan! What's the point of getting married when I'm eight thousand miles away

(*PIKA comes to, finds his bearing, discovers bondage,*

Frantic, he tries to grab pocket knife to undo bondage,

Girls lunge away from him.)

CHRIS (*cont.*) Get in, get in, back of the,

PIKA Let me go.

ADIEL We are here to help.

CHRIS Adiel!

PIKA You tied me up.

ADIEL You were being difficult at first. Look. Medicine. For you.

PIKA Stay there. Let me see inside the box first.

ADIEL See, just bandages and ice packs.

CHRIS I say we go inside the office and lock the door.

ADIEL You do that if you want to.

PIKA They cut off my ear.

ADIEL Yes, I know.

CHRIS Adiel this is not safe.

ADIEL You are bleeding. We can help you stop the blood. Can I come closer? We can help you.

(*PIKA lowers the blade.*)

ADIEL (*cont.*) Can you put that down please?

(*PIKA puts the blade down. Close, tho.*)

ADIEL (*cont.*) Thank you. I am Adiel. What is your name?

PIKA Pika.

ADIEL Okay Pika, let us sit you up, can you lean your head this way, good. You must not lie down, okay?

(ADIEL unties him.)

CHRIS Adiel what are you insane?

ADIEL You poison your parents and I am insane?

CHRIS This is a bad idea. Worse than my Tunisia idea, in fact, we won't have to go to Tunisia, because we will be dead anyway.

ADIEL Come here.

CHRIS Dead!

ADIEL Chris I need your help, come here.

CHRIS Dead.

ADIEL Stop saying dead and keep this rag on his head. You must apply pressure, we cannot do anything until he stops bleeding. We cannot go to Tunisia until he stops bleeding.

(CHRIS reluctantly goes to ADIEL and the boy. Takes over the rags.)

CHRIS Oh god oh jesus this is oh wow—

ADIEL You can put more pressure, you must be firm.

CHRIS How do you know all this.

ADIEL In my country, you have to learn to do more than just make pretty things.

CHRIS That's why I'm saying, we should go to Tunisia. Where are you going!

ADIEL To get water!

CHRIS Come back here. Come back here! Adiel, get back here right-

*(She's gone.
Silence.)*

CHRIS *(cont.)* Let's just, get this…

(CHRIS pushes the blade away kinda sorta subtly, PIKA is rigid.)

CHRIS *(cont.)* No, I'm not gonna, I just wanted to,

(The blade is out of easy reach.)

CHRIS *(cont.)* I'm Chris.

PIKA Yes.

CHRIS What happened? Your *(gestures, ear)*, I mean you don't have to say if you don't want to—

PIKA I tried to run away and then he catch me and then I run away again.

CHRIS Does it hurt?
Do you want something? Lemonade?
Or, Oreo?

(PIKA stares at the Oreo for a bit before taking it. He eats the Oreo in silence.)

PIKA There is a hole in the roof.

CHRIS Yep.

PIKA What happened?

CHRIS Don't know. We woke up one morning and there was this dead bird on the pews, and a hole in the roof above it. I like it, kinda like a skylight. Lets the breeze in, and you can see the stars in the night,

(ADIEL's back with a bucket of water.)

ADIEL How are we doing?

CHRIS Great.

(She checks beneath the rag.)

ADIEL Little bit longer.

(ADIEL preps the bandages, alcohol swabs.)

PIKA I like it too. The people in this church can pray, see God directly, and pray.

ADIEL Hm?

CHRIS The hole. He likes the hole in our roof.

ADIEL Do you like to pray?

PIKA The Commander, he makes us pray very very much. In the morning, in the night, the other chidren, they are not so committed. I am committed. But I want to look at the sky when I am talking to God. Not to close my eyes, or bow my head like the Commander wants.

CHRIS What do you pray about?

ADIEL You can let go now.

(CHRIS lets go. ADIEL wets the rag, cleans the clots of blood around his lobbed off ear.)

PIKA My soul.

CHRIS Your soul?

PIKA I pray for my soul. I have done many bad things.

ADIEL Now this will hurt a little, hold on to Chris if you want to.

*(He does.
Alcohol swabs. Dab dab, while blowing gently,
Wince wince.)*

ADIEL *(cont.)* Good boy, almost finished. Good boy.

PIKA I am not a good boy.

ADIEL No? Chris can you help me cut this tape.

CHRIS Yeah. Of course.

PIKA In the bush, I dream, my soul is shrinking, like a little raisin, tiny like one rain, and it disappears away into the ocean. God does not hear me in this ocean. I do not hear Him.

ADIEL Well you are not in the bush, you are not in the ocean, you are here with us, in our church. And He is very happy you are here, Pika.

PIKA No. I am lost. I am surrounded by bad souls and I cannot breathe cannot remember who I am and now I am also bad soul. I am a very bad soul and cannot remember how to pray I cannot remember His voice I cannot remember how to talk to him. I am a terrible bad soul and so He has forgotten about me. He has forgotten.

(*PIKA cries, and cries.*
Cries like a thirteen year old boy cries when he is very scared.
He cries, and cries.)

CHRIS Pika, how old are you?

PIKA Thirteen.

CHRIS Okay, so when I was a kid, even younger than you, I had this thing about a piano. Obsession.

One day, my dad's like, Chris, I got a surprise for you, I'm like, IT'S A PIANO

he reaches behind and gives me, well,

he's cut out a cereal box, and built a small piano out of the cardboard.

He plays, singing the notes he's playing, like, "doon doon doon doon doon doon doon doon."

What do I do? I snatch it, tear it all up.

Soon as I did it I knew I did something bad, because the look on his face was–

And I watch him pick up the pieces, go to his office, close the door.

I'm thinking, he's gone. He hates me. He'll forget me and find another daughter in my place,

Finally I can't take it any more so I go knock on his door, crying "Daddy, I'm sorry"

Door opens, and you know what I see? The piano.

He's been in there this whole time, putting the piano back together.

He goes, "doon doon doon doon doon doon doon," and while I'm crying snot and tears, he lifts me onto his lap, says, "Chris, this is all we have, for now. It's small and fragile, so easy to break.

but look, I fixed it. Every time we break something, it's okay, long as we fix it. And I did. So it's okay."

(*The boy has stopped crying.*)

PIKA That is the most bad thing that you did?

CHRIS Ha. No. I wish.

PIKA I do not know how to fix my soul.

CHRIS Maybe someone else is fixing it, you just can't see yet.

(*CHRIS finds a blanket or throw, wraps around the boy.*
ADIEL activates an ice pack and places it on his wound.)

ADIEL Here, this is cold, press it to your bandages, yes like that. The blood is not completely stopped, so you must not lie down yet, alright?

PIKA Thank you.

(*ADIEL waits for PIKA to settle, and then takes CHRIS aside.*)

ADIEL If we go, you might never see your father again.

CHRIS I know.

ADIEL You might never be able to fix it, with either of them.

CHRIS I know.

ADIEL Once we leave, we cannot return. We cannot undo what we are about to do. Do you understand this?

CHRIS Adiel, once I get on that plane with them I cannot come back.

ADIEL Ok.

CHRIS !

ADIEL Not Tunisia. We can go down to the city. It will be easy for us to find something to do in the city. Much easier than me trying to cross the borders without a passport.

CHRIS Great. Yes. Okay.

ADIEL First I must go home.

CHRIS What? No.

ADIEL I cannot just leave,

CHRIS I don't think it's safe to be outside right now,

ADIEL I have to let them know that I am leaving, that I am not, Taken,

CHRIS We could leave them a note, here?

ADIEL My auntie will be very heartbroken, she must be allowed to be so, in private.

CHRIS I'll come with.

ADIEL No.

CHRIS I don't think this is a good idea Adiel.

ADIEL I know this town. The shadows, the paths. I'll be fine.

(*CHRIS takes gun from where it was hidden.*)

CHRIS Take this.

ADIEL Chris–

CHRIS Just, in case. Please be careful.

(ADIEL leaves. With gun.)

PIKA You are leaving?

CHRIS Yeah. Do you think she'll be okay?

PIKA Why are you leaving? Is this a bad township?

CHRIS No. No, it's pretty great, nice township-, The men that you were running from, they've gone? You think?

PIKA Maybe. Are you running away too?

CHRIS Kind of.

PIKA You do something bad?

CHRIS No. Yes, maybe, I don't know, depends on what you decide is bad.

PIKA I did something bad. I did many things bad. I do not want more bad things, so I run away. They catch me, but then I run away again. If they catch me again, I will be like meerkat

(PIKA does an unexpected impression of a meerkat.)

PIKA *(cont.)* two big black holes at the side of the head.

CHRIS Oh.

PIKA You said you are going to the city.

CHRIS Yes.

PIKA Can I come with?

CHRIS With us? Huh, wow, I don't know, Pika—

PIKA If I stay in this township, or alone somewhere else, they will find me.
And then I become meerkat. Or maybe they kill me. Mostly they kill second time finds.

CHRIS Where's your home? Wouldn't it be better to go home?

PIKA I do not remember, I was taken when I was ten. Three years ago. Even if I do find my home again, my family will not want me because I am bad.

CHRIS Look, that's tough, but—

PIKA If I am with other people who are family, they cannot make advance.

CHRIS We aren't your family.

PIKA I can help with many things. I am trained for battle I can steal foods or climb over walls and trees I can defend you and your friend Adiel. I can do many many things. If you are worried about my bad soul, I promise you I will fix it.

CHRIS How do you fix a bad soul?
I mean, it's not about your soul, good or bad, it's just, we don't know each other, we can't just start living together. Maybe if you stay here, talk to my dad in the morning, he might help you out, but maybe not, our pastor won't be in such a soul fixing mood after his only child runs away.

PIKA Your dad is the pastor?

CHRIS Yup.

PIKA Why are you running away? All your problems can be solved here.

CHRIS Yeah, no. Look, I don't know how God or pastors do it, but I know how the real world does it.

PIKA Do what?

CHRIS Fix your soul.

PIKA The real world has powers to fix the soul?

CHRIS Sure.

PIKA Who is the real world?

CHRIS You know, countries, governments, people. In South Africa, they had a truth and reconciliation committee, they made it international, everyone could tap in on the hearings. It was super successful and nearly everyone's souls were fixed. The president won the Nobel Peace Prize for it.

PIKA How is it done? Do you know how to do it?

CHRIS Sure. It's not that hard. It's just some people listening to other people after a time of, bad things, and then, for the criminals—deciding whether or not to forgive, for the victims—deciding how to rehabilitate, restore, make better. They also decided who were the criminals who were the victims.

PIKA Who has the power to decide?

CHRIS The people.

PIKA There is just two of us.

CHRIS So I will be the people. And we can put your hearing on tape, and if we find more people, they can weigh in.

PIKA I don't understand why you have the power.

CHRIS Me neither, but it seemed to have worked for them, it's worth a shot? I mean, I am the pastor's kid so maybe I can gather forces from the real world and the God world.

PIKA I did many bad things.

CHRIS Here, put your right hand on this Bible.

PIKA More bad than breaking a piano.

CHRIS Come on, can't hurt to try?

*(He does.
CHRIS hits rec.)*

CHRIS *(cont.)* Do you, Pika the ex-soldier, solemnly swear to tell the whole truth and nothing but the truth so help you God.

PIKA Ok.

CHRIS It is January 1st, year 2000, we are gathered here today for the public hearing of ex-soldier Pika, who has applied for absolution from the bad things of his past. My name is Christina Jennifer Englewood and I will be representing the people. Pika, tell us what you have done.

PIKA Everything?

CHRIS Everything.

PIKA I cannot remember everything. It is very very long list.

CHRIS Then pick one of the worst.

PIKA I do not want to tell. You would not like me. You would not want to take me with you.

CHRIS Pika we're doing this so we might be able to.

PIKA Ok.

CHRIS Go on.

PIKA There was a man, he was a soldier of the army too. He was high ranks, he ate with the Commander but he was discovered, of helping girls escape the army. The man was tied up to a tree. The Commander called some names, and each soldier whose name was called must come and cut a piece of the man off with the machete while the man was still alive. When My name was called, there was not very much left to cut off so the Commander order me to cut off the head. I did. It was not easy because I was still new and did not have strength with machete. And then after I cut off the head the Commander order me to throw the head in the air and catch it three times, like this, like this, like this. And then kick it like a soccer ball like this. Then we sing the song, *Polo polo Yesu larahe, Yesu lara woko ki i bal ayee mi tiyu tic palala oo wa ito.* His head roll on to the road, that is where we left it.

CHRIS Wow.

PIKA Do you hate me now?

CHRIS No.

PIKA Do you think it worked?

CHRIS How do you feel?

PIKA Terrible.

CHRIS It is the decision of the people to grant absolution to ex-soldier Pika. May your soul find peace in this court's ruling. How about now?

PIKA A little better. Does that mean I can come with you?

Chris gets close to the mic on the tape recorder.

CHRIS Yes.

PIKA Yes?!!

CHRIS We have to talk to Adiel, but, she's the easy one.

(CHRIS *takes out cassette and presents it to PIKA.*)

PIKA Thank you. Thank you.

Hugs.

CHRIS Yay family!

CHRIS (*blows on her blower*) Yes!

(PIKA *grabs the blower and flings it away.*)

PIKA What is that!

CHRIS I'm sorry.

PIKA They will come here. Why did you do that! // They will come here.

CHRIS Sorry I wasn't- It's been a while, your people have probably left. Adiel went out on her own, there's no way she would've gone outside if she thought they were still –

(*Someone rattles the door.*)

CHRIS (*cont.*) That's Adi-

(PIKA *yanks her down.*
Finger to his lips, and creeps along towards the window, takes a peek.
He sees.)

CHRIS (*cont.*) Who—

(PIKA's *frightened eyes shut her up.*
They look for a place to hide,
More sounds, rattle door,
CHRIS *gestures up there!*
They climb up on to the roof.
Door is knocked in.
A soldier enters.)

SOLDIER Pika...

(SOLDIER *looks around.*)

SOLDIER (*cont.*) Pika...?

(SOLDIER *notices the bloody rags, water.*)

SOLDIER (*cont.*) Pika. You know there is no-where to go. Nobody else wants you. Come now. Let us go home. Nobody needs to know about our adventure tonight, it'll be our little secret, eh?

(*Hurried footsteps come closer.*)

CHRIS Adiel!

(PIKA *shushes her, holds her back, shakes his head.*
ADIEL *runs in through the broken doorway.*)

(She stops dead in her tracks when she sees the soldier.)

SOLDIER Hello.

ADIEL If you were looking for shelter, there was no need to break the door. The house of our Lord is always open.

SOLDIER This one was closed and locked.

(SOLDIER holds up the bloody rag.)

SOLDIER *(cont.)* I am looking for a lost soldier. I think he is here?

ADIEL I don't know. I hope you find what you are looking for.

(SOLDIER blocks her path.)

ADIEL *(cont.)* I was simply passing by and I saw the broken door.

SOLDIER I see.

ADIEL Good night.

SOLDIER Where are you going so late in the night?

ADIEL Just out for a walk.

SOLDIER With a travel bag?

ADIEL Yes.

SOLDIER Running away, like my lost soldier? Or even With my lost soldier?

ADIEL Just out for a walk.

SOLDIER I see. We are going to make this a game.

(SOLDIER takes out a weapon, probably a machete.)

CHRIS Fuck, no,

PIKA Shh!

SOLDIER I do not like games.

(PIKA starts to climb down the side of the wall - outside.)

CHRIS What are you doing!

(PIKA shushes her violently.)

SOLDIER I ask again. I am looking for a lost soldier.

ADIEL I think I am looking at one.

SOLDIER You think you are? How old are you?

ADIEL Twenty. Five.

SOLDIER Are you lying?

ADIEL No.

SOLDIER That is unfortunate. If you were younger I could take you with me. Now I have to kill you.

It's a joke.

(PIKA appears in the window or doorway, so that ADIEL spots him.

He gestures: roof.)

SOLDIER *(cont.)* I don't like to kill beautiful girls. If I can help it.

So last chance. Where is Pika?

(CHRIS starts climbing down the way PIKA went.

A slip, CHRIS makes a sound.

SOLDIER hears, turns towards the sound with his machete-)

ADIEL He left.

SOLDIER What?

ADIEL I saw him outside the window just a few moments ago.

(SOLDIER starts to leave)

(PIKA leaps into the shadows.)

ADIEL *(cont.)* Let him go. He is poisoned. Broken. He does not care about this country. I do. Let me come with you.

SOLDIER You want to come with me?

ADIEL I want to help, take care of you.

SOLDIER You want to take care of me?

ADIEL Yes.

(PIKA climbs back up to the roof.)

SOLDIER Whoever has taught you how to lie, has done a very good job.

ADIEL Or maybe I am not lying.

(ADIEL undoes his buckle.

PIKA re-appears to CHRIS.)

PIKA Psst. Psst!

(He has a rock. She helps.)

SOLDIER You are a strange little girl.

ADIEL Is it so strange to be attracted to a powerful man?

SOLDIER You are attracted to me?

ADIEL Yes.

(Her hands in his pants.

SOLDIER's hands slide where she has hidden the gun.)

ADIEL *(cont.)* No. Not yet. Down there.

SOLDIER Giving orders already–

(SOLDIER finds the gun on ADIEL.)

SOLDIER *(cont.)* What is–

Ha.

Good game soldier.

ADIEL It's not mine. I forgot it was even there // I promise you,

SOLDIER Were you going to shoot me?

ADIEL No no of course not –

(Sudden movement,

SOLDIER leaps towards ADIEL,

PIKA falls on top of the man with the rock aimed for his head.)

PIKA AAAAAAAAAH!

(Bam.)

SOLDIER Wha- What is, you-

(PIKA bashes in the skull of the soldier, repeatedly.
Bambam bambam bambambambam –
Stands back.
Is he dead?

Absolute stillness.

CHRIS is the first to move on the roof.
ADIEL and PIKA start.)

CHRIS It's me, just me. Chris.

ADIEL Chris.

CHRIS I'm so sorry. I'm so sorry. Imsosorrys-
osorry -

ADIEL I thought you were, // I didn't know,

CHRIS I wanted to but // I couldn't,

ADIEL Pika?

PIKA I am okay.

ADIEL I thought you were, I didn't know
what // you were, where,

CHRIS You were so brave, so brave, I'm so //
sorry Adiel I didn't know what to, Pika, and

(CHRIS embraces ADIEL.)

ADIEL It's okay, I understand. Everything's alright, it's alright. Shh…

(CHRIS kisses ADIEL like life and death.)

PIKA What are you doing.

ADIEL Pika.

PIKA What were you, you were, you were doing like a man and his wife.

CHRIS She Is my wife.

ADIEL Chris don't-

PIKA That is a sin and abomination and evil in
the sight of God. God has saved your life
tonight, God has saved three of our lives tonight and in his house you will make sin,
dirty in sin -

ADIEL Pika,

PIKA Do not touch me you are a filthy sinner
dirty sinner abomination.

(PIKA grabs a gun.)

ADIEL Pika that is not what God wants -

(Bang.)

PIKA You do not know what God wants.

(ADIEL falls.)

CHRIS No.
No no no no no.
What did you do. What is, What was-
What's going on I don't,
Adiel look at me, hey, look, up here, come
on Adiel.
Adiel! Adiel please look at me please please
look at me Adiel–

(PIKA gets closer to ADIEL.)

CHRIS *(cont.)* Don't you fucking dare.

(CHRIS gets gun.)

PIKA I can help, let me—

(Bang. She missed.)

PIKA *(cont.)* Chris. Please I -

(Bang. She missed.
Bang bang bang Bang bang bang Bang bang bang
Bang bang bang.
Pika has run out during the bangs.

CHRIS still shoots, without ammo.

Bang bang bang click click click click.

CHRIS alone with ADIEL in the church.

PIKA alone with himself, somewhere else.)

PIKA *(cont.)* **Polo polo Yesu larahe**
Yesu lara woko ki i bal ayee mi tiyu tic
palala oo wa ito[3]
Polo polo Yesu larahe
Yesu lara woko ki i bal ayee mi tiyu tic
palala oo wa ito
Polo polo Yesu larahe
Yesu lara woko ki i bal ayee mi tiyu tic
palala oo wa ito

A very angry sad battle cry.
Whose?

★

PART II

The ensemble minus CHRIS
A single tentative voice, gradually grows into more sound, more joy

ALL but CHRIS **Polo polo Yesu larahe**
Yesu lara woko ki i bal ayee mi tiyu tic palala oo wa ito
Polo polo Yesu larahe

Yesu lara woko ki i bal ayee mi tiyu tic palala oo wa ito
Polo polo Yesu larahe
Yesu lara woko ki i bal ayee mi tiyu tic palala oo wa ito

Day.
The church is the same church, only cleaned up, moderned up church.
The church is beautiful; a lot of it has changed, but it somehow feels the same.
The hole in the roof is now replaced with a skylight.
The church is decorated with wild flowers
And somewhere, a tea set. The tea in the pot has gone cold.

PAUL "Everybody knows, in this story, the traveler is met with some ill fate. He is beaten, robbed, and then left half dead along the road. He is lying in the ditch bleeding to his death. Not long before first the priest, somebody like me, he passes by, sees the man in pain! Will he save him? No. He takes off. Second the Levite, somebody like our deacon Abuu, he passes by and sees the man in pain! Will he save him? No, he is going off as well. Third the Samaritan, somebody like the political criminal, somebody that we all hate all together, somebody we believe is a bad man, he passes by. And boom, he of course, helps the dying traveler.

And we all think about this little story, that it is a teaching about kindness.

About moral and ethical responsibility. About being nice. But, really? Is Jesus spending all this creative energy to tell us to be nice? Come on now, we know, we know we must be nice. Not just those of faith, but everybody knows this, if you are a person, you know that it is a good thing to try and be nice to another person, especially if that person is naked and bleeding at the side of the road.

To understand what Jesus is really talking about, we must understand that this story is an answer to a question asked by some scholar in the crowd. The scholar asks the question, who is this "neighbor" that we must love. In fact, what is love?

Is love a feeling? A sensual pull toward one certain human being?

A little chemical released into our bodies that drains the brain of oxygen, and pumps the heart like the phone on vibration, so that all of your blood flows, races through all the veins in your body, makes you think about that person only, is that love? If that is love, I do not know if my wife will appreciate Jesus asking me to love all my neighbors so much."

(He laughs at his joke.
RUTH has entered at some point.)

PAUL *(cont.)* That is a good joke. Let me write this one down.

RUTH I don't get the joke.

PAUL Ruth!

RUTH Why am I in your sermon as a joke?

PAUL What happened? Do you know what time it is?

RUTH Ai yai, you know, I met somebody on the street, pastor –

PAUL You met somebody on the street is why you are so late for our date?

RUTH A date? African husbands do not date their African wives.

PAUL This African husband does. Who did you meet?

RUTH What is this! Tea? You made tea! And flowers. This man has stolen all the flowers of Africa to put them in our church.

PAUL The aunties of the congregation brought them over for our celebration. I just bunched them artfully and placed them around the church. For our tea.

RUTH You are very proud of your tea.

PAUL And my flowers.

RUTH So many flowers.

PAUL I was inspired.

RUTH Yes?

PAUL Yes, by a beautiful lady with the regretful habit of forgetting the time on her wedding anniversary.

RUTH It is only our second one. I have to do it more than three times for it to be a habit.

PAUL So next year it will be a habit.

RUTH Ah, already you are giving up on me?

PAUL Never. Pastor is not allowed to give up on members of his church. Not even his wife.

Come. Sit. Let us have some very old very lukewarm tea.

(They sit. He pours the tea in each cup.)

RUTH Thank you.

PAUL Okay so you sit there, and I will–

RUTH Where are you going?

PAUL I am going to give you my wedding anniversary gift.

RUTH What? Pastor, we agreed we are not giving gifts this year.

PAUL I know, but I had a very good idea for a gift. Here is your Bible.

(He goes to the pulpit.)

PAUL *(cont.)* Now let us turn to the Gospel of Luke chapter ten verses twenty-five to thirty seven.

RUTH Pastor what are you doing?

PAUL I am giving you a sermon.

RUTH Your anniversary gift is a sermon?

PAUL Yes.

RUTH Your very good idea of a gift is to make me sit still and listen to your practicing your sermon.

PAUL No. I am delivering the sermon. For you. And then, tomorrow morning, I shall do a re-run for the rest of the congregation so you can show off your very romantic pastor husband.

RUTH Is this the sermon where I am a joke?

PAUL You are not a joke, you are referred to as a person who-, ag it is funny in context.

RUTH And this funny romantic sermon, is how long?

PAUL I don't know, about thirty, forty, or fifty minutes?

RUTH Fifty minutes?!

PAUL I am telling you Ruth, when God gave me the idea for the sermon I knew in my heart it is a love letter directly to you. By the time I am done you will not remember how long it was, you will be so moved that you will ask me to marry you again or leave me to be a nun for Jesus, one of the two.

RUTH Every sermon you prepare makes me want to leave you for Jesus Pastor, as you practice on me, every Saturday. But I have this one problem, you see, I do not want your beautiful sermon to be interrupted, and, this person that I met on the street, he is a member of this church and so I invited him to our tea.

PAUL Oh. Why?

RUTH Because he is leaving this township to-night and so I said he must come to the church to receive your blessing before he goes.

PAUL On our anniversary day? Who is this?

RUTH Remember you do not give up on any member of the church.

PAUL Who is this.

RUTH I met Francis

PAUL Francis.

RUTH You do not give up on any // member-

PAUL No.

RUTH You // just said so yourself

PAUL Francis? Ruth you cannot be serious, Francis is no member of this church?

RUTH He was one of the first people of this township to call you pastor, how is he not a member of your church?

PAUL He is leaving? That is a good idea.

RUTH Good idea? He is being chased out of his own hometown. Thin as a stick, bruises everywhere and he has bandages on his wrists,

PAUL He has what? Ag the stupidness of this boy.

RUTH I gave him a hug and he just started crying. For a whole hour he just held my hand and cried. Pastor we must help him. He needs your guidance.

PAUL I gave my guidance. He rejected it.

RUTH He does not follow your orders one time and we must all abandon the man?

PAUL God's orders, not mine-

RUTH We are His church not His military.

PAUL Church, military, it does not matter, if we let that boy in here it will break this community. If I say yes to him, I am saying no to everybody else, Ruth. Did you see last month during the whole situation, our attendance was cut in half?

RUTH If a man has hundred sheep and one of them wanders away, won't he leave the ninety-nine others on the hills and go out to search for the one that is lost?[4]

PAUL In this township the ninety-nine others are lost too. We have only just begun to find them. I cannot risk the souls of this whole church for one stupid boy.

RUTH Then nobody else needs to know,

PAUL It's not // about,

RUTH just let us show him God has not forgotten him. Paul please. He said he didn't want to come unless he knew you said yes. I said I will text him.

PAUL Ruth,

RUTH I already texted him.

PAUL Ai yai.

RUTH This is my anniversary wish. And now I owe you two gifts. Anything you want.

PAUL My wife is the pastor. I am just the pretty man with the deep loud voice.
Okay.

RUTH Okay?!

PAUL I will talk some sense into him and then make you fall in love with me again with my super sermon.

RUTH I am always falling in love with you again.

PAUL Ah you just say that because you got your way.

(*RUTH gives him an awesome hug.*)

RUTH Paul. I promise you. To this boy you are the miracle man from God. Thank you.

PAUL Ha. I had my fair share of miracle people from God. Happy anniversary.

(*CHRIS is lingering at the door.*)

RUTH Oh hello!

CHRIS Sorry. I'm-

(*CHRIS starts to leave.*)

RUTH No, no please stay.

CHRIS No I was just,

PAUL Hello!

CHRIS Hi.

PAUL Are you needing assistance?

CHRIS Excuse me?

PAUL You are looking like you are lost. What are you looking for?

CHRIS Do you have to be looking for something to be lost?

PAUL Generally yes, I think so.

RUTH I have seen you before, yes?

CHRIS Oh. I don't-

RUTH You were here every day this week, at our church.

PAUL Every day? I did not know! Hello I am the pastor of this church.

CHRIS I'm not a creepy person, I was just looking. Around.

RUTH I did not think you were a creepy person. I thought what is this beautiful *mzungu* lady doing here, and I was so very curious but you never came inside so I left you alone.

CHRIS Thank you.

PAUL Are you alright?

CHRIS Hm?

PAUL You are standing at the door like a child who has done something naughty, would you like to come inside?

CHRIS Um, yeah. Sure.

(*CHRIS takes one step in.*)

RUTH Welcome to our church.

CHRIS *Apwoyo matek.*

RUTH You are very welcome!

PAUL That is very good!

CHRIS Ha, thanks. I know two things. Thank you and *Jal – le.*

RUTH That is very very good!

PAUL Those two phrases will take you far in this country.

CHRIS That has been my experience.

RUTH I am the pastor's wife, Ruth.

PAUL And I am the pastor's wife's husband, Paul.

CHRIS Christina. Hi.

PAUL So what bring you to our township? Are you working with a NGO?

CHRIS No I'm just visiting for a few days. I grew up here.

RUTH Are you sure![5]

CHRIS Long ago, as a kid.

PAUL You were here as a child?

CHRIS My parents were, missionaries.

RUTH Are you sure!? It was a very difficult time for our country.

CHRIS I think we left before it got really bad. But this was our church. Built it, brick for brick.

RUTH What? This was your church? That is fantastic! Pastor this was her church!

PAUL Yes! Wonderful wonderful.

CHRIS I wondered if it would still be here, wasn't sure−

RUTH We are all still here. You built a very strong church.

CHRIS The building, at least.

RUTH Ha! I must ask you-, There is this one, a little picture on the corner.

CHRIS Little picture?

RUTH Yes yes it is like a small banana with three circles inside, Please, come come!

(*They find a little heart engraved into the corner stone.*)

CHRIS That's, we did it. Three smiley faces, and our initials at the bottom of each face – me, my mom, my dad. And then I drew a heart around the three. I was eight, so it's a bit, not a heart but.
The first brick we laid.

RUTH Ag! I made up so many stories about what this one could be!

CHRIS My dad had a thing about documenting.
He would've loved to see this.
He should've seen this.
It might've, helped.

RUTH Our doors are always open whenever he would like to visit.

CHRIS Oh he can't. He's dead. Last month. He died.

RUTH Are you alright?

CHRIS No, I'm [fine]

(RUTH gives her a very awesome hug.
CHRIS steps away.)

CHRIS *(cont.)* Oh, no. Please I don't,
We weren't that close, barely talked for like ten years, strangers, almost, really.
Actually, sorry, I'm just here to, it's a weird-, actually, what I need to ask you –

RUTH Please, how can we help?

CHRIS I have my dad, his ashes, he left it in his will that we bury him here,

PAUL Here. Here at our church?

CHRIS It's weird.

RUTH Yes it is a little bit strange. That you would bury your dead in our church.

CHRIS It's not like a coffin, he's in a tree seed.
So it would be a seed grave. Not really a grave grave.
He was a weird guy
and he wanted to be a tree at this church.

RUTH A tree.

CHRIS This grows into a tree. Mahogany.

RUTH Haw.

CHRIS I think he thought, he might finally find some peace, if he came back.
And I thought hey, okay I'll fly eight thousand miles to plant him in a ditch in Africa and maybe we'll have some kind of cozy posthumous father daughter moment closure all that kind of-
I'm just the proxy. You don't have to say yes.

RUTH Of course we say yes

PAUL Ah,

RUTH It is a tree! I think that will be beautiful in the garden.

PAUL Ruth we do not have a garden.

RUTH So the first pastor of this church will be the very first resident of our new garden.

PAUL I do not know if our African soil will be kind to your tree, but yes it would be an honor.

CHRIS Oh god, Thank you.

RUTH When do you want a burial? Ceremony?

CHRIS Oh! No no. We did the funeral, everything, it's fine

PAUL So, you want for us to plant the box with your father in it?

CHRIS Unless you want me to dig the hole, I could dig the hole,

RUTH Don't worry about that one. You must be so tired. Here, sit down. Would you like some tea?

PAUL Ruth didn't you say we had another guest soon.

RUTH Oh he will be a few minutes. We can have some tea and a chat with Christina. She has come such a long way. I will bring more cups. And we should brew more tea.

CHRIS Actually I'm okay, I just wanted to –

RUTH We will take care of you, it is no worry.
The house is just over there. But of course you know that!

(RUTH leaves.
Quiet.)

CHRIS Thank you, for the *(gestures to the tree seed)*

PAUL Of course. How did he pass?

CHRIS Fatigue. Didn't know people could die of fatigue. He just, got tired of living.

PAUL He must have loved this church very much.

CHRIS He did.
What happened to your [gesture: ear]

PAUL It went missing.

CHRIS Oh.

PAUL Every other person in this country has something or other missing from their face.

CHRIS Of course. I'm sorry. I didn't mean to pry. Sorry.

PAUL I think I will go help my wife with the tea. Sometimes she forgets to turn the stove off et cetera.

(PAUL leaves.
CHRIS is alone.
The space. The Skylight. The Space.)

RUTH I had no idea today would turn into such a party!

(RUTH and PAUL enter.)

PAUL Yes, unfortunately we have a guest coming, in a few minutes.

RUTH Pastor what is that.

CHRIS Oh that's fine, I don't have to stay –

RUTH Stay! Stay! Don't mind our pastor, Chris. He likes to joke. It is only funny in context. Come sit down, both of you, we are floating around like dust clumps. Chris tell me everything, / there are so many rumors of this church –

CHRIS I don't remember much, rumors?

RUTH Because of these rumors nobody would come! For the first three months our entire congregation was two people. And I was one of the two people.

PAUL Ruth,

RUTH And then Pastor visited every single home in this township. He went door to door, and still these people would not come. What were they saying, Pastor, somebody died in the church, on the day of the // millennium, killed herself or got herself killed –

PAUL The *Acholi* are superstitious people, they always are saying something happened –

RUTH Everybody has a different version of the story, ai yai how did your father deal with these people, eh?

CHRIS I, don't know. He's dead so. How did you guys end up here?

RUTH This is the question I ask every day of myself! I am originally from the city but I was seduced by this terrible man. I had this big idea that I would help this country. Oh yes, I will march myself to the nearest trauma center I would educate and help all these broken minds from their war troubles –

PAUL Let us stop boring our visitor // with the history, and –

RUTH Of course I very quickly understood I was a stupid girl with more fears then skills. I was so ready to quit and run away until this one came along. After all he has been through, he tries to teach me about Jesus, and get me to go to church with him, sing Jesus songs, but the big trap was this one, Chris, he tells a story to me.

PAUL Do you want to see more of the church Christina.

RUTH After I tell my homerun story. When we were getting serious, and I am weighing the good things and bad things about this man – Chris, you know the process I am talking about.

CHRIS Of course.

RUTH So I am thinking, mmm he's a little bit small, he is a little bit nerd, he is little bit no money and so on,

PAUL Ruth do we have any ice, I am thirsty for some ice water –

RUTH Yes, in the kitchen. Anyway so I am on the seesaw a little bit and he knows this so he takes me to a beautiful lake, put me on a boat like in the American movies yes? And he tells me this story.

PAUL Ruth, don't-

RUTH Na uh uh! Girl talk time. If you are embarrassed cover your ears while I show off my romantic pastor huband, eh?

Okay, so once upon a time there is this man, who loved his wife so so much,

and one day the wife really really wanted a piano.

But the man, he was a poor man, so he could not buy a piano. So he collects scraps of cardboard from the market, and he makes a small piano, of the discarded boxes. And then he gives it to his wife. The wife is very very disappointed. So much that she will tear up the piano that he took so very long to make just for her. The wife leaves the house and he thought ah, there she goes, she will find a man who can give her a real piano. But the man cannot forget her. He cannot stop himself from fixing the broken piano. And every day he is playing this piano with his voice, "doon doon doon doon doon doon doon doon," praying for her return.

Finally the wife returns, very guilty. But to her great surprise she finds at the window, the piano, it is fixed. She cries and says I'm sorry, but he says, "my love it is okay. I fixed it."

"Ruth," this man says to me now, "We will break many things but I promise you, I will always always find a way to build it again, if only you can be brave enough to stay." Boom, Curtain fall, end of story thank you for playing ladies, Pika belongs to me.

CHRIS I thought your name was Paul.

RUTH It is. But I call him Pika, it is his African name.

PAUL Ruth could you give us a moment alone?

RUTH Alone?

PAUL Please.

RUTH Pastor, stop being so peculiar.

PAUL Just, please, could you

RUTH Chris, my husband is so strange sometimes, we will ignore Pika's –

PAUL My name is not Pika pleasepleasepleasepleaseplease will you Leave.

RUTH …

PAUL Please.

RUTH I-

PAUL Could you.

(RUTH leaves.
Silence.)

CHRIS You look good.

PAUL Thank you. You too.

(Silence.)

CHRIS I like what you did. With the church. The skylight.

PAUL Mostly it was Ruth.

CHRIS She's lovely.

(Silence.)

PAUL Are you, married?

CHRIS No.

PAUL It is different in America, the time of marriage I think. Here we like to marry our woman earlier.

CHRIS Is that a joke?

(Silence.)

PAUL What do you want. Why are you here?

CHRIS My dad died. He wanted,

PAUL That is why you are here? The only reason to come all the way-

CHRIS I don't have to explain anything, to you, of all people,

PAUL If you have returned to revenge–

CHRIS Revenge?

PAUL If you have returned so to to ruin // this church

CHRIS Why would I want to ruin-

PAUL -it won't work I have already told them everything.

CHRIS Wow okay well That's bullshit.

PAUL I have told them Everything.

CHRIS Everything?

PAUL Everything they need to know.

CHRIS Your wife doesn't know very much.

PAUL I have experienced many atrocities, they do not need to hear -

CHRIS About who died? On the millennium, emptying this church for the past decade and half?

PAUL You left. You and your people left and I came back.

You do not know how difficult for me it was to come back // to face this empty church

CHRIS So why? Why? Why did you?

PAUL I am good for this community. They // see hope,

CHRIS It's sick! What you, the hole, up there, is it

PAUL We needed // more light

CHRIS - some kind of shrine? Some kind of- More Light?

PAUL It is just a window on a roof–

CHRIS No it is not.

PAUL I am trying to fix what is broken, the church, this township,
You break something, it is okay if you try to fix it, you said that to me, we can fix everything, with God's help,

CHRIS No you can't. No amount of windows on a roof can fix what you broke.

PAUL But I will keep trying, we must keep trying, like your father did for you -

CHRIS Some guy duck-taped some paper together to shut his daughter up and then some years later he died, it's not some grand metaphor to build your new life on, forgetting the people you've fucked over–

PAUL Forget? For-, Every night, hundred bleeding bodies, in my dreams // they come together

CHRIS Please I don't need your dreams in my -

PAUL Yours, and Adiel's

CHRIS Stop don't say her name please you // don't get to -

PAUL That is my night every night, Forget? I cannot forget. Do not talk of things you do not know, Chris, // you do not know my troubles, every night -

CHRIS I think I can talk about whatever the fuck I want why are you here at my church?

PAUL Not your church my church it is my church You left!
God's church. It's God's church and God has forgiven me, that is the only way I got better Not farms not people, but Grace, The only way how I am now a good man.

CHRIS Well Good for God but you did not kill God You killed people and they can't forgive you because they are dead and Dead Can't Forgive.

PAUL I came to this church hoping, at first, I did not know if she had lived,

CHRIS She didn't.

(Silence.)

PAUL Perhaps it was the wrong choice, sick, as you say.
But I had to come back, make it good again, this is where, somebody was happy about me
you were happy about me even when you knew how bad I was

CHRIS Happy? Were you there? Pika you are the only human on this earth I have aimed and shot // a loaded weapon

PAUL You missed. Every shot. A whole round of bullets at point blank and every bullet missed.

CHRIS Because I was sixteen and didn't know how to shoot a gun.

PAUL You missed because you did not want to kill me.

CHRIS I Do want to. Did, want to.

PAUL You said yes to me.

CHRIS What?

(PAUL leaves, maybe to the office.)

PAUL You said family, you were happy so happy, you tried to help, remember, you wanted so much for my soul

CHRIS What are you // talking about?

(He returns, tape recorder, from somewhere-)

CHRIS *(cont.)* I never, What is that. What are you, why do you have that, this is, // that's not yours, It's not yours

PAUL You were the first person to say yes to me. You said absolution,

CHRIS No.

PAUL - you said yes.

CHRIS Okay, fine I said yes, and then you killed the one person that

PAUL I have killed more than one people, you already knew this. How is it different than what you already said yes to? You are coming here to my church, with your father's ashes, because you are sad, // hurt, struggling -

CHRIS Back the fuck off about my father

PAUL Struggling to bury what is dead, trying to make better what is hurt, we are doing the same thing -

CHRIS We are not doing the same thing -

PAUL Yes we are. But you, you are lost in your hurt, you treasure your hurt like it is the castle that makes you special. I am sorry for your suffering but I cannot let my people pay the price for your brokenness. Fight your

battles on your own soil and let me fight mine here.

(Silence.)

CHRIS I just want to plant my dead dad and leave, okay? I've wasted my entire adult life trying to leave, this church. I just want to leave.

PAUL So. Leave.

*(Silence.
Francis enters.)*

FRANCIS Excuse me - Hello I am looking for the pastor, do you know where he is?

CHRIS -
He's -

FRANCIS Wait I've seen you before?

CHRIS What?

PAUL Francis-

FRANCIS Pastor! This is, oh what is your name, Sarah. Melissa.

PAUL Now // is not a good

FRANCIS Jennifer?

CHRIS Chris.

FRANCIS Like the Kardashian?

CHRIS Um. No. Like short for Christina.

FRANCIS Christina! Of course! You were very close with my cousin, Adiel-

PAUL Francis you // must leave us

CHRIS Francis.

FRANCIS You have not changed at all how are you // how is your family!

(FRANCIS gives her an awesome hug.)

PAUL Are you deaf boy, I said Go!

FRANCIS Pastor.

RUTH Francis, come.

PAUL Ruth.

RUTH Let us make ourselves some tea in the house

FRANCIS But I thought, Ruth your message, you said -

RUTH Come, we talk more inside the // house while we wait -

FRANCIS But you did not invite me? Pastor? You do not want me here?

PAUL What do you want me to say? You shout out your deeds all around the town, // deliberately go against my advice

FRANCIS No Paul I did not tell anyone, // nobody was supposed to know.

PAUL Nobody was supposed to know? God knows everything.

FRANCIS I was not talking about God,

PAUL Why are we not talking about God? Talk about God. Because it is Him you are hurting,

FRANCIS I am sorry that it is hurting God, hurting so many people that I love,

PAUL You are not sorry.

FRANCIS What do you want me to do? I cannot help who I am.

PAUL Then I cannot help your homo ways heading to hell, but I will not have that in my church.

CHRIS You can't be serious.

PAUL Christina, this is not your battle, stay out.

CHRIS Not my- are you fucking kidding me?

RUTH Christina, please, I think you must / come back later.

PAUL Francis and I must get through this together, you have no place –

CHRIS You're doing to him what you did to me.

PAUL //That is different.

CHRIS I think I have a place.
How is it different?

PAUL I am different. I cannot let my personal guilt blind my judgment in the leadership of this // church, I –

CHRIS You killed my wife.

Silence.

CHRIS *(cont.)* We saved your life and you killed her because I kissed my fucking wife.

RUTH What?

FRANCIS Wife? Paul? What // is this one. Ruth?

CHRIS This is not that different, Pika.

PAUL // My name is not Pika!

CHRIS Nothing's changed, you're still a murderer and I am still stuck in that same shithole you've put me in.

PAUL You put yourself there.

RUTH Pastor what is she // talking about

PAUL All the sins you have committed against the Lord,

CHRIS My Sins?

PAUL your decadence,

CHRIS What is my sin, Pika. Patching up your face after you put a gun to my head? Letting you run after you shot a bullet into Adiel–

PAUL I do not cling // to my past with your enthusiasm

FRANCIS Adiel?

RUTH Who is // Adiel?

FRANCIS No, Adiel died here. She shot herself after killing a soldier, Paul and Ruth came only last year–

CHRIS What do you say every Sunday Pika, to This Community, Thou shalt not lie? Thou shalt not kill? Thou shalt not kill a person, return to the scene of the crime fourteen years later and damn their cousin to hell?

FRANCIS You were here?

CHRIS And when you're looking out at these people who trust you and love you and willingly lap up the bullcrap you're feeding them, do you feel Any Guilt? Shame?
or has the Grace of God taken care of that too.

RUTH Pika. What are these people saying?

PAUL Ruth please, take Francis, away, // Chris and I must

FRANCIS You were the soldier.

CHRIS Chris and I must what? What more // do you want with me?

RUTH Come Francis we will talk to pastor after, // I promise, Francis

FRANCIS You killed her. We all thought, but it was you? This whole time it was you?

PAUL I am not perfect, I do not know everything, but every sin is washed clean if –

CHRIS What if I took a gun and blew out your wife's guts, think we could // clean that up too?

PAUL Shut up about // my wife! Shut up!

RUTH Okay Pika // look to me

CHRIS If I murdered your wife?

PAUL That is in the past

RUTH It is //alright, I am here, see? Pika look to me.

PAUL Stop talking about the past

CHRIS If it's in the past why are you here.

PAUL I am trying to fix it!

CHRIS You are kicking this man out onto the streets, to fix what you did to his cousin?

FRANCIS How are you a pastor?

RUTH Francis this is enough –

FRANCIS How is a man like you a pastor at my church?

PAUL I am no longer your pastor, man! I am no longer your- Get out. Get //out get

RUTH Paul let us // go, we shall go for a walk, a nice

PAUL I am no longer your pastor this is no longer your church–

FRANCIS And somehow you have the power to tell me, I am going to hell?

PAUL I do not care where you go get out Get Out

FRANCIS I trusted you. I gave you my secret. But you hated me.

RUTH Francis. Leave.

FRANCIS You hated me before you even knew me.

RUTH Get out.

(*FRANCIS smashes a window.*)

RUTH (*cont.*) What are you doing!

PAUL Francis.

FRANCIS No.

(*FRANCIS picks up a piece of glass.*)

FRANCIS (*cont.*) I am not leaving. You want to save my church from my dirty dirty sins this is how you will do it.

(*FRANCIS extends the glass towards PAUL.*)

PAUL What are you doing man.

FRANCIS Do it.

RUTH Francis, stop this stupidness!

(*FRANCIS swings his weapon around to RUTH.*)

FRANCIS Shut up stay // there.

PAUL Ruth stay back!

FRANCIS You know how to do it. Do it. I'm not the first homo you killed in this church. You can't make me leave my home, everything I know and not pay for it, you can't kick me out turn your eyes and wait for somebody else to bash my head in, I am not going to wait for that, you do it. Do It.
Okay I'll do it. You watch.

(*FRANCIS presses the glass to his own throat.*)

RUTH Francis!

CHRIS Francis, there are better ways to fight this.

PAUL This is not what God wants.

FRANCIS I do not want your God anymore.

PAUL You know that is not true.

FRANCIS Do not tell me what I know. You are a liar. You are a joke.

(*He presses.*)

RUTH Francis, look to me.

FRANCIS This church is a joke.

RUTH I was wrong
I was wrong to ask you to leave.
Pastor is wrong to ask you to leave.
No more. We will do this to you no more.

FRANCIS No more.

RUTH I promise you.
We will work this problem out together.

Give that to pastor.
Please, Francis.
Death is so final.
Right? You know this.

(*A breath.*
FRANCIS gives the bloody glass piece to PAUL.
RUTH hits him.
Wherever she can however she can.
slap slap slap—)

RUTH (*cont.*) Idiot! Stupid stupid boy, you stupid boy, don't you ever do that again, don't you ever even think about doing something like that again! Ever again / Do you understand? Stupid. Stupid stupid boy, I will kill you if you do that again, understand? Stupid idiot stupid

CHRIS Hey hey, it's okay. It's okay, we're good, he's okay we're fine. Calm down, breathe, okay? Come, just take it easy. Everything's alright, it's alright. Shh…

(*RUTH hugs on CHRIS tightly,*
a replica of sixteen-year-old CHRIS's embrace
with ADIEL 14 years ago.)

PAUL Get away from my wife!

CHRIS –

RUTH –

PAUL Get away from my wife Get away from my wife

(*PAUL bolts towards them and shoves CHRIS away viciously.*)

PAUL (*cont.*) Get away from my wife

(*Shove Shove.*)

PAUL (*cont.*) I said get away from my wife!

(*PAUL grabs CHRIS, glass piece still in hand.*)

RUTH Pika No!

(*RUTH gets in between PAUL and CHRIS.*)

RUTH (*cont.*) No.

(*He stops.*
No one moves.
PAUL steps back, glass piece still in hand.)

PAUL (*cont.*) Everybody knows.
Everybody knows…

RUTH Paul.

(*like a memory exercise*)

PAUL Everybody knows, in this story, the traveler is met with some ill fate. First the priest sees the man in pain will he save him No.

Second the Levite sees the man in pain will he save him No. Third the Samaritan, somebody that we all hate, somebody we believe is a bad man,
who is the bad man?
Start again. Everybody knows in this story, the soldier is met with some ill fate. First the No, not a soldier, a traveler, he is a traveler the man the Traveler is beaten, bled, and then left alone by the tree tied to the tree there is no tree
Haha, pastor's brain is so sleepy today.

RUTH Paul look to me.

(RUTH steps towards him but PAUL moves away.)

PAUL Everybody knows! There is no tree.
First
The Priest, the pastor, I am a pastor now. Everybody knows,
He passes by, sees the man in pain! Will he save him? How can he save him?
He is dead
He is not dead!
He is lying on the, where is he lying. Why is he lying.
LOVE.
Drains the oxygen, pumps the heart, the blood flows, races through
spills on to her clothes on to this floor on to no, LOVE. Love, is patient love is kind it does not,
Love is love is
The blood
of the tree
a gift.
to one who does not deserve.

(PAUL sees CHRIS.)

PAUL *(cont.)* Do you hate me now?

(PAUL places the glass piece in her hands.)

You said yes You said You said You will fix You are a joke. This church is a joke. Everything is still broken and You

RUTH Paul. Come. Please.

(PAUL leaves the church.

Echo of Rain Falling
Into…
Very Early Morning.
The sun is not yet up.

RUTH in the middle of the church.

Perhaps where we first found ADIEL.)

(Perhaps she is praying.
Perhaps she was listening to the tape recorder,
Either way, that is what she holds in her hand,
like a bible or a rosary)

(CHRIS comes to the doorway, her carry-on in tow.)

CHRIS Hi.
RUTH Christina.
CHRIS How are you?
RUTH –
CHRIS Is Paul,
RUTH He has not returned yet.
CHRIS Oh.
RUTH He will return.
CHRIS I'm sorry.
RUTH What can I do for you?
CHRIS I just wanted to leave this with –
RUTH I am very sorry Christina but I do not think we must do that for you. You must bury your dead where it affects You.
CHRIS Oh, no, that wasn't what-, I agree. It would be weird to know your dad is growing into a tree in someone else's backyard.
RUTH I am sorry we cannot help.
CHRIS No don't be. He can find peace in my backyard. When I have one. We'll be fine.
That's not why I'm here,

(A cardboard piano.)

CHRIS *(cont.)* Couldn't sleep, so I just, I'm not so good with crafts, but.
I'll just leave it here, gotta head out, to catch the bus, Francis is waiting at the,
RUTH Francis?
CHRIS Um, yeah. It's, we're on the same bus and, it'd be nice to catch up. So.

(CHRIS turns to leave)

RUTH He listened to this one. So much. He listened to it every month sometimes every day
I never did ask.
It is up to the wife to keep the secrets that our husbands try to keep from us.
A secret flies out to me, and I think must catch it,
I must be a part of his ribcages and hold them together.
I did not know my silence was suffocating him also.
He is not a bad man, Chris.

He is trying so very hard to be good.

CHRIS He's lucky to have that. You.

RUTH I am lucky to have him.

I wish you both safe travels.

CHRIS Thank you.

Happy Anniversary.

(CHRIS leaves.

RUTH alone, in church.

RUTH turns tape over.

Rewind.

Hits play.)

TAPE This is the wedding of Christina Jennifer Englewood and Adiel Nakalinzi. January 1ˢᵗ, Year 2000. I, Chris Blank, take thee, Adiel Nakalinzi, to be my wife, ugh, that's such dumb word.

To be my wife…

(Tape continues under
as the four come together in hymn:)

Just as I am, without one plea,
But that Thy blood was shed for me,
And that Thou bidst me come to Thee,
O Lamb of God, I come, I come

Just as I am, though tossed about
With many a conflict, many a doubt,-
Fightings and fears within, without,
O Lamb of God, I come, I come

Just as I am, of that free love
The breadth, length depth, and height
** to prove,**
Here for a season, then above,
O Lamb of God, I come,

TAPE With this ring I thee wed, with my body I thee worship, and with all my worldly goods I thee endow: //In the name of //In the name of the Father, and of the Son, and of the Holy Ghost. Amen. //Amen.

Notes

1. "Hymn 313," Words by Charlotte Elliott, Music by William B. Bradbury.
2. "Unchained Melody" by Righteous Brothers
3. Heaven Heaven Jesus save us, Jesus saved us from sinning I have accepted to work with you till death
4. Excerpt from Matthew 18:12 (NLT)
5. This phrase is used interchangeably with "Really!" in the Ugandan dialect.

Chitra Banerjee Divakaruni

Biography

Chitra Banerjee Divakaruni is an award-winning and best-selling author, poet, activist and teacher of writing. Her work has been published in over 50 magazines, including *The Atlantic Monthly* and *The New Yorker*, and her writing has been included in over 50 anthologies, including The Best American Short Stories, the O. Henry Prize Stories and the Pushcart Prize Anthology. Her books have been translated into 29 languages, including Dutch, Hebrew, Bengali, Russian and Japanese, and many of them have been used for campus-wide and city-wide reads. Several of her works have been made into films and plays. She lives in  Houston with her husband Murthy and has two sons, Anand and Abhay, who are in college. She loves to connect with readers on her Facebook page.

Born in Kolkata, India, she came to the United States for her graduate studies, receiving a Master's degree in English from Wright State University in Dayton, Ohio, and a PhD from the University of California, Berkeley.

Divakaruni teaches in the nationally ranked Creative Writing program at the University of Houston, where she is the Betty and Gene McDavid Professor of Creative Writing. She serves on the Advisory board of Maitri in the San Francisco Bay Area and Daya in Houston. Both are organizations that help South Asian or South Asian American women who find themselves in abusive or domestic violence situations. She served on the board of Pratham, an organization that helps educate underprivileged children in India, for many years and is currently on their emeritus board.

Divakaruni has judged several prestigious awards, such as the National Book Award and the PEN Faulkner Award. She is, herself, the winner of a number of awards, including the American Book Award.

Two of her books, *The Mistress of Spices* and *Sister of My Heart*, have been made into movies by filmmakers Gurinder Chadha and Paul Berges (an English film) and Suhasini Mani Ratnam (a Tamil TV serial), respectively. A short story, "The Word

Love," from her collection *Arranged Marriage*, was made into a bilingual short film in Bengali and English, titled *Ammar Ma*. All the films have won awards.

Artistic statement

The first two decades of my life when I lived in India, I did not write anything. I never thought I had a story to tell, let alone that the story would be of interest to anyone. It was immigration that made me into a writer.

Immigration turned my known world upside down and inside out. In coming to America from a traditional Indian family, I found myself in a place that was very different, a place that was at once exciting and scary, limitless in its opportunities and claustrophobic because of the things that were out of my reach. From this place, I saw India, for the first time, much more clearly than before.

When I lived in India, I was immersed in the culture. I never thought about it. Living in America, especially in those early years, I thought about India a lot: what I appreciated about it, what I questioned about it. What I missed so deeply that it was like a physical ache inside me.

I was also aware of America in a new, hypersensitive way. People who had lived in America all their lives did not see what I noticed—the strangeness, the wonder, the pleasures and dangers of America. I have tried to convey some of that in *Arranged Marriage*, an immigrant story much like mine, much like that of hundreds of people around me. In some ways, it is the story of America, only this time told through Indian American voices.

My hope in writing *Arranged Marriage* was to make the story familiar, to make the characters and the hopes with which they traveled halfway across the world sympathetic to readers. For readers to see that as human beings we all want the same things: to love and be loved, to be safe, to be happy. One of the most valuable aspects of America is its amazing and wonderful diversity. But not everyone embraces this diversity, especially when the country is going through hard times. I hoped that readers of my book would be encouraged to appreciate our multicultural heritage.

For my South Asian readers, my hope was that they would see themselves reflected thoughtfully in literature, and that that reflection would empower them. This is crucial, I believe, for the health of every community.

When *Arranged Marriage* was given an American Book Award, I was delighted because I felt that now some of these hopes with which I wrote the book would actually come true. When "Clothes," a story from the collection, was picked up and transformed into a play, I was additionally delighted. I felt this new medium would draw more viewers to it and spread the message of diversity in a very powerful, visual fashion.

Production history

Clothes was a collaboration of the New WORLD Theater and the Mount Holyoke College Department of Theater. It was adapted to theater by Roberta Uno from the eponymous short story by Chitra Divakaruni, from her collection, *Arranged Marriage*. It premiered February 2000 at the Mount Holyoke College Rooke Theatre in South Hadley, Massachusetts with the following cast: Purva Bedi, performer; Aparna Sindhoor, performer; Saavitri Ramanand, musician; Ram Nath, musician; David Nelson, musician. Roberta Uno was the director; Aparna Sindhoor, the choreographer; original score composed by Sukanya Prabhakar, composer; Harley Erdman, dramaturg; Leandro Soto, set designer; John T. Howard, lighting designer; Kevin Brainerd, costume designer; Emily Stork, Malea Jochim, stage manager; Emma Donoghue, assistant state manager; Suzanne Hayden, technical director. *Clothes* also toured, including to the Jacob's Pillow Inside/Out series.

2 *Clothes*
Chitra Banerjee
Divakaruni

Based on the short story "Clothes" by Chitra Banerjee Divakaruni from *Arranged Marriage*. Adaptation by Roberta Uno.

Characters

Note: This dance drama was conceptualized for two actors with Bharatanatyam dance skills accompanied by live music, which underscores nearly continuously throughout.

NARRATOR, DEEPALI, FATHER, SOMESH, MOTHER-IN-LAW
Actor One
MITA Actor Two, principal dancer

Scene I

(*The Women's Lake in an Indian village. Women's Lake Dance begins, featuring both women. BATHING DANCE. Both wear white costumes that, through lighting, transform to different colors during the play. Actor One steps out to narrate.*)

NARRATOR The water of the women's lake laps against my breasts, washing the hot nervousness from my body. The waves make my sari float up around me, wet and yellow, like a sunflower after rain. (*Becomes DEEPALI; she is washing MITA's hair.*) Today my friend Deepali is washing my hair with special care, so it will glisten with little lights.

MITA Because today is a special day, the day of my bride viewing! (*MITA begins singing.*)

DEEPALI E, Mita, are you deaf?

(*DREAM DANCE begins and continues under DEEPALI's following dialogue.*)

DEEPALI Look at you, dreaming about your husband already, and you haven't even seen him yet! Mita? Well answer me? Does he have a brother? Maybe I can marry him and we can still be like sisters? E, Mita? This is the third time I'm asking you the same question! Well, forget it. Who cares

about a friend from a small Indian village when you're about to go live in America. (*DREAM DANCE ends.*)

MITA I want to deny it, say I'll always love her.

NARRATOR But already the activities of our girlhood seem to be far in the past, the colors leached out of them, like old sepia photographs. His name is Somesh Sen, the man who will be my husband.

NARRATOR/MITA (*together*) Somesh Sen. Father had told me about him.

(*FATHER approaches MITA*)

FATHER He is coming all the way from California, my daughter. Why, that is halfway across the world! What a great honor for our family! Let me show you where your future home will be, if you are lucky enough to be chosen.

(*FATHER picks up globe from his table. MITA is at once fascinated and reluctant to look.*)
See, here where is says United States of America, this bright pink shape.

(*MITA touches the globe, shivers.*)

MITA (*to herself*) How far I'll be going—to the other side of the earth! (*To audience*) Following a stranger to a land whose customs would be alien to me. Would I ever see my dear parents again? "Don't send me away,"

I want to cry. Father knows how afraid I am. But he is as helpless as I am.

FATHER *(distressed)* Mita Moni, little jewel, don't cry. *(Puts his arm around MITA)* He's a good man. Comes from a fine family. He will be kind to you. A new life is beginning for you. You will like being a married woman. I know it. How many new things you'll see, things I have never seen in my life. See, here is the special sari I bought for you to wear at the bride viewing.

(Spotlight changes, turning MITA's costume and surroundings to dawn.)

NARRATOR It was the color of dawn, of new beginnings. It was the most expensive sari I had ever seen, and surely the most beautiful. Pale pink, like the early morning sky over the women's lake. It was embroidered all over with tiny stars made of real gold thread.

(BRIDE VIEWING DANCE over the following)

NARRATOR It is a sari to walk carefully in. A sari that could change one's life.

MITA I stood holding it, wanting to weep. *(Dances with slow-dawning joy)* I knew that it would dazzle Somesh into choosing me to be his wife.

MITA *(Stops dance to address audience)* I know now that every woman's destiny is to leave the known for the unknown.

(LEAVING-FOR-UNKNOWN DANCE begins; dance sequence is drowned out by the slowly increasing roar of an airplane landing. MITA spins into the unknown. Blackout.)

Scene II

One year later. The interior of a different airplane. MITA's dance movements morph to convey unease and disconnection.

NARRATOR When the plane takes off, I try to stay calm, like father does when he practices yoga. But my hands clench themselves on the folds of the sari. When I force them open, I see they have left damp blotches on the delicate, crushed fabric.

My sari is red, because red is the color of luck for married women. The same color as the marriage-mark on my forehead. But, it's hard for me to think of myself as a married woman. The syllables rustle uneasily in my mouth, like a stiff satin that's never been worn.

(MITA stops suddenly to express astonished dismay.)

NARRATOR/MITA *(together)* Mrs. Sumita Sen.

(PLANE DANCE begins. MITA grows more assured, excited about the future.)

NARRATOR Somesh has to leave for America just a week after the wedding. He had to get back to the store, he explained to me. The store. It seems more real to me than Somesh - perhaps because I know more about it. It was what we had mostly talked about the night after the wedding, the first time we were alone together, on our bridal bed of flowers. His bedroom was dark, with only a little glimmer of moonlight from the window.

(SOMESH and MITA sit on the ground, facing each other. He touches her arm, MITA flinches back. He removes his hand.)

SOMESH *(In a light tone, as though nothing were wrong)* You won't believe it, Mita, until you see it for yourself. It's open 24 hours each day, 7 days a week. And can you guess what it's called? 7-Eleven!

(SOMESH gestures to paint for her a picture of the store. The light changes MITA's costumes and surround to soft-green—the color of her night sari. Projected 7-Eleven objects float onto back screen, surreal and larger than life.)

MITA 7-Eleven. It's a strange name, exotic, risky.

MITA All the stores I know are piously names after the gods and goddesses—Ganesh Sweet House, Lakshmi Vastralaya for Saris—to bring the owners luck!

SOMESH We sell all kinds of amazing things in the store—apple juice in cardboard cartons that never leak, American bread that comes in cellophane packages, already cut up; even the potato chips come in a canister, each grainy flake curved exactly like the next! But do you know what people like most?

(MITA shakes her head, a look of amazement on her face.)

SOMESH Beer and wine! They're the most popular items in America.

MITA *(In shocked surprise)* No!

SOMESH *(Takes her hand, laughing)* I can see you're going to have to get over your traditional ways. A lot of Americans drink, you know. And really, there's nothing wrong with it. When you come to California, I'll get you some sweet white wine and you'll see how good it makes you feel.

(SOMESH caresses MITA. She closes her eyes and tries not to jerk away because it is her wifely duty.)

MITA *Bite hard on your tongue,* my friend Madhavi has advised. The pain will keep your mind off what's going on down there.

(MITA bites her tongue, crying out in pain. SOMESH stops. Gently reassures her.)

SOMESH Shhh. It's OK. We'll wait until you feel like it.

NARRATOR He smiles away my apologies and starts telling me more about the store. All night we lay side by side on the big white bridal pillow, talking, and I thought, father was right, he is a good man, my husband, a kind, patient man. And so handsome, too.

MITA I breathe in the scent of his American cologne and feel luckier that I have any right to be.

NARRATOR The night before he left, Somesh confessed that the store wasn't making any money. In the half-dark his face looked young, apprehensive, in need of protection. I'd never seen that on a man's face before. Something rose in me like a wave.

MITA *It's all right,* I say, as though to a child, and pull his head down to my breast. *I won't be disappointed. I'll help you.* And a sudden happiness fills me.

(7-ELEVEN DANCE)

NARRATOR That night, I dreamed I was at the store. Soft American music floated in the background as I moved between shelves stocked high with brightly colored cans and elegant-necked bottles, polishing them until they shone.

(Dream shifts to grey of plane interior again. A long journey.)

NARRATOR Now, sitting inside this metal shell that is hurtling through emptiness, I try to remember how gentle my husband's hands had been, and his lips, surprisingly soft, like a woman's. How I've longed for them through those drawn-out nights while I waited for my visa to arrive. He will be standing at the customs gate, and when I reach him, he will lower his face to mine.

MITA *(Stops dance and addresses audience)* We will kiss in front of everyone, like Americans, not caring, then pull back, look each other in the eye, and smile.

(Airplane touches down to California Girls song. Blackout)

Scene III

(Six months later. SOMESH's apartment in California. Freeway overpasses seen through window bars. MITA enacts trying on clothes, SOMESH watches her from a corner, applauding, sometimes coming forward to help her. Camaraderie and intimacy are deepening in their relationship.)

NARRATOR Late at night I stand in front of our bedroom mirror, trying on the clothes Somesh has bought for me and smuggles in past his parents. I model each one for him, clasping my hands behind my head and pouting my lips just like the models on TV. We're breathless with the suppressed laughter of conspiracy- Father and Mother Sen must not hear us.

I'm wearing a pair of jeans now, marveling at the curves of my hips and thighs which have always been hidden under my saris. A close-fitting T-shirt outlines my breasts.

MITA The T-shirt is sunrise-orange, the color of joy, of my new American life. Across its middle, in large black letters, is written GREAT AMERICA. I thought the letters referred to the country.

SOMESH No, it's the name of an amusement park! I'll take you there, Mita Sweetheart, as soon as we move into our new apartment.

MITA That's my dream—moving out of this two-room apartment.

NARRATOR The apartment where it seems to me if we all breathed in at once, there would be no air left. Where I must cover my head with the edge of my sari and serve tea to the old women who come to visit Mother Sen.

SOMESH *(In a quiet argument)* But I'm their life. They've always been there when I needed them. I could never abandon them at some old people's home.

MITA You're constantly thinking of them. But what about me? I want to scream. Then I remember my own parents. I beat back my unreasonable desire and nod agreement.

(PAPERWEIGHT DANCE)

NARRATOR Even in bed Somesh and I kiss guiltily, listening for the giveaway creak of springs. I feel caught in a world where everything is frozen in place, like a scene inside a glass paperweight.

MITA I stand inside this glass world, watching helplessly as America rushes by.

(Dance ends.)

NARRATOR Somesh has bought me a cream blouse with a long brown skirt.

(Light changes, turning MITA's costume earth-color.)

SOMESH They match beautifully, like the inside and outside of an almond. *(smoothing the skirt, helping her button the shirt)* This is for when you start working. But first I want you to start college, get a degree, perhaps in teaching.

MITA Do you really think I can?

SOMESH Of course.

MITA *(Addresses audience)* But I have a secret plan.

(7-ELEVEN DANCE reprise solo over the following narration.)

NARRATOR What I really want is to work in the store. I want to stand behind the counter wearing this cream and brown skirt set and ring up purchases. The register drawer will glide open. Confident, I will count out green dollars and silver quarters. I will dust the jars of gilt-wrapped chocolates on the counter, the Neon Budweiser waterfall at the window. I will charm the customers with my smile, so that they will return again and again just to hear me telling them… *(Dance out.)*

MITA Have a nice day. Have a nice day. Have a great day! But the store, this store I've never really visited, isn't making much money yet. That's why they've let the hired help go.

SOMESH We can't move until the store shows profits. Because we must continue to take care of my mother and father's expense. That's why I'm taking the graveyard shift.

MITA That horrible word, like a chill hand up my spine.

(FEAR DANCE)

MITA I lie awake those nights, picturing masked intruders in the back of the store, like I've seen on the police shows Father Sen sometimes watches.

SOMESH *(Laughing, shaking her arm)* But Mita, there's no reason to worry. We have bars on the windows and a burglar alarm. And remember, the extra cash will help us move out that much quicker. *(Light shifts MITA's white costume to a rainbow.)*

MITA I'm wearing a nightie now, my very first one.

NARRATOR It glides over my hips to stop outrageously at mid-thigh. My mouth is an O of surprise, my legs long and sleek from hair remover I asked Somesh to buy me last week.

MITA The legs of a movie star! *(SOMESH moves forward to hold MITA.)*

SOMESH You're beautiful.

MITA Do you really think I am?

SOMESH Very beautiful. The most beautiful woman in the world.

MITA His fingers are taking the pins from my hair, undoing my braids. The escaped strands fall on his face like dark rain.

SOMESH Please don't turn off the light. I want to keep seeing your face.

(SENSUOUS DANCE to blackout, music continues to city sounds, as music fades, gunshots.)

Scene IV

(A few months later. SOMESH's apartment in California, projection of freeway overpasses seen through window-bars. MITA stands very still, facing away from audience, in the middle of the empty room. Lighting is stark white, blinding. As scene progresses, the NARRATOR will remove MITA's jewelry and the lighting will grow dim, the silhouettes of skyscrapers etc. fade away, leaving prison-like window bars.)

NARRATOR *(Speaks in a sleepwalker's voice)* I must hurry. Any moment there'll be a knock at the door. They are afraid to leave me alone too long, afraid I might do something to myself.

I try to put on the borrowed sari I am supposed to wear. But it spills through my disobedient fingers. There are waves and waves around my feet.

MITA White. Widow's color, color of endings.

(BRIEF WAVES MOVEMENT)

NARRATOR There's a cut, still stinging, on the side of my right arm. It's from the bangle-breaking ceremony. Old Mrs. Ghosh, who's a widow herself, took my hands in hers and brought them down on the bedpost, so the glass bangles I was wearing shattered and multicolored shards flew out in every direction. Some landed on the body that was on the bed.

MITA *(Stops and addresses audience)* I can't call it Somesh. He is gone already.

(DEJECTION DANCE)

NARRATOR All the women in the room were crying except me. Mother Sen approached me. I watched her as though from the far end of a tunnel.

MOTHER-IN-LAW *(Puts a tentative hand to touch her back)* Oh my dear, my dear. I can't bear to look at you in these widow's clothes, without the red marriage sindur on your forehead. *(turns and listens to other women mourners)* What a superstitious lot you are to blame her. It isn't because of her ill-luck that Somesh was killed. It has nothing to do with her! *(Turns to MITA again)* God curse the man who came into the store last night, to whom a handful of dollars was more important than my son's life! Who took everything so easily. And from us also. Now what is left for us?

(Slowly MITA turns but doesn't look at her.)

MITA *(Aloud, but without looking at MOTHER-IN-LAW)* He wanted me to go to college. To choose a career.

MOTHER-IN-LAW Dear daughter, you must forget those dreams. You are our daughter, our only child now—you must come back with us to Calcutta. This country—it's too dangerous. Like a mirage, it lures us in only to drown in a lake of quicksand.

MITA *(to herself)* Next month we would have had $4000 in our savings book. Next month we could have moved out.

MOTHER-IN-LAW My dear, you must not worry that you are alone now. We'll take care of each other, protect each other from the bitter world. You have a home with us for the rest of your life.

MITA *(to herself)* For the rest of my life!

NARRATOR It made me dizzy.

(FACELESS PARADE DANCE. Images begin flashing faster and faster as NARRATOR speaks. These will be images referenced throughout the play - objects from the store, clothing advertisements, roller coasters, etc. MITA's dance will grow frenzied and desperate.)

NARRATOR A faceless parade straggles across my eyelids. All those customers at the store that I will never meet. A classroom of smiling children who love me in my cream-and-brown American skirt. The savings book where we have $3605.33. His lips unexpectedly soft, woman-smooth. Elegant-necked wine bottles swept off the shelves, shattering on the floor.

MITA I know Somesh would not have tried to stop the gunman.

MITA *(Moves forward, shadowed by SOMESH)* I can picture his silhouette against the lighted Budweiser sign, hands raised. He is trying to find the right expression to put on his face, calm, reassuring, reasonable.

MITA/SOMESH *(together)* Ok, take the money. No, I won't call the police.

MITA His eyes darken with disbelief as his fingers touch his chest and come away wet.

MITA I yanked away the cover. I had to see. I'd expected blood, a lot of blood, the deep red-black of it crusting his chest.

(HORROR DANCE)

NARRATOR But they must have cleaned him up at the hospital. He was dressed in his silk wedding kurta. The musky aroma of the aftershave someone must have sprinkled on the body didn't quite hide that other smell, thin, sour, metallic.
The smell of death.

(In this next session, NARRATOR is to enact MITA, so that there are two MITAs on stage, one dancing her present grief, one going back in time, remembering, acting out the drowning incident.)

NARRATOR Sometimes, bathing in the women's lake, floating with the sun beating down on my closed eyelids, I would think, it would be so easy to let go, to drop into the dim brown world of mud, of water weeds fine as hair.
Once I almost did it. I curled my body inward, tight as a fist, and felt it begin to sink. The sun grew pale and shapeless. The water, suddenly cold, licked at the insides of my ears in welcome. But in the end I couldn't.
How vividly it comes to me, this memory I haven't called up in years. The desperate flailing of arms and legs, the wild animal trapped inside my chest, clawing at my lungs. The day returning to me as searing air, the way I drew it in, as though I would never have enough of it.

(Music stops.)

MITA That's when I know I cannot go back. I don't know how I'll manage, here in this new dangerous land. I only know I must.

NARRATOR Because at this very moment widows in white saris are bowing their veiled heads, serving tea to in-laws. Doves with cut-off wings.

(MITA'S DANCE)

(In this final section, NARRATOR and MITA should move together, slowly, stylized movements of growing confidence and grace, their movements synchronized. Should be choreographed so that at times—and especially at the end—one of them stands exactly behind the other as though two parts of MITA's identity have come together. Underscoring music continues through end.)

NARRATOR I am standing in front of the mirror now, tucking in the sari. I straighten my shoulders and stand taller.

MITA Take a deep breath.

NARRATOR Air fills me—the same air that traveled through Somesh's lungs a little while ago.

MITA The thought is like an unexpected, intimate gift.

NARRATOR I tilt my chin, readying myself for the arguments of the coming weeks.

MITA In the mirror a woman holds my gaze, her eyes apprehensive yet steady.

NARRATOR She wears a blouse and skirt the color of almonds.

(Underscoring instruments drop out, only the swelling, climbing voice of the vocalist trails. Blackout.)

Marissa Chibas

Biography

Marissa Chibas is a writer and performer. She is the recipient of the 2015 TCG Fox Fellowship in Distinguished Achievement. Her solo performance, *Daughter of a Cuban Revolutionary*, produced by the CalArts Center for New Performance (CNP), has toured the U.S., Europe, and Mexico. For CNP, Marissa coadapted the award-winning production  of Gertrude Stein's *Brewsie and Willie* and played Edgar in *King Lear,* a production that toured to the Frictions Festival in France. Marissa has acted in over 50 productions and two dozen American premieres, including *The Keening*, by Umberto Dorado, at the ART in Cambridge, *Two Sisters and a Piano*, by Nilo Cruz, at the McCarter, and The Mark Taper Forum productions of *The House of Bernarda Alba* and Eduardo Machado's *The Floating Island Plays.* On Broadway, she performed in *Abe Lincoln in Illinois* and *Brighton Beach Memoirs*, as well as off Broadway and in many prominent resident theaters, including Arena Stage, Alley Theater, and the Yale Repertory Theatre. Her silent film/performance piece, *Clara's Los Angeles*, was presented at REDCAT's NOW FEST and the San Diego Latino Film Festival. Marissa is on the Theater School faculty at CalArts where she heads Duende CalArts, a CNP initiative that collaborates with innovative Latin@ and Latin American artists to create adventurous performance. For Duende, she conceived and wrote *Shelter,* which premiered in April 2016 in Los Angeles and was subsequently performed at the Kennedy Center. *Shelter* focuses on the Central American unaccompanied children who are seeking asylum in the U.S. She is working on a performance piece entitled *The Second Woman,* opening in the fall of 2016 at the Bootleg Theater in Los Angeles.

Artistic statement

Telling these stories is both an act of defiance and of reconciliation. I am defying those that have excluded my father and others from Cuban history, and I seek reconciliation with my ancestors who continually disturbed my waking and dreaming life until I finally wrote and performed this play. It is an honor to unearth and give voice to those lost and forgotten. This play taught me the healing effect for both the audiences I performed as well as myself—of bringing to light what has been kept in shadow.

I write from a sense of urgency. During a recent talk back for *Daughter of a Cuban Revolutionary*, I was asked if I regretted that politics had been such a big part of my life. I responded that I thought not being political was a luxury I know nothing about. Most of the people I know have no choice but to be political in order to survive and to make their futures, and the futures of those they love, better. I create work that responds to the urgent needs my various communities grapple with— whether it be identity, immigration, or aging. I am dedicated to revealing complexities that reject polarized views of left/right, black/white, for/against. I demand that my work challenge easy answers, codifications, and misconceptions.

Daughter of a Cuban Revolutionary voices stories erased from Cuban history. My father, Raul, cowrote the 1957 Cuban manifesto. Each time I perform this play, I claim his place in the Cuban struggle against tyranny. Another dominant figure in the play is my uncle, Eduardo Chibas, who was the leading candidate for the 1952 Cuban presidency. He committed suicide during an impassioned live radio broadcast a few months before the election. His legacy haunted me as a child and to this day has tremendous impact on the Cuban community, both on and off the island.

The other central figure is my mother, Dalia, runner-up Miss Cuba 1959. In fact, my father was a judge at the pageant, which is how they met. I used to joke to friends that in my Cuban family things never happened, they OCCURRED! Being the daughter of a Cuban revolutionary and a beauty queen meant having a grand share of drama and hilarity. My solo performance has been a chance to bring forward some of these combustible elements that make up my life as well as that of my family. I share these revolutionary stories through a personal lens and the personal through the prism of the revolution.

Everywhere I have performed *Daughter of a Cuban Revolutionary* I have been struck by how many people approach me afterwards to tell me their tales of exodus. They either lived through something similar or are inspired to bring to light the journeys of their own families. More and more, our world seems to be made of migrants and those in exile. The story of exile is of increasing interest—so many people have been uprooted and forced to adapt to a new country and its ways. It is moving for me to see the effect of this deeply personal play on others with very different backgrounds. I am grateful *Daughter of a Cuban Revolutionary* is able to speak to their struggle.

I end the play listing the various things I am the daughter of. In this gesture, I claim who I am and what I stand for. As much as Cuba is and always will be a sacred land for me, I am also aware that "I am the daughter whose deep roots travel far beyond homeland and geographical borders." What I seek as an artist are those deep roots, to connect with my audience in a way that reaches their hearts, and to inspire soulful reflection. The recent historical events that have opened the way between the U.S. and Cuba have left me cautiously optimistic. It is a great dream of mine to be able to share these stories in the land of my ancestors and to see the Cuban people emerge from this transition more empowered and able to forge their own new identity as a sovereign nation. Perhaps that day will come soon.

Production history

Daughter of a Cuban Revolutionary was produced by the CalArts Center for New Performance and premiered at REDCAT in 2007. The play toured to the Darryl Roth Theater in NYC for INTAR, Teatro Lobo in Miami, Teatro Experimental in Guadalajara, The Edinburgh Fringe Festival, Encuentro 2014 at LATC, and Arts Emerson in Boston. The production was directed by Mira Kingsley, and the dramaturg was Anne Garcia Romero. The play was written and performed by Marissa Chibas.

Original design team included Dan Evans (Set), Rebecca Marcus (Lights), Colbert Davis (Sound), Adam Flemming (Video), Karen Murk (Costume), and Victor Sandoval (Stage Manager).

3 *Daughter of a Cuban Revolutionary*
Marissa Chibas

As the audience enters MARISSA is standing with her back towards the audience facing the set down stage center. The stage is either covered in sand or has 10 or so rocks placed in different parts of the perimeter of the stage. A large trumpet speaker lies on its side downstage right. This is a set element that she uses throughout the play, sitting on it and using it in a variety of ways. There is a video screen upstage and across the space.

We hear a sound collage of voices, music, Eddy Chibas's last speech, etc.—all audio elements of Marissa's family and Cuban American life. As the sound texture increases she slowly lifts her right leg up and places it on the stage. She turns to face the audience. She is wearing a green army jacket, green pants and underneath, a white buttoned long sleeved shirt. On her neck is tied a bright scarf, a white handkerchief in her pocket. During the following sequence MARISSA spins slowly upstage. The text in bold is said while in gestures of drowning.

MARISSA So, what is this place? I am astonished *(gasp of breath)* I am drowning. So, what is this place? A cave. No...much more. I am swimming in a cave with a fifty-foot waterfall in the Venezuelan Amazon on my honeymoon with a tour party of six and an indigenous guide, named Stanley. I am also in the thrall of something within - my past overwhelms me, drags me down, calls on me to remember. **Cuba acuerdate!** My life passing before me, spinning through this space like a whirlpool. **I am swallowing water, I can't keep my head above the water line, I can't breathe**. I submit to the power, my heart's center, Cuba calling on me to remember the forgotten stories of my people, my family, the legacy of exile - **Grab on to the wall of the cave, I can't, my hand is slipping** - joy, hope, despair

all nurtured in the womb of what I know of as Cuba. There's nothing to hold on to here, nothing solid to pull me to safety. I can stay here in this timeless place. I can let the cold fluid fill my mouth and lungs. Should I release in to this timelessness? **Cuba, remember.** I can just keep gulping until the waterfall swallows me whole. It's this moment that is hard to pull away from and call out for help, this extended-time moment. **I'm drowning.** It's so tempting to stay, to let myself drown. **Cuba, acuerdate.** The cave walls have parted and I have never been anywhere like this. I am not afraid. I am in this eternal second between worlds and it really can go either way.

(We see the sugar cane footage from "I am Cuba" projected across the space. MARISSA is consumed full body by the image. MARISSA continues to move across the space engaging with the image behind her. The text in bold below is said by the woman Raul meets in Union Square. She has a heavy New York accent.)

MARISSA *(MARISSA hums "Siboney" by Ernesto Lecuona.)*
My father used to play me that song while regaling me with of stories from his youth. My father Raul was first imprisoned at the age of 15 by the Cuban dictator Machado. He had been handing out leaflets promoting social democratic change. His brother Eddy, my uncle, had been imprisoned a month earlier for political reasons and Raul wanted to follow in his big brother's footsteps. Whatever Eddy did, Raul wanted to do. Eddy was Raul's super hero in the flesh, moving up in the ranks of student revolutionaries and making a name for himself as a political writer and leader. After Raul's prison term, his parents, who were part of

Cuba's elite upper class, sent their fifteen year old son to the U.S. in the hopes that the political climate and Raul would both cool off. While there he stayed with his Tia Conchita in Washington D.C. and made trips by train to New York City, which at that time was a twelve hour ordeal.

YOUNG RAUL Union Square, New York City, 1932

The Great Depression
Constant activity
Fiery voices, young and old, some with American accents many from foreign lands
Can I be a part of this?
Hot dogs get your…
To the North – Guardian Life Insurance
To the West – Amalgamated bank
To the East – Union Square Bank
To the South – a huge Wrigley's chewing gum sign
Cruu Cruuu
A group gathers around a large tree
One young woman speaks –
Here in America the greatest, the richest country in the world, where we have boundless resources and stockpiles enough to feed the entire Nation, ten million people are unemployed and struggle each day to-
She has a beautiful voice, nice legs
One group after another, all ages, all races, from every corner of the globe, they gather here to
Galvanize, embolden, inspire this generation on to new paths
Build a better world
We think that capitalism cannot survive
A new concept
We are seeking a new world order
May I speak
Anyone here can speak
My name is Raul Chibas. I am from Cuba. I…excuse me this is, speaking in public is not as easy for me. My brother, Eddy, is much better at this.
Go on, what have you got to say?
Our struggle in Cuba began in March of 1927 when president Machado extended his term and a constitutional amendment was made to accommodate him. Since that act against democratic principles, the students of La Habana University have been fighting this regime no matter the consequences. Many of us have had to flee. One of the leaders, Julio Antonio Mella, was hunted down and killed in Mexico City by Machado's men. The artist Diego Rivera heard his last words, "I am murdered by Machado, I die for the revolutionary cause." My brother Eddy is also a leader in this fight. He speaks of our struggle with a clarity and passion I wish I possessed. As for me, I am here because I was arrested for distributing literature against the disappearance of my friends. I was taken to the Principe Fortress and was beaten. I was in prison one month. Many of my friends have disappeared without a trace. One of my brother's best companions, Angel Alvarez, was taken last January by the police. He helped me escape to this country. Angel was brutally tortured. We appealed to the American Ambassador to save his life. The Ambassador assured us that Angel's life would be protected. Angel was murdered that very day. But we will continue our struggle for true liberty. Thank you for hearing, for letting me speak

MARISSA Si, me acuerdo, I remember, me acuerdo his mad love affair with the Big Apple. It was this trip, it was bohemian New York that formed him, rooted him in the ideals that would last his lifetime.

Twenty five years after that day in Union Square; after the Machado regime; after the first Batista regime; after 11 years of a very flawed democracy; and during Batista's second dictatorship, an endless parade of corrupt or extremist leaders, then the 1957 manifesto written by Fidel Castro, Felipe Pasos, and my father Raul.

(We hear in voice over the following text from the 1957 manifesto.)

El 12 de Julio, 1957 de la Sierra Maestra
Where the sense of duty has united us, we make this call to our compatriots. The time has come in which the nation can save itself from tyranny through the intelligence, courage and civic responsibility of its children. Our greatest weakness has been division and tyranny. To unite is the only patriotic act at this hour.
To unite in that which the political, revolutionary and social sectors that fight dictatorship have in common. And what do political parties of the opposition, revolutionary sectors and civic institutions have in common? The desire to put an end to a regime of coercion, to the violation of individual rights,

to the infamous crimes, and to find peace for which we all yearn through the only means possible, which is the democratic and constitutional channeling of the country. Do we, rebels of the Sierra Maestra, not desire free elections, a democratic regime, a constitutional government? It is because we desire these more than anyone that we are here.

RAUL You know what you don't do. You don't start your final day thinking that it is your last. A long drive. A very long drive. It is August of 1957. I am Raul Chibas, for the moment at least. I am 41 years old. I am in a patrol car. My cousin Robertico is sitting beside me; and we are on a ride to our deaths. A month ago I co-wrote a manifesto for the Cuban revolution. Fidel recently gave me orders to leave the Sierra, where I had been fighting with him and other rebels, to go to the U.S. and to bring back weapons. In La Habana, while making arrangements to leave the country, I was captured by Batista's police. One of them, Alfarro is driving this patrol car. I know Alfarro by reputation. Many of my friends have died at the hands of this butcher, and now it is my turn. It is 3am. The streets are deserted. There is the only the monotonous hum of the patrol car and the sight of the headlights sweeping away the darkness ahead of it. The silence is broken every now and then by Alfarro or his goon turning around to tell Robertico and I how much they are going to enjoy killing us. They are really looking forward to it, they tell us. The plan is to take us to a lake on the outskirts of La Habana and shoot us in the head. Then they will load our bodies onto a plane and dump them over the Sierra to make it look as though we died there in combat and not here in the city at the hands of these assassins. My mind is passing over many thoughts and memories. How did I get here? I know I am a dead man. In a few moments time my life will be over. Strange. I believe in what I am dying for. Alfarro has pulled up to a gas station. He's making a phone call. He doesn't want to use the radio in the patrol car in case some sympathizer picks up the signal and tries to rescue us. He's come back. We keep driving. We are at the intersection for the road to the lake. We turn in the opposite direction. Maybe there's a chance. We pull up to the plaza in front of the castle of Atarez, a place known

for its torture chambers. More police officers. They taunt us, jeer at us, wave their guns in our faces. Alfarro and the other one get out of the car. A man lunges forward. My heart nearly stops. He says something incomprehensible, ludicrous to me. He asks me about Trucutú Longa. Now, Trucutú Longa is a football player who has no neck. He is named after a cartoon character who also has no neck. Why this man is asking me about Trucutú Longa with all the casualness in the world at a moment when I am about to be killed is so ridiculous so absurd to me. I don't even know Trucutú Longa! He moves away and a tall imposing man takes his place.

VOICE 'Do you know who I am?'

RAUL 'No.'

VOICE 'I am Ventura.'

RAUL He said this as though expecting the earth to shake.

VOICE 'You know that you are a dead man, don't you.'

RAUL 'Yes, I know.'

He pulls out his gun and points it towards my head. I cannot look away. I cannot breathe. Time has stopped. Suddenly something comes over the radio of the patrol car. A strange combination of words, some kind of code. The police officers and Ventura all lean in. They break off and begin to yell and curse loudly and I think, if they are upset it must be good for me! It is not convenient to kill me tonight. Orders are to take me to the prison. They don't want another Martyr. I spend two weeks in there. Screams all day and night. The faces of my torturers. The sneakers I do my calisthenics in. Odd combinations of memories and fears mixed in one nightmare. When I get out I am interviewed by the press. My captors make sure that my visible wounds have healed. I manage to get out of the country, to the U.S. where I make the appropriate contacts and fly back with the newly purchased weapons on the first successful guerilla nighttime flight. Mission accomplished.

RAUL I will tell that story often and remind my daughter that without that radio signal, without the interception of that radio signal I would have been killed and her birth would not have happened. I am erased from Cuban history. I am conspicuously left out of the list of rebel comandantes at the Museum of the Revolution in La Habana. I have been airbrushed out of Cuban history.

(Video imagery of the Sierra, opening footage from "I am Cuba" mixed with Raul's photos and water. MARISSA floats with the images. She takes on the position in the cave with her arms outstretched. She peels away the green army jacket and by the end of the sequence leaves it downstage right.)

MARISSA Si, me acuerdo. I remember that I owe my existence to a radio signal. I remember a great divide. I remember being at a beach when I was a child, and playing with a little girl and when her mother asked me my name she took the little girl away while screaming obscenities at me. My mother later explained that there were those who hated my father for his involvement in the revolution. But I never understood exactly. Raul always said that he would fight the revolution all over again, although he was tragically disappointed in the outcome. Change was necessary. He often said that he had not traded one dictator to replace it with another. Si, me acuerdo, I remember. We're having a party!

MARISSA August 1969. I live with my Cuban American family at 90th Street and Columbus Ave. on the island of Manhattan. From our 20th story window I can see the GW building and the little globe on top of another building that tells the weather by a colored light. Red means rain, white snow, and green a clear day. We're having a party, and not just any party. My sister Dee Dee and I are extremely excited, we've been promised by my mother's friends, Anais and Elena a dance lesson. Our first real dance lesson. We want so much to learn those graceful moves these gorgeous red nailed women make. When they are not dancing they are telling sad stories and looking lost, but when they dance they look like goddesses. We want that. We want to look like goddesses.

I woke up to the smell of onions, garlic and lemon sautéing and Sergio Mendes and Brasil 66 playing in the background. Our guests are about to arrive. My father methodically pierces the olives with colored toothpicks. My mother, Dalia, is primping her large bouffant hairdo with the help of the mirror over the bar. They are drinking whiskey sours and the fragrance perfumes the whole room. Peanuts and olives are laid out on the coffee table, the Spanish tiled bar, and the dining table. The buzzer from the lobby sounds. We wait for those first guests as they make their way to the elevator, up the twenty flights and to our front door.

Hola

Buenas Noches, como estan ustedes?

Dame tu abrigo

Mira la vista!

Ding dong

Buzz

Ya estan llegando todos

Soon the other guests arrive.

Al fin el trafico estan de madre

Ay que elegante

Un daiquiri por favor

Anais in a super duper mini hot pink skirt. She sits on a bar stool popping olives in her mouth, drink in hand and telling jokes. This bar stool is no match for my voluptuous nalgas, and I spill over on all sides. Elena enters in her trademark black tailored suit and see-through white silk blouse.

She puffs her cigarette, eyes slightly closed, Garbo style.

Scotch on the rocks por favor.

Dee Dee and I run around passing drinks and hors d'oeuvres in our matching skirts and go-go shirts, and are constantly hugged and pinched and praised.

The paella is ready

click clack click clack to the kitchen

The party divides into two factions

The living room – Bueno rrrrooooorrooooo

The kitchen – Ayyyhheeeeayyy

Sangria

the sounds of people laughing and talking and needing to keep making sound.

Some of these guests have been in the U.S. for several years, some are recent Cuban immigrants, but all come with a thirst to experience something familiar, a reprieve from feeling like an alien.

(Benny Moré's "Santa Isabel" plays over one of the radios. During the following section MARISSA learns to dance to the music.)

ELENA Time for your first real dance lesson

She kicks the speaker

Benny More

Don't move

The first step is to listen

You aren't allowed to move until the rhythm creeps into your body. The way into the music is through the entire body

Keep the torso still and let that rhythm move through you until it reaches your nalgas

MARISSA My pelvis has a life of its own.

Anais' moves are round and sensual. Her nalgas stir the room into a frenzy. Dee Dee takes on her style and is Anais' special pupil. I take after Elena. Her signature move is to call the music further in with a hand gesture. She also teaches me the thrill of the slight hesitation, to hold back just for a moment and then fling myself wildly back in the rhythm.

They clap and encourage us.

I see my father and mother dancing. My father barely moves but is always in rhythm. My mother has the moves. She shakes her hips and glances around the room to see who is watching her. I witness something that I rarely see on their faces, joy. Oh yes, I remember, it is the communal pleasure of living in these sounds that make our hearts and bodies swell with ecstasy. We know something about these sounds, we understand them, they are a deep secret within us, a kind of ancient language that we share.

A group of men in the midst of a heated discussion about Cuba begin to shout uncontrollably. The insults begin to fly and the dancing stops short. The yelling reaches its climax when one of the guests threatens to leave in a barrage of escalating screams. Elena's lone female voice pierces through all the others: "Oye! Stop it! We didn't come here to fight. Este exilio nos tiene locos. This exile is killing us! There's enough fighting between us. We came to laugh and dance and forget our problems for a few hours. So be quiet and let's dance!"

(A dance to send away the bad spirits. MARISSA takes on Dalia's persona. She begins as though speaking over the exuberance of the party. The text in bold is said in the voice of her Uncle Juan.)

DALIA Hola, I am Dalia Colominas. First runner up Miss Cuba of 1959. Everyone says I should have won. All the judges afterward told me, they said 'Dalia tu debias haver ganado'. The girl who won, her father is a famous poet and that's why they gave her the crown and not me. I am so mad that I run up to my hotel room and refused to go to the party. Ay, I have this beautiful suite all to myself. With eight brothers and sisters I really appreciate having this room for the week.

Well, losing is disappointment. Then the judges come to my room and offer me the same prizes as the girl who won. That makes me feel better so I go down to the party. That's when I meet Raul Chibas, a comandante of the revolution. He is in his guerilla outfit, like all the rebels are doing. They have just won and come down from the mountains and everyone is feeling you know happy and optimistic. There are celebrations all night in the street and Raul and Camillo Cienfuegos have both come to the pageant party. Camillo is handsome, he is very handsome. You know like Gary Cooper handsome. He is a pilot with the 26th of July movement. He will die a year later in a plane crash. A lot of people will think that Castro had him killed because he was so handsome and charismatic and could be a competition. I don't know. They are, Raul and Camillo, are both at the pageant party and I see that all the girls are around Camillo so I go and talk to Raul. He isn't as good looking but he is very charismatic and intelligent... His brother, Eddy Chibas, was a famous politician who had his own weekly radio program. I remember hearing that show. Everyone did. It was on Sundays at 8pm and you could walk down any street in Cuba and hear Eddy Chibas's voice because everyone tuned in. He was very popular, especially for those who had nothing to lose. He would denounce corrupt government officials to expose the graft, you know, the stealing that was going on.

One day an informant told Eddy about someone in the government who was stealing money from the treasury. The informant promised him proof for the following week. Eddy made the denouncement on his radio program and said that he would present the proof on his next show. But the informant took off, mysteriously, and was nowhere to be found. And so Eddy lost credibility. They made fun of him in the newspapers. He was still the front runner for the presidency...but then one Sunday, on his radio show, Eddy made an impassioned speech and at the end shot himself, committed suicide.

No one knew what happened to this inform-ant, some doubted there ever was one, others thought Eddy was set up. Yo no se. He was a lost hope... Of course this was all when I was very young, just a child really. Raul is 17 years older than I am. Raul looks so distinguished in the outfit of a comandante. He has traveled so much and I love hearing about the Châteaux of the Loire and Mont Saint-Michel and New York. I love hearing about architecture of other cities. I want to study architecture but here in Cuba, at this time, it isn't something a woman can study. Raul knows so much about these things I dream about. He is on top of the world; his life dream has been won. Cuba es libre.

One of my pageant prizes was a trip to N.Y. This is my first time here and I want to do and see all I can. Raul decides to follow me here and I don't tell him not to. But he is so mad because my mother made me bring my brother Juan as a chaperone. So, everywhere Raul and I go in N.Y; the Metropolitan Mu-seum, Carnegie Hall, walking down Fifth Ave., Juan is right between us! Ay, Raul is so mad. And, my brother Juan, bueno somos de Matanza and he is very loud and not shy! My mother gave him strict orders and he is following them like a good soldier.

Don't get so close to my sister!

Or he see's something that excites him, like Rockefeller Center **Mira Nanny! Estamos en Rockefeller Center! Vamos al Show!** and everyone in the streets turns around to look at us. Raul is one of the shyest people - not the shyest... he is spending the whole trip chasing me, embarrassed, and frus-trated. For me this trip is... a beginning. I am seeing a life I never knew was possible. It is better than the movies. And the women are so elegant and free and... cosmopolitan! When we get back to Cuba Raul still pur-sues me. One day I get a phone call from Raul to go down to his office. As soon as I walk in someone bolts the door behind me. I look around the room and there is Raul smiling devilishly. Standing next to him is a man. Raul introduces the man as a justice of the peace. Then he says, well, come on, this is the time. We're getting married. Yes, of course I was in a little shock, I mean... this is a little strange don't you think? A surprise

wedding, a surprise for the bride! But that's how he is. When he makes a decision... that is it. Raul and I will leave Cuba in August of 1960 for what we think will be a short time. I will hear of my mother's death by telephone and be unable to go to her funeral. I will raise two daughters. I will be married 17 years then divorce. I will declare myself a cosmopolitan woman and fight for my free-dom. On my last days I will tell my daughter Marissa, I love you...put on some lipstick.

(MARISSA has taken off the scarf and placed it downstage center.)

MARISSA Si me acuerdo. I remember my moth-er's beauty, love of glamour, and fighting spirit. I remember seeing Raul as a man be-tween worlds; not a communist nor a cap-italist, not happy nor sad, neither a man of faith nor an atheist. After the revolution, when it became clear the direction the coun-try was headed in, and key positions were being given to the communist faction of the coalition of fighters that won the revolution, Raul has an audience with Castro. In this meeting he speaks his mind and insists that Fidel acknowledge the manifesto and the democratic principles outlined in that doc-ument. Castro listens, says little. Raul leaves the meeting knowing his days are numbered and prison or worse is a certainty. He flees under cover of night in a seventeen-foot catamaran and lands in the Florida Keys. *(MARISSA jumps off stage.)* Raul will never see Cuba again. Did I inherit his inability to land, his need for flight, his tortured soul? Where did that begin? Was it the loss of his beloved brother, was it losing Eddy that broke his heart? Did I break his heart, am I like Eddy? Did I inherit my uncles...? Oh no. Si me acu-. Can we stop this-? Can we stop this now?

(Harsh sounds. Video of whirlpool type imagery, storms, crashing waves etc. MARISSA comes back to downstage left corner of stage and waves handkerchief behind her.)

MARISSA The clock pulses bright red - 4 am. I've been tossing and turning for at least two hours. The shadows in the room are eerie and unsettling. I move slowly to-wards the bathroom and my eyes focus on what at first seems to be an apparition. On the roof of the building in front me is a figure, a man in a white suit frantically waving and shouting something. He's frantically waving at me. He is terrifying. The man in the white suit stomps the ground of the roof. Oh my god, I'm not imagining this, am I? I feel totally naked and then realize that, yes; in fact I am totally naked. I move away from the window. My heart is pounding wildly. I begin to think how much the man on the roof oddly resembles my Cuban uncle Eddy who has been dead for over thirty years and who I only know from photos but yes it sure does look like him. Odd. How is this possible? I look again on the roof. Where is he? But I saw him? He couldn't have disappeared? I saw him! Where is he? Where is he? *(Confusion and then light bulb!)* Duh! I have to go there!

I need to go there, to Cuba. I need to reclaim, to seek what was lost to find meaning to restore something to find out about my families' history in Cuba that I know absolutely nothing about to have fun to be exotic to feel at home somewhere to go to Mecca to hear those cadences and rhythms to get some information to go to the places I've been hearing about all my life to have the molecules in my body stirred and shaken to delve into dangerous territory to say oh yeah I've been to Cuba to not feel like an idiot when asked "why haven't you ever gone there?" To prove something to see my family there to know more about my uncle Eddy to record the old timers still in Cuba before it's too late to find out if I really have anything at all to do with that place to have a pilgrimage.

(MARISSA holds the speaker.)

La Habana, 1993.
Pouring rain. This is the height of what is now called the "special period". The Soviets are now the Russians and aid from that lost empire has been cut off abruptly. Blackouts and food shortages are part of the countries daily life.
Neither Raul nor Dalia wanted me to come here. But I had to. I am the first of my family to go back and on this tempestuous day in August I am going back to a place I have never been.
Santo Suarez, Cuba
A large run down colonial house.

I meet my Tia Amelia and her family, my family. I am treated like royalty as they offer me the best of the little they have. I take out the gifts I have brought them; they laugh and joke as I tell them about the antics of their U.S. family. Tia Delia still stops family gatherings with her "visions," Tio Juan still works as a janitor in the same NY office building he has been cleaning for the past 30 years and still refuses to get a telephone so his sisters won't bother him and Dalia is still a wild social butterfly. They are wrapped in my stories of Yuma, that's what they call anything new, cool, or from the U.S. Eso es Yuma!
My Tia Amelia glows with wisdom and resignation. They all make light of the difficulty of their situation and proudly share the results of their clever resourcefulness – homemade paint, jerry rigged back up power for the outages, recycled skate boards made out of old roller skates and blocks of wood.
I take my Cuban family to a Paladar, a clandestine restaurant in a private home. I see my young cousins eat cheese for the first time. I see my families faces light up when the Paella arrives. I feel a weight descend on us at the end of the meal.
I am beginning to understand the code that Cubans speak with, the glances and mime used to avoid being overheard saying something counter revolutionary. No one can afford to speak freely here. It is an atmosphere that makes my rebellious spirit want to shout in the streets. But I don't.
The National Archives La Habana. I hold in my hand photograph after sepia toned photograph of people I do not recognize and whose stories are a mystery to me. These strangers are my family - a lost world. They are deteriorating in my hands. They look out at me with a fixed gaze, peer into my soul. If only my father were here to tell me who these people are and to release me from their haunting eyes. Do any of their features remind me of particular living family members? Are those my sister Dee Dee's eyes? Gloria's glance? Raul's air? The back of the pictures offer no help, no mention of when the photographs were taken or where.
The damp musty scent of decay
My back aches
Muscles tighten

I cannot breathe
My head swims, spins, is pounded on
I look for an opening
Arms stretch towards the wooden chair in
front of me
Darkness

(The sound of a crackly radio.)

MARISSA I meet my father's cousin Arturin.
He is living in a dilapidated apartment that
has been devastated by a flood. You can see
the mark about halfway up the wall where
the water reached. There are three pictures
on the wall. One of Arturin's mother, one
of his father, and one of Uncle Eddy. Each
has the mark of the flood running across
them. Arturin's apartment is filled with old
radios. The hallway leading to his living
room is lined on either side with stacked,
old, broken radios. Arturin tries to fix
them. He keeps them whether they work
or not.
Arturin was my Uncle Eddy's typist. He
typed nearly every speech that Eddy made.

ARTURIN Yo trabajé con Eddy, algunas veces
hasta las 2 de la mañana!

MARISSA You were a part of history, parte de la
historia Cubana.

ARTURIN Si. Todavía hace Raul su calisthenics?

MARISSA Si, Raul still does his calisthenics.

ARTURIN Muy bien, muy bien. Yo también.
A mi me robaron el otro día. Unos jóvenes.
Estaba caminando después de ver a mi
espiritualista. Me golpearon, me quitaron
todo! Lo poco que tengo.

MARISSA How awful that such a kind and gentle
man was robbed and beaten. Lo siento mucho.

ARTURIN Ven. Ven.

MARISSA Arturin takes me down his small
corridor and into the kitchen. There are
radios stacked here too. From behind an
old wooden wall clock he pulls out a small
tattered cardboard box. Pieces of cardboard
crumble to the ground.
Arturin lifts out a small pin with Eddy's image from his presidential campaign, then a
yellowed handkerchief with Eddy's initials,
finally some audio tapes with large green
lumpy mounds of mold on them… and one
clean one.

(Wagner music.

MARISSA reveals Eddy's glasses.

*Eddy footage. MARISSA places Eddy's glasses
on her head.*

*This text is heard first with Eddy Chibas's voice
from the original recording in Spanish. That recording plays under the section above. MARISSA
first begins as if translating and eventually becomes
Eddy Chibas.)*

EDDY Five centuries ago the Tribunal of the
Inquisition cried at Galileo, "Liar and de-
ceiver! Present proof that the earth moves
around the sun!" Galileo could not present
the physical proof of the obvious fact and
was condemned, but kept repeating, firm in
his moral conviction, "But it moves! But it
moves!"
Five years ago I accused the Minister of
Education of stealing the monies for school
materials and breakfasts and of fomenting in
Miami an empire of real estate. The minister and all his leaders stormed in crying,
"Liar! Slanderer! Present the proof!" I could
not present the physical proof that they were
stealing the money from the National Treasury, but I kept repeating, firm in my moral
conviction, "They are stealing it! They are
stealing it!"
Last Sunday, from this same tribunal of
orientation and combat, I presented to the
people irrefutable proof of the enormous
corruption of the current regime: photographs of schools and hospitals in misery
contrasted with the ostentatious palaces of
governors that not long ago lived in poverty.
My words of this past Sunday did not have
the resonance required by the grave situation. Cuba must awaken, but my knocking
was not, perhaps sufficiently strong. We will
continue to call upon the conscience of the
Cuban people.
Cuba has a great destiny reserved in history,
but she should achieve it. Cuba has seen her
historical destiny frustrated until now by
the corruption and blindness of her governors whose thoughts have always soared at
ground level.
The only governing body capable of saving
Cuba is that of the Party of the Cuban People, Ortodoxos!
Forward fellow Ortodoxos! For economic
independence, political liberty and social
justice! Let us sweep away the thieves of
government! Ethics over greed! People of

Cuba arise and go forth! People of Cuba awaken! This is the final pounding on your door!

(MARISSA reaches her arm upwards and brings it down hitting her stomach as a gunshot is heard.)

EDDY I died on August 16th, 1951 shortly before my 44th birthday. My party, the Ortodoxos will never again have prominence. I will be a figure claimed by both Cuban exiles as well as those in Cuba. My suicide will create a political vacuum that will allow the dictator Batista to impose a successful military coup and the election of 1952 will never take place. It will be the end of democratic elections in Cuba. At the one-year anniversary of the triumph of the revolution, Fidel Castro will give a speech at my grave and state that the revolution began with Eduardo Chibas.

(Below the text in bold is MARISSA as an older RAUL.)

MARISSA Me acuerdo, I remember being haunted by the overwhelming presence of this man, this uncle, this legend whose tragic suicide hovered over our family. Eddy's photograph, which hung in whatever hallway or closet served as my father's office, lunged towards me defiantly. I knew I could never repair the depth of that loss. As a young adult I tried to get as far away from Cuba and the longing for that lost world as I could.

Me acuerdo, I remember one crisp fall day when I was in college trying to muster the courage to tell Raul that I'd found faith. I was raised on "religion is the opiate of the masses." Raul himself had been an altar boy and that experience turned him off to religion forever. I found a quiet place of peace and comfort with the Quakers.

Que? Los Quakers? Que es eso?

They believe that there is that of God in everyone.

Bah! Fanatics!

Well no, or else you would have heard of them.

How can there be a God that allows so much suffering that tolerates hunger?–This is the worst thing you could have done to me.

(Breath)

(Video image of Raul. Each line indicates a different voice in the hospital room.)

MARISSA Me acuerdo un hospital. I remember my father's hospital room. He is dying.

(Breath)

Many voices
Clicking heels along a long corridor
Que te dijo el doctor
The sound of a baby whining
Take him into the garden downstairs
Claro que esta aburrido aqui
Who put on this CD?
That it's soon and…

(Breath)

Did she bring more straws? He looks thirsty.
…y que– it's something like drowning, which…
So, this guy Papi knew from the Sierra is coming up now. I don't know him but he said he fought with Papi and insisted on coming up…

(Breath)

The phone rings
Hello, oh hi…Yes…thank you
Everything ok?
Yes, but…
We need more straws
OK, I'll get them
Por favor Capitan Ochoa, entra

CAPITAN Permiso

(Pause)

Mira Raul

(Pause)

I was in the Sierra with your father. We fought together. I was in prison after the revolution, like so many who dared question. They kept me in a ditch, that's how I lost my sight. I was there 27 years.

(CAPITAN begins to move the speaker diagonally downstage right.)

Te acuerdas Raul – Do you remember the Sierra? Do you remember when you first arrived there and immediately the planes came overhead and began shooting? You took cover at a nearby Campo. Remember the large trees that embraced and sheltered you. You moved on when you thought it was safe and scaled the side of a mountain where you met up with Fidel and the rest of us. More planes attacked, B26's began to fire. As soon as they stopped we all talked enthusiastically and optimistically about the future.

Remember how after each attack we felt renewed by having survived, and when our companeros fell, our souls swelled with the need to continue and fight?

And when we marched into San Lorenzo y Los Lajiales where we saw the grove named, Mango de las Mujeres, for the women hung and burned alive from those trees while fighting for independence from Spain.

Everywhere we marched and hid from fire held out our history to us with outstretched arms. The ghosts whispered through the hot humid air of the righteousness of our cause. We were not afraid. We were among those that live in no time, that trail eternally along the mango groves and sing of…revolution.

Te acuerdas how in the midst of the destruction and devastation we felt unparalleled hope for the future? How we were fueled by the campesinos who greeted us warmly and fed us and joined us, and how the stories of the heroes in the city filled us with strength and pride.

Do you remember the overwhelming feeling of the Nation, those in the cities and those of us fighting in the mountains, rising up as one voice to crush the dictatorship that had oppressed us for so long?

I remember how much you believed that there was a better way, a way that rejected the notion of the necessity of poverty and ignorance. That rejected disproportionate wealth.

(He stomps the ground and gestures upwards.)

I remember you Raul. I remember. Me acuerdo!

Now untie yourself from the pier and behold, Axe!

I remember you. Me acuerdo!

Todos vuelven a la tierra en que nacieron
Al embrujo incomparable de su sol
Todos vuelven al rincón donde vivieron
Donde acaso floreció más de un amor.
Axe! Ningun Cubano deber morir afuera de Cuba. Axe! Yo lo veo, lo veo alli! Lo veo en Cuba! Axe! Axe! Axe!

MARISSA What was that? Who was that guy? Papi? He's gone, he's gone.

(MARISSA slowly takes off the white shirt during this next sequence.)

Bajo el árbol solitario de el pasado
cuantas veces nos ponemos a sonar
todos vuelven para la ruta de el recuerdo
pero el tiempo de el amor no vuelve mas
Beneath the solitary tree of the past
How often do we find ourselves dreaming
We all return by memories road
que santo el amor de la tierra
que triste la ausencia que deja el ayer
How sacred is the love of the earth
How sad the loss of yesterday
que santo el amor de la tierra…

(MARISSA sets the shirt down center and in the next sequence collects Eddy's glasses and handkerchief, then Raul's jacket.)

MARISSA Before leaving La Habana I stop at a tourist shop and buy 12 medallions representing the Orishas. At that time I knew nothing about the Orishas, only know that they are the West African gods whose stories were carried to Cuba by the slaves brought there. Each African God has a Catholic Saint as a counterpart. I decide to wear this medallion with the name Ochun carved on the back, this one who wears a cascade of yellow flowers. The others I give away to my friends. When I return home I ask my mother who Ochun is. She tells me that her Catholic counterpart is La Caridad del Cobre, the patron saint of Cuba. How interesting. Of all 12 medallions I pick her. Is she known for anything in particular? Oh, yes… she saves people from drowning.

(MARISSA sets down Dalia's scarf with the other things. She has made an altar on the speaker with the clothing items she has taken off during the course of the play. She is wearing a bright colored no sleeved shirt.)

The Cave. As tempting as it is to stay here, I choose to call out for help. My guide, Stanley, reaches me in time and pulls me out of the water. *(She coughs, finds her breath.)* I feel the damp earth beneath me and am grateful — so grateful to be here.

Yo me acuerdo. No me puedo olvidar. Soy a hija de Raul y Dalia.

I am the daughter who sprang from the thoughts of Eddy Chibas.

I am the daughter of ocean breezes, and the New York IRT subway, of croquetas and hamburgers, of Celia Cruz and Duke Ellington.

I am the daughter whose deep roots travel far beyond homeland and geographical borders.
I am the daughter of miles de valseros, thousands of Cubans who have drowned trying to make their way to Yuma.
I am the daughter of those who question the time when democracy and capitalism became inextricably bound.

I am the daughter of those in Cuban prisons who dared demand their human rights.
I am the daughter of those Latino's in the U.S. currently being terrorized.
I am the daughter of those who seek justice and liberty wherever that may be.
Soy hija de un revolucionario Cubano
I am the daughter of a Cuban Revolutionary

Danai Gurira

Biography

Danai Gurira is an award-winning play-wright and actress. As a playwright, her works include *Eclipsed* (six Tony Award Nominations: Best Play, NAACP Award; Helen Hayes Award: Best New Play; Connecticut Critics Circle Award: Outstanding Production of a Play), *In the Continuum* (OBIE Award, Outer Critics Award, Helen Hayes Award), and *The Convert* (six Ovation Awards, Los Angeles Outer Critics Award). Her newest play, *Familiar,* received its world premiere at Yale Rep in 2015 and premiered in New York at Playwrights Horizons in 2016. She is a recipient of the Whiting Award, a Hodder Fellow, and has been commissioned by Yale Rep, Center Theatre Group, Playwrights Horizons, and the Royal Court. She is currently developing a pilot for HBO. As an actor, select credits include the Tupac Shakur biopic *All Eyez on Me*, Marvel's upcoming film *Black Panther*, Michonne on AMC's "The Walking Dead," *The Visitor, Mother of George*, and Isabella in NYSF's *Measure for Measure* (Equity Callaway Award). Gurira is an Ambassador for the ONE Campaign and founder of LOGpledge.org, an awareness building campaign focused on the plights of women and girls around the globe. She is the co-founder of Almasi Arts, which works to give access and opportunity to the African Dramatic Artist (almasiartsalliance.org). Born in the US to Zimbabwean parents, Gurira was raised in Zimbabwe and holds an MFA from Tisch, NYU.

Artistic statement

I was enthralled by an image I saw in *The New York Times* in 2003 of women in the Liberian war right when it was at its climax. There were some women rebel fighters who were getting attention in the Western press because no one had ever seen anything like this. I was raised in Africa and I had never seen anything like it, women with AK-47s, dressed very hip and looking formidable. I was keen to pursue that story and put it on the stage one day. When I get bit by that bug and the story is saying, 'You must tell me,' I then go through a process that is often painful, and arduous, and long—and joyful!—of submitting to the story until I prove a worthy enough vessel to get it out.

The idea of calling it *Eclipsed* was about saying there is great light in these breathing, vivid characters who have personality and flavor. They are not statistics. The idea is that their light has not been destroyed, it's been blocked. An eclipse is temporary. So, the hope in the title is that we will eventually start to see these women's faces, to hear them and know them.

Production history

The world premiere of *Eclipsed* was produced by Woolly Mammoth Theatre Company (Howard Shalwitz, Artistic Director; Jeffrey Herrmann, Managing Director) in Washington, D.C., on August 31, 2009. The play was directed by Liesl Tommy. The scenic design was by Daniel Ettinger, the lighting design was by Colin K. Bills, the costume design was by Kathleen Geldard, the sound design was by Veronika Vorel, and the production stage manager was Rebecca Berlin. The cast was:

THE GIRL	Ayesha Ngaujah
HELENA	Uzo Aduba
BESSIE	Liz Femi Wilson
MAIMA	Jessica Frances Dukes
RITA	Dawn Ursula

Eclipsed was produced by Center Theatre Group (Michael Ritchie, Artistic Director; Charles Dillingham, Managing Director) in Los Angeles, on September 13, 2009. The play was directed by Robert O'Hara. The scenic design was by Sibyl Wickersheimer, the lighting design was by Christopher Kuhl, the costume design was by Alex Jaeger, the sound design was by Adam Phalen, the original music was by Kathryn Bostic, and the production stage manager was Amy Bristol Brownewell. The cast was:

THE GIRL	Miriam F. Glover
HELENA	Bahni Turpin
BESSIE	Edwina Findley
MAIMA	Kelly M. Jenrette
RITA	Michael Hyatt

Eclipsed was produced by Yale Repertory Theatre (James Bundy, Artistic Director; Victoria Nolan, Managing Director) in New Haven, Connecticut, on October 23, 2009. The play was directed by Liesl Tommy. The scenic design was by Germán Cardenás, the lighting design was by Marcus Doshi, the costume design was by Elizabeth Barrett Groth, the sound design and original music was by Broken Chord

Collective, the dramaturg was Walter Byongsok Chon, and the production stage manager was Karen Hashley. The cast was:

THE GIRL	Adepero Oduye
HELENA	Stacey Sargeant
BESSIE	Pascale Armand
MAIMA	Zainab Jah
RITA	Shona Tucker

Eclipsed had its New York premiere at The Public Theater (Oskar Eustis, Artistic Director; Patrick Willingham, Executive Director) on October 14, 2015. The play was directed by Liesl Tommy. The scenic and costume design was by Clint Ramos, the lighting design was by Jennifer Schriever, the sound design and original music was by Broken Chord Collective, and the production stage manager was Diane DiVita. The cast was:

THE GIRL	Lupita Nyong'o
HELENA	Saycon Sengbloh
BESSIE	Pascale Armand
MAIMA	Zainab Jah
RITA	Akosua Busia

Eclipsed was developed with the support of McCarter Theatre Center (Emily Mann, Artistic Director) and developed by the Ojai Playwrights Conference (Robert Egan, Artistic Director).

    Eclipsed opened on Broadway at the Golden Theatre on March 6, 2016. The producers were Stephen C. Byrd, Alia Jones-Harvey, Paula Marie Black, Carole Shorenstein Hays, Alani Lala Anthony, Michael Magers, Kenny Ozoude, Willette Klausner, Davelle, Dominion Pictures, Emanon Productions, FG Productions, The Forstalls and MA Theatricals. The artistic team and cast remained the same as The Public Theater production.

4 *Eclipsed*
Danai Gurira

To the courageous women of Liberia and of every war zone. To my Auntie Dora, your light will never dim in our hearts.

Characters

THE GIRL	Fifteen
HELENA	Late teens/early twenties
BESSIE	Mid–late teens
MAIMA	Mid–late teens
RITA	Forties

Setting

Liberia: Bomi County, a LURD rebel army camp, 2003

ACT I

Scene 1

LURD Rebel Army Camp Base. HELENA and BESSIE, 'wives' of a Commanding Officer, sit. It is a dilapidated shelter; it may once have been someone's decent home. It is riddled with bullet holes and black soot and mortar residue, it is a partially indoor enclosure. Piles of used ammunition litter one corner. The enclosure is well organized, however, with obvious areas for cooking, sleeping and bathing. A tattered Liberian flag hangs on the back wall.

Lights up on HELENA sitting on a metal tub, styling BESSIE's wig.

BESSIE is six and a half months pregnant. They look offstage.

HELENA *(Getting up.)* Does dat look like the CO to you?

BESSIE Sorry! I tought I smell him, he has dis smell, I can smell it, can't you smell it? Maybe it just me who know his smell well well. Let's leave ha for few minute.

(HELENA pushes her over and lets THE GIRL out from under the tub.)

BESSIE *(To THE GIRL.)* Sorry.

(Pulls her wig off, goes and sits down next to tub again.)

BESSIE Can you finish? *(Indicating hair.)* It making my wig not sit right.

HELENA Come. *(Starts to finish braiding BESSIE's hair.)*
(To THE GIRL.) So den whot happen when he go back?

THE GIRL Oh, ya, dere dis one joke I no tell you, one time de servant call him, he say, he say, 'You sweat from a baboon's balls.' *(Laughing.)*

(HELENA and BESSIE are quiet.)

HELENA Whot dat?

THE GIRL It baboon sweating in de, de man parts – den he calling him dat.

HELENA Oh...ahh...ahh ha, ya dat funny, dat funny.

BESSIE So in de end he stay wit de African wife?

THE GIRL Wait! He lovin de American gal so she say no den he go back to Zamunda in Africa.

HELENA Where Zamunda – I neva hear of no Zamunda.

THE GIRL It not real.

HELENA Oh.

BESSIE Why he no be from Liberia?

THE GIRL I don't know. So he come back and dey have a big, big weddin.

BESSIE Wit de African gal!

THE GIRL WAIT! So we all tinking it wit de African gal and she walking wit de big wedding dress.

BESSIE African wedding dress?

THE GIRL Ahhh…no…it woz de white one.

BESSIE Oh…dose ones borin.

THE GIRL Ya. So he looking sad sad cause he tink it gon be de African one – and den, and den she get to de front and it NOT! It de American gal!

BESSIE So…de American gal win.

THE GIRL NO!! Dat de woman he love.

HELENA But he could have been wit me or you or ha – but de American tek him. And you say he Prince wit lot o money. He could have been wit poor African gal, den she can hep ha family. You say ha fada have restaurant – so she no need dat hep. I no like dat.

THE GIRL NO! It movie – it not real, it just a story.

HELENA I no like dat story. I goin –

(HELENA jumps and puts tub roughly over THE GIRL, and sits on it, BESSIE resumes her position. Both look up at a man and watch him, they jump into line as though in an army formation. BESSIE responds to him, gestures at herself, puts on her wig and walks out, following him – the audience cannot see him. HELENA watches them go, and lets THE GIRL out from under tub.)

THE GIRL How long I stay unda ere like dis?

HELENA How long? Don't know right now.

THE GIRL How long you been ere for?

HELENA Long time. Long, long time. Dey no let me go after de first world war, dey been keeping me for years.

THE GIRL Since you was how old?

HELENA Young.

THE GIRL Ten years, twelve years, fifteen years, whot?

HELENA Ten – fiftee – ten years.

THE GIRL And how many years you got now?

(BESSIE enters, goes and wipes between her legs with a cloth, comes and joins them, pulls off her wig and sits back down for HELENA to finish braiding.)

HELENA Lots of dem.

THE GIRL Whot? Whot dat mean?

BESSIE It mean she old! If she knew how many years she had she would have told you a long time ago.

THE GIRL You no know how many years you got?

HELENA I neva say dat.

BESSIE So how many den?

HELENA Enough to pull your head bald you no shut your mout.

THE GIRL Do you wanna know? Maybe we can figure it out.

HELENA No, dat's fine.

THE GIRL Don't you want to know? I don know, I just tink we should know who we are, whot year we got, where we come from. Dis war not forever.

HELENA Dat whot it feel like.

THE GIRL Ya, but it not. I want to keep doing tings. I fifteen years. I know dat. I want to do sometin wit myself, be a doctor or Member of Parliament or sometin.

BESSIE A whot?

HELENA So whot has dat got to do wit how many years I got?

THE GIRL It go hep you to know alla your particulars.

HELENA Okay – so how you go figure it out?

THE GIRL Okay. When did dey bring you ere? Which war woz it?

HELENA It de first one – I say.

THE GIRL So dat woz 1990 – no?

HELENA I tink so, I no know.

THE GIRL I tink it woz. So –

HELENA No, but it not happen like dat, I was in Nimba County, and Doe men come and dat when I first taken.

THE GIRL Ya, dat de same time.

HELENA Oh, okay.

THE GIRL So how you get to be wit dese rebels when you was attacked by Doe men?

HELENA Dey find me in de bush when I run.

THE GIRL And you been wit dem since den?

HELENA Ya.

THE GIRL No time you get away from dem?

HELENA *(Shakes her head.)*

THE GIRL You remember whot your age when dey catch you?

HELENA I was small small.

THE GIRL Before you bleed.

HELENA Ya.

THE GIRL So, maybe you had twelve, or thirteen years.

HELENA Ya.

THE GIRL So den you now maybe *(counting on her fingers)* – twenty-five years.

BESSIE Whoaw, see, she old.

HELENA You not so young. How many year she got?

THE GIRL You no know?

BESSIE I tink I about nineteen.

THE GIRL Why?

BESSIE Because dat when a woman got de juices to have baby and I got baby.

HELENA She so stupid oh.

THE GIRL When dey bring you?

BESSIE I was living in de nort and Taylor men everywhere, den de rebels come and start de fighting – dats when I woz taken. But I tink I been ere since I woz almost a woman.

HELENA She been ere not too long time.

THE GIRL You in de nort – I tink dat fighting woz just few years ago.

HELENA How you know all dese ting?

BESSIE Ha fada woz in de army.

HELENA Oh…

THE GIRL I just know when de army go where – I hear my fada and moda talking and – *(THE GIRL goes quiet, looks away, almost in a trance of silence.)*

BESSIE So how many years I got?

(THE GIRL doesn't answer, curls up in a corner and looks away.)

BESSIE Hey, whot ha problem oh?

HELENA Leave ha. She may be tinking on tings dat happen.

BESSIE Plenty, plenty happen to me, I neva look like dat.

HELENA SHUT it, jus go do sometin, go see – he coming.

BESSIE He no comin, I tek good care of him. I wanted him to sleep so he not go come back again. I mek sure he finish good and thorough. You gon finish my hair?

HELENA It not easy oh! You got de original African kink! And look at dis comb – it look like it be run ova by truck! You need a new one oh!

BESSIE When he go back to war I go ask for one – I need new wig, too.

HELENA You do oh. Dat one more nappy dan your head.

BESSIE No it not. It still mek me look like Janet Jackson oh.

HELENA You crazy.

BESSIE It does, plenty people tell me dat.

HELENA Like who?

BESSIE Like CO.

HELENA CO neva eva say nice ting like dat. He no know how.

BESSIE He no say nice ting to YOU. He say it to me.

HELENA Watch your mout oh. You forgetting who Number One. Just because he jumpin on you also –

BESSIE Plenty, he jumping on me plenty.

HELENA Dat no mean he like you betta.

BESSIE Whot it mean?

HELENA It mean –

(HELENA jumps runs and puts the bath over THE GIRL. The man enters, the women fall in line. HELENA points at herself. She goes out and glimpses at BESSIE as she does. BESSIE paces, looking agitated. HELENA enters.)

HELENA Tought you say you put him to sleep.

BESSIE Whot he wont?

HELENA None a your concern. Startin tomorrow, cook only half of de cassava and save de rest.

BESSIE Why? Who comin?

HELENA People comin. Dat all you need to know.

BESSIE Whot he tell you? *(Sucking her teeth.)* Who comin to eat all our food? We only have small sma –

HELENA Jus do as I say. Now come I finish your hair.

BESSIE *(Suddenly in a huff.)* No! I go finish it myself.

HELENA Dat fine for me! I love to see dat!

(BESSIE sits, attempting to finish her hair, can't balance mirror, can't see what she is doing, tries to comb it, comb flies out of her hand.)

BESSIE Shit man.

HELENA You fine?

BESSIE Leave me.

(THE GIRL knocks on tin bath.)

HELENA Oh! *(Quickly uncovers her.)* I sorry. You okay? I tink he gone for de night now, you sleep under dere, but we put some stone dere to keep it up so you can breathe.

THE GIRL Tanks.

HELENA We gon figure sometin betta for you in de morning.

(HELENA prepares a bed for THE GIRL and puts her to sleep under tub, prepares herself, and starts to get under covers. BESSIE still struggles with hair.)

THE GIRL Tanks.

HELENA You sure you fine?

BESSIE I FINE!

HELENA Good. I gon sleep.

BESSIE So sleep.

(HELENA goes to bed while BESSIE keeps trying to comb her hair. BESSIE gasps in frustration, HELENA chuckles quietly.)

Scene 2

BESSIE now asleep with hands still stuck in hair. HELENA is asleep. The tin bath now upturned, THE GIRL is gone. Middle of the night. HELENA wakes up, looks around for THE GIRL, can't find her anywhere. HELENA shakes BESSIE awake.

HELENA Where de gal?

BESSIE Hmmm?

HELENA Wake up or I go trash you! I say where de gal?

BESSIE I no know, I sleep.

HELENA Shit, shit, shit, shit.

(THE GIRL walks in looking dazed.)

HELENA Whot wrong wit you?

THE GIRL *(Doesn't respond.)*

HELENA Where you go to?

THE GIRL *(Doesn't respond.)*

HELENA Whot de matta? I say where you go? Whot did I tell you bout going by you self. You know whot dey gon do to you, dey find you? Do you know? Eh! Speak oh! Who dis gal tink she is eh? You know whot I do to protec you? You betta treat me wit respec, I wife Number One to Commanding Officer General. Dat mean, he trust me de most – I even tell oda men whot to do – if I tell him about you he go –

THE GIRL He already do it.

HELENA Whot? Whot you mean? He already do whot?

THE GIRL *(Numb.)* He already do whot you talking about – he know I ere. *(HELENA is silent, stunned. BESSIE looks on.)*

HELENA You meet him?

THE GIRL Ya.

HELENA He know I keeping you?

THE GIRL Ya.

HELENA Where he now?

THE GIRL He sleep, he told me to come back and go sleep. He catch me when I go to do wet.

HELENA Whot I tell you about going outta dis compound eh? Whot I tell you. Shit. We gon get it in de morning.

BESSIE You go get it, I neva say we keep ha from him.

HELENA Was it jus him? I say was it jus him?

THE GIRL Ya.

HELENA You bleed?

THE GIRL Ya.

(HELENA goes to basin, brings a wet cloth, kneels next to THE GIRL.)

THE GIRL I wash already.

(HELENA and BESSIE look on at her, shocked, confused.)

HELENA You okay?

THE GIRL Jus let me sleep, I say I fine, whot number I is?

HELENA Whot number whot?

THE GIRL Whot number wife? He say dere is a rankin.

HELENA Ah, ah…number four, you number four.

THE GIRL Whot number is she?

HELENA Tree.

THE GIRL So who Number Two?

(HELENA and BESSIE look at each other for a moment.)

HELENA She no ere right now.

THE GIRL Hmm…you show me tomorrow whot I do around ere.

HELENA Ya, I show you.

THE GIRL Can I sleep ere now? I no have to hide under dat now. *(Indicating tin bath.)*

HELENA Ya…ere *(Handing her a blanket.)*

(THE GIRL takes the blanket, lies down, and closes her eyes. HELENA and BESSIE watch her in confusion.)

Scene 3

Next day, BESSIE is washing soldiers' clothes in a basin and hanging them on the line, HELENA walks in with a bucket of water balanced on her head. She takes it down and pours it into the basin, then joins BESSIE in washing clothes.

BESSIE I tink she a witch oh.

HELENA Are you stupid?

BESSIE She go come in ere talking, 'Hep me oh!' Den she go lay wit de CO, it not even grieve ha! And she askin whot number is she – she act like he not just jump on ha, and she neva know man before! De first time for me I was crying for two days, he not dere, I crying, he come to get me, I cryin, he doin it, I crying, he stop, I crying, I go sleep, I crying, I was vex. She act like she got no problems. Like notin bad jus happen.

HELENA Coz she not like you, dat's all.

BESSIE No, she got sometin off. Maybe she goin off an she not showing it. I go watch ha close close. Whot you tell CO?

HELENA I say she woz hiding wit de small soldier.

BESSIE He believe?

HELENA He no mind, he got ha now. *(BESSIE stops suddenly and gasps as the baby moves, HELENA watches her.)* You alright?

BESSIE No, I no alright, I no want it. I gonna hate it.

HELENA No you not. It gon be nice to have a small one ere.

BESSIE Are you crazy? It meking me fat oh! You can have it den…why you neva have one, Number One? You been ere for long time. You neva get baby? You can't born?

HELENA *(She scrubs clothes harder.)* Go check on dat gal, I go finish dis.

BESSIE Why I go check on ha all de time? She FINE. I tol you she woz go be fine, you worry bout ha too much – when I first come you no –

HELENA Jus DO AS I SAY!

BESSIE *(She stops.)* You too harsh man. Fine, I go.

(THE GIRL walks in with firewood, humming a mellow tune to herself. BESSIE and HELENA look on, BESSIE looks over at HELENA for a long moment, goes back to scrubbing clothes.)

BESSIE *(To THE GIRL.)* You alright?

THE GIRL Ya.

BESSIE You fine?

THE GIRL Ya.

BESSIE You sure?

THE GIRL Ya?

HELENA Shut it, Number Tree.

BESSIE I checking. Like you tol me.

HELENA *(Sucks her tongue loudly at BESSIE.)* You know how to make fire? *(THE GIRL nods.)*

HELENA Good, do dat ova dere.

(She points at fire pit. THE GIRL goes to build fire, HELENA goes with her, watches her closely.)

HELENA Is you sure you fine? It betta den whot happen to some of de gals out dere, all de soldier get to have dem. Wit us, it just de CO. I know it no feel good right now, but it gon get betta – you gon get use to it – you alright?

THE GIRL I fine.

(THE GIRL succeeds in lighting fire.)

Scene 4

A week later. THE GIRL and BESSIE are eating. HELENA comes in with a plate of food. She throws it away, then starts to make a different meal.

BESSIE Whot? He no want dat? *(Rushing to retrieve the plate.)*

HELENA He acting like he got a spirit or sometin.

BESSIE He vex? Whot he saying?

HELENA He saying de food it taste funny and he tink someone or some spirit trying to kill him. He put a curse on hisself. How God gonna bless a man when he killing moda an chile and stealin and chopping. Den he wonda why he scared of spirits. He want me to make more food and to put dis in it. *(She holds up small pouch.)* He really scare coz o de people comin.

THE GIRL Whot's dat?

BESSIE It from de medicine man. It go make so dat no bullet can touch him. *(To HELENA)* Whot people?

THE GIRL How it go do dat?

BESSIE Dat whot medicine can do – don't you know? You no see de rebels dey got de marks on dere arms where dey put de special juju? Dat whot hep dem not get killed when dey fight. *(To HELENA)* Whot people comin?

HELENA *(Briskly preparing the meal.)* He gettin more and more mad oh. He actin like bigga devil. And he teking juju, den he keep saying stupid ting like, 'Oh, de monkey Charles Taylor, he got to die, I gon get him'. He don know who Charles Taylor is, whot he done or whot he gon do when he gone. Just talking a lot o notin. But I know why he like dis – he scare coz de women comin – dey gon mek him face hisself.

(HELENA takes food out.)

BESSIE WHOT?! Whot you mean? Whot she mean? WHOT WOMEN COMING?! Sometin off oh. He tekin his juju and she mekin me cook half de cassava. Sometin off. She no gon tell me dough. I gon watch dem close close. Tink dey can jus be hiding ting from me. I been ere LONG time! I can know all de same ting she know…see whot happen I no doin all de ting I do ere, whot dis place gon be like, I –

(HELENA comes back with several different items in her hands: dresses, shoes, scarves, a radio, a book.)

(Dancing with glee.) Ohhhh, dat whot I like to see, Number One, dat whot I like. I need some new tings, it been too long. Any high heels, some nice wig or sometin, dis one is finished, oh!

HELENA I gon get de rest. Number Four come hep me. DON'T TOUCH! Keep on doing whot you doin, notin happening ere.

(HELENA and THE GIRL exit.)

BESSIE *(Calling after HELENA.)* Don't be sour, oh, I ready for some new tings, just tell me whot I can have and not have. Now dat Number Two gone, I can go second right? Right?

MAIMA You sound happy I gone, Number Tree, it alright dough, I know you miss me much much.

(MAIMA enters from the other side of the compound, sharply dressed in tight jeans, a slinky top and a bandana, her AK-47 rifle slung snugly over her shoulder. She carries a sack of rice.)

BESSIE Whot you doin ere?

MAIMA Where I supposed to be?

BESSIE Somewhere doing some stupid ting.

MAIMA I a soldier and dis an army camp, so where else am I supposed to be?

BESSIE You no solider.

MAIMA Whot?

BESSIE I say you no soldier, you a wife like us.

MAIMA I woz a wife like you. Den I wake up. Ere, I bring special gift. *(Drags in a bag of rice.)*

BESSIE Is dat RICE! Oh! Dat so good oh we no have rice in long time oh! *(Catching herself)* But, if you want me to tank you, it not happenin – I know where you get it.

MAIMA You no worry bout dat, just cook it for us.

BESSIE You no know how to cook now?

MAIMA I no cook, dat de job you do. I know you missin me while I out dere, fighting for freedom, so I tought I go pay you visit, let you know I okay, we can have some good food togeda.

(HELENA enters with a few more looted items; she sees MAIMA and is visibly unnerved by MAIMA's presence.)

HELENA Whot…whot you…whot you wont ere?

MAIMA Ain't you glad to see me? Stop pretending you no glad to see I alive.

HELENA I not pretending. Whot I want to know is whot you wont.

MAIMA See, look how we be treating one anoda! I coming, bringing gifts from war and –

HELENA *(Getting composed again, but still not able to look at MAIMA.)* We no need no gifts.

MAIMA You talking like you got a spirit oh! I bringing rice. RICE!!! When woz de last time you see some rice eh?

HELENA Keep it, we got plenty cassava.

BESSIE But –

MAIMA Okay, I tek it to Commando Trigger's wives. I wonted you to have it first – but –

BESSIE *(Rushing over to HELENA's side.)* Can't we just tek it – she not bad no more, she trying to do good, maybe dis gift from GOD… PLEASE Number One, I so sick o cassava – I so SICK of it – PLEASE, just let ha leave it.

HELENA *(Ignoring BESSIE, to MAIMA.)* You still ere?

MAIMA Okay, I takin it. You wont to act like you loving on God so much, you neva hear of FORGIVENESS? Dat when you forget de past and give people new chance. You can't do dat, hah? *(She starts to lug rice out, she glimpses over at THE GIRL, who is looking at her intently.)* Who dis?

HELENA No one.

MAIMA Dis de new wife eh? You number Four? I Number Two. Where you from?

BESSIE How you kn –

MAIMA I know evertin that happens around ere, you don know dat by now? Where you from little gal?

THE GIRL Kakata.

MAIMA You likin it ere? Number One treatin you nice nice? She good at dat – in de beginning.

BESSIE We treatin ha betta dan you would, you have beat ha and shave ha head by now.

MAIMA Stop talking stupid oh, why don't you beat dis rice like a propa little commandant wife.

HELENA Don't do notin, Number Tree. Number Two, you ca –

MAIMA Disgruntled.

HELENA Whot?

MAIMA I have a nem of war now and it Disgruntled.

HELENA I no care bout whot you call yourself – just go. GO!

MAIMA Oh, so it still like dat eh? You gon kick me out like dog oh? Okay…okay…dat fine, I leave de new family be… for now…but I go come back. *(To THE GIRL)* Little gal, you let me know you need sometin okay? Number One de Great aint de only one got tings to teach. Dey go tell you, I can do ANYTING.

(MAIMA leaves.)

HELENA *(Sucks her teeth ferociously as she makes sure MAIMA is gone.)* Tink we gon trow a party for ha or what.

THE GIRL She got gun.

HELENA *(Sharply.)* SO?

THE GIRL *(Cautiously.)* Whot she do?

BESSIE Mmmm, she bad oh, *(very quickly, almost manically)* when I first come, me and ha we use to be good, good friends, she good wit hair oh, and she used to mek my hair nice, nice – dat woz de nicest my hair eva – *(she glances at HELENA)* – ah…ah…den she no like dat she not de one CO trust de most – because he be trusting on Number One because dey been togeda long long – den she start to get not nice – she like to fight too often oh, she no like dat he liking me and calling me first when he come from war – den a NEW gal come – dat when it get ugly oh –

HELENA Number Tree.

BESSIE Dis new gal woz cute oh. Even I getting jealous small small. And she have dis long hair, I no know how ha hair it growing like dat when she black like me oh! Maybe she a witch – dat whot I tinking now.

HELENA Number Tree.

BESSIE Den, I say oh, she go get CO all de time and all de tings he giving me gon go to dis little ting. But Number Two get too jealous oh. Den one day de CO come back from fighting and he got plenty tings. Den he call Number Four. Dat even vex me oh! Number One, she no mind. She no mind noting. Den –

HELENA NUMBER TREE – shut it oh!

BESSIE She ask – she ask whot happen.

HELENA You telling ha plenty oda tings dan whot happen.

BESSIE Okay – I go say it quick – I go say it quick. Okay, so den – where I woz? Oh, so den – *(suddenly remembers and laments)* oh, de rice, Number One, de rice!! Okay, sorry, sorry – so den Number Two see Number Four come back wit alla dese tings and she get new skirt, she get new dress, she get dese sandals, plenty, plenty tings. Den Number Two vex oh – so she wait till we all sleeping den she jump on Number Four – and remember I say Number Four little oh! So Number Two, she beat ha and tek ha tings, she give ha sabou! All dat nice hair she got – GONE – she beat ha face hard oh – in de morning ha face all swollen she looking bad – den when CO call for ha – she scared to tell him it Number Two – coz den Number Two go really finish ha propa, so den she say it a soldier but she no know who coz it dark – den CO tink she loving on anoda soldier so he kick ha out of dis compound. He no like to see his women loving on oda men. So den she go to anoda compound and in de next compound de women are not for one man in particular – dey fo everyone – so now she in bad way oh, all de soldier be having ha. Den Number One real vex and Number Two and ha, dey be treating each oda bad – so den Number Two she go get into de army to fight – and me I no know how she do dat or WHOT bad ting she doing to people out dere and –

HELENA You finish?

BESSIE Ya, I finish oh – she ask.

THE GIRL She a woman in de army?

HELENA She devil, dat all…devil. You stay away from ha oh. Okay?

THE GIRL Okay.

(HELENA sorts all the looted items out and carefully examines each one, folding the clothes with precision after carefully looking them over. Every now and then HELENA looks over her shoulder abruptly and BESSIE backs up.)

BESSIE You find a good wig?

HELENA Get back, I say I go sort tru it. *(She picks up a book.)* Don't know whot he want me to do with dis, it a joke or sometin?

BESSIE *(Taking it.)* I don't know. It a big ting oh, ere, let me tek it, it go keep de fire burning long time.

(THE GIRL jumps up and grabs at it as BESSIE is about to chuck it.)

THE GIRL I want it! If dat okay.

(BESSIE and HELENA look at her long and hard.)

HELENA You know how to use it?

THE GIRL Small small.

BESSIE Where you learn to use it?

HELENA Your ma and pa send you to school?

THE GIRL Ya…my ma…she mek sure I get book learning.

HELENA When?

THE GIRL I start five years ago.

HELENA So you can read and write and do all dem book ting?

THE GIRL Ya…

BESSIE Where you go to school? Where you find school in Liberia? She lying, she crazy oh!

HELENA Shut up ya mout. Dere still are some school left, and she come from near Monrovia, de fighting only been dere small, small time. It about sometin?

THE GIRL *(Examining the book.)* Ya…

HELENA Whot it about? Book tings or interesting tings?

THE GIRL I have to look, de front is tore off… it about a man.

HELENA Whot man?

THE GIRL *(Reading.)* Bill Clint – o. Bill Clinto –

BESSIE Bill Clinto –

HELENA A white man?

THE GIRL *(Reading more inside.)* Ya, he white. He from America.

BESSIE You sho he white? Dere lots of Liberians in America. Maybe he American from Liberia or Liberian from America.

THE GIRL No, I tink he American from America.

BESSIE So all dat big ting, it just about dat one man?

THE GIRL I have to read it first.

BESSIE How you gon read all dat ting? It go tek up all your eyesight, mek you blind.

HELENA You stupid. You no go blind from too much book.

BESSIE How you know? You no read.

HELENA You no read either!

BESSIE Number Four, you tell us, can you go blind from book?

THE GIRL I not sure, but I neva heard of dat.

BESSIE Dat don't mean it not happen. *(Sucking tongue loudly and goes to her corner.)* Can I have my clothes please!

HELENA Hold on. Are dose pictures?

THE GIRL Ya, dere lots o dem.

HELENA Let's see. *(THE GIRL opens the book and they proceed to look at pictures in the center of it.)* Ya, he white man. He most sure white man. Dis look like it he wife. I wonder if he need anoda.

BESSIE You want white man now?

HELENA I no want NO man but how I go survive I don't have one? If I have one I rather have Clinto and not de one I be having now.

BESSIE How you know he a good husband?

HELENA You can tell, he good, he go get his wife nice new ting – see how she dressed? Not old ting he steal from civilian. And he gon go places wit her and hold ha hand. He dances wit ha. Dat a good husband.

BESSIE You want de CO to dance wit you and hold ya hand?

HELENA *(Sucks her tongue loudly, ignoring her.)* Read some of it to us, Number Four. I want to hear about Clinto.

THE GIRL *(Reading.)* Oh, look he come to Africa, dis him in Uganda.

HELENA Oh, he holding African beby.

THE GIRL He is, it say de beby name Bill Clinto – dey nem it afta him.

HELENA Eh, Number Tree – you nem you beby afta Clinto maybe he go come rescue you.

BESSIE *(Sucking her tongue.)* He see me, he gon forget dat white wife. She betta not let him come ere.

HELENA Read some.

THE GIRL *(Reading.)* Okay, 'Bill Clinto– in de White Hos. Presid– ' Ah dat word too hard. 'Presi-dental work in de – '

HELENA Oh, it sounding boring oh.

THE GIRL WAIT – it gon get good, just give me a few min –

(She stops abruptly, they jump into formation, THE GIRL is called by CO off stage, she slowly and carefully puts the book in a corner and goes out. HELENA goes back to sorting out clothes, she silently puts a couple things aside for THE GIRL next to her book and gestures for BESSIE to look at the rest.)

BESSIE Wait, wait, wait minute. How you go give ha stuff first before me? I have bigger rankin dan ha! How she gon get when I no look yet? I taking whot I want from dere – *(BESSIE starts to go towards THE GIRL's stuff, HELENA blocks her.)*

HELENA Eh, eh, eh, don't you dare. Dat MY stuff dat I GIVING to ha. So you IS going second. Tek whot you want. But don't you let me find you taking no ting from Number Four.

(BESSIE backs up, sucking her tongue, she is thoroughly annoyed, goes over to pile and takes all of the items into her corner.)

BESSIE Dis ting was like it was made for me man! *(Putting on an African print top and matching skirt.)* I look like de first lady.

HELENA *(Barely looking up.)* Hmmhmm.

(THE GIRL comes back in, walking strangely. She crosses, takes water from nearby bucket, grabs cloth, goes to remote corner and cleans under her skirt.)

BESSIE He quick wit you, he be taking too long with me dese days.

HELENA Shut yo mout.

BESSIE Whot? Dat mean he be liking ha more – or she doing sometin dat mek him feel too good. Whot you do, Number Four? I want him to go quick quick wit me too.

HELENA LEAVE HA!

BESSIE I no know WHOT your problem is wit dis little gal. She notin special. She your chile or sometin? We all do it, she used to it now. See, look at ha, *(THE GIRL is in her corner, reading her book intently.)* she fine.

Scene 5

Two evenings later. Newly looted radio playing, BESSIE dancing to a few bars of a track.

RADIO Dat woz Awilo de jam number one across West Africa! Miss Economic Community of West African States, Miss ECOWAS happening dis Saturday in Accra, Ghana, where we get to love on our West African beauties. DON'T MISS IT!!! Youssou N'dour and Seun Kuti will be entertaining us all night long!

(Signal starts to fade out.)

BESSIE Oh, shit man *(She frantically turns the dial.)* Oh, don't stop talking DJ Jay D!!!!

Number One, come hep me get signal, it stop workin – it – *(BESSIE stops abruptly, sees MAIMA watching her in a corner. MAIMA is highly amused, with her AK-47 rifle slung around her back.)*

MAIMA Don stop for me Number Tree, you having disco all for yourself oh!

BESSIE Whot you doing ere now?

MAIMA Can't I visit my sistas wit no reason?

BESSIE *(Agitated.)* Whot you wont?

MAIMA Eh, eh! You wont to be harsh like dat oh! Fine, ere, I bring special gift for de new gal, *(Holds up a pretty cotton dress.)* she look like she still wearing tings she run tru de bush in.

BESSIE *(Suspiciously.)* What you want eh? You tryin to do some stupid ting, I know you oh. Leave ha, she don need no dirty dress.

MAIMA I tryin to tek good care of odas. Dat whot I know to do. Even if you ones don't. You de ones letting ha walk around like she livin wit lizards in de rocks.

BESSIE You don know how to do notin nice for no one. You betta go before Number One come back.

MAIMA Oh, ya, where is Number One de great?

BESSIE She getting wata, she no gon wanna see you.

MAIMA I no care whot she wont, I my own boss now, I no trying to mek ha happy.

BESSIE Just go oh, go fight to mek free Liberia or whateva you doin.

MAIMA Eh, eh, eh, don't talk what too deep for that nice empty head of yours oh. I IS fighting for a free Liberia. If you can carry one tought in dere, carry dat.

BESSIE LEAVE ME OH!

MAIMA Eh, why so vex? Fine, here de dress, you mek sure you give ha. If I see it on you, I gon have to tek it back.

(MAIMA exits. BESSIE impatiently watches her leave, grabs dress, looks it over, holds it to her body and places it against herself. She then puts it in her corner and attempts to look occupied just as HELENA and THE GIRL enter. THE GIRL has a bucket of water balanced on her head, HELENA walks in behind her.)

HELENA Whot your problem oh?

BESSIE NO! No problem! No problem!

HELENA *(Staring at her suspiciously.)* We bring wata, Number Tree heat cassava. Number Four, read Clinto.

THE GIRL Okay… *(Excitedly retrieving the book from her corner.)* so where we woz? Oh… Clinto woz at odds wit de entire government, wit de senate and de house – now both wit Repub – li – can maj – o – ity and seeking his blood if possible.

BESSIE AHH! Dey gon kill him?

HELENA NO! Dey can't kill de big man o America!

BESSIE Dey kill Doe.

HELENA Dat in Liberia oh! Dat no happen in America!

BESSIE Dey kill Doe.

HELENA Dat in Liberia oh! Dat no happen in America!

BESSIE Liberia and America de same oh! Liberia started by America! My great great grandmo –

THE GIRL I no tink dey talking bout killin killin. I tink dey talking bout stressing him.

HELENA/BESSIE Ooooh.

THE GIRL President Clinto woz still ad – ada – adamant – ly – denying his affair with Monica Lewi – sky, and Congress when –

HELENA Wait, wait, wait oh. Who is Congress and why he want to catch him and whot is affair wit Monica Lew – is – sky?

THE GIRL I tink Congress it like government, like ministers, but dey no have to answer to him.

HELENA Oh, okay – so dey can say whot happen to de big man o de country?

THE GIRL I tink dey vote and den dey can say yes or no to de big man. But dere anoda one – de, where dey now, *(Leafing through book.)* de Judi – s – a – ry, dey like oda ministers.

HELENA Why dey need so many?

THE GIRL I don know. Maybe it to mek sure many people can have say.

BESSIE So who Monica now?

HELENA She Number Two, no?

THE GIRL I tink so – but he not supposed to have a Number Two.

BESSIE Oh, that like my Pa – he only have my Ma, but den dis witch come and mek him look at ha den –

HELENA Number Four – can you keep reading.

BESSIE Oh, wait – why dey want to stress de big man?

HELENA Oh, ya?

THE GIRL Dey no like him – dey from anoda group – like he LURD like us and dey wit Charles Taylor men.

BESSIE Ooooh.

HELENA Ahh…okay.

THE GIRL *(Reading.)* It seemed de con – se – kence in mind woz to remove him from his pre – si – den – tal role –

HELENA Wait –

BESSIE To whot?

THE GIRL Dey want to mek him no be big man no more.

HELENA Why? Because he have a Number Two?

THE GIRL Ya, den he lie.

BESSIE Why dat gon mek him not be big man no more?

THE GIRL I don know.

HELENA Imagine we have dat ere – dere be no one to rule de country oh!

BESSIE I tell you, if Clinto see me, he gon want me oh.

THE GIRL My pa only love on my ma.

HELENA How you know?

THE GIRL I KNOW. He good husband. He tell me only be wit man who loving on me.

HELENA He no know dis war comin when he tell you dat.

BESSIE Keep reading. I wan de part when he come to Africa.

THE GIRL *(Suddenly agitated.)* No, I tired now.

HELENA Tek dis to dem.

(Hands her freshly cooked fufu. THE GIRL exits.)

BESSIE She get sour quick oh!

HELENA She missing family, dat all.

(THE GIRL returns.)

THE GIRL He say he wan to see you.

(HELENA exits.)

BESSIE You miss your pa and your ma?

THE GIRL Ya…*(Tears brimming.)* I wan my ma.

BESSIE I tink mine dead. But I tink I go find my broda when it ova. *(HELENA re-enters, with a few new loot items.)*

BESSIE NO!! He get more? When dey go fight?

HELENA Dey been gone two days.

BESSIE Oh. I no realize. Whot he bring?

HELENA Tek, I don want anyting.

BESSIE TANK YOU! *(She grabs things from HELENA, sorts through them ravenously.)* Oh, dis is NICE! Oh, I no like dat, whot is DIS! He crazy oh, he tink we grandmodas, ere Number Four.

(THE GIRL takes pile, a packet of hair extensions fall to the floor.)

BESSIE Oh, I wont dat! I no see dat!

HELENA Eyy, you let ha have it so now it hers.

BESSIE She no want dat anyway!

THE GIRL I wouldn't mind –

HELENA Ah, den it hers Number Tree, you already have your hair done anyway.

BESSIE NO! I need it – I higher rankin dan ha!

HELENA Ya and you give it to ha so now it ha's.

BESSIE I no agree.

HELENA So whot? I Number One and I say –

BESSIE If she de big man of dis compound den whot are we?

THE GIRL Whot are we whot?

BESSIE We de ministers, no?

THE GIRL Oh, we de Sen-ate and de Judiciary.

BESSIE So I as de Sen-ate – say 'no' to de big man.

THE GIRL Okay, den I as de Judiciary, I say 'yes'.

HELENA So whot I say go – de extensions are for Number Four.

BESSIE Shit man. *(Goes to her corner, scowling at THE GIRL and HELENA.)*

HELENA Come I braid it for you Number Four.

THE GIRL Oh…okay

(THE GIRL goes to sit down; when called by CO, points at herself and goes. BESSIE sulks in corner, HELENA leans back and closes her eyes, BESSIE starts to inch toward HELENA, watching her as she does, she gets close to extensions, and attempts to take them.)

HELENA Don't even.

(BESSIE, retreats, deflated.)

BESSIE It no fair, I NEED those, I having baby and I gon get bigger and ugly, I need my hair to look nice at LEAST.

HELENA You not gon get ugly.

BESSIE Yes I is, you know how des women look when dey have beby, dey face go big like it got air and dey eyes go small like bird and dey lips go wide like dis and dey look BAD. I want to use de hair to cova my face small, small.

HELENA You gon be fine. De CO not gonna jump on you so much.

BESSIE I know, dat de one ting. He gon be on Number Four PLENTY, coz he no jump on you no more and – ah… ah…whot I say? I no mean to say like dat whot I –

HELENA Just go sleep.

BESSIE Okay. *(She goes and lies on her mat.)* You tink Clinto's Number One angry wit him?

HELENA Ya.

BESSIE You tink dey all living togeda nice nice now – like us?

HELENA I no know – I no tink dey do it like us. I tink de women can leave.

BESSIE Number Two leave…

HELENA She no leave, she just fightin wit dem now. Dat not de leaving I mean.

BESSIE Ya. Dat true.

HELENA Number Tree?

BESSIE Ya?

HELENA You been savin de cassava like I tell you?

BESSIE YA! Tell me whot happening. What you keeping keeping de cassava for?

HELENA I gon cook it all in de morning.

BESSIE WHO COMIN?

HELENA Neva matta. No one you gon find interstin. Number Tree?

BESSIE Ya?

HELENA Sleep.

BESSIE Fine.

(THE GIRL enters, goes and wipes between her legs, and curls up on the mat. HELENA blows out torch.)

Scene 6

Next day. At camp, by the compound, RITA, a member of Liberian Women's Initiative, an upper-class, well-educated woman; throughout she occasionally speaks 'Liberian English' like the women in the camp but her proper English often takes over. She is relatively new to the struggle for peace and functions awkwardly in this rough terrain. She approaches HELENA, who is pounding cassava with a mortar and pestle.

RITA How tings?

HELENA *(Surprised.)* How tings? How you come follow me out ere? I got to finish dis *(Indicates cassava.)* You need sometin?

RITA No, ah… I just… I… I wanted to see how things going out here.

HELENA Whot?

RITA And to tank you for de cooking it was very good so tank you.

HELENA You off oh?

RITA Whot you mean?

HELENA How you go tank me for cookin? Dat whot I do, dat whot we do ere, how you tank for dat, you off oh.

RITA That not all you can do – dere much more you could do – no one should expect that from you. *(Beat.)* I know I am not really meant to be out here *(Looks around cautiously.)* My colleagues like to follow some rigid protocol when we meet with the COs. But I believe we should take every opportunity to meet you gals. Rita –

(Rita looks around the compound, intrigued, horrified. She has obviously never been in a place like this before.)

HELENA Well, you betta go. *(Beat.)* How you come here? How it okay for you to come here? Why he let you in, treat you good, give you our cassava, not mek you a wife like us?

(Beat.)

RITA Okay. *(Beat.)* Well, we are a part of a large network of women peace makers, it is our mission to end dis war. Right now we are negotiating with the factions to immediately obey the ceasefire, to put down their guns. The only way to do that is to come to these different warlords and talk them down. *(Beat.)* They have been doing this for a long time, they – ah – *we* have quite a reputation in de country now, it allows *us* to come and go like how you see.

HELENA Why he so scare of you?

RITA He isn't scared of us.

HELENA He is! He told no one do notin to de Peace women when dey come, he no treat no one else like dat. And he been using his juju a lot just now. Dat how I know he scare de most, when he using dat stuff. It mek his spirit go quiet. So ya, he scare of you.

RITA Well good. GOOD. They scare of us, maybe we can actually get them to the point where things change and they stop acting like BEASTS, trying to treat us like we village girls they rob from de bush.

HELENA *(Coldly.)* Is dat right.

(An awkward pause ensues for a few beats.)

HELENA Why you do all dat stuff?

RITA Why? Why you tink? You happy with Liberia as it going? You tink dis a nice place? Look at de tings going on my dear! Look at where YOU are! You tink it normal you wifing some dirty self-proclaimed general in de bush? You tink it normal a boy carrying a gun killing and raping? You think it okay dere no more schools, no more NOTIN! I had to WALK my son from Kakata to the Ivory Coast just so he could stay in school!

HELENA Okay, you don have to get vex.

RITA Sorry... I...

(A few beats pass, HELENA stores ground cassavas, RITA starts to look around curiously.)

RITA So...do ah...any other gals comin around lately?

HELENA *(Suspiciously.)* Why you asking me dat?

RITA If I...if I could get you out of ere – would you go – would you go with me?

HELENA Go where?

RITA You can go to school, you can –

HELENA Where I gon go to school?

RITA I can get you in a camp in Cote D'Ivoire or –

HELENA Where dat?

RITA Ivory Coast.

HELENA Oh. So why you calling it sometin else?

RITA No mind. Why would you not go?

HELENA I don know.

RITA Would it be a hard choice? If I could get him to agree, would it be so hard to leave this?

HELENA No...but ...

RITA You happy ere?

HELENA No, but dis is war and I whot else I gon do?

RITA You know all the things you can do if you go to school, the ways you can improve your life! You can get your own business, own your own house, take care of your children –

HELENA I no have children.

RITA But you might have them! Things could be over soon, you have to think about whot your life can be.

HELENA I no know, I wife Number One I been wit him for long, long time. I tek care o him, I–

RITA The war ends – are you still wife Number One?

HELENA I... I no know who I is out of war – dat not whot I get to tink about.

RITA I am going to hep you – it is going to end.

HELENA I got tings to do ere, tings no gon happen propa I go. I tek care o CO. I have rank ere now. I can tell de small small boys whot to do. I care for de oda women. And dere lots o tings we doin ere now – we even reading book in de compound.

RITA Whot book?

HELENA It about de big man of America, Clinto.

RITA Clinton?

HELENA Ya. And his government. And Monica his Number Two and how de Judiciary and Senate and Starr trying to stress him. *(RITA laughs.)* We no know if he stop being big man because of his Number Two or not – we no get dat far yet. You know whot happen? If you know don't tell me notin.

RITA I no gon tell you. But you know that happen long time ago oh. Five years or so.

HELENA We no mind, it still good story, don tell me whot happen. *(Beat.)* But, you know, when I look at you, you know all dese book tings – I do wan to learn – I neva go to school – I do want dat. It just… I just don know if I can learn now – I getting old to be sometin different.

(HELENA walks out, taking the cassava with her. RITA watches her for a bit, thinking. She grabs a stick, and starts to write in the dust. HELENA reenters.)

HELENA Whot you doin?

RITA Writing my name. Whot's yours?

(HELENA stares at RITA for a long beat.)

HELENA My nem? Numba One.

RITA The one your ma and pa give you!

HELENA NO. I wife Numba One to the Commanding Officer of LURD Army – I –

RITA WHAT DID YOUR MOTHER CALL YOU?

HELENA I – I neva use it – I –

RITA You MUST know it. Tell it to me – now.

HELENA It… it… I can't.

RITA *(Seeing HELENA is shaken.)* Okay, it's okay, just whisper it to me, try. *(RITA holds HELENA close, putting her ear to her.)* Come on gal. *(HELENA whispers something inaudible into RITA's ear.)* That's beautiful! Here let me show you whot that look like – *(RITA writes HELENA's name in the dirt.)* There – you do it – *(Hesitantly, HELENA takes the stick and writes out the same letters.)* Good… good… very good *(HELENA finishes writing her name.)* That your name. You just do it.

HELENA No lie?

RITA No lie.

HELENA It not that hard!

RITA No, it not! Now let me show you what each letter it is –

HELENA I can't believe OH! I do book ting! *(RITA laughs.)* I gon tell de new gal! *(RITA stops dead, stands up.)*

RITA Whot? Whot new gal?

(Lights.)

Scene 7

THE GIRL enters, humming a tune, she picks firewood and places it in a wheelbarrow. After a moment she picks up a stick, starts writing something in the dirt with it, MAIMA enters, unseen by THE GIRL, she watches her for a beat and then:

MAIMA So you city girl eh?

THE GIRL *(Startled.)* Yah.

MAIMA I know Kakata well well. I get supplies from dere all de time. You run for long time?

THE GIRL *(Cautiously.)* Some… some days.

MAIMA Ya, dat hard eh. But you look strong oh. Like you got a lotta powa!

THE GIRL Powa?

MAIMA Ya. I can see your eyes, dey got fire! And your arms and legs – dey strong oh.

THE GIRL *(Giggling, embarrassed.)* No!

MAIMA Yes! You got to tap dat powa oh. You tink God give all dat to you for notin? You tink God let you survive for notin? You got to do de tings you called to do oh. Is dis it? Picking firewood in de bush? Dis whot your powa for?

THE GIRL I… I don know. *(Giggles again.)*

MAIMA Whot? Whot so funny oh?

THE GIRL It just… it just… Number One say you devil, but you talking like you prophet.

MAIMA Number One say dat eh?

THE GIRL Hmmhmm! *(She continues to giggle. MAIMA laughs too, though in a different tone.)*

MAIMA Ya… ya dat funny oh. *(Beat.)* How you like *Numba One*?

THE GIRL She fine.

MAIMA *(Lighting a cigarette.)* She kick me out oh. Ya… Some stupid gal was lovin on anoda soldier who beat ha. Den she gone tell Numba One dat it my fault she get trown out – Numba One believe ha and not me – She crazy oh.

THE GIRL What about de sabou?

MAIMA HA! So dey tell you already. Dey not gon tell you how dey getting all dose tings de CO bring from war eh? How he getting dem *(Taking a long drag on her cigarette. Then vexed.)* He giving WORSE den a sabou! HA! But dey wann act like dey clean o all sin or sometin. You trust who you want. Like Tupac say, Only God can judge me. *(Putting out her cigarette.)*

THE GIRL So where you get dis den? *(Tugging on jeans.)*

MAIMA Kakata.

THE GIRL And dis. *(Indicating earrings.)*

MAIMA Dis… dis from de big city.

THE GIRL You get tings from de big city!

MAIMA Ya. *(Laughs.)* Plenty tings. Didn't you like de dress?

THE GIRL Whot dress?

MAIMA What? Dat STUPID gal. I go fuck ha up good. *(She sucks her teeth.)* I brin you dress. So you can look betta dan dis. So you can look good like me. Don worry, let ha have it. Whot you wont? Tell me whot you like.

THE GIRL Nail varnish.

MAIMA Ah, which color – you look like you like de red one, or de purple.

THE GIRL Pink.

MAIMA *(Laughing.)* Okay. Dat good! You have to decide whot you wont. Dis is war, how you gon survive? Dis is how *(Indicating gun.)* – den you can prospa – you can get every color of de rainbow nail varnish, it no matter whot happening. And most important – no man gon touch you. *(Examines her closely.)* So de CO he like you, ha? He jump on you a lot? You like dat? Look at me. Is dat whot you want? Hmmmhmm? Did you like dat?

THE GIRL No.

MAIMA *(Militarily.)* Whot?

THE GIRL NO.

MAIMA So whot you gon do? Let me tell you de last time a man jump on me. In fact, I can't remember, all I know is he not know I have gun. He dead now. No one gon jump me again. Now, I choose who I lovin on. Because of dis. Whotever you wan, it's yours. Just go get gun.

THE GIRL I can't… no…

MAIMA It easy right now – dey need soldier – dey so desperate for fighter now, dey tek baboon if dey could teach it who to fire. Ere, *(Hands her gun.)* try it – hold it.

THE GIRL I don –

MAIMA TRY.

THE GIRL *(Takes gun.)* It heavy oh.

MAIMA Now hold it like dis and you point it forward – Now fire.

THE GIRL No, I scare.

MAIMA Scare of whot? FIRE! GIRL FIRE!!

(THE GIRL fires the gun. She gasps, panting. Adrenaline flooding her system. MAIMA, pleased, affectionately strokes her head.)

Scene 8

At camp. Next day. HELENA is cooking and intermittently changing the channels on the temperamental

radio. THE GIRL is painting her nails. BESSIE is leaning against a crate, eyes shut, breathing hard.

BESSIE *(To HELENA as HELENA changes radio channels.)* Wait – dat good song – WAIT – Dat music oh! Whot your problem? Let de songs play oh!

HELENA I not looking for music.

BESSIE Whot you want den?

HELENA Neva matta.*(Beat.)* I want to know whot happenin.

BESSIE Where? What happenin wit whot?

HELENA Wit de WAR.

BESSIE You got a spirit dat too strong oh. So you want to hear dose people just talkin and talkin?

HELENA Yes. It called *news*.

BESSIE Who –

HELENA SHHHH your mout oh!

RADIO …as fighting intensifies approximately one hundred women all dressed in white marched to the U.S. Embassy in Monrovia calling for immediate and direct intervention by the U.S. government leading to… *(Radio crackles and dies.)*

HELENA *(Sucks her teeth.)*

BESSIE And we coulda be listening to music all dat time oh! *(Changing position with discomfort.)* Was dat one a de peace women I saw you talking to?

HELENA Ya.

BESSIE Like de ones who come last time?

HELENA Ya.

BESSIE Dat who woz comin?

HELENA Ya.

BESSIE Oh dat borin oh. Why she talking to you? I tought dey not talking to us, just to de CO. I tink dey witch oh, dey can talk to CO like dey men or someting.

HELENA Dey not witch.

BESSIE Whot? So why dey can do dat? Dey got some strong juju. Dey off oh.

HELENA No. Dey been workin on dis stuff for long time from de city so de CO have to show dem respec dat all.

BESSIE Ya coz dey witch.

HELENA Not everyone witch!

BESSIE *(She adjusts her position with difficulty.)* Ahhh…senate want to pass bill. It de – 'No work when baby coming' bill. I can't do notin – I hate dis, I HATE DIS!! I no feel good Number One.

HELENA Stop talking like you a small chile, you go HAVE a chile, act like it oh!

BESSIE I shoul neva listen to you, I no want dis ting.

HELENA You go have it, and you go love it, cause dat whot a moda do.

BESSIE I no want to BE no moda. You say you go tek care of it. You betta. An you KNOW you go tek care of it if it got a face like dat ugly fada of it. Read Clinto Number Four.

THE GIRL I no tink he too ugly.

(HELENA and BESSIE stop and stare at THE GIRL curiously.)

THE GIRL He got a big nose, dat is true, but he no too ugly, his eyes and his mout not too bad.

BESSIE Dere sometin wrong wit you. Really someting wrong oh.

HELENA And where you get dat from? *(She indicates the nail varnish.)*

THE GIRL Whot?

HELENA DON 'whot', whot you tink? Dat ting you holding in your hand.

THE GIRL Oh…dis wos gif.

BESSIE Gif from who?

HELENA EEEEY! You no ask ha notin! I wife Number One ere ha? So shut ya mout. A gif from who?

THE GIRL Dey tol me not to tell.

HELENA TOLD YOU WHOT? I no tink you understand where you are. You are in my territory, little gal, I am de 'Commanda In Chief' in dis ere country of dis compound – EVERYONE do like dey is tol, dey follow command. You don wanna see wha –

THE GIRL Dat not whot she tol me.

HELENA Whot?

BESSIE Whot she say?

HELENA Whot you say?

THE GIRL I SAY…dat not whot she tol me.

HELENA Who? Who tell you WHOT?

THE GIRL She tell me dat she woz de one de CO love de most even dough you wife Number One.

HELENA Oh, of COURSE –

THE GIRL DEN, den, she watch how you always mek it so everyting go tru you, jus like when de loot come de oda day and you de one who decide who get evertin firs and you decide who get whot

HELENA HA!

THE GIRL AND she say she bring me nicer tings dan whot you get and Number Tree steal whot you bring me and –

BESSIE *(Hastily.)* She a LIAR oh! She lyin Number One, I tell you true –

HELENA She back again? WHERE she be?

THE GIRL She go again, wit de soldier, she go to fight.

HELENA Where you see ha?

THE GIRL Out dere when I go to get de firewood.

HELENA So whot? You like ha? You wanna fight now eh? You wanna be in de army?

THE GIRL I tinkin about it.

HELENA She tinkin about it.

BESSIE Tinking!

HELENA You no know notin little gal! NOTIN. You tink you can fight, you go do dat, you go see whot happen to you – de ting you go end up doin out dere. You wanna kill a man, a woman, a small small chile? You wanna do dat, hey?

THE GIRL No, but I no gon do dat.

HELENA How you no gon do dat? You go do whot da commanda tell you go do. If he tell you go kill dat village and bring him tree wives, you go have to do dat.

THE GIRL She no say dat, she say –

HELENA She go say good ting coz she wan you to be like ha, but she LYING to you.

THE GIRL No, she tell me she get whotever she wont from de civilian, she tell me she only go for Charles Taylor men, not de modas and de children.

BESSIE Let ha go! She crazy oh!

HELENA SHUT YA MOUT! You no know whot you talking about little gal. Dey go mek you do all de ting you see when you and you family have to run, all dose ting and worse. Do you know whot she do? Whot dese soldier do? Whot dey done in my presence? Dey gon mek you slit a moda's stomach and tek out de beby to see if it boy or a gal. Dey gon mek you –

THE GIRL *(Explosively.)* I NO GON DO NO TING LIKE DAT!!! But if I soldier, I no have to stay ere no more!

HELENA It betta ere den –

THE GIRL NO it not. Look at ha! She gon have his beby! I NO WANT DAT!!

HELENA We can stop dat, dere is dis leaf you can chew –

THE GIRL I NO WANNA CHEW NO LEAF! I want him to leave me alone. I just want to get AWAY FROM HIM! Now she gettin big, he gon jump on me all de time, he no want you no more, and I no want dat! If I got a gun, don nobody gonna fuck wit me no more. I wan dat.

HELENA Dat whot she say? No one fuck wit ha now?

THE GIRL Ya, dat whot she say. And dat whot I wan.

(She gets up, walks out.)

★

ACT II

Scene 1

Two days later. The middle of a shootout. MAIMA fires some shots in the direction of random gunfire. They crouch close to the ground. THE GIRL holds her gun close to her body and stares on. She attempts to prep her gun and it gets stuck and she falls, struggling to unjam it.

MAIMA Okay, listen good oh! Check de ammo for any dents in cartridges. Now, when you put de magazine into dat hole dere – put dat forward lip of de magazine into de hole first. Ya. And be sure de magazine it flat down. *(THE GIRL dislodges magazine and does as instructed.)* Good. Now you pull de charging handle to de back, all de way…all de way and release. You have to know how to do dat quick quick.

THE GIRL Okay.

MAIMA Now come *(THE GIRL hesitates, starring at the carnage in front of her in distress.)* COME.

(THE GIRL cautiously approaches her.)

MAIMA You see dat one dere?

THE GIRL Ya.

MAIMA Dat de enemy – now fire him.

THE GIRL Why?

MAIMA Whot?!

THE GIRL Why we firing dem? Why…why dey choppin de men like dat? Why can't we just let dem go somewhere, run away, why –

MAIMA I don't know whot you talking about. To me, dat is de ENEMY. Do you know dey harboring lots of Charles Taylor men ere? Do you know whot dey could do to you? Dose are de monkeys who kill our mas and rape our grandmodas.

THE GIRL But dey just living ere – dey –

MAIMA EEEEYYYY! *(Grabs her face and looks deeply in her face.)* LISTEN TO ME! Dose are Charles Taylor's monkeys! Dat who we fightin. We are fighting de monkey Charles Taylor. He eating and drinking and living like a king in a land of paupers. We drive him out.

And we gon keep on putting on de pressure. He scare of us. We gon do him worse dan dey do Former President Samuel K. Doe. We gon catch him and dress him like a woman before we kill him. We gon restore Liberia to its rightful people. You understand, de enemy, de enemy is no longer human being. Okay?

THE GIRL Okay.

MAIMA *(Redirecting their attention to the fighting.)* Now…see dat one?

THE GIRL Ya.

MAIMA Fire him. Do like I show you, NOW.

(After much hesitation she shoots with her eyes closed.)

MAIMA Ah, come on – *(Holds gun in direction of man.)* Fire again. FIRE.

(THE GIRL shoots.)

MAIMA Good gal. Now you doin sometin, you hepin us get closa to freedom. One monkey at a time. You don't go nowhere. Stay down okay?

(MAIMA gets up and goes. Moments later MAIMA returns.)

Okay, it's ova. You do good. You do good, good. Round up de young gals.

THE GIRL Whot young gals?

MAIMA You'll see dem as you walk around. Round dem up. Dat's your job.

THE GIRL Where we gon tek dem

MAIMA Back to de camp.

THE GIRL For whot?

(MAIMA doesn't respond.)

THE GIRL Whot? For de generals? *(MAIMA doesn't respond.)*

THE GIRL NO, no no no no no. How can we do dat to dem – den de same ting dat –

MAIMA You want it to be you? You want to do it in dere place? Dey won't mind, dey will tek anyting. Dey is beasts and beasts need to be fed. It dat simple. We have to provide dem wit fresh meat or dey go find it some oda way and you don't want to be dat oda way, do you?

THE GIRL But I thot you say dat –

MAIMA You feed dem, you not get eaten. Dat simple. Go and get de gals or I go have to tell dem you want to replace de gals today. Is it you or dem? Dis is how you survive, you understan? So is it you or dem, Number Four?

THE GIRL Don't call me dat.

MAIMA Den go get de gals. If you want a name of war, act like a soldier and HUNT. Go. Go on gal. Go. GO.

(*They stare at each other for a long moment and THE GIRL goes.*)

Scene 2

One month later. MAIMA leads RITA to a make-shift latrine in the army camp, MAIMA's gun firmly clutched. RITA wears a T-shirt with the words, 'DI-ALOGUE DIALOGUE DIALOGUE' across the front.

MAIMA So right now I looking to find some sound system. It right ere. (*Pointing at latrine with rifle.*) You know dose in high demand, oh.

RITA Is dat right? (*Trying to mask a grimace as she examines latrine, positions herself, and squats to urinate.*)

MAIMA Ya! See, you women from de city you tink we backward out ere, we know whot is happenin, we got radio, Bose, evertin out ere.

RITA Ohhh!

MAIMA (*Runs to RITA, pulling rifle into position.*) Whot matta?

RITA Notin. I just almost fall in.

MAIMA Don't do dat, you gon get a shit bath you fall in dat! I sure you used to betta, you women from de city, but dis all we have ere.

RITA Dat fine, dat fine. (*Adjusting her clothes, coming out from latrine area.*) Thank you.

MAIMA So. You got some tings to sell from de city? Some rice, some cloth, tings like dat? We can mek our trade on a regular. You come and bring tings from de city den I gon sell it out ere in de bush. One a my men he heping me sell. We can do good business. You got some tings?

RITA No, noting.

MAIMA Noting? You say you was business-woman.

RITA I was. I woz in big business, big, big business. Not whot you tinkin. (*Almost reminiscent, almost with pride.*) I had a petrol station, two supermarkets, a hair salon – you know dat woman at all the important events with de big, big head wrap and a lot of makeup? Dat woz me. (*Beat.*) I doing different work now.

MAIMA Whot? Dis peace ting? Dat not gon bring you no profit oh! You woz doing good oh! We could have work togeda! It best to work wit de system, and right now – de system it war.

RITA De war gon end, it gon end soon –

MAIMA How you know? De fightin getting stronga! LURD is getting bigga! We tekin more an more!

RITA I know, people are dying, for no reason. De fighting getting closa and closa to Monrovia. It real bad now. We was just ere a mont ago and we had to come back again. Your CO got to stop dis. He got to tell his army to stop.

MAIMA Stop for WHOT?! Dis whot we got to do to get rid of de monkey Charles T –

RITA Charles Taylor not de only problem. We see de villages you LURD be tekin ova, modas, grandmodas and children dying. Dat got to end too, don't you tink? Aren't you tired? Don't you want to go home to your family? To move forward? Where you from?

MAIMA I from Liberia.

RITA Whot is your name, the one your family give you?

MAIMA See, I know whot you women try to do. You trying to mek us weak. You want us to start to feel like little gals crying – 'Ooh, I lost my ma, ooh, ooh, I lost my pa, dey hurt me, dey rape me'. I no do dat no more, go to de villages if you looking for stupid gal like dat. I hep mek women strong. Dat whot I do. You want cryin little ladies, go to de Commandant wives. Me, I no care about –

RITA Do you miss your ma? What did she wont for you when you get big?

MAIMA EH, EH! Who you tink you talking to? YOU, you women, you come up in ere like you – (*Gaining her stride.*) We all know de REAL reason you doin dis – no man wont you so you got notin else to do but botha us – you need a man? Let me try see I can find you one. It may be hard! You not so fresh no more

RITA (*Aghast.*) You rude little ting. (*Explosively.*) You who runnin around witout a tought in your head, showing off wit dat stick dat kill people. And trading your pussy for profit –

MAIMA (*Agitated.*) EH EH EH! WHO YOU TINK YOU TALKING TO? You know de tings I go do to you, you not protected by de Commanda?

RITA (*Regaining her composure.*) Okay, okay, okay... I apologize for whot I just said. I do. I do. (*Beat.*) I ask you about your moda, about your name because you don't wont to lose dat, you must neva lose dat. (*She reaches out to touch MAIMA, MAIMA backs up violently.*) When I lose ha...those LURD boys just tek ha. Dey knock me down with their guns and drag ha away. I busy shouting, 'Do you KNOW WHO I AM!' Dey didn't care who I woz. I woz just another woman to be abused. And she had tings, tings she wanted to do, to be, she wanted to be a businesswoman like me or something. And it MY fault because I know that I could have protected her better than that. I should have gone to Ivory Coast or Ghana or something. I stayed ere because I wont to profit from war, tinkin somehow my money gon keep me safe. It didn't do noting for me dat day. How long you tink you can mock God before He mock you back?

MAIMA Who you talkin about? (*Beat.*)

RITA My...my daughter... I talking bout my daughter. So please, please trust, I ere to hep – I suffering too.

MAIMA LURD tek ha?

RITA Yes.

MAIMA Ha. So dat why you ere. Actin like you ere for peace talks. Dat why you coming out all de time, talking wit us even though de oda women you wit stay at de CO compound. Actin like you care bout us – you just lookin for your daughter ere. HA! Well, I not ha, so you can get offa me oh.

RITA No you not ha. You certainly not. (*Beat.*) But I am also ere to hep.

MAIMA Hmmmhmmm!

RITA I am! And I looking at you right now. And I wont to know – who is your moda and whot is your nem; I gon give you shit until you see whot you doin is gon kill you and your heart gon cut and God gon mock you back and –

MAIMA God not gon mock me! He heping me, coz I hep myself. So don't you worry about me. Go look for your daughta and leave us be oh. (*MAIMA starts to walk out, turns back.*) Ha, how I gon learn from you oh? Whot you teach your daughta not hep ha. If she had learn wit me, wit dis, (*Indicating rifle.*) maybe she still be around

(*MAIMA mockingly gestures 'After you' with rifle. RITA after some hesitation starts out, with MAIMA following behind.*)

Scene 3

The next day. Army Camp, THE GIRL, rifle in hand, dressed sharp in a tight pair of pants and matching shirt, new hairstyle.

THE GIRL 'Firm your jaw! FIRM YOUR JAW! You can't be tinking about mama and deddy anymore! Listen to me – I am now you moda, your fada, your grandmother, your great grandfather, your ancestors, your Creator, your Jesus and your Allah. You belong to me. You will be listening to me all de time. You will do whot I say, when I say do. Touch your nose – I say touch your nose – good. Good. Stand up! Sit down! Stand up again! Good. Now, there will be no crying, no galie talk and no period cramping ere. I am your Superior! You will be doing what I say when I say do!' (*To MAIMA.*) Den I say some gon be wife and some soldier.

MAIMA (*Emerging from behind her.*) Dat good! Dat good oh! You get betta about it!

THE GIRL ... Ah...ya, it getting betta wit de gals. I just remember whot you tell me –

MAIMA (*Pleased.*) Whot? Whot I say?

THE GIRL Dat dis is war, and you can't tink too much and God keeping my conscience for me – it gon be clean and new when dis ova.

MAIMA Dat good oh!

THE GIRL Tanks!

MAIMA So where you workin?

THE GIRL De check point, wit Rambo.

MAIMA Whot you do?

THE GIRL (*Excitedly.*) Oh ya! I just tell dem – you can't tek dat big bag a rice all dat way! Den I say, just leave it here, I'll tek care of it. When I see woman wit nice cloth, I just tek whot I like from ha, den I say, 'Proceed tru de check point, proceed!' Look, I get some Timberlands – dey a bit small, but I stretching dem out. Dey just do whot I say do! Den dis one man – I fire him. He had too much money – we jokin – we call him Charles Taylor's son! But we scare he got too many connection so I had to fire him.

MAIMA Whot you got for me?

THE GIRL *(THE GIRL hands her half of a wad of money.)* And I save you sometin. Look at dis. *(Hands her a shirt she took off a civilian.)*

MAIMA I no like dat.

THE GIRL Oh, sorry.

MAIMA But dis is good oh, you acting like solider afta a short time oh! How long you been wit me?

THE GIRL Ah…about a mont.

MAIMA See! You doing real good job oh! I woz worrying about you, now I see everytin fine oh!

THE GIRL Ya, I okay. *(Beat.)*

MAIMA You lovin on someone?

THE GIRL Huh?

MAIMA I say you lovin on someone?

THE GIRL NO.

MAIMA You want to?

THE GIRL *(Bewildered.)* I… I don know.

MAIMA You need to be lovin on someone – it go hep you be protected. You chose someone you like, high rankin – den I hook it up.

THE GIRL I tought you say if I have gun –

MAIMA You have to have someone – it hep. Den you can start your business like me. Right now, I lovin on tree men. If I not lovin on no man I not gon have de tings I want. I just gotta mek sure I wit a man of high ranking. And one of dem he got high ranking. De oda one, he got good business but de third one, he de one I like, he de one got my heart. *(She giggles like a girl in love.)* De one wit high rankin, he got many women, but I his favorite dough. He give me de most tings when he come home from war. But whot I really want, whot I looking for right now is a four wheel drive, one a my men teach me how to drive so now I go buy and sell and go back and forth to Monrovia. You need one. We will find you one. Okay.

THE GIRL Ya…okay.

Scene 4

Two weeks later. RITA and HELENA at camp, in compound. The compound looks markedly more sparse, with the cooking station manifesting clear signs of neglect. HELENA fiddles with the radio which now has an elaborate makeshift antenna attached to it.

RADIO …the LURD rebels are now closing in on Monrovia, having taken over eighty percent of Lib – *(Unintelligible.)* …intensive fighting for the past six weeks since early June… *(Unintelligible.)* …displaced citizens in the sports stadium… *(Unintelligible.)* … while the peace talks in Accra are at a deadlock the… *(Unintelligible crackle ensues, HELENA finally turns it off.)*

RITA Da fightin so bad I don't even know how we going to get back. How de CO actin?

HELENA He actin mad oh. He say dey tekin Monrovia den dey gon live in Charles Taylor's hos. Dey talking about Charles Taylor hos an we no got notin ere. Lots a dem in my unit gon and not coming back.

RITA You seen dat gal yet?

HELENA No, but my small soldier been wit ha. He saying she still close, say she looting civilian plenty. She getting de gals for de commandas too, she –

RITA My God. AHHHH! Who she wit?

HELENA Number Two – she calling haself sometin foolish now like Misgruntle or sometin.

RITA Disgrunted?

HELENA Ya.

RITA Dat Number Two?

HELENA Ya, you meet ha?

RITA Ya…I meet ha. *(Under her breath.)* Oh my God.

HELENA She devil, she do bad tings. But Number Four not like ha. Number Four she…she special gal…she read to us –she tell us tings she wont to do – she –

RITA You find out where she from?

HELENA Ahh…she say Kakata.

RITA Ha.

HELENA She say ha fada woz in de army dere – but she talk about ha ma de most, ha ma –

RITA And she got book learning?

HELENA Ya. *(Beat.)* Who knows where dey be now? I been praying for Number Four.

RITA *(Turning away.)* Hmm, okay.

HELENA Whot…you no pray?

RITA Ahh…no…no I don't. And these women I am working with, they…they prayer warriors oh. I'm not into all dat. I'm not…good…

HELENA *(Delicately.)* Okay, you wanna to try?

RITA *(Very hesitantly.)* Ah…not…not really… ah…

HELENA It not gon do you notin harm oh. It mek me feel betta. I see you got sometin heavy on you – praying it mek tings not so heavy.

RITA *(Stares at HELENA for a long moment. Finally.)* Okay… okay, you…you go ahead.

HELENA Okay. *(HELENA kneels and takes RITA's hand.)* God, bring Number Four back, protec ha, keep ha safe in body and mind, convic her heart to come back to sense, show ha your love *(Beat.)* and I pray for Mama Peace, Lord, that she might know ha work it not in vain. We pray in Jesus His love precious Amen.

RITA *(Beat.)* Amen. *(Beat.)* Thank you.

HELENA Tank you.

(BESSIE walks in, heavily pregnant, with a new but shaggy wig that covers most of her face.)

RITA I have to go – oh…hello!

BESSIE *(To RITA.)* Oh, good, you ere again! You bring cassava?

HELENA Number Tree –

RITA No…ah….no I don't have anything actually.

BESSIE NOTIN! We no got no food oh! Why you come ere and you no hep –

HELENA NUMBER TREE!

RITA You have no food? Noting?

BESSIE NOTIN!

HELENA *(To BESSIE.)* EEEYYYY!! *(To RITA.)* He…he gon bring some…we'll have sometin soon.

RITA Goodness…

BESSIE Well you can read us book at leas! I missin Clinto!

RITA Ah…ah…of course, of course… oh my goodness how are you – you haven't been eating – *(Indicating BESSIE's belly.)*

BESSIE *(Handing book to her.)* Oh dat. *(Indicating belly as though it isn't attached to her body.)* Dat fine! De olda woman from de next compound is midwife. Read, just small small.

RITA Okay… *(Opening book.)* Just a little. Do you know where you were?

(BESSIE and HELENA look at her blankly.)

Whot woz the last thing you remember hearing?

HELENA Oh, he woz to go to court, den he get to not go.

RITA Okay, *(Leafing through book.)* let's see.

BESSIE You tink we send him letta, he gon get it?

RITA You want to send Bill Clinton a letter?

BESSIE Ya. I just wont to tell him I glad he still de big man and I like his story.

HELENA She mad oh! She tink de big man of America gon read letta from us.

BESSIE Why he not? America our fada – we founded by Americans – so he our big man too.

RITA That is true but…uhhh…about that – I should tell you something…

HELENA About whot?

RITA About Clinton being the big man…

BESSIE Oh, ohh, oh oh.

HELENA Whot your problem oh?

BESSIE I do wet – but I no do wet.

RITA Oh my goodness. Where de midwife? We tek ha?

HELENA Ya, she not far, grab ha arm.

(They help BESSIE up, her wig falls to the ground as they escort her out.)

BESSIE My wig, oh, get my wig!!! I need it to cova my face small small! De wig oh!

Scene 5

A week later. THE GIRL rushes in and falls to her knees, weeping and attempting to pray.

THE GIRL Our fada – Who are in – sometin… hollow your nem, de kingdom dat be yours…de kingdom dat be yours come – on eart and in…sometin, for de powa…you de powa…

(MAIMA enters.)

MAIMA You do good work. So you get your nem today.

THE GIRL *(Wiping tears away quickly and sitting up.)* Whot dat?

MAIMA De nem dat mek you a soldier.

THE GIRL Okay.

MAIMA Ya, so tell me, why are you fightin?

THE GIRL *(Reciting what she has been taught.)* We are fighting for de liberty of de people.

MAIMA And who are we fighting?

THE GIRL We are fighting de monkey Charles Taylor. He eating and drinking and living like a king in a land of paupers. We drive him out. Once he gon, we stop. And we gon…and we gon…

MAIMA …keep…

THE GIRL We gon keep on putting on de pressure… we gon keep on putting on de pressure…

MAIMA He scare of us. He neva gon come out and fight like a man. He wont to hide behind all his security. We gon strip him of all a dat. We gon do him worse dan dey do Former President Samuel K. Doe.

THE GIRL Former Samuel K. Doe

MAIMA We gon catch him and dress him like a woman before we kill him.

THE GIRL Sorry.

MAIMA Jus keep learning it. If any of de Commanders come to you dey go be vex you don know dose tings. So why is you fighting? Choose sometin you want to fight for.

THE GIRL My moda.

MAIMA Why?

THE GIRL I...she just who I want to fight for.

MAIMA Whot you want for her?

THE GIRL I want ha to be happy, to be blessed by God.

MAIMA You gon fight for your ma? You go see justice served so you ma and all de mas of Liberia blessed and not in pain no more?

THE GIRL Ya.

MAIMA Den dat your nem.

THE GIRL Whot?

MAIMA Moda's Blessing. *(Beat.)*

THE GIRL *(Searching.)* I tink...I tink I cursed.

MAIMA Whot? You tink you whot?

THE GIRL I CURSED. She curse me, she say, she say 'Devil bless you', and now I, I, I can't remember whot my moda she look like! I can't remember! I go, I go get de gals like I always do afta fighting, but dis one, she looking all nice in ha nice cloth, she acting like she betta dan me, I wanted ha to shut ha mout, to show me respec. She kept saying, 'Devil bless you!' Now she keep coming back to say dat to me, in my head, she won't shut up her mouth! Den I say okay, I can fight this ting, I just remember my moda saying 'God bless you' – and dis thing gonna disappear. Den, den, I can't see my moda no more! I can't hear my moda no more! I just hear dis gal! *(Beat.)* I had just wanted to shut ha up. I tought... I tought... It neva happen like dat before, I got system. De men have to come to me and discuss which gal dey want, I give dem one. I tell dem – dis gal special, she your wife, she only go wit you. But wit dis one – I didn't protec ha like I usually do – I just let dem tek ha, because she woz talking too much. *(Beat.)* Dey do it right in front of us at de camp, dey don't care, dey don't care dat

God right dere, dat He can see whot dey do. Dey just keep jumpin and jumpin on ha, it five o dem and I see she too small, she just little, small small den me. I want to say stop but I scare dey gon come to me if I say sometin. *(Beat.)* I see she stressed, she start to vomit – it look like rice or oats or sometin, den ha eyes start goin back. I can't move; den, den, ha eyes just go still, she starring right up to de sky and she not moving; de fifth one he just keep going till he done. *(Beat.)* She got blood everywhere, dey leave ha lying dere and tell one o de small soldier to go get wata so dey can wash deyselves, dey tell me and anoda small soldier to trow ha in de riva, I just do like dey say, I too scare to say noting. I tek ha arms and he tek ha legs, she still bleedin and bleedin, ha eyes still looking up, I no look at ha no more. We drop ha in de riva and I pray, I pray dat God bless ha soul, dat He no blame me for whot dose men do. But it my fault she dead, and she tell me 'Devil bless you', and now I can't even see my moda no more! I cursed. I got dis sin on me and I gon go to de devil straight.

MAIMA EYYYY!!! FIRM YOUR JAW. *(Slapping her.)* I say FIRM YOUR JAW! I say firm your jaw, FIRM IT. *(Hitting her and beating her continuously, passionately.)* Don't you eva, *(Beating her.)* EVA *(Beating her more.)* come to me wit dose STUPID stories – you understan? You got to be STRONG! Dis is war little gal. And you a soldier. *(She stops beating her but holds THE GIRL's jaw firmly in her hand.)* Whot does a soldier do in war? SPEAK!

THE GIRL Dey fight.

MAIMA Ya, dey fight. We winning, we even stronga and stronga now. So you betta fight little gal. You Moda's Blessing now, you SOLDIER, you understan?

THE GIRL I understan.

(MAIMA releases THE GIRL abruptly and roughly escorts her out.)

Scene 6

Same evening. BESSIE at camp, with an infant strapped to her back, she sings to herself, as she coos at her baby, and sweeps the compound – THE GIRL enters and stands silently in the corner, her face obscured by the dark. BESSIE finally sweeps at THE GIRL's feet.

BESSIE *(Startled.)* FUCK SATAN, HEP JESUS! Number Four! How you gon come on me like dat?

THE GIRL I sorry.

BESSIE Whot you doing ere, Number Four? I not see you for long time. I thought you Commander General by now!

THE GIRL Moda's Blessing.

BESSIE Huh?

THE GIRL My nem, it…it Moda's Blessing.

BESSIE Okaaaay. So whot you wont?

THE GIRL You getting beby?

BESSIE Hmmhmm.

THE GIRL Oh, he sweet oh!

BESSIE It a gal.

THE GIRL Oh, ya, oh I see ha betta now, she look like you. She pretty.

BESSIE Tanks. I like ha. I did not tink I woz go like ha, but I do. She no look like him, she a small small me! How I no gon love ha? I look at ha, and she look at me wit dose eyes and all dat stuff coming out ha mout after she drink milk and I say, If any body do sometin to my chile, ever – dat de only ting dat gon mek me pick up de gun and fire you, den I curse you, curse you to de devil. Dat when I gon go to de medicine man for true and get some o de juju dat go hurt someone, dey go wake up with no privates or sometin. Dey go fire dey self – dey be so vex. *(Beat.)* I neva felt a love like dat, you know. I kill and curse for ha. And I tink God will be on my side. I sure of dat. How you? You should get beby, it feel good.

THE GIRL No, I can… I don wont dat. Where Number One?

BESSIE She wit de CO.

THE GIRL I go wait for ha. Ere, I bring gif.

(She pulls out a large cassava root.)

BESSIE That so good oh, cassava! It been too long oh! *(BESSIE grabs the cassava root and rushes to cooking station. She searches for a knife to peel and chop the root.)*

THE GIRL *(Looking around.)* Whot dis? *(She picks up a tattered piece of paper.)*

BESSIE Oh, dat dis ting Number One keep doin – she learn to write sometin, she keep writing it ova and ova – she going mad oh! Guess whot we learn about Clinto? He not de big man no more! It a Bush. A bush! Dat his name – a Bush! Like in de bush – you know?

THE GIRL Ya, I understan.

BESSIE Dat funny oh!

THE GIRL Ya. Where Number One?

BESSIE I tol you she wit de CO. Whot vexing you?

THE GIRL Notin.

BESSIE Okay. *(Goes back to peeling.)*

(RITA rushes in, excited, looks around for HELENA.)

RITA Where's Number One?

BESSIE SHE WIT DE CO! Whot wrong wit you people oh!

RITA I have to tell you all something. *(Notices THE GIRL.)* Oh…

BESSIE She Number Four.

THE GIRL *(Automatically.)* Moda's Blessing.

RITA Oh…oh God…oh God… *(RITA, trembling and fighting tears, advances towards THE GIRL.)* It not ha…it…it not ha…it not. *(Shaking her head and looking to BESSIE in mournful agony.)*

BESSIE Whot you talking oh?

RITA Ah…ah…ahhhh…ah…noting. Noting. *(Collecting herself for several beats. To THE GIRL.)* Rita Endee, I am a member of the Liberian Women Initiative for Peace –

THE GIRL Oh.

RITA So…so whot is your name?

THE GIRL I tol you – I –

RITA Whot is your real name – the name your mother and father gave you?

THE GIRL *(Struck.)* Oh…

(HELENA enters, a dazed look on her face, she looks over the compound, not even taking RITA and THE GIRL in. Methodically, almost robotically, she starts to pick up things and pack them up.)

BESSIE Whot you doing?

HELENA Hmm?

BESSIE Whot you packing for, Number One?

HELENA Helena. H-E-L-E-N-A. Helena. Dat my nem. I not sure about my last nem, I tink it Sowa, Sona, or sometin. I tink it Sowa. I need to remember all dese ting now. Where I from? Buchanan? Whot I go do now? Whot I go do now? *(Starts laughing.)*

BESSIE You go mad oh?

HELENA *(She finally takes in the room.)* He call me over, he say sit down. All de years I be wit him, he neva have me sit down. Maybe sit on him, but neva he sit me down to talk to me like human to human. Den he say, 'De war ova, Charles Taylor go to Nigeria, you can go. Pack your tings and go. We going home.' Den he get up and walk away. Dat it.

All dose years, he tek all dose years, he mek me leave my chile when we running from Taylor men, he, he mek my chile die in de bush, all alone – he mek it so I no get born no more, he mek me so sick my stomach broken, den he go just trow me away like dat. I cook every meal he eat, I know all de secret of his unit, everyting, but he just go spit me out like dat, like I someone he just meet yesterday. *(Starts to laugh.)* I scared oh! He say, 'you can go'! I can just go, wherever I want – de war it ova! Do I have ma? Do I have pa? I no know, 'You can go', I don know whot GO means! Whot it mean? I tink, I tink I gon go to Monrovia, sell tings, get a business, but I wont to go to school, I wont to learn to do sometin, to read like you Number Four – you can be member of Parliament now! Did you hear me? We can all GO! Let's GO, Ma Peace! I can go now! You free, Number Four – you no have to fight no more. Don't do no bad tings no more – dat not you, gal, dat not how God mek you. He mek you good gal.

(HELENA hands THE GIRL her book. THE GIRL slaps HELENA hard, grabs her rifle and points it at HELENA's throat, pushing her back until the rifle is touching HELENA's throat. She releases almost primal sounds of aggression, her eyes flashing something verging on demonic. She stands there, seeming to will herself to drop the gun and pull the trigger simultaneously. RITA stands petrified, then seems to will herself to advance towards THE GIRL, and speak to her softly.)

RITA Gal…gal…listen to me. I am a member of Liberian Women for PEACE. I gon hep you gal, I gon hep you – You don't wan to do this. Dis is not you, dis not whot God make you for.

THE GIRL Whot he mek me for?

RITA Good tings, he mek you for so many good tings. Look at her, she wants to read now – why? Because of you, because of you my daughter.

(THE GIRL looks over at RITA, searching, THE GIRL breaks down, drops her rifle and drops to her knees and weeps. RITA removes rifle, drops to her knees also and gently strokes her back, THE GIRL crumples into RITA's arms. RITA clings to her with yearning compassion. Silence ensues for several beats. BESSIE's baby starts to cry.)

RITA *(Stroking THE GIRL's back, to BESSIE.)* How is she?

BESSIE She fine.

RITA She's just a few days old huh?

BESSIE She young, young.

RITA Whot's her name?

BESSIE Clintine.

RITA Oh, Clementine – that's Fre –

BESSIE NO! Clintine.

RITA Clintine?

BESSIE Ya.

RITA Okay, that, that's lovely. We need to move. The Commander General is letting you go – these camps are dismantling so I can get you all some help. There is a truck we are catching – about fifteen minutes from ere. We rounding up as many of you women as we can, but there is no time! We have to go now. There is still some fighting so we have to get to the main road really carefully. But the major crisis is over, Taylor is gone! So I am going to take you gals to a camp – further north, near Guinea –

BESSIE I tink I go stay.

HELENA Whot you say?

BESSIE I go stay wit CO.

HELENA Stay to do whot?

BESSIE He de fada of my chile, he de only man I know to be wit for long time. Whot I go do out dere? I can't learn to do tings, dat not me.

HELENA So you go follow CO around wherever he go?

BESSIE Ya, I go home wit him. He like lovin on me, he no gon mind. *(MAIMA rushes in.)*

MAIMA Moda's Blessing, so you run ere like beby eh? Let's go.

RITA Where are you trying to take her?

MAIMA Dat not your problem – she soldier.

RITA Taylor is gone.

MAIMA I know dat. Dat don mean it ova. His monkey soldiers still everywhere. Whot dey tink? Dey tink we go just stop now?

RITA You got to stop, it ova! The ECOWAS forces are killing any rebels still fighting. They are going to have disarmament and you have to turn in your weapons –

MAIMA Dey can turn in dey modas! I not letting my gun go for notin. Moda's Blessing – LET'S GO!

BESSIE Leave ha! She gonna stay wit Ma Peace and Helena.

MAIMA Wit who?

HELENA Wit me. It ova oh. Just stop, you should just stop it while you can.

MAIMA Shut your mout. Stop for whot? Den whot? No way. And since when you care about whot happen to me eh?

HELENA I always care about you. Dat why I can stand to see de tings you doing. But you can stop now, it ova.

MAIMA *(Stares at HELENA for a long beat. Finally.)* FUCK YOU! Moda's Blessing —

HELENA Leave ha, Maima.

MAIMA Whot you call me?

HELENA I call you your name.

RITA De war ova, get back to who you woz. You go back out there fighting, you not gonna make it.

MAIMA You God? NO! So you no know notin about whot gon happen to me. YOU NO KNOW. DIS WHOT I KNOW TO DO. *(Breaking.)* WHAT YOU TINK EH? WHAT YOU TINK? YOU TINK I GONNA BE LIKE MY MODA begging at de refugee camps, pleadin around for a cup a rice den dey just jump ha till she dead when dey supposed to be protecting ha? Tink I gon let dem treat me like I is notin! NO WAY! DAT NOT MY STYLE, DAT NEVA GON BE ME! *(Desperately.)* MODA'S BLESSING COME ON! COME WIT ME! LET'S GO! You gon stay? *(Beat.)* You stay, you gon wish you come. You stay, you no gon have NO-TIN. You just go back to being weak little gal. *(She leaves sucking her teeth.)*

(Silence for a few beats as they watch MAIMA go, RITA shaking her head.)

RITA *(To THE GIRL.)* You gon be okay. You can find your family now.

THE GIRL I don't tink I have any, my pa dead and my moda, dey, dey tek ha and den dey —

(THE GIRL stares at BESSIE — her face immobile. The women all stare back at her in a prolonged silence, absorbing all that isn't said in full understanding. Finally.)

RITA We have to go.

HELENA Okay —

BESSIE Okay. Bye.

HELENA Bye. Stay wit God eh, don't stay wit CO forever— he gon waste you.

BESSIE I be fine.

RITA Whot is your name, my daughter? The one your mother and father gave you?

BESSIE Oh, dat? It…it Bessie.

RITA Good, okay Bessie, I cannot just leave you — please, come, you can —

BESSIE I be fine. I be fine. I wan stay. Dat whot I wont.

RITA Okay… *(RITA gives up. To HELENA and THE GIRL.)* Come, we have got to go now. Here, let me help you. *(She helps HELENA gather up her things.)*

(RITA and HELENA exit. THE GIRL goes and grabs her book, stumbles on her gun, stops, picks it up and looks at it and looks after where MAIMA exited. She stands there with book and gun in hand behind BESSIE who sits on the floor with her daughter, cooing her and singing to her gently. THE GIRL doesn't move, seemingly transfixed to the floor, unable to walk in either direction. Random gunshots can be heard in the distance. As BESSIE sings, the lights fade out.)

BESSIE Clintine, Clintine, you so pretty like mama — Clintine, Clintine!

Quiara Alegría Hudes

Biography

Quiara Alegría Hudes is a playwright, strong wife, and mother of two, barrio feminist and native of West Philly, U.S.A. Hailed for her work's exuberance, intellectual rigor, and rich imagination, her plays and musicals have been performed around the world. They are *Water By the Spoonful*, winner of the Pulitzer Prize for Drama; *In the Heights*, winner of the Tony Award for Best Musical and

Pulitzer finalist; *Elliot, A Soldier's Fugue*, another Pulitzer finalist; *Daphne's Dive*; *The Good Peaches*; *Miss You Like Hell*; and *The Happiest Song Plays Last*. Hudes is a playwright-in-residence at Signature Theater in New York and is the Shapiro Distinguished Professor of Writing and Theater at Wesleyan University. Originally trained as a composer, Hudes has done some deep dives into marrying live music and drama. She has collaborated with renowned musicians including Nelson Gonzalez, Michel Camilo, Lin-Manuel Miranda, Erin McKeown, and The Cleveland Orchestra.

Artistic statement

As a playwright, I have the ongoing honor, and sometimes nagging chore, of doing interviews to publicize various productions. The question I get asked most frequently in interviews is this: "Are you a Latina playwright?" A few common variations on this are: "What is a Latino artist?" and "Do you write Latino plays?"

Well, yes, I am Latina. And yes, I am a playwright. But this question always feels like a trap to me. If I say yes, then I give the interviewer a neat little corner to tuck me away into, I give the reader an excuse to not consider me a mainstream writer. I become a writer with an asterisk, a writer who needs an explanation. Of course, if I say, "No," then I'm a liar.

Sometimes, especially in short interviews, I get asked follow-up questions that go like this: "Are you a woman playwright?" "Are you a Jewish playwright?" And sometimes these sorts of questions take up so much time that I don't get asked a single question about the content of the play I've created. I don't get the opportunity to speak as an artist, but instead as someone who's vexingly undefinable, whose identity is slippery and therefore not to be trusted, as someone who does not fit easily into a checkbox and therefore who might confuse the readers.

If I'm in a very good mood, these questions intrigue me. More often, they set my blood boiling. Perhaps I get defensive feeling that, because I'm of mixed cultural heritage, the interviewer is simply dressing up a different question that he doesn't have the balls to straight up ask: "Are you an authentic Latina?" Or, more simply put, "What are you?" A question which often makes me want to throw a pot of steaming caldo santo right in the asker's face. As if such a question can be answered in one palatable talking point. "Yes, I grew up scraping the pegao from the bottom of abuela's caldero, therefore I am a Latina artist." Identity is extraordinary and rich and sensitive and, yes, painful, and I don't have to break it down for you, Mr. Interviewer. It's not my responsibility to educate you, Mr. Interviewer, on "what" I am or "what" Latino is. Go to Wikipedia and ask me a real question.

Or *is* it my responsibility, my job, to educate the public about my most private histories, the secrets in my soul, the links in my DNA? About my colonial roots, my Taino roots, my conquistadorized, and Holocausted roots? Perhaps we must all carry that mantel of having to explain ourselves, and seize it as a real opportunity.

When these same interviewers sit down at the interview table with Edward Albee or Tracy Letts or David Lindsay Abaire, all heroes of mine, do they ask these writers: "Do you consider yourself a white playwright?" I've never read an interview where a white author has to justify or explain his identity or why it is that he writes for white actors. Certainly, I think I'd squeal from wicked delight if one of them were ever asked, "Do you consider yourself a male playwright?"

So here, today, amongst you fellow travelers, you readers who were attracted to this collection of plays for your own emotional and intellectual reasons, I will answer this question once and for all. So that next time I'm asked this question, I've got my answer on hand.

Interviewer says, "Are you a Latina playwright?"

I respond, "My fellow Latino artists, we are the dreamers and the agitated nightmares. The insomnia and the spa. Irrational bewitchers. Deserts who brew tropical storms. We are annihilators of reason and embracers of duality. We use paint like cop cars use sirens. We use our limbs and knees, our pencil strokes and timbales to steer great ships through agitated seas. Spelunkers of the human heart's deceits. We eat trash and shit gold. We are the word stupid misspelled s-t-o-o-p-i-d. Daydreamers, ruminators. We stand in our ancestral kitchen, stirring the magma. Lighting the match at the base of the volcano. We are hackers of the status quo. Saturation bursters. We show up to the water balloon toss but our latex is filled with honey and mud. We bathe in baroque pipe organs and dry our drenched skin with haiku. Syncopators. Sixty-niners. Smut mouthed calla lilies. Fabricators of crystalline reality. Unhappy prisoners, jilted strivers, we fall off the edge of the cliff and as we plummet we happen to crack open a Neruda poem or hit play on a Lila Downs song and our landing is cushioned. We repair our broken ankles and climb the cliff again. Every day in the rehearsal room, at the writing desk, facing the canvas—cliff climbers, we, with no ropes or rigging to shield us from gravity. We are glass-paneled walls facing the sea. Glass-bottomed boats that reveal cumulus clouds. We are the ninety-nine percent of the forty-seven percent of the whole damn caramel flan. We are the edible desert, a mouthful of sand. We are the rot that bears the ripest fruit. We are the canaries in the cage in our tia's dark living room. The sun-faded flags dangling from papi's rear view mirror. We are machos weeping for want of love. Cancer patients who are belly laughing for joy. We are montunos possessed by Baptist gospel chords. Chopin nocturnes that are *blao!* thunderstruck by Chango. We are the hump-backed abuela who lifts the car with one finger. The moreno chiles who crave lo mein. We are lickable lightning."

After a pause, I follow up with a question of my own: "Did you get all that?"

Production history

Elliot, A Soldier's Fugue was written and developed with the support of a Page 73 Playwriting Fellowship. An early version of *Elliot, A Soldier's Fugue* was presented at Miracle Theatre in Portland, Oregon, in September 2005, directed by Olga Sanchez.

Elliot, *A Soldier's Fugue* was premiered on January 4, 2006, and was given its world premiere on January 28, 2006, by Page 73 Productions in New York, under the artistic direction of Liz Jones, Asher Richelli, Nicole Fiz, and Daniel Schiffman, at the Culture Project. The productions were directed by Davis McCallum. The cast was as follows:

ELLIOT	Armando Riesco
GINNY	Zabryna Guevara
POP	Triney Sandoval
GRANDPOP	Mateo Gómez

The set design was by Sandra Goldmark, costumes designed by Chloe Chapin, music by Michael Freedman, and lighting designed by Joel Moritz.

5 *Elliot, A Soldier's Fugue*
Quiara Alegría Hudes

Characters

ELLIOT serving in Iraq, 1st Marine Division, 19

POP Elliot's father, served in Vietnam, 3rd Cavalry Division, various ages

GRANDPOP Elliot's grandfather, served in Korea, 65th Infantry
Regiment of Puerto Rico, various ages

GINNY Elliot's mother, served in Vietnam, Army Nurse Corps, various ages

Set

The set has two playing areas. The "empty space" is minimal, it transforms
into many locations. It is stark, sad. When light enters, it is like light through
a jailhouse window or through the dusty stained glass of a decrepit chapel.
The "garden space," by contrast, is teeming with life. It is a verdant sanctuary,
green speckled with magenta and gold. Both spaces are holy in their own way.

Production notes

Fugues

In the "fugue" scenes, people narrate each other's actions and sometimes
narrate their own. For instance:
ELLIOT A boy enters.
(Elliot enters.)
GRANDPOP Clean, deodorized.
Some drops of water plummet from his nose and lips.
The shower was ice cold.
(Elliot shivers.)
Elliot's action should mirror what the narrator, Grandpop, says. The
narrator steps in and out of the scene as necessary.

Pop's letters

Pop's letters are active and alive. They are not reflective, past-tense
documents. They are immediate communication. Sometimes the letters are
shared dialogue between Pop and Grandpop, but it should always be clear
that it is Pop's story being spoken.

Music

Flute. Bach, danzónes, jazz, etudes, scales, hip-hop beats. Overlapping lines.

Other

Please do not use actual barbed wire or vines in the wrapping scenes. The stage directions in these moments are an important part of the soul of the piece, but should not be staged literally.

Punctuation notes

// : Indicates dialogue entry of following character

1/FUGUE

(The empty space, very empty. A pair of white underwear is on the ground. That's all we see.)

GINNY A room made of cinderblock.
   A mattress lies on a cot containing 36 springs.
   If you lie on the mattress, you can feel each of the 36 springs.
   One at a time.
   As you close your eyes.
   And try to sleep the full four hours.
POP A white sheet is on the mattress.
   The corners are folded and tucked under.
   Tight, like an envelope.
GRANDPOP Military code.
   The corner of the sheet is checked at 0600 hours, daily.
   No wrinkles or bumps allowed.
ELLIOT A man enters.

(ELLIOT enters in a towel. It's 2003. He's 18.)

GRANDPOP Clean, deodorized.
   Some drops of water plummet from his nose and lips.
   The shower was ice cold.

(ELLIOT shivers. He picks up the underwear.)

GINNY He performs his own military-style inspection.

(ELLIOT looks at the front and back of the underwear. No apparent stains. He sniffs them. They're clean.)

ELLIOT Nice.

(ELLIOT puts them on under the towel, removes the towel.)

POP There's little bumps of skin on his arm.
   His pores tighten.
   His leg hair stands on end.
   Cold shower spray.

(ELLIOT drops to the ground and does 10 push-ups. He springs to his feet and seems invigorated.)

ELLIOT One two three four five six seven eight nine ten. Rah!
POP The mirror in the room reflects a slight distortion.

(ELLIOT peers into the mirror—the audience.)

GINNY The chin.
   The teeth.
   Uppers and lowers.
   The molars.
   The one, lone filling.

(He clenches his jaw, furrows his eyebrows. Holding the face, he curls a bicep, showing off a round muscle.)

ELLIOT *(To the mirror adversary.)* What? You want to step? You're making Subway hoagies. I'm a marine. Who are you?

(He shakes out that pose. Now, he smiles like a little angel into the mirror.)

ELLIOT *(To the mirror mommy.)* Mami, quiero chuletas. Pasteles. Morsilla. Barbecue ribs. Sorullito. Macaroni salad. Sopa de fideo. When I make it back home, you gonna make me a plate, right? A montón of ribs. But no pigs feet. Ain't no other Puerto Rican on this earth be cookin no pigs feet.

(ELLIOT shakes out that pose. He leans in, an inch away from the mirror. He pops a pimple. He wipes it on his underwear. He scrutinizes his face for more pimples. There are none. He fixes his nearly-shaved hair. He stands in a suave posture, leaning sexy. He blows a subtle kiss to the mirror.)

ELLIOT You know you like it. Navy nursee want mi culito?

(He turns around, looks at his butt in the mirror. He clenches his butt muscles and releases. Then he does this about 10 times in a quick succession, watching the mirror the whole time. He stops.)

POP Blank.
   He's nervous about something.

GRANDPOP He will board the ship to Iraq at 0700 hours.

(ELLIOT starts to put on his uniform under...
The room is empty. A towel is on the floor.)

GINNY A room with steel doors.
Steel walls, steel windows.
The room sways up and down.
Hammocks on top of hammocks swing back and forth.

GRANDPOP The room is inside a boat.
That's on the ocean to Vietnam.

GINNY The floors of the USS Eltinge are inspected at 0530 daily.

POP and GRANDPOP Military code.
No dirt allowed.

GINNY But the floor is wet.
It's the Pacific Ocean, seeping inside.

POP A young man enters.

(POP enters. It's 1966. He wears a uniform and catches his breath.)

GINNY The 0400 deck run was hot.
The shower will be warm.
640 muscles will relax.

GRANDPOP Military code.
No bare chests.

(POP untucks his shirt, unbuttons it, throws it to the floor.)

POP *(Imitating a drill sergeant under his breath. Faux southern accent.)* Keep up the pace, Ortiz. You can't hear me, Ortiz? Are you deaf, Ortiz? Corporal Feifer, is Corporal Ortiz deaf?

GRANDPOP Military code.
No bare feet.

(He takes off his boots, peels off his socks.)

POP You're the best damn shot in the marines, Ortiz. You could kill a fly. Does your momma know what a great shot you are?

GINNY Reflect honor upon yourself and your home country.

(He peels off his undershirt.)

POP Where are you from, Ortiz? What's your momma's name? Eh? Is she fat like you? Your momma got a fat ass, Ortiz?

(ELLIOT is fully dressed. He salutes the mirror.)

ELLIOT Lance Corporal Elliot Ortiz Third Light Armored Recon Battalion First Marine Division. Mutha fucka.

(POP finds a paper and pencil. He taps the pencil, thinking of what to write.

ELLIOT checks inside his duffel bag.)

GINNY The duffel is heavy full of boots and pants.
A map of Iraq.
A Bible with four small photographs.

GRANDPOP Military code.
No electronic devices.

ELLIOT Got my walkman.

GRANDPOP Military code.
No valuables.

ELLIOT My Nas CD. Jay Z. Slow Jams. Reggaetón 2002.

POP April 12, 1966...

(ELLIOT opens a little green Bible, looks at photos.)

ELLIOT My photos. Mom. In your garden.

(He kisses the photo. Finds a new one.)

Grandpop. Senile old head.

(Taps the photo. Finds a new one.)

Pops. With your beer-ass belly.

POP *(Writing.)* Dear Pop...

ELLIOT *(Still to the photo.)* When I get home, we gonna have a father and son. Chill in mom's garden. Drink some Bud Light out them mini cans. I don't want to hear about no "leave the past in the past." You gonna tell me your stories.

(ELLIOT puts on headphones and starts bobbing his head to the hip-hop beat.
POP continues to write under...
The room is empty. A towel is on the floor.)

GINNY A tent.
No windows, no door.
Walls made of canvas.
A floor made of dirt.
The soil of Inchon, Korea is frozen.

GRANDPOP 16 cots they built by hand.
Underwear, towels, unmade beds.
Dirty photos.

GINNY That is, snapshots of moms and daughters and wives
That have dirt on them.

GRANDPOP A boy enters.

(GRANDPOP enters. It's 1950. He's wearing heavy soldier clothes. He rubs his arms for warmth. He puts on additional clothing layers.)

GINNY His breath crystallizes.
His boots are full of icy sweat.
The 0500 swamp run was subzero.

(GRANDPOP blows into his hands for warmth. He bends his fingers.)

GRANDPOP One two three four... five. My thumb is as purple as a flower.

(He pulls a black leather case from his cot. He opens it, revealing a flute. He pulls out pieces of the flute, begins to assemble them, cleaning dirt from the joints.)

Ah, this Korean dirt is too damn dirty. We lost another man to frostbite this week. These guys deserve some Bach. Light as a feather,

POP *(Finishing the letter.)* Your son,

GRANDPOP free as a bird.

POP Little George.

(GRANDPOP puts the flute to his lips, inhales, begins to play. The melody of a Bach passacaglia.

POP folds up the letter, puts it in an envelope. Addresses the envelope.)

GINNY Military code.
Make no demands.
Military code.
Treat women with respect.
Military code.
Become friends with fellow soldiers.
No rude behavior.
Pray in silence, please.

(POP drops the letter, lays down, sings himself to sleep. It overlaps with GRANDPOP's flute and ELLIOT's head-bobbing.)

POP 1234
We're gonna jump on the count of four
If I die when I hit the mud
Bury me with a case of bud
A case of bud and a bottle of rum
Drunk as hell in kingdom come
Count off
1234[1]

(ELLIOT skips forward a few tracks on the walkman. He finds his jam. Head bobbing, feeling it.)

ELLIOT Uh, uh.
And when I see ya I'ma take what I want so
You tryin to front, hope ya
Got ur self a gun
You ain't real, hope ya
Got ur self a gun
Uh, uh, uh, uh. //
I got mine I hope ya... uh, uh
You from da hood I hope ya...
You want beef I hope ya...
Uh, uh, uh, uh.
And when I see you I'ma
Take what I want so
You tryin to front, hope ya...
You ain't real, hope ya...

Uh, uh, uh, uh.[2]

POP 1234
We're gonna change on the count of four
If my heart begins to bleed
Bury me with a bag full a' weed
A bag full a' weed and a
Bottle of rum
Laugh at the devil in kingdom come
Count off
Bud bud bud bud
Bud bud bud bud

(It is three-part counterpoint between the men. Lights fade, counterpoint lingers.)

2/PRELUDE

(The empty space. A flashbulb goes off.)

SPORTSCASTER VOICE Thanks, Harry. I'm standing outside the Phillies locker room with hometown hero Lance Corporal Elliot Ortiz. He'll be throwing out tonight's opening pitch.

ELLIOT Call me Big El.

SPORTSCASTER VOICE You were one of the first marines to cross into Iraq.

ELLIOT Two days after my eighteenth birthday.

SPORTSCASTER VOICE And you received a Purple Heart at 19. Big El, welcome home.

ELLIOT Philly!

SPORTSCASTER VOICE You're in Philadelphia for a week and then it's back to Iraq for your second tour of duty?

ELLIOT We'll see. I got until Friday to make up my mind.

SPORTSCASTER VOICE Did you miss the city of brotherly love?

ELLIOT Mom's food. My girl Stephanie. My little baby cousin. Cheese steaks.

SPORTSCASTER VOICE Any big plans while you're home?

ELLIOT Basically eat. Do some interviews. My mom's gonna fix up my leg. I'm a take my pop out for a drink, be like, alright, old head. Time to trade some war stories.

SPORTSCASTER VOICE I hope you order a Shirley Temple. Aren't you 19?

ELLIOT I'll order a Shirley Temple.

SPORTSCASTER VOICE Big Phillies fan?

ELLIOT Three years in a row I was Lenny Dykstra for Halloween.

SPORTSCASTER VOICE A few more seconds to pitch time.

ELLIOT Hold up. Quick shout out to North Philly. 2nd and Berks, share the love! To my moms. My pops. I'm doing it for you. Grandpops—videotape this so you don't forget! Stephanie. All my friends still out there in Iraq. Waikiki, one of these days I'm going to get on a plane to Hawaii and your mom better cook me some Kahlua pig.

SPORTSCASTER VOICE Curve ball, fast ball?

ELLIOT Wait and see. I gotta keep you on your toes. I'm gonna stand on that mound and show ya'll I got an arm better than Schilling! Record lightning speed!

3/ PRELUDE

(The garden. GRANDPOP opens a letter and reads. POP appears separately.)

GRANDPOP and POP May 24, 1966

POP Dear pop,
    It's hot wet

GRANDPOP cold muddy

POP miserable. Operation Prairie has us in the jungle, and it's a sauna.

GRANDPOP One hundred twenty degrees by 1100 hours,

POP you think you're gonna cook by 1300. Then yesterday it starts to rain.

GRANDPOP Drops the size of marbles—

POP my first real shower in weeks. Monsoon. They said,

GRANDPOP "Get used to it." Corporal shoved a machete in my hand and told me to lead.

POP He's the leader, but I get to go first!

GRANDPOP I cut through the vines, clear the way. We get lesions,

POP ticks,

GRANDPOP leeches.

POP At night we strip down, everybody pulls the things off each other. We see a lot of rock ape.

GRANDPOP They're bigger than chimps and they throw rocks at us.

POP They've got great aim! You just shoot up in the air, they run away.

GRANDPOP At night you can't see your own hand in front of your face.

POP I imagine you and mom on the back stoop, having a beer. Uncle Tony playing his guitar. My buddy Joe Bobb,

GRANDPOP from Kentucky.

POP He carries all his equipment on his back, plus a guitar, and he starts playing these hillbilly songs.

GRANDPOP They're pretty good.

POP I think Uncle Tony would like them. I pulled out your flute and we jammed a little. C-rations, gotta split,

POP and GRANDPOP Little George.

4/ PRELUDE

(GINNY in the garden.)

GINNY The garden is 25 years old. It used to be abandoned. There was glass everywhere. Right here, it was a stripped-down school bus. Here, a big, big pile of old tires. I bought it for one dollar. A pretty good deal. Only a few months after I came back from Vietnam. I told myself, you've got to *do* something. So I bought it. I went and got a ton of dirt from Sears. Dirt is expensive! I said, when I'm done with this, it's going to be a splitting image of Puerto Rico. Of Arecibo. It's pretty close. You can see electric wires dangling like right there and there. But I call that "native Philadelphia vines." If you look real close, through the heliconia you see anti-theft bars on my window.

Green things, you let them grow wild. Don't try to control them. Like people, listen to them, let them do their own thing. You give them a little guidance on the way. My father was a mean bastard. The first time I remember him touching me, it was to whack me with a shoe. He used to whack my head with a wooden spoon every time I cursed. I still have a bump on my head from that. Ooh, I hated him. But I was mesmerized to see him with his plants. He became a saint if you put a flower in his hand. Secrets, when things grow at night. Phases of the moon. He didn't need a computer, he had it all in his brain. "I got no use for that." That was his thing. "I got no use for church." "I got no use for a phone." "I got no use for children." He had use for a flower.

There are certain plants you only plant at night. Orchids. Plants with provocative shapes. Plants you want to touch. Sexy plants. My garden is so sexy. If I was young, I'd bring all the guys here. The weirdest things get my juices going. I sit out here at night, imagine romances in the spaces between banana leaves. See myself as a teenager, in Puerto Rico, a whole different body on these bones. I'm with a boyfriend, covered in dirt.

When I was a nurse in the Army Nurse Corps, they brought men in by the loads. The evacuation hospital. The things you see. Scratched corneas all the way to. A guy with the back of his body torn off. You get the man on the cot, he's screaming. There's men screaming all around. Always the same thing, calling out for his mother, his wife, girlfriend. First thing, before anything else, I would make eye contact. I always looked them in the eye, like to say, hey, it's just you and me. Touch his face like I was his wife. Don't look at his wound, look at him like he's the man of my dreams. Just for one tiny second. Then, it's down to business. Try to keep that heart going, that breath pumping in and out, keep that blood inside the tissue. Sometimes I was very attracted to the men I worked on. A tenderness would sweep through me. Right before dying, your body goes into shock. Pretty much a serious case of the shakes. If I saw a man like that, I thought, would he like one last kiss? One last hand on his ass? Give him a good going away party.

Just things in my mind. Not things you act on. With George, though. We had a great time when he was in the evacuation hospital. I stitched his leg up like a quilt and we stayed up all night smoking joints. Everyone in the hospital was passed out asleep. The first time George got up and walked to me. I took his head in my right hand and I kissed him so hard. That kiss was the best feeling in my body. Ooh. You see so much death, then someone's lips touches yours and you go on vacation for one small second.

Gardening is like boxing. It's like those days in Vietnam. The wins versus the losses. Ninety percent of it is failures but the triumphs? When Elliot left for Iraq, I went crazy with the planting. Begonias, ferns, trees. A seed is a contract with the future. It's saying, I know something better will happen tomorrow. I planted bearded irises next to palms. I planted tulips with a border of cacti. All the things the book tells you, "Don't ever plant these together." "Guide to Proper Gardening." Well I got on my knees and planted them side by side. I'm like, you have to throw all preconceived notions out the window. You have to plant wild. When your son goes to war, you plant every goddam seed you can find. It doesn't matter what the seed is. So long as it grows. I plant like I want and to hell with the consequences. I planted a hundred clematis vines by the kitchen window, and next thing I know sage is growing there. The tomato vines gave me beautiful tomatoes. The bamboo shot out from the ground. And the heliconia!

(She retrieves a heliconia leaf.)

Each leaf is actually a cup. It collects the rainwater. So any weary traveler can stop and take a drink.

5/ PRELUDE

(The garden. GRANDPOP opens a letter and reads. POP appears separately.)

POP October 7, 1966

GRANDPOP Dear Dad and all the rest of you lucky people,

POP Got my next assignment. All those weeks of waiting and boredom? Those are the good old days! They marched us to Dong Ha for Operation Prairie 2. I'm infantry. Some guys drive, go by tank. Infantry walks. We walk by the side of the tank. Two days straight, we've been scouting for body parts. You collect what you find, throw it in the tank, they label it and take it away. Where they take it? You got me. What they write on the label? It's like bird watching. You develop your eye.

GRANDPOP Don't show this letter to mom, please. And don't ask me about it when I get home. If I feel like talking about it I will but otherwise don't ask.

POP Today this one little shrimp kept hanging around, chasing after the tank. Looking at me with these eyes. I gave him my crackers I was saving for dinner. I made funny faces and he called me dinky dow. That's Vietnamese for crazy, I guess. Dinky dow! Dinky dow! He inhaled those crackers then he smiled and hugged my leg. He was so small he only came up to my knee.

6/ FUGUE

(The empty space.
Two wallets are on the ground.)

GINNY In my dreams, he said.
Everything is in green.
Green from the night vision goggles.
Green Iraq.

Verdant Falluja.
Emerald Tikrit.

(ELLIOT enters. He puts on night vision goggles.)

ELLIOT *(To imaginary night patrol partner.)* Waikiki man, whatchu gonna eat first thing when you get home? I don't know. Probably start me off with some French toast from Denny's. Don't even get me near the cereal aisle. I'll go crazy. I yearn for some cereal. If you had to choose between Cocoa Puffs and Count Chocula, what would you choose? Wheaties or Life? Fruity Pebbles or Crunchberry? You know my mom don't even buy Cap'n Crunch. She buys King Vitaman. Cereal so cheap, it don't even come in a box. It comes in a bag like them cheap Jewish noodles.

GINNY Nightmares every night, he said.
A dream about the first guy he actually saw that he killed.
A dream that doesn't let you forget a face.

ELLIOT The ultimate Denny's challenge. Would you go for the Grand Slam or the French Toast Combo? Wait. Or Western Eggs with Hash Browns? Yo, hash browns with ketchup. Condiments. Mustard, tartar sauce. I need me some condiments.

GINNY Green moon.
Green star.
Green blink of the eye.
Green teeth.
The same thing plays over and over.

(ELLIOT's attention is suddenly distracted.)

ELLIOT Yo, you see that?

GINNY The green profile of a machine gun in the distance.

ELLIOT Waikiki, look straight ahead. Straight, at that busted wall. Shit. You see that guy? What's in his hand? He's got an AK. What do you mean, "I don't know." Do you see him?

(ELLIOT looks out.)

We got some hostiles. Permission to shoot.

(Pause.)

Permission to open fire.

(Pause.)

Is this your first? Shit, this is my first, too. Alright. You ready?

GINNY In the dream, aiming in.
In the dream, knowing his aim is exact.
In the dream, closing his eyes.

(ELLIOT closes his eyes.)

ELLIOT Bang.

(ELLIOT opens his eyes.)

GINNY Opening his eyes.
The man is on the ground.

ELLIOT Hostile down. Uh, target down.
(Elliot gets up, disoriented from adrenaline.)

GINNY In the dream, a sudden movement.

ELLIOT Bang bang. Oh shit. That fucker moved. Did you see that? He moved, right? Mother f. Target down. Yes, I'm sure. Target down.

GINNY Nightmares every night, he said.
A dream about the first guy he actually saw that he killed.

(POP enters, sits on the ground. He's trying to stay awake. He looks through binoculars.)

GRANDPOP In my dreams, he said.

GINNY Walking toward the guy.

(ELLIOT walks to the wallet.)

GRANDPOP Everything is a whisper.

GINNY Standing over the guy.

(ELLIOT looks down at the wallet.)

GRANDPOP Breathing is delicate.

GINNY A green face.

GRANDPOP Whisper of water in the river.

GINNY A green forehead.

GRANDPOP Buzz of mosquito.

GINNY A green upper lip.

GRANDPOP Quiet Dong-Ha.

GINNY A green river of blood.

(ELLIOT kneels down, reaches to the wallet on the ground before him. It represents the dead man. He puts his hand on the wallet and remains in that position.)

GRANDPOP Echo Vietnam.

POP Joe Bobb. Wake up, man. Tell me about your gang from Kentucky. What, back in the Bronx? Yeah, we got ourselves a gang, but not a bad one. We help people on our street. Like some kids flipped over an ice cream stand. It was just a nice old guy, the kids flipped it, knocked the old guy flat. We chased after them. Dragged one. Punched him til he said sorry. We called ourselves the Social Sevens. After the Magnificent Sevens.

GRANDPOP Nightmares every night, he said.
A dream that doesn't let you forget a voice.
The same sounds echoing back and forth.

POP Guns? Naw, we weren't into none of that. We threw a lot of rocks and bottles. And handballs. Bronx Handball Champs,

1964. Doubles and singles. Hm? What's a handball?

GRANDPOP The snap of a branch.

POP Shh.

GRANDPOP Footsteps in the mud.

POP You hear something?

GRANDPOP Three drops of water.
A little splash.

(POP grabs his binoculars and looks out.)

POP VC on us. Ten o'clock. Kneeling in front of the river, alone. He's drinking. Fuck, he's thirsty. Joe Bobb, man, this is my first time. Oh shit. Shit. Bang. *(Pause.)* Bang.

GRANDPOP Whisper of two bullets in the air.
Echo of his gun.
A torso falling in the mud.

POP Got him. I got him, Joe Bobb. Man down. VC down.

(POP rises, looks out.)

GRANDPOP Hearing everything.
Walking to the guy.
Boots squishing in the mud.

(POP walks to the second wallet.)

Standing over the guy.
The guy says the Vietnamese word for "mother."
He has a soft voice.
He swallows air.
A brief convulsion.
Gasp.
Silence.
Water whispers in the river.

POP and ELLIOT Military code.
Remove ID and intel from dead hostiles.

(POP kneels in front of the wallet. It represents the dead man. He reaches out his hand and touches the wallet.

ELLIOT and POP are in the same position, each of them touching a wallet. They move in unison.)

POP The wallet
The body
The face
The eyes

(ELLIOT and POP open the wallets.)

ELLIOT The photo
The pictures
Bullet

(ELLIOT and POP each pull a little photo out of the wallets.)

POP Dog tags
The wife

ELLIOT The children

(They turn over the photo and look at the back of it.)

Black ink

POP A date

POP and ELLIOT Handwriting
A family portrait

(They drop the photo. They find a second photo. Lights fade.)

7/ PRELUDE

(The empty space. A flash bulb goes off. ELLIOT is in a TV studio. Harsh studio lighting is on him.)

PRODUCER VOICE ABC evening local news. And we're rolling to tape in three, two…

ELLIOT *(Tapping a mike on his shirt collar.)* Hello? What? Yeah. So where do we start?

(He presses his fingers against his ear, indicating that a producer or someone is talking to him through an ear monitor.)

My name? Elliot Ortiz.

(Listens.)

Sorry. Lance Corporal Elliot Ortiz, 3rd Light Armored Recon Battalion, 1st Marine Division.
(Listens.)
What? How was I injured?

PRODUCER VOICE *(Impatient.)* Someone fix his monitor. Don't worry, Mr. uh, Ortiz. Just tell us the story of your injury, would you?

ELLIOT Okay. Well. I was on watch outside Tikrit. I don't know. I feel stupid. I already told this story once.

PRODUCER VOICE You did?

ELLIOT Just now. In the screen test.

PRODUCER VOICE Right, right. That was to acclimate you to the camera.

ELLIOT It loses the impact to repeat it over and over.

PRODUCER VOICE Was it scary?

ELLIOT People say, oh that must be scary. But when you're there, you're like, oh shit, and you react. When it's happening you're not thinking about it. You're like, damn, this is really happening. That's all you can think. You're in shock basically. It's a mentality. Kill or be killed. You put everything away and your mentality is war. Some people get real gung ho about fighting. I was laid back.

PRODUCER VOICE Yes, Mr. uh Ortiz. This is great. This is exactly it. Let's go back and do you mind repeating a couple sentences, same exact thing, without the expletives?

ELLIOT Say what?

PRODUCER VOICE Same thing. But no shit and no damn.

ELLIOT I don't remember word for word.

PRODUCER VOICE No problem. Here we go. "But when you're there, you're like, oh shit, and you react."

ELLIOT But when you're there you're like, oh snap, and you react.

PRODUCER VOICE "You're like, damn, this is really happening."

ELLIOT You're like, flip, this is really happening.

PRODUCER VOICE Flip? Do people say "flip" these days?

ELLIOT You're like, FUCK, this is really happening.

PRODUCER VOICE Cut!

ELLIOT It's a marine thing.

8/ PRELUDE

(GRANDPOP in the garden.)

GRANDPOP Of everything Bach wrote, it is the fugues. The fugue is like an argument. It starts in one voice. The voice is the melody, the single solitary melodic line. The statement. Another voice creeps up on the first one. Voice two responds to voice one. They tangle together. They argue, they become messy. They create dissonance. Two, three, four lines clashing. You think, good god, they'll never untie themselves. How did this mess get started in the first place? Major keys, minor keys, all at once on top of each other. *(Leans in.)* It's about untying the knot. In Korea my platoon fell in love with Bach. All night long, firing eight-inch Howitzers into the evergreens. Flute is very soothing after the bombs settle down. They begged me to play. "Hey, Ortiz, pull out that pipe!" I taught them minor key versus major key. Minor key, it's melancholy, it's like the back of the woman you love as she walks away from you. Major key, well that's more simple, like how the sun rises. They understood. If we had a rough battle, if we lost one of our guys, they said, "Eh, Ortiz, I need a minor key." But if they had just got a letter from home, a note from the lady, then they want C major, up-tempo.

"Light as a feather, free as a bird." My teacher always said the same thing. Let your muscles relax. Feel like a balloon is holding up your spine. He was a gringo but he lived with us rural Puerto Ricans. Way in the mountains. He was touring in San Juan with his famous jazz combo, fell in love with a woman, never left. We accepted him as one of our own. He was honorary Boricua. "Light as a feather, free as a bird." I said, you know, if I get any lighter and freer, I'll float to the moon. But that's how you learn. By repeating. Over and over. At Inchon my right hand was purple with frostbite, I developed a technique for left-hand only. In Kunu-Ri? Every night we took our weapons to bed, like a wife. One night I shot myself in the shoulder. So I mastered the left-hand method.

Elliot always wanted to know. "Abuelo, tell me a story." About life in the service, about Puerto Rico. "Abuelo, how old were you when? How old were you when this, when that?" Carajo, I don't remember! All I know is what music I was playing at the time. When I started school, when I was a boy, helping mom in the house, it was etudes and scales. The foundations. The first girl I "danced with," it was danzónes around that time, mambo with a touch of jazz. But in Korea, I played Bach only. Because it is cold music, it is like math. You can approach it like a calculation. An exercise. A routine.

At the airport, I handed the flute to little George. I thought, he needs a word of advice, but what is there to say? I sent him to boot camp with a fifty dollar bill and a flute. That he didn't know how to play. But without it my fingers grew stiff. I started losing words. Dates. Names of objects. Family names. Battles I had fought in. I started repeating words as if I was playing scales. Practice. Bookmarks to remind myself. "Inchon, Inchon, Inchon." "Korea, Korea." "Bayamón." "Howitzer." "Evergreen."

9/PRELUDE

(The garden. GRANDPOP opens a letter and reads. POP appears separately, in a good mood.)

POP November 30, 1966

Did you ever notice a helmet is an incredibly useful item? I got a wide range of artistic and practical uses for mine.

GRANDPOP Today I took a bath, if you want to call it that, out of my helmet. The newer ones have two parts.

POP If you take the metal part out, you can cook in it. Tonight we had two cans of tuna. And hamburgers in gravy. Hess' contribution?

POP and GRANDPOP Ham with lima beans.

POP Everyone empties out their cans. Make a little blue campfire with some minor explosives. Voila,

GRANDPOP helmet stew.

POP So that's our Thanksgiving feast. The guys are singing carols. They're in the spirit! Jingle bells
Mortar shells
VC in the grass
Take your Merry Christmas
And shove it up your ass

10/ FUGUE

(The empty space. Two cots are there.
ELLIOT lies on the ground. GRANDPOP, GINNY and POP wrap ELLIOT's legs in barbed wire. They entangle ELLIOT in this position, trapping him. ELLIOT lies helpless.)

GINNY A road outside Tikrit.
A mile short of Saddam's hometown.

GRANDPOP Cars are allowed out, but not back in.

POP The boy was standing guard.

GRANDPOP He saw an incoming car.

GINNY The headlights approached.

POP He fired into the car.

GRANDPOP The horn sounded.

POP The car collided into the barricade.

GINNY The concertina wire slinkied onto his legs.

GRANDPOP Two seconds ago.

ELLIOT Sarge! Sarge! Waikiki!

GINNY Seventy four thorns dig deep into his skin.

POP Seventy four barbs chew into his bone.

GRANDPOP It is not a sensation of rawness.

GINNY It is not excruciating pain.

POP It is a penetrating weakness.

GRANDPOP Energy pours out of his leg.

GINNY Like water from a garden hose.

ELLIOT Sarge!

POP The boy knows he is trapped.

GRANDPOP He doesn't know he is injured.

GINNY He does a military style inspection.

(ELLIOT reaches up his pants leg.)

GRANDPOP His hand enters the warm meat of his calf.

ELLIOT Oh shit. Stay calm. Put the tourniquet on. Lay back. Drink a cup of water.

(ELLIOT pulls a strip of cloth from his pocket. He wraps it like a tourniquet around his thigh. Tight.)

GINNY Forty one percent of all injuries are leg wounds.

POP Military code.

GRANDPOP Carry a tourniquet at all times.

GINNY Instructions in the event of rapid blood loss.

GRANDPOP One.

ELLIOT Stay calm.

POP Two.

ELLIOT Put the tourniquet on.

GRANDPOP Three.

ELLIOT Lay back.
Four... Four?

GINNY Drink a cup of water.

ELLIOT Someone get me a cup of water.

POP Stay

GRANDPOP Calm
Put

POP Tourniquet

GINNY Lay

GRANDPOP Back
Drink

POP Cup

GINNY Water

ELLIOT Hello? Stay calm. Put a beret on. Fall away. Drink a hot tub. Fuck. Stay with me, Ortiz. Big El going to be okay. Hello? Big El okay. Right?

POP Fast forward pictures.

GINNY Mom

POP Pop

GRANDPOP Grandpop

POP Fast forward.

GINNY Grandpop

GRANDPOP Pop

POP Mom

GINNY Rapid shutter motion.

GRANDPOP Frames with no sound.

GINNY Moving lips, no words.

ELLIOT Mom

POP Pop

GRANDPOP Grandpop

ELLIOT Stay calm. Lay back. Smoke a cigarette.

(He pulls a cigarette out of his pocket.)

Anyone got a light?

(He smokes the unlit cigarette.)

POP Instructions if wounded while alone.

GRANDPOP Call for help.

POP Signal commander.

GINNY Call for your corpsman.

POP Identify yourself.

ELLIOT Sarge! Waikiki! Big El down. Big El down.

POP His blood congeals in the sand.

GRANDPOP His fingertips are cool.

GINNY He enters a euphoric state.

GRANDPOP The boots,

ELLIOT Beautiful.

POP The barbed wire,

ELLIOT Beautiful.

GINNY The stars,

ELLIOT Beautiful.

GINNY In the event of extended blood loss.
    Reflect on a time you were happy.
    When have you felt a sensation of joy?

ELLIOT Mom…
    Pop…

(ELLIOT remains injured under…
POP enters and lays on a cot.)

GRANDPOP An evacuation hospital.
    Made of a Vietnamese monastery.
    Ancient windows with no glass.

GINNY Through the window, views of Vietnam.
    That look like views of Puerto Rico.
    Mountains.

ELLIOT Mountains.

GRANDPOP Waterfalls.

ELLIOT Waterfalls.

GINNY All different colors of green.
    Rock formations.
    A few bald spots from the bombs.

GRANDPOP The wood floor is covered with cement.
    The cement is covered with water and blood.
    The cement is cool.
    The blood is cool.

ELLIOT Cool.

(ELLIOT nods off, going into shock.)

GINNY A woman enters.

(GINNY enters, approaches POP's cot.)

    Hey.

POP Nurse Ginny. Still on duty?

GINNY Shh. Don't wake the babies.

POP Can't sleep?

GINNY Yeah.

POP Me too.

GINNY Nightmares. Weird stuff, I kept seeing your leg. I thought I should check up on you.

POP It itches, but you know. The guy next to me's got no left leg at all.

GINNY I was thinking, a private physical therapy session.

POP Sounds good.

GINNY Clean you up.

(GINNY lifts up his pant leg. There is a big gauze patch there. She slowly pulls back the gauze.)

POP That's as far back as it goes. The rest is stuck to the gauze.

GINNY We're all out of anesthetic. I'll be gentle.

(She works on his wound. He is clearly in physical pain.)

    Twenty eight stitches.
    Two diagonals.
    The first time she touched the man's wound,
    A pain pierced up through her index finger.
    Through her knuckle.
    Wrist.
    Forearm.
    Elbow.
    Humerus.
    Shoulder.
    The pain jolted in her veins.
    Exploded in her vital organs.
    Pancreas, lungs, brains, spleen.
    Planted itself between her legs.
    She touched the blood on his skin and had the desire to make love to the wounded man.

POP Ay dios mio. Fuck.

GINNY Think of the time in life you were happiest.

POP Why?

GINNY You forget the pain.

POP It's not pain. It fucking itches!

GINNY Sorry.

POP Sorry.

(Pause. GINNY covers the wound. She pulls down his pant leg. She sits on top him.)

GINNY Is it too much weight?

POP Please, crush me to death.

GINNY There's too many bells and whistles in hospitals. To be a nurse is easy. Give a dog a bone.

POP Reach into my pocket.

GINNY Lance Corporal Ortiz.

POP Go ahead.

(She puts her hand into his pocket. She feels around.)

GINNY What am I looking for?

POP You'll know when you find it.

(She removes her hand from his pocket. She's holding a joint.)

Medicine.

GINNY Anesthetic.

(GINNY lights the joint. They pass it back and forth. Between inhales, they touch each other.)

GRANDPOP Through the window, views of Vietnam.

That look like views of Puerto Rico.

Mountains.

Green.

Stars.

Bamboo.

Little huts up the mountainside.

POP *(Stoned.)* I got one. I was a little boy in Puerto Rico. Bayamón. I had this ugly scrappy dog. We used to run around scaring my dad's roosters. One of the roosters got pissed and poked the dog's left eye out.

GINNY What was his name?

POP Jimmy.

GINNY Jimmy? Jimmy!

(ELLIOT shivers.)

ELLIOT Ugghhh…

POP Shh. Did you hear something? The operating room.

GINNY No, it's the monkeys. There's a whole family of them that live in the tree.

POP They're not rock ape are they?

GINNY What's rock ape?

POP Big, brown, and ugly.

GINNY Rock ape!

(They laugh. She suddenly gets off of him and walks to a far corner of the room. She still has the joint.)

GINNY Tonight you're going to do like Jesus did. You're going to get up and walk on water. Defy all the odds. And I'm going to do like a circus tamer. Like someone who trains dogs or exotic animals. If you're a good tiger and you do your trick and you don't bite, you get a reward. If you do your dolphin tricks, I give you a fish.

POP Seafood is my favorite.

GINNY Walk to me. See if you can make it.

POP Not even a hand out of bed?

GINNY If you want a taste of this ripe avocado, you got to pick it off the tree all by yourself.

(POP struggles to get up. This is a difficult, painful process. He slowly makes his way across the room.)

POP Shrapnel.

In the ligaments.

In the soft-hard knee cap.//

ELLIOT Stay

POP In the spaces between stitches.

Shrapnel from a mortar bomb.//

ELLIOT Back

Lay

POP Splinters that fragment within you.

Wobbling within your guts.

Creating ripples in your bloodstream.//

ELLIOT Home

(POP arrives at GINNY. He falls into her. They kiss.)

ELLIOT Signal

Elliot Ortiz

(GINNY and POP stop kissing.)

POP Do you heal all your patients this way?

ELLIOT Elliot Ortiz.

GINNY Let's go outside and watch the monkeys.

POP No, really. You do this a lot?

ELLIOT Elliot Ortiz.

GINNY Think you can make it outside?

POP Give me a hand this time.

ELLIOT Ortiz.

GINNY There's a gorgeous view of the moon.

(They exit, slowly, carefully, in each other's arms. They pass in front of ELLIOT, who is shivering.)

ELLIOT Mom?

Pop?

11/ PRELUDE

(The empty space. ELLIOT wears big radio station headphones.)

RADIO VOICE You're listening to WHYY, member supported radio, welcome back. I'm having a conversation with Elliot Ortiz, a North Philadelphia native who graduated from Edison High in 2002. So, Elliot, you're seventeen years old, just finishing boot camp, and the President declares war. What was going through your mind?

ELLIOT I was like, okay then, let's do this.

RADIO VOICE You were ready. Is it exciting to be a marine?

ELLIOT People say, oh, it's like a video game. Oh, it's like the movies. Naw. Base is the most depressing place ever. You wake up, go outside, you see rocky sand mountains. That's it. Rocks. Sand. You gotta drive 30 minutes to find a Wal-Mart. I just mainly stay on base, rent a lot of movies.

RADIO VOICE But not base, let's talk about Iraq. Did you see a lot of action?

ELLIOT Yeah.

RADIO VOICE Were there times you were scared?

ELLIOT The first time I heard a mortar shell. That scared the crap out of me. Literally.

RADIO VOICE And you were injured. Tell me about that.

ELLIOT It's a long story.

RADIO VOICE What sticks out in your mind? About the experience?

ELLIOT I got two corrective surgeries. They'll send me back if I want.

RADIO VOICE To Iraq? Will you go?

ELLIOT I mean, my leg is still messed up but. I'm not trying to stay here and work at Subway Hoagies. "Pardon me, sir, you want some hot peppers with that roast beef?"

RADIO VOICE What do the troops think about politics? Do they support the war?

ELLIOT Politics? Nobody cares about that. People drink their sorrows away. You hear people running down the hallway like, "F this!" "F that!" "Kill raghead!"

RADIO VOICE *(Slightly changed tone.)* Editor flag last remark. *(Back to interview.)* Both your father and grandfather served in the military.

ELLIOT My pop was in Vietnam, Marine Corps. Three purple hearts.

RADIO VOICE It must be something else to trade war stories with your father.

ELLIOT He doesn't bring up that stuff too much.

RADIO VOICE Some say there's a code of silence after returning home.

ELLIOT My mom's got a box of his old letters, his uniform, dog tags. Our basement flooded and everything is in piles down there. But I was like, "Mom you gotta find that stuff."

RADIO VOICE What about your grandfather?

ELLIOT He was in Korea. He was a flute player. He'll be like, "I played Mozart in the north when everyone had frostbite." He's got two or three stories that he just tells them over and over. He's got old-timers.

RADIO VOICE Alzheimer's?

ELLIOT Right.

RADIO VOICE You must have felt a great deal of pressure to enlist.

ELLIOT Naw, I didn't even tell them. I just went one day and signed the papers.

RADIO VOICE Just like that.

ELLIOT Dad was actually kind of pissed, like, "The Marines is no joke. The Marines is going to mess with you."

RADIO VOICE So why go then?

(No answer.)

Why did you enlist?

ELLIOT I was like, Dad was a Marine. I want to be a Marine. I really did it for him.

12/ PRELUDE

(The garden. GINNY holds a large yellow envelope stuffed full of papers. She pulls out one sheet at a time. GRANDPOP appears separately, reading a letter. POP appears separately. He is incredibly happy, slightly drunk.)

POP April 4, '67
    To my pop back in the Bronx aka "Little P.R.",
    The evac hospital was like Disney Land. Real beds.

GRANDPOP Clean sheets.

POP Fresh pajamas. The women there? I met this one nurse, Ginny. Nurse Ginny. So let me ask you.

GINNY "Nurse Ginny."

POP How old were you when you fell for Mom?

GRANDPOP Did you know right away she was your woman?

POP I'm serious old man, I want answers. Got back to the platoon this morning. The guys were still alive, which is a good feeling. We had a big celebration.

GINNY "Helmet stew."

POP Hess' mom sent a package with wood alcohol. Stuff she made in the bathtub. Awful stuff.

GRANDPOP We got drunk.

POP Joe Bobb pulled out his guitar. I pulled out your flute. I made a big official speech, told them the whole story. You're a decorated veteran,

GINNY "Bird watching."

POP you served in Korea, back when they kept the Puerto Ricans separate. How you played the same exact flute to your platoon. Then when I enlisted you handed me the flute and said,

GRANDPOP "You're a man. Teach yourself how to play."

POP Joe Bobb showed me a hillbilly song. I showed him a danzón. The keys are sticking, it's the swamp. Low D won't budge, two of the pads fell off. Here's my little plan I'm putting together.

GRANDPOP Get home safe.

POP Marry nurse Ginny.

GINNY "C-rations."

POP Have a son, give him the flute. One flute, three generations. Aw man, right now Joe Bobb is throwing up all over. The smell is bad. It's the wood alcohol.

GRANDPOP Tell Mom my leg is okay.

GINNY "Date unknown."

POP And sorry I didn't write for so long.

13/ PRELUDE

(The garden, at night. ELLIOT stands in the garden. POP's letters are on the ground.)

ELLIOT My little green Bible. Every soldier has something you take with you, no matter where you go, you take that thing. Waikiki had a tattoo of his mom. Mario had a gold cross his grandma had gave him. He wore it around his neck even though it was against the rules. I kept the Bible right inside my vest pocket. I had a picture of Stephanie in it, like a family portrait with all her cousins. My senior prom picture with all the guys. A picture of Mom and Pop. I looked at those pictures every day. Stared at those pictures. Daze off for like two hours at a time. *(Pause.)* The first guy I shot down, I kept his passport there.

One night, I don't know why, I was just going to kill my corporal. He was asleep. I put my rifle to the corporal's head and I was going to kill him. All I kept thinking was the bad stuff he made us do. He was the kind of guy who gets off on bringing down morale. Like making us run with trench foot. Trench foot is when your feet start rotting. Because of chemical and biological weapons, we didn't take our boots off for 36 days straight. When I finally took my boots off, I had to peel my socks from the skin. They were black, and the second they came off, they became instantly hard. Corporal made us run with trench foot. Run to get the water. Run to get the ammo. Everyone was asleep and I was ready to pull the trigger. Waikiki woke up and saw what I was doing. He kicked my arm like, "Eh, man, let's switch." So I looked at my pictures and slept, he went on watch. The next day me and Waikiki were running to get the water and he was like, "Eh, man, what were you doing last night?" I was like, "I don't know." He was like, "It's alright. We'll be out of here soon."

After I got injured, when my chopper landed in Spain. They pulled me out of there. They cut. My clothes were so disgusting they had to cut them off my body. My underwear was so black. The nurse had to cut it up the sides and take it off me like a pamper. The second she did that, it turned hard like a cast of plaster. You could see the shape of everything. Everything. It looked like an invisible man was wearing them. She threw it like a basketball in the trash. When the guys had finally found me, they had stuffed my leg full of cotton rags. The nurse counted one two three then ripped all the cotton out. I thought I was gonna die. I broke the metal railing right off the stretcher.

They didn't have underwear to put on me so they put a hospital gown instead. The kind that opens in the back and you can see the butt. I was still on the runway. The chopper took off, my gown flew up over my face, but my hands were tied down so I couldn't do nothing. I was butt naked in the middle of everybody. Next thing I know, someone pulled the gown away from my face and I saw this fine female looking down at me. When I saw her, it was like angels singing. *(He imitates angels singing.)* Like, *aaaaaaah.* So what's the first thing that's gonna happen to a guy? She saw it. I was so embarrassed.

The sponge baths I got while I was over there? They give you a sponge bath every other day. The first time. Once again, it was another fine female. It was four months since I seen one. Most female officers, out in the field, they don't look like this one did. So something happened, you know what happened. She was sponging me down and saw it and was like, "You want me to leave the room?" After three days she got used to it. She would be chatting, changing the subject. When you catch a woody with an officer, who you have to see everyday in Spain? The day I left she was like, "Yo, take care of your friend."

When I first landed in Philly, Chucky and Buckwheat met me at the airport. They came running up to the gate like, "Did you kill em? Did you kill em? Did you have a gun? Did you have a really big gun?" I was like, nah, don't you worry about none of that. Don't think about those things. I was trying to forget, but that's how they see me now. That's what I am. That's how Stephanie sees me. And the guys.

On the airplane flying home. All I could think was, I have to talk to Pop. Hear his stories. He used to tell stuff from the war but looking back, it was mostly jokes. Like he swallowed a thing of chewing tobacco and puked for three days. He took a leak off a tank and a pretty Vietnamese lady saw him. He never sat me down and told me what it was like, for real. The first night I got here, I was like, Pop, I need to hear it from your mouth. That was Monday. He was like, we'll talk about it Tuesday. Wednesday rolled around, I'm like, Pop I'm only home a week. Did you have nightmares, too? Every single night? Did you feel guilty, too? When you shot a guy? Things he never opened up about. Finally I got him real drunk, I'm like, now's the time. I was like, did you shoot anyone up close? Did you shoot a civilian? Anything. He threw the table at me. Threw his beer bottle on the steps. Marched up the stairs, slammed the door.

Seeing Mom, it takes so much stress off. She laid me down, and worked on my leg in an old fashioned way. Went to the herb store, got all her magic potions. The gauze bandage, it hardly came off. I could peel it back like a inch. The rest was infected, stuck to the gauze. At night, it itched so bad I had to scream. Mom laid me down in her garden, she told me to relax. Breathe in. Breathe out. Breathe like a circle. She told me to close my eyes and imagine the time I was happiest in my entire life. Then I felt her fingers on my leg. That felt so good. Hands that love you touching your worst place. I started to cry like a baby. I don't know why. It's just, I forgot how that feels. Like home. The tears were just coming. She put aloe and all sorts of stuff in there. I could tell she was crying too. She knows I been through a lot. She understands.

(GINNY enters. She begins to braid vines around ELLIOT's body, from the garden. She wraps his body in intricate, meticulous ways. She adds leaves and other flora. This is a slow process. It lasts until the end of the scene.)

It's a hard question. Of every second in your life, nail down the best one. I started playing memories, like a movie in my mind.

The prom. Me all slicked out with the guys, in our silver suits. Matching silver shoes. Hooking up with Stephanie. All the different places me and Steph got freaky. In her mom's house. On top of the roof for New Year's. This one time I took Sean fishing down the Allegheny. He farted real loud. He ripped a nasty one. All the white dudes, in their fisherman hats, they were like, "Crazy Puerto Ricans. You scared the fish away."

The first time I ever went to Puerto Rico. With Mom and Pop. We drove around the island with the windows rolled down. I was like, damn, so this is where I come from. This is my roots. This one time we stopped at Luquillo beach. The water was light light blue, and flat like a table, no waves. Mom was like, "Pull over, George, and teach me to swim." We swam in there like for five hours. Pop was holding mom on the surface of the water. He would hold on, like, "You ready? You ready?" She was like, "Ay! Hold on, papi! I'm gonna sink!" And he would let go and she would stay, floating, on the top. She was so happy. It looked like they were in love. Then you could see the moon in the water. It was still day but she floated on the moon. I could live in that day forever. See them like that every day.

After Mom fixed my leg, she was like, "I got a gift for you. Something important." She gave me a fat yellow envelope. Crusty and old. She was like, "Burn this or read it. It's up to you." I sat out in the garden, started pulling letters out of the envelope. It was all of pop's letters from Vietnam.

(POP enters the garden.)

POP Date unknown

ELLIOT I read every one. All night, I didn't hardly move.

POP Dad,

I just want to say I'm sorry.

ELLIOT I was like, Pop, I fucking walked in your shoes.

POP I threw your flute away.

ELLIOT Pop, we lived the same fucking life.

POP All these thoughts were going through my head like thinking about the Bronx, you, Mom.

ELLIOT It's scary how much was the same. Killing a guy. Getting your leg scratched up. Falling in love.

POP They got Hess and Joe Bobb.

ELLIOT Nightmares. Meds. Infections. Letters to your father.

POP One instant. Their bodies were covered with dust. Tree bark. Their eyes.

ELLIOT Even ripping them up, taping them back together. It was like the feeling from Puerto Rico, but not a peaceful feeling.

POP It was like shoot someone, destroy something. I threw your flute in the river.

ELLIOT You see all the shit you can't erase. Like, here's who you are, Elliot, and you never even knew.

POP You can't sit around and feel sorry for yourself or you're gonna die. I had to do something, so that's what I did.

(POP's letter is done.)

ELLIOT Pop's up on the second floor, got the AC on, watching TV. Probably smoking weed. Probably doesn't even know I seen his letters. I know he won't even come to the airport tomorrow. He'll just be like:

(POP speaks directly to ELLIOT.)

POP Well, you chose it so good luck with it. Don't do anything stupid.

(ELLIOT is tangled in vines. Lights fade.)

14/FUGUE

(The empty space.
Three duffel bags are on the floor.)

GINNY A runway.
The Philadelphia airport tarmac.
July 2003 is dry and windy.
Two seagulls fly even though the ocean is miles away.
Luggage carts roll in one direction,
Taxiing planes in another.
The windows are sealed to airtight, noisetight.
People crowd around the departure monitors.

ELLIOT A man enters.

(ELLIOT enters.)

Cologne is sprayed on his neck.
A clean shave.

(ELLIOT looks at his watch.)

0700 hours.
Thinking in military time again.
He fixes his short hair.

(ELLIOT fixes his short hair.)

Grabs his life.

(ELLIOT picks up a duffel bag.)

Inside his bag are two fatigues his mother ironed this morning.
Fresh sorullito from Grandmom.
Still warm, wrapped in two paper towels.
Grease-sealed in a plastic bag.
A naked photo from Stephanie.
In the photo she is smiling and holding in her stomach.
Her skin is brown.
The hair on her body is brown.
She is blinking, her eyes half closed.

GINNY San Juan Bay.
A boarding ramp.
A transport ship to South Korea
Via Japan via Panama Canal.
September 1950 is mild.
The water is light light blue.
And flat like a table, no waves.

GRANDPOP A boy enters.

(GRANDPOP enters. He stands beside ELLIOT and picks up another duffel bag. GRANDPOP waves goodbye to his family, offstage.)

Slacks pressed.
Hair combed.
Family standing at the rails.
His wife wears a cotton dress.
Sweat gathers in her brown curls.
On her hip, Little George.
His five year old son.
A boarding ramp.
Corrugated steel.
His first ride on the ocean.

(GRANDPOP picks up his duffel and freezes.)

GINNY A runway.
The Newark Airport tarmac.
August 1965 is unseasonably cool.

(POP enters. He stands beside ELLIOT and picks up a duffel bag.)

POP A boy enters.

(He looks at his watch.)

9:15 a.m.
He will never get used to military time.
He grabs his life.
At the bottom of his duffel, good luck charms.
A red handball glove.
A bottle of vodka from the Social Sevens.
Two pencils and paper.
A long corridor.

A gray carpeted ramp.
A plane to Parris Island
To a ship to Vietnam.

(POP picks up his duffel and freezes.)

ELLIOT The bag
   The duffel
   The photo
   Stephanie
   Teeth
   Jazz
   Calvin Klein
   Fubu
   Flute
   Helmet

36 springs
Ink
Heliconia
Handwriting

(ELLIOT grabs his duffel, steps forward.)

He walks down the gray carpeted ramp.
Boards the plane to Camp Pendleton.
Where he will board his second ship to Kuwait.
Where he will cross the border north into Iraq.
Again.
Happy he has an aisle seat.
Going back to war.

Notes

1. Based on traditional military cadences
2. From Nas, "Got Yourself A Gun"

———————————

Meena Natarajan and Ananya Chatterjea

Biographies

Meena Natarajan is a playwright and director and the Executive and Literary Director of Pangea World Theater, a progressive, international ensemble space for arts and dialogue. She has led the theater's growth since its founding in 1995. As a playwright, her scripts have been professionally produced both in India and the U.S. She adapted Farid Ud-din Attar's 12th-century poem, *Conference of the Birds*, into a dramatic script for Pangea World Theater for its founding production in 1996 and again in 2009 and 2016. A staged reading of the play was pro-

duced by Silk Road Theatre in Chicago in 2013. An excerpt of her play *Without My Country* received a reading at the Women Playwrights International Festival in Greece in 2000. Her production, *Partitions*, dealing with the anti-Sikh riots in the '80s and the partition of India in 1947, performed as part of the Playwrights Center's New Stage Directions Series in Minneapolis in April 2002. Other plays include: *The Inner World,* based on 2000-year-old Tamil poems of love and war, *Rashomon* based on Akutagawa's short stories with playwright Luu Pham, *Etchings In the Sand*, with choreographer Ananya Chatterjea and plays commissioned by the Advocates of Human Rights, Amnesty International and Praxis International. Meena received a Twin Cities International Citizen's Award in 2001 for her work in Pangea. Her work *From The Ashes* toured to the first National Asian-American Theatre Festival in New York, 2007. She was commissioned to write a play, *No Expiration Date*, on Aging, Sexuality, and Mindfulness by the Program of Human Sexuality at the University of Minnesota. She has been awarded grants from the Minnesota State Arts Board, Theatre Communications Group, and Playwrights Center. Meena was awarded the Visionary Award for mid-career leaders from the Minnesota Council of Nonprofits in 2013.

Ananya Chatterjea is a choreographer, dancer, and thinker who envisions her work as a "call to action" with a particular focus on women artists of color. She is the Artistic Director of Ananya Dance Theatre (www.ananyadancetheatre.org). The company's work, described as "people powered dances of transformation," proceeds both through concert performances and through participatory performances in nontraditional spaces, where audiences become cocreators of movement explorations with the dancers. Ananya is the recipient of a 2012 McKnight Choreography Fellowship and a 2011 Guggenheim Choreography Fellowship. She was honored with a citation for Outstanding Dance Educator from the MN Sage Awards. Her most recent work *Roktim* was described as being characterized by "cohesive, precise movement vocabulary" and a "unique aesthetic" that "found a fresh liveliness in the agriculture sweatshop nightmare" (*Star Tribune*, 9/20/15). Ananya toured this work recently on a State Department funded tour to Ethiopia, and presented *Roktim* as the keynote performance at the Crossing Boundaries Festival in Addis Ababa at the National Theater. Her work *Moreechika, Season of Mirage* was remarked upon as "all powerful…but Chatterjea's choreography also leaves room for brutal beauty and vulnerability" (Star Tribune, 9/9/12), and toured to the Harare International Arts Festival, Zimbabwe (2012). Ananya is a Professor of Dance at the University of Minnesota and teaches courses in dance technique and theories of performance.

Artistic statement

Etchings in the Sand is an exploration of memories, fragments of the past that remained with us as we traveled across continents. The creative process and the thematic focus were very different than our typical working modes. Neither of us had worked with autobiography as such a clear jumping off point as we did in *Etchings*. Moreover, without necessarily having planned for it to be so, we implicitly agreed to move away from the usual "burdens" of representation artists of color are urged to bear within the parameters of a neoliberal multiculturalism, and to create without explicit references to the political imperatives that press upon us. Instead, we created from a deeply personal store of memories and played with layering memory images from different places and times. In this, we came to invest in a reflection upon memory itself, our friendship, and how we move between past and present everyday.

Memories became a doorway into our present. Remembering became a practice, flowing in current time, creating another layer of memories in a friendship between two women, South Asian, diasporic, immigrants, artists. Remembering parts of our pasts even as we grappled to come to terms with some of the memories that surfaced, and bits of the pasts of our ancestors as we remembered them, was a way of documenting stories that had moved us through our journeys, and now lived with us. We came to commit to active remembering together—something we seldom have time for in the hectic pace of our lives—as a way of tracking our journeys across time and place. And we realized that while there were hoards of little remembrances that slip their way in our consciousness as we go about our work, there was also the process of dedicating some time to intentionally conjuring up and reliving memories, and allowing these to inform our present.

In the end, we realized that this deeply personal project became about carving out space. By creating an artistic project for ourselves, we refused to fit into the groove popular for "third world women." We claimed complex subjectivities through the fragmented narrative of memories, even as we insisted on articulating histories that were very different from each other. We came to understand that the project of remembering, however fictionalized, and recreating moments of our lives as theater, is one that is permeated with a subversive politics of resistance. It is one that needs to be paid attention to, for this is often how we transform major historical narratives that fail to acknowledge our lived realities. We remember feminist writer Urvashi Butalia as she talks about the value of oral histories: "…people locate their memories by different dates, or different timeframes, than the events that mark the beginning and end of histories, their narratives flow above, below, or through the disciplinary narratives of history. They offer a way of turning the historical lens at a somewhat different angle, and to look at what this perspective offers."[1] Our performed remembered fragments had not narrated any major historical events, but they had mingled time frames as they exist in our experiencing, and they had captured particular moments in the fleeting history of a constantly changing cultural context. The value, for us, is beyond words.

Production history

Etchings in the Sand was originally premiered at Pangea World Theater in Minneapolis June 1–11, 2000, directed by Dipankar Mukherjee at The Little Theater, Hennepin Center for the Arts. Meena Natarajan and Ananya Chatterjea performed in the dance narrative.

6 *Etchings in the Sand*
Meena Natarajan and Ananya Chatterjea

Scene I

Stage. A big square drawn in powdered chalk on the floor. The beginnings of a hopscotch (kit-kit) game. As the play proceeds, this disintegrates. At the back of the stage, a clothesline with clothes and on one corner, a mound of earth.

From off stage, these questions are heard almost riding on top of each other. As the questions near the end, both MEENA and ANANYA come on stage and finish the squares of the hopscotch game that they will play. They finish the pattern in silence, humming notes from an Indian folksong and playing as they do and they start the game. They repeat the questions again as they play kit-kit/hopscotch. The second time, the last line is repeated once by MEENA and once by ANANYA.

MEENA Is this moon above our head the same one that shone its brilliance the night we left?

ANANYA Is it the same one that shimmers in the starless sky in our new home?

MEENA And why did we decide to leave if our hearts are still here?

ANANYA Where is the child I used to be?

MEENA Why does the darkness answer me with the same questions I throw out into this unlimited night?

ANANYA Does the father who speaks to you in your dream die again when morning comes?

MEENA And when you die, do your dreams die too?

ANANYA Which doorway do I stand in watching time go by?

MEENA And aren't we lent to this earth for a short time?

ANANYA Does memory remember the history raining down on it?

MEENA Which crack in the earth contains my story?

ANANYA Which crack in the earth contains my story?

MEENA Which crack in the earth contains my story?

ANANYA Which crack in the earth contains my story?

(As the last line ends, ANANYA throws the stone over her shoulder into a mound of earth. She looks at the earth, notices something bright and starts digging in the earth, pulling out photographs, earrings, jewelry, little objects and lingering over them. She brings a necklace over to MEENA and they laugh over it. ANANYA goes back to the mound of earth. The digging starts to get more and more frantic. Breeze. ANANYA in a corner digging mud frantically. MEENA watches this and something about the frantic digging and picking up of a piece of clothing disturbs her. She backs away and the clothes touch her face. She touches each article of clothing. As ANANYA lays her head to rest on the mound of earth, MEENA says the following lines.)

MEENA There are places in our memory which are forgotten. Like places, which we visit once and never return to, they are neglected, left vacant, and decay in our infinite search for other memories. Yet we look for them, scrabbling in the dust of time to recapture that fragrance that once was, not even knowing what it is that we are searching for. And there are those other memories that refuse to die, that refuse to leave, that persist in spite of our efforts to forget them, that hang like clothes in the wind, some tattered and torn and others new and whole.

Scene II

Choreographic movement, ANANYA moves/dances across stage. The dance of the past, raindrops, catching them, being tossed, picking flowers, throw back in an effort to go over, going from one corner to the other. Stuck in the past.

MEENA sits in front of the audience weaving cloths or threads of different colors, braiding them into strands while this dance goes on.

Scene III

Memories. Photographs. The recounting of memories from the past, near past so that there is a kaleidoscope of memories: starts slowly but becomes quicker and quicker as the two women cut each other's memories with ones of their own. This has to sound cohesive and whole with one person's memories riding on and being triggered by the other's.

MEENA I see in my mind's eye my grandmother. When my mother was a little knot of flesh in her belly, I see my grandmother sitting in her chair on a verandah in Ipoh, surrounded by her maids, Chinese and Indian. In sepia, this remains etched in my memory. This is the same chair that my mother sits fourteen years later, waiting patiently for the family hen to hatch a little brown egg on her lap. My grandmother steps out into the yard in her sari that is nine yards long and picks a lychee. She slowly unpeels the thick, un-yielding skin with her fingernails. She bites into the soft tender fruit and laughs as its yield of sugar liquid drips down her chin. She steps then into the kitchen, the kitchen from which my mother is shooed away by the cook fourteen years later. Is that where my memories begin? Or does it begin some years after that? My mother standing next to my father for the first time when my father's family goes to see her at her father's home. My mother, five feet, looking up at my father who is six one. The second time they meet, they dare not look at each other, it is too public. This is their wedding day. Or even before that when my grandmother and grandfather ages 9 and 12 sit next to each other in India, him dreaming of his kites and her playing with her dolls. The sacred fire rises to the heavens in front of them in a single gesture as they are tied in a knot for the next 67 years.

ANANYA Or perhaps it begins when my father arrives in Lucknow, that city of palaces and dances, to see my mother for the first time. As he travels the many miles in the train from Calcutta to Lucknow, the air seems to get clearer and clearer and the road ahead is ripe with the future. While he fills his waiting hours with sleep, does he dream of the sun? This is the same train that my brother and I are in a few years later as we go back again and again to Lucknow. I sit with my nose pressed to the windowpane, watching Mithul and Rajkanna running in the green fields alongside. The same Mithul and Rajkanna, old friends who now comfort my daughter when she is alone. Or perhaps my memories begin this moment as I watch my daughter and wonder, did this piece of magic ever rest in my stomach? My daughter chattering on incessantly about me, then herself, then the teacher, then the cat, jumping identities with facile assurance. Today, I am the keeper of her memories and I will tell her soon about these summer days and about the days when, a little baby in her bassinet, she learned to coo and gurgle, responding to every sound I made. She's excited, we said excitedly, by learning to converse.

MEENA Sitting on the beach in Madras in the early dawn with my mother and aunt in the water, fully clothed, letting the waves wash the past away, and then return to the sea and come back and return again. I look at my mother, committing every feature to memory, note the creases in her forehead and cheeks. She looks at the sea. I look away at the land.

ANANYA That kalboishakhi norwester that burst through calm lowering skies spinning the coconut trees lining the horizon in a mad dance. The jingle of bangles mother rushing to shut all the windows, fighting the gusts of the wind and the pieces of hail that came splintering into the house anyways. And mother says,

MEENA What a house your father has built, full of cheap materials, no way to keep out the rains, and these relentless storms!

ANANYA A minute later, rain rushes in and ma and I drenched to the skin, laughing and laughing, almost like sisters.

MEENA What must I do with those clothes I carry from continent to continent? Clothes of the living, clothes of the dead, clothes to smell and touch and feel?

ANANYA What must I do with those little wisps of remembering in my mind?

MEENA What must I do with these wisps of remembering?

ANANYA Star light start bright I wish I will I wish I would get the wish I wish tonight.

MEENA Name your desire.

ANANYA And I wish for those green slippers I saw on that pavement in Delhi.

MEENA It's yours.

ANANYA I could swear I told nobody about that wish, and still sometimes, magically enough daddy and mummy knew, and before you even could guess that they had actually un-wrapped your heart in the middle of the night when you were sound asleep and the slippers were there in the morning.

MEENA Star light start bright I wish I will I wish I would get the wish I wish tonight.

ANANYA Name your desire.

MEENA I wish.................

ANANYA Name it.

MEENA I wish........ I could bring the dead back to life.

ANANYA You can.

MEENA And I wish.... that last day on the bus, the two of us sitting next to each other, two seeds from the same body, she falling asleep, her head resting on my shoulders, the feel of her skin against my arm, feeling her breath fan in and out … and I pushed her away.

ANANYA But you didn't. You let her rest.

MEENA I did.

ANANYA Star light start bright I wish I will I wish I would get the wish I wish tonight.

MEENA Tell me.

ANANYA I wish I wish I could say - I still love you.

MEENA You can.

ANANYA And I remember every touch, every gesture, every loving word, every violent word, every betrayal.

MEENA I remember legacies of silences.

ANANYA I remember the arch of a neck, whispers of eyelashes, the trembling of skin on skin,

MEENA Intimate gestures of hands.

ANANYA Fingers that trace stories.

MEENA Stories that fill the night with longings.

ANANYA Wishing for the stars

MEENA on starless nights, such as this.

ANANYA Those little star bindi's that ma made and stuck on my forehead.

MEENA To wish for the light on dark monsoon days.

ANANYA Brownness of Calcutta monsoon days, muddied and waterlogged

MEENA The smell of heavy rubber raincoats

ANANYA Plastic Slippers, rubber boots

MEENA The smell of wet earth after a downpour

ANANYA The whole world washed clean of its old news

MEENA Raag Malhar in the afternoon and it's stopped raining.

ANANYA White jasmine buds on black hair.

MEENA Walking down paths paved with Gul-mohar flowers in spring

ANANYA and the roads turning a flaming orange

MEENA Spring followed by baking summer af-ternoons, followed by cool Novembers.

ANANYA Fire crackers at five a.m. on October dawns, loud enough to wake the dead

MEENA And hiding under the bed with two cushions pinned to two ears, watching legs that walk to and fro.

ANANYA Touching the guru's feet before a performance

MEENA Feet and palms full of henna that smears on pillows, bedsheets, hair, skin

ANANYA Pattern of teeth marks on skin on a water-stained terrace in Calcutta

MEENA Poems of passionate love written on palm leaves in another tongue two thousand years ago.

ANANYA Stories told at mealtimes by aunts, surrogate mothers.

MEENA And English sonnets by fathers on sul-try nights as stars, the pole star, the little and great bear slowly inch their way across the sky.

ANANYA The nomadic sea under that sky.

MEENA Speaking of endless arrivals and departures.

ANANYA Sand towers that tremble and vanish with the waves.

MEENA Speaking of endless departures and arrivals.

Scene IV

There is choreographic movement again. ANANYA moves/dances across on stage. This time the walk signifies both past and future. The past is invested with feeling. Being wrapped up in the past. Welcoming the future. Looking at present and taking present into oneself.

MEENA Is this my human dawn or dusk?

My arrival foreshadows her departure.

My departure augurs your arrival.

And in the space and time between entry and exit

Moments filled with farewells, greetings, dedications, memories,

migrations, exiles, nights, days, dreams, future, victories, defeats

Moments ripe with restless wonderings

vibrating on the edge of oblivion and renewal

Moments exhaling into the peripheries of an unlived hour.

Is this my human dusk or dawn?

Scene V

Family. What unlikely families we become here in a new place. Creating of new rituals with old roots. ANANYA and MEENA put little pieces of the past such as old photographs, old necklaces, and bags full of beads and old memories all over the stage. Final moment: ANANYA looks at a photograph. It triggers off something she wants to share. She runs and tells MEENA. Lights on both. They laugh at something together. Creation of new memories.

Note

1. Urvashi Butalia, *The other side of silence: Voices from the partition of India*, 1998, Viking/Penguin Books India Ltd.: New Delhi, p. 10.

Lameece Issaq and Jacob Kader

Biographies

Lameece Issaq's play, *Food and Fadwa,* co-written with Jacob Kader, received its World Premiere production at New York Theatre Workshop in 2012 (also a recipient of a 2011 Edgerton Foundation New American Play Award). Her other plays include: *"A" Date*, *Samia's Cup*, *Neighborhood Nightly News* (The New York Arab American Comedy Festival); *Nooha's List*, part of *Motherhood Out Loud* (Hartford Stage, The Geffen and Primary Stages). Lameece is the Artistic Director of the Obie Award-winning Noor Theatre, a company dedicated to supporting, developing, and presenting the work of the-atre artists of Middle Eastern descent. As an actor, Lameece has appeared in her own play *Food and Fadwa* at New York Theatre Workshop, as well as in *The Fever Chart*, The Public Theater; *The Black Eyed*, New York Theatre Workshop; *Girl Blog From Iraq: Baghdad Burning*, Barrow Street Theater/Edinburgh Fringe Festival (Stage Theater Award Nomination, Outstanding Ensemble); and *Stuff Happens*, The Public Theater (Drama Desk Award, Outstanding Ensemble). Issaq holds an MFA from the University of Texas, Austin. She is also a member of the League of Professional Theatre Women, The Dramatists Guild, AEA and is a 2016 NYFA Finalist in Playwriting. Lameece is currently co-writing the film *Abraham* with Jacob Kader.

Jacob Kader has experience in writing, directing, and producing film, video, and theater. He received his Masters of Fine Arts in directing from Columbia University in 2009. His feature script *Small Victories* received faculty honors at Columbia and was selected for RAWI-2009 (Royal Jordan Film Commission/Sundance Institute's Screenwriting Lab). His short thesis film, *Quarter Magic*, screened in the 2010 Columbia University Film Festival and most recently at the 2011 Twin Cities Arab Film Festival. He lives in Brooklyn with his family.

Artistic statement by Lameece Issaq

My work investigates the universal experiences of isolation and loneliness, and what coping mechanisms we use to bear the unbearable. With humor and humanity, *Food *and Fadwa* examines these experiences through the lens of one woman's overactive imagination. I am also invested in telling stories about the Arab world and its people; namely, creating nuanced portraits that are accessible and authentic. *Food and Fadwa* was written, in part, as an antidote to the average American's understanding of Palestinians and their circumstances, and the often one-sided stories told in our media and entertainment.

Artistic statement by Jacob Kader

Drawing from his background as a Palestinian-American with Muslim and Mormon roots, Jacob Kader's work as a playwright and screenwriter explores themes of hyphenated ethnicity, cultural and religious identity, and stories of migration. With *Food and Fadwa*, he and Lameece Issaq sought to portray a powerful and conflicted main character with deep connections to her family's land, and also focus on how the Israeli Occupation of Palestine has a multifaceted effect on the everyday lives of Palestinians.

Production history

Parts of *Food and Fadwa* were first read in May 2007 as a part of the "*Aswat*: Voices of Palestine" reading series, produced by NIBRAS and New York Theatre Workshop.

The play was developed at New York Theatre Workshop's artist summer residencies, both at Vassar College during the summer of 2008, and the following summer at Dartmouth College.

In July 2011, Noor Theatre teamed up with Mizna, an Arab-American Arts organization based in Minneapolis, to produce a workshop production of *Food and Fadwa* at Pangea World Theater.

During the spring of 2012, *Food and Fadwa* had its World Premiere at New York Theatre Workshop, co-produced with Noor Theatre. The play was a part of NYTW's 2011–2012 mainstage season.

World premiere production information

Directed by Shana Gold
Cast: Maha Chehlaoui, Lameece Issaq, Kathryn Kates, Arian Moayed, Laith Nakli, Heather Raffo and Haaz Sleiman
Assistant Director: Noelle Ghoussaini
Dramaturg: Nancy Vitale
Set Design: Andromache Chalfant
Lighting Design: Japhy Weideman
Sound Design: Jane Shaw
Costume Design: Gabriel Berry
Production Stage: Manager Lindsey Turteltaub

7 *Food and Fadwa*
Lameece Issaq and Jacob Kader

Characters

FADWA FARANESH	30, Palestinian woman. Single, living in Bethlehem.
BABA	75, FADWA and DALAL's father. Olive farmer. Vibrant and well in FADWA's memories, but in reality suffering from Alzheimer's disease.
DALAL FARANESH	25, FADWA's younger sister. Engaged to Emir. Teaches music.
EMIR AZZAM	25, Engaged to DALAL. A mechanic in Jerusalem.
YOUSSIF AZZAM	30, Palestinian living in New York City. EMIR's older brother.
HAYAT JOHNSON	30, Palestinian-American living in New York City. FADWA and DALAL's first cousin. An ambitious chef and restaurateur.
AUNTIE SAMIA	65, She is sister to BABA; Aunt to HAYAT, DALAL and FADWA. Lives next door. Widowed, no children.

Setting

FARANESH house in Bethlehem, West Bank. A recent spring. Over a two week period.

Language notes

Arabic is translated in the text in bold brackets with colloquial terms in italics. Use English when not comfortable with Arabic.

> "Though the works of the human race disappear tracelessly by time or bomb,
> the sun does not falter in its course;
> the stars keep their invariable vigil.
> Cosmic law cannot be stayed or changed,
> and man would do well to put himself in harmony with it.
> If the cosmos is against might,
> if the sun wars not in the heavens
> but retires at dueful time to give the stars their little sway,
> what avails our mailed fist?
> Shall any peace come out of it?

Not cruelty but goodwill upholds the universal sinews;
a humanity at peace will know the endless fruits of victory,
sweeter to the taste than any nurtured on the soil of blood."

Pramahansa Yogananda

My Soul tonight loses itself in the silent heart of a tree, standing alone, among
the whispers of immensity.

Tagore

ACT I

Scene 1

Lights up on FADWA, standing center stage behind a long marbled counter. She is in a housedress and bandana. To her right is an antiquated stove, circa 1960, behind her a fridge, sink, counter, and cabinets. Upstage center-left a hallway leads to the rest of the home. Stage left, a living area and the front door entrance/exit of the home. Upstage right a pantry and grape vines clinging to the old walls of the home. Stage right, a dining area, and the backdoor entrance/exit of the home, which leads to the neighborhood and fields beyond. FADWA addresses the audience.

FADWA Hello and welcome to another episode of *Food and Fadwa, Echlit'l Hob*. I am your host, Fadwa Faranesh! I am honored to have you in my little kitchen. Today we are kicking off our wedding week series! You all know my little sister Dalal is getting married next week. And we will be having lots of visitors, including my beloved Youssif, coming all the way from New York! Many of my American viewers are New Yorkers, so special "shout out" to you. And Youssif, if you're watching, you better get here hungry, *wella*, I'm making all your favorites! Ok. A crash course on Palestinian weddings: parties. A party three days before the wedding, a party two days before the wedding, a party to take a break from the parties before the wedding. And for every party, FOOD! No food, no respect. Bad food, bad reputation. You will be the laughing stock of Bethlehem. It is vicious. *Yallah*, let us start the *mezza*. Appetizers. Our first dish, my favorite. *Baba Ghanoush.*

(She puts on old battered oven mitts and reaches into the oven to retrieve a pan of roasted eggplant.)

Here we have pre roasted the eggplant. It should be totally charred on the outside, and totally cooked on the inside.

(She continues preparing the dish.)

After the eggplant cools, you will peel off the skin to reveal the tender tendrils of this fleshy vegetable. You will then scoop, scoop, scoop. And mash. Mash to a pulp. Do you know what it means, *Baba Ghanoush*? "Spoiled old daddy." Because the creator of this dish would mash up eggplant to feed her to her father, who was old and toothless and could not chew. *Meskeen.* **[Poor Man.]** But he was picky. He did not like this boring, plain eggplant. Eat this? Are you crazy? *Arruf!* **[Gross!]** He wanted zest—life, in his food! And so began the culinary wizardry: A touch of *tahini* for a creamy robustness, a squeeze of zesty lemon, a clove of garlic for bite and spice, and *viola!* Transformed from this plain eggplant—into a smoky sensation that he loved. Spoiled old man!

(She finishes and tastes it.)

FADWA Let's add a dash of salt—

(Tasting it)

Mmm. Needs one more thing. What is it? Anyone? It is only the most important ingredient in an Arab kitchen.

(Holding up a bottle of olive oil.)

Zeit Zaytoun. Oil of olives. Extra virgin. Like me. Now, just a pour a little—

DALAL *(O.S.)* Fadwa?

EMIR *(O.S.)* Foo Foo! Smells good!

(FADWA stops cold. Enter DALAL wearing a lovely dress.)

DALAL Hi *habibti*. Were you talking to someone?

FADWA Eh, no no. Just cooking.

(Enter EMIR, in grease stained coveralls, carrying boxes filled with gifts.)

EMIR Feed me, woman!

FADWA Yes, your highness. What's in the boxes? Gifts from the kids?

EMIR The kids, the whole school. *Willik*, half the West Bank!

FADWA Look at all that.

EMIR This isn't even everything! We had to leave most of it at the checkpoint.

FADWA Checkpoint? In the neighborhood?

DALAL Yes, the mobile one near the school. The army set it up last week.

EMIR I feel more secure.

DALAL They were searching everyone. Taking things. Like during the incursions.

EMIR Even the box of pastries! I should have eaten it all.

DALAL I got the cutest gift, a necklace with a garnet. The soldier took it and put it on his soldier girlfriend! Right in front of me!

EMIR It was the right thing to do. I don't want you wearing jewelry from strange men.

DALAL It was from my student! He's *twelve!*

EMIR You fell in love with *me* when I was 12. It could happen again.

(DALAL smacks EMIR.)

EMIR Hey, at least they let you keep the poem—

DALAL *Wellek,* shut up Emir!

EMIR Where is it? Ah. Ehem. "Dear Miss Dalal: You fill up my heart, With the music you teach. Most beautiful lady in Bethlehem's reach. I hope I can visit you in New York one day, And recite the sweet notes you taught me to play. Love, Wissam." Aaawwww.

DALAL Give it to me!

(EMIR dodges DALAL's grabs.)

EMIR Visit you in New York! Totally hot for teacher!

(DALAL still tries to grab the letter, EMIR holds it away.)

EMIR Oh oh oh! "PS I will never forget you. You're the only one for me." In love with her!

DALAL *Hmarr* [jackass]!

EMIR But not as much as I am. And on our wedding night, I'm gonna show you how much. Actually, can I show you right now?

(EMIR tries to grab her.)

DALAL Hush!

(Enter BABA in his pajamas, a robe, and slippers.)

BABA Fadwa?

DALAL Hi Baba. How are you, *habibi?*

FADWA Hungry?

EMIR Starving.

FADWA Not you.

BABA *(Patting his pockets.)* Where is my wallet?

FADWA Did you lose it again Baba?

DALAL It probably fell out of your pocket, *habibi,* we'll look around.

BABA I need my wallet.

FADWA What for Baba? There's nothing in it!

EMIR A man needs his wallet.

DALAL It has pictures of Mama!

FADWA I know—

DALAL Check under his chair.

EMIR I'll check the fridge.

DALAL Emir! Help us look.

EMIR I am!

DALAL For the wallet!

EMIR Ooh, are these leftovers? Ew, is this fresh?

(A knock on the door as AUNTIE SAMIA enters carrying pots of food and produce.)

SAMIA Alo!

DALAL Hi Auntie! Do you know where Baba put his wallet?

(SAMIA shakes her head "no" with a click of her tongue, starts patting down BABA who becomes annoyed. A silent fight ensues.)

EMIR *(Rummaging through the fridge)* Is there ice cream? Wait—That's weird—

(EMIR pulls the wallet out of the freezer and holds it up.)

EMIR In the freezer. Between the lamb and the...lamb. Uh, here, *Ami.* Nice and, eh... cold.

(BABA snatches the wallet from EMIR and shuffles offstage.)

EMIR He loves me. He really does.

DALAL Auntie—

SAMIA ZEIN!

BABA Stop following me woman!

DALAL I'll be there to help in a bit.

SAMIA Ok. But tonight Arab Idol.

DALAL Auntie—

FADWA Oh! That girl from Kuwait was voted off last week. So sad.

EMIR Thank GOD. She was the worst! Every time she opened her mouth, it's like a quail giving birth.

DALAL Quails don't give birth.

EMIR Exactly.

FADWA I loved her—she's a wonderful singer.

EMIR What? You can't hear!

DALAL Can we talk about this later? Auntie, just go check on your brother, please.

(SAMIA exits.)

DALAL Fadwa, did you give Baba his pills yet?

FADWA No, he has to eat something first.

DALAL He needs to take them at the same time every day, we've been through this.

EMIR I'll get the rest of the stuff out of the car.

(Exit EMIR.)

DALAL Fadwa.

FADWA What is that medicine even doing for him, *yanni?* It's worthless.

DALAL It keeps him from doing things like that.

FADWA What, from misplacing his wallet sometimes?—

DALAL That wasn't just misplacing, Fadwa—

FADWA He needs something other than pills, pills, pills. I've been taking him out for long walks lately—

DALAL He needs medication.

FADWA He needs fresh air and exercise—

DALAL That doesn't help with his confusion—

FADWA Yes it does.

DALAL And, why is he still in his pajamas? It's after noon.

FADWA He hates being changed, Dalal, I don't want to agitate him—not when I have so much to do.

DALAL He needs to stay on a routine, like the doctor said. It helps him.

FADWA Don't tell me what helps—I'm with him all day.

DALAL I know you are, but these things have to be done properly. After I leave, you'll have to do them on your own.

FADWA After you leave, I won't have a hundred wedding guests to cook for!

(Enter EMIR on his cell phone carrying a box of stuff and DALAL's oud hanging by the strap around his chest.)

EMIR *Wallay himmak,* brother. **[Don't worry, brother.]** We'll see you tonight. Welcome home, Youssif! *(Hanging up) Hamdillah,* he just landed in Jordan.

FADWA *Hamdillah,* but I hope they don't hold him too long at the border.

EMIR Eh, it's nothing. Another 7, 8 hours. Maybe 30. Big deal?

(EMIR goes to the stove and starts picking at the food.)

FADWA Get away from the food. You're filthy!

EMIR I was at the garage all morning under Abu Rami's farting Fiat, what do you want?

DALAL I want you to go home and get cleaned up. We have our meeting with the priest tonight—

EMIR It's lunchtime! I'm eating this.

FADWA That's for the wedding!

EMIR This *hashweh* isn't! And this chicken—

FADWA That's for dinner. When Youssif gets here, then you can eat.

EMIR WHAT? I could die in the meantime!

FADWA Don't touch anything. I want things to be nice for Youssif.

EMIR My god, Youssif. Everything Youssif.

DALAL *(Warning)* Emir.

FADWA The man hasn't had any decent cooking in over two years. Since before he left. *Haram.*

EMIR The man runs one of the best restaurants in New York City. He eats better than any of us. Gourmet, *habibti.*

FADWA Gourmet *wella mish* gourmet. This is home cooking. Nothing better. He knows that.

EMIR Ooooh, trying to lure him back home with a pot of *hashweh?*

DALAL *Khalas* Emir.

FADWA It's time he came home. Long overdue.

EMIR He's making money.

FADWA That's not everything. He needs family. Friends.

EMIR Over. Rated. Anyway, soon he'll have me and Dalal. And Foo Foo, soon you'll come too, *inshallah.*

DALAL I wish.

FADWA Maybe…we'll see…

EMIR You can be my personal chef. I think you'll enjoy it very much.

FADWA I'm already your personal chef.

EMIR I'm glad you know your place. Now do your duty.

(EMIR holds out a plate.)

FADWA I told you not yet.

EMIR You sound just like Dalal. *Ya* Allah **[My God]**, house full of prudes.

FADWA I'm hiding this.

(FADWA takes the pot of hashweh and exits.)

EMIR *(Yelling after her)* I hate you!

DALAL *(Glaring at EMIR.)* Emir.

EMIR What? I didn't touch anything.

DALAL Don't tease her about Youssif.

EMIR Oh come on, I was just playing with her.

DALAL It's still sensitive.

EMIR She's fine now.

DALAL No she isn't. You know they haven't been talking.

EMIR They'll work it out.

(Enter FADWA carrying a couple bottles of olive oil.)

FADWA Still here?

EMIR I'm waiting for lunch.

DALAL *Yallah,* let's go. You still need to finish the student housing forms.

EMIR My little soon-to-be PhD. I can't wait to call her doctor...*Wallah,* I can't wait to go. No more dirty garages—

FADWA No, just dirty dishes—

EMIR Washing dishes, bussing tables—I'll do it all, I don't care. And trust me, your cousin will move me up in no time.

DALAL Don't expect Hayat to promote you before you've even started.

EMIR She made Youssif general manager in less than two years.

FADWA He earned that position. Give the man some credit.

EMIR I give him credit for getting in good with Chef Hayat! Her cookbook is a bestseller!

FADWA Oh please.

EMIR She sent me a copy.

FADWA She sent everyone a copy!

EMIR She sent everyone a copy?

FADWA Revising our family recipes and calling them authentic? *Yanni,* who is buying this crap?

DALAL Foo Foo, she did go to one of the best culinary schools.

FADWA *Kus imm il* one of the best culinary schools! She's selling lies, I can't stand it!

(FADWA gives the eggplant a beating.)

DALAL Don't take it out on the wedding food. Please! I don't want to eat your fury!

EMIR Me neither. But, I'll take what I can get.

DALAL You, stop dilly-dallying. *Yallah,* I'll meet you at the church in a few hours.

EMIR I am not wearing a tie.

DALAL You have to make a good impression on the priest. You still haven't bothered to meet him. The wedding is less than a week away! Out.

EMIR Yes, sergeant.

DALAL *(Holding EMIR at the door)* Look, soldiers.

EMIR I'll catch a ride with them.

DALAL Just go out the back.

EMIR For you, anything. *(Kisses DALAL on the cheek. Begins exiting.)* Bye, Foo Foo. Thanks for "lunch."

DALAL Be careful.

EMIR Don't worry.

(EMIR exits. DALAL stares out the window.)

DALAL *Ya Allah,* I'm so sick of them!

FADWA Just worry about your wedding.

SAMIA *(O.S.)* Dalal. *Yallah.*

FADWA Go help Auntie Samia before she comes in here and starts yelling.

SAMIA *(O.S. Yelling) Ya banat! Kaslaneen!*

FADWA Too late.

DALAL Coming!

SAMIA *Dalal! Willik Dalal!*

DALAL Coming, coming! *Ya Allah,* coming!

(DALAL exits. FADWA starts to clean the mess she made, pauses, looks up at the audience.)

Scene 2

Same day, evening. Lights up on FADWA.

FADWA Good evening, and welcome back to *Food and Fadwa!* For those of you just joining in, we've been cooking up scrumptious appetizers for the wedding—I hope you're taking good notes! We were just adding some olive oil to a few of our dishes here. This is a kind of wonder condiment in my family. It isn't just used for cooking. It's used for sore muscles, ear aches, hair conditioner. My father, my Baba, says that olive oil could cure any illness except the illness of death. He tells a story about...

(Lights rise on BABA of FADWA's memory. He faces the audience:)

FADWA/BABA Adam

BABA Adam, of Adam and Eve, was deeply distressed due to his recent fall from grace and expulsion from the Garden of Eden. He wasn't accustomed to the aches, and pains of his new physical form. And he was a whiner. He had the nerve, if you can imagine, to render up his complaints to God, begging for mercy. Our infinitely compassionate Creator pitied the poor, suffering Adam and so sent his messenger, the Archangel Gabriel, to his rescue. Gabriel, in his celestial splendor, descended from heaven with the most magnificent offering the earth had yet seen: an olive tree. He gifted the ailing Adam with the precious sapling, instructed him to plant it and harvest the fruits for oil, promising it to be the panacea for all afflictions. We are born of Adam, Fadwa. We have inherited his afflictions, and so must we take his cures. I drink everyday, half a glass-

FADWA/BABA I will live long life!

(Lights down on BABA.)

FADWA My Baba is obsessed with olive oil. You see this bottle? *(She holds up a bottle.)* Camera one, can I have a close up on the bottle? Thank you, Mike, you are so cute. You see, it says *Zeit Zaytoun't Zein.* Zein's Olive Oil. Zein, my father. My Baba Ghanoush. It is the only olive oil we are allowed to use. Straight from my grandmother's groves.

FADWA My Tayta-

BABA Your Tayta- *(Lights up on BABA)*—was very devoted to her olive trees—to a fault. Even pregnant, she stood in her groves for hours, picking olives until the moment her water broke! The closer her contractions became, the more she picked! And as a mother knows when to birth her child, a farmer knows the exact moment to harvest. Pick the olives too soon, and they are bitter. Pick them too late, and they are weak and useless… Tayta was devoted to the well-being of all her children, human and fruit alike.

FADWA My Baba-

BABA Your Baba—Baba was born under a majestic, ancient olive tree-

FADWA -Under which Tayta nursed him for 40 days straight.

BABA I refused to suckle in any other location.

FADWA There, under the shelter of that resplendent evergreen, my Baba found comfort—

BABA —Experiencing the perfect symbiosis between man and nature, even as a tiny newborn.

FADWA But my poor Tata was totally freezing her breasts off!

BABA Every time she tried to move from that tree, I would scream.

FADWA She tried everything to assuage her stubborn baby.

BABA Toys, whistles, bells—

FADWA Nomadic dancers, donkey rides-

BABA Nothing!

FADWA Finally she resorted to singing—

BABA A risky idea, given her atrocious singing voice—

FADWA -And was able to move his little heart with the sweetest of songs—*Ah Ya Zein.*

(BABA begins to play the oud.)

Slowly she moved from the tree to the house, singing these lyrics over and over again: *Ah Ya Zein—*

BABA/FADWA *AH YA ZEIN AH YA ZEIN IL-AABEE-DEEN, YA WARD, YA WARD IMM-FATAH-BAYN-IL-BA-SA-TEEN. AH YA ZEIN*

FADWA Oh you beautiful

BABA *AH YA ZEIN IL-AABEE-DEEN*

FADWA Oh you beautiful amongst the worshippers.

BABA *YA WARD*

FADWA You a rose

BABA *YA WARD IMM-FATAH-BAYN-IL-BA-SA-TEEN.*

FADWA You a rose that bloomed in the gardens.

FADWA *AH YA ZEIN, AH YA ZEIN*

(Lights down on BABA. Enter YOUSSIF.)

YOUSSIF Bravo, *willik,* bravo!

FADWA Oh my god!

YOUSSIF Are you giving a concert?

FADWA Don't you knock?

(They kiss each other on the cheek and immediately start talking over each other.)

FADWA/YOUSSIF How was your flight/How are you—

FADWA/YOUSSIF Fine—You must be tired/Fine. How's your dad?

FADWA/YOUSSIF He's ok—/I'm ok—

FADWA/YOUSSIF It's good to see you./It's good to see you.

FADWA I'm glad you're home.

YOUSSIF Me too. *(Beat.)* You're hair got long.

FADWA Yeah…

BABA *(O.S.)* Fadwa?

FADWA Yes?

(BABA shuffles on stage holding a small plant.)

BABA Olive oil, Fadwa. Please. For the plant.

(FADWA takes BABA a bottle of olive oil. He rubs some oil on the plant's leaves.)

BABA Because they are dry. *(He rubs a bit on his temples. Points to his head.)* Because it is lost. There. You are very sweet my little one. You will grow to be 20 feet tall and I will visit you in the field. You will not be in this…eh, this ...eh... for much longer. Yes. You will grow to be 20 feet tall. Like my other trees. My trees...*(Spotting YOUSSIF.)* Hello.

YOUSSIF Uh, *Amo*, it's me, Youssif. Youssif Azzam. Do you remember me?

BABA Eh? Youssif? *(Recognizing)* *Walek, habibi* Youssif! **[Oh, my dear Youssif!]** *Shta'tilak, Amo!* **[I missed you, Son!]** And Fadwa also misses you.

YOUSSIF I miss her too, *Amo.*

BABA You finally come back to marry her, eh? Okay! You have my permission! *Mabrook!* **[Congratulations!]** We'll make a party here for you. You will be a beautiful bride. Did you tell Mama? She'll be so happy. Now. *Weh'it a zoor Il shajar.* **[It's time to go tend to the trees.]** I want to pick some olives. Special for the party. Youssif, you come also and pick, huh?

YOUSSIF Ok, *Amo*...eh, sure.

BABA Where is my...my...Bring me...the thing that holds the olives, *habibti.*

FADWA Your bucket?

BABA Yes, that. *(He stops and looks around.)* Where am I?

FADWA Baba, you're home.

BABA No.

FADWA Baba—

BABA I must go home.

FADWA Baba, you are home.

YOUSSIF Come on, *Amo*, I'll take you.

BABA Okay.

YOUSSIF Wow, you're still strong! *(To FADWA as he walks BABA around the kitchen)* Come on, Fadwa. We're going home. *(They walk, slowly, finally stopping at Baba's chair.)*

YOUSSIF Ok, *Amo.* We're here.

BABA *(Looking around, nodding his head.)* Good. Good.

FADWA Get some rest before dinner.

(BABA exits.)

FADWA Wow. Thank you.

YOUSSIF I've heard it helps to play along.

FADWA Sometimes he's fine. Other times...I don't know.

YOUSSIF Emir's been telling me. I always ask. *(Spots the tabla)* Is that my tabla? The one your father gave me?

FADWA He thinks it's a bucket for olive picking.

(She flips it over and hands it to him.)

YOUSSIF Man, I miss playing—especially with him. *(Thumps on it.)* Such a great sound. Can't find them like this in New York.

FADWA Then why did you leave it here?

YOUSSIF I thought I would come back for it.

FADWA I thought so too.

(They share a brief look.)

EMIR *(O.S.) Walak ya Kelb!***[Hey you bastard!]** Where's my brother?!

YOUSSIF *Yil 3an deenak*, Emir! **[Damn, Emir!]**

(Enter EMIR and DALAL. EMIR is wearing a necktie.)

EMIR Well, well, well look who's back from *Amreeka!*

YOUSSIF Still haven't grown into your big mouth, huh?

(YOUSSIF and DALAL kiss on the cheek.)

DALAL *Hamdillah 3al salaami!* **[Thank God for your arrival.]**

YOUSSIF *Allah ey salmik*, Dal Dal.

EMIR *(Splitting them apart)* Hey, hey, hey, easy! You never give me that many kisses!

DALAL I don't want you to get too excited.

EMIR You got here fast, man. How long did they keep you at the border?

YOUSSIF Five hours. Nothing.

EMIR Lucky bastard. All right, let's feed this man. Where's that *hashweh? Yallah.*

YOUSSIF There's *hashweh?*

EMIR She's been depriving me all day, this woman. No one could eat till you got here. No one.

YOUSSIF I am the guest of honor. And I am older than you.

EMIR Much older. Ancient. Prehistoric. Look at this leathery, withering face. *(He grabs YOUSSIF's face.)* My brother is home. *Hamdillah.*

(Enter SAMIA.)

SAMIA *(Seeing YOUSSIF, she runs to him.)* Youssif! Ya habibi! Ya habibi! Ya habibi!

(SAMIA kisses him about 50 times.)

YOUSSIF *Ehlan ya Samia!* [Hi dear Samia]. How are you *Khalto?*

(SAMIA, practically in tears, grabs FADWA and YOUSSIF'S hands and connects them, looking back and forth at them, beaming. YOUSSIF is moved, but slightly uncomfortable.)

FADWA Eh, Dalal, help me finish getting everything on the table.

YOUSSIF I'll help.

DALAL No, no. Emir, set the table.

EMIR I'll just sit here so you know where to put the food.

DALAL Emir.

YOUSSIF Let me help you.

EMIR No no no, you relax old man.

(EMIR jumps up to help. In the kitchen everyone bustles around to get dinner on the table. SAMIA sings cheerfully.)

FADWA Hummus?

DALAL Got it.

FADWA Salad?

SAMIA Yes.

FADWA Wait! Salad needs salt. Mix that. Please.

EMIR *(Sniffing the air.)* For God's sake, what is that? *(Sniffing YOUSSIF.)* Stetson? Old Spice?

YOUSSIF Armani.

EMIR *Walaw!* Excuse me.

FADWA It smells nice.

EMIR Oof Please! For sissies. You know what I use, old man? Three drops of German motor oil, slice of lemon.

DALAL Maybe you'll use soap someday.

EMIR She can't keep her hands off me.

(He pinches her side.)

FADWA Auntie, get the good silverware—

YOUSSIF No please, don't trouble yourself.

FADWA It's ok, it's ok—

EMIR Forget it! Who cares? Let's eat!

(Everyone sits. EMIR fills his plate with food to begin eating.)

DALAL *(Smacking his head.)* Savage! Can you wait please? We still need to say grace.

EMIR God knows how I feel about food. Amen.

(DALAL takes away his fork.)

DALAL Dear heavenly Father. Thank you for this wonderful meal. Please bless those who provided it, those who made it and those who are about to eat it. Thank you for our home, our health and for Youssif's safe arrival—

FADWA *Hamdillah.*

DALAL Please bless all of our family members, both here and living abroad—

HAYAT Especially those living abroad.

(HAYAT, beautifully dressed, carrying two suitcases, leans against the doorway smiling. A beat. DALAL and HAYAT scream.)

DALAL Oh my God!

FADWA Oh my God.

DALAL Hayat! *Willik,* Hayat!

HAYAT Look at you! You're a woman!

(EMIR joins in the screams.)

HAYAT Emir! Hi hi hi!!! My little Prince!

EMIR Little Prince? A king! Come give me a hug!

DALAL I can't believe you're here! I thought you couldn't come!

HAYAT I just couldn't miss your wedding, sweetie. No way!

YOUSSIF You weren't supposed to be here for a few more days.

DALAL You knew she was coming?

HAYAT I told him not to tell! I wanted to surprise everyone!

FADWA Well you did! Wow.

HAYAT Foofs! Give me a hug! You look ... good. Nice doo-rag, girl!

EMIR Who-rag?

HAYAT Hi Auntie Samia! Oh my God, you haven't aged!

SAMIA I know.

HAYAT You and my mother have the same skin—ugh, Gorgeous.

SAMIA Faranesh sisters— very pretty! But your mother was the wild one. You come over, I tell you stories.

HAYAT *(Taking SAMIA's hands.)* Oh I will. I'm sorry about your husband—I know it's been some time since he passed—

(SAMIA smiles and gives her a big hug.)

SAMIA It's ok, it's ok. Life.

HAYAT Where's your dad? At the olive press?

EMIR There's nothing left to press—

FADWA No, he's in his room. He's—

HAYAT Uncle Zein!

FADWA He's ill, Hayat. Please greet him later.

HAYAT I know he's ill, but...I just thought—

DALAL It's ok, *habibti,* you can see him in a bit. He's just resting now. I'm sure he'll be happy to see you.

HAYAT I just—I didn't realize—My mom made it sound like he was fine.

DALAL She did?

FADWA When was the last time you spoke to her?

HAYAT Oh, God, when was the last time I spoke to Mama. You guys probably talk to her more than I do. And we live in the same city.

SAMIA No. No good. *Tsk tsk tsk.*

DALAL Well, people get busy. How was your flight? When did you get in?

HAYAT About two hours ago. It was hectic. I flew direct to Tel Aviv and they held me for, like, 15 minutes while they checked my passport. Awful.

FADWA 15 minutes is awful?

HAYAT I'm not used to being questioned like that.

DALAL No, *habibti*, of course not. A lot has changed since you were here last. I cannot believe I am looking at my cousin right now!

HAYAT I know!

DALAL We'll share a room, like when we were kids!

HAYAT Oh, sleepovers

EMIR I love sleepovers.

DALAL Emir, take Hayat's suitcases into my room. Fadwa, do we have clean linens?

FADWA Um, yes…

DALAL Can you go put them on the extra bed in my room?

HAYAT Oh you don't have to do that now, Foofs.

FADWA It's ok.

(FADWA exits, followed by SAMIA. EMIR goes to pick up the suitcases.)

EMIR My God, what the hell is in here, cement?

HAYAT Presents, darling, wedding presents.

EMIR Mind if I take a peek?

HAYAT Don't you dare!

EMIR Dalal!

(DALAL picks up HAYATs other bag and runs after him.)

YOUSSIF So, what happened? I thought you couldn't come till Thursday.

HAYAT Well, they moved my Food Network event so I switched some things around to be here earlier! I wish we were staying together.

YOUSSIF I know, but…I have to talk to Fadwa.

HAYAT Right. You're adorable.

YOUSSIF *(Playfully.)* Try to resist the urge to flirt with me.

HAYAT *(Winking at him.)* I'll try.

(Enter EMIR and DALAL.)

EMIR Folks let's eat! Fadwa! *Yallah!*

(SAMIA enters.)

FADWA *(O.S.)* I'll be there in one second.

DALAL My God, Hayat, I love your outfit. When we get to New York, Bloomingdales!

HAYAT Dalaly, when you get to New York, I will take you everywhere!

EMIR Fadwa! Come *on!*

(Enter FADWA.)

FADWA *(Serving spoon in hand.)* Yallah, come sit everyone. Give me your plates.

DALAL Hayat, sit and eat something.

HAYAT What's for dinner there? *(Peeking into the pot.)* Oh, rice and meat? It's kind of a heavy meal—I mean it's like 11am my time!

DALAL Foo Foo, make a plate for Hayat.

HAYAT Well, ok, but not too much. Thank you, that's great. *(Pointedly sniffing the food.)* Hmm.

EMIR Fadwa, this is MUMTAZ! **[FANTASTIC!]**

FADWA Thank you, Emir. Youssif?

YOUSSIF A little more. A little more.

HAYAT *(HAYAT looks at him and pats her belly.)* Take it easy. Gotta stay trim…

YOUSSIF One more.

HAYAT All right, we'll go for a run tomorrow.

EMIR *Shoo* run? Run where? Run here and you'll get shot. Why not scale the separation wall while you're at it? Now *that's* circuit training. Run for your life! It's the West Bank Workout!

HAYAT That wall is—I have no words. I mean, I always knew—but seeing it. It's shocking.

YOUSSIF It's our national landmark!

EMIR Yep. Our Great Wall of Palestine!

HAYAT It's practically in your backyard.

DALAL It's in everyone's backyard.

EMIR Yes, we own at least a kilometer.

YOUSSIF Let's have a drink. *Arak* anyone?

EMIR I'll take a double!

(EMIR pours two drinks.)

HAYAT I mean, that thing, that God forsaken monstrosity—Is that legal? I can't believe the UN let this happen.

(EMIR and YOUSSIF raise their glasses.)

YOUSSIF To the Separation Wall!

EMIR The Security Wall!

YOUSSIF A Mere Fence!

EMIR A Virtual Gate!

YOUSSIF/EMIR To The Wall!/To The Wall!

(They drink. EMIR pours two more shots.)

HAYAT I saw the protesters out there when I was coming in. Good for them.

YOUSSIF *(Raising his glass.)* 307 miles longer than the Berlin Wall!

EMIR 14 feet taller!

YOUSSIF/EMIR To The Wall!/To The Wall!

(They drink.)

HAYAT Knock it off you two! This is serious. They've completely jailed us in…

EMIR Brother.

YOUSSIF Brother.

EMIR Drink with me in honor of my Jerusalem permit.

(EMIR takes out an ID card. YOUSSIF grabs it.)

YOUSSIF This expires tomorrow! 11:59 PM tomorrow night!

EMIR Bravo, you still remember your Hebrew!

YOUSSIF *Ken. Ken!* **[Yes.]** Permit, I will drink to you.

EMIR Permit! For you, I drink!

YOUSSIF/EMIR Permit!/Permit!

HAYAT Expires? Can't you renew it?

DALAL He tried. The military denied him.

HAYAT Why did they deny you?

EMIR Dalal...

DALAL When he tried to renew it, the military started asking him questions, like about people in the neighborhood. There's this woman down the street who's an activist—they wanted information on her. He told them he didn't know anything—

EMIR I *didn't* know anything! I fixed her car once.

DALAL They wanted him to find things out, act as an informant.

EMIR Never.

DALAL A few days later, his permit was denied.

HAYAT Why do you even need a permit? Jerusalem is like, 15 miles away?

YOUSSIF Five.

HAYAT Five miles?

DALAL It *used* to take 10-15 minutes to get there. Now, more like 5 hours, with the checkpoints and roadblocks. But that's only if you're lucky enough to have the permit.

HAYAT But why do you need a permit?

(Everyone begins a historical explanation, talking over one another.)

EMIR Enough! Let me explain to our American visitor here. Move your plates. Fadwa, Dalal hold these.

(He hands them the hummus and salad.)

DALAL Eh, what are you doing?

EMIR Okay. This table here is all of the West Bank. Let us say this hummus represents Area A—let's just put a few dollops here and there.

FADWA *Yee,* what are you—

EMIR And now these little piles of rice are Area B—

YOUSSIF And these little pieces of napkin are Area C—

FADWA *Ya Allah,* you're making a mess!

EMIR Visual aids are very important. Now, Area A—the hummus—are areas run by the Palestinian Authority. Supposedly. Authority on what—God knows. The piles of rice, Area B, are areas that are Palestinian run but with Israeli *security.* Area C, the pieces of napkin, are areas that are Israeli controlled. And all of these little pieces of chicken are undetermined areas.

YOUSSIF *Yanni,* areas that are up for negotiation—

EMIR In other words, Israeli.

YOUSSIF And these bits of salad are the Israeli settlements—

EMIR And all of this salt—those are checkpoints. Hundreds of them sprinkled all over the place—

HAYAT I think I'm getting it...

YOUSSIF And don't forget the wall—these cups are the wall. We need more cups.

EMIR This fork will be the permit.

YOUSSIF Genius brother.

EMIR Now Bethlehem is here, in Area A, in the hummus. If you want to get from hummus to hummus, you don't need a fork. You can just use bread.

HAYAT What does the bread represent?

EMIR Nothing. It's just the best way to eat hummus.

DALAL It doesn't make sense!

FADWA It's oversimplified!

EMIR It's *Oslo!* So, if you want to go from hummus to rice, you still don't need a fork. And, Area C, what's Israeli controlled, doesn't need bread or a fork because no one wants to eat napkin.

YOUSSIF Exactly.

FADWA What?

DALAL I'm confused.

HAYAT It's making sense! So where is Jerusalem in relation to all this?

EMIR Jerusalem is here, in the undetermined space, the chicken.

HAYAT Which you need a fork for!

EMIR *Aywah!* Exactly!

HAYAT And no matter what, you always have to go through the salt—the checkpoints!

EMIR That's right. Smart girl! See before, we didn't need forks. We just ate chicken with our hands. But they said, "You people are a bunch of animals! How can you eat chicken with your hands? You must use forks!"

HAYAT And tomorrow your fork expires.

EMIR Yep. *(His smile fades.)* Tomorrow is the last day I will be permitted to enter the Old City. If you need me, I can be found at the Wailing Wall, wailing.

(YOUSSIF pours two more drinks.)

YOUSSIF Al Quds!

EMIR Al Quds!

EMIR/YOUSSIF Al Quds!/Al Quds!

DALAL Emir, that's it for you. Time to clean up this… map.

EMIR Yes, my Goddess.

HAYAT Oh, wait, what about Gaza?

EMIR Gaza? Different menu. Fadwa, dinner was magnificent.

YOUSSIF Delicious as usual.

HAYAT It was, thank you, Foof. What's in the *hashweh*? Nutmeg, I'm guessing? *(FADWA nods. HAYAT is not too impressed.)* It's good.

(SAMIA rises to start cleaning.)

HAYAT So, Auntie, are you still next door? I want to come hear those stories—

(SAMIA shakes her head yes. Her cell phone rings.)

SAMIA *(On phone)* 'Alo? No Miriam, I can't go. Arab Idol is on in half hour.

(SAMIA fishes a cigarette out of her pocket and goes to light it.)

DALAL —Auntie, don't you dare smoke that in here—

SAMIA Aren't you watching? You better vote!

(SAMIA gives an irritated tsk, and exits shaking her head.)

EMIR Hayat, tell us about your award!

HAYAT Oh, it's no big deal, really.

EMIR She's so humble!

YOUSSIF It is a big deal. Show them the feature in Oprah Magazine. Did you bring a copy?

HAYAT I did! *(She goes to her oversized designer bag, pulls out the magazine and hands it to EMIR.)* Um, page 56, I think.

(SAMIA slips back into the house.)

EMIR "Ethnic Authentics We Love and Admire: Chef Hayat Faranesh."

FADWA Faranesh?

HAYAT Yeah, I'm using my mom's name now. Better for PR. My dad's kinda ticked off about it, but his name is way too Anglo! I mean, Johnson? Chef Hayat Johnson? I don't think so!

EMIR "The James Beard Award-winning chef shares a few of her favorite recipes with O

this month." Amazing! Look at this picture of you—very nice!

HAYAT Oh, thanks sweetie. The award is a great thing, it really is, I mean, some people say it's like an Oscar for chefs, but the important thing is—well, it's big news, actually—Youssif, I'm telling them now—

YOUSSIF Just give it a day—

EMIR No, tell us now!

HAYAT Well, the award generated a lot of buzz and interest, and thankfully, investors who want to put up the money for a new place!

DALAL That's great, Hayat.

HAYAT Yes, and I've asked this guy—*(Pointing to YOUSSIF.)*—to be my business partner.

FADWA Really?

HAYAT But I need a third man. Guess who I'm thinking of?

EMIR Bono!

HAYAT You!

EMIR What?

HAYAT Yeah.

VEMIR You're kidding? Ours?

YOUSSIF Well, we still have a lot of details to take care of—

EMIR But our own restaurant again, Youssif?

YOUSSIF *Inshallah*, it will work out this time.

EMIR You know what would bring in a lot of people? If we call it Emir's Palace.

(Enter BABA.)

DALAL Baba, look who's here! Hayat! From America! Your sister Jamila's daughter.

HAYAT Hi Khalo! Habibi, I've missed you! *(HAYAT goes to hug him.)* The last time you saw me I was still a teenager. Do you recognize me?

BABA *(Staring at her blankly.)* I don't think so….

FADWA *Yallah*, it's time to eat something, Baba.

EMIR Here, *Amo*. Whatever you don't eat, I will.

(EMIR tries to hand him a bowl of food, but Baba knocks it out of his hand.)

BABA No! I will not take food from this thief!

DALAL Baba? It's Emir, my fiancé.

BABA I know Emir! Emir the thief! You stole money from me! I saw you!

FADWA Baba, no. /Of course he didn't.

BABA Get out! /Get out or I will show you! Out!

(BABA wields his slipper.)

EMIR *Amo*, I got your wallet from the freezer. I would never—

BABA Out I said!

YOUSSIF *(Dramatically)* Emir, how dare you steal from the family! Get out! Don't come back!

HAYAT Oh God! You guys are drunk!

EMIR No, really. Deniro, please continue.

YOUSSIF Out! But first, apologize.

DALAL He didn't do anything.

YOUSSIF Just to ease his mind, *habibti*. Emir! Apologize!

EMIR Eh, sorry.

YOUSSIF You're not very sincere.

BABA No, he's not. That is why I hate him.

EMIR *(Melodramatically)* Amo, I am so sorry from the bottom of my unusually brave heart. Please accept my apology and forgive me, beloved elder!

DALAL Ok, you see Baba? He didn't mean it—

EMIR —I am the most despicable thief alive. I must REPENT!

DALAL EMIR!

YOUSSIF That's better! Right, *Amo*? Better?

BABA Give me my money back!

(Everyone looks to EMIR.)

EMIR Eh, how much did I take?

BABA You know how much!

EMIR *(Pulls some change out of his pocket.)* Right. Here are two shekels and an American nickel.

BABA 50 shekel!

EMIR Sorry, I steal from so many people, I can't keep track.

YOUSSIF Give this to him.

BABA Wait till I tell your mother what a thief you're marrying!

EMIR *Amo*. This is 50 shekel and I'm very sorry.

(BABA looks at the money. He takes it and shuffles away.)

BABA Fadwa. I want to go to bed.

FADWA Ok, Baba. I'm so sorry Emir.

BABA *(O.S.)* Fadwa! Where is my pajama?

FADWA Coming.

(FADWA exits after BABA.)

HAYAT Oh my God. I had no idea. I feel so stupid.

EMIR You feel stupid? I'm a criminal!

HAYAT Dalal, if there's anything you need, anything I can do—please, let me.

DALAL You're doing enough just by being with us.

HAYAT I'm so happy to be here. *Yallah,* let's get this place cleaned up.

(Lights down as EMIR, YOUSSIF, DALAL, and HAYAT clean up.)

Scene 3

Next day, early morning. FADWA speaks to the audience:

FADWA Good Morning, Gentle Viewers and welcome to another episode of *Food and Fadwa*. It is 9am Holy Land Standard time and we are up very early to do some necessary wedding prep. But first we need to have breakfast. We don't want the bride getting cranky or the cameraman passing out from the low blood sugar. Right, Mike? Now. This is a little breakfast treat we call *mana'eesh*. *Mana'eesh* is like a warm bath and a fireplace and a hug all rolled into one savory, delicious bite. First, we roll out the pita dough and spread on it a mixture of olive oil and *za'tar*. *Za'tar* is a seasoning made of dried ground thyme, sumac and sesame seeds. *(She spreads the oil and za'tar mix onto the dough.)* Now we bake. My Youssif goes crazy for *mana'eesh,* crazy!

HAYAT *(O.S.)* I mean it's just an option. One of many.

(Enter DALAL and HAYAT.)

HAYAT *(In bad Arabic)* Sabah il Care! Morning Foof!

DALAL Hi!

FADWA Hello. You're up early.

HAYAT I'm still jet-lagged. Thought I would take advantage of it!

FADWA There's *mana'eesh*.

DALAL Thank you.

FADWA Take some to Emir before he goes to work.

DALAL He left already. He went at 4 this morning to get in line at the checkpoint.

FADWA He never leaves that early.

DALAL It's his last day in Jerusalem. He wants enough time to say goodbye to everyone.

FADWA Is Youssif up?

HAYAT Oh, he's exhausted, sweetie, he's still asleep. But, I'm sure he'll be by later if he can. He's got a lot of people to catch up with. I've got something for you, Fadwa.

(HAYAT exits.)

FADWA Uh, so how was your walk with Baba?

DALAL It was good.

FADWA See?

DALAL We didn't go far, just around the neighborhood. But Baba did well.

FADWA Good!

DALAL He's on the front porch with Auntie Samia, trying to play his oud...I hope it comes back to him.

FADWA *Inshallah.*

DALAL He has to play at my wedding.

FADWA *Inshallah.*

(Enter SAMIA chatting away on her cell, heading for the kitchen.)

SAMIA *(On phone)* Miriam, this kid from Tunisia is the best singer in the competition. *Wallah,* I will kill someone if they vote him off!

FADWA Auntie—

(SAMIA gives a slight wave and continues babbling.)

SAMIA *(On phone)* Uh huh. Uh huh. Exactly.

FADWA Auntie, I need you to—

(SAMIA nods violently and waves her hand to shut FADWA up. She retrieves a bowl and a few bunches of parsley from the kitchen, and heads back to the front porch.)

SAMIA *(On phone)* Yee, the Saudi boy? He gets the most votes every week because he's from the biggest country. They don't care if he can sing or not! Makes me sick.

(SAMIA exits.)

DALAL Obsessed.

FADWA What time is your dress fitting? I just need to get some things done before we go—

DALAL Oh, don't worry about it. Hayat's coming with me. You have enough to do.

(HAYAT returns with a pile of very colorful dresses, and goes to dump them into FADWA's food covered hands.)

HAYAT Fadwa, for you! Ooh, are your hands clean? That one's Chanel.

DALAL Chanel?

HAYAT I never wear them. I thought Foofs might want a few. You, I'll take shopping once we get to the city.

FADWA I don't need these, Hayat, I—

DALAL You still need a dress for the wedding.

FADWA I have one.

DALAL The black one? It's 15 years old.

FADWA What? It's timeless.

HAYAT *(Picking a dress from the pile.)* This one would look great on you.

FADWA What is that, a headband?

DALAL Try it on!

FADWA No! I don't like it!

HAYAT *(Picking out a very colorful, puffy sleeved frock.)* What about this?

FADWA I don't understand it.

HAYAT Come on girl, just try it.

DALAL Don't be silly, go try them. *Yallah,* go!

(FADWA exits.)

HAYAT Girl needs a make-over. I mean that in a good way. She's pretty. She needs some fixing up is all.

DALAL She works very hard. And with my father...

HAYAT I'm serious about taking him with us. It's totally doable. There are special clinics, drug trials, music therapy—*(DALAL looks hesitant.)* Of course, talk to Fadwa. See what she thinks.

DALAL I will.

FADWA *(O.S.)* Ugly!

DALAL Show us! *(To Hayat.)* Wouldn't those treatments be expensive?

HAYAT My money is your money. What good is it sitting in a bank when my uncle is suffering? Please, please.

(Enter FADWA in the puffy sleeved frock.)

FADWA I feel weird.

DALAL It's pretty!

HAYAT It's a few seasons old, but who would know here?

FADWA It's too short.

DALAL Try the other ones.

HAYAT No pressure, Foo Foo. Ease into it. Keep them for now and see if there's one you like.

FADWA I like my dress better.

(FADWA shuffles off.)

HAYAT Stubborn, as always.

DALAL Very. But what about a visa? It took 6 months to get Emir's and mine.

HAYAT Medical visas are faster. And I know a congressman who'd do anything for a good meal. We'll get him a visa.

(FADWA re-enters.)

FADWA Get who a visa?

DALAL/HAYAT Nobody./Your dad.

FADWA What does he need a visa for?

HAYAT To come to the States.

FADWA He's sick in case you haven't noticed. He can't travel.

DALAL No, for medical treatment...

HAYAT Just to see what else can be done about his dementia.

(O.S. we hear some strained plucking of the Oud.)

DALAL Did you hear that?

HAYAT Sounds a bit…off…

DALAL It's something! That's it, Baba. Keep going.

(DALAL hurries offstage. FADWA resumes cooking. HAYAT walks about, inhaling deeply.)

HAYAT God, I miss this house. Mmmm…smell is the same as always…that combination of sweat and *za'tar* takes me back. Must be in the walls. *(Taking inventory of the kitchen.)* Same pots, same pans! I don't know how you manage with this stuff. The cookware that is available now is astounding, Foof.

FADWA I don't need those things.

HAYAT The furniture! Same. These chairs have to be more than three decades old. There is this picture over at Youssif and Emir's mom's place—totally framed and everything—of you and Youssif, you're about five, I think, sitting together on the same chair—this very one—with your arms around each other. It is *the* perfect picture of puppy love.

(The sound of an actual song being played is heard offstage.)

HAYAT Is that your dad playing?

FADWA It's Dalal.

HAYAT I feel terrible that I haven't seen you guys in so long. God, since your mom's… funeral. Fifteen years…it just goes by. I always want to get back here—but I don't have time to do anything! Ask Youssif, I'm always swamped! And my latest book has kept me *so* busy. Rewrites and contracts and editing. My editor *forbade* me from leaving the city, *habibi*. For. Bade.

(FADWA is silent, her attention on the food.)

HAYAT Your mom was the reason I started cooking. I still make the date cookies she taught us how to make when we were kids. My favorites. I put the recipe in my cookbook—Auntie Lena's Date Delights.

FADWA But you changed the recipe.

HAYAT Oh, just a smidge. A few things here and there, but basically the same. I do it all the time! I love to play. You know, I'm happy to show you a few new tricks for the wedding. I created this amazing recipe for *tabbouli* with currants and white truffle oil. It's brilliant.

FADWA Sounds delicious, Hayat.

HAYAT Youssif *loves* it. Best tabbouli he's ever had.

FADWA He said that?

HAYAT I can tell…

FADWA Can you?

(HAYAT starts to leave.)

HAYAT Well, I promised Youssif and Emir's mom I would help with the wedding favors. Candied almonds in a white mesh sack. When will that tradition die?

FADWA It's the sentiment. Hard bitterness shelled in sweetness. Like marriage.

HAYAT Romantic. I'll see you later, then? When I come back we're gonna make some new eats, Fadwa. It'll be fun.

FADWA Yes, fun.

HAYAT Unlike when we were kids…

FADWA Uh huh.

(HAYAT exits.)

FADWA Today's episode of Food and Fadwa was brought to you by: Hayat! A self-absorbed toxic agent designed to choke, irritate and manipulate! Hayat! Good for spoiling any and all joyful moments of merriment from birthdays to anniversaries! Now fully equipped with a worthless collection of cookbooks, Hayat is the perfect spoiler for all your celebratory needs. Order your Hayat today and get free shipping and handling and a free fat ass! Offer available in Palestine only. Hello and welcome back. Our next dish, *Tabbouli!* Auntie! Parsley!

(AUNTIE SAMIA enters with a bowl of chopped parsley.)

FADWA Here comes my Aunt with the pre-chopped parsley! Thank you, *Amto* Samia, for this beautifully de-stemmed and chopped parsley. You can go home now. *Yallah, kishi.* **[Come on, move it.]**

(AUNTIE SAMIA shuffles off muttering under her breath and shaking her head.)

FADWA She wants to be on the show, but….she's very moody. Next on the menu: *tabbouli*. This traditional Arabic salad made of parsley and bulgur wheat sounds deceptively simple. But do not be fooled. This dish is a test in tediousness. It requires patience.

(Grabbing a bunch of parsley and begins to pick it off the stem as she speaks.)

FADWA First, we de-stem. Please, de-stem. Do not put stems in the *tabbouli*. I will kill you. We are not farm animals. Now we can chop. Chop finely. Slowly. Don't be lazy. Do not betray the parsley with your own agenda. And don't rush! When you rush, the food suffers. Or you will, when you cut off a finger! You deserve it! No one wants to eat hastily made food! Recipe for indigestions! Look, now, how fine it is, how soft and loveable. Same with the bulgur. It starts dry, hard, lacking edibility. But after it has soaked in the warm womb of water, it softens. Now, the two may unite. Parsley is so strong that it can grow in the bitter cold, and then sprouts in the early spring, when everything else is still asleep. Because of this, it is thought to be a symbol of new beginnings. Parsley is an amazing gift from nature. *Tabbouli* is a perfect dish to serve at a wedding. It does not need adornments or updating. It is authentic and true to the culture from which it comes. *(She mixes the bulgur with the parsley.)* Now we can add some chopped tomatoes and cucumbers and green onions—of course mint. Beautiful! Look at those colors!

(Lights shift. BABA, in real time, enters trying to sing Fairuz's "Habaytak Tenseet Alnowm." He can't remember the words, but is doing pretty well.)

BABA *(Singing)* Anna habaytak, habaytak. Breakfast, *ya* Fadwa? *(Continuing singing) Habaytak...tenseet...tenseet...* **[I loved you until I forgot...I forgot...]**

FADWA *Al nowm...anna habaytak habaytak* **[the sleep...I loved you, I loved you]**

BABA/FADWA *(Remembering) Anna habaytak, habaytak!* **[I loved you, I loved you!]**

(BABA and FADWA sing along softly. BABA peeks into the counter, shakes his head and smiles, retrieves two plates, sets them on the table and sits. FADWA brings a spread to the table—all the while the two sing. They are well synchronized: she stands at the table cutting cucumbers into discs; he puts a few on his plate, and a few on hers. She cuts up the manaeesh; he places them on his plates and hers. She pours tea; he puts sugar in both mugs. And on and on...It's a quiet, little ritual just between the two of them. On harder days, BABA can't always swing it, but it's a good day so far.)

BABA Sit, sit.

FADWA Yes, Baba.

(FADWA sits and they eat.)

BABA Excellent. Very, very good.

FADWA Thanks, Baba. More?

(BABA shakes his head no with a tsk and continues eating. FADWA stops and watches him for a moment. BABA eats serenely, then catches FADWA watching him. He smiles, sweetly pinches her cheek and goes back to his food.)

BABA It's ok, my Fadwa. Everything is ok...

(Enter DALAL.)

DALAL You did really well, Baba.

FADWA Come eat.

(DALAL goes to the table and nibbles off of the plates.)

BABA Get your mother, she should be here too. Why doesn't she eat with us anymore? Is she angry with me?

FADWA No, she's not angry with you, *Yaba.*

BABA I should go see.

FADWA Baba, just finish your food—

BABA I'm finished. It was very good.

DALAL Baba, here. It's time to take your pills.

(BABA takes down his pills and exits. FADWA starts clearing the plates.)

DALAL He's been doing that more and more. Asking for Mama...

FADWA Well—

DALAL I can't watch it. He needs help.

FADWA I'll call his doctor.

DALAL I don't mean here, I mean in the States. He needs better care. We could take him together.

FADWA I don't think it will help.

DALAL Listen, Hayat spoke to some doctors and she thinks—

FADWA —And what we're a bunch of idiot *falaheen* from the village? We don't know better, *yanni?*

DALAL We don't know better!

FADWA I do. I know his rhythms, his moods, more than anyone.

DALAL But Hayat said-

FADWA Hayat said. She hasn't talked to her own mother in God knows how long and now she's telling me what's best for my father?

DALAL He's my father too. We need to make decisions about his life together, Fadwa.

FADWA Baba's life is here, Dalal, he will be lost anywhere else.

DALAL *(Quietly.)* Soon he won't know the difference.

FADWA Yes he will.

BABA *(O.S.)* Fadwa? *Willik,* Fadwa! She's not here.

FADWA I'll be right there, Baba.

DALAL This conversation isn't over.

FADWA Go to your fitting. Don't forget Hayat.

BABA *(O.S.)* Fadwa?

FADWA Coming!

(FADWA exits. DALAL sighs. Lights down.)

Scene 4

Same day, late afternoon. YOUSSIF enters and goes directly to the pot to taste the food as nobody is around. Enter FADWA.

YOUSSIF *(Embarrassed)* I followed the smell from my house. Oh, *mloukiyi*. My favorite.

FADWA I know. Probably still needs something.

YOUSSIF No, *nothing*. It's perfect. *(He savors the taste.)* Always, perfect.

(YOUSSIF goes to the counter and grabs a handful of fresh herbs.)

YOUSSIF I love *the* smell.

FADWA *Shoo,* you don't have mint in New York?

YOUSSIF Not *like* this. From the garden?

FADWA What's left of it.

(YOUSSIF picks up a bottle of olive oil.)

YOUSSIF "Zeit *Zaytoon't* Zein."

FADWA We have about a dozen bottles left.

YOUSSIF You *should* preserve them.

FADWA They're meant to be used.

YOUSSIF Not by my family. Remember when your dad refused to sell to our restaurant?

FADWA Well, no, he wanted your dad to pay double because of what we did, remember?

YOUSSIF That's right! Your father went straight to my father and told him "If Youssif is going to waste my olives, you will pay double for the oil!" I got in so much trouble.

FADWA So did I. Worst summer of my life.

YOUSSIF But it wasn't our fault. We didn't even start it! It was that annoying neighbor kid who used to follow us around everywhere— that total pain in the ass. And we tried to hide from her in your dad's trees, but she found us so we had to pelt her with unripe olives. She just stood there, crying and getting a stoning! What a *heblah!*

FADWA That wasn't a neighbor. That was Hayat.

YOUSSIF Really? Are you sure?

FADWA Yes, I'm sure! She and my Aunt Jamila were visiting from the States and she wouldn't leave us alone for one second!

YOUSSIF Oh *God*, that's right! *(Laughing)* I can't believe it was Hayat! Wow. Well she's changed a lot since then.

FADWA Not that much. Remember how she tried to blame everything on me? She didn't want to get you in trouble, so she told my father that you were trying to defend her—

YOUSSIF But he didn't believe her—

FADWA No, because he saw us in the tree and she was on the ground, crying her head off! And there were olives everywhere! Remember how they got stuck in her hair, sort of hanging off like beads?

(YOUSSIF and FADWA laugh.)

FADWA That *was* funny.

YOUSSIF What were we, 12?

FADWA Yeah.

BABA *(O.S.)* Get away from me, Samia. Get away!

FADWA Baba, *what's* going on in there?

BABA *(O.S.)* Get away I said!

YOUSSIF I'll go check on him.

(YOUSSIF exits. FADWA looks up at the audience, a twinkle in her eye.)

FADWA *Mloukiyi* was once thought to be a sexual stimulant and was even banned by an Egyptian ruler in the 10th century for its passion inducing effects! This little, leafy vegetable? Better be careful to whom you serve it. *(She stirs the pot, smelling and tasting.)* Mmm. Food is very impressionable. It will take on the qualities of whatever mood the preparer is in. So, here's a tip. Try talking to your food. Say to it, "You are beautiful! You are healthy and I love you and have always loved you—*(Talking into her pot. LIGHTS Shift.)* You taste good and you smell good—

(YOUSSIF re-enters.)

YOUSSIF *Flattering* the food? Is that your secret?

FADWA It helps.

YOUSSIF Maybe I should have another bite, just to make sure it's working.

FADWA *3ala 3yani, habibi.* **[literally means "on my eye", figuratively "anything for you"]**

(She hands him a spoonful.)

YOUSSIF Oh, yeah. It's definitely working. Fadwa, there's something—

(HAYAT enters.)

HAYAT Oh, hi. I thought you'd be here. I was just at your mom's to see where you were.

FADWA Where's Dalal?

HAYAT Still getting fitted, it took forever. There were three other women in front of us, so we left to get mani/pedis from the dressmaker's cousin? We get back to the fitting and everyone's sitting around drinking coffee! Hello? How 'bout some time management, folks?

YOUSSIF They have their own system.

HAYAT Dalal sent me home. I walked past an army jeep at the end of the block.

YOUSSIF I saw that earlier.

HAYAT It's creepy. (*Peering into FADWA's pot.*) Ooh, *mlkoukiyi*. Your favorite.

YOUSSIF No one makes it better.

HAYAT You know, it's best when you sauté the chicken with a bit of ginger first, gives it a little Asian flare—

FADWA Keep your flares to yourself. This is pure Arabic.

HAYAT Habibi, don't be closed! In my cookbooks, I do all kinds of fusions.

FADWA (*Under her breath*) How about fusing your lips together?

(*FADWA exits.*)

HAYAT Youssif.

YOUSSIF I—I just need to find the right moment.

HAYAT Honey, come on, just tell her.

YOUSSIF I am…I will. It's harder than I thought.

HAYAT Sweetie, we have a life together. Whatever feelings you have—it's nostalgia! (*Putting her arms around him.*) We're building something amazing together. (*Peering into him.*) My sweet, sweet, sensitive man. Look, I'm here for you and I support you. But she deserves to know. If you care about her, you'll tell her.

YOUSSIF I have to tell her in my own way.

HAYAT I know, baby. I love you.

(*Enter FADWA. She stops cold at what she sees: HAYAT and YOUSSIF standing very closely, her hand on his face.*)

FADWA Youssif?

HAYAT I'll leave you two alone.

(*HAYAT exits.*)

YOUSSIF Fadwa.

FADWA I don't understand—I

YOUSSIF Fadwa, I—

FADWA Are you serious? Is that serious?

YOUSSIF I'm sorry, but please hear me out—

FADWA Don't come near me. Do not come near me.

(*Enter HAYAT.*)

HAYAT There are soldiers all over the place- they're telling people to get inside.

(*The sound of rapid gunfire and sirens.*)

HAYAT —Oh my God!

(*An announcement over a loudspeaker repeats the following in Arabic and English in an Israeli accent.*)

ISRAELI MILITARY ANNOUNCEMENT MAMNOU'A AL-TAJAWOOL! MAMNOU'A AL-TAJAWOOL! THERE IS A 24-HOUR CURFEW EFFECTIVE IMMEDIATELY. CLEAR THE STREETS! YOU ARE UNDER A 24-HOUR CURFEW UNTIL FURTHER NOTICE. ANYONE LEFT ON THE STREET WILL BE ARRESTED.

(*Sound of rapid gunfire. SAMIA runs in.*)

YOUSSIF God damn it.

(*Enter DALAL in her wedding dress.*)

DALAL Is Emir home yet?

FADWA No, Emir's not back. Are you ok?

DALAL (*Out of breath.*) There are tanks and soldiers everywhere.

HAYAT Oh my God. We have to go. We have to get out of here.

DALAL You can't go anywhere. They are arresting anyone who is caught outside.

(*YOUSSIF shakes his head no.*)

HAYAT We can't leave? Not even to go two blocks?

YOUSSIF Not until they lift the curfew.

HAYAT (*Getting hysterical*) When will they lift the curfew?

YOUSSIF Nobody knows. When I was here last they shut down the whole city for months.

HAYAT This is bullshit! I'm an American citizen, I will not be told to stay inside! I'm going!

FADWA Bye Hayat! See you later.

(*More sounds of gunfire. The loudspeaker blares.*)

ISRAELI MILITARY ANNOUNCEMENT RETURN TO YOUR HOMES! ANYONE CAUGHT IN PUBLIC WILL BE ARRESTED!

(*Enter BABA*)

BABA Fadwa?

(*Lights down as FADWA, HAYAT, YOUSSIF, SAMIA, and DALAL, in her wedding dress, look toward BABA.*)

END OF ACT I.

★

ACT II

Scene I

It is early evening. Day 5 of curfew. Lights up on FADWA.

FADWA Good evening and thank you for tuning in to *Food and Fadwa*. It is the fifth day of our special curfew series. The topic today: Rationing! This is a very valuable skill. Let's say, for example, you are being forced to stay in a house, with some of your most annoying relatives. Some talk on the phone all day, others don't shower, others flirts with your boyfriend. You cannot get away from them. And worse, they are eating all of the food! But you cannot go out to buy more-you are under house arrest! What will you do? You must be prepared! How to cook when facing starvation due to military incursion: A three-step guide. One: storing and canning food for future use. Two: finding creative ways to serve less food with the magic that is food presentation! And three: rationing. You see here, I have portioned food for each family member according to their needs. *(She holds up a little container that says "Hayat.")* This one for example, doesn't need too much. You must know the art of food rationing. And you will learn it right here, live from Bethlehem. Do you know what it means, Bethlehem? *Beit LaHem,* we call it in Arabic. It means, "House of Meat." Yep. In Aramaic and Hebrew, it means, "House of Bread." So you see, it really makes no sense that someone should go hungry here. We are the house of bread and meat. We are living inside a sandwich!

(Enter DALAL, still in her wedding dress.)

DALAL *(On her cellphone)* No, no, no. *(She puts her hand over the receiver and speaks to FADWA.)* Emir's mom wants to postpone the wedding!

(FADWA motions at her as if to say "what are you talking about?" and DALAL waves her off.)

DALAL I know, but they could lift the curfew tonight and—just tell them we'll let them know tomorrow morning. No, not yet...I'm sure Emir's fine... he'll find his way back. Yes, I'll let you know. Ok. *Yallah, bye.*

FADWA *(Firmly.)* Take the dress off.

DALAL No.

FADWA It's been five days.

DALAL *(Simply.)* I am sending a message to God.

FADWA I hope He gets it soon. Your message is beginning to smell.

DALAL I am getting married, Fadwa. Tomorrow is my wedding day and I am getting married. *(Shaking her fists at the sky) Sam3een?* **[Do you hear?]** Married! I am *not* postponing. *(FADWA gives DALAL a look.)* What? We postpone and what? We find ourselves broke and Emir runs off to America and I am stuck here alone forever?

FADWA What are you talking about?

DALAL I cannot end up like you! *(Catching herself)* I'm sorry, Foo Foo. I didn't mean it. I'm just worried about Emir and—I'm so sorry. I don't even know what to say to them. I can hardly look Youssif in the eye.

FADWA *Khalas,* forget it.

DALAL Where is everyone?

FADWA Auntie wanted to bathe Baba, but he thought she was a soldier trying to strip search him, so Youssif pretended to arrest her. She's sitting on the bathroom floor, her hands tied up in toilet paper. Youssif is bathing him now and Hayat just walked in. She's singing to them in Arabic.

DALAL *Yee.*

FADWA I know. I had to leave.

(Enter HAYAT rubbing a sore spot on her arm.)

HAYAT Your father threw a bar of soap at me. A fresh bar. With edges! Christ!

DALAL Are you okay?

HAYAT It's fine. It just shocked me a little. How's Emir? Have you heard from him?

DALAL Not since the day before yesterday. He couldn't tell me where he is. They're hiding somewhere, him and two guys. I'm so worried. I've been calling him all day. No answer.

HAYAT Maybe his phone died.

DALAL Maybe they found him. God, what if they found him and took him to jail?

FADWA Nobody took him, *habibti.* This is Emir we're talking about. He's wily.

HAYAT This is ridiculous. We're not fucking animals! They have to let us out eventually. For food at least, my God. *(HAYAT goes to the counter.)* What are these containers with everyone's name on them? What happened to all the wedding food?

DALAL Fadwa?

FADWA Inside the containers.

DALAL What?

FADWA Sorry, Dal Dal.

DALAL What about all the stuff in the freezer? We couldn't eat that?

FADWA We have to eat what will spoil first. The frozen stuff I'm saving.

DALAL What if they lift the curfew in time for the wedding? What will everyone eat, Fadwa?

FADWA *Habibti*, I can always make more. Right now we have to eat what we have. There are six of us here.

HAYAT Oh, sweetie. Don't worry. I can make a banquet out of nothing. I'll take care of everything.

FADWA I've taken care of it.

DALAL I might as well eat, I haven't had anything all day.

HAYAT Me neither.

(DALAL takes a long, bright orange, chef-style apron out of a drawer and puts it on over her wedding dress. She grabs two clean forks from another drawer and hands one to HAYAT. They sit at the table and nibble from DALAL's container.)

FADWA You look ridiculous.

DALAL I don't want to stain the dress.

YOUSSIF *(O.S.)* Yes! We will leave her there until she rots!

(Enter YOUSSIF with BABA.)

DALAL Na3eeman!

HAYAT Nice and clean! Looking good, uncle.

FADWA *Yallah*, Baba, come sit.

(BABA shakes his head "no" and heads for the recliner.)

YOUSSIF Someone needs to check on Samia.

FADWA Dalal, make sure Baba eats something.

(FADWA exits.)

YOUSSIF Your father is wearing me out. I'm starving. Is there anything left?

HAYAT Here, Baby, have some of this. Come.

(YOUSSIF sits and eats. BABA picks up DALAL's oud, and plucks a few strings.)

DALAL *Yallah*, Baba, play! Let's try this again, you can do it! *Aywah!* **[That's right!]** *(Singing.) Da da dee dee dee dee da da da da da.*

(BABA puts the oud down, agitated, stands up and begins nervously pacing back and forth near the window.)

DALAL Baba?

HAYAT Is he okay?

DALAL *Yallah*, let's sing something, *habibi*.

(DALAL snaps her fingers and dances her way to BABA. BABA slows down his pacing and stares out the window, rocking back and forth while DALAL sings.)

DALAL *(Singing) Sana tayn, Sana tayn, Santayn ooh enna estenak, 3ala ay, 3ala ay tooh-jounrni, mish moumkin ansak. Yallah, Baba!*

(FADWA enters and watches.)

HAYAT I've never heard that verse before—

DALAL *Sanatayn, Sanatayn—*,

HAYAT Honey, translate.

DALAL *Sanatayn ooh enna estenak—*

YOUSSIF Um…"Two years, two years that I've been waiting for you"—

DALAL *3ala ay, 3ala ay tooh-journi, mish moumkin ansak—*

YOUSSIF "Why did you abandon me? It is impossible to forget you." Um…something like that.

(DALAL ends the song. BABA smiles wistfully as he looks out the window. YOUSSIF and FADWA glimpse at each other.)

HAYAT That is so sad. Arabic songs are depressing.

FADWA Come, Yaba, have some dinner.

(BABA turns and looks at all of them, shakes his head violently, and looks back out the window. He straightens himself up and walks briskly out of the room.)

FADWA Baba you have to eat!

DALAL I'll take him something. Hayat, come help me.

HAYAT I'm coming.

(DALAL grabs a container of food and exits with HAYAT. FADWA and YOUSSIF are alone.)

YOUSSIF Fadwa can we talk about this now? You can't keep giving me the silent treatment. I'm sorry.

FADWA I thought you still wanted to make it work between us.

YOUSSIF I did, but…I couldn't do it anymore. You made your decision, Fadwa.

FADWA I didn't make a decision! You told me America would be temporary. Temporary—

YOUSSIF Things changed—

FADWA Things changed for me too—

YOUSSIF I know, I tried to accommodate you in every way I could—

FADWA You abandoned me.

YOUSSIF I didn't abandon you. I left to make us a life—

FADWA You could have done that here.

YOUSSIF Fadwa, I had nothing. *Nothing.* Everything my family had was gone. My father's restaurant, all his years of work and sacrifice, lost.

FADWA Youssif—

YOUSSIF It was my responsibility.

FADWA There was nothing you could have done to save it—there was a war!

YOUSSIF War, occupation, it doesn't matter. I failed. I had to leave, you know that—

FADWA But you promised you would come back—

YOUSSIF Don't put this all on me. You promised you would visit me, and you didn't. You wouldn't.

FADWA I *couldn't.* All I wanted to do was get on a plane and leave this shit behind, but I couldn't leave him. He needed me!

YOUSSIF I needed you! My God someone else could have looked after him for a change! I would have given anything to just be with you for a day, an hour—

FADWA Then you could have come home!

YOUSSIF *Ya Allah* I am so sick of hearing that! I am so sick of it!

FADWA Do you understand? I am his caretaker, not Dalal or Samia—me. He relies on me for everything—

YOUSSIF I never meant for you to take care of him on your own! Why else do you think I stayed in the States? So I could work, and save and provide a home for you—a place where you could bring him, and we could take care of him together.

FADWA Youssif, I can hardly convince the man to change his clothes. How did you expect me to convince him to change his entire life! I can't just take a deluded man to a place that is completely foreign to him and just start over.

YOUSSIF Foo Foo—

FADWA Don't call me that.

YOUSSIF Everything I was doing was for you. Every shit job, every minute of overtime— the only thing that kept me going was you. It was all for you—for us—

FADWA Then why didn't you wait for me?

YOUSSIF How long was I supposed to wait??

FADWA I didn't know we had a time limit—

YOUSSIF I sent money, I bought you plane tickets, I spoke to doctors, I called and called and called. Like an idiot. And sometimes, I wouldn't hear from you for days or weeks—

FADWA Because I had my hands full, day and night. I thought you understood—

YOUSSIF I did, but—

FADWA You were supposed to stand by me, even if it was hard, even when I couldn't call back sometimes or come visit. Because that is what people do when they love each other. I needed you to be there for me and be strong, not make me choose between you and my father.

YOUSSIF That's what you think? *(FADWA doesn't answer.)* I'm sorry, Fadwa. I can't do this. Nothing I could do was enough. I had to move on, you were killing me.

FADWA Your life is so easy there.

YOUSSIF You don't know what it was like for me. I had no one. Hayat was there for me.

FADWA You went to her because it was easy!

YOUSSIF It is easy, Fadwa. Not everything has to be so difficult.

(BABA wanders onstage toward the door with the tabla in his hands, flipped over like a bucket. He is wearing a straw hat, pajamas, a robe and worker boots. He opens the door and stares outside. A SHOT is fired toward the house. Everyone freezes. BABA stands there.)

BABA *Kus imko! Klab! Sharameet!* **[Fuck you! Dogs! Sons of whores!]** Goddamn animals!

(Another GUNSHOT.)

FADWA Baba! Get inside!

BABA It's time to harvest!/ Everything will rot!

FADWA Get away from there, Yaba—

BABA *(To the outside)* This is our land! Go to hell! You hear me? Hell!

(YOUSSIF runs to the door and shuts it reaching for BABA's arm.)

YOUSSIF *Amo,* it's too dangerous to go now.

BABA Who are you? Don't touch me! Fadwa, bring me my gun!

FADWA Baba, you don't have a gun.

(Enter DALAL and HAYAT)

BABA My gun, *binti!* **[daughter!]** They want my trees!

YOUSSIF *Amo! Amo,* eh, I have your gun.

BABA You? Give me!

DALAL What's going on?

YOUSSIF It's in the other room. Let's take a look at it.

BABA Yes. I will show them.

DALAL Wait, wait. Give him his medicine.

FADWA We ran out this morning.

DALAL What?

YOUSSIF I'll keep an eye on him for now. We'll figure something out. *(To BABA) Yallah Amo.*

BABA *Yallah, ya binit.* Fadwa!

FADWA Yes, Baba.

(YOUSSIF, FADWA and BABA exit. HAYAT goes to the window.)

DALAL Be careful.

HAYAT Soldiers shooting at the house?

DALAL It was probably settlers.

HAYAT You're kidding?

DALAL They're much worse. I think I'll sleep out here tonight. I can't sleep next to Auntie Samia anymore. Her snoring…

(DALAL checks her cell phone.)

HAYAT Anything from Emir?

(DALAL sighs and shakes her head no.)

HAYAT I'm sure he's fine, sweetie.

(DALAL takes off the apron and lies on the couch.)

HAYAT Aren't you uncomfortable in that dress?

DALAL It's the only thing that's *giving* me comfort. It was my mom's. I wish she were here.

HAYAT Me too. She always made me feel so welcome. She was an angel.

DALAL Yeah…

HAYAT Auntie Lena. She was so good to us. The only one who was actually kind to my mother. Your dad too, but the women around here. God. But Lena … no judgment. You're so much like her.

DALAL I know. It's the cheeks!

HAYAT No. It's the kindness. *(Crying.)* I'm sorry.

DALAL We're all under a lot of stress, *habibti.* Go get some sleep. *(They hug.)* If you can stand Samia's snoring symphony.

HAYAT I can sleep through anything. I live in Manhattan. Goodnight, *habibti.*

DALAL Goodnight.

HAYAT And thank you.

(HAYAT exits. Lights dim.)

Scene 2

A few hours have passed, it is just before dawn. DALAL is sleeping on the couch in her wedding dress. BABA shuffles into the kitchen, but stops when he notices DALAL sleeping. He gingerly approaches her. He stares at her. He begins to touch her face, her lips, and hair.

BABA Lena…*habibti* Lena…

(He kneels down and gently kisses her on the lips, caressing her body and hair. DALAL wakes.)

DALAL Hmm? Emir?

(BABA looks at her. She opens her eyes.)

BABA Lena. *Elbi,* Lena. **[My beloved Lena.]** Lena.

(He leans down again to kiss her. DALAL pushes him and jumps up.)

DALAL No no no. No, Baba. It's me. It's Dalal.

BABA You look so beautiful, *habibti. (He grabs her and brings her close to him like a lover and begins to kiss her on the neck.)* My beautiful wife…come to bed… *(She manages to push him away.)*

DALAL No, Baba. Stop that. Look at me. I'm Dalal. Dalal, your daughter, remember?

BABA *(Gripping her tightly)* Stop playing with me, Lena.

DALAL No. *No.* Fadwa! Stop it! STOP IT! BABA! Let GO! Fadwa! Youssif!

(FADWA runs in, followed by YOUSSIF.)

BABA Don't be afraid. My wife! My beautiful wife!

(DALAL breaks free. YOUSSIF blocks BABA from her.)

DALAL I am your *child.*

(FADWA holds DALAL. BABA stands there staring. SAMIA and HAYAT enter.)

BABA *Habibti. Habibti,* don't cry. I'm sorry. *(To FADWA)* Why does she cry?

DALAL I can't take it.

(A loud crash is heard offstage. Everyone freezes.)

HAYAT What was that? Oh my God, is someone in the house?

(The loud sound of something falling to the ground and breaking.)

EMIR *(O.S.)* Goddamnit! Stupid plant.

(EMIR appears in the doorway holding the plant he knocked over.)

EMIR Good morning!

DALAL Emir! Oh, Emir!

(DALAL runs to him and hugs him. The following overlaps.)

HAYAT Oh thank God/

YOUSSIF Where the hell were you/

SAMIA *Habibi,* thank God/

FADWA Emir/

EMIR I'm fine, *habibti,* I'm fine. *(Pulling her out of the hug to look at her.)* What is this? Did I miss the wedding?

HAYAT Oh no! He's not supposed to see her in that! Bad luck.

EMIR *Yee!* Not bad luck! We don't need any more of that! Ok, I close my eyes. Here. Now I don't see you. *(Sniffing)* But I smell you. My God you stink!

FADWA She's been wearing that for almost a week!

EMIR *Willy, felaHah!* **[Little peasant girl!]** You smell like a Bedouin gypsy.

DALAL *(Laughing)* Stop it! This is a symbol. You see? It brought you back to me. On our wedding day!

EMIR It did. Is this your mating scent?

(DALAL hits him and tries to hug him.)

EMIR No, no, please! I can't take it!

YOUSSIF Where were you? What happened?

EMIR I was coming through the checkpoint from Jerusalem when they called curfew. But I couldn't get back here, so I snuck up into the hills, which is a real party with all the crazy settlers, but the Bedouins showed us where to hide. Anyway, we kept hearing rumors that they were going to lift the curfew, but they didn't. *Khalas,* I couldn't take it anymore. I waited until nightfall and snuck back in. Lured and protected by your magical stench.

DALAL *(Hitting him on the arm.)* You could have been shot.

EMIR I'm like a silent cheetah. At night, no one can see me.

BABA I don't believe it.

EMIR Hi *Ami!* Did you miss me?

BABA *(Very calmly observing EMIR.)* I know you.

EMIR *Nuskur Allah!* **[Thank God!]** He remembers! Come, let me hug you.

BABA First my money, now my Lena.

EMIR Lena?

BABA Thieving collaborator!

FADWA Go change. Now. Go change, go change, go change—

HAYAT Come on, sweetie.

(DALAL, SAMIA, HAYAT exit.)

EMIR *(Cautiously approaching BABA.)* Amo. It's me, Emir. And that woman, that smelly woman, is your daughter. My fiancé. I know this is hard for you. We are going to do everything we can to make you happy and comfortable. Okay? You are like a father to me and I love you.

(EMIR grabs BABA by the shoulders firmly and looks into his eyes.)

BABA It's hard; it's very hard. Please take care of my Lena.

EMIR I will.

BABA My Lena, my Lena, my Lena…

(BABA shuffles over to the window and stares out.)

YOUSSIF Emir, go clean yourself and get some rest. We're throwing you a shaving party tomorrow.

FADWA Party?

YOUSSIF We can't have the wedding, but we can still celebrate.

FADWA There isn't much, but we can pull something together. We still have *knafi!*

EMIR My favorite! I haven't eaten in three days.

FADWA There's a bit of *hashweh* left. From last week.

EMIR Finally, she offers me *hashweh.* I had to be half dead, but *yallah,* I got my wish.

FADWA *(Handing him a plate.)* Here, *habibi.* Sorry, it isn't much.

EMIR Are you kidding? This is a feast! Now, if you'll excuse me, I'm going to eat this while I sleep and shower. Goodnight brother! Goodnight sister! The prince has returned! Goodnight!

(Exit EMIR)

YOUSSIF I'll stay with him. Get some sleep.

(FADWA exits. BABA is still staring out of the window.)

BABA Lena…Lena…

YOUSSIF *Amo?* Come help me with this, eh? *Yallah.*

(YOUSSIF brings the pot and plant that EMIR knocked over and sits next to BABA on the ground.)

YOUSSIF Here, put some soil on the bottom of this pot—*aywah,* that's it. You're a pro, *Ami.* I remember how much you used to work— plowing, pruning, picking. Every day, up before sunrise, spending hours and hours in the groves. Just keep working and working and working.

BABA Lena...

YOUSSIF It's good to keep busy. Keeps the mind quiet. *Ya Allah,* I wish I could take you to New York with me. It feels good there. We could go to a baseball game and sit really high up in the stands and just feel the openness, the freedom. I never understood the game but in the summer, it's the best. Sit in the sun, drink beer—sometimes I bring hookah and we pass it around the stands. Everyone smoking *argili* and watching the Mets lose. It's glorious! You would love it. *(Watching BABA'S hands.)* You're doing a beautiful job, *habibi.* Beautiful. There, finished.

(BABA stares at the plant, he touches a leaf, and then hangs his head and cries. YOUSSIF holds him.)

It's ok, *Ami,* it's ok.

(Lights down.)

Scene 3

Same day, early evening. The place is tidy and looks as if an effort has been made to make things pretty. FADWA is preparing sweets and coffee, while laughing to herself and pretending to speak to people in front of her. She holds up food and models it. Enter HAYAT. She stops and watches FADWA.

FADWA And, *this,* Gentle Viewers, is *knafi.*

HAYAT Uh, did I interrupt something?

(FADWA says nothing, but chuckles to herself in reference to the comment. She rolls her eyes and connects back to the audience as if to say "Isn't she annoying?")

FADWA Delicious, crispy and sweet on the outside. Oozing with cheese on the inside...

(HAYAT goes to the fridge and retrieves a pitcher of water to pour herself a glass.)

HAYAT Do you need help with anything? *(FADWA doesn't answer.)* Fadwa?

FADWA A poet once said, "To eat the pastries of Arabs is to make a person's life serene and happy and keep away evil."

HAYAT Okay, whatever.

(HAYAT starts to exit, but then turns around and observes. YOUSSIF enters, heading toward the fridge. HAYAT stops him, and points to FADWA. They both watch.)

FADWA Never will you walk into an Arab home and not find pastries. Never! Absolute dishonor. We always have something in the freezer ready for baking. This pan, for example, was made eight months ago. Perfectly preserved and ready for consumption.

(SAMIA enters to see HAYAT and YOUSSIF watching FADWA. She reprimands them silently.)

DALAL Foo Foo? Have you seen my silver heels? *(Enter DALAL in a beautiful purple dress. Looking back and forth between YOUSSIF and HAYAT and FADWA.)* What's everyone doing?

(FADWA turns around to everyone.)

HAYAT Look amazing. I thought Emir was getting a shave and we were all supposed to stand around and watch.

YOUSSIF It's more than that—we're celebrating his last days as a single man—we're cleaning him up, so to speak.

DALAL Now go change! You too, Foo Foo. *Yallah.* Party starts in ten!

(DALAL grabs FADWA and they exit. SAMIA looks at HAYAT and YOUSSIF reproachfully and exits.)

HAYAT See? Fadwa does that all day, and everyone ignores it like it's totally normal!

YOUSSIF It's just what she does, it's endearing.

HAYAT It's borderline psychotic! It freaks me out.

YOUSSIF She's just imaginative.

HAYAT *Artists* are imaginative! She's nuts!

YOUSSIF Fadwa is kind of an artist.

HAYAT In what way?

YOUSSIF In the food-way.

HAYAT Oh, come on.

YOUSSIF No one can do what she does.

HAYAT I resent that. What, because she can roll a few fucking grape leaves?

YOUSSIF Hayat, please.

HAYAT No, what is so earth shattering about her food? There's no creativity, it's the same old boring shit!

YOUSSIF It's just got something...

HAYAT You know, if you want her so badly, just stay here! Stay in this backwards, war-torn den of depravity—I don't care! I can't stand this anymore.

YOUSSIF I'm not saying that—

HAYAT Well what are you saying?

YOUSSIF Hayat, come on. Look at what these people are going through. And despite all of it, they are doing the impossible to make sure you're comfortable—

HAYAT I know that, Youssif, and I'm doing my best to be helpful and stay out of the way!

YOUSSIF *(Gently)* Of course you are, *habibti*, you've been very gracious… but just have a *little* patience. Come here… Come on, come here. *(He holds her.)*

HAYAT I'm sorry, sweetie. I'm just…

YOUSSIF *Khalas.* I know this is hard for you; we'll get out of here soon, I promise.

(YOUSSIF kisses her forehead and holds her a moment. Enter FADWA in a red dress looking beautiful. YOUSSIF, rather startled, stares at her.)

YOUSSIF Wow.

HAYAT Make up your mind.

(HAYAT exits.)

YOUSSIF Hayat!

(FADWA goes to the counter and starts cutting up the dessert. YOUSSIF continues to look at her. Enter EMIR, DALAL, AUNTIE SAMIA and BABA. AUNTIE SAMIA gently leads BABA to his chair where she covers him with a blanket.)

EMIR Alright, let's do this! Well, well who's that pretty woman?

DALAL Doesn't she look beautiful?

EMIR What happened to Fadwa? Hey, lady, can you cook?

DALAL I've never seen that dress! Have you been hiding it?

FADWA No. I just…I bought it a long time ago.

DALAL When? For what?

FADWA Nothing. It doesn't matter.

(YOUSSIF pulls a chair into the center of the stage. Enter HAYAT.)

YOUSSIF *Yallah, yallah.* Let's start!

(SAMIA begins a traditional Arabic incantation, which is a call to the groom, preparing him for a life of marriage. SAMIA does an ululation. EMIR is placed on a chair. YOUSSIF dresses him in a long bib, the kind used in a barber shop.)

YOUSSIF Ready brother?

EMIR If you cut me, I kill you.

YOUSSIF Then you better not move or speak!

(YOUSSIF covers EMIR's face with shaving cream. Everyone starts to clap hands and sings "Ehlik Ya Halak," the groom's shaving song. BABA, still sitting in his chair, gives notice to the dancing and singing. He begins to smile. He slowly starts to stand and clap his hands along. No one has noticed quite yet. YOUSSIF finishes shaving EMIR, and pulls him up onto the chair.)

BABA Now you look like a man! Dalal, my oud! Youssif, get the tabla! Emir, *habibi*, dance with your fiancé!

(BABA picks up his oud and begins to play. As the clapping dies down, BABA'S version of "Ah Ya Zein" begins and he too starts incantations. He walks over to the speechless group as he plays, looking utterly joyful. EMIR hops off the chair and seats BABA in it. BABA plays oud while YOUSSIF plays tabla. EMIR takes DALAL's hand and dances with her, as everyone claps along. BABA starts singing "Ah Ya Zein." SAMIA balances a liquor bottle on her head and dances between the bride and groom. FADWA and HAYAT stand away from each other and clap along. SAMIA takes the liquor bottle off her head and pours shots of "Arak" into tiny glasses, and starts handing them out. Everyone lifts glasses into the air as BABA continues to sing and YOUSSIF continues to play. As they take down their shots, BABA's singing begins to stumble, followed by his playing. Finally, he stops.)

YOUSSIF *Amo?* What happened?

BABA I don't know.

(BABA stares at the oud a while longer.)

FADWA Baba?

BABA My name is Zein. You must call me Zein.

(BABA puts down the oud, grabs the tabla and shuffles off stage, followed by FADWA and SAMIA. HAYAT, YOUSSIF, DALAL and EMIR are silent. Lights fade.)

Scene 4

About an hour later. HAYAT, YOUSSIF, DALAL and EMIR sit around the table, eating knafi, and drinking Arabic coffee. EMIR is comforting DALAL.

EMIR His playing was a blessing, *habibti*.

HAYAT It was! It was beautiful.

DALAL But he can't stay in the house like this. And he needs medicine.

HAYAT We're gonna get him out of here. This is no place for a man that sick.

EMIR What is she talking about?

HAYAT We're taking him with us. To New York.

EMIR *Inshallah* he's gonna live with us? *(DA-LAL hits him.)* What? The man wants to kill me.

HAYAT We'll figure something out. My mom can help. She needs to get to know him again.

DALAL She won't recognize him.

EMIR She won't recognize *him?* He'll probably think she's Ariel Sharon.

(YOUSSIF laughs, HAYAT hits him. DALAL hits EMIR.)

DALAL That's not funny!

HAYAT So not funny!

YOUSSIF Well, she is a little bloated looking—

HAYAT Rude!

(EMIR and YOUSSIF laugh. Enter SAMIA.)

SAMIA *(On phone.)* I know *habibti*, this is very stressful.

(SAMIA gets herself a coffee and lights up.)

DALAL Auntie, not in the house!

EMIR Where is she supposed to go? Give the lady a break.

SAMIA *(On phone)* No, it's not fair. Our cable isn't working either. Call your cousin in Jordan and find out who was voted off the show. *Wallah*, I'm suffering from this.

DALAL Unbelievable.

HAYAT I thought American Idol was a bad idea.

(Enter FADWA.)

EMIR You're missing all the fun, Foo Foo!

DALAL How's Baba?

FADWA He's ok. He's sleeping on the floor of his bedroom.

DALAL On the floor?

EMIR The floor is like a feather bed. I slept on a hill of stones for days. This is what we learn when we're in hiding. Skills, people. Skills. Speaking of which, flip your cups.

DALAL Oh no.

HAYAT What?

YOUSSIF My brother has the "gift" of clairvoyance.

EMIR Sadly, Youssif did not inherit this talent.

YOUSSIF I got the good looks and charm.

EMIR These things fade, my child. When you can determine the destiny of another human being simply by glancing at their used up coffee grounds—*that* is an immortal skill. You see, friends, I received a holy transmission from my Great Aunt Soraya at the tender age of 7. She possessed the—how do you call it—the Divine Fire. Something only I was fit to inherit.

DALAL *Bella zanakha, Emir!* **[Stop being silly, Emir!]**

EMIR Shhhh. Do not disturb the flow. *(Closing his eyes and taking a deep breath.)* Dalal, you shall be first, my lady.

(EMIR takes DALAL's cup, makes chanting/humming sounds as he cradles it dramatically in his hands.)

EMIR Mmm. Yes, yes, yes. Your marriage to a handsome man will be rudely interrupted through no fault of your own. You will have children. Eight of them. All named Emir. Foo Foo. I don't even need to see your cup. You will make me a cake. It will be delicious. Samia, your cup.

(SAMIA's phone rings, and she waves EMIR off violently while she answers it.)

SAMIA *(On phone.)* Ah, Mariam? Anything? No! No! The Tunisian? Oh no. Oh no. Life is very unfair.

(SAMIA cries and exits. Everyone reacts to the news of the Tunisian.)

EMIR Your turn, brother, hand it over. *(EMIR takes YOUSSIF's cup.)* Oooh, too bad, too bad. Baldness, nose hairs, halitosis. Tough break. Good luck, brother.

HAYAT Come on, be serious.

FADWA Yeah, Emir, be serious. Isn't there something in there about settling?

EMIR Eh, no, no. My vision cannot be spoken out loud.

HAYAT I'll start cleaning up.

DALAL I'll help.

EMIR Is there any more *knafi*?

FADWA *(Peering into YOUSSIF'S cup.)* Oh, look at that. I'm right.

YOUSSIF *(Warning)* Fadwa.

HAYAT Ok, I think this is ready to be washed now.

(HAYAT grabs the cup from FADWA.)

FADWA Does he love you?

EMIR You know, maybe I'll sleep outside. I miss the dirt.

FADWA Ask him. Youssif, do you love her?

HAYAT Are you totally delusional? I am in a *relationship* with this man!

FADWA You ought to have higher standards, Hayat. No woman should have a relationship with a man who doesn't love her.

YOUSSIF Fadwa, watch yourself.

HAYAT Excuse me?

DALAL *(Trying to calm things down)* Ok, ok—

FADWA Excuse you? No, I don't excuse you. Funny how you cannot seem to find your own man. You're just like your mother.

DALAL Fadwa! Shut up!

FADWA Thank God she took her filthy ways and left. Are you sure you know who your father is?

(Everyone starts talking over each other. Do not wait for the characters to finish their dialogue.)

DALAL *Khalas, Foo Foo!*

HAYAT You little village bitch!

YOUSSIF Hayat!

HAYAT Exactly the reason my mother left!

FADWA Why? Because she ran out of married men to seduce?

HAYAT YOU are the reason people leave this hellhole! You don't allow people to breathe! You're worse than any wall, any curfew, or any occupation! No wonder Youssif left you.

(FADWA goes to attack HAYAT. EMIR grabs her and holds her back. YOUSSIF is standing in the middle of them, holding HAYAT at bay. SAMIA enters with BABA standing behind her watching the fight.)

FADWA He left me? He left me, *ya kelbi?*

HAYAT Deal with it!

FADWA How long have you been planning this?

HAYAT Oh planning? Really—

FADWA You think you are so much better than everyone!

HAYAT Fucking grow up Fadwa, grow the fuck up!

FADWA You're nothing! You're a liar *kus ocht illi khala'ik!* [essentially, "fuck the sister of the woman who bore you"].

HAYAT I am so SICK of your bullshit! I mean pretending you're on a goddamn cooking show! You're out of your fucking mind!

FADWA The man doesn't love you! He will never love you! Let go of me!

HAYAT You're not enough for him.

FADWA I'll kill you!

(FADWA, trying to get EMIR to release her, kicks him in the knee.)

EMIR Ouch! Animals!

YOUSSIF *(At the top of his lungs)* STOP THIS NOW!

(The electricity SHUTS OFF, leaving them in the dark.)

YOUSSIF Shit.

DALAL *Ya Allah*, not again.

EMIR This is romantic.

DALAL There are candles around here somewhere.

FADWA *Khariyi.* [Shithead.]

HAYAT I understood that.

FADWA Good.

DALAL Enough. Emir, come help me look. Emir! Where are you?

EMIR I'm coming—goddammit, I'm limping. You two should join the army. Maniacs. *(Sounds of rummaging.)* What the hell is this? A drill? Where's the flashlight?

DALAL There's one in the pantry—

EMIR Here's one!

HAYAT What the hell is going on?

EMIR Listen, the Israelis are just helping us go green.

(EMIR turns it on. The flashlight begins darting around. It's hard to tell in all of the commotion and cacophony, but BABA gently walks out the back door of the home.)

SAMIA Here, here. Candles. *(She lights two.)* Ok, everyone to bed.

EMIR Dalal and I will share a bed out of consideration for the guests.

DALAL Emir, take the couch.

EMIR Yes, sergeant.

SAMIA Fadwa, Hayat—Shame on you both. To your rooms.

(HAYAT, DALAL, SAMIA and FADWA exit.)

EMIR Some match!

YOUSSIF Unbelievable.

EMIR *Yanni*, Fadwa is an ox, my God. I think she dislocated my knee!

(YOUSSIF goes to the window.)

YOUSSIF The neighbor has his generator on, but no electricity on the rest of the block. I should call Mama.

EMIR I talked to her earlier, she's fine. At least her sisters are with her, thank God.

YOUSSIF I'm glad our father isn't alive to see this.

EMIR He would have turned on the gas generator and sold shawarma to the whole neighborhood, shit, he probably would have sold them to the soldiers. I miss him.

(They share a laugh. EMIR sits on the chair. YOUSSIF on the couch.)

YOUSSIF Me too. I'm a *hmarr*. A complete jackass.

EMIR Not a complete jackass.

YOUSSIF I should have told Fadwa sooner.

EMIR Yeah, what were you thinking?

YOUSSIF I wanted to tell her face-to-face.

EMIR That is very noble of you.

YOUSSIF I just...I thought Fadwa and I could have some time to... I don't know... resolve things. This is my fault.

EMIR You did your best. And so did Fadwa.

(YOUSSIF pours them each a drink from the bottle of Arak and they toast.)

YOUSSIF It was a good night.

EMIR It really was. Except for the part where Fadwa tried to rip Hayat's face off. But the rest, very nice.

YOUSSIF Congratulations, Emir. *Mabrook, elf mabrook.* **[a thousand congrats.]**

(They toast, drink, and try to rest.)

FADWA *(O.S.)* No, he's not in his room.

DALAL *(O.S.)* Did you check the other room?

FADWA *(O.S.)* He's not there.

EMIR What now?

(DALAL and FADWA enter.)

DALAL Is Baba out here?

EMIR I don't think so.

FADWA Baba!

(HAYAT and SAMIA enter.)

SAMIA Zein!

DALAL Baba!

EMIR Amo!

YOUSSIF *Amo!* Where is his tabla?

HAYAT *(O.S)* It's not in his room.

(HAYAT enters. DALAL notices the back door open.)

DALAL Why is the door open?

(FADWA goes straight for the door. EMIR chases her to hold her from going out.)

FADWA Baba! Where are you? Baba! Are you out here?

EMIR Foo Foo, get inside—

FADWA We have to go look for him.

(FADWA tries to go back out, but EMIR grabs her. They struggle, but EMIR gets her back in the house.)

EMIR Fadwa, no!

FADWA What if they arrest him and he gets agitated, he won't understand—

EMIR Maybe he went to my mother's?

YOUSSIF I'll call her.

HAYAT Just start calling everyone you know. Get the word out.

(EMIR and YOUSSIF dial their phones.)

HAYAT We'll know more in the morning.

(YOUSSIF goes to the radio, turns it on to hear ongoing news in Arabic. Everyone listens with rapt attention. FADWA sits at the dining room table and stares toward the back door. The characters blow out their candles and clear the stage as the radio stays on continually, to indicate the passing of a few days as the lights rise into day. FADWA blows out her candle.)

END OF ACT II.

★

ACT III

Scene I

Lights rise. Morning on the tenth day of curfew. FADWA stands at the counter.

FADWA *(Whispering to her audience.)* Good morning. Today is the tenth day of our ongoing curfew series and our topic this morning is fasting. Yes, today, you have tuned into *NO Food and Fadwa!* Fasting is a sacred practice.

Baba says- *(She looks to the back door.)* -that sometimes we are too spoiled—we forget how much we've been given. We must fast to remember to be grateful...

(Enter YOUSSIF carrying a crate of olive oil.)

YOUSSIF Foo Foo, are you ok?

(Enter EMIR, DALAL, HAYAT, and SAMIA.)

EMIR I'm dying of thirst—

YOUSSIF They turned off the water.

EMIR Terrific.

HAYAT There's a bottle in the pantry. I filled a couple. I thought this might happen.

DALAL I'm starving.

YOUSSIF There's this.

DALAL Olive oil?

HAYAT Come on, everyone. It's nourishment. *(Pouring oil into several cups.)* Here. Take sips.

EMIR Mmm. Buttery yet fruity, with notes of almond and strife. Dalal, *yallah.*

DALAL I can't. I feel sick.

EMIR You need strength.

(DALAL's cell phone rings.)

DALAL Emir, get it.

EMIR Hello? Hi Mama.

DALAL Again? The woman is draining my battery.

EMIR *(On phone)* No we haven't heard much— there were reports that maybe someone spotted him, but—yeah. Any word about the curfew? Really? Maybe in a few hours? Okay, call as soon as you hear. Bye, love you.

YOUSSIF Just have to keep waiting.

HAYAT We've called everyone we know here and back home for help. The word is out. *(HAYAT goes to FADWA with a cup of olive oil.)* Foo Foo? How about just a bit? *(FADWA doesn't answer.)* Youssif, you have to do something.

YOUSSIF Fadwa, drink this.

(FADWA stares off toward the window.)

YOUSSIF Come on, just a little bit.

(FADWA continues to stare off.)

DALAL Just leave her.

EMIR *Shoo* leave her?

YOUSSIF Fadwa.

DALAL Leave her, just leave her!

EMIR Why are you yelling?

DALAL Maybe she doesn't want to talk to him!

EMIR We can't just let her sit there and waste away!

HAYAT Ok, everyone, just. Let's try to get along.

DALAL I don't want to get along. I don't want get along.

(The phone rings.)

EMIR *(On phone)* Mama, good news? Excuse me? Oh, Shalom. I'm sorry sir, what did you say—

(Lights shift. On one corner of the stage, BABA of FADWA's memory emerges, as EMIR speaks on the phone. Characters are still, except BABA.)

BABA To appreciate God's great bounty, simply look, Fadwa, at the blessed olive tree. Its very branches a symbol for peace, its fruit a holy gift.

(Illustrating with his hands.)

BABA You see, there is a wide sort of tube that runs down the length of the trunk; it contracts and expands, pumping sap through the trunk and the branches, giving the tree life. Do you understand, Foo Foo? The tree has a heart. That tube serves as its heart. What is a heart but the center of a man's compassion and capacity for love? A tree loves. It has compassion for man. It gives us its breath so that we may live; teaches us to be rooted and steadfast and gives shelter to all who seek it...

EMIR Where? I see. Thank you very much, sir, for the call.

(EMIR hangs up.)

BABA To seize an ancient olive tree is like a confiscation of memory...

(BABA of FADWA's memory exits and the lights fade.)

EMIR They found your father. I'm so sorry.

(DALAL runs into the back bedroom.)

EMIR Dalal!

(EMIR exits. HAYAT exits. YOUSSIF kneels next to FADWA.)

YOUSSIF Fadwa.

FADWA He went to find his trees...so he could remember...

YOUSSIF What do you mean? Fadwa?

(SAMIA approaches gently.)

FADWA He went to his trees...

AUNTIE SAMIA That's right, *habibti,* he did. *(to YOUSSIF)* You can't imagine what it was like. Tanks and bulldozers surrounded his groves. It was harvest time—we were all there. It's a celebration—you know how we've done this for generations. We stood and watched as the army uprooted every tree. There was no reason, or warning. Just...waste. The soldiers told us to go, but my brother wouldn't move. He is very stubborn...very strong. But when he came home, he just sat in this chair...just staring.

He didn't speak. When he finally did, weeks later, it was to ask where he was…He left to try to remember.

(SAMIA shakes her head sadly and exits. FADWA starts to cry.)

YOUSSIF I'm sorry, I wish I was here…*ya Allah*…I'm so sorry…

(YOUSSIF holds FADWA and slowly aides her off-stage. The electricity returns bringing the home out of darkness. The lights shift as the front door opens, the indication being the family has been to the funeral. DALAL and EMIR carry olive tree saplings and place them around the house, then quietly exit. SAMIA and HAYAT enter with flowers, setting them down. HAYAT clears a few things and exits. SAMIA exits through the backdoor.)

Scene 2

Lights up as FADWA enters, carrying trays of food. Enter HAYAT.

HAYAT You know, I cook to feel better too, sometimes.

FADWA I'm just arranging. This is all from Youssif's family, and some other neighbors.

HAYAT I don't know how they managed it. Just two days ago no one had anything. Can I help?

(FADWA nods and the two silently arrange food together.)

HAYAT My mom was so happy to hear he passed peacefully.

FADWA It was good to talk to her.

HAYAT It made her feel like she was with us.

(Enter DALAL in black.)

DALAL I think I packed everything I own. Hayat, you're sure about the flight?

HAYAT Everything's taken care of sweetie—the airline rebooked our flights no problem.

DALAL I wish we had more time…tomorrow feels too fast…

HAYAT I'll help you finish packing.

(HAYAT exits.)

FADWA Dalal?

DALAL It's just so many things at once.

FADWA In six months, you'll come back and we'll have the wedding and I'll make you the most beautiful feast…

DALAL Maybe we should stay—Emir can figure something out, we can live here with you—

FADWA Oh, please, you two will drive me crazy! No, you have to go.

(Re-enter HAYAT carrying three packages of maxi-pads.)

HAYAT Sweetie, are you serious? Are you opening a drug store? There are ten more in her suitcase!

(DALAL, FADWA and HAYAT begin laughing.)

DALAL Stop it! What if they don't have them?

HAYAT What do you think, that we all sit around on towels in a red tent?

DALAL No, I mean that's my brand!

(EMIR and YOUSSIF enter. YOUSSIF carries a paper bag.)

EMIR *Bonjour* lovely ladies.

YOUSSIF *Marhaba.*

DALAL Ok, put them away, *willy!*

YOUSSIF Put what away?

EMIR Oh you won't be needing those for much longer. I plan on keeping you pregnant for at least ten years.

DALAL Oh hush!

HAYAT I am not letting you pack these!

EMIR See? She's on my side.

DALAL You still can't touch me for another 6 months!

EMIR Oh, no, no, no. In America, we don't need the marriage part! That's why we're going!

(EMIR, HAYAT and DALAL exit.)

YOUSSIF These are some of your father's things. *(Out of the paper bag he removes BABA's tabla.)* He was holding it, beside the tree, where they found him. That's what they said.

FADWA Keep it.

YOUSSIF No, no.

FADWA It was yours to begin with.

(YOUSSIF takes the tabla.)

YOUSSIF I looked up to your father… I loved him very much.

FADWA He loved you too.

YOUSSIF What's holding you here, Fadwa? You're free to go anywhere now…

FADWA This is home. And someone has to find a home for these little trees.

(They look at the plants and trees.)

YOUSSIF Yes. Someone does. Well, we leave early so…

(YOUSSIF opens his arms and FADWA goes to him.)

YOUSSIF You're my best friend.

FADWA You're mine too.

YOUSSIF *Habibit elbe, inti.* **[You are the love of my life.]**

(She releases him from the embrace, and touches his face. YOUSSIF exits. FADWA turns to the audience.)

FADWA Thank you for tuning in to the final episode of *Food and Fadwa, Ecklit il Hob.* We have had quite the gastronomic journey! Right, Mike? Don't be upset, you'll find another job! If you cannot say goodbye, you cannot have a new hello. My father used to say that for a new tree to grow, it must be planted in a clean, fertile field, free from rotting roots, trunks or weeds. Once it grows and takes full root, you'll have served it well. When its leaves fall and its trunk begins to rot…let it die with dignity. Say goodbye with grace, and then, begin again. So long, sweet friends, and may you have a safe and blessed journey. Remember, no matter what you eat, the most important food of all is *ecklit'il hob.* The food of love.

(Lights down on FADWA as she takes a plant, unwraps it, and plants it in the earth.)

Dionna Michelle Daniel

Biography

Dionna Michelle Daniel is a new American playwright, actress, and vocalist from Winston–Salem, North Carolina. A strong-willed, passionate artist with southern charm, she blends her love of poetry and song into her plays. As a true southern girl who spent most of her life in northwestern North Carolina, her writing tells stories of home. Her work addresses social and political issues surrounding the African-American experience and exposes the viewer to the purveying social injustices and inequalities permeating our community. Although her work focuses on Black bodies and Black voices, her powerful voice and nuanced  words are felt from people of all backgrounds. She believes in education through art, and in its power to reach hearts and change minds indefinitely. Her goal is not to offer solutions, but to pose many questions in hopes of starting a dialogue with her audience. For the past four summers, she has returned to Winston–Salem, North Carolina, working as the presentation development specialist for the Authoring Action organization, where she mentors youth in spoken word poetry and performance. Dionna is currently pursuing a bachelor of fine arts in acting from California Institute of the Arts (Class of 2017) with a minor in creative writing. At CalArts, she serves as the artistic director of the Black Arts Collective. She also graduated from the competitive high school program at the University of North Carolina School of the Arts with a concentration in acting. She attributes all her accomplishments to her loving parents Ray and Francina Daniel who have supported her every step of the way.

Artistic statement

Every human being has a moment when their soul cries, "Enough is enough!" *Gunshot Medley* was the product of one of those moments. While staying with my parents in North Carolina during the summer of 2015, I watched racial tensions fester in the South after the Charleston church massacre. As the news of these nine deaths played across my television screen, my body began to overflow with an array of emotions. Each life of another African-American person that has been lost to racism and police brutality reopens the wound of grief Black America has endured for centuries. While their nine faces flashed on CNN, I was shattered. I was angry. I was broken. Enough was enough, but I didn't know what I could do. Where was I supposed to channel my pain in times of intense mourning?

During that time, I vividly recall the fury in my bones when white men rode up and down my street with huge Confederate flags hoisted onto the backs of their pick-up trucks. The Confederate flags that some Southerners kept tucked away in closets, chests, and attics due to shame were now proudly displayed on porches and flag poles all throughout North Carolina. However, this was nothing new. All throughout my life, the Confederate flag was made visible in many different ways. It is just that after Charleston, my instances of encountering this symbol of racism and ignorant pride tripled.

One day while visiting one of the oldest cemeteries in Winston-Salem, North Carolina, I came across a segregated graveyard that housed the bodies of both African-American slaves and white Confederate soldiers. The section where the Confederate soldiers were buried was well kept while the slaves' graves were hidden from view. In the slave section, there were three tombstones with the names Betty, Alvis, and George. All that was left were their first names and the dates of their deaths. All of the deaths preceded the Emancipation Proclamation. The moment I saw those names and dates etched into stone, my soul knew I must tell their stories.

My goal is to reconstruct the way in which the slave narrative is told, showing another perspective of what it means to be black in America. It is a call to action. It is an illustration of a mother's love for her children. It is a story of many generations and the perseverance of the human spirit. To my black brothers and sisters, I want to offer hope to you and our generations to come. We must honor the lives that have been lost to hatred, racism, and police brutality throughout the span of America's history. This is for the ancestors, the newly departed and the ones who have always been looking over us.

Production history

Gunshot Medley premiered April 29, 2016 at the CalArts New Works Festival. Collaborators involved in the New Works workshop production of *Gunshot Medley* included: Dionna Michelle Daniel (writer, director, High Priestess of Souls), Amandla Jahava (Betty), Patrick Bucknor (Alvis), Darius Booker (George), Sam Sewell (Sound Design & Music Director), Chardonnay Napier (Costume Design), Marcus Doyle (Scenic Design), Victor Murillo (Lighting Design), Baily Johnson (Stage Manager), and a four man folk band consisting of Elias Pearlstein, Kris Rahamad, Devin Burgenbauch, and Tanner Polednak. *Gunshot Medley* is currently being developed into a full-length play.

8 *Gunshot Medley*
Dionna Michelle Daniel

Characters

BETTY Twenties, the one who cleans the mess.
ALVIS Late teens, the one who unearths that which is stained.
GEORGE Early thirties, the one who dreams while awake.
HIGH PRIESTESS OF SOULS The wind, incarnate of the Yoruban Orisha Oya.

Setting

The Hereafter

Playwright's notes

All music must be played with a live band. The band must include an African drum, a banjo, a violin and a double bass. Italicized lines indicate songs. All lyrics included within the script are American folk songs/spirituals and are within public domain. The four characters listed must be played by black actors. The use of names with blank spaces signifies that something profound is bubbling within the emotional lives of the characters. The director and actors should discover what actions fill those spaces.

Punctuation notes

//: Indicates dialogue entry of following character

Scene 1

The stage is blanketed in dirt. Far in the distance lies the graveyard. The gates to the cemetery lie on the other side. The sun is fixed right below the horizon. Band plays instrumental of "My Country Tis' of Thee." BETTY, alone, scrubs the ground. She wrings the cloth. Rustle of the wind. HIGH PRIESTESS OF SOULS enters and hums along with the band. HIGH PRIESTESS positions herself between the band and the actors. She presides over the Hereafter, a land of perpetual twilight.

Gunshot Medley.

(BETTY drops to her knees and scrubs. ALVIS enters running.)

ALVIS Betty! Betty! Betty girl!

BETTY Alvis quit ya hollerin'. You tryin' to raise the dead?

ALVIS Betty girl, you so silly. Raise the dead? You of all people know the dead don't need raisin'. They around all the time. Every time I hear the wind, that scary kind of wind that whistles and makes the leaves shake. That scary kind of wind you hear in autumn time. When I hear it, I know the souls are rustlin' and they ain't sleep no more. And when I hear music, that good type of music that rattles my bones to the center. Ya know the kind I'm talkin' about! Whenever I hear good music, I know the dead can't stay dead for long without wantin' to dance.

(ALVIS grooves.)

ALVIS The dead can't stay dead. They just gettin' a little shut eye for a second.

BETTY Well just keep it down. I don't want to hear George mouth today. You want to make him mad again?

ALVIS I ain't scared of George! What he gonna do? He all talk and no show.

BETTY That's what you said last time before he kicked your ass and left you in that plot.

ALVIS I lost my footin' and fell.

BETTY Mmmhmm. Well, what you hollerin' about this time Alvis? You found somethin' new out in the yard?

ALVIS Yes ma'am! Nothin' much but...

(ALVIS pulls out a toy gun.)

ALVIS Put your hands up where I can see 'em. Pow Pow!

BETTY What the fuck Alvis! What the hell is your problem?

ALVIS *(Laughing.)* You so funny Betty! This just a little toy. A child's gun. It ain't gonna do nothin'.

BETTY It ain't the gun, it's the fact you didn't warn me or nothin'. You don't play games like that with people.

ALVIS I'm sorry. Just a joke...Pow Pow!

BETTY ...

ALVIS But I brought it back because I want you to clean it for me. Look at the stains.

BETTY Nah Alvis. I'm through with you today, scarin' me like that. You funny honey.

ALVIS I said I was sorry.

BETTY Nope.

ALVIS Please Betty! It's my new toy. I can play cowboys and Indians. Cops and robbers. I'll catch all the bad guys. Wipe it clean for me.

BETTY Fine, as long as you don't pull that mess again.

(BETTY wipes the toy gun. BETTY sees.)

BETTY

ALVIS

ALVIS You looking real sick Betty.

BETTY Alvis?

ALVIS Yes.

BETTY Go bury it.

ALVIS But—

BETTY That was a child's gun but...

ALVIS But what?

BETTY Just go bury it.

ALVIS But—

BETTY !

ALVIS ...Ok Betty.

(ALVIS leaves. Rustle of the wind. HIGH PRIESTESS OF SOULS hums. BETTY caresses her rag. Enter GEORGE.)

GEORGE Betty girl, you still cleanin' things that boy brings in from the graveyards?

BETTY Sometimes. I tell him to go back and bury the things he don't need to be holdin' onto. I tell him to bury the stained ones. He been wanderin' too far nowadays. I'm scared he'll find somethin' out there and start rememberin'. But he always come back though. Always excited when he find somethin'. Always as loud as can be. He wake you up from that long nap you've been takin'?

GEORGE You know good and well don't nobody sleep round here.

BETTY Well I ain't seen you at your post in a while, so I thought you was sleepin' for good. Thought you was dead dead but I guess—

GEORGE Betty, I quit!

BETTY Quit what?

GEORGE My post. I ain't ever goin' back again.

BETTY How you just gonna quit?

GEORGE Because I just said so.

BETTY You lost your mind? You can't quit now. Everythin's all shook up over there. I know you feel it in the air.

GEORGE If I don't quit now, when should I? It'll all go on forever. Day after day. Month after month. Yes, I feel it in the air. I hear it. The wind's singin' and I'm listenin'. That's why I'm quittin'. Betty, I've got to change folk! The bodies keep pilin' up. You keep doin' your job. Alvis keeps doin' his. It never stops.

BETTY George, you doin' good work here. Where's your lamp? Go get it. Who's gonna be the one to lead 'em home? You know what I said bout my mama. Wise woman she was. She used to say the ancestors be the ones to look after those on earth and those who tryin' to pass to the other side.

GEORGE You think this is what she was talkin' about? Look at you! Ain't you tired? Tired of scrubbin'? Tired of wastin' time? I'm quittin' to change somethin'. I was at my post the other day and the wind was rustlin' in the treetops. I heard the wind sing to me and I floated off in what felt like a dream. You know how I miss dreams. Dreamin', wakin' up with brand new eyes. Ain't dreamed in a long time but the other day it was as if I was dreamin' while awake. I saw these folks and they was workin' and it wasn't none of the labor we was used to doin'. It was the back breakin' kind. And in my dream this one man rose up from the rest and he had a loud voice like the crackle of thunder. He spoke and the people heard him and they rebelled against their captors. Then the wind whispered to me and she proclaimed it was a vision of the past. It had all been done before. So it can be done now and I'mma do that! Gonna make my way back and lead.

BETTY Mmmhmm.

GEORGE You think I can't do it?!

BETTY Didn't say nothing. Just said mmmhmm.

(Rustle of the wind.)

HIGH PRIESTESS *Steal away, steal away, steal away to Jesus*
Steal away, steal away home
I ain't got long to steal away
My Lord, He calls me
He calls me by the thunder
The trumpet sounds within-a my soul//
I ain't got long to stay here

GEORGE You hear it Betty? You hear the wind? She sounding real pretty and I can feel something comin'. I'm gonna help deliver it!

(Gunshot Medley. GEORGE snaps out of his daydream and leaves. BETTY drops to her knees and scrubs.)

BETTY George?

(Rustle of the wind.)

Scene 2

The sun is still fixed in its same position, as always. BETTY scrubs. She wrings the cloth. She caresses the cloth. Rustle of the wind.

HIGH PRIESTESS *Children, go where I send thee,/ How shall I send thee?/ I'm gonna send thee one by one/ One for the little bitty - baby/ Born, born, born in Bethlehem./ Children, go where I send thee,*

BETTY *How shall I send thee?*

HIGH PRIESTESS *I'm gonna send thee two by two/ Two for Paul and – Silas/ One for the little bitty - baby/ Born, born, born in Bethlehem.*

HIGH PRIESTESS and BETTY *Children, go where I send thee,/ How shall I send thee?/ I'm gonna send thee/ three by three/ Three for the Hebrew children/ Two for Paul and Silas/ One for the little bitty - baby/ Born, born, born in Bethlehem./ Born, born, born in Bethlehem.*

BETTY Little brown baby,/ If this land were mine/ I'd crown you sole empress of the land,/ prince of this kingdom./ Itty bitty baby,/ with skin baked in the grit,/ the soil of Africa mixed with Carolina clay./ Brown baby,/ Rattlin' feet that danced inside of me,/ I got to learn how to craft a bullet-proof child,/ a warrior child./ Baby, they using your skin for target practice/ but you are magic in my eyes./ A mother's eyes./ A mother's hands./ A mother's womb./ I lay down the foundation for you,/ clear and clean the land for you to walk on solid ground./ Won't let no one tear you down!/ The love you stand on is solid ground.

(Two Gunshots. BETTY drops to her knees and scrubs. ALVIS enters running.)

ALVIS Betty! Betty! Got somethin' for you Betty! And I sho' did like the song you was singin'.

BETTY What you got Alvis?

ALVIS It ain't much. Something real small but I think it's beautiful. Look how pretty this paper is. Look at all the colors.

BETTY Skittles?

ALVIS Nah, I think you pronounce it skeee-tles. It was lyin' beside this tin can that read Arizona but the can wasn't as pretty. It didn't have all the colors of the rainbow, so I left it out there in the dirt. Can you clean it Betty?

BETTY It's a piece of paper and it's stained.

ALVIS I know it's stained. Why you think I brought it for you to clean?

BETTY It's not worth cleanin'.

ALVIS But it's so pretty…

BETTY Don't give me them eyes.

ALVIS …

BETTY Go now!

ALVIS …

BETTY Damn!

(She wipes the Skittles wrapper. BETTY sees.)

ALVIS What's wrong?

BETTY

ALVIS You seein' somethin'?

BETTY Go bury it Alvis.

ALVIS But—

BETTY Go back to the yard and bury it.

ALVIS I will, but—

BETTY Not today. I'm tired and my heart's heavy.

ALVIS But you always say your heart's heavy.

BETTY 'Cus it is. Now go!

ALVIS I will, I will. But before I leave I got somethin' else for you. Guess what I heard down in the yard? I picked up this new song. I swear music always be gettin' better and better as time passes.

(ALVIS sings a funk love song like Mary Jane by Rick James.)

ALVIS Make me wanna dance. Them songs about love put me straight in my feelings. You know *Rollin' in My Sweet Baby's Arms*?

BETTY Nah.

ALVIS *Well, I ain't gonna work on the railroad/ I ain't gonna work on the farm/ I'll lay around the shack/ Till the mail train comes back/ And roll in my sweet baby's arms./ Well, I'm rollin' in my sweet baby's arms/ Rollin' in my sweet baby's arms/ Lay around the shack/ Till the mail train comes back/ Then I'll roll in my sweet baby's arms./ Well, now where were you last Saturday night/ While I was a lyin' in jail/ Hey, you're walkin' the streets with another man/ Wouldn't even go my bail./ Well, I'm rollin' in my sweet baby's arms/ Rollin' in my sweet baby's arms/ Lay around the shack/ Till the mail train comes back/ I'll roll in my sweet baby's arms.* Love is the only thing that lasts. That and music, and when you hear good music you start dancin', so I guess you could say dancin' lasts forever too. Music is home. It like a warm coat. You slip it over you in the winter time and it feels quite good. Bein' in the middle of music feels real good. And love feels good. And *lovin'* feels even better. All of them you can't see but you sho' can feel. Just like the wind. And the wind is music to my ears. And music… I'm goin' in circles. Betty, why you ain't stop me?

BETTY I liked what you was sayin'.

ALVIS Sho' nuff?

BETTY Mmmhmm.

ALVIS Well, I like that you liked what I was sayin'. I like that you listen to me. Unlike George. Matter of fact, where is George? I ain't seen him in what it feels like a month.

BETTY Yesterday. A month. A year. It all the same here.

(GEORGE enters defeated. He is dressed in all black, militant attire.)

ALVIS Speak of the black devil himself. George! Hey George! (*Laughing.*) Look at them clothes you got there George! Don't you look nice. Know what, I got a song for you! *"Oh, what brings you here so late?" said the knight on the road.*
"I go to meet my God," said the child as he stood.
And he stood and he stood.
And it's well that he stood.//
"I go to meet my God," said the child as he stood.

GEORGE Alvis, shut it.

ALVIS That song about a lil boy meetin' the devil who's dressed up as a knight—

GEORGE Alvis, not today—

ALVIS (*Laughing*) George you black! You black as night! George, that song about you!

BETTY Stop tellin' corny jokes. What's wrong with you George? You don't look how you left.

GEORGE Betty, I stood there. I stood and petitioned and yelled and hollered and proclaimed. I exhaled all my dreams to them so they could breathe with new eyes. Stood on them New York streets, each corner of Harlem. I stretched out my voice for miles and miles. I went back with the sole purpose to lead my people but days turned to months and months drifted into years and people were listenin' but no one actually heard what I was sayin'.

BETTY What was you sayin' to them?

GEORGE Go back! Get as far away from this land as possible and stay away. Hop on a boat, plane, swim, goddamn, sprout wings for all I care, just get out! How do we ever expect to be free here? There has to be an Exodus. We should be given our own nation. Our own land.

ALVIS To tell you the truth, forty acres and a mule didn't help no one George.

GEORGE Not land here! Land back home!

BETTY Home?

GEORGE Africa!

ALVIS That ain't my home. It ain't your home either. George, you don't even know what Africa looks like.

GEORGE I seen it in past dreams, land of my ancestors.

ALVIS That don't mean it's your home. This is your home. This soil is where they laid your bones.

GEORGE My home ain't a place where I don't belong.

ALVIS Sure you belong. You got country bumpkin written all over you. You got Appalachian folk music flowin' through your veins. It's all up in your DNA. Tobacco and cotton. Sweet tea and humidity. You so country it ain't even funny. You just feelin' stuck. Stuck and tryin' to build a bridge across the water—

BETTY Basically George, it sound like what you were preachin' ain't what the people wanted to hear. It ain't what they need.

GEORGE But that wasn't the only time I went back. Y'all know, I'm not one to give up so easily. Big dreams I got, though my eyes are weary from no sleep. I made new plans. "My people take up some guns," I said. "Arm yourselves," I said. Goin' back all them times taught me that if you want to be heard, you got to make a lot of noise or no one listens. But even when they listenin', I'm not sure if they heard it. Better go back to my post now, huh? Better go light my lamp and—

(Rustle of the wind. HIGH PRIESTESS hums.)

BETTY

ALVIS

GEORGE

GEORGE There she goes again. Ain't failed me yet! Gonna make em' see with brand new eyes. See y'all on the other side.

(GEORGE leaves.)

ALVIS George! George—

BETTY Don't try wakin' him up from that dream. Don't want him to trip and fall.

ALVIS Guess that explain why it feel like I ain't seen him in a month.

BETTY A few hours. A month. A year. It's all the same here.

(Gunshot Medley. ALVIS hurries back to the graveyard. BETTY drops to her knees and scrubs.)

Scene 3

The sun, still in its same position. Twilight. BETTY scrubs. She wrings the cloth. She caresses the cloth. Rustle of the wind.

HIGH PRIESTESS : *I was standing by my window/ On one cold and cloudy day/ When I saw the hearse come rolling/ For to carry my mother away/ Will the circle be unbroken/ Bye and bye Lord, bye and bye/ There's a better home awaiting/ In the sky Lord, in the sky/ Oh, I followed*

close behind her/ Tried to hold up and be brave/ But I could not hide my sorrow/ When they laid her in the grave / Will the circle be unbroken/ Bye and bye Lord, bye and bye/ There's a better home awaiting/ In the sky Lord, in the sky.

BETTY Brown baby,/ Wish you would've met my mama./ Cornrow headed queen, crown of black kinks, fields of flowers for hair,/ earth woman with them tobacco stained hands./ Tobacco… tobacco…bacca…tobacco Rebecca./ Hear that name?/ Tobacco stains lingerin' on Rebecca's hands./ Brown baby,/ wish you would've met your auntie./ Onyx lady, obsidian lady, midnight lady with that star twinkle skin./ Rainclouds over the two of us./ The tears I shed when sissy was stolen from me./ Big mouth, sistah gal./ Shut your mouth, sistah gal./ Dumped your body in the river, sistah gal./ From fightin' back, sistah gal./ Didn't want him to touch her like that, sistah gal./ Flood in my heart when they fished her body out that river./ Sistah gal wouldn't shut her mouth./ When he touched her, she bit back./ They sent me away because they thought I'd bite back./ Snake sistah. Serpent sistah. Venom sistah./ They tried to silence you with the river's tides./ Dragon sistah. Phoenix sistah./ Full of fire, full of red./ Blood sistah, bleeding and bleeding/ each cycle the moon becomes whole again,/ womb breathing fire,/ bleeding and breathing./ Sistah gal, it was the two of us,/ but you were the wiser./ They've tried to extinguish our fire, sistah./ Brown baby,/ Grow fangs, sink in those teeth,/ And set fire to all you see.

(Two Gunshots. The ground shakes, the dead turning over in their graves. The band stomps feet to BETTY'S work song.)

BETTY Dig a hole dig a hole in the meadow/ Dig a hole in the cold cold ground/ Dig a hole dig a hole in the meadow/ Gonna lay darling Corey down.

(Gunshot Medley. BETTY scrubs. ALVIS enters running.)

ALVIS Betty! Betty! Betty! Got somethin' for ya!

BETTY Wipe all that chicken grease off your lips.

ALVIS You so funny girl! Always callin' me out and stuff. You remind me of the girl I loved once. Did I tell you her name?

BETTY You keep changin' her name each time.

ALVIS Ain't the name that matter's it's the feelin'. Listen! *Oh, once I lived in Old Virginny/ To North Carolina I did go/ There I saw a nice young lady/ Oh, her name I did not know/ Her hair was black and her eyes was sparkling/ On her cheeks were diamonds red/ And on her breast she wore a lily/ To mourn the tears that I have shed/ Oh, when I'm asleep I dream about her/ When I'm awake I see no rest/ Every moment seems like an hour/ Oh, the pains that cross my breast/ Oh Molly dear, go ask your mother/ If you my bride can ever be/ If she says no, come back and tell me/ And never more will I trouble thee*

BETTY That song ain't bout you or no girl you was in love with. You was born and bred in North Carolina. Name one street in Virginia! You ain't walked on one of 'em.

ALVIS Main Street.

BETTY Every city got a main street.

ALVIS Now look! It's a story about me and the girl I loved. It becomes my story when I sing it, especially if I put all of my feelins' in it. But I truly did love a girl and man, was she dark! Real black and real beautiful, and she was always callin' me out on the silliest things just like you do! Betty, how come you never talk about the man you loved? You must've been in love before you came to live with us.

BETTY Nah.

ALVIS Sure you was. Stop lyin'. You start grinnin' the moment the word love slides out my mouth. And that do be a lot.

BETTY More times than I can count.

ALVIS So, go ahead and spill it.

BETTY Well…there was one before I was sold to live with y'all.

ALVIS Go on…

(Rustle of the wind. The spell is cast. BETTY and ALVIS are rocked by the wind into the arms of their past loves. They grasp air.)

HIGH PRIESTESS : *Black is the colour of my true love's hair./ His face so soft and wondrous fair/ The purest eyes and the strongest hands/ I love the ground on where he stands/ I love my love and well he knows/ Yes I love the ground on where he goes/ And still I hope that the time will come/ When he and I will be as one/ Black is the color of my true love's hair/ Of my true love's hair/ Of my true love's hair.*

BETTY So yes. I know what love looks like, sound like, how it feel. His voice was honey, smooth and rich. He was not too tall, not too short. I'd see him from across the fields and we'd shoot looks at each other. And I imagined us free…in fields. Not tobacco fields but fields of flowers. Dandelions to be exact. The freest thing I ever did see was a dandelion scattered to the wind. All her body floatin' to wherever the breeze takes her, sproutin' new roots wherever she decided to land. I'd wish us in dandelion fields and like the flowers we'd be rescued by the wind… Oh god, let me stop.

ALVIS No, no, no, keep going, please!

BETTY Nah. You've heard enough. But go on, you brought somethin' for me I'd reckon. Somethin' to clean?

ALVIS No, not to clean.

BETTY That's a first.

ALVIS This time I brought things to show you.

BETTY Ok?

(Instrumental of a song like Kendrick Lamar's "Alright" begins to play. ALVIS dances a popular dance move like the Soulja Boy.)

ALVIS Oh and this one!

(ALVIS does the dab.)

BETTY : You look so funny!

ALVIS What you talkin' bout? I look good. Damn, I swear music gets better and better each year. And the dance moves Betty! I picked up these moves down in the yard. Heard the wind rustlin' and singin' these new tunes. And I heard this song that said "Nigga, we gon' be alright!"

(ALVIS grooves to the music and sings along.)

ALVIS You can't deny it. That's some good shit.

BETTY *(Grinning.)* Mmmhmmm.

ALVIS But I found something else out there.

BETTY Ok?

ALVIS Well I, I was down by the other… well, it's small but it—

BETTY I don't have all day.

(ALVIS whips out a Confederate flag.)

BETTY Nigga, why'd you bring that here?

ALVIS Now don't be mad but guess where I found it?

BETTY I don't care where you found it? Why'd you bring that here?

ALVIS I found it in the yard but on the other side of the graveyard, by our graves. Not on our graves, but pretty damn close. It was planted on the graves of the white Confederate soldiers. Did you know someone planted bushes near us Betty? I'll be out walkin' for miles, days at a time, but I don't ever go by our graves. I promise. Ain't been on that side of the graveyard in a while but today I did. Had to hop over a bush to get to our tombstones. We're hidden behind the trees and leaves and bushes. Don't be mad that I went over there Betty. I know you said not to but I had to. Just look at it! It's brand new. A little dirty, but it's not stained. Look at it! Can you believe someone still honors them? Someone still believes in Dixie. Dixie ain't dead. Not here in the South. Dixie ain't ever been dead. This whole country is Dixie. The stars and stripes just the rebel flag with make-up on her face.

BETTY Alvis, I told you to stop goin' out to our graves. Last time you bout lost your mind. Started mutterin' things. Left your post. Started talkin' crazy. You know what happens when you start rememberin'.

ALVIS I was only obeyin' the orders of the wind. I heard her singin' a real sad song about a church and a congregation.

(Gunshot 1. Rustle of the wind.)

HIGH PRIESTESS *Here in the Vineyard of my Lord*
I hope to live and labor,
And be obedient to my God
Until my dying hour.
I love to see the lilies grow//
And view them all a standing
Here n the right place while here below,
Just as the Lord commanded.

ALVIS And then the thunder came, said the wind and the congregation was no more. Nothin' but gunshots and blood. And as she was singin', I saw it all so vividly.
They let the devil into the church but they didn't know. Like that song I told George about.

(Gunshot 2.)

HIGH PRIESTESS *We ofttimes meet both night and day, //*
A faithful band of pilgrims;
We read, we sing, we preach and pray,
And find the Lord most precious

ALVIS The devil prayed with them. They welcomed him with love. How could they have known? Then the ringin'… the ringin'…. they were all gone. No more congregation.

(Gunshot 3)

HIGH PRIESTESS *But while we sing this song of love*
Our hearts are deeply wounded, //

Perhaps we all may meet no more
Here in a congregation.

ALVIS South of here, cross the border, the wind told me about the ringin'…

(Gunshot 4.)

HIGH PRIESTESS …*(Hums.)*

ALVIS The ringin'…the ringin' by the coast. A ringin' in Charleston. I heard it, bitter melody, and when it hit my ears somethin' broke inside of me.

HIGH PRIESTESS …*(Hums.)*

(Gunshot 5.)

BETTY I heard it too. Nasty melody in my ear. I just don't know if anyone on the other side heard it.

HIGH PRIESTESS …*(Hums.)*

(Gunshot 6.)

BETTY I heard the cries. I heard the ringin'. I hear it all the time. It's just that this one reminded me how much it all hurts my soul. My heart is so heavy.

(Gunshot 7.)

HIGH PRIESTESS : *But if on earth we meet no more, / I hope we'll meet in heaven, / Where congregation ne're break up, / But dwell in sweet communion. / Where all the ransomed church of God/ Shall meet no more to sever, / With not a sorrow, pain nor tear, / sing one sweet chord forever*

(Gunshot 8 and Gunshot 9.)

BETTY
ALVIS

(ALVIS hums along with High Priestess.)

ALVIS Reminds me of us. Remember it Betty?

BETTY Alvis, you feelin' some type of way?

ALVIS Feelin' fine but….somethin' inside me…. somethin's broke…

(ALVIS hums.)

BETTY Alvis, get rid of that flag and stay away from our graves. Alvis, snap out of —

ALVIS I'm fine! Every now and then I like to see where my bones lay.

(ALVIS hums.)

ALVIS The sun's been setting for a mighty long time. But no night. Never night. Remember what stars and the moon look like Betty? I don't.

BETTY Alvis, no need to be rememberin' right now. Go back to your post and bury that flag.

(ALVIS hums.)

BETTY I know you heard me Alvis!

ALVIS The dead can't stay dead for long, Betty. I've never been dead dead. Neither you or George. Always been stuck in the space between. Here in the twilight. Always hearin' the ringin'. Always the diggin'. Always the wipin' and scrubbin'. Always been stuck. Remember us? Remember what it was like to be alive? Remember what it felt like to sleep. Remember what it felt like to love? Remember what it felt like to eat? To get beat? To be spat at? To be poked and touched and branded? Remember when I untied your body from the post Betty? All that red spilled. Remember being tied to the whippin' post? Remember them beatin' that first baby out of you? Remember?

BETTY Don't bring that up now. My heart's already heavy. I don't want to think about them right now—

ALVIS My heart's heavy too! Cold and turned to stone. I ain't diggin' graves no more! You can't keep buryin' these things.

BETTY You see me buryin' anythin'? I'm not buryin' nothin'. I clean it all up.

ALVIS You scrubbin' but nothin's been cleaned! You blind? Nah, you just ain't rememberin'? Remember George's body? I remember George's body. I remember takin' him down from that tree. Eyes bulgin' from his sockets! Rage festerin' inside me! Remember when I gave birth to my anger and they hung me from that very same tree? Remember Betty? Remember bein' the last one of us alive? No one there to protect you. I wanted to be there for you. I said to myself, the next time they did those horrible things to you, I'd kill them all. But I was dead and gone. Witnessin'. Watchin'. What more could I do? And I watched the red spill everywhere. I watched you get beat till your heart gave out. That's why I can no longer bring myself to see. I ain't stupid and I ain't blind. I choose not to see. 'Cus I watched till that dead child flowed out of you—

BETTY Alvis stop speaking all of this! My heart is heavy—

ALVIS Flowed out of your butchered body. All that red. Two dead babies you never got to raise, Betty! Remember? And remember him? How those babies came to be? How that white man used your body and then beat you for bringin' life into the world. Remember how you told me that same type of thing happened to your sister and that's why

you were sold to live with us? Remember? No respect for yawls bodies! No respect! Y'all think Alvis all fun and games but when I start rememberin'—

(BETTY is broken.)

ALVIS Betty?

BETTY

BETTY

ALVIS I'm sorry. I really am. Don't cry. I'm not tryin' to hurt you. Never would I hurt you. I just wish I could've been there for you like I had for George. Since I couldn't be there for you, I got to find a way to be there for the others, the ones still livin' who're already stuck and don't even know it. Betty, don't cry. Listen to the wind. Hear her? See, we gon' be alright. We gon' be alright! Listen Betty. Don't you cry. There's something more than this. More to life than this. More to death than this. Buryin' ain't helpin' no one. Scrubbin' ain't either. There's somethin' else out there. I got to go Betty girl. Justice is callin'.

(ALVIS leaves on a mission.)

BETTY Alvis? Alvis! You and George can't leave me here alone.

(Gunshot Medley. BETTY drops to her knees and scrubs. She stands and wrings the cloth. Gunshot Medley. BETTY drops to her knees and scrubs. The gunshots are continuous, fireworks. BETTY scrubs trying to clean all the red. As she wipes the dirt, she begins to uncover bits of a large stained Confederate flag buried under the same soil she's been scrubbing this entire time. Transfixed, she names those who have passed while she scrubs.)

BETTY Jesse Washington. Emmmett Till. Kimani Gray. Ousmane "Monte" Zongo. Ramarley Graham. James Brissette. Malcolm Ferguson. Rekia Boyd. Malissa Williams. Tarika Wilson. Dakota Bright. Manny Loggins. Everybody's somebody's child. Everybody's somebody's child. Jesse Thorton. Tyisha Miller. Timothy Russell.….

(Obsessively, she says the names as she scrubs. Rustle of Wind. HIGH PRIESTESS hums, casting her spell. The ground shakes. Twilight begins to fade into night. The past and present all coincide at the same time. Rustle of the wind. The band strikes up "My Country Tis' of Thee." GEORGE enters in a suit. He stands elevated. Fireworks. Gunshot Medley.)

GEORGE *(Reminiscent of Martin Luther King Jr.'s "I Have A Dream Speech.")* I'm here today in hopes that this meeting of sister and brotherhood will go down as one of the greatest demonstrations of unity this country has ever seen. Today I am here because it is more than evident that the descendants of African slaves in this country have never been free. It is evident that although they toiled in the smoldering heat and their children toiled in that heat, and although their children's children toiled, not once have reparations been paid. I come here today with a deep sorrow in my soul. The sorrow of centuries of mothers' tears. Centuries of fathers' anguish. I stand here while the streets are littered with the blood of a mother's child, while the leaders of this great nation refuse to acknowledge the epidemic at hand. The expendability of black life that is sweeping the nation. This epidemic is nothing new. It has been here since the nation's inception. The birth of this nation was a complete seizure. We live on a pirate's land. Looted and stolen from the native peoples whose roots were long erected here millennia ago. We populate a country that once profited from earthly crops such as sugarcane, cotton, and tobacco. Now we have traded in those crops for an industrial crop. The gun. We inhabit a country whose bread and butter is the formation, implementation and clean up of wars. The profit of artillery...of bullets...of rifles. My people, I wish to say let freedom ring from the hilltops, from the valleys and from the mountainsides but when you live within the borders of a pirate's nation, how can you ever be free? Safe? There is a ringing throughout this country. Do you hear the gunshot medley? Do you? Do you hear the beckoning of the wind? She sang me a lullaby and rocked my soul to sleep last night. And last night I had a dream. After all these years and decades and centuries, I finally dreamed again. I shut my eyes and dreamed of all the peoples. Not just the black ones of this land but all of them. They all woke up with brand new eyes and they breathed fire onto their chains. The system crumbled like the walls of Jericho. I had a dream that all of us set fire to this land and in the ashes was love. A wise friend of mine

believed that love was the only thing that lasts. A dear friend that in life and death sang nothing but songs of love, for what weapon can survive in a land built of the foundations of love. It is solid ground. So I know you may not hear me. I know you don't hear me. But at least you're listening. At least you're listening.

(He descends the steps. Gunshot. He's pinned against the wall. A shadow of a noose is casted behind him. GEORGE is dead dead. BETTY continues scrubbing, the names becoming louder, the Confederate flag becoming more visible.)

BETTY Alton Sterling. John Crawford. Oscar Grant. Michael Brown. Akai Gurley. Sean Bell. Tamir Rice. Aiyana Stanley-Jones. Patrick Dorismond. Timothy Stansbury. Everybody's somebody's child. Everybody's somebody's child. Joel Acevedo. Kendrec Mc Dade...

(ALVIS enters running. He wears modern clothes such as jeans, sneakers, and a hoodie. He carries a gun and a bloody American flag. He shows BETTY what he's accomplished. She doesn't see him. She is transfixed in her task. He sees GEORGE'S body. He sees the noose. ALVIS tries to wake GEORGE but GEORGE is dead dead.)

ALVIS

ALVIS

ALVIS

(ALVIS points gun at audience. Gunshot. He falls to his knees, drops gun and raises both hands in surrender. Gunshot. He freezes. ALVIS is dead dead.)

BETTY Eric Garner. Philando Castille. Ezell Ford. Corey Harris. Darrien Hunt. Roshad McIntosh. Everybody's somebody's child. Everybody's somebody's child. I'm tired. Brown baby, I'll always love you with all the love I could ever give but my soul's tired. This ain't my mess to clean. But, you gon' be alright. You hear that? The wind. She singin' me a lullaby. Time to rest. Time to dream. Goodnight, baby. Night.

(She begins to leave her post. She drops cloth. Gunshot.)

Blackout.

Tammy Haili'ōpua Baker

Biography

Tammy Haili'ōpua Baker is a Hawaiian Language perpetuator via the medium of the stage as an ultimate metaphor for traditional culture's transcendence into the fast-evolving western world. Her works have been produced locally and toured internationally, the most recent being *Lā'ieikawai*, the inaugural Hawaiian theatre production at Kennedy Theatre at University of Hawai'i at Mānoa (UHM). She has been consistently recognized as Hawai'i's most culturally progressive playwright, nearly sweeping the Hawai'i State Theatre Council's Po'okela Awards in 2015 and selling out Kennedy and Hawai'i Theatre at record rates. As an associate professor in the Department of Theatre and Dance at UHM, Baker is the director of Hana Keaka, the new Hawaiian Theatre program, focused on perpetuating traditional *mo'olelo* (stories, history) via modern theatre. Her work centers on the development of an indigenous Hawaiian theatre aesthetic and form, Hawaiian language revitalization, and the empowerment of cultural identity through stage performance. In addition to advocating for the elevation of Hawaiian performance practices, she also teaches courses in Pacific and Indigenous theatre and playwriting. Baker is the artistic director of Ka Hālau Hanakeaka, a Hawaiian medium theatre troupe. Originally from Kapa'a, Kaua'i, she now resides in Kahalu'u, Ko'olaupoko, O'ahu.

Artistic statement

The ability to share the stories of my people is a privilege. My role as a playwright/director is similar to the role of the *pa'a mo'olelo*, or storyteller, in traditional Hawaiian society. Pa'a mo'olelo are the conduit for communicating the history, values, and teachings from one generation to the next. I am honored to carry this *kuleana* (responsibility) as a playwright utilizing the stage as a platform for conveying our *mo'olelo* (stories, history) in today's modern world. I believe it is vital for our stories to be (re)told so that our challenges and triumphs are recognized and celebrated. The plays that I write are also a means to honor our ancestors, cultural practices, and language.

In 1995, I wrote and directed *Kaluaiko'olau: Ke Kā'e'a'e'a o nā Pali Kalalau* for a hero from my island home of Kaua'i. This was the beginning of my journey as a playwright and the development of the modern practice of *hana keaka* (Hawaiian medium theatre). The majority of the plays I've written are based on traditional *mo'olelo* with the Hawaiian language as the foundation of the play. *Hana keaka* incorporates traditional Hawaiian performance forms such as *mele* (song), *oli* (chant), *hula* (dance), and *ha'i mo'olelo* (storytelling) into the theatrical presentation. In addition to storytelling, *hana keaka* is a tool for raising and empowering Hawaiian consciousness. Through mounting of these theatrical productions, we've reclaimed historical events, contributed to the Hawaiian language revitalization movement, and inspired our fellow *Kānaka Maoli* (Native Hawaiians). *Hana keaka* represents the indigenous voice of our Hawaiian archipelago in the domain of theatre.

Over the years, I've explored my voice as a playwright authoring plays in Hawaiian, English, and Hawaiian Creole English (HCE), otherwise known as Pidgin. Like many of my generation who grew up on Kaua'i, Pidgin was my first language. In my life, I've battled the negative stigmas associated with Pidgin speakers. Often thought of as less intelligent than our English speaking counterparts. HCE/Pidgin language is a part of my identity that I will always maintain. As a multiethnic playwright from Hawai'i, I feel compelled to honor the diverse communities that make up our landscape. Therefore, I appreciate the opportunity to write plays in Pidgin that represent and resonate with the Pidgin speakers in my community. These plays express a local worldview that is encapsulated in the unique vocabulary, idioms, and phrases only found in HCE. Frowned upon for many decades and formerly referenced as broken-English, HCE/Pidgin has recently been recognized as an official language of the State of Hawai'i.

He Lei no Kākā'ako: Woven Memories weaves together stories of today addressing the issues that former and current residents of Kākā'ako encounter in this rapidly evolving neighborhood. The play is an opportunity to offer perspectives on the transformation and loss in the community, to examine the challenges we face, and to celebrate the diverse tapestry that we know as Hawai'i. At the time in which this play was written, there was a shift in the community to reclaim Kākā'ako for the local people. Although there has been a lot of positive change and energy in this community, serious social issues remain unresolved, with the growing house-less population that occupies Kākā'ako Park and the numerous development projects popping up in the area. A goal of this play was to create a space for dialogue amongst community members. In fact, *He Lei no Kākā'ako: Woven Memories* was presented in concert with two other plays written specifically for this place in a warehouse on Lana Lane in Kākā'ako. This event coincided with the painting of large art murals that the Honolulu arts community and a sector of those with a vested interest in

Kākaʻako's future supported fervently. Following the performances discussion ensued with the audience members and the artist involved in the project. The community engagement and the candid discussion was a healthy exercise that was long overdue.

I walked away from the Kākaʻako Co-Lab experience feeling that collectively we had raised awareness in the broader community for this *wahi pana* (special place). The attention that the project received was an indicator of success. Struggles would continue but our work had generated a wave of conversations about the state of affairs in Kākaʻako, its history, and most importantly, its future. Personally I had felt a connection to this place; however, a couple of months would pass by before I would learn that my ancestors had lived on the very lane where this production took place. In researching census reports for a genealogy project, I stumbled upon my great grandmother's home on Lana Lane accommodating 14 members of the Cain-Kaʻilihiwa ʻohana in 1940. This little discovery of family history confirmed the connection I had felt throughout the scripting and production process. Was this coincidence? Was it fate? Our kupuna lead us to where we need to be. They reveal knowledge when we are ready to receive. I believe this play illustrates my calling and *kuleana* as a *paʻa moʻolelo* to serve my community. *He haliʻa, he aloha, he lei no Kākaʻako. Ke aloha nō.*

Production history

In association with Interisland terminal Kumu Kahua Theatre produced *He Lei no Kākaʻako: Woven Memories* as a part of Co-Lab Kākaʻako, originally performed off-site in a warehouse on Lana Lane in Kākaʻako. The production was directed by John Wat, cast included Donna Blanchard, Charles Kapahu Timtim, and Alan Okubo. The play was also performed at the Network of Ensemble Theatres (N.E.T.) National Summit in 2013 and the Summit Fest 2013 in Honolulu.

9 *He Lei no Kākā'āko: Woven Memories*
Tammy Haili'ōpua Baker

Characters

Scene 1: Woven Memories
LEIALOHA (garland of love) Female 30's

Scene 2: My Precious Child
KALEIHI'IPOLI (garland held close to the bosom) Female 40's

Scene 3: Come Home
ALDEN Male 60's retired chief of police
KAWAO Son of Alden, late 30's
LOKE (rose) Female 40's police officer

Scene 4: A Garland Undone
LEINANI (beautiful garland) Female late 20's

Scene 5: Celebration
ADELINE Older Portuguese woman late 60's
VIVIEN Portuguese woman 50's
BERNARD Older Portuguese man late 60's

Scene 6: Times Past
ROBERT Older Portuguese man 80's, former resident of Kākā'āko

Scene 7: Aloha and Art
LEI (garland) Female mid 20's
WENDY Female mid 20's

Scene 8: The Refrain of My Song
KAMALEI (garland child, name of a star) Female early 20's
DIRECTOR Haole male 50's
ASSISTANT DIRECTOR Male/female 30's

The multiple characters in this play may be performed by four actors, two females and two males.

Setting

The stage is bare. Lighting is used to isolate areas of the stage and create the different environments.

Minimal props are used to distinguish character and location changes.

Scene 1: Woven Memories

(LEIALOHA enters with a lei in her hand. She adorns herself with the lei placing it on her neck.)

LEIALOHA He lei no Kākāʻako[1]
Memories woven through the generations
Highs and lows
Laughter and tears
Birth and death
Darkness and light
Light and darkness
Joy and sadness
All of it held together
Entwined, wili ʻia[2]
A fine weave
One moment compressed upon the other like selected pieces of fern that create the foundation for a lei. The ferns depend on one another. Each one fastened together, they become strong. Collectively, they are the lei.

(Her fingers gently stroke her lei.)

This lei is my family, we are of this ʻāina.[3] For many generations we like the ferns have depended on one another. With each new generation the lei expands, new life is added and wili pū ʻia[4] into the existing lei. The babies are adornments for our elders to wear on their shoulders like a well-manicured lei. Some lei are fancier than others attracting a lot of attention. Making others envious of the beauty or the scent of the flowers strung together. Like the ferns Kākāʻako is fragile. Our ecosystem, our community is inevitably impacted by invasive species and foreign traffic. How do we respond to this change? How do we thrive in a place that is no longer the home it once was? How do we maintain our identity and the traditions of our people when the landscape and the future of our ʻāina is in the hands of developers who want to build. They abandon the needs of the local people to turn a profit for their company. This once thriving community was destroyed by industrialization. Now the developers and politicians offer affordable housing. Who will live in the high-rise apartments? This kind of living detaches people further from the land. Will the apartments be occupied by kamaʻāina? The people of this land? Or will it be the new home for more malihini?[5] The patches of fern fade, pala.[6] Just like the reclamation project of 1948 with the construction of the massive seawall and the eventual backfilling of our reefs here from Olomehani street to Kewalo Basin. The new development projects will change the landscape of Kākāʻako forever.

Memories and stories are all we have left about this place. My grandparents called this location home. They raised nine kids here. They would fish and gather food from the reef buried under the concrete that thousands of cars drive over each day. Only through memory can we reconstruct the beauty of this ʻāina. My grandmother had a garden where she grew fruit and her favorite flowers, gardenias and plumerias.
Delicate flowers
A sweet fragrance
The recognizable scent of my grandma's garden

(LEIALOHA removes her lei and lifts it up to the sky.)

This lei is for you grandma.

(LIGHTS OUT.)

Scene 2: My Precious Child

(Dark dimly lit Kākā'āko Park at night. A homeless woman, KALEIHI'IPOLI, sits near the pavilion wall cradling her baby in her arms. She whispers to the baby and softly strokes the child's delicate face. She slowly scans the park as she cuddles her baby near her bosom. KALEIHI'IPOLI sings to her child.)

> KALEIHI'IPOLI E HI'I LEI Ē, HI'I
>   LEI Ē
> E HINA UKA Ē,
> HINA I KAI Ē.
> E KU'U KAMA HO'I Ē,
> E MĀLIE Ē.

(She takes a deep breath smelling her baby's head as she pulls her baby into her bosom. She delivers a soft kiss on baby's forehead.)

Pupuka[7], 'ae. You know how much Mommy loves you. Mommy loves you so much, more than you'll ever know. Shhh, Mommy is here to protect you, yeah. Things are so different now. Not like when I was a little keiki.

(KALEIHI'IPOLI's body stiffens.)

KALEIHI'IPOLI This place isn't what it used to be. So much has been lost, so much change. I remember my granny taking us to the mission house museum for story telling, swimming at Kewalo Basin with my cousins and even- I remember going to Kamaka 'ukulele factory. That uncle over there, he was related to Granny, he would cut us fruit to eat when Granny would go to talk stories with her cousins over there. They would kanikapila.[8] There was no need for a radio. All of them talented musicians. So many have passed on. My granny's voice was like the gentle kolonahe[9] wind caressing the curves and folds of the mountain range. Her voice made me feel safe. She would always sing to us wherever we went. Good times, never had to worry about our safety.

(She hears some one, twitches and clutches her baby to her chest in a defensive manner.)

What you mean? No! No, no! You can't take my baby from me. You have no right to take her from me. Get away, get away from me.

(She stands up.)

You have no right! I don't care who you are, state agency, bureaucratic rubbish, CPS, I don't care who you are. You have no idea what is right for me and my child. This is my child. I gave birth to her and I am raising her to the best of my ability with the resources that I have. *(Pause.)* No! Absolutely not. We are not homeless. I provide shelter for my child. We are not homeless. I don't care who made a report, they don't live with us. You are not going to tell me how and where to raise my child.

(She shifts back and forth pulling away.)

This is ridiculous. We have a home. This is our home. It might not have four walls but this is our home. I grew up here, this is my community. House-less does not mean homeless! We belong to this 'āina.

(She picks up a bag or two clutching baby in her arms.)

(To BABY.) No worry Honey, Mommy's isn't gonna let anybody hurt you. Nobody is gonna take you from me. I promise you baby. Nobody will- Mommy's gonna take good care of you.

(She jerks backward as if someone is trying to take her baby away from her. She nearly falls. During the following dialogue KALEIHI'IPOLI tightly grabs both ends of the blanket which seems to hold a swaddled baby pulls it apart in front of her revealing the empty blankets. She breaks down crying.)

KALEIHI'IPOLI No! My baby! My baby!

(The crying turns into absurd laughter and then silence. She wearily bundles the blankets together to resemble a baby again. Brushing the cheeks of her imagined baby, she softly sings.)

> E HI'I LEI Ē, HI'I LEI Ē,
> E HINA UKA Ē,
> HINA I KAI Ē,
> E KU'U KAMA HO'I Ē,
> E MĀLIE Ē.

(BLACKOUT.)

Scene 3: Come Home

(LIGHTS UP. Early morning at Kākāʻako Park. KAWAO stretches taking different ʻai[10] positions. He practices breathing patterns used by lua[11] practitioners. On the opposite side of the stage KAWAO's movements are mirrored by an older man, his father ALDEN. They move in a rhythmic synchronized fashion sharing similar breathing patterns. When the routine is complete, they each take a deep breath.)

ALDEN Hoʻoponopono[12], it is time.

(KAWAO is seen praying.)

KAWAO E huikala mai iaʻu e Ke Akua. E huikala mai i koʻu mau lawehala.[13] Mahalo Ke Akua for all of your blessings, for keeping me alive to live another day, for being with me in times of darkness. I thank you Ke Akua. Please Ke Akua, e hōʻike mai i ke ala hele kūpono e hele aku ai.[14] Mahalo.

(KAWAO bids farewell to his park neighboors.)

Okay Smokey, aloha. See you fellas later. Kay Aunty Merna, aloha. No forget your insulin today, heh. *(Answering.)* Yeah, yeah, yeah I be back when I pau work. Kay aloha Braddah Rick. *(Pause.)* Shoot!

(KAWAO crosses to the street heading to UFC Gym B.J. Penn when he thinks he recognizes a car passing by. His gaze follows the car. He takes a deep breath and moves closer to the sidewalk.)

(To himself.) Ke Akua, you move quick!

(ALDEN exits car and approaches KAWAO. They stare at one another.)

ALDEN Eh Boy.

(KAWAO nods as emotions swell within.)

KAWAO Eh Dad.

ALDEN It's been a long time.

KAWAO Yep.

(They both nod nervously eventually extending their arms and embracing. Both men release their embrace. They attempt to regain composure.)

ALDEN You look healthy. Good shape.

KAWAO You too… *(Playful.)* for one ʻelemakule.[15]

ALDEN Heh?

KAWAO Nah, only joking.

(ALDEN smiles. Silence.)

So I was on my way to work.

ALDEN Yeah, yeah, yeah. Okay.

KAWAO And-

ALDEN I heard you was working.

KAWAO Yeah. Trying my best.

ALDEN That's good. Good.

KAWAO So how's Mom?

ALDEN She doing alright.

KAWAO She okay?

ALDEN Yeah.

KAWAO Good, good.

ALDEN Kawao, we need to talk. I not here for argue with-

KAWAO Dad, I no like be late for work.

ALDEN I understand. *(Pause.)* Listen Boy, it's time for hoʻoponopono.

KAWAO *(Nodding in agreement.)* Hoʻoponopono, I like fix things-

ALDEN I'm glad you feel that way. Look son, you made some bad choices and-

KAWAO Dad, I pau[16] carrying this burden. I no like-

ALDEN Try listen to me first.

KAWAO I listening.

ALDEN I know you think that I wasn't there for you when you needed me and that I could have stopped what was going on. But you had to learn your lesson.

KAWAO Learn my lesson.

ALDEN I couldn't just stand by and pretend my boy was going fix himself. I was praying for change, but nothing. Things only got worse. You made life so difficult.

KAWAO Life is complicated.

ALDEN Complicated! How you think things was for me everyday at the station? Getting calls for racketeering and extortion only to realize that my son was one of the derelicts running the ring. Shame, boy!

KAWAO I know I disappointed you and shamed our family. But no matter how many times I apologize it hasn't been enough. I'm sorry-

ALDEN I'm sorry too, Boy. Sorry for ever thinking that you knew-

KAWAO Dad I no like fight with you.

ALDEN I hear that's what you doing now. *(Shaking his head.)* Fighting.

KAWAO I training.

ALDEN You never have enough of that?

(KAWAO retreats.)

You need a real job.

KAWAO This can be a real job.

ALDEN A real job has a paycheck, a legal pay-check so that you can provide for yourself.

KAWAO Training helps me focus. Getting in the ring let's me release.

ALDEN Release all your anger?

KAWAO Maybe.

ALDEN You cannot fight for the rest of your life.

KAWAO Maybe I can, maybe that's who I am.

ALDEN That's not who you are!

KAWAO E kala mai[17] but, you don't know me.

ALDEN I know that using your hands to beat men up is not a career. You not pau beating people up for money? I thought that was part of the reform efforts inside.

KAWAO I'm a warrior.

ALDEN ʻAʻole.[18] A warrior is an honorable title.

KAWAO Koa ke koa, hele i mua.[19]

ALDEN Is that what you learned in prison? That's what they teaching you, that all the Hawaiians behind bars are warriors? Come on. What, they making one stable of cauli-flower ear fighters and calling you warri-ors! That's not reform, that's not preparing you for society when you get out. How are you supposed to assimilate back into the community? They should be teaching you guys real job skills to prepare you for when you get out.

KAWAO Nothing can prepare you for getting out.

ALDEN Job skills can. Teaching you how to get a real job.

KAWAO I have a job.

ALDEN Are you collecting a paycheck? A legal paycheck where they record your social security number and make you pay taxes. If not, you can't call that a job. Just like you can't call this a home.

KAWAO What's this about?

ALDEN I don't like hearing from my friends that my son is living at Kākāʻako park. They tell me, "No worry, he looking good."

KAWAO So this is about **you** then? Not about me, not about me getting a job and it's not about where I'm living. It's about your im-age and what your friends saying about your family.

ALDEN My image? Our whole family's image was tainted.

KAWAO Tainted and stained. I get it, I spilt the wine on Tūtū's white table cloth. Fine, I take complete responsibility for shaming the ʻohana.

ALDEN Shame! I've worked so hard to rid our family of shame.

KAWAO So have I. *(Pause.)* Dad, I found one way to wash out each and every stain, Ke Akua.

ALDEN Why Boy, why?

KAWAO Why-

ALDEN I thought I came to terms with all of this.

KAWAO How come you never came to visit me? And why now? Why you coming to see me now? I been out for over a year now and-

ALDEN You cannot be living here.

KAWAO You not going answer my question?

ALDEN This is not your home.

KAWAO I disagree. I'm maʻa[20] to this place, spent many days over here surfing Incinerators and Kewalo's. We even had one headquaters down here-

ALDEN Don't bring that stuff up. I know you probably spent more time over here than at home. Boy, you don't wanna be here. You need a roof over your head, a bed to sleep in-

KAWAO *(Laughing.)* A bed. I don't know what it's like to sleep on a bed. I not sure if I can.

ALDEN Son, I am here to make things right.

KAWAO I've prayed for this day. I've prayed con-stantly for forgiveness, especially for you to forgive me.

ALDEN My Boy, I forgave you a long time ago.

KAWAO Seriously?

ALDEN ʻAe, I just haven't been able to forgive myself.

KAWAO *(Quoting scripture.)* Wash me thoroughly and repeatedly from my iniquity and guilt and cleanse me and make wholly pure from my sin.

ALDEN Psalm 51.

KAWAO ʻAe. *(Pause.)* Give it to Ke Akua Dad. In him we have redemption.

ALDEN And salvation. Forgive me son.

(ALDEN reaches out to his son.)

KAWAO Yes, I forgive you. I love you Dad.

ALDEN Come home Boy.

KAWAO Mahalo.

(They embrace. During the following dialogue and number of City and County officials and officers from the Honolulu Police Department (HPD) ar-rive at the park to issue eviction notices.)

ALDEN I've felt like a hypocrite every Sunday preaching to the community about forgiveness and aloha. And yet I never made the effort to hoʻoponopono things with my own flesh and blood, with my son.

KAWAO We need to have a hoʻoponopono with the enitre ʻohana.

ALDEN *(Placing his hand on KAWAO's cheek.)* Create in me a clean heart Ke Akua and renew my spirit.

KAWAO *(Looking around.)* Dad what's going on? What is City and County doing here? HPD too, what's going on?

ALDEN Ke Akua forgive my shortcomings and failings, behold my affliction and my pain and forgive all of my sins.

KAWAO Dad! What is this?

ALDEN This is a pule.[21]

KAWAO No, not your pule. This! Look at them. They coming to evict us? The day before Thanksgiving? Is this why you're here?

ALDEN No. I mean yes. No. I am here to hoʻoponopono and invite you to come home.

KAWAO You don't want another police report in the family's name, heh?

ALDEN What kinda question is that? Your mama wants you to come home. I want you to come home.

(City and County official (LOKE) is heard on side of stage.)

LOKE So listen up, you all are in violation of Hawaiʻi state law. You are currently residing on state property. If any of you have children, you may qualify for assistance through the McKinney-Vento Homeless Assistance Act.

KAWAO What about Aunty Merna? Her diabetes is really bad. And Ricky, he no more legs and Smokey them. What's gonna happen to them?

ALDEN Who is Aunty Merna? Who are these people?

KAWAO They're my ʻohana over here.

ALDEN I am your ʻohana. You not related to those people.

LOKE Let's make this easy. You must vacate the premises immediately. If you do not remove yourselves and your possessions, we will remove them for you.

KAWAO I can't just leave them.

ALDEN Yes, you can. You have a home to go to.

LOKE As you can see I am not alone. Honolulu Police Department is here to assist in the process. You must break down all tents and structures. Let's move.

KAWAO Home?

(LOKE approaches the men.)

LOKE Sirs, I would advise you both to leave the premises as well. This may get a little ugly. They don't always cooperate with us.

KAWAO They don't have a choice.

ALDEN Of course ma'am.

(LOKE moves on. ALDEN pulls his son to the side.)

KAWAO You have a choice. Make the right choice.

LOKE *(Off-stage.)* Tents must go! I am not going to argue with you. This isn't your home!

ALDEN Son, come home.

KAWAO *Home?* I can't-

(KAWAO turns and moves to exit.)

ALDEN Kawaonahele Kaʻōpio.

(Upon hearing his name KAWAO stops and turns to his father.)

KAWAO Eō[22].

ALDEN E hoʻi mai.[23]

KAWAO *(Nods.)* A hui hou kāua.[24]

(KAWAO crosses to exit.)

ALDEN A hui hou aku nō.[25]

(On opposite sides of the stage both characters take deep breaths and move insync. BLACKOUT.)

Scene 4: A Garland Undone

(LEINANI enters reciting poetry.)

LEINANI Oh my dear anthurium blossom
Your heartshaped body withstands the elements
You stand firm in the gusts of wind
Oh tail flower, so beautiful in my sight

I beckon you to hold on to our garland of love
A garland that we created, entwined with care...
I never meant to hurt you. I tried to stay. I tried to hold on. The truth is the harder I worked at holding on, the quicker it unraveled. Hemo,[26] our lei came apart. The lei

that we created together that we vowed to protect and cherish. One moment we were secure and the next there were wilted flowers scattered on the floor. There was no reason for me to stay anymore. We grew apart. You had...you would travel a different path. And I, I'm a different kind of flower. We thought an anthurium and a plumeria could be together, it wasn't meant to be. You simply can't make a lei of anthuriums and plumeria. They don't match. Their bodies don't fit one another. As much as the plumeria tries to embrace the anthurium, the ridged flower refuses to conform. Its core has no flexibility. Seemingly open and hospitable, its waxed broad blade reveals its true self. It's a striking flower, irresistibly beautiful but lacks compassion. It isn't like the plumeria; bright, fragrant and sensitive. The plumeria is a social flower. She enjoys parties, being with her family and friends, and she refuses to be kept cooped up in the house all day long. I will no longer live under your dictatorship. This plumeria was meant to dance in the radiant sun.

We agreed to be equal partners in this relationship. We had the best intentions to be supportive of one another's work and outside interests too, but you weren't able to be my pillar of support. Perhaps it was a conflict of interest. I failed too. I couldn't support you completely, like with your job. The development company you work for created a monster. You translated the intimate details of my family history into dollar signs and profits. How dare you use the family information that I shared with you for the advancement of that wicked boss of yours to acquire property that was stolen from my great-grandparents! Betrayal, you chose your path and hurt me deeply. *(Overcome with emotion.)* I now question everything that we shared...the lei that we wove together over the last five years, ua hemo. *(Gathers herself and takes a deep breath.)* It isn't always clear what one's motivation is in a relationship. I believe that my intentions were pure and I still have aloha for you, my anthurium. Although it seems you walk on the dark side, I wish you the best. I now know that we were never meant to be.

(She sings and gestures hula movement with her hands.)

> ALOHA 'OE, ALOHA 'OE
> E KE ONAONA NOHO I KA LIPO
> ONE FOND EMBRACE,
> A HO'I A'E AU
> UNTIL WE MEET AGAIN[27]

(LIGHTS FADE TO BLACK.)

Scene 5: Celebration

(LIGHTS UP on the Kewalo Holy Ghost Society meeting. Members purchase tickets for the chance to crown their granddaugther queen of the Holy Ghost Parade.)

ADELINE Give me ten.

VIVIEN Ten?

ADELINE My granddaughter not getting any younger. It's this year or never.

VIVIEN *(Collects the money.)* Benzer der.[28]

BERNARD Começar, começar, começar.[29] Aloha everyone and thank you all for attending our meeting tonight. We have much work ahead of us as we plan the upcoming Kewalo Holy Ghost Parade even though we not in Kewalo anymore and we not gonna be marching through Kākā'ako like before.

ADELINE It's okay Bernard. We still celebrate. *(Poses with her hands.)* We still dance the charmarita!

BERNARD Thank you Adeline. So everyone has purchased their tickets.

(The crowd cheers a "yes".)

ADELINE Give me ten more tickets, Vivien.

(The women exchange money.)

VIVIEN Here you go, Adeline. Good Luck.

(VIVIEN includes the final slips of paper into the bowl and hands it to BERNARD.)

BERNARD We will begin. Remember the seventh dominga names the queen. We already have our Portugal native to carry the flag. Obrigado Augusto for being our Portugal born brother.

(The crowd claps.)

Vivien.

VIVIEN I'll go first.

(VIVIEN reaches into the bowl and pulls up a blank slip of paper.)

Oh well. Four more to go.

(She pulls again. And happily raises it up into the air.)

Number five.

BERNARD Congratulations, your family will have the honor of carrying St. Christopher.

ADELINE Wonderful. My turn.

(BERNARD gestures to ADELINE to come to the bowl.)

Por favor[30] Sweet Jesus. For my Christine.

(She pulls her first slip of paper.)

Aye.

(She shakes her head and pulls four more slips of paper.)

Ai cu dez.[31]

VIVIEN Be patient. You have five- no, fifteen more to go.

BERNARD Yes, you might pull number six and carry the Sacred Heart of Jesus.

ADELINE I need to pull the seventh dominga for my neta.[32]

(She pulls. Everyone looks.)

No.

(Her hand enters the bowl and swirls the slips of papers about. Slowly her hand emerges from the side of the bowl.)

Aye!

(Blank slip. The crowd reacts. She crosses her heart.)

In the name of the Father, Son and Holy Spirit.

(She whispers a prayer to herself and takes a deep breath. ADELINE carefully places her hand in the bowl and closes her eyes. The others look at

one another. Taking another breath ADELINE removes the slip of paper and doesn't look at it. She looks at VIVIEN's face. She jumps around.)

ADELINE The seventh dominga? Jesus Cristo. Amen! *(Looking at the slip of paper.)* Aye ya yai! Aye merda![33] Oh thank you Sweet Lord Jesus! Aye so much work now. Never mind, how many years I was hoping for this.

BERNARD Oh Adeline relax bum bye you have a heart attack or something.

VIVIEN Congratulations!

ADELINE Thank you! Something told me for buy plenty tickets tonight on my way here. I know that was my Lord Jesus talking to me and he answered my prayers. I tell you Jesus he's listening. He's always listening to us. He a kind and generous Lord. Amen, hallelujah, praise his name. He gave me another miracle today. God bless all of you here tonight. This is the best Holy Ghost Society in Honolulu, in the state probably. And I am dancing the chamarita this year knee replacement surgery and all! Oh amen!

(Everyone laughs.)

VIVIEN Kay who's next we still gotta pull for the Sacred Heart of Jesus and talk about all the plans, food booths, malasadas, mass and everything.

ADELINE Oh I think we going pink this year. That was my mother's favorite color. Pink carnations! Pink carnation bouquets for the young ladies. We can put carnations in the hair with baby's breath...

BERNARD Alright who's next?

VIVIEN So exciting Adeline. I love pink carnations. And if you no more enough granddaughters you can borrow some of mine.

BERNARD Great, come on down Sylvia.

ADELINE We can make double carantion lei for Father Patrick them.

BERNARD Sylvia-

(Charmarita music fills the room. Ladies are dancing. FADE TO BLACK.)

Scene 6: Times Past

(ROBERT an older Portuguese man sits downstage center. He looks warily at the teenager speaking to him.)

ROBERT So how come you like interview me for? *(Pause.)* Oh...and what you going do with the interview when pau?[34] *(He listens.)*

This is for one school project. Eh too good your school let you come talk to people like me. But you know what, I nobody. People no know me, just one regular guy from Kākaʻako. *(Pause.)* Ah, I guess so, we go do the interview liʻdat. You seem like one good kid. What you like know? *(He listens to the question posed.)* What is special about this place? Plenty things. Before days, this was one of the choicest neighborhoods for live in, good kine people, tight community, most of us living over here was related somehow. We either cousins or somebody married in the family related to you somehow, you know what I mean. Like my cousin Charlie, he was in love with our third cousin Sylvia and never even know until we seen our other cousin Caroline at the Kewalo Holy Ghost Parade looking for her mother, my Aunty Linda. Caroline when kinda like Charlie so when she seen him and Sylvia making anykine with each other she figure that's her chance for make her move. Caroline when for tell Charlie's mother that he was hooking up with Sylvia and how they not supposed to be together because they cousins. But she's one babooze because her and Charlie was related more close. They was second cousins. That never stop them from dating and having one baby. Poor thing, little bit off my nephew. Where we was? *(Beat.)* Oh yeah how come this place is special to me…I guess cause I had grow up over here, spent most of my life over here. I get plenty memories about this place. Small kid time we come home from school and book ʻum to the beach right after school. We would go surfing, pick ʻopihi[35], make anykine with the wahines. That was some good times. This was one good place, safe. We all knew each other. You know we never even lock our doors before in this neighborhood. Nobody make trouble. That's not true, had some donkeys but we used to take care of that. My uncle was police captain and my other uncle was- well we not talk about that. Let's just say Kākaʻako was one pretty safe place to be. *(He listens to the next question.)* It's hard sometimes. We never like leave but we never own the property, yeah. Was lease kine. So when the state had they plans for make Kākaʻako one business district, pau the houses went. We never have choice, even the school over here and our church on Queen, pau. And you look this place now, just like we never was here. All these memories of our home, it's like was on one other island or something. I don't know, make me sad sometime. That's probably why I never like do this interview with you. It's hard, just like they went erase us, they when erase the community, the people that was here. We the people that made Kākaʻako. *(ROBERT is emotional. Takes a deep breath.)* Sorry boy, uncle pau talk. You take care now. Aloha.

(LIGHTS FADE as ROBERT rises to exit.)

Scene 7: Aloha and Art

(LEI and WENDY enter a parking lot full of vendors and art projects. They look around.)

LEI This is so cool.
WENDY I guess so. What do they call this?
LEI Honolulu Night Market.
WENDY Lot's of food booths. I like food.
LEI And look at the artwork.
WENDY It's like a craft fair.
LEI With live art! That's cool.
WENDY Since when are you into art?
LEI I've always liked art-
WENDY Sure you have.

(LEI looks back at WENDY.)

What's his name?

LEI Who?
WENDY Come on, spill. Art is the furthest thing from your mind. You failed ceramics sophomore year. We're not here for the art.
LEI We're here for the artist.
WENDY That's what I thought. Who is he?
LEI He's from here.
WENDY I don't think you're ready for another relationship.
LEI What you-
WENDY Lei, you and Maka broke up two weeks ago. How can you even be thinking of hooking up with someone new? This is time for you. Why don't you think about taking care of yourself…I don't-
LEI I thought you were my friend.

WENDY Lei, I am your friend that's why I'm being real with you. An artist? He's not gonna want to be in a committed relationship. That's why you and Maka broke up.

LEI Stop talking about Maka. Let's have fun tonight. Look, I like the vibe here. People hanging out, new energy in the streets, art murals in progress. Let's have a drink. I'm gonna have fun tonight.

WENDY And at the end of the night we're leaving together.

(LEI hesitates.)

LEI Yeah.

WENDY Lei…remember our rule.

LEI I remember. *(She spots the artist.)* Over there, the one up on the ladder. He's the artist that I came to see.

WENDY You're not gonna be his next art project.

LEI Come on he's really cool, all of this new arts market and artist in the streets of Kākaʻako is what he does. He runs this non-profit teaching kids to use art as a way to express themselves and to repair this community. You'll like him.

WENDY He's kinda handsome.

LEI I know.

WENDY Remember our rule. You not making artwork with him tonight!

LEI Girl, you need to relax.

WENDY No! After one session of finger painting with him, who's gonna clean up the mess and put all the paints away? Me, not him.

LEI Interesting how you thought we would be doing finger painting tonight.

WENDY I'm serious. *(Pointing at LEI.)* That canvas is not available for new art. She needs time to–

LEI Where's your aloha sister?

WENDY Aloha?!

(LEI pulls WENDY towards the mural.)

LEI I got an A+ in Aloha 101.

WENDY Please!

LEI Let's see how I do in Art 101?

WENDY Remember–

LEI This community needs our love and support. The artists are reinventing Kākaʻako. It's a place for us, this generation, to make it our own. Show some aloha…

WENDY You don't always have to embody your name.

LEI That was rude.

WENDY Okay, we'll meet your artist friend but like I said–

LEI Yes, I'm going home with you tonight.

WENDY Let's go Miss Leialoha. He better have one friend.

LEI Aloha, it's the golden rule.

WENDY Right!

> LEI and WENDY HE ALOHA AU IĀ ʻOE LĀ,
> KOU PĀPĀLINA LAHILAHI[36]

(WENDY hits LEI on her backside referring to her "rosy cheeks." They exit as the LIGHTS FADE.)

Scene 8: The Refrain of My Song

(Camera rolling as KAMALEI sits enjoying a cocktail.)

KAMALEI We're embracing change. We celebrate the transformation of Kākaʻako. Urban Island Culture. It's a new place for us kamaʻāina[37] to enjoy. A place to live. A place to play. A place–

DIRECTOR Cut. Let's take that again and try to hit Urban Island Culture. *(Pause.)* One more thing, say the word *kamaʻāina (Mispronounced.)* for me.

KAMALEI Kamaʻāina.

DIRECTOR One more time. We need to pronounce it correctly. *(Attempting to sound Hawaiian.)* Kamaʻāina, punch that glottal stop.

KAMALEI *(Exaggerating.)* Kamaʻāina.

DIRECTOR Good. You have the perfect look for what we're trying to convey here. Local, but not too local to alienate others.

KAMALEI *(Taken aback.)* Mahalo.

DIRECTOR Where's my P.A.? Send a special 'thank you' to the casting agent. Let's roll again.

ASSISTANT DIRECTOR Quiet on the set. Kākaʻako Development commercial take four.

DIRECTOR Roll it.

ASSISTANT DIRECTOR On three. One—two—three. Rolling.

DIRECTOR Action.

KAMALEI We're embracing change. We celebrate the transformation of Kākaʻako. Urban—Island—Culture. It's a new place for us kamaʻāina to enjoy. A place to live. A place to play. A place to call home with affordable housing for you and me.

DIRECTOR Cut. That's a wrap. *(To KAMALEI.)* Good job miss. *(To ASSISTANT DIRECTOR.)* Consider the units sold. Who wouldn't want to live next door to her, right?

(KAMALEI is a bit offended by the comment. DIRECTOR and ASSISTANT DIRECTOR exit. KAMALEI fakes a smile and waves goodbye.)

KAMALEI *(Imitating the director.)* "Punch that glottal stop." I feel like punching his face. Frickin' haole. As if I don't know my language. Who's the kama'āina? Damn malihini![38]

(She removes the flower tucked behind her right ear and looks at it.)

That felt like prostitution. *(Beat.)* What am I selling? This place is so far gone. It's a concrete jungle. We're selling a piece of concrete, it's not like I'm promoting the sale of sacred 'āina. Kākā'āko was ruined a long time ago. Local people were driven out to build this industrial area that eventually fell apart. Maybe the developers will make something out of this run-down area. Transform the neighborhood.

There's been a lot of movement here recently. The local artists are all over the rebirth of Kākā'āko. They're reclaiming this place and the new art murals here are cool, but affordable housing? Yeah right! *(Mocking the previous commercial dialogue.)* "A place to live. A place to play. A place to call home for you and me?" Not even! How many locals, kama'āina, will actually live here? How many want to live here? Or could potentially afford a place here? *(Pause.)* I can only speak for myself. I'm not celebrating the Kākā'āko metamorphosis nor am I looking to move to town where you constantly smell sewage because there isn't the proper infrastructure for all of the high-rises that are being built and the masses of people moving here. That's what happens when they choose to backfill our ponds and reefs. The salt ponds of times past will never be restored here in Kākā'āko. We'll never be able to gather limu[39] or fish in the ponds our ancestors kept. *(Beat.)* Aloha 'āina seems like an absurd term here with all of the exploitation and desecration this place has experienced. To be quite honest, it's difficult to feel aloha for the cement and gravel that makes up this unattractive landscape.

Ha'ina 'ia mai ana ka puana.[40] The new Kākā'āko will attract more newcomers to this city lifestyle.

Oh how I ponder the meaning of this land. Kākā'āko means dull, slow, crooked, underhand, mean, unfair, or, fraudulent. Auē e Kākā'āko ē,[41] the implications of your name. Minamina wale ke ka'a ahi kau lewa.[42] Regretful is the current status of this land with excessive buildings and the unnecessary 5.2 billion dollar rail.

At one time you were a thriving community providing for our royalty and the many malihini who came to these shores. Once the land of Boki,[43] and now, 'oki loa![44]

Ho'ōla i ke kaiāulu.[45] The efforts of Kamehameha are admirable. Salt, Six Eighty, and sustainability to create community. "Our Kākā'āko," the urban-island-lifestyle.

(KAMALEI gestures as if dancing hula with the closing lines.)

He hali'a, he aloha, he lei no Kākā'āko.[46]

(Fade to black.)

Notes

1. A garland for Kākā'āko.
2. Braided or twisted together.
3. Land.
4. Twisted together.
5. Foreigners.
6. To rippen or to become rotten.
7. Literal translation=ugly, Hawaiians use this term to ward off jealous on-lookers.
8. To play music, to jam.
9. A gentle, pleasant breeze.
10. Strokes or hold positions.

11. Hawaiian martial arts.
12. To make things right.
13. Forgive me, Lord. Forgive my many sins.
14. Please show me the proper path to travel.
15. An old man.
16. Done, finished.
17. Excuse me/pardon me.
18. No.
19. Be a warrior, go forward.
20. Accustomed, used to.
21. Pule=prayer/to pray.
22. Yes.
23. Return (home).
24. Until we meet again./See you later.
25. Until we meet again indeed.
26. To come undone.
27. Song by Queen Liliʻuokalani
    Farewell to you, farewell to you
    The charming one who dwells in the shaded bowers
    One fond embrace,
    ʻEre I depart
    Until we meet again
28. Bless her.
29. Let's begin.
30. Please.
31. OMG. (lit. There ten asses.)
32. Granddaughter.
33. Oh Shit (pronounced= merdersh)
34. Finshed.
35. Limpet, shell fish.
36. Traditional song, Pāpālina Lahilahi.
    I love you, and your dainty or rosy cheeks.
37. Native born, child of the land, host.
38. Foreigner.
39. Seaweed.
40. Tell the refrain of my song.
41. Alas Kākāʻako.
42. Regretful is the rail.
43. Boki is a supernatural dog guardian of Kākāʻako.
44. Completely done.
45. Give new life to the community.
46. Memories, love, a flower garland for Kākāʻako.

Nikkole Salter

Biography

Ms. Salter is an OBIE Award-winning actress, dramatist, educator, and advocate who has written 6 full-length plays, been produced on 3 continents in 5 countries, and been published in 15 international publications. Her work has appeared in over 20 Off-Broadway, regional, and international theatres, and the Crossroads Theatre production of her play *Repairing a Na-*  *tion* (directed by Marshall Jones, III) was taped for the second season of the WNET program *Theatre Close-Up*, which aired on NYC's channel THIRTEEN, WLIC, NJTV, and streamed on the internet. Ms. Salter is a 2014 MAP Fund Grant recipient, a Eugene O'Neill Theater Center National Playwrights Conference semi-finalist, a two-time Playwrights of New York (PoNY) Fellowship nominee. She is also cofounder of The Continuum Project, Inc., a non-profit organization that uses the arts to promote community enrichment and empowerment (www.the ContinuumProject.org). The CP's first initiative, The Legacy Program, was featured on Dr. Henry Louis Gates, Jr.'s PBS program *Finding Your Roots*.

Ms. Salter is an active member of the Actors Equity Association, the Screen Actors Guild/American Federation of Television and Radio Artists, and the Dramatists Guild, and sits on the Board of Directors of the Theatre Communications Group. She received her BFA in theatre from Howard University and her MFA from New York University's Graduate Acting Program. More information is available at www.NikkoleSalter.com.

Artistic statement

Horace Mann, the father of public education in America, said, "Education, then, beyond all other devices of human origin, is the great equalizer of the conditions of men...[The Common School] will open a wider area over which the social feelings will expand; and if this education should be universal and complete, it would do more than all things else to obliterate factitious distinctions in society." Unfortunately, the American system of public education has fallen short of creating Mr. Mann's vision of an America free of "factitious distinctions." We exist in a time when our apparent social, economic, political, religious, and ideological positions have Balkanized – or perhaps have merely been revealed to have always been deeply divided. Those divisions are the cause for the ever-ensuing battle for hierarchical positioning in a more and more severely stratified society, rather than, as Mann suggested is best, the use of equal public education to move closer to an integrated ideal. *Lines in the Dust* is my exploration into why these divisions and this stratification – these lines – exist and, through the lens of public education, what impact they have had, and continue to have, on urban African American communities and the American promise of freedom, justice, and equal opportunity and equal access to the American dream of upward mobility.

Production history

Lines in the Dust was commissioned by Luna Stage in West Orange, NJ; Cheryl Katz, Artistic Director. It received its World Premiere in October 9–November 9, 2014 at Luna Stage (Cheryl, Artistic Director; John Penn Lewis Managing Director) in West Orange, NJ. This production was directed by Reginald Douglas with the following designers: Set, Deborah Wheatley; Props, Brianna McIntyre; Lighting, Mike Riggs; Costume, Deborah Caney; and Sound, Julian Evans; Fight Direction, Dan O'Driscoll. The Production Manager was Liz Cesario, the Stage Manager was Dan Viola, and the Assistant Stage Manager was Courtney Labossiere. The cast was as follows:

DR. BEVERLY LONG	Dorcas Sowunmi
DENITRA MORGAN	Erin Cherry
MIKE DiMAGGIO	Rick Delaney

10 *Lines in the Dust*
Nikkole Salter

Characters

DR. BEVERLY LONG, Ed.D, PRINCIPAL
In 2009: a haughty 42-year-old African American, mother, educator, and ex-Assistant Superintendent for Curriculum and Instruction for Newark Public Schools in Newark, NJ looking to pick up the pieces of a major career faux pas.

In 2010: a refined 43-year-old African American, mother, educator and the Interim Principal of the Millburn High School in Millburn, NJ, struggling to reconcile her occupational duty with her moral obligation to her original home community.

DENITRA MORGAN
In 2009: a down-to-earth 37-year-old African American mother, community college graduate, and an LVN at an urgent care center recently denied the last suitable school option for her daughter, scrambling for alternatives.

In 2010: a determined 38-year-old African American mother, community college graduate, and an LVN at an urgent care center striving trying to maintain her daughter's position at Millburn High School under false pretenses.

MICHAEL DiMAGGIO, P.I.
In 2010: a charming and resourceful 64-year-old Italian American grandfather, high school graduate, retired lieutenant detective for the Millburn Police Department, freelance licensed private investigator, and a new member of the Concerned Citizens Council of Millburn Township actively participating in securing the safety and status of his neighborhood.

Settings

Early spring 2009:
House for sale, Millburn, NJ.

October/November, 2010:
Millburn High School, Beverly's Office, Millburn, NJ.

House for sale, Millburn, NJ.
Denitra Morgan's home, Newark, NJ.
Millburn Township School Board, Millburn, NJ.

Punctuation notes

// : Indicates dialogue entry of following character

★

ACT I

Scene 1

Essex County. Millburn, NJ. Early Spring, 2009. The grand foyer of a house for sale at the close of a grand tour. There's a small table with a vase of beautiful flowers, a small tray of cookies, copied spec sheets and an open registry perhaps behind a barrier of some sort. Perhaps there's an "open house" banner, a picture of a realtor, a single helium welcome balloon, and/ or a visible "for sale" sign. DENITRA MORGAN [37] is babysitting the tray of cookies while checking out the features of the room. BEVERLY LONG [42] enters as if to leave. Beverly inadvertently drops her spec sheet while preparing.

DENITRA Hey. You dropped your…?
BEVERLY *(A gesture signifying, "My?")*

(BEVERLY hands DENITRA the spec sheet.)

BEVERLY Thank you. *(Almost to herself)* Not that I need it. Since there's *(Subtly mocking the realtor)* "<u>very little</u> room for negotiation."
DENITRA Yes. *(With the same subtle mockery)* "Very little."

(Their eyes meet. BEVERLY steps closer to DENITRA.)

BEVERLY *(Beat)* You heard in there – // What she – ?
DENITRA Oh, yes. I heard.
BEVERLY *(Aware of the possibility of being heard)* I thought maybe it was me – that I was being –
DENITRA No, it wasn't you. She was being very –
BEVERLY *(Imitating)* Eight <u>hundred</u> ninety nine <u>thousand</u> // and <u>very</u> little room –
DENITRA *(Imitating)* And very little room – Yes!
BEVERLY As if I couldn't possibly –
DENITRA As if neither of us could.
BEVERLY As though we were obviously –
DENITRA Like she knows how much –
BEVERLY But she doesn't know.

DENITRA How could she know?
BEVERLY She assumes.
DENITRA Well, we know what happens when one assumes.
BEVERLY And her look, like:

(DENITRA imitates the realtor's look.)

DENITRA Like, "this is directed toward you"?
BEVERLY Yes!

(DENITRA steps closer to BEVERLY.)

DENITRA Did you pick up on – what'd she say in the kitchen? *(re-enacting)* "Millburn's not the most diversecommunity.Butwhereitlacksindiversity it makes up in safety." // Some such nonsense.
BEVERLY Yes, I did.
DENITRA I had to look to my right and my left like, "No she –"
BEVERLY I know!
DENITRA Like it was a selling point! Like nothing was wrong with –
BEVERLY I had had it when she said, *(re-enacting)* "In Millburn one doesn't have to worry about urban vandalism or drugs." Like there are no // drugs in Millburn! Give me a break!
DENITRA Drugs in Millburn! Are you serious?! What planet – ?
BEVERLY She's delusional.

(They laugh loud, then quickly acknowledge their volume.)

DENITRA And "urban's" just a euphemism for –
BEVERLY Oh, I know.
DENITRA "Owner-occupied   neighborhood." "No forced busing in schools."
BEVERLY Mmm, hmm.
DENITRA I know what that means.
BEVERLY That coded, covert way of –
DENITRA That's why I – I turned to my daughter and said, "Let's take a walk."

BEVERLY I thought you'd left.

DENITRA Oh, no. We don't run from stupid. Cower to ignorance. No. I told Noelle, "We don't need her to give us a tour. Go and see all you want to see. Every cabinet. Every closet. Every fixture. This is a house open to the public, that's what 'open house means,' and you, sweetheart, are part of the public. Have a cookie. Venture forth."

BEVERLY Good for you.

DENITRA And I dare that woman to say something to my child.

BEVERLY She won't.

DENITRA She better not. *(Shaking her head in disbelief)* In 2009.

BEVERLY I know. You'd think by now –

DENITRA You'd think.

BEVERLY There's a black man in the White House.

DENITRA I know.

BEVERLY Do we look like we're some poor rag-a-muffins out the projects of Newark?

DENITRA *(Blinks)*

BEVERLY No. We're clearly two beautiful, capable, educated black women. I have a degree. I have three!

DENITRA *(Blinks again)*

BEVERLY What if I wasn't from Jersey? If I'd never been to Millburn? This lady would lead me to believe that that kind of thinking is indicative of this town, right?

DENITRA *(Beat)* Yeah.

BEVERLY I've got half a mind to write a letter to the state realty board.

DENITRA You think that would make a difference? Please. I ain't got time to be writing letters and forging battles. I got a child to raise.

BEVERLY Me too.

DENITRA Who has the energy to be convincing – ? At the end of the day I see it as her loss. I know I'm a lovely person.

BEVERLY As am I.

DENITRA You are.

BEVERLY So are you.

DENITRA We are lovely people.

BEVERLY Clearly. *(Beat)* House is overpriced, anyway. It's been listed on the market nearly a year.

DENITRA I guess that's what happens when there's *(mocking)* "very // little room for negotiation."

BEVERLY *(mocking)* "little room for negotiation."

(They laugh.)

BEVERLY *(Vocalized exhale)* Well, thank you for confirming that *I* wasn't being –

DENITRA No, no, you –

BEVERLY 'Cause for a while there I thought maybe I was –

DENITRA No that *agent* was – I'll corroborate your story.

BEVERLY Well, thank you.

DENITRA You are quite welcome.

(BEVERLY extends her hand to shake.)

BEVERLY Beverly.

DENITRA Denitra.

BEVERLY Pleasure.

(They shake.)

BEVERLY Have you been in the market for a while?

DENITRA *(Beat)* No. Not long. *(Beat)* Not sure I'm moving anywhere, really.

BEVERLY What's got you looking? The schools?

DENITRA *(Beat)* Yeah. She is starting high school in the fall, so…

BEVERLY Where is she now?

DENITRA Where is she going to school?

BEVERLY Yes.

DENITRA *(Beat)* Maplewood. Right over in – That's where we live. Maplewood.

BEVERLY Nice.

DENITRA We like it.

BEVERLY Maplewood schools are good. I know Columbia High puts up some good numbers.

DENITRA Yeah, they do. *(Beat)* But I wonder if Millburn's better. Did you know, they're named number one in the county? Students do better on the SAT and AP tests, so they get into better colleges. 99% graduation rate. 40% of Millburn graduates go to top four-year universities – 10% of their graduates were accepted to Ivy Leagues from last year, and –

BEVERLY You do your homework.

DENITRA Oh, I always have. I don't play when it comes to education.

BEVERLY *(Secret revealed)* My son will be a sophomore at Millburn High in the fall.

DENITRA Okay. So you already –

BEVERLY I just like to get a feel of what people think – I'll be working for the district.

DENITRA Oh. Okay. Hey, that's a good strategy. Work for the district. I wish I had thought – Are they still hiring?

BEVERLY *(Laughing)* Oh, I don't –

DENITRA Do they need a – a corporate attorney? "Will work for quality education."

(They laugh.)

BEVERLY I wish. There is no such perk. Employees have to live here too.

DENITRA Really?

BEVERLY If you want a good school, you have to pay: property taxes or private school tuition, pick your poison. I say, at least with the former, you get some equity.

DENITRA Gotta pay if you wanna play.

BEVERLY At least we can. Imagine if we were stuck in other, worser – if we couldn't afford to –

DENITRA Yeah.

BEVERLY I don't know what those parents do. "Hope" it works out? Pray?

DENITRA *(Chuckling)* Beg, borrow, lie, cheat their way…

BEVERLY Of course they do. Wouldn't you?

DENITRA *(Beat)* Yeah, I guess I would.

BEVERLY I definitely would. What parent wouldn't? I probably shouldn't be saying it, but… If I had to? You'd better believe it. Absolutely.

DENITRA Do what you gotta do.

BEVERLY Do what you have to do. I'm just glad I'm fortunate enough to be in a position where I don't have to make those kind of decisions.

DENITRA *(Beat)* Yeah. Me too.

Scene 2

SCHOOL BELL.

VO This is breaker five, breaker five reporting from the west entrance, over.

Lights up. A year and a half later: Monday morning, October 18, 2010. BEVERLY's office. Millburn High School, Millburn, NJ. All around is organized evidence of an administrator overwhelmed. MIKE DIMAGGIO stands reading the information on a bulletin board hanging from the wall - newspaper articles, letters, etc. Principal Beverly Long, Ed.D enters. MIKE gives her his attention.

BEVERLY *(Into the walkie talkie)* Breaker five maintain your post and secure the west entrance. Students must only be able to enter and exit through the main building at dismissal. Copy?

VO Copy that.

BEVERLY *(To MIKE)* Sorry about the wait.

MICHAEL No prob.

BEVERLY Perimeter walk took longer than we expected. More safety protocols. It's like just when we've implemented one policy, another –

MICHAEL Another one pops up. Like termites outta the woodworks. I know how that goes.

BEVERLY I just have to email a quick update to the superintendent, then we'll get started.

MICHAEL Sure. Sure. Take your time.

(BEVERLY types for a few moments.)

MICHAEL *(Beat)* Is the uh… Is the principal gonna be joinin' us?

(BEVERLY finishes.)

BEVERLY *(Beat)* I am the principal.

MICHAEL You're the…?

BEVERLY Yes.

MICHAEL *(Beat)* Ah, Christ –

BEVERLY It's alright.

MICHAEL Ah, man. They should tell ya – they just –

BEVERLY It's fine.

MICHAEL Nobody said – At the district office, they just hand you your paperwork and throw you in the deep end. "You're meeting with the principal. Monday. Two thirty." Boom. But they don't tell ya who or what or who –

BEVERLY Why don't you have a seat, Mister…?

MICHAEL Christ. Where are my man - DiMaggio. Mike DiMaggio, at your service.

(He extends his hand to shake. She accepts.)

BEVERLY Glad to meet you.

MICHAEL Same.

(BEVERLY continues to organize and settle during—)

BEVERLY You'll have to excuse the *(a gesture signifying, "mess.")* This past month things have been a little - Parents, the media, police. My office isn't usually -

MICHAEL You don't have-ta apologize to me. I worked in a police precinct with fifty guys. You ain't seen mess.

BEVERLY You were a police officer?

MICHAEL Lieutenant detective.

BEVERLY Oh.

MICHAEL Millburn PD.

BEVERLY Oh. Wonderful. So you're familiar with –

MICHAEL Oh, yeah. I got thirty five years on these streets.

BEVERLY Thirty-five. Wow. That's…

MICHAEL Now, I bet you I know what you're thinkin'.

BEVERLY You do?

MICHAEL You're thinkin', "How's a handsome, interesting fella like myself – who don't look a day over forty – how' did I manage to get in thirty-five years on the job?"

BEVERLY *(Beat)* That was exactly what I was thinking.

MICHAEL Some people got good genes. What can I say?

BEVERLY True.

MICHAEL Black ain't the only thing don't crack, eh?

(MIKE laughs. BEVERLY does not.)

BEVERLY I assume you've done this work before.

MICHAEL Private investigation?

BEVERLY For schools specifically.

MICHAEL Oh, yeah. I've done plenty-a - Truancy, border hoppin' -

BEVERLY Border hopping?

MICHAEL Oh, sorry - s'What we call school residency fraud in the field.

BEVERLY Oh.

MICHAEL Yeah, I've been freelancing for the past six years. All over Jersey. I could do it with my eyes closed.

BEVERLY Don't do that.

MICHAEL Oh, I didn't mean I actually close my - // I mean it's second nature -

BEVERLY Because these circumstances are not your ordinary -

MICHAEL No, I understand. What's going on here isn't your regular - it's serious.

BEVERLY To say the least.

MICHAEL s'A shame something like this has to happen to get people to wake up, stop livin' in airy-fairy land and realize they've gotta be - People think because they're a couple-a towns over and there's a Trader Joe's they're immune to the kind-a stuff that happens over there. But nobody's immune. There's no wall keeping them over there and us over here. It's just a line. A line in the dust. And once that line gets crossed, once that outside element gets in…then we've got ourselves a problem.

BEVERLY Yeah.

MICHAEL Like now: they're sayin' the shooting of your student? They're sayin' it could be gang related.

BEVERLY There's evidence that suggests it was gang related?

MICHAEL Well, his bein' from Newark, for one.

BEVERLY That doesn't make him a gang member.

MICHAEL See, that's the common miscon - He don't haveta be a gang member for it to have been gang "related."

BEVERLY You've lost me.

MICHAEL He could-a had a brother, or a // cousin -

BEVERLY Brother?

MICHAEL Or a cousin - somebody close who - I mean, think about it: A *boy*, born and raised in the *projects* in *Newark*, not knowing no gang members? No uncles, no friends, no neighbors - *nobody*? That's like… s'Like sayin' you work in a strip club don't know no strippers. Bein' a inmate don't know no prisoners.

(MIKE chuckles.)

MICHAEL It ain't impossible. But it ain't likely. Shooting was basically a drive-by. s'Got gang M.O. written all over it.

BEVERLY God. That's the last thing I need.

MICHAEL I know. s'Like as if the kid bein' here - hikin' up the property taxes wasn't enough. Now you could have a potential public safety issue on your hands.

BEVERLY You think?

MICHAEL Yeah. It's like - Case in point: Just a few weeks ago right here in Millburn. It was all over the news. Husband's at work on Wall Street. Wife's home alone with the kid. Black guy busts into the house. Bang. It's her worst nightmare. He robs 'em, roughs her up in front of her kid. Knocks her down the basement stairs. Thank God he didn't rape her. Kill her. Fled the scene. Little did he know, the whole thing was caught on the nanny cam. APB went out. They found him in New York. Cuffed 'im. Brought 'im back to Jersey. And where was he from? I'll give you a hint: it's here in New Jersey. In Essex county with us. And it ain't Irvington. Just take a wild -

BEVERLY Newark.

MICHAEL Surprise, right? The suspect was from the good old city of bricks. See, that's the issue. The outside element. And it's like this kid, Marvin -

BEVERLY Malik.

MICHAEL *(A gesture that signifies, "Exactly.")* Yeah, Malik, God rest his soul. Nobody's child should be … it's beyond… I can't even imagine… but it's the same thing. That outside element makin' its way in.

BEVERLY I don't know. He was a good kid. I just can't // wrap my mind around -

MICHAEL Hey: he may've been a good kid, he might've been the lovechild of Mr. Rogers and Mary Poppins, but good kid or not: falsifying government documents and stealin' public services is a crime. A felony in some states. Don't matter what kind-a kid he was. It's the law. The law's the law.

BEVERLY You're right.

(Beverly's cell phone rings. Beverly checks it.)

BEVERLY I'm sorry. It's my son. I have to - in case it's // an emergency.

MICHAEL Of course.

(MIKE helps himself to a framed picture on her desk during the following.)

BEVERLY *(Into the phone)* Jordan? You okay? *(Beat)* No. Go to the library. *(Beat)* No. Wait in the library. Start your homework. I'll be done within the hour, okay. *(Beat)* Uh, you're welcome. *(Beat) (Mocking him)* Thank you, Mommy. Bye.

(BEVERLY ends her call.)

MICHAEL 'sThis your son.

BEVERLY Yeah. That's my baby.

(BEVERLY restores the picture.)

MICHAEL Baby? He's taller 'an you. He's a Millburn Miller?

BEVERLY Yep. Junior now.

MICHAEL Must be cool, having your mom as the principal.

BEVERLY I get the impression he'd rather not be around me all day.

MICHAEL Crampin' his style, huh?

BEVERLY That's the impression I get. *(Beat)* Okay -

(The telephone rings.)

BEVERLY Jesus.

(BEVERLY picks up.)

BEVERLY Excuse me. *(Into the phone)* Principal Long. *(Beat)* Ah... No, no. Hold him. I'll be right out.

(BEVERLY hangs up.)

BEVERLY *(To MIKE)* I'm sorry. If you'll excuse me for one moment. I have to confer with my vice principal before dismissal.

MICHAEL Of course.

BEVERLY I'll be right back. 'Tis the life.

(BEVERLY exits. MIKE sits for a while. He rises to peruse the room looking BEVERLY's accolades and framed photos. He sees her degrees.)

MICHAEL *(Reading)* "Princeton." Huh.

(He looks at another framed award.)

MICHAEL *(Reading)* "The New Jersey State Association of School Administrators recognizes "*Doctor*" Beverly Long for her distinguished service in enhancing the educational program of a New Jersey public school." Hunh.

(DENITRA enters, shocking MIKE. She carries a letter.)

DENITRA Knock, knock? Beverly? *(Beat)* Oh. I didn't - *(beat)* I'm sorry. *(Beat)* Hi. Is Principal Long here?

MICHAEL Not unless she changed her name to Casper.

(MIKE chuckles.)

DENITRA *(A gesture signifying, "who?")*

MICHAEL The friendly ghost?

DENITRA *(A facial expression signifying, "what the hell are you talking about?")*

MICHAEL Probably before your time. *(Beat)* She uh, she stepped out.

DENITRA Oh. *(Beat)* Did she say when she'd be back?

MICHAEL Your guess is as good as mine.

DENITRA *(To herself)* ...Great.

MICHAEL I don't think she'll be long... if you wanna stick around. I don't mind. I'd rather not be in the principal's office by myself anyhow. Too many bad memories, eh?

(MIKE laughs. DENITRA does not. DENITRA considers, then decides to stay. MIKE picks up the paper. DENITRA whips out her smart phone. They settle in. Moments pass.)

MICHAEL I can divide the paper. If you'd like.

DENITRA I can actually get it on my *(a gesture indicating her, "smart phone.")*

MICHAEL Oh. *(Beat)* I don't see how anyone can read on those little screens.

DENITRA It is hard sometimes.

MICHAEL If you'd-a told me thirty years ago that people'd be reading the news on little hand held gadgets I'd say you lost your mind. I don't think I'll ever be able to get used-ta - I need the actual paper, you know. Nuts and bolts.

DENITRA I hear ya.

MICHAEL But I guess I better get used to it, eh? The local papers can barely stay in business. Everything's gonna be on that thing.

DENITRA It's going that way.

MICHAEL What I don't like about - Only the big news guys can really get a followin' on those things. They're all well and good, but they're not gonna report on the little guy. They're all here now, 'cause-a the shooting, but the regular affairs of Millburn, they don't report on those.

DENITRA No, they don't.

MICHAEL So how will people stay informed of what's going on in their own communities? Everybody's so concerned about what's going on in Iraq. People don't know what's going on in their own - s'Like - Do you live here in Millburn?

DENITRA Yes.

MICHAEL Okay. Do you know about the BP oil spill out there in the Gulf of - ?

DENITRA Yes.

MICHAEL Yes, of course, right? Can't miss that one. You hear about that mosque they wanna build on Ground Zero?

DENITRA Yes. I've heard that.

MICHAEL Okay. Do you know about the zoning ordinance hoopla, right here in town??

DENITRA *(beat)* No.

MICHAEL See. You know what's going on in the Gulf of Mexico, in New York City, I bet you'd know what was going on in Afghanistan before you'd know what was going on in your own backyard.

DENITRA What's the hoopla?

MICHAEL Well, there's this synagogue over on Jefferson and Old Short Hills Road - you know just past the - when you drive up Old Short Hills a little past the middle school?

DENITRA Right.

MICHAEL Right there - it's pretty residential, right?

DENITRA Yes.

MICHAEL That's 'cause the zoning board passed ordinances that make it so that the area stays residential. But this synagogue wants to come and violate the ordinance and build a sixteen thousand square foot building smack dab in the middle - bam - with no regard to - just bam. They only got 75 worshipers! Why do they need so much space?

DENITRA I don't -

MICHAEL 'Cause they don't just wanna pray. Yeah. I went around - I'm a part of this organization, the Concerned Citizens of Millburn? - I did some investigatin' for 'em - I drove around a couple-a times and I saw 'em erectin' tents, caterin' trucks, balloons -They said that it was just a place for worship - but clearly *(a gesture and sound signifying, "it's more than that.")*

DENITRA Oh.

MICHAEL They got 50 to 70 cars parked all around. A complete mess. The traffic! The safety! The noise! It's just…The ordinance clearly states all buildings of public assembly built in that area have to have so much space between it and the houses. It's got to be on a 3-acre plot. Is that plot three acres?

DENITRA No?

MICHAEL Not even close. Yet and still, they want the zoning board to ignore the ordinance and approve their application to build. Now, is that right?

DENITRA No.

MICHAEL No, it ain't. *(Beat)* Now, personally, I could care less whether or not they pray there or do what ever they do. s'None-a my business. Mazel tov. I'm Italian Catholic. Ain't nobody's business where I say my Hail Marys, you know what I mean? But the issue is bigger than them: the community is designed to be a certain way. If the zoning board breaks the rules, what's to stop other folks from… Next thing you'll know, you'll have people comin' in from God knows where - And I don't know about you, but the last thing I need-a be worried about is whether or not my community is gonna be livable in the next twenty years, you know?

DENITRA Yeah.

MICHAEL s'Why I stay involved. s'Why you gotta stay involved. Read the local paper not that little gadget about what's going on in Baghdad.

(He offers the paper. She accepts. The PA system comes on with two tones.)

VO *(A student)* Good afternoon Millburn High. These are your PM announcements for October 18th. 2010. Be advised: all after school activities will remain suspended throughout the week. Stay tuned for Principal Long.

(A scuffle is heard as they exchange positioning. BEVERLY clears her throat.)

BEVERLY *(Voice over)* Good afternoon students, this is your principal. As a reminder, the campus remains under security alert. All high alert dismissal procedures still apply. As you leave today, please make it your business to arrive quickly and safely to your final destination. For those of you whose parents are picking you up, please go directly to their cars to alleviate any unnecessary traffic. For those of you driving, please drive safely and obey all posted signage. Remember that you are not obligated to talk to any lingering reporters, and that, if you see one on school grounds, please tell a teacher or an administrator immediately. *(Beat)* As you venture home, reflect on all you learned today. And remember, your education is the preparation for your future. Failing to prepare, is preparing to fail. Don't leave for tomorrow what can be done today. This is your principal.

(They simultaneously snicker at BEVERLY'S PA announcement - perhaps for different reasons, but joint laughter nonetheless. The PA system clicks off.)

MICHAEL *(Beat)* Whatdya think about the whole shebang going on here? I assume you know about the shooting and -

DENITRA Of course. I think it's horrible.

MICHAEL Yeah.

DENITRA It's sad. It's a shame what happened to -

MICHAEL Yeah. And I tell ya, the Concerned Citizens? They told me they had been fighting for the school board to audit enrollment for years! These non-resident kids have been here for years moochin' off-a - all while the school board's cryin' broke! The Citizens were trying to tell 'em, "If you stop paying for these out-of-towners, you'd have the money in your budget for -" But did they listen? No. And now look what happened.

DENITRA Yeah.

MICHAEL Some people gotta learn the hard way, eh?

DENITRA Unfortunately.

MICHAEL Here. Take this.

(He hands her a flyer. She accepts.)

MICHAEL I don't know if you're into town politics or whatever. That's the community association I told you I'm a part of. The Concerned Citizens of Millburn. You may've seen us? We recruit sometimes outside the post office?

DENITRA No. *(Slight beat)* But I don't go to the post office much.

MICHAEL We have newcomer meetings at the Bauer Center in Taylor Park every other Friday night at 7pm. Right after work. Since the shooting, people've been comin' outta the woodworks to join. We're lookin' to get as many people involved as possible. And we want it to be a diverse group, you know? A united front. Everybody who lives here who cares. You should come if you can.

DENITRA Is this like the neighborhood watch?

MICHAEL No. No. Our mission is to *(he reads from the flyer)* "inform residents about the decisions being made that negatively affect the future of our town."

DENITRA Okay.

MICHAEL Everybody's gotta be actively involved. Everybody. You can't complain what happens if you don't get involved.

DENITRA True.

MICHAEL Whereabouts do you live?

DENITRA *(Beat)* Us? Oh. We live -

(BEVERLY returns.)

BEVERLY Alright. Let us -

(The dismissal bell rings.)

DENITRA Bev - Hi, Principal Long. I -

BEVERLY Denitra?

DENITRA I'm sorry to -

BEVERLY Were we supposed to meet?

DENITRA No, no. This isn't a scheduled -

BEVERLY Is everything alright?

(DENITRA quickly pulls BEVERLY away from MIKE.)

DENITRA You tell me.

BEVERLY Tell you what?

DENITRA What'd she do?

BEVERLY What'd who do?

DENITRA *(Beat)* You don't know what I'm talking about.

BEVERLY I haven't the faintest idea -

DENITRA Isn't the principal the only one with the power to suspend students?

BEVERLY Suspend? Who?

DENITRA Noelle.

BEVERLY What?

DENITRA Yes.

BEVERLY Okay. I... I'm almost done here. Give me a few moments to finish up with Mr. DiMaggio, and I'll be right with you. Okay?

DENITRA Thank you.

BEVERLY It'll be alright.

DENITRA I'll just *(a gesture signifying, "be out here.")*

BEVERLY That's good.

(DENITRA exits. MIKE watches.)

BEVERLY Crazy. The perfect crazy end to the perfectly crazy Monday.

MICHAEL Well, you know what they say:

BEVERLY What's that?

MICHAEL When it rains, everything gets wet.

(MIKE laughs. BEVERLY finally chuckles.)

BEVERLY *(Beat)* Why don't we...?

MICHAEL Let's do it.

BEVERLY Where'd we leave off?

MICHAEL At the beginning.

BEVERLY Right.

MICHAEL Everything starts with the enrollment analysis report.

BEVERLY What's that?

MICHAEL It's a - Essentially, what I do is, basically, I take all the names from your rolls - every single student - and I plug 'em into a database of public records - tax assessors, postal service, that kind-a thing. And the computer'll spit out a report - all the addresses associated with those names in the public record.

BEVERLY Okay.

MICHAEL Then I'll compare those addresses to the addresses from the registration information you have on file for each student.

BEVERLY Okay.

MICHAEL You follow? I know it's a little complicated -

BEVERLY I'm followin'.

MICHAEL Then the computer'll spit out another report of the discrepancies - all the names where the address they claim with you is nowhere to be found in the public record. That'll be the basis of my investigation.

BEVERLY Got it.

MICHAEL They say to expect anywhere between 1 and 2 percent of the total enrollment.

BEVERLY What's that? That'll be, what?

MICHAEL Somewhere between 14 and 28 students.

BEVERLY Oh. That's it? That's not - I mean, one student is one too many, but that's certainly not the epidemic they'd have us think -

MICHAEL Well, I'm expecting more. Millburn's gone without an enrollment purge for a while, from what I understand.

BEVERLY That's right.

MICHAEL So, there'll probably be a lotta names rollin' in from the fraud hotline. // There'll be more.

BEVERLY Oh, we're not doing that.

MICHAEL What?

BEVERLY The fraud hotline.

MICHAEL You're not doing a fraud hotline?

BEVERLY No.

MICHAEL Why not?

BEVERLY Families are complying. Almost ninety percent have submitted their documents on time. I don't think the results we'll get from any hotline are worth creating an environment where we're pitting student against student, neighbor against neighbor.

MICHAEL How's a hotline pittin' - ?

BEVERLY It's just not the kind of environment - We've already gone through a shooting. We don't need to go through a witch hunt too. In all honesty, I'm hoping any remaining violators quickly realize that this is serious and just withdraw their children before the board meetings...save us all the time, the money.

MICHAEL Hey, hey! You tryin' to put me outta business here?

(MIKE chuckles. BEVERLY looks.)

MICHAEL I'm just bustin' your ba - Pullin' your leg.

BEVERLY I'd actually love to put you out of business, Mr. DiMaggio. I'd love for this whole thing // to just...

MICHAEL Hey, I'd love for it to be that nobody hadda be - But, the rules is as they are and there's always gonna be somebody willing to break the rules, right?

BEVERLY Unfortunately.

MICHAEL *(Beat)* What the district really needs to do is think about investin' in a permanent P.I. position.

BEVERLY *(Beat)* A P.I., say, like you?

MICHAEL You could do worse.

BEVERLY I don't know where we'd get the budget.

MICHAEL Lemme ask you: How much does it cost here, per student per year? Ball park?

BEVERLY Seventeen thousand. Give or take.

MICHAEL The district could lose *seventeen grand* on one kid stayin' in school who don't belong!?

BEVERLY As long as the district doesn't hire another teacher or add a classroom it really doesn't cost a full -

MICHAEL But generally speaking. Seventeen.

BEVERLY Yes. Generally speaking.

MICHAEL So say if a hundred kids end up bein' non-residents, that's what? One point seven million dollars could be saved, right?

BEVERLY In theory.

MICHAEL Lets' say it would cost the district twenty grand to retain a guy like me every year. Hypothetically speaking.

BEVERLY Alright.

MICHAEL But I could potentially save you one point seven million. See how I did that?

BEVERLY I did.

MICHAEL Spend twenty thou' to save a million? Kickin' out two non-resident kids would more'n pay for the retainer fee. Got a buddy contracted with a district up in Bergen County. They got the same problem. Parents lyin' left and right. He nabs at least five to ten kids every year per school. The service basically pays for itself. Here:

(He hands her his brochure.)

MICHAEL I made this brochure to share with the higher-ups. It breaks it all down. Results you can expect in a year. Two. Five. I'm sure with your endorsement -

BEVERLY Thank you.

MICHAEL Having a P.I. on staff is a deterrent in and of itself.

BEVERLY As it stands, I'm really focused on this current crisis. Once we make it to solid ground, then I can think about –

MICHAEL Sure, sure. s'Just something to put on your back burner.

BEVERLY Will do.

(BEVERLY places the brochure in a desk, or somewhere that makes it clear it will never see the light of day.)

BEVERLY So, what are our next steps?

MICHAEL Next step is basically I get started on my report then hit the field. Start knockin' on doors.

BEVERLY Do you need any support, any supplies, anything from us?

MICHAEL I could use a hotline…

(MIKE chuckles, BEVERLY does a little.)

MICHAEL Just kiddin'.

BEVERLY If you need anything else, please don't be shy.

MICHAEL Me? Shy? *(A gesture signifying, "fughettaboutit.")*

BEVERLY Alright. See you next Monday for an update. You can schedule with Mrs. Madison on your way out.

MICHAEL Sure thing.

(BEVERLY opens the door for MIKE to leave.)

BEVERLY Come on in.

(DENITRA enters as he exits. MIKE salutes DENITRA in the exchange. BEVERLY shuts the door before MIKE is able to say a formal goodbye.)

BEVERLY Now, what happened?

DENITRA The truancy office called me this morning to say that Noelle was suspended indefinitely as of last Friday.

BEVERLY What?

DENITRA Yes. And she's been sittin' in the office all – she's been crying, texting me like crazy. I was stuck at work, I couldn't –

BEVERLY Wait a minute. She was suspended?

DENITRA Yes. I told her to come talk to you, but she said the man wouldn't let her leave. He wouldn't even let her go to class to turn in her homework! When I finally get here, he hands me this and –

(DENITRA hands BEVERLY a letter. BEVERLY looks it over.)

DENITRA And I'm like, "What's this?" And he says –

BEVERLY Did you submit your updated residency documents?

DENITRA Of course. Weeks ago. Way before the deadline. I gave them copies of our property taxes. Utilities. Affidavit. Everything. I gave them to Noelle to turn in. What more do they want? My birth certificate? Blood?

BEVERLY Did she turn them in?

DENITRA I assume so. I mean, what else would she do with them?

BEVERLY Do you have your time stamp receipt?

DENITRA That's just what he – No. We never got a receipt.

BEVERLY When you turned the documents in, Ms. Scibetta gave a receipt that she time stamped as proof of submission.

DENITRA I never got any receipt.

BEVERLY She would've given it to Noelle when she turned them in. Did you ask her?

DENITRA Even if she did give it to her, which Noelle wholeheartedly denies, we're talking about a girl who has lost her house keys 4 times in one year. She's lost the pants to her Easter suit. Pants. This is the person we're asking to produce a receipt from weeks ago?

BEVERLY Alright.

DENITRA Don't you all have a record? I asked him to review his records to verify and he refused. Talkin' 'bout I have to go to the district offices. I don't have time to go to nobody's – I said, "Lemme see Beverly first, 'cause these people are crazy." It's always something.

BEVERLY Let me check…

(BEVERLY types then scrolls through files on her computer. DENITRA nervously watches for a moment, then—)

DENITRA It's not like Noelle's an incoming student. She's been here a year. To suspend her for some paperwork? This is ridiculous. Havin' her sit out of class? Interrupting her education for –

BEVERLY I don't even see a record logged for her. Let me…

(BEVERLY types and scrolls. DENITRA crosses to see BEVERLY's computer screen.)

DENITRA That happened last year with her transcripts, remember?

BEVERLY God, I hope this is not an indication – I don't know how much more I can impress upon them the importance of consistent and accurate records. Our work is being audited. I cringe to think…If there are errors in Noelle's record, a child we know has residence, how many other students –

DENITRA I can't afford to be leavin' work to come up here every time.

BEVERLY You? I can't afford these kinds of mistakes. Not now. I'm being blamed for enough as it is.

(BEVERLY continues to look on her computer.)

DENITRA Blaming you for what? *(Referring to the newspaper clipping on the bulletin board)* For…?

BEVERLY Yeah.

DENITRA What? No.

BEVERLY You don't believe – ?

(BEVERLY stops. She hesitates, then reaches for a letter and hands it to DENITRA. DENITRA opens it and reads.)

BEVERLY Got served this morning.

DENITRA Served? As in sued?

BEVERLY Negligent endangerment. That's the charge.

DENITRA What?

BEVERLY Yeah.

DENITRA Is this against the district, the school or – ?

BEVERLY Oh, no. I'm named specifically. As "principal." Suddenly I'm principal. When I want budget changes, I'm just the interim principal. When I want to implement new programs, I'm interim principal. But when folks are being indicted? Now I'm in charge.

DENITRA Oh, hun.

BEVERLY It's their rationale that kills me. They're saying I negligently allowed this boy into the school, and his "lethal presence" endangered their children. It's just *(a gesture signifying, "absurd.")*

DENITRA My God.

BEVERLY Like I was supposed to know that his parents were lying? Now they're saying he was in a gang or –

DENITRA Who are these people suing you?

BEVERLY Parents. A group of parents who have been out to get me since the shooting. Before the police report even revealed Malik's residence they were –

DENITRA The PTO?

BEVERLY No, they're not the PTO. The PTO is very supportive. No, these parents? They're a part of the concerned citizen's something. I don't know what they're calling themselves.

DENITRA The Concerned Citizen's Council of Millburn Township?

BEVERLY *(Beat)* Yeah. How do you…?

(DENITRA shows her the flyer MIKE gave her.)

BEVERLY Where did you get this?

DENITRA The man who was here.

BEVERLY The man who just left?!

DENITRA Yeah. He asked me if I live in town and told me that they were concerned citizens recruiting –

BEVERLY You're kidding, right?!

DENITRA No. He was telling me about –

BEVERLY He's a part of this?!

DENITRA Yeah.

BEVERLY This is the group that – They want me out, Denitra!

DENITRA Are you sure?

BEVERLY Am I sure!? At the last school board meeting, that they bum rushed, one of them stood up, said he represented the citizen's council or whatever and called for my resignation!

DENITRA What?!

BEVERLY Yes. He hijacked the entire public question portion of the –

DENITRA But they can't call for your resignation. Who are they?

BEVERLY They can't, but they have influence. They make a lot of noise and nobody wants to – They're the ones behind the enrollment audit. They lobbied the PTO. They lobbied the school board until they gave in for fear of their threats to sue if they didn't – And they're suing anyway! They're the reason the board agreed to hire a – *(beat)* Oh my God, and he gave you this. They hired him as the private investigator, but he's a part of –

DENITRA Okay. Don't jump to any –

BEVERLY No, you don't understand, Denitra. People are bunkering down. Since the shooting it's been nothing but damage control and positioning. Everyone making sure that they won't be – And now they've got me sleeping with the enemy. They're trying to set me up to take the fall.

DENITRA Don't go off the deep end –

BEVERLY What should I do? Legally? What can I do in your professional opinion to protect myself?

DENITRA *(Beat)* I don't - It's not...it's not my kind of law. I do -

BEVERLY What kind of attorney do I need?

DENITRA … Civil? I don't -

BEVERLY But I should get my own attorney, though, right? Not rely on the district's counsel?

DENITRA You probably should. Get your own. Definitely.

BEVERLY I will.

DENITRA That's best.

BEVERLY *(Beat)* Can I ask you something?

DENITRA Sure.

BEVERLY And be brutally honest.

DENITRA Of course.

BEVERLY Do you think I'm doing a good job as principal?

DENITRA Yes.

BEVERLY Have you heard any parents say, any teachers, staff relay that they have a problem with my leadership?

DENITRA No. Why would you think - ?

BEVERLY Some people are saying it.

DENITRA Who?

BEVERLY I got wind that Mr. Ludlow said so. Publicly. In the district office. That things have gone "downhill in the last year." Knowing that I've only been here a year. So he's basically saying -

DENITRA Who is he? I mean -

BEVERLY He's head of security.

DENITRA Well, of course _he_ would - he's just trying to save himself from - You can't get yourself worked up over gossip and claims and citizen's groups. People are going to talk. But people have your back. Hundreds of people in this community showed up to Malik's vigil. They know it's not your fault. It's a bad situation, but you're handling things very well.

BEVERLY Please tell that to the district.

DENITRA I will.

BEVERLY And the PTO.

DENITRA I will.

BEVERLY And the Concerned Citizen's Council of Millburn.

DENITRA Them, we might have to beat up.

(BEVERLY laughs.)

DENITRA Don't make me take off work and come down to one of those meetings.

BEVERLY *(Laughing)* Stop -

DENITRA I'll take off my earrings, put on my boots, get the Vaseline. Just point 'em out.

(BEVERLY laughs.)

BEVERLY Thanks.

DENITRA Girl, please. But, at the risk of sounding contradictory, you can't be too cautious. Especially now that there's an actual claim filed. Watch everybody. Even your staff. You don't know what they're doing, what they're saying, when you're not around. How they may be inadvertently sabotaging you, i.e. "losing documents." How's the song go? "They smile in your face…"

BEVERLY And stab you right in your back.

DENITRA Trust and believe that each and every one of these folk would chose themselves over you if they had to.

BEVERLY *(Beat)* God. If I wanted drama I would've stayed in Newark.

DENITRA *(Beat)* You were in Newark?

BEVERLY Yep. Sure was.

DENITRA You never told me that. When?

BEVERLY Right before I took this position, actually.

DENITRA As a principal?

BEVERLY No. As "Assistant Superintendent for Curriculum and Instruction."

DENITRA *(Beat)* Fancy.

BEVERLY Handpicked by the Governor.

DENITRA Really?

BEVERLY Yep.

DENITRA What happened?

BEVERLY *(Beat)* I quit. *(Beat)* I've never quit anything in my life, but I quit that. Sure did.

DENITRA Why?

BEVERLY *(Beat)* Because I didn't go to undergrad, grad and post grad to spend my days getting cursed out at board meetings by parents who call you sell out for trying to defend them, and colleagues who throw you under the bus for telling the truth. I earned more than that. I deserved better. Jordan deserved better too.

DENITRA Wait: you had Jordan in school there?!

BEVERLY How would it have looked if I, who was responsible for making sure the kids were being taught the right things the right way, if I had my child in another school district?

DENITRA People do it. I bet half the Newark staff lives in Glenridge and Montclair. I bet none of them send their kids to Newark schools.

BEVERLY And I know why. Have you ever spent some time in a Newark high school?

DENITRA *(Beat)* No. I mean, I've heard some things…

BEVERLY Part of my job was to walk through every school in the district to observe teachers. Elementary and middle schools were generally fine. Jordan went to Hawthorne Elementary. Excellent school. But high school? Something shifts. I remember being on a walk through in Jordan's high school, the bell rings to switch classes and out pour the students. And it's the usual thing, but this day something was… I don't know I just… The conversations amongst the kids were just - n-word this. B-word that. F-this. Right in front of adults. They didn't care. I heard a teacher in the distance shout, "Get yo' a-word to class." And this was them on their best behavior, I mean, they knew we were coming to walk through. Lots of lingering. Lots of on-the-corner loitering. A security officer a little too friendly with one of the little girls for my taste. Then I think to myself, he's not but twenty years old. He most likely graduated from there two years ago.

DENITRA Probably.

BEVERLY There were lots of kids, an innumerable amount, not carrying anything at all, which means they had no books, no homework to turn in, nothing with which to take notes or carry handouts or store materials they received, no paper and pen even. And this was not because they all had laptops or tablets or anything, like the students here. The bell rings for class to start, passing is over, but no one's in a rush. Just shuffling along. I decide to sneak away from the walk to peak in on Jordan's class - I kept him out of the general population. He was in "honors academy," I made sure. And I never tell him when I'm going to pop up, so he'll always be on his best -

DENITRA I do the same thing.

BEVERLY - and I get to his class and what do I see?… All the boys are lined up on one side of the room, girls on the other, facing the wall, spread eagle while two security officers wand them down. Another walks through the aisles of the class looking through their bags… for contraband. The teacher's entering grades, and I tell her who I am and I ask her, "What's going on here?" Figuring there was a serious incident of violence. But she casually says, "Random security check." They pick a classroom at random every morning. Like numbers out of a hat. They got my baby on the wall doin' the pat down perp walk - he's done nothing wrong, and what killed me was that this was normal. All of it - the hallways, the cursing, the low expectations, the loitering - The kids were used to it. I had become used to it. The teacher was used to interrupting her lesson for random security checks. I mean, this was a classroom - supposed to be a learning space, a safe space, but there they were spread eagle…and not at all bothered by it… laughing even. And I realized: My son was being indoctrinated into _prison_ culture because of my career aspirations. I pulled him from that school that same day and quit the next. Just packed my stuff up, and walked away. Right in the middle of curriculum approval. I didn't even finish presenting to the board. I didn't want to be associated with that mayhem, not one more minute. My Princeton bud told me about what happened here with the previous principal -

DENITRA What happened?

BEVERLY He was called out for uttering some very non-PC words. And rather than deal - After nineteen years he was more than vested - So, he just *(a gesture signifying, "let it go.")*

DENITRA Wow.

BEVERLY So, he left. And I was told they were looking for "diverse candidates," right?

DENITRA To save face.

BEVERLY Yes. But I couldn't even think about the tokenism - I mean, my whole life *(a gesture signifying, "I've been token-ized")* - I believe I was chosen for the Newark job, in part, because I was - Well, I should say it wasn't just my ability. Well, I shouldn't say -

DENITRA I get it. You cover all their bases. Female. Minority.

BEVERLY Yes. But I always do my best.

DENITRA Of course. That's what we do.

BEVERLY Despite the *(a gesture signifying "tokenism")* - I still saw this as an opportunity. So, I went for the position and I got it. And I never looked back. And now, just when

I thought I rescued my career from being completely derailed - pow. The irony is I did all of it to keep Jordan away from that, and here he is having the experience anyhow.

DENITRA Yeah. *(Beat)* Did Jordan know? About the boy's address?

BEVERLY He says no. He may've. They were friends. There are only 8 black boys in the entire school. They gravitated toward each other.

DENITRA How's he holding up?

BEVERLY He's... conflicted. In many ways. A student said something insensitive about Malik, kids just repeat what they hear at home, and Jordan went off on the boy. I asked him why. He said it was like he was defending himself by defending Malik. That people look at them just the same. Then he gets angry because he knows people look at them like they're the same. He showed me this viral email someone stuck in his locker - about how to treat black people when they see them walking on the streets in Millburn. It said to call the police. No matter what they're doing, if you see a black boy call the police. So I don't let him walk home. He waits in the school library to drive home with me. I'm trying to get him to talk about, to process...He said to me the other night, "Mom, why does it matter where you go to school, as long as you go?"

DENITRA What did you say?

BEVERLY I said, "That's the way it is." I mean, I didn't want to get into zoning and districting and redlining and steering and home rule -

DENITRA Of course.

BEVERLY How's Noelle taking it?

DENITRA I think she's okay.

BEVERLY Her poem at the vigil was just amazing.

DENITRA Thank you. She did a good job, didn't she?

BEVERLY I think everyone was stunned.

DENITRA *(Beat)* Why?

BEVERLY Not that she couldn't... I just think that's the most anybody's heard from her. I mean, I knew *(a gesture signifying, "she was capable")* -

DENITRA I tell her she needs to stop being all shy. "You can't spend all your time in the office with the Principal if you wanna -"

BEVERLY She'll get out there. She will. In due time. I try not to pressure her. I remember what it was like when I was her age. High school is scary. But I bet now? So many people came up to her after she read. The poem was so... "He wanted to learn so he could be free. May that spirit live on in you // and in me."

DENITRA "And in me."

BEVERLY I mean, just *(a gesture signifying "moving.")*

DENITRA I know.

BEVERLY Where does a fifteen year old get that wisdom, that - ?

DENITRA I don't know. I think the situation....I think it just touched her heart.

BEVERLY Did she know him?

DENITRA I don't think so.

BEVERLY The way she was able to... It brought me to tears.

DENITRA Yeah... me too.

BEVERLY "He wanted to learn..."

DENITRA Yeah.

BEVERLY *(Beat)* How is she doing in her classes?

DENITRA Good. It'll be better than last year, I'm sure. She took her first trigonometry exam last Friday, but she wasn't in class today to see how she did. And, oh, she said she's decided where she wants to go to college.

BEVERLY She did?

DENITRA She wants to go to Princeton, like you.

BEVERLY Does she? Really? Aww...

DENITRA I should've known she wouldn't want to follow in my footsteps.

BEVERLY Oh now.

DENITRA It's true. It's always, "Principal Long, this." "Principal Long, that." She really looks up to you. I think she didn't come in here and tell you she was suspended like I asked her to because she didn't want you to be disappointed in her.

BEVERLY I'm not disappointed! It was a clerical error. It's not her fault.

DENITRA I know, but -

BEVERLY Oh, she should have come to me. She knows she can come to me, by now, doesn't she? After all we've been through?

DENITRA You'd think.

BEVERLY Tell her not to worry her little head. We'll clear it up.

DENITRA Speaking of which: what do I need to do?

BEVERLY Right. All you need to do is re-submit the documents.

DENITRA What about the deadline?

BEVERLY Don't worry about the deadline. Have Noelle bring the documents to my office tomorrow, first thing.

DENITRA Okay. First thing.

BEVERLY I'll ask Mrs. Madison to walk them over when she makes her trip to the district offices. She'll get them logged. Tell them it got separated from the batch somehow.

DENITRA Okay. And what about the suspension? She can't miss any more school. And I don't want this on her record. Suspended students don't go to Princeton.

(BEVERLY writes a note.)

BEVERLY Once her name is re-instated the suspension will be removed from her record. Until then, give Noelle this. *(BEVERLY hands DENITRA the note.)* She'll have to carry it with her to her classes. Tell her not to lose it. Or forget it. Teachers are instructed to follow protocol – and they do. No one wants to lose their job behind... They will send her out.

DENITRA I'll staple it to her chest.

BEVERLY And I thank you for bringing this issue to me first and not the district. I don't need these kinds of mistakes getting out.

DENITRA Girl, no problem. I didn't want to go over there anyhow. *(Beat)* Now let me go get her, and get home.

BEVERLY I'm right behind you.

DENITRA Tell Jordan I said, "Keep your head up."

BEVERLY I will.

DENITRA And, hey: No matter what none of these folks got to say, remember: you're doing a good job, Beverly.

BEVERLY Thank you, Denitra.

DENITRA No problem.

BEVERLY And Denitra?

DENITRA Yeah.

BEVERLY If you could shoot me some names of some attorneys, I'd appreciate it.

DENITRA *(Beat)* I'll see what I can do.

BEVERLY Thanks.

(DENITRA exits. BEVERLY takes a breather. She picks up her cellphone and dials. She continues to grab her things to leave during—)

BEVERLY *(Into the phone)* Jordan? *(Beat)* It's time to go. Meet me at the car. *(Beat)* Okay.

(BEVERLY ends the call, gathers her things, exhales and exits.)

Scene 3

A week later. Monday, October 25, 2010. Principal BEVERLY LONG, Ed.D's office at Millburn High School, Millburn, NJ. She sits with MICHAEL DIMAGGIO, private investigator. There's a box of pastry box of pizelles visible. He hands her a report and begins to speak. She shushes him, and takes her time reading a bit. Then:

BEVERLY So how many in total?

MICHAEL Forty-nine.

(Beverly leafs through the report.)

BEVERLY That's more than the "fourteen to twenty-eight" you said –

MICHAEL I told you there'd be more.

BEVERLY What's the margin of error?

MICHAEL *(Beat)* There's no error. The report don't lie.

BEVERLY Nothin's a hundred percent.

MICHAEL

BEVERLY What's forty-nine, in terms of the total enrollment? Percentage wise?

MICHAEL Three in a half percent of the total enrollment.

BEVERLY Not that high.

MICHAEL It's above average.

BEVERLY I mean it's still not as much of a problem as people –

MICHAEL I know a lot of residents who'd say it's still a problem.

BEVERLY What I mean is that not everyone you identified in this report will be in violation. You said seventeen were already cleared from your investigation this past week. That leaves...what? Thirty-two more the report may be wrong about.

MICHAEL The report isn't "wrong." The information is always accurate. The database can't interpret... It always gets a little hard to figure out who lives where when there's divorced parents, or families with multiple properties. Like this one –

(He hands her a document.)

MICHAEL I gotta figure out first what the at-home situation is. But I think they might be rentin' the apartment, just long enough to use the address.

BEVERLY On what basis did you arrive at that conclusion?

MICHAEL It's empty.

BEVERLY The apartment's empty?

MICHAEL Yeah. Landlord, said they pay the rent, but never moved anything in.

BEVERLY So you're saying people do that just to - ?

MICHAEL Oh, yeah. My buddy out in Bergen County? He says sometimes, the well-to-do ones, when they get confronted, you know, "Take your kid and pay up, or move to town?" They just rent apartments.

BEVERLY If they can afford to rent, why not just pay for private school?

MICHAEL Hey: Your guess is as good as mine. Maybe they're just intent on comin' here. Who knows?

BEVERLY *(Beat)* Isn't this case one of the seventeen you said were cleared?

MICHAEL *(Beat)* Yeah… It's basically clear - there are a few loose strings -

BEVERLY You just said you're not sure if they're legitimately in town. I'd say that's pretty unclear to me.

MICHAEL I just need-a confirm - For the most part -

BEVERLY Are the seventeen clear "for the most part" or clear?

MICHAEL

BEVERLY They either are, or they're not.

MICHAEL There's just a few loose strings.

BEVERLY So when you reported seventeen today, that was a false report? To what? Make it look like you accomplished more than you actually -

MICHAEL No. No, it - Seventeen are basically clear.

BEVERLY These are people's lives, Mr. DiMaggio. I cannot go to the board with "basically."

MICHAEL They'll be confirmed. The investigation is not over. They'll be -

BEVERLY They must.

MICHAEL *(Beat)* They will.

(BEVERLY reviews the documents, marking them with questions and notes. Moments pass.)

MICHAEL Pizelle?

BEVERLY No. Thank you.

MICHAEL Sure? They're good. From Calandras.

BEVERLY *(Beat)* The bakery in Newark?

MICHAEL Yeah. You know it?

BEVERLY I do.

MICHAEL Ah, it's my favorite. To this day. I go down every once in a while. Pick up a box. Just like Grandma's. *(Beat)* Have one.

BEVERLY No, I -

MICHAEL They're delicious.

BEVERLY That's alright -

MICHAEL Oh, c'mon. They're good.

BEVERLY I try to stay away from sugar.

MICHAEL Oh, not you too! Since when did sugar become - ? My daughter and me were in Costco. I'm pickin' up a box-a candy for the trick-or-treaters. I love the kids. I'm the guy on the block that gives out the good candy - the whole bar, not the just bite sized - kids love me -

BEVERLY I'm sure they do.

MICHAEL Hey, somebody's gotta keep the dentist in business, eh? So I'm pickin' up the bars. Know what my daughter gets to give out? *(Beat)* Kale chips. Ever had a kale chip?

BEVERLY No.

MICHAEL Don't. It's like eatin' newspaper. I say to her, "Give the kids a break! It's the only time they can eat junk. Let 'em have a candy, they're kids for Christ's sake." It's just a little sugar. It won't kill ya.

(MIKE offers again. BEVERLY rejects the offer.)

MICHAEL Ah, you're no fun. *(Beat)* More for me.

(MIKE takes a pizelle. He drops crumbs.)

BEVERLY Napkin?

MICHAEL No. I'm alright.

BEVERLY *(Beat)* No, have a napkin.

(BEVERLY gives him a napkin. MIKE accepts.)

BEVERLY Alright. So, Mr. DiMaggio -

MICHAEL You've gotta stop callin' me Mr. DiMaggio. Call me Mike. Mr. DiMaggio is my father.

BEVERLY Your father?

MICHAEL What, I'm too old to have a father.

BEVERLY No, I didn't mean –

MICHAEL Well, I am. I am too old. And let me tell ya, he's still tryin'-ta tell me what to do. I say to him this morning, "Dad. I think the gravy's got too much salt." He says to me, "Hey. Shut your mouth when you're talkin' to me." Ninety years old.

BEVERLY *(A gesture signifying, "Wow.")*

MICHAEL They don't make 'em like that anymore. Contadini dalla Calabria.

BEVERLY What's that?

MICHAEL Ah…Farmers from Calabria. The old country. Italy.

BEVERLY Oh.

MICHAEL They came when my father was a boy. My grandfather worked as a laborer. Neither of 'em could read or write in English when they came to Newark. Neither finished school in Italy they were so poor. And they built themselves up.

BEVERLY Oh, so you're from Newark?

MICHAEL Am I from Newark? Can't you tell? I was Nicky Newark himself. The original tough guys. Cigarettes in the cuff of my t-shirt and everything. I may live in Millburn now, but I ain't no white collar, Wall Street, tree-hugger type.

BEVERLY How long have you been in Millburn?

MICHAEL Oh, long time. Since '71, '72. After I was discharged. Came home. Newark had gone to - Newark was destroyed. After the riots in '67 - before your time.

BEVERLY The year I was born.

MICHAEL Okay so you -

BEVERLY I remember. The aftermath.

MICHAEL Yeah. So, after that I hadda move my parents out to Nutley. Was there with them for a while. Then I got on the force here. Got married. Bought a place. Been here ever since. Over 30 years now.

BEVERLY You like it here.

MICHAEL What's not to like? It's the best place to raise a family. They don't call it one of America's greatest towns for nothin'.

BEVERLY No, they don't.

MICHAEL That's why we gotta make sure it stays that way. Stay involved.

BEVERLY *(Beat)* Oh, so you're involved? In the community?

MICHAEL Yeah. I was so-so before, but after the shootin'…I think everybody's gotta be involved if we're gonna - If we don't take care-a our community, who will, you know?

BEVERLY *(Beat)* So, what do you do to - ?

MICHAEL Do?

BEVERLY What does your community involvement entail?

MICHAEL What do you mean?

BEVERLY What activities - Is there any particular cause you champion or - ?

MICHAEL No, not really. I'm a part of a group - reallysmartpeople,youknow?Sharpasknives. Committed.

BEVERLY And what do you all do?

MICHAEL We look at everything pertainin' to - Zoning board, school board -

BEVERLY School board?

MICHAEL Yeah.

BEVERLY What about the school board?

MICHAEL Honestly, I don't know much - I just joined up a couple-a weeks ago. But I know they're very involved. Naturally, I didn't sign up for the school board committee - bein' the P.I. and all. I thought it'd be a conflict of interest.

BEVERLY I would think so. *(Beat)* But I'm sure they ask you questions. For the inside track?

MICHAEL Naw. They wouldn't -

BEVERLY Oh, I'm sure they do.

MICHAEL They wouldn't - even if they - I wouldn't. My investigations are confidential. I know what the rules are.

(BEVERLY looks at him and considers for a few moments, then decides to proceed.)

BEVERLY Good. *(Beat)* Why don't we…

MICHAEL Of course.

BEVERLY We had six voluntary withdrawals this past week.

MICHAEL They're makin' my job easier, huh?

(BEVERLY hands MIKE documents of the withdrawn students.)

MICHAEL Let me see here…

(He looks them over.)

BEVERLY And, other than the seventeen, you say you identified three non-residents this week?

MICHAEL Sure did. Lemme just… okay. Here we go. *(Beat)* I give you our first offender Brandon McGuire. Twelfth grade.

(MIKE pins the picture of a Caucasian boy on the bulletin board and gives Beverly the file to read. She refers to the documents in the file during—)

MICHAEL Said he lived on Nottingham. According to the county, house does belong to the McGuire's. But not the same first names as listed on his registration form. Other McGuires. Kid walks there after school, but gets picked up around 6pm, presumably by the father. The kid looks just like 'im. Followed the car. They let off at a house in Springfield, get this, where a Deborah and Jackson McGuire, the people listed as his parents on the registration form, are also listed as owners. I suspect the kid is domiciled in Springfield in the parents' home. I think the Millburn address belongs to his paternal grandparents.

BEVERLY Are we certain the grandparents don't have guardianship?

MICHAEL Certain? No. I don't think he sleeps there. Never seen him leave the house in the morning for school or nothin'. I doubt it.

BEVERLY Let's be sure before we recommend restitution.

MICHAEL And expulsion, right?

BEVERLY His parents are gonna want him to finish here. He's been here three years already, this is his fourth. What's one more year? For continuity?

MICHAEL Continuity-shmontinunity.

BEVERLY If they can pay, of course.

MICHAEL If that's the case anybody from anywhere, as long as they have the money can come. It's not just the money, is it? It's about the community. This school here is for the kids here. 'sHow it's always been. We've gotta recommend expulsion too, in my opinion. Send a firm message. If they can afford to pay to come here, they can afford private.

BEVERLY Alright. Expulsion and restitution.

(MIKE places the folder in the expulsion pile.)

MICHAEL *(Beat)* Number two: Jada Dower. Ninth grade.

(He posts another photo of an African American girl and hands the file folder to BEVERLY.)

MICHAEL Said she lived on Morris Turnpike. Went there, and get this: it's a market! Not a bodega where you can live over top. A supermarket! No housing whatsoever unless you're livin' on aisle two with the cabbages. Followed her one night. Kid lives in East Orange. Walks to an apartment building on South Munn Avenue. I'd have to follow her once more to confirm. But she definitely don't live in Millburn. She races to the bus station when the bell rings.

BEVERLY Okay.

MICHAEL At least she's only been here a little over a month. She won't owe much. Expulsion, restitution?

BEVERLY Yes.

(MIKE moves the folder to the pile.)

BEVERLY *(Beat)* And the third?

MICHAEL Two for the price of one: Marcus and Omar Meyer. Tenth and eleventh grade.

(He posts another photo and hands the file folder to BEVERLY.)

MICHAEL Said they lived on Cedar. Looked it up. Old Jewish couple owns it. Followed them two nights in a row 'cause I couldn't believe it. Kids live all the way in Ironbound. Ironbound. Three buses. The 70, the 25 and the 34S. Gets off at Walnut and Jefferson. Go into a home on Oliver Street. I have pictures of 'em eatin' dinner through the window… They live there. And s'funny. People do the craziest… So, they go outta their way to put the Millburn address on the registration form, right? But the mother, she still lists her employer as Merry Maids. Their mother's a domestic. I had a hunch, so I call the Merry Maid's office, pretend I'm a client, turns out, the house at the Millburn address is a house on her cleaning list. That's probably how she got the address.

BEVERLY Wow.

MICHAEL I know. To just use someone's address!?

BEVERLY Who's to say they – What if the owners know?

MICHAEL *(Beat)* You know, that's a *(a gesture signifying, "good point")* …. And if they do, shame on them. Come to think of it, it wouldn't surprise me. The Jews are always the ones lettin' people in. Did the same thing in Newark when I was growin' up. People don't remember, but the whole Weequahic section in Newark? It was Jew at first. And they kept lettin' it out, lettin' it out. Look at it now. They'd rent to anybody. Sell to anybody. They didn't care. s'Long as they're makin' money. They're the ones, after they let the community go to hell in a wastebasket – they're the ones who burned out their own property for the insurance money. And then they all took that money and moved to Livingston. They don't tell you that, little known history fact, do they?

BEVERLY No.

MICHAEL That's how it happens. s'A cryin' shame. I try to warn people – I was talkin' to a parent, and she was thankin' me. *Thankin' me* for investigating. She said she didn't want this town to end up –

BEVERLY You were talking with the parents?

MICHAEL Sure.

BEVERLY Why would you do that, Mike?

MICHAEL Whatdya mean?

BEVERLY If you tell people who you are, isn't it difficult to be underground?

MICHAEL *(Beat)* She was a resident. I won't be investigatin' her.

BEVERLY I'm no detective or expert or anything, but don't private investigators have to maintain their anonymity? Should you be talking to the parents?

MICHAEL The community interview is a perfectly sound pre-surveillance investigation technique. And if there's not going to be a hotline –

BEVERLY Oh, God.

MICHAEL How else am I going to get tips?

BEVERLY Who says you have to get tips? I didn't hire you to follow tips. I hired you –

MICHAEL Woah, woah, woah. You didn't hire me at all. The board hired me.

BEVERLY *(Beat)* With my recommendation.

MICHAEL Regardless. I was hired to do a thorough job.

BEVERLY If everybody knows who you are, how will you be able to do a thorough job?

MICHAEL Listen: I know how to do my job. I've been a detective probably almost as long as you've been alive, okay? *(Beat)* And I had some solid tips come through from my interviews this week. For example: David Parks, not on the list. Tip said he dropped the kid off one night after a study session in –

BEVERLY David's legitimate.

MICHAEL Informant said he lived in Orange. Orange is all over his registration form, public records. Clear as day: Orange.

BEVERLY He does live out-of-district. David has special permission. He's an athlete. *(Beat)* It's in his file.

MICHAEL *(Beat)* Oh. They give special permission?

BEVERLY Yes. For extenuating circumstances. Health. Safety. Legacy…

MICHAEL And basketball.

BEVERLY In this case football, yes. To give the coaches room to recruit the best talent.

MICHAEL Christ. Alright. I'm gonna need a list-a those special permission kids. I don't wanna be spinnin' my wheels here.

BEVERLY I'll email Mrs. Scibetta. She'll get you a list. There aren't many. Just a few.

MICHAEL You know 'em?

BEVERLY I'm familiar. I don't know everyone for sure, but –

MICHAEL Any of these ring a bell as special permissions? *(Pulling out a photograph)* Grace Lee?

BEVERLY Uh… no, I don't –

MICHAEL *(Pulling out a photograph)* Jeremiah Frankel.

BEVERLY mmm…No.

MICHAEL *(Pulling out a photograph)* Noelle Morgan?

BEVERLY

MICHAEL *(Beat)* 10th grade. Informant said her kid overheard Noelle mention something at their tennis meet? She's on the red flag list I think too. Lemme –

(MIKE cross references his list.)

BEVERLY Is she?

MICHAEL Yeah. Clear as day. Red flag, see?

(BEVERLY looks at the list for a few moments.)

BEVERLY This…this is wrong.

MICHAEL The report's never wrong.

BEVERLY No, there's a mistake.

MICHAEL She's special permission?

BEVERLY *(Long beat)* You know, I don't… Maybe… I'm not…

MICHAEL *(Pulling out a photograph)* *(beat)* What about Tabitha Spencer?

BEVERLY You know, come to think of it, I don't think I can really be sure about any of them.

MICHAEL *(Beat)* Alright.

BEVERLY Yeah. We should wait – You should hold off until we get the official list.

MICHAEL *(Beat)* Alright… I'll wait on the special permissions. So many lists! Red flag, special permission –

BEVERLY Actually, all of these, from your interviews, you should hold off on all of these. Until we get the official list. Just focus on the others from the report. Those'll be the ones the board is expecting to hear about, anyhow. Anything else is just icing on the cake. Leave these leads – Tabitha, Jeremiah, Noelle, etcetera – leave them alone.

MICHAEL *(Beat)* Aye, aye, captain.

BEVERLY Good. So, that's it? That's today's…?

MICHAEL Yep, that covers it. We should have the full report next Monday the latest. Just in time for Wednesday's board meeting.

BEVERLY Great.

(MIKE packs up to depart.)

MICHAEL *(Beat)* And, uh, I wanted to let you know. I've been working on a presentation. For the board meeting. I figured it could be the intro, you know, before we reveal the recommendations. I have it in power point presentation. Lots of pictures and stuff. It can be an intro, that way, if they have any questions about methodology or whatever have you, they can ask me directly, you won't have to be put on the spot.

BEVERLY Sounds good.

MICHAEL And, if you want, I can do the whole presentation. Just so, if they have any questions about the surveillance or –

BEVERLY Yes, that's – yes. That sounds great.

MICHAEL Alright. Good. That's good. *(Beat)* You alright?

BEVERLY I'm fine.

MICHAEL Alright. *(Beat)* Monday.

BEVERLY Monday.

(MIKE pauses to observe BEVERLY, then exits. BEVERLY immediately picks up the red flag list. She looks for Noelle's name. BEVERLY picks up the phone and presses the intercom button.)

BEVERLY Mrs. Madison?

VO Yes?

BEVERLY Hey. I need a copy of all of the registration documents for Noelle Morgan. The proof of residency docs too. The ones you took over to the district office last week?

VO I remember. Okay. When do you need them?

BEVERLY Like, now.

VO Now. Okay. I'll get them now.

BEVERLY Great. Thanks. I also need you to clear the rest of my schedule for today. I have to make a personal run.

VO *(Beat)* Okay. Will do.

BEVERLY *(Beat)* Thanks.

(BEVERLY "hangs up" the intercom speaker. She grabs her belongings, the red flag list and exits.)

Scene 4

A half-hour later that afternoon. BEVERLY opens the door to the same open house. Perhaps a different Open House sign, or a different realtor's picture decorates the grand foyer. BEVERLY looks in amazement.

BEVERLY Hello? *(Beat)* Anyone?

(BEVERLY surveys the space. BEVERLY exits the house and stops on the porch area.)

BEVERLY God damnit, Denitra.

(BEVERLY exits.)

BLACKOUT.

★

ACT II

Scene 1

That evening, an hour or so later. PRINCIPAL LONG holds the red flag list and a copy of the proof of residency documents. She approaches DENITRA's door. She stands without knocking. DENITRA enters the living room with scrubs on, preparing to leave. She talks into her cellular phone.

DENITRA *(Into the phone)* Okay. There's meatloaf in the oven for when you get home. You come straight home after and call me from the house phone. I'll be at my class, then I picked up a shift. *(Beat)* And Miss Milagros will be checking in.

(PRINCIPAL LONG knocks.)

DENITRA *(Beat)* Alright. Let me go. Somebody's at the door. *(Beat)* Love you.

(DENITRA hangs up the phone.)

DENITRA Who is it?

BEVERLY *(Beat)* *(from outside)* Beverly.

DENITRA *(Beat)* Who?

BEVERLY *(Beat)* It's Beverly, Denitra. Principal Beverly Long.

(DENITRA freezes. Moments pass. DENITRA finally opens the door. The women stare at each other for some time.)

DENITRA Come in.

(BEVERLY boldly enters. She takes in the modest apartment in disbelief. She turns her attention to DENITRA. Moments pass.)

BEVERLY You used that house. And you've been here the whole time, haven't you?

DENITRA *(Beat)* Yes.

BEVERLY I've got to give you credit. You had me fooled. I've been running through our encounters in my mind. The first moment we met, freshman orientation, all the meetings about Noelle's classes, scanning my memory for indications, clues that I missed. But no. Nothing. I thought we were connecting. I thought you were the real deal.

DENITRA What does that mean? The real deal?

BEVERLY Legitimate residents. *(Beat)* For the record, I want you to know I believed in your charade so much, that even then, with evidence staring me in my face, I gave you the benefit of the doubt. I said, "Maybe she decided to pay the eight hundred ninety nine thousand," and actually went to see for myself. *(Beat)* Tell me something, indulge me, for a moment: How did you think this would work out? What was the plan?

DENITRA The plan was she'd go to a good school. I'd work and finish my bridge program to get my RN license. She'd go to college. I'd past my certification exam and get a better job. That was the plan.

BEVERLY And how's that going for you?

DENITRA It was going fine. I didn't anticipate an enrollment audit.

BEVERLY What did you plan to do if you got caught? Did you have a plan?

DENITRA I honestly didn't think I would.

BEVERLY No?

DENITRA I did my research. People do this everyday. All over the country.

BEVERLY Then I'm sure you also discovered it's illegal, Denitra. It's a crime.

DENITRA

BEVERLY God.

(Moments pass.)

DENITRA So what now?

BEVERLY What do you mean?

DENITRA You're going to report us?

BEVERLY Shouldn't I?

DENITRA Are you?

BEVERLY It's bad enough you've lied. But you've got Noelle lying too. What kind of parent –

DENITRA Noelle doesn't know.

BEVERLY What?!

DENITRA She doesn't know.

BEVERLY *(Beat)* Oh, my God, Denitra. Why? Why would you – ?

DENITRA I didn't want her to develop a complex.

BEVERLY What kind of complex is she going to have when they find out? She's going to be humiliated. You think the kids – do you think the *parents* don't already suspect that she's a non-resident just because she's black?

DENITRA I didn't want her to feel like she didn't belong.

BEVERLY She doesn't.

DENITRA She does. Look at her grades now. She can do the work.

BEVERLY But she must know she's not supposed to – that she's supposed to go to school in her neighborhood.

DENITRA She knows that.

BEVERLY So, what did you tell her?

DENITRA *(Beat)* She thinks she's in a gifted and talented pilot program.

BEVERLY Oh my God.

DENITRA That's all she needs to know.

BEVERLY Unbelievable. What would you have done if she wanted to invite one of her little friends over or – ?

DENITRA You think after seeing their houses, she's going to want to invite them to hers?

BEVERLY Weren't you worried she'd say something to her classmates – her friends?

DENITRA You know she doesn't have any friends at that school. Why do you think she spends her lunch periods volunteering in your office? Or in the student store? She doesn't hang out. She works. She studies. She goes to tennis practice. That's it. She's not there for friends. She's there to get an education.

BEVERLY *(Beat)* Why didn't you tell me?

DENITRA How could I have told you, Beverly?

BEVERLY How could you not? You looked me in my face, on multiple occasions, and lied to me.

DENITRA I lied to them.

BEVERLY No, you lied to me. "Can Noelle go home with you after practice, I'm stuck at work preparing *briefs* for *court* tomorrow." I can't believe I asked YOU for legal advice!

DENITRA What do you want me to say?

BEVERLY The truth! She never turned in those documents 'cause you never gave them to her to turn in, did you? And foolishly, blindly, I swept that under the rug for you!

DENITRA I'm sorry, Beverly. Is that what you want?

BEVERLY No. What I want is not to be a part of your lie. 'Cause you're being investigated. FYI. The private investigator has you on his list. He'll be following you and looking into your affairs. And do you think he's going to miss that I slipped your documentation - this forged, fake, PhotoShopped documentation - into the pile after the deadline? No. When he notices, you think he's going to take it as pure coincidence?

DENITRA Tell them you didn't do it.

BEVERLY What?

DENITRA It was a human error, a mix up - someone put it in the wrong place -

BEVERLY No, Denitra - You've made me an accessory. You intentionally sabotaged - you talk about my staff, they weren't the ones I should be looking out for to stab me in the back. What were you thinking?

DENITRA I wasn't thinking about you.

BEVERLY

DENITRA I was thinking about my daughter -

BEVERLY Oh, please -

DENITRA I was thinking she's going to have a chance -

BEVERLY Please.

DENITRA Oh, now you don't have time for a sista's thoughts? Just yesterday, when you thought I was middle class with a law degree, you could listen. But now you know I'm from Newark -

BEVERLY You're not the only one from Newark, Denitra. I'm from Newark. Raised in Scudder Homes on Bon Ton Potato Chips and quarter water. It wasn't the White House, but it wasn't - There were good people there. And, yes, we had it hard, but we grew up fine and none of us forge government documents. Spare me your urban sob story.

DENITRA Where'd you go to high school?

BEVERLY What does that matter?

DENITRA I bet you were one of those special Negros they plucked from the hood concrete to refine. I bet you were a part of some pet integration program where they bused you out to some white suburban bliss -

BEVERLY So what if I was?

DENITRA You think you're better than me, Beverly? With your three degrees?

BEVERLY Please.

DENITRA You think I didn't work hard enough? You think I don't deserve - ? *(Beat)* I was

damn near the top of my high school class. Right here in this same neighborhood. I was a cheerleader. Volleyball. In youth and government. I did everything by the book. I thought I was going to Harvard! I couldn't figure out how I was the best thing since sliced bread at my school, but I couldn't break a thousand on the SATs. How I was acing three AP classes my senior year, but couldn't pass the national AP tests. Why, when I'm forced to settle for Essex County College, they have me in remedial math and English. How can you graduate high school and need remedial anything? I couldn't even register for some of the classes in my major 'cause I didn't meet those academic standards. I spent two years in remedial. Embarrassed 'cause I told everyone I was going to Harvard be a lawyer! And look at me! Look at me! "What was I thinking?" I was thinking I didn't want that for Noelle. I want her to _know_ that she meets the _highest_ standards. I wanted her to be able to go to a top four-year institution where they prepare kids to be the leaders of this world. Not the people who take your order. That's what I was thinking. And I'm sorry. I'm sorry you got caught up. It was not my intention. But I was not thinking about you.

(Moments pass.)

BEVERLY You gotta withdraw her, Denitra. Tomorrow. People are withdrawing. They walk away voluntarily before the board meeting and there's no penalty. No harm, no foul.

DENITRA I can't do that.

BEVERLY What other options do you have?

DENITRA You tell me.

BEVERLY None.

DENITRA Withdraw her and what? Where's she going to go to school?

BEVERLY Enroll her at her home school.

DENITRA No.

BEVERLY It's not that bad. // You'll find some outside -

DENITRA It's not that bad? Would you let Jordan go back?

BEVERLY

DENITRA Oh, I get it. It's not that bad for _us_. That's what you're saying.

BEVERLY They're going to catch you. It's just a matter of time.

DENITRA Are you worried about me, or are you worried about you?

BEVERLY That's not fair.

DENITRA Why ain't it?

BEVERLY I have a career –

DENITRA You mean the one where you leave the moment you see how much kids in Newark need? The moment you realize it's not going to be easy.

BEVERLY Excuse me?

DENITRA If you gave a damn about these kids you'd-a never left. But you did. Because you could. Well, some of us can't, Beverly. We don't have that option. If people like you would have the presence of mind to see what they're doin' – to stay and help build this community, we wouldn't need them. If you'd see it as your responsibility… if you'd see yourself in me. But you don't. Shove more programs down our throats. We don't want your program. We tired of people gettin' paid feedin' us some damn pity program! We want your love. Your commitment. Your respect. Your pride.

BEVERLY I resent that. I have done more than most people would even think to do. I had given my life to helping people just like you –

DENITRA Like me?! // (*A gesture signifying, "No she didn't just say, "people like you""*)

BEVERLY – but I do things the right way, Denitra. The right way. If you want to sneak around and break the law with your child, go ahead. But I did not sign up to be a part of this. There are real consequ – We could face fines. We could go to jail!

DENITRA I'M NOT SCARED-A JAIL!!! My goal is not to stay out of jail. That's not the worst thing that could happen for me. My goal is to get Noelle a good education. So, the worst thing that could happen to me is that she doesn't get one.

BEVERLY And what about me?

DENITRA What about you?

BEVERLY I'm implicated.

DENITRA I know! You the one gave me the idea!

BEVERLY *I* gave you the idea?!

DENITRA Yes. When we met. At that house.

BEVERLY Please, you were at that house scouting addresses to use. // I didn't give you any –

DENITRA No, I wasn't.

BEVERLY Yes, you were.

DENITRA I wasn't –

BEVERLY Then why were you there?

DENITRA (*Beat*) Once, maybe twice a month we dress up and I take Noelle to an open house in a ritzy neighborhood. We get dressed up and we decide who we'll be - doctors, or news anchors, or attorneys. We pretend that's who we are and we go to these houses and fancy restaurants and I expose her to the possibilities – how some people live and work and sleep. Some people have granite countertops and crown molding and marble floors and walk-in closets. That's a possibility. We'd go and I'd tell her, "Imagine you live here. Imagine you own it. See yourself paying for it and let yourself feel like it's yours. Remember how it smells, how it feels. And know in your heart that you're going to be there one day." That's why we were there. And then when you said… you affirmed in me that I should do whatever it takes - a good parent does whatever it takes, right?

BEVERLY

DENITRA I did. And she's thriving now. She struggled her first year, but she's thriving now. (*Beat*) Beverly, you're already involved. I didn't mean for you to be, but you are. Even if I withdraw, they're gonna find out and take you to task. Noelle withdrawin' is not the solution to your problem. (*Beat*) So you hate me? Fine. Hate me. Hate me all you want. But don't not help her stay, 'cause you hate me. (*Beat*) You left all those other boys and girls spread eagle against the wall. You don't have to leave Noelle there too.

Moments pass.

DENITRA (*Beat*) Alright. That's fine. (*Beat*) Sometimes I wonder. I fight so hard to give her what you were given - GIVEN, not earned. That BS about working hard and pulling yourself up by your bootstraps is just that, BS. Opportunity isn't just about merit. It's about positioning. You weren't better than the thousands that didn't get picked. You weren't more capable. Someone let you in. That's it. You can have all the talent in the world, but if no one lets you in… I've spent this entire time wanting her to be picked. But I'm starting to wonder, for what? 'Cause what's the point of getting in if you're telling me, the best she could hope for is to turn out like you.

BEVERLY

DENITRA You…you do what you need to do. I've got to go to work, so…I'm already late.

(*DENITRA prepares çto leave. She stops when BEVERLY starts to speak.*)

BEVERLY Write… write a formal letter petitioning the district for special permission. For an inter-district transfer on an academic basis. Date it for this past August. Say that Noelle's advanced in math and science and there's no robotics program at your home school. Make sure you mention the award she got last year. Give it to Noelle, and tell her to put it in my hand, don't leave it anywhere with anyone, don't talk about it, nothing.

DENITRA What's that gon' do?

BEVERLY I'll try to get her name on the special permissions list. If she is granted special permission from the district, she'll automatically be lifted off the P.I.'s radar. And she'll actually legitimately be in the school.

DENITRA Okay.

BEVERLY I'll do my best to push the request through the proper channels. I'll try to keep her out of the audit report. *(Beat)* I'll try. That's all I will do.

DENITRA Okay.

(BEVERLY goes to leave. DENITRA stops her.)

DENITRA Thank you.

(BEVERLY looks at DENITRA, then leaves.)

Scene 2

A week later. Monday, Nov. 1, 2010. In the office of Principal BEVERLY LONG. MIKE has index cards while he rehearses his PowerPoint presentation. He clicks his clicker and a slide projection appears of a chicken and an egg.

MICHAEL What comes first: the chicken or the egg?

(He clicks to reveal another slide of a typical suburban American school and community street.)

MICHAEL Or rather: What comes first: the school or the community?

(He clicks to reveal another slide of a schoolhouse.)

MICHAEL The quality of the public schools is proven to be the single most attractive amenity for homebuyers across America. Having a great school attracts economically stable families and businesses to your community, thus keeping the property value high.

(He clicks his clicker and another slide appears of an upper middle class suburban family home.)

MICHAEL At the same time, communities that have high property values also have higher property tax contributions to their schools. And everybody knows schools that have more money have better education, and the parents tend to be more involved because they've made a substantial investment.

(He clicks his clicker and another slide appears of the word, 'fraud'.)

MICHAEL School Residency Fraud devalues schools and communities because the people coming haven't made an investment. They're not givers, they're takers. Students with a low investment have a lower respect for the school, lower achievement, and the parents are not involved. So your school can quickly go from one like this…!

(He clicks to reveal a slide of a pristine school with mostly happy white faces and bodies.)

MICHAEL …to one like this…

(He clicks to reveal a slide of a derelict school with metal detectors and only troubled black and brown faces and bodies.)

MICHAEL Which means your community can go from looking like this…

(He clicks to reveal a slide of a pristine suburban neighborhood with mostly happy white faces and bodies.)

MICHAEL To one that looks like this…

(He clicks to reveal a slide of a horrible neighborhood with boarded up buildings and only troubled black and brown faces and bodies.)

MICHAEL …like that. *(He snaps his fingers.)* Since the unfortunate murder of that young man last month, I'm sure you can see, how quickly the residency fraud issue can go from a fiscal issue to a public safety issue. When people are from your neighborhood, they're accountable to the community. People know you and you know them. But when people are not residents, when no one knows them and they don't know nobody, how can you hold them accountable? You can't. *(Beat)* So, who can protect your community from non-residents?

(He clicks onto a glowing picture of himself.)

MICHAEL A licensed Private Investigator can.

(He clicks to reveal another slide of the Old First Ward in Newark, 1950s.)

I'll tell ya a little story: I'm born and raised in Newark. The old First Ward. Seventh Avenue. My father bought a home on the G.I. Bill the year I was born. And it was a nice place to grow up. Real great memories of my home neighborhood. The bakeries. The butcheries. Frankie Valli and Sinatra - he wasn't from Newark, he was from Hoboken - but he came to Newark to get his bread from our neighborhood, so we claim him. I can still smell the onions and garlic hitting the pan every Sunday morning for the tomato sauce. I can still see my father's grocery. It was beautiful. But my father's generation made a mistake. As certain other people started migrating to the city, they let those people strike fear in their hearts. They let the city build the Columbus Homes - a federal housing project - right in their community. They let the real estate agents blockbuster 'em, so they were sellin' their property at a loss just to be able to get outta dodge. Then the riots happened. So, when I got outta the service in '68, wha-did I come home to? Newark was worse than the war zone I left. The entire community was unrecognizable so many had left. And why'd they leave? Why didn't they stay and fight? If I'da been there, I'da fought. My father's ninety years old, he's still heartbroken. He loved his home. He worked hard for it. He loved the First Ward. I did too. Today, my beloved community has a highway running through it. The 2-80. What was once all Italian is now full of Puerto Ricans. Other than a few surviving businesses - the famous Calandra's Bakery - s'like we weren't even there. Why'd they let those people, the government and whoever else interfere with our lives, I'll never understand. All that history. All that pride. Lost forever.

Now, you've got a good thing goin' here in Millburn. A real good thing that's been built by the folks came before you for you. And everybody can see that. And I tell-ya, they're gonna come and try-and take it. It's easier to take than to build your own. I ask you, are you gonna take this opportunity to do everything you can to fight to keep Millburn? Or are you going to let it go it to a bunch of people who don't even live here? The choice is yours.

(He clicks to reveal the chicken and egg slide.)

So what comes first, the chicken or the egg? It's neither.

(He clicks to reveal another slide of a Millburn high school.)

Schools come first.

Thank you. *(Beat)* Then I hope there'll be a bunch of clappin'.

(MIKE turns the lights on to reveal PRINCI-PAL LONG sitting.)

MICHAEL So?

BEVERLY *(Beat)* This is for?

MICHAEL The intro.

BEVERLY To our presentation to the board?

MICHAEL Yeah. Whaddya think? You think - ?

BEVERLY I think it's -

MICHAEL Too long?

BEVERLY I think you could use more -

MICHAEL Pictures?

BEVERLY Facts. Charts. Graphs. The board will like facts. School residency fraud statistics.

MICHAEL You mean like how many cases - ?

BEVERLY Yeah. And in comparison to other areas.

MICHAEL Okay. I see that. I can look into that. Most states don't keep that kind of data. I know the feds don't. *(Beat)* But other than that?

BEVERLY I think just facts.

MICHAEL Just facts.

BEVERLY No images.

MICHAEL No pictures?

BEVERLY No.

MICHAEL The pictures are what's gonna make it come alive for 'em.

BEVERLY Well -

MICHAEL Other than that it's just a bunch of numbers.

BEVERLY No, I think they'll get it.

MICHAEL I want to appeal to their emotions.

BEVERLY That emotion being?

MICHAEL What do you mean?

BEVERLY The emotion you want people to feel from your presentation?

MICHAEL ...Impassioned.

BEVERLY Impassioned.

MICHAEL I want them to feel the importance of the issue.

BEVERLY Okay.

MICHAEL I want them to be worried. There's an emotion.

BEVERLY Worried about?

MICHAEL Their futures.

BEVERLY Because you think they should be worried?

MICHAEL Absolutely. Don't you?

BEVERLY Yes, we all should be *concerned* about the future of our schools. But what I don't think we should feel is afraid. And right now, those pictures, they make me feel like you want me to be afraid -

MICHAEL No –

BEVERLY Afraid in a very specific way. The images are very –

MICHAEL I'm not trying to scare anybody.

BEVERLY They're very biased.

MICHAEL *(Beat)* You think I'm biased?

BEVERLY No, I didn't say you – I think the pictures you chose, and how you present them create a very biased look –

MICHAEL These are real pictures.

BEVERLY I'm sure, but the way you present them –

MICHAEL What way? In a slide show?

BEVERLY No. Back to back and in juxtaposition to – It makes it seem as if the thing they should be afraid of is the ghetto.

MICHAEL Yeah.

BEVERLY *(Beat)* Yeah?

MICHAEL *(Beat)* Aren't you afraid of that?

BEVERLY Excuse me?

MICHAEL You live here in Millburn, right?

BEVERLY I do, but I'm not –

MICHAEL You don't want to live there do you?

BEVERLY No, but –

MICHAEL Because you're afraid.

BEVERLY No.

MICHAEL Get outta here.

BEVERLY I'm not afraid of the ghetto.

MICHAEL Come on, Bev.

BEVERLY Excuse me?

MICHAEL Of course you are. We all are. Nobody wants that.

BEVERLY Nobody wants to live in a flooded area either, but we don't use pictures of floods to get people to move to the desert.

MICHAEL Huh?

BEVERLY And please refrain from calling me Bev. You may be fine with Mike, but I am not fine with Bev. Do I look like a Bev to you? No. Address me as Dr. Long. Principal Long. Mrs. Long. But never Bev.

MICHAEL What's your issue?

BEVERLY Those pictures and only those pictures make it seem as though there's nothing good in those environments. I think it paints a lopsided picture.

MICHAEL It shows what can happen when people don't take care.

BEVERLY It makes it seem like Black people are the only ones who "don't take care."

MICHAEL What, you'd prefer I throw in some Latino's. Some trailer trash? Then it'd be alright?

BEVERLY Yeah. Then throw in some guidos and guineas. Why not? And some chinks and some paddys and some gypsys and some hicks and hillbillies. Then why not some towel heads and some kikes and spics and some red necks, and some African booty scratchers and whoever else, then we'd be even! That'd be great!

(A few moments pass. BEVERLY breathes.)

BEVERLY I apologize. That was inappropriate. *(Beat)* I said all that to say, that I'd prefer that you didn't use any images. You can only present to the Board Wednesday if you create an appropriately professional presentation that sticks to the facts.

MICHAEL *(Beat)* Fine.

BEVERLY *(Beat)* Thank you.

MICHAEL *(Beat)* I mean, I'm gonna haveta rework the entire –

BEVERLY I'm sure you can do it.

MICHAEL *(Beat)* Fine.

BEVERLY So on Wednesday, you'll do your intro and I'll present the cases and recommendations, then we'll take questions.

MICHAEL *(Beat)* I think I should present the cases.

BEVERLY Why would you think that?

MICHAEL 'Cause they're mine. The Board hired me to do 'em, so they should hear the results of 'em from me.

BEVERLY The board will hear the cases from me. This is my school. These are my students. I'm the principal.

MICHAEL Interim principal.

BEVERLY *(Beat)* Principal, nonetheless. If you have a problem with that, please let me know. I'm sure we can find a replacement.

MICHAEL

BEVERLY Great. Last week we had 17 non-residents, 3 violators, 2 withdrawn. And this week you have?

MICHAEL

BEVERLY And this week you have?

MICHAEL *(Beat)* 15 are non-residents. 12 are fine. I know 5 of the 15 withdrew voluntarily so that leaves 10 violators.

BEVERLY So I'll start by saying, we identified twenty non-residents.

MICHAEL Yes.

BEVERLY And that's what? Two percent of enrollment?

MICHAEL You're the genius aren't you? *Doctor* Long?

BEVERLY

MICHAEL It's about one and a half percent.

BEVERLY *(Beat)* Who are the 10 from this week?

MICHAEL *(Beat)* First up, Noelle Morgan, 10th grade.

BEVERLY *(Beat)* Okay.

MICHAEL Been investigatin' the student for the last couple of days.

BEVERLY Weren't you waiting to see if she was on the special permissions list? I thought I told you to hold off.

MICHAEL You did. And I was, but then I noticed a couple-a interesting things.

BEVERLY Things like?

MICHAEL When I thought about it, I realized, special permission students shouldn't make the red flag list. Why? 'Cause they don't lie about their address. They don't gotta, they got special permission. Noelle's registration form lists a house in Millburn. But public record says Newark. She lied.

BEVERLY Not necessarily. Maybe she's recently moved.

MICHAEL Thought about that too. The house that she says was her residence is listed on the market - but the parent is not the seller. And the house had been on the market for almost 2 years. Which leads me to the logical question: where does she live? When looking into this question I found something else interesting. When we left last week, I actually went to Ms. Scibetta and asked for her to get me a special permission list - I didn't wanna bother ya. Sometimes things go so slow in your office. CP time, I guess. I figured I'd get it from her myself. But then, later in the week, you sent a list over and there was a difference. The special permission list she gave me had no Noelle. But the one you gave me, Noelle. So I went up to the district office to see what that was about and found out that she recently applied for special permission... which is odd. Why would a child already enrolled apply for special permission - isn't that something you do before school starts?

BEVERLY Not necessarily.

MICHAEL But then something else happened I found most interesting. I saw that her updated residency documents ain't have no time stamp on 'em. Most kids, they turn 'em in and the office stamps 'em to prove that they were on time, but these, nothing. See? Nothin'. It's like somebody slipped 'em in to the pile after the fact. Who could do that? *(Beat)* Then I saw you at the address listed on her registration form -

(He pins the picture of Beverly onto the bulletin board.)

MICHAEL Which is odd, because you just closed on a house here last year. You're already in the market for a new one? Your husband may be a big shot engineer, but according to your taxes you don't have enough for two houses in Millburn. So, I ask myself, how does all this link up? Why would you be at this address? Who would have the authority to slip in documents late? Who could add her name to this special permissions list? *(Long beat)* Then I looked into where you were before you came here. Assistant Superintendent for Newark Public Schools. *(Beat)* You think I'm stupid? I've been doin' this a long time, lady. *(Beat)* What is she your student or something? Is that what you're doing? Smugglin' in kids from Newark.

BEVERLY No. I'm not smuggling -

MICHAEL What were they? Your students? Malik? Noelle? Is that -

BEVERLY No! I didn't know either of them. I didn't know Malik didn't live -

MICHAEL But you know Noelle doesn't?

BEVERLY *(Beat)* I've come to know, yes.

MICHAEL And you're helpin' her.

BEVERLY *(Beat)* You don't know what she's facing.

MICHAEL It doesn't matter what she's facing. That's not our problem.

BEVERLY Well, maybe it should be.

MICHAEL What?

BEVERLY Maybe it should be everyone's problem. Those kids in Newark -

(MIKE dismisses BEVERLY, and decides to turn and address her.)

MICHAEL No, no, no, no, no. Newark ain't one of these underfunded - our tax dollars have gone above and beyond - They get nine hundred million dollars from the state to educate those kids. Plus a hundred million from that Facebook Zuckerberg guy and the damn kids still can't read and write up to par. So, where's our money goin'? Down the toilet, that's where. They don't want to learn!

BEVERLY They DO want to learn!! All children want to learn! Noelle wants to learn! Look at her grades! She went from almost failing last year, to finishing near the top of some of her classes. But what's going to happen if she's thrown back into that environment?

MICHAEL If they don't like the environment, they're the ones should fix it.

BEVERLY Have you ever seen a kid, a good kid, a capable kid, ready to learn. Like a sponge. Have you ever seen a kid like that relegated to a bad situation?

MICHAEL Then they should move! // Move and – !

BEVERLY They can't afford to!

MICHAEL They should save! // Like we – !

BEVERLY The children can't save. The kids can't do anything about whatever situation they're in. And I've seen kids – bright, intelligent kids – limited to the culture of that. It rubs off onto you. It changed them. And when I asked them why they let it, they said… they'd said people would accuse them of acting white. For being responsible. For being articulate. They "accused" them of trying to be white – trying to be better than what they are – as if what they *are* is… So to prove to them she is black she will dumb herself down. She will, at least subconsciously accept, that smart qualities are exclusively white things. And in efforts to maintain what little grasp she has on her identity as a black person, she'll come to believe in a devalued understanding of herself. Some people might say, well, shame on her for not being stronger. They would say she's made a choice and feel no pity. But what we require that girl to have to do, to rise up beyond all that – we'd never ask your kids to do. They don't have to battle crime and violence and metal detectors and police brutality and gang members and child care facilities for the children of teenagers, and no lunch money, and *generations* of under and miseducation and low expectations and black faces saying, "stop acting white, how dare you try to be more," and white faces saying, "get back to your town, you're black, you aren't good enough to be here with us." Your children didn't. Your grandchildren won't. They don't have to make it out of anything to get what they need. They can spend their whole lives right here and prosper and // grow if they want to –

MICHAEL That's 'cause we participate in our communities. We hold our representatives accountable. If those parents bothered to show up to a school board meetin' or two, they –

BEVERLY It wouldn't matter.

MICHAEL Oh, what a cop out – So, they don't have no responsibility for –

BEVERLY The state runs their school system in Newark. It doesn't matter how much the parents participate, the state decides how to spend the money.

MICHAEL Yes! The money. *My* hard earned – ! You know how much Newark high schools get per kid? Twenty-three thousand dollars. Our kids? Seventeen. Those kids get six thousand dollars more per kid and still they –

BEVERLY It doesn't cost more to teach them. It costs more to keep them there.

MICHAEL I ain't keepin' them anywhere.

QPL Yes, you are. We all are.

MICHAEL How? How am I –

BEVERLY They need special programs, special services. That's what costs – the concentration of poverty costs money to maintain. That's the problem. Not the kids. The cost would be lower if the schools were integrated, if all the schools had kids from all socio-economic backgrounds. If it's truly about money for you, you would call the representatives you hold so accountable and you would say, "Integrate the districts by county. It would cost tax payers less." Or you'd have Millburn sign up for the state School Choice Program, so that the school could *receive* money to let students from other districts come.

(She refers to the phone.)

BEVERLY So, call your representative and tell them that that's what you wanna do. You want to let kids in Newark come to school here 'cause it will lower your tax burden and give the school a source of unrestricted income. Since that's your chief concern. The money.

(Moments pass.)

BEVERLY You don't want to do that, do you?

MICHAEL

BEVERLY 'Cause you don't want them here. You're paying to keep them away from us. That's where the money's going. *WE* are paying to keep them over there.

MICHAEL

BEVERLY Do they deserve that? Does Noelle deserve that?

MICHAEL

BEVERLY Can you at least admit that no child, no matter where they're born, deserves to be confined to that?

MICHAEL

BEVERLY Okay. Okay. At least wait for the results of the special permission petition go through. See what the district has to say. It may be a moot point if they –

MICHAEL

BEVERLY It's only one girl, Mike. One girl getting a chance that she deserves. One girl.

MICHAEL Principals are supposed to do what's best for the school, for the community. Not individual students. Right?

BEVERLY

MICHAEL The people of Millburn trusted you.

(MIKE picks up his belongings, including his camera.)

BEVERLY Okay. Wait a second. Just wait –

(MIKE goes to leave.)

MICHAEL We both have jobs to do. I'm going to do mine. You should do yours. While you still have one.

(MIKE exits.)

BEVERLY Mike.

Scene 3

Later that afternoon, after school. MIKE is posted outside DENITRA's house. DENITRA comes storming out. She catches him in a moment of being unaware.

DENITRA Excuse me?

(MIKE is startled to attention.)

DENITRA Yes, you. Can I have a word with you?

MICHAEL *(Beat)* Hey – You're the –

DENITRA Yeah, remember me? I know who you are, what you do.

MICHAEL What are you doin' – ?

DENITRA Are you following my daughter?

MICHAEL *(Beat)* Your daughter? Wait a minute: you live here.

DENITRA She walks into the house, freaked out, 'cause she says a white man has been following her. Are you some kind of pervert?

MICHAEL

DENITRA I'm talking to you!

MICHAEL I ain't gotta respond.

DENITRA You ain't gotta respond? You do, sir. You do have to respond, when you're following people –

MICHAEL I'm on public property.

DENITRA I don't care where you are. You cannot follow a child. That's harassment. That's against the law!

MICHAEL It is not against the law.

DENITRA If you have a problem with me, sir, then follow me, but what you will not do is follow my child, you pervert, I'm calling the cops.

MICHAEL *(Scoff)*

DENITRA That funny to you? You think I won't?

(DENITRA dials.)

MICHAEL I think that the cops in Newark got more serious stuff to attend to.

DENITRA *(Into the phone)* Hello. Yes. Clinton Street. There is a pervert following my teenaged daughter. Yes. *(Beat)* He's an old white man. Can't miss him. He's the only white person in a 10-block radius. *(Beat)* Yes, he's threatening! He's following my – *(She hangs up.)* I'll take your picture. Post it with the pedophiles.

(DENITRA uses her phone to prepare to take a photo.)

MICHAEL Do not take my picture.

DENITRA Oh, I'm taking your picture, buddy.

MICHAEL Do not take my –

(She snaps a shot.)

DENITRA How's it feel, huh? How's it feel for someone to violate your space, huh? You ain't the only one can take pictures. I got a damn camera too, how 'bout that. And I'ma post 'em. All over Facebook. *(Announcing it to the community)* The pedophile following my child!

MICHAEL I ain't no pedophile. I'm a private investigator well within the legal limits, in public spaces –

DENITRA She's a child. How'd you like it if I go follow your kid around –

MICHAEL My kid ain't breakin' the law, lady. // My kid ain't breakin' the law. I raised law abiding citizens. I didn't teach my kids to lie and cheat to get –

DENITRA My kid ain't breakin' the law! You wanna follow somebody?! Follow somebody your own size, dammit. I don't give a damn about your kids! You racist –

MICHAEL Oh, now I'm a racist! // Of course –

DENITRA Yes.

MICHAEL You people kill me with that. A person says the truth, does what the LAW says to do and he's a racist? NO! You're the racist! // A racist quack s'what you are! A criminal –!

DENITRA I can't be racist. I can't be a – What's my crime? // Wanting to educate my daughter?!

MICHAEL Stealing! Stealing's your crime – !

DENITRA How do you steal free education!?! She's entitled to a – It's our civil right!

MICHAEL Whatdya talkin' about civil – ?! You're not doing this for your civil rights! You're not marching for anybody, but yourself. Civil rights! Martin Luther King would be turning over in his grave to see you. You're nothing like they were. They were upstanding. They wore suits and spoke proper English. They took care of their homes and paid their taxes and prayed to God! Look at what you people did to Newark!

DENITRA I didn't do this to Newark! // I didn't make Newark – I just live here. I take care-a my –

MICHAEL Look at the buildings still boarded! You know what used to be there? A five and dime. And there? A sandwich shop. And around the corner? A grocery. My father's grocery. You claim your civil right!? What about our civil rights!!

DENITRA I'm not trying to take your rights! I'm trying to give my daughter a chance.

MICHAEL By scammin' the system!

DENITRA She's just going to school! What do you lose by her going to a better school?!

MICHAEL Everybody can't go to Millburn High, lady! You go in your neighborhood. That's the law.

DENITRA You don't care about the law.

MICHAEL I've spent my whole life upholdin' the law, lady. // My whole life!

DENITRA You bend the rules all the time. When it suits you. You and your citizen's group.

MICHAEL When do we bend the rules?

DENITRA With that those Jewish synagogue people.

MICHAEL No, they're the ones trying to break the law, lady. Get your facts straight.

DENITRA Oh, I looked it up. There have been other places of worship in Millburn that don't meet the zoning ordinance, but were allowed a variance. But when the Jews asked for a variance, suddenly it's against the law. Then, when the Jewish people took y'all to court for applying the law differently, what did y'all do? Y'all lobbied to _change_ the law – to keep them out! You don't respect the law.

MICHAEL

DENITRA You're a coward – a COWARD – standing behind your "law" when you know, YOU KNOW the laws ain't fair!!!

MICHAEL // Say what you wanna, lady – say whatever you wanna to make it seem –

DENITRA Them laws ain't for everybody. They don't protect me!! They don't benefit me! They're for you! They're all for you! To keep you high on the hill while my daughter grovels for scraps!

MICHAEL If your daughter ends up groveling for scraps it'll be 'cause she turned out to be nothin' but a welfare queen, lyin' and cheatin' the system, just like her mother!

(DENITRA slaps MIKE. They are both silent and still. She realizes what she has done. She is stunned at her own action. So is he. Many moments pass.)

MICHAEL *(Beat)* I didn't mean your daughter wouldn't…I didn't –

DENITRA My daughter…is going to be…great. She's gonna be great.

MICHAEL *(Beat)* I didn't mean your daughter –

DENITRA *(Stoney)* You stay the hell away from Noelle. Don't you be followin' her no more. You stay the hell away from my child or I will…try me.

(DENITRA enters her apartment and leans on the door, realizing what she has done. She grabs her things and exits.)

Scene 4

That night, an half-hour later. BEVERLY's office. BEVERLY prepares to leave for the evening. DENITRA enters with trepidation.

DENITRA Beverly? I caught you.

BEVERLY *(Beat)* What are you doing here?

DENITRA I went to your house and your husband said you were still at school, so I thought I'd –

BEVERLY What's wrong?

DENITRA I didn't hear from you. About the special permission. Did she get it?

BEVERLY That's what you came all the way up here for?

DENITRA Now I'm coming "all the way up"? Newark is fifteen minutes up Springfield Avenue, Beverly.

BEVERLY I just mean you could've called.

DENITRA Did she get it?

BEVERLY *(Beat)* No. There's a moratorium on approvals until after the audit. *(Beat)* I'm sorry.

(DENITRA takes a breath.)

DENITRA *(Beat)* Okay. Okay.

(A few moments pass.)

DENITRA Okay. Well, first of all, I want to say thank you –

BEVERLY Denitra –

DENITRA I've never had anyone, no teacher no administrator, do as much for Noelle as you have. And I know we're not friends, that we're not - Thank you for trying.

BEVERLY Why are you talking like this?

DENITRA I just want you to know I'm grateful…and that I never intended to cause you any trouble.

BEVERLY What's done is done.

DENITRA There's more. Something happened between me and the private investigator.

BEVERLY

DENITRA He was following Noelle and she came into the house. She was scared. She didn't know who he was and I -

BEVERLY What happened?

DENITRA And I went out to confront him and I -

BEVERLY No.

DENITRA We got into an altercation.

BEVERLY

DENITRA I'm not worried about him. I just thought I should let you know. Since I knew you have to work with him.

BEVERLY I doubt I'll be working with him, after -

DENITRA I'm sorry.

BEVERLY No, it's not you. We had already… He found the registration documents I had slipped into the pile, so…

DENITRA Oh, my God, Beverly. They fired you?

BEVERLY No. But they will.

DENITRA I'm so sorry.

BEVERLY *(A gesture signifying, "let it go.")* It is what it is.

DENITRA What are you going to do?

BEVERLY What can I do? Wait and see. *(Beat)* But for you? There's still something you can do.

DENITRA What?

BEVERLY I know you don't want to hear it -

DENITRA Just tell me straight.

BEVERLY *(Beat)* I recommend that you take this last opportunity to withdraw her.

(BEVERLY hands her papers.)

BEVERLY Sign and pull her before the board meeting tomorrow. Once she's on record, there's nothing you can do.

(DENITRA looks at the papers. Moments pass.)

DENITRA I guess at the end of the day we gotta accept it, huh?

BEVERLY *(Beat)* It's not what you want, but there are other options. There are some good high schools in Newark - University, Technology - I can call some people I know to try to cash in some favors. Or she can re-apply to some charters next year and -

DENITRA You mean so they can play the lottery with her life again?

BEVERLY *(Beat)* We'll find something else.

DENITRA When?

BEVERLY As soon as we can.

DENITRA She doesn't have time. This is her time. Right here. Right now.

BEVERLY Going to school in Newark is not the end of the world. There are lots of students who graduate, go to college, and have careers. Fine lives. It's not an automatic condemnation to -

DENITRA No! You don't - you don't know what I went through. That school robbed me of my future. I put in my all and it -

BEVERLY You still have a future. // You can be -

DENITRA No, I don't.

BEVERLY Yes, you do.

DENITRA There are no thirty-eight year old undergraduates at Harvard, Beverly. There's a window, a window of opportunity you have to seize if you're going to be… Mine has come and gone. That's not going to happen to her. I can't let it happen to her. I can't -

BEVERLY Okay, okay -

(DENITRA looks at the papers.)

DENITRA I can't sign these. I won't be the one to cut her off.

BEVERLY Alright.

DENITRA I want her to win.

BEVERLY So do I. But we broke the law, Denitra.

DENITRA *(Beat)* Rosa Parks broke the law. Sojourner Truth broke the law. Frederick Douglass learned to read and broke the law. Why should we respect a law that don't respect us?

BEVERLY

DENITRA Help me so that she can win.

BEVERLY I don't know what else to - I've done what I can do -

DENITRA You could do something else. If you want her to do well, if you want her to have a shot -

BEVERLY I do. What?

DENITRA *(Beat)* You can take her.

BEVERLY

DENITRA *(Beat)* I want you to take her.

BEVERLY

DENITRA *(Beat)* I want you to take guardianship of Noelle.

(A few moments pass.)

BEVERLY *(Beat)* Denitra. You don't even know what you're saying, you - wait to see what happens tomorrow - wait and see -

DENITRA No. I can't wait for them to decide what happens to us. We decide our fate. We decide. Not them.

BEVERLY

DENITRA I thought about it. I'd...I'd be okay with it if I knew that she was getting her education. *(Beat)* Will you?

BEVERLY

DENITRA You and your husband are stable. Even if they fire you, you still live in Millburn. You could take her, and then they couldn't make her go. They'd have to take her and she can finish and go on to...to be like you.

BEVERLY I am not the be all and end all, Denitra.

DENITRA You got a good life.

BEVERLY Do I?

DENITRA Look at your house. You have a career. You have a family. You have nice things. You're comfortable.

BEVERLY Yes. And I'm glad for that, I'm not going to lie. But that's... Let me tell you what happens, Denitra... I've accomplished all this, but I haven't seen my family in over a year. Jordan doesn't know his cousins in Newark. Wanna know why? Because...because I'm ashamed of that. Because I look down on that. That's the residue... I was just like Noelle. My mother was just like you. I got lucky. I left home, I went to a good school, but it was hard. I sat in classrooms or in empty stairwells at lunch I felt so alone. If you let her go, she may end up feeling like...like she doesn't belong with you. Like you're beneath her. She won't want to feel that way, but she will, not in her mind, in her marrow. She will feel that she doesn't belong here. But she won't belong there either. She will be a floater, trying to anchor herself with her accomplishments and her stuff when all she really wants to do is feel like she's okay being in her own skin. This is not just good school versus bad school. This is choosing between the possibility of being successful and her sense of self. *(Beat)* Choosing my way won't - Being with me, won't necessarily be better for her, Denitra. It may mean better schools, better jobs, but not necessarily better for her as a person. She can stay with you, and we'll make sure she has outside academic support and she can have –

DENITRA No.

BEVERLY Listen to me –

DENITRA If we have to choose, being ashamed is better than being stuck. It's better than being in this situation. It's better than being like me.

(DENITRA breaks.)

BEVERLY Denitra. Ain't nothin' wrong with you. Nothing's wrong with you.

DENITRA Shhh…..

(DENITRA gathers herself.)

DENITRA I know it's a lot to answer now. I know you have to speak to your family. Just, please, think about it. Think about it, please. Please.

BEVERLY Okay.

Scene 5

Afternoon. Wednesday, November 3, 2010. Millburn Board of Education school residency fraud hearing. The lights are dimmed around MIKE and his projection screen. MIKE fingers index cards and takes in the board room attendees for some time. BEVERLY sits at a table nearby. DENITRA enters. MIKE takes them in. He takes in the audience as the members of the school board and community. He clears his throat. Finally, he clicks his clicker and a slide appears of a chicken and an egg.

MICHAEL What comes first: the chicken or the egg?

(He clicks to reveal another slide of a generic school house alongside a generic community.)

MICHAEL Or rather: What comes first: the school or the community?

(He clicks to reveal another slide of a white classroom teacher and mostly white students engaged in learning.)

MICHAEL What's the number one reason families choose to live in a certain neighborhood? It's the schools. A good school, it attracts good people and good business, keeping the property value high.

(He clicks his clicker and another slide appears of a grand suburban house for sale.)

MICHAEL Conversely, communities that have high property values usually have higher tax revenue. And everybody knows schools that have more money... have better education, and the parents tend to be more involved because they've made an investment.

(He clicks his clicker and another slide appears of the word 'fraud'.)

MICHAEL School Residency Fraud... puts an undue burden on a community - making there be more people to serve than the system was designed to take. So your school can go from one looking like this:

(He clicks to reveal a slide of a classroom filled with an adequate number of students.)

MICHAEL ...to one like this...

(He clicks to reveal a slide of an overcrowded school.)

MICHAEL And with crowded classrooms, student test scores can go from ones like this…

(He clicks to reveal a slide of high grades.)

MICHAEL …to ones like this…

(He clicks to reveal failing grades.)

MICHAEL Like that. *(He snaps his fingers.)* And once the grades go, once the quality of education is questionable, everything else is out the window. *(He clicks again to reveal a personal picture.)* But a licensed Private Investigator can make sure your schools stay strong. I'll tell ya a little story: I'm born and raised in Newark. I got such great memories, sometimes I forget we were poor. Sometimes, poor as dirt. I didn't know it. 'Cause I loved my community. My family. My friends. I don't know how my parents did so much with so little. But, somehow, I was able to get a good education in my neighborhood. I didn't have to leave it to have that chance. I didn't have to choose between my family, my community and my future. And, though my father worked two, sometimes three jobs, he did everything in his power to make sure we got an education, 'cause he wanted us to have a better life. He didn't have to break the law to give us that chance. *(Beat)* But if that was the only way he felt he had to make sure we…I think he would've. *(Beat)* And I got an education, and I was able to do better than him. And give my kids an education, and they're doin' better than me. I'm proud of that. *(He looks to DENITRA.)* Every parent wants their kid to be able to do better. Every teacher - *(He looks to BEVERLY.)* every principal worth her salt wants every child to be able to have their fair shot at havin' better. Unfortunately, not everybody has that chance. Sometimes it's beyond their reach. And it breaks my heart, 'cause it ain't the kids' fault. It's our fault. The adults. It's the law. Unfortunately, it's the law. And the law's the law.

(He clicks onto a glowing picture of himself with his credentials listed.)

MICHAEL For those-a you don't know me, my name is Michael DiMaggio and I'm a retired lieutenant detective and a licensed private investigator. You contracted my services to investigate and confirm the domiciled residences of your one thousand four hundred and eight students. It was a pleasure to serve this community.

(MIKE opens his file to reveal the final report. He looks at it for some moments. He looks at the audience for some moments. Then—)

MICHAEL *(Beat)* I'll now leave you with Principal Long to relay the details of our investigation and her recommendations for each. Principal Long?

(BEVERLY, stunned, looks to MIKE. After a few moments, she rises. He hands her the list. She looks at the list and at the board room attendees. She clears her throat.)

BEVERLY Uh, thank you, Mr. DiMaggio, for that … for that introduction. *(Beat)* Mr. DiMaggio conducted an electronic enrollment evaluation, community interviews and surveillance which helped him identify the students in violation. *(Long beat)* First. Lauron Baker, ninth grade. Recommended expulsion and restitution.

(As BEVERLY calls off the names, pictures are projected by MIKE.)

BEVERLY Jada Dower, ninth grade. Recommend expulsion and restitution. *(Beat)* Marcus and Omar Meyer, ninth and tenth grade. Three years in violation. Recommended expulsion and restitution.

(She stops and looks at the page. BEVERLY looks at MIKE. BEVERLY looks to DENITRA, then the boardroom attendees.)

BEVERLY Noelle Morgan, tenth grade… One year in violation. Recommended expulsion and restitution.

(DENITRA exits and BEVERLY watches her go. BEVERLY continues to read the names and each child appears. The lights contract around BEVERLY as she is left alone with the images of the children called (and perhaps more) swirling around her.)

BEVERLY Tabitha Spencer, tenth grade. One year in violation. Expulsion and restitution. Miranda Morris, eleventh grade. Two years in violation. Expulsion and restitution. Brandon McGuire, twelfth grade. Three years in violation. Expulsion and restitution…

Scene 6

That night, hours later. DENITRA's apartment. There's a knock at the door. DENITRA walks to her door and peers through the peep hole. She opens the door. BEVERLY stands.

DENITRA Come in.
BEVERLY Thank you.

(DENITRA enters the home, BEVERLY follows.)

DENITRA Can get you something to drink?
BEVERLY No, thank you.
DENITRA *(Beat)* Can I take your coat?
BEVERLY No. I'm okay.
DENITRA Okay. *(Beat)* Congratulations. I mean, on keeping your job. That's really great.
BEVERLY Yes.

(A few moments pass.)

DENITRA Okay. Well, uh… you said you // wanted to talk to me about something.
BEVERLY Listen, I hope you understand why I couldn't omit her –
DENITRA Oh, no. I get it. I understand.
BEVERLY I couldn't condemn the other 19 and not –
DENITRA I know. I know.
BEVERLY I'm sorry.

(A few moments pass.)

DENITRA Did you give any thought to…what we talked about… in your office?
BEVERLY Yes. Yes, I did.
DENITRA *(Beat)* I'll understand if you decided you can't.
BEVERLY *(Beat)* I decided I would.
DENITRA *(A gesture signifying, "You will?")*
BEVERLY *(Beat)* I talked it over with my husband. Jordan was excited. And we were set to do it, but…
DENITRA You were going to do it, but?
BEVERLY It's more complicated than I thought and –
DENITRA Beverly, whatever needs to happen – I thought about what you said – it's never too late to –
BEVERLY No, that's not it.
DENITRA Then, what?
BEVERLY *(Beat)* How much money do you make a year?
DENITRA *(Beat)* Why?
BEVERLY It's important.
DENITRA About thirty-five, forty thousand a year. What? Why does that matter?
BEVERLY I went the county offices and the district to get the paperwork I'd need to take guardianship of Noelle and enroll her under my address. And when I looked it over… You can't just transfer guardianship to me – transferring just so that she can go to school

is illegal. You have to prove that you can't take care of your child. Financially, mentally, that you need someone to intervene.
DENITRA *(Beat)* Okay. So what do I have to - ?
BEVERLY You'd have to…you'd have to lose your capacity to earn as much…or there has to be a medical issue or something in order to legally –
DENITRA How much money do you have to make?
BEVERLY *(Beat)* You have to be at the state poverty level. They won't let me take her and enroll her unless… You have to prove. And they're going to look. After everything that's – there's no way they're not going to look.

(A few moments pass. DENITRA starts to laugh hysterically.)

DENITRA God! I couldn't make this up! It's just –
BEVERLY Denitra.
DENITRA You know hard I worked to make that much money a year? You know how many hours, how much feces, and blood and piss and puss and God knows –
BEVERLY I know –
DENITRA I mean, what else do they want from me? Seriously. What else? I'm willing to give you my child! What more?
BEVERLY We'll think of something else. We'll –
DENITRA We?
BEVERLY Yes.
DENITRA No. Go home, Beverly. You tried.
BEVERLY No.
DENITRA Go home.
BEVERLY No. I am here. I'm here, Denitra. I'm not going anywhere. I'm here.

(DENITRA breaks. BEVERLY lets her have her moment. She recovers. They sit. DENITRA takes the documents. She looks them over, then stops. They sit in silence. Many moments pass.)

BEVERLY There's got to be a better way.
DENITRA This… all this… this is bigger than us.
BEVERLY *(Beat)* No. _People_ made it this way. _People_ can change it. We can change it.

(Moments pass.)

BEVERLY It's gonna be alright.
DENITRA
BEVERLY *(Beat)* It is going to be alright.
DENITRA *(With hope and hopelessness)* Yeah.

(Lights Fade.)

Tanya Saracho

Biography

Tanya Saracho was born in Los Mochis, Sinaloa, México. She is a playwright and television writer who's worked on *How To Get Away With Murder*, HBO's *Looking*, *Girls*, and *Devious Maids*. Saracho was named Best New Playwright by Chicago Magazine and is a proud member of The Kilroys. Saracho's plays have been produced at Primary Stages in NYC (upcoming), 2nd Stage in NYC, Denver Theatre Center, Oregon Shakespeare Festival, The Goodman Theater, Steppenwolf Theater, Teatro Vista, Teatro Luna, Fountain  Theater, Clubbed Thumb, NEXT Theater, and 16th Street Theater. Saracho was named one of nine national Latino "Luminarios" by Café Magazine and given the first Revolucionario Award in Theater by the National Museum of Mexican Art. She is the founder of Teatro Luna (the first all-Latina Theatre Company in the nation, now defunct) as well as the founder of ALTA (Alliance of Latino Theatre Artists). Plays written include: *Fade, Hushabye, Mala Hierba, The Tenth Muse, Song for the Disappeared, Enfrascada, El Nogalar* (inspired by *The Cherry Orchard*), an adaptation of *The House on Mango Street* for Steppenwolf, *Our Lady of the Underpass, Kita y Fernanda*, and *Quita Mitos*. Saracho currently has works in development with Starz, Two Rivers Theatre, and South Coast Repertory.

Artistic statement

I grew up in this world—in the world that *Mala Hierba* inhabits. That border world where class and gender and sexuality all intermingle in a big bowl of what it means to live at the edge of two cultures. The "trophy wife" is quite the staple here. It's one of the few models of femaleness I had growing up in the Rio Grande Valley— that of the "trapped woman." The notion of a woman trapped by her station and her aesthetic has stayed with me. Those cultural and national ties that bind so much that they stifle a woman's truth—that has been, and will remain, a constant exploration of my work.

Production history

Mala Hierba has had staged readings at: The Atlantic Theatre, Playwrights Horizon (in conjunction with Clubbed Thumb), The Public Theatre, Victory Gardens Theatre, and About Face Theatre. It received a production at 2nd Stage in New York City for its Uptown Series and it went into development at HBO for an adaptation into a TV series.

Original production information

Cast

MARI	Roberta Colindrez
YUYA	Sandra Marquez
LILIANA	Marta Milans
FABIOLA	Ana Nogueira

Crew

Director: Jerry Ruiz
Scenic Design: Raul Abrego
Costume Design: Carisa Kelly
Lighting Design: Jen Schriever
Sound Design: Jill BC DuBoff
Fight Choreography: Thomas Schall
Production Stage Manager: Lori Ann Zepp
Stage Manager: Alisa Zeljeznjak

11 *Mala Hierba*
Tanya Saracho

Characters

LILIANA   Late 20's–Early 30's. Wife of border magnate. Always decked out; always impeccable: This is the trophiest of "Trophy Wives." Lili's got that kind of charm that can't be taught. She was born in Mexico to a proper Mexican family.

MARITZA   Same age as Liliana. Mari is a visual artist based in Chicago with South Texas roots. Her friends in the Lesbian community might call her a "boi" or a "stud" and she wouldn't mind it. She has a few tattoos she loves, some she regrets. She loves fiercely and is fiercely loyal.

YUYA   Older than Liliana by at least 12 or 15 years, but perhaps older. Yuya raised Liliana and her siblings and served that household until she imported herself to Liliana's new household when she married. Yuya is usually smarter than anyone in the room, but she hides her resentment well. Hey, she knows her place.

FABIOLA   The very entitled 25-year-old fresa daughter of Liliana's husband. This girl has always had everything and has seldom been told "no."

Time

The span of one week, late this Spring

Place

Sharyland, Texas in The Rio Grande Valley

Punctuation notes

// : Overlapping is very important – these women talk like people talk: over one another. Every // cues the following line of dialogue. Please adhere to this.

Scene 1

THURSDAY MORNING: The Cantu's master bedroom. This is a decadent room, with a big wooden bed and matching bedroom furniture. 1000 thread-count sheets, that sort of thing. The best that money can buy and also the tackiest money can buy. Alright, not tacky but these people have had Versace furniture back when it was in style, knowhatImean? It's just too much, too fabulous, this house could definitely be on MTV's cribs. Lots of creme colors and lots of wood. Gilded things. It's morning. The bed is unmade, and it's seen something major: the sheets are all rumpled and disheveled and there are belts everywhere. Like seven of them, strewn across the floor and the bed. Two are fastened to the bed as restraints. Fastened to the posts. LILIANA is getting dressed as YUYA enters.*

YUYA A mira pues, I thought you were still in there showering.
LILIANA Come help me with this.

(YUYA helps zip her up.)

YUYA Que purty, this color. Is this from the big box that came yesterday?
LILIANA Yes. All the other dresses are disgusting, though. Will you send them all back?
YUYA Tu y tus Internet addictions. Yeah, I'll send them back. No pero, it does look purty on you, this color.

(LILIANA goes to sit by the vanity and absentmindedly picks up a belt from the bench and hands it to YUYA. The belt is nothing, just a belt. YUYA picks and puts away belts during the next exchange.)

LILIANA I also got it in rosita and lilac but both made me look too... Texan.
YUYA Oooh, lilac would look purty with your green eyes.
LILIANA Maybe I'll keep that one.

(A crash is heard in the garden. Your general metal-chairs-on-table crash.)

LILIANA Puta madre, Yuya! All morning these men have been // with the banging and the—
YUYA They're just unloading the chairs and the tables. I just went to supervise. It's fine. // Que quieres que te diga, it's going to be noisy like that.
LILIANA Pero que relajo se traen!
YUYA It's looking real good down there though. You'll see right now when you go down.
LILIANA It better look amazing. It better look like a pinche editorial in a pinche magazine with all the money I'm spending.
YUYA It will, todo mundo will be talking about it. You'll see.
LILIANA Oh, God I hope so.
YUYA This room es todo un desmother. I'm going to change these sheets, okei? Should I put on the satin ones that he likes?

LILIANA Ay, no Yuya. Those make me feel so Scarface.
YUYA The peach ones then.
LILIANA Which peach? Oh, the creme? Si, pon esas Yuya.[1]

(YUYA goes about redressing the bed.)

YUYA Adivina[2] who came last night?
LILIANA Porfavor, crees que no me di cuenta?[3] The whole neighborhood heard her come in in the middle of the night. Driving in like a manica, stomping around like a pinche elephant.
YUYA Es una malcriada.[4]
LILIANA I don't want to say anything because you know, because I feel bad for her, raised by mother after mother.
YUYA Please. I have kids okei? And they only turned out to be good kids because I gave them sus buenos guamazos[5] if they ever got sassy with me. Which is exactly what this girl was missing. With kids you can't be afraid to make a fist.
LILIANA No, if I ever have kids, I'm never going to hit them. If I ever have kids voy a razonar con ellos.[6]
YUYA Yeah, razonar like this with them.

(makes a bitch slap movement)

No te digo,[7] that's the only way. If not you'll turn out big brats like this one.
LILIANA Me da lastima.[8]
YUYA You feel bad for that brat?
LILIANA A little.

(YUYA continues making the bed.)

YUYA She didn't never go to sleep. Se fue[9] straight to the study to the computer, she was still up when I get up this morning y viene y me dice en[10] la kitchen "I want eggs benedict. But with fresh mozarella instead of ham. Make it." Asi nomas,[11] "make it." And she never says my name neither, siempre se le olvida.[12] How long have I worked here and she don't remember my name? Every dog's name she remembers, pero el mio ni maiz paloma.[13]
LILIANA You know what a big fuss they made when I brought you asi que dale las gracias[14] that she even talks to you. Just don't...
YUYA Oh, I know. I know. Please, you know that I know how to act. Twelve years working for your family, I know how to act.
LILIANA I know, just...please, porque va con el cuento con Alberto.[15]
YUYA *(to herself)* "Eggs Benedict"...Pinche huerca.

LILIANA *(about earrings)* The gold or the silver?

YUYA Gold. Aunque the silver looks good too.

LILIANA I have a million things to do before to-morrow. We have to call the bakery and order a whole new cake. Alberto changed his mind about the red velvet, now he wants tres leches for the party cake. But he still wants it to be five tiers. I can't tell him tres leches doesn't hold up in tiers. It would be mush.

YUYA Just get him a tres leches para el solito y dale a[16] everybody else red velvet.

LILIANA Oh, because it's as simple as that, verda? You know how he is. He'll check and then, well, we don't want him to get how he gets at his own birthday party. The bakery is going to have to work it out. And I'm sorry that they have a day to make a whole new cake. Pero a ver como le hacen. That is not my problem. Por eso se les paga lo que se les paga, verdad?[17]

(beat)

Santo Dios, que desmadre.[18] If his 55th birthday is this much trouble I don't want to know what will happen when he turns 60. Me va a dar un infarto.[19]

YUYA We'll see if you're around for that.

(a dirty look from LILIANA)

Digo, si Dios nos da vida.[20] You never know what will happen.

LILIANA No te pases conmigo,[21] cabrona. You think I don't know what you mean? What people say? I know I'm married to Henry The Eight.

(She throws a brush at YUYA)

COMO ME VAS A DECIR ESO?[22]

(consciously quieting down)

I don't need this shit from you, Yuya! Five years I've lived tip toeing around this pinche family and I don't need you for eggshells right now. Not you too, pinche cabrona.[23]

YUYA I'm sorry. I didn't mean it like that-

LILIANA Claro que[24] you meant it like that. Vibora.[25]

YUYA Disculpame.[26] I wasn't-

LILIANA *(throwing another brush at her)* Con esa pinche lengua de vibora![27] You viper!

(FABIOLA enters without knocking.)

FABI Anybody know if there's an art supply store in this hicksville? I want to paint.

LILIANA Fabi! Hola muneca! Llegaste bien?[28]

(The two kiss on the cheek and FABIOLA throws herself on the freshly made bed.)

FABI Yeah, sorry I didn't call you guys. I got here like at 6 actually, but I grabbed dinner with some friends. Did you know there's a P.F. Chang's here now? // Finally, something other than fucking taquerias and Whataburgers. And then we went to this wanna-be beer garden place. I'm like, alright McAllen, don't try so hard. But then it was like two am and I was like, fuck, I guess I better get home.

LILIANA Yes, since last year…

LILIANA Yuya, eso es todo. Gracias.[29]

(YUYA exits)

How was the drive?

FABI What do you mean how was the drive? It was a drive. What am I going to tell you? I drove, I stopped to pee, I ate cheetos in the car.

(A beat.)

FABI Can we please talk about the fucking madness going on downstairs? All those men everywhere. I could barely come up the driveway.

LILIANA They're setting up for your dad's party.

FABI Obviously. But do they have to be in everybody's way? // Hey, what are you wearing tomorrow. What are you wearing to dad's thing?

LILIANA I'm sorry about this Fabi.

LILIANA *(She takes a quick beat)* Ah, I have a couple of options…

FABI Can I see?

LILIANA I don't… do I have them all here? Let me see. *(goes into the closet)*

FABI I didn't bring anything that I like and forget trying to find something here. Por favor. I'll end up with a cowboy hat or something…and ropers.

LILIANA *(emerging from closet with two dress bags)* I was thinking this red one, because it's going to be hot. I don't want to, you know, I don't want to sweat, so no sleeves. But really I think I'm going to wear this white one because I love the-

FABI Oh, my god. No, you're going to let me wear the white one. Where did you get this?!

LILIANA I ordered it.

FABI Where from?

LILIANA Online.

FABI From where? I love it!

(FABI takes off her clothes to try it on. LILIANA gives a quick sigh, she obviously wanted to wear that one.)

LILIANA I don't even remember. You know how you get to shopping online and you have like a thousand opened tabs and you just click buy and…yeah, I don't remember.

FABI Shuddup, this fits me like a glove. Look at this. Do you have gold shoes?

LILIANA Aaah, I think so.

FABI Oh, I really like how it looks. You don't mind do you?

LILIANA No, como crees.[30]

FABI You sure?

LILIANA Please, no. I was going to wear this red one anyway.

FABI Ok, great so I got the dress, now for the shoes.

LILIANA Yeah, let me show you, what I got…

FABI Hey, so you got a new car, huh?

LILIANA *(Slight "oh no" beat. She knows what's coming.)* …yeah. You saw it.

FABI How can one miss it? It's like taking up two spaces in the garage.

LILIANA Yeah, it's a little ridiculous, isn't it?

FABI I love it.

(pause)

LILIANA Yeah, I love it too.

FABI Yeah.

(pause)

LILIANA While you're down, if you want to you can drive it.

FABI Could I?

LILIANA Of course. It's such a smooth ride.

FABI I know. I drove it out to get a shake last night.

LILIANA You what?

FABI I was dying for a shake, like dying—I'm probably getting my period—and the keys were right there. So I was like, let me check it out. And you're so right, it's like butter. I feel so tall in it. I don't know how easy it can be to have something like that in Houston, like so big, you know? But it's like butter. The seats. Ah, so comfy. And I like all the stuff on the dash.

LILIANA Yeah, it's like you're driving a space ship, isn't it?

FABI I want it.

LILIANA I have no doubt that- Alberto wouldn't even blink if you asked him for one. How long are you down for? We can go to the dealership together-

FABI I like that one. *(pause)* I like, totally fell in love with it. The color.

LILIANA …ah, my little truck…

FABI Not so little. Your little… big truck. *(Pause. LILIANA's trying to deal with the knot in her throat.)*

LILIANA *(Ah, man, this hurts)* No.

(beat)

YOUR big truck.

FABI What? No way.

LILIANA Yes, please. *Your* truck.

FABI Are you serious?

LILIANA Fabiola. Of course. You're the one that's up there in Houston-

FABI Like for real, for real? You'll give me your car? Title transfer and everything?

LILIANA Claro. No se diga mas. I didn't buy it, right? // You're the one up there working so hard. And studying so hard, you know? Of course. Come on.

FABI Nope. But your good taste did choose it.

FABI Why are you the best? You are my favorite of my dad's wives, you know that? Totally mean it.

LILIANA Oh, that means so much to me, Fabi. De verdad.[31]

FABI I'm super serious. You know I didn't get along with that gringa he fucking brought back from Arizona. // Ugh. Arizona is the new Alabama, it's a fucking toothless hicksville.

LILIANA Oh, I know. No, yeah, I know.

FABI Nasty fucking gringa with no class.

LILIANA I know.

FABI I mean it. You're like…you're almost like a sister to me, but like not.

(She pulls out the keys from the pocket of her sweatpants on the bed)

So, all mine?

LILIANA Well, we just have to run it by Alberto.

FABI Oh, I know you'll convince him. You're the best!

(Big hug)

Oh, and the best taste in clothes. Hands down.

(About the dress)

Thank you, mil! It looks good, no?

LILIANA Way better than it would've looked on me.

FABI Shuddup, don't say that. I'll give it back to you tomorrow. Ok, I'm going to go get a raspa. That's the one thing I crave from here.

In Houston the closest thing we get to it is a slushy but I tell people, I don't want a fucking neon red slushy that taste likes sugary ass, I want a fucking raspa like with the shaved fucking ice from the valley. That's what I want. If I could learn to shave ice myself, I'd totally eat that for breakfast, lunch and dinner.

(beat)

Oh, guess who I ran into this morning? Same bright idea, I guess, we were both getting a shake. Maritza Perez. Do you remember her?

LILIANA Mari Perez?

FABI Yes! Oh, my god she looks amazing. She was a sore thumb standing there with all her like… I don't know. Gear. She's like all emo or something. Anyway, apparently she was living in Detroit.

LILIANA Chicago.

FABI Yeah. Chicago and she's visiting because, actually, I don't know. She told me but I wasn't paying too much attention. Anyway, she's here for a little while. So I invited her to dad's thing tomorrow.

LILIANA You what!

FABI She's your friend, right?

LILIANA I haven't talked to her in like decades.

FABI Oh, she told me she saw you at some wedding? Or a funeral?

LILIANA I mean, sure. She, she knew my brother and she came down for the memorial but I'm sorry I didn't really talk to her, I literally passed her in the hallway… I didn't really talk to her…

FABI Well, now you get a chance to catch up.

(about the dress)

Hey, thanks again. It fits like a glove.

(exiting)

You know what? I'm going to do something nice for you cuz you've been so badass with me. What flavor raspa do you want?

LILIANA I don't really…

FABI Vanilla! I'm going to get you vanilla. So I can have a taste. *(Exits.)*

(LILIANA sits down on the bed, the air has been popped out of her chest. Lights go down.)

Scene 2

FRIDAY NIGHT: The master bedroom. We hear the dull sound of a party down below. Clinking and

music and the occasional cackle, etc. You know, party shit. LILIANA enters in her red dress. She looks amazing in it, she's a little sweaty though. She digs in a vanity drawer for a packet (not bottle) of pills from Mexico. Tafil to be exact. She pops one in her mouth and chases it with the glass of malbec she's brought with her. A little while before YUYA enters with a similar pack.

YUYA I couldn't find // your purse.

LILIANA I found some.

YUYA Me encontre este paquete[32] in the kitchen. You had another stash behind the diet pills.

LILIANA Ah, thank God I have foresight. Should I take two? No porque luego[33] I'll fall asleep or something. I don't know what to do? I want to take the whole freaking box. He hates the band. He hates it.

YUYA He's over that. He forgot about it as soon as he yelled at you.

LILIANA I hope so. I hope he forgot. Osea ojala because during the toast all I kept thinking is, chingada madre[34] he's going to start yelling as soon as he sees we couldn't make a five tier tres leches.

YUYA It's just cake.

LILIANA Como que[35] it's just cake? It's not just cake.

YUYA The governor loved the red velvet. Les dimos tres pieces.[36]

LILIANA I know. It's the only thing that saved me. Did you see his son? He looks like a movie star now. There was a time, long time ago, there was a time I thought we'd end up married.

YUYA Nombre,[37] you don't want to move back to Mexico and be a governor's wife. They're killing governors right now. La mafia is making a video game of beheading them for points.

LILIANA Ay, Yuya! Porque me traumas?[38]

YUYA Me? The news trauma! They traumatize you every day at six o'clock. People don't even know if what they're watching is the news or some video game con good graphics. Blood everywhere.

(beat)

He did get so handsome though. He got tall. Maybe he won't got into politics like his dad.

LILIANA Please, they're all politicians. His entire family. There's no way. Let's stop talking about him. If Alberto notices the little looks he's been giving me, no para que quieres…. Do I look okay?

YUYA He was watching you like this.

LILIANA He was, wasn't he? I'm not just imagining. Good. Oh, but his wife es una mustia.[39] Did you see her? No hips. No boobs. Dark. Ugh. De donde saco a esa indita?[40]

YUYA I didn't believe it was his wife at first.

LILIANA I know! Yo aqui como que "Hola! Mucho gusto." Guacala.[41]

YUYA At least the one thing you can say is that you're always the prettiest one everywhere you go.

LILIANA (*Still messing with her hair.*) At least we can say that.

(*beat*)

You like my hair like this? Should I wear it down?

YUYA No, he told you to wear it up. Luego se enoja.[42]

LILIANA That's true. But I always feel so old with it up.

YUYA You don't look old. Se te ve bien.[43]

LILIANA I know, but it makes me feel like I'm thirty eight or something. Over the hill.

(*A knock on the door.*)

LILIANA Si? Adelante.[44]

(*MARITZA enters the threshold, not the bedroom yet, but her presence is like hot vapor in the room. LILIANA jolts up.*)

LILIANA Yuya, ve a ver si se ofrece algo abajo. Andale ve.[45]

(*pause*)

MARITZA Hey, Yuya. How you been?

YUYA (*Ignoring MARITZA, to LILIANA.*) I think maybe you should go downstairs and see if Alberto wants to dance now. Andaba diciendo before that he wanted to dance.

LILIANA Yuya, go downstairs, I said.

YUYA I think maybe you should come too.

LILIANA No te lo vuelvo a repetir![46] Go check on the guests! Go!

(*YUYA exits glaring at MARITZA.*)

MARITZA Bye, Yuya. Nice seeing you too.

(*Very pregnant pause. Like 9 months pregnant.*)

LILIANA Hi.

MARITZA Hi.

(*pause*)

Great party.

LILIANA Thank you. Been planning it half the year. Did you see who we got to play?

MARITZA I know. Fancy.

LILIANA Alberto hated them in person. They sound different in person.

MARITZA I thought they sounded good. Speakers were a little loud though.

LILIANA I don't think anyone one noticed that. I mean, you know about that sort of thing, but I don't think… people seemed to be enjoying themselves.

MARITZA They always do at these things, no? All the decadent food and endless drinks.

LILIANA Let's hope so.

(*pause*)

MARITZA You look amazing.

LILIANA Thank you. Thanks.

MARITZA You really do.

LILIANA Thanks. You look…I like your blazer. It's like 80's, right?

MARITZA I guess.

LILIANA Aren't you hot in that? It's too hot for a blazer. No te estas asando?[47]

MARITZA Alberto's wearing a blazer.

LILIANA I'm sure he's cooking in it. I'm sure all the men are cooking in their blazers. That's why it's good to be a woman in weather like this, because we can wear things like this and not cook in blazers.

MARITZA Well, if he can cook in his blazer; I'll cook in my blazer.

LILIANA I should have gotten giant fans to put everywhere, or cooling stations.

(*A pivot*)

MARITZA I've been here a week.

LILIANA Maybe we should go downstairs. Everyone will wonder where I went.

MARITZA A week, Liliana.

LILIANA Want to try a fun drink? They designed it just for the party. It's like a mai-tai but better.

MARITZA I've been sitting on my ass for a whole fucking week asking myself, "Did that phone call really happen?"

LILIANA I want to go downstairs.

MARITZA Sitting there at my cousin's, who is too polite to ask, "What the fuck are you doing down here?" and me sitting there wondering the same fucking thing.

LILIANA Que malhablada eres, eh.[48]

MARITZA (*quickly*) What? See, don't start doing that.

LILIANA Shut up, I hate it when you act like you don't understand. You speak Spanish.

MARITZA Since when do I speak Spanish? You won't ever fucking believe that I don't.

LILIANA Well, why don't you? It's never made sense to me. Your last name is, what it is. Your parents speak it. You look like you do. I mean, it just makes no sense to me.

(quick beat)

Can we please go downstairs?

MARITZA What am I doing here, Liliana?

LILIANA I don't know, to be honest. I didn't invite you, not to be rude, but I didn't invite you. So… I don't really know what you're doing here.

MARITZA Oh, really? You didn't invite me?

LILIANA Not to the party. No.

MARITZA Shut the fuck up! What am I doing in Texas?

LILIANA Could we talk tomorrow? Wait, no because…Could we talk on Monday? I'll meet you at your cousin's on Monday.

MARITZA You want to wait to fucking talk until Monday?! // I'm supposed to just sit on my ass waiting for you until Monday, when I've been down here for a fucking week with you avoiding my phone calls, just sitting on my ass.

LILIANA Ssshhhh….sssshhh…calmaditacalmadita….please, Mari. Please.

(She goes to lock the door.)

Ssshhhh.

MARITZA I'm not your fucking puppet Liliana.

LILIANA Porfavor no levantes la voz.[49] Someone will hear you. This is not how I wanted this to go. // I promise you this is not how I wanted this to go.

MARITZA And how exactly did you want this to go when I get a phone call in the middle of the night where you sound as if the sky is fucking falling falling…

LILIANA No seas exagerada. You take everything so seriously. Sometimes I take an Ambien // and I just get—

MARITZA Jesus fucking Christ. Are you serious right now?

LILIANA Listen. Let's go downstairs. Let's just make the best of it and enjoy the party, vale?

MARITZA This is you on the phone, "please come down, Mari. You're the only person I can turn to, Mari. Please, please, Mari." You said that—among other things. So my stupid ass gets on the first plane, which is not cheap, Liliana. I get on the first plane

because I think "fuck, Liliana's about to die or something" and here I am – almost a fucking week because for whatever reason you're now avoiding me and have locked yourself up in your fucking, in your fucking narco compound – do you know how enraging that is? // you ignoring my texts and my facebooks and my fucking emails?!

LILIANA Please please keep your voice down.

LILIANA I'm sorry. You're right. I shouldn't have called you like that in the middle of the… I'm sorry. I promise you, everything is fine. I don't know what I was talking about. Just, just ignore everything I said, okay?

(A knock at the door.)

Oh, fuck me. Quien?[50]

FABI *(off)* Lili, these shoes suck. I need to look for new ones.

LILIANA What? Ah, yeah, hold on.

(to MARITZA) Just… please. Yes, you're right, I owe you an explanation. Tomorrow. Or ah, Monday. I promise.

MARITZA Fucking puppetmaster.

(LILIANA unlocks the door and opens it. FABI is a little drunk.)

FABI Where the hell did you get these shoes from? They are cheap as hell. The strap is slicing my heel. Only cheap shoes do that. Oh, hey. What are you guys doing in here? What you don't want to be downstairs // dancing to that Gadawful…

LILIANA I was looking for a headache…for an asprin for Mari, only stronger and we were, you know, catching up.

FABI Were you?

(Taking out some coke.)

That's nice. It's good to catch up with friends.

(To MARI) You want a bump?

(pause)

MARITZA Sure.

LILIANA What? Mari, don't. Oh, god.

(Goes into the closet)

I'll look for some shoes for you. I'll see if I have some shoes.

FABI Nice hair on her, huh? Hello, prom 1997. Why does she do her hair like that? She tries to so hard. Poor thing.

(bump)

Oh, my god. It's so fucking hot out there.

(bump)

Let me see your ink.

(MARITZA shows FABI her tattoo. Mari bumps.)

FABI I like that. I like the style cuz it's not too obvious, you know? But it's still a flower. What kind of flower is that?

MARITZA It's a lily.

FABI Right. I want like a big arm sleeve tattoo one day. Like from here to here.

MARITZA Really?

FABI Not really. But wouldn't that be cool?

MARITZA Are you the tattoo kind?

FABI Are you kidding? Look at this.

(She lifts her dress and pulls down her panties)

It means "bullshit" in Chinese. Or like the equivalent.

MARITZA Nice.

(LILIANA enters to FABI pulling down her panties. She enters with tons of shoes. She spills them on the table.)

LILIANA Fabiola, que haces?

MARITZA She's showing me her bullshit. Or the equivalent.

(Fabi's delighted with Mari)

LILIANA I brought everything out, everything I think that goes with that dress. I mean, you could do color if you wanted because it's white.

FABI Maybe I'll just go barefoot. What do you think?

MARITZA Do it.

FABI I need a fucking pedicure, though.

MARITZA Nah.

FABI Yeah? Barefoot?

(bump)

So where did you find that design?

MARITZA *(re: tattoo)* What? This?

FABI Yeah, who drew it? I might want a flower like that. Like right here.

MARITZA I drew it.

FABI You drew that? That's like really good.

MARITZA Well, thank you.

LILIANA Maritza is actually an amazing artist, I mean, do you still do your art thing?

MARITZA Unfortunately. Yeah. I never learned to do something respectable with my life.

LILIANA She's being modest but she's actually kind of famous, right?

MARITZA I wouldn't use the term famous.

FABI Shuddup, are you serious?

MARITZA Your *stepmother* here is being kind. I have a gallery. And yeah, some people like my work. But I wouldn't say that makes me famous.

FABI Shuddup, that's amazing. Dude, I paint. I do.

MARITZA Oh, yeah?

LILIANA She makes these like, huge canvas things with–

FABI Shuddup. I love it. Ok, you have to take a look at my stuff.

MARITZA Sure.

FABI Lili, who knew that you had cool friends! Like, who knew.
(offering coke) Lili?

LILIANA I don't…no thanks.

FABI Oh, right. Pills are your thing.

LILIANA De que hablas?[51]

FABI I don't blame you, to deal with my dad you need like an I.V. of Xanax to like drag around with you. My dad, as soon as you start to be emotional about anything-shit you could be watching Oprah or like a Disney movie with puppies and who doesn't cry at that, you know? But you start crying and it annoys my dad so much that he'll literally pop a pill in your mouth. I mean, like he'll take out a pill, pull down your jaw and pop the fucking Tafil in your mouth. All those pills right there? Reynosa. They're all from Mex. He doesn't need a prescription. He's got everyone sedated with those fucking pills, right Lili?

LILIANA Everybody takes those. I only take it here and there when I'm stressed. Tafil is for children anyway, I just take the child dose.

FABI Pop two in your mouth: grown up dose. Pop three:

(snores)

This party sucks. The music is atrocious. I told my dad that that band was shit.

LILIANA Did you?

FABI It's shit. Mari, let's go do something. You seem like a fun girl. Let's go look for trouble in this shithole of a town. What do you think?

MARITZA *(pause)* Ok. I'm down.

FABI Awesome.

LILIANA I don't know if you should… Mari and I were catching up since… she's leaving tomorrow.

FABI Are you leaving tomorrow?

MARITZA Maybe.

FABI Ah, well if you're leaving then we should definitely go party, you know?

MARITZA Like I said…I'm down.

LILIANA But we didn't get to catch up. We were…we didn't get to catch up and I haven't talked to you in so long and we were catching up.

MARITZA Maybe I'll stay till Monday then. We can catch up later.

LILIANA Why don't we catch up now?

FABI (*laughing*) -sounds like the two of you are saying you want some ketchup. Like for fries.

(*laughing*)

Come on, let's peace out. Liliana, tell Papi I had to go. That I just had to go because this music, it's making my ears bleed. Ok?

LILIANA He's going to be angry.

FABI Well, make sure he's not. You're so good at calming him down.
(*To MARITZA*) I've never seen anyone calm him down the way she does. I don't know what she does.
You got like fairy dust. Ok, let's go. Ciao ciao.

(*FABI exits. MARITZA lingers.*)

Maritza!

MARITZA Monday.

(*LILIANA looks like a wet dog or something. No air in her chest again. A moment.*)

Scene 3

FRIDAY INTO SATURDAY: The back deck of the Cantu's huge patio. There are beautiful equipales with the family crest and lots of fabulous patio décor. It's like tacky but fabulous, you know? Firstly with a touch of Northern Mexico including some Tapatio pieces (like the equipales and some big talavera vases) but also with a little Southwest/American comfort thrown in there, like stuff from the Sharper Image. There's one of those electronic, self-contained fire pits and the wavy light from the pool reflects onto the deck, giving it a sort of glow. LILIANA is sitting in the dark, although it's not that dark since the pool is lit and the Texas moon is smiling. She's eating a bowl of Fritos with lime juice and salsa Tabasco. She licks her fingers every so often. Maybe she uses an exprimidor de limones to put more lime on the Fritos. She's got the cordless house phone and her cell phone and checks it a couple of times. It's like 3 or 4am, dude it's mad late. She should be in bed. YUYA enters after a while.

YUYA That's gonna put a big hole in your stomach.

LILIANA This is my second bowl.

YUYA Shoot, I'm going to have to roll you up the stairs.

LILIANA Shut up, Yuya. Fuck, why don't I smoke? If I smoked I'd be super skinny.

YUYA Maybe you should take it up. No porque luego the man upstairs, he wouldn't like the smell.

LILIANA Verda? My hair would reek. Ok, we need a better plan to make this little belly be flat again. It needs to go down like this, not stick out like that. Guacala, I'm so gross.

YUYA I didn't want to say it, but you are getting a little wide right here in the middle.

LILIANA Shut up, don't say that to me, Yuya. Are you serious?

YUYA Have I ever lied to you?

(*Freaked out pause*)

LILIANA Oh, my God you're right. I think I'm growing some back fat. Do you see? I'm getting back fat and love handles. Que trauma.

YUYA The best was when you used to throw up, that's when you look the best.

LILIANA Yeah, I looked so good then. You could see my bones right here. But my breath smelled so bad and you know… I kept getting dizzy everywhere.

YUYA Plus your hair…

LILIANA Oh, I know. I thought I was in that movie *The Craft* all of a sudden. Like that girl washing her hair in the school shower and she's like washing it and it's coming off all over her hands. Callate, no me lo recuerdes.[52] Imagine if I lost my hair?
I'd be so ugly.

(*YUYA nods in agreement. A quick moment.*)

Maybe we need to go back to Monterrey for those injections again because that totally worked. I was so skinny with the injections because I couldn't keep anything down. But we need to find a doctor who doesn't make me break out into hives. I don't know what was in that stuff, but the last time we went-

YUYA Uy, you looked like the swamp thing.

LILIANA I did. Shut up, Yuya. Stop stressing me out.
(*Eats more Fritos.*) Ya ves como me tienes?[53] Here I am eating trash. But why does it have to be so fucking good?

YUYA You gonna rot your guts.

LILIANA Good, maybe I'll get an ulcer and not get hungry.

YUYA Luego[54] you're gonna be complaining in the morning que acid reflux this and que acid reflux that.

LILIANA What are you talking about, it is morning. It's going to be light out in a couple of hours.

(beat)

Ah, I hate it when Fabiola's here. I fucking hate it when she comes down. Right when we got Alberto calm and… you know, appeased and mansito, aqui vienes esta pinche huerca…[55]

(beat)

I'm going to have to give her the car, you know? Hija de su puta madre.[56]

I'm going to have to give her my fucking truck.

YUYA I don't know. Her daddy no esta muy happy with her.[57]

LILIANA Oh, please. He always does whatever she wants in the end. Always gets her way. Nadamas saca la mano[58]

(stretching out her hand)

"Please, Papi. Papito porfavor."[59]

(beat)

Wait.

(Goes to look through the glass door)

Imaginate si nos cacha Alberto. Porfavor Diosito que no se despierte.[60]

We're all fucked if he wakes up and sees his Porsche missing. How did she find the keys? I don't even know where he keeps the fucking keys. Me lleva…[61]

YUYA Para que te preocupas por ella?[62]

LILIANA Como que porque me preocupo?[63]

YUYA I don't understand why you're sitting out here todo worried about her.

LILIANA She's got his car, Yuya. Estas mensa?[64] She's got his car.

YUYA Alla ella, that's her problem.

LILIANA *(raising her voice then catching herself)* It's everybody's problem. He wakes up and notices that she's gone with his brand new—I mean, the man hasn't even gotten to drive it, we went around the neighborhood for ten minutes.

YUYA He took you to the beach in it.

LILIANA Well, yes, he took me to the beach in it. Still.

YUYA You're not mad because she took his car, tu 'tas enchilada cuz she went off with Maritza, to who knows where.

LILIANA Yuya.

YUYA Am I saying the truth here?

LILIANA Mejor te callas Yuya.

YUYA You are out here in the middle of the night waiting because you can't stand that // your little friend there…

LILIANA I'm going to throw this bottle at you // let it splatter and hit you with hot sauce in the eye!

YUYA Andale.[65] Throw it and wake him up.

(LILIANA puts the bottle down. Glares at YUYA. Silence.)

You think I say this to make you mad or something.

LILIANA I know you say it to make me mad.

YUYA Lili, if he ever gets wind of-

(In a flash LILIANA has gotten up and is holding YUYA by the face. Tight. One hand on her throat maybe. This shuts YUYA up. For a moment.)

LILIANA Shut up! Cierras el hocico or do I shut it for you?!

(pause)

YUYA He'll kill you.

LILIANA I know he will.

(pause)

YUYA You think I don't have feelings and that I don't feel anything and that when we clean you up in the morning from, from whatever he does to you at night-

LILIANA Te estas pasando, Yuya.[66]

YUYA Hey, I've been married too.

LILIANA I doubt your husband had my husband's appetite, I doubt it very much.

YUYA I know. Por eso digo[67] that I'm not just saying this to be some jerk or something. Lili, you're like my daughter. To me you're like a daughter.

LILIANA I know.

YUYA You know that's the truth. And my job is to take care of you. When I saw her here, in your house. It's just bad business // to have her here.

LILIANA Just stop talking, Yuya.

YUYA I knew there would be trouble. There can be trouble if you don't just, send her away. You need to send her away.

LILIANA I tried.

YUYA No. You can't half ass try. You gotta send her away.

LILIANA Oh, like I have any power over whether she comes or goes. She doesn't listen to me. Nobody listens to me.

(Sound of garage door)

The door-the garage door.

(YUYA gets up to go see)

Wait, don't go. Wait until she goes upstairs or she goes to get online. I just want to make sure the car is the garage.

YUYA She probably left wrappers and things y sabra Dios que tanto.[68]

I'm going to have to go in there and clean it up.

LILIANA Yeah, we clean it up when she goes to-

YUYA The keys. We need the keys from her. Si no la jodimos.[69]

(Suddenly FABIOLA bursts out onto the deck, as she's taking off her top. She's followed by MARITZA.)

FABIOLA ...because they don't fucking trust me with house keys like if I'm nine years old! It's like gestapo nation up in here.

(re: shirt.)

Help me take this off.

(MARITZA helps her with the shirt.)

MARITZA Fabi, I think you should call it a night.

FABIOLA No, come on, the pool it's heated. We'll swim and it'll be so perfect.

(FABIOLA notices the other women)

OhmyGod, what are you two doing here. Like little gargoyles.

(to YUYA) Oh, yes perfect, you! Hey! Will you make us some-

(to MARITZA) Do you want tuna fish? I am like feenin' for some tuna fish with lots and lots of mayo right now. Like a vat of mayo. Do you want some?

(to YUYA) Will you go make us some. Like right now.

(YUYA gets up to go)

YUYA Do I bring you something to drink?

FABIOLA Yes, you bring us something to drink. What are we going to eat the sandwiches with nothing to drink? Mari, what do you want to drink?

MARITZA I'm good. I don't need anything.

FABIOLA Oooh, freshly squeezed lemonade. With like the whole thing of sugar, pour the whole jar of sugar in there. Con Topochico. Go.

(YUYA exits)

Let's jump in now because we die if we eat and then swim. Isn't that what they say? That you'll get like a cramp in your stomach and die.

MARITZA Maybe we should chill for a little bit.

FABIOLA Fuck that, I thought we were going to jump in.

LILIANA Fabi, maybe you shouldn't. Your dad can wake up.

FABIOLA Fuck him. He didn't even pay attention to me at the fucking...Did you see how he's treating me?

LILIANA Que esperabas? It really hurt him when you left in the middle of his party.

FABIOLA I came down for him, didn't I? I was there at the fucking party. Oh, God he's such a fucking...

(about the Fritos) What the hell is this?

MARITZA It's Fritos with lime and hot sauce.

FABIOLA That's disgusting.

MARITZA It's actually really really good.

FABIOLA No way. Let me taste.

(eats)

This is like...gross good.

MARITZA I think um... we have a little situation with the car.

LILIANA What do you mean with the car?

MARITZA I think, you're going to have to call a tow truck. But maybe not.

FABIOLA Oh, it's not even that serious, I just didn't want to figure it out this late-

LILIANA Where's the car?

MARITZA That's why I gave her a ride-

LILIANA Where's the car.

MARITZA It's at the bar.

FABIOLA We left it in the parking lot.

LILIANA What happened to it?

FABIOLA The freaking tree. There shouldn't be trees in parking lots, it's so fucking stupid. You put a tree in the middle of a parking lot, you're going to run into it when you're backing up.

It's like simple geometry.

MARITZA The headlight got a little beat up-

LILIANA Backing up?

MARITZA Sort of. I mean, the left brake light too.

LILIANA Dios mio, que va a decir tu Papa?

FABIOLA Fuck him. It's a fucking car. A fucking obvious ass Porsche, hello. Can you get any more obvious than that. My dad is so fucking obvious about everything. This fucking

house, his fucking cars, his little wives—no offense Lili, you know I adore you, but he's such a fucking douche. You know what's a good classy fucking car? A Bugatti. That's a real fucking car. Have you seen those cars? Have you seen them?

MARITZA No.

FABIOLA You would die.

MARITZA *(To LILIANA)* I can take it to my cousin's in the morning.

LILIANA Could you take it to him right now?

MARITZA I can't wake him up right now.

LILIANA Could you take it first thing? Alberto leaves for Guadalajara for the whole weekend and he won't be back until Tuesday and if we are lucky he won't notice when Chuy drives him to the airport in the morning.

FABIOLA You know what? Let's go wake Papi. Papi! I'm going to wake him and tell him that I took it and I rammed it into a tree. Papi! I don't care. Papi!

LILIANA We don't want to do that, Fabi. De verdad.[70] We have three days to make it right, y que suerte porque si se entera tu papa que andabas-[71]

FABIOLA I don't care. You think I care? Tell him. I'll tell him as soon as he wakes up.

LILIANA Fabiola!

FABIOLA Are we going to jump into the pool here?

MARITZA Not right now, Fabi.

FABIOLA My buzz is like…

(makes womp womp sound)

How long does it take to make tuna sandwiches for God's sake?

(beat)

Lili, I love that color on your nails. You're cool, you know that? I like you. Mari, Lili is my favorite of my dad's wives.

MARITZA Yeah, you said that.

FABIOLA He's had some bad fucking bad taste, straight up. There's no one like my mom, man. No one like my mom. No offense, Lili. You're like awesome. But some of these… ugh. I hate white people. There. I said it. I hate white people. I would never date a white guy. I mean a white Mexican, sure. But like, a white American? Yuck. Would you date a gringo, Mari? A gringa.

MARITZA I date all kinds. I take people as they come.

FABIOLA Yeah, I do too. I mean, yeah. I don't really hate white people. Come on, I live in Houston. How would I hate white people?

(beat)

I want to visit you in Chicago.

(Oh, man, sloppy drunk now)

I like you, Mari. I like you a lot. I'm coming to Chicago. I'm so coming to see you for sure.

MARITZA Yeah?

FABIOLA Yeah.

LILIANA It's very cold in Chicago. It's like sub zero in the summer.

MARITZA Is that why you've never been to Chicago? Because of the temperature? I mean, you've never been to Chicago, have you?

LILIANA Why would I go to Chicago? There's nothing in Chicago for me. There's nothing…what's there in Chicago. I rather go to like, New York, if I'm going to go somewhere freezing cold.

MARITZA New York is not as cold as Chicago.

LILIANA Exactly.

FABIOLA *(about Frito's plate)* I want to like, lick this plate.

MARITZA Told you it was good.

FABIOLA Fuck Yuya. Why is she taking so long? Am I going to have to carry these sandwiches out myself?

(exits)

LILIANA You want to go follow your girlfriend over there?

(MARITZA smiles big)

All of a sudden you're BFFs, the two of you? What you could possibly have in common with that girl-

MARITZA She's actually not bad once you get her to calm the fuck down. She has a lot of potential.

LILIANA Oh, she has a lot of potential? She has a lot of potential.

MARITZA Why are you getting all worked up?

LILIANA I'm not getting all worked up.

MARITZA I think you're tweaking // out a little bit.

LILIANA Ugh, I'm going to…I'm going to take this bowl and bust open your head right now. I want to fucking beat you over the head with this.

(MARITZA smiles super big.)

Stop smiling. Stop it. I hate you.

MARITZA No you don't.

LILIANA *(Diffused. A beat)* I do. Te deteste. *(beat)* Pinche Mari. How bad is the car?

MARITZA I mean I'm not going to lie, it's not like he won't notice if you don't get it fixed. There's a big hole in the headlight and the brake light is dangling.

LILIANA What the hell was she doing? Why was she driving? Why did you let her drive?

MARITZA Hey, I brought her back in one piece, OK? But I'm not her baby sitter. You can't baby sit that.

LILIANA Mari?

MARITZA Yeah?

LILIANA I think you should go.

MARITZA Yeah, I think I should go too. We don't want old boy coming down in his bathrobe finding me here. I think Fabi's OK and she's in your capable hands now. Going to peace out now.

(starting to leave)

Lovely seeing you–

LILIANA No, I mean you should go. Go back home.

MARITZA You know that's not going to happen until we talk. I've sat around all week waiting for a word from you.

LILIANA There's nothing to talk about. Everything's actually fine.

MARITZA I'm not leaving until we have a proper talk. And I promise you, this will the the last time we talk, Liliana. // The last time. Because I'm not doing this shit again!

LILIANA God. Not here, please. Shhhhh. Keep your voice down, Maritza. Please…

(Silence. MARITZA stares at LILIANA. For like a long time. After a while YUYA enters with the tuna sandwiches and the keys to the Porsche.)

YUYA She passed out.

(Holding out the keys.)

Are you all still eating the sandwiches?

LILIANA Nobody's eating sandwiches, Yuya! Here give me these.

(Grabs keys from YUYA.)

Mari, I'll meet you super early at your cousin's right after Alberto leaves. His flight leaves at eight so he'll be leaving around seven, six thirty. I'll text you when I'm on my way.

MARITZA I might forget to have my phone on.

LILIANA Don't joke with me right now, Maritza.

MARITZA Come on. When have I failed you? *(pause)*

YUYA *(Picking up FABIOLA's t-shirt from the ground.)* I think we should move this girl upstairs before she drools or guacarea en el[72] sofa.

LILIANA Yeah, you go take her upstairs, Yuya. I'm walking Mari out.

(YUYA exits with a glare at MARITZA.)

MARITZA When have I failed you?

(LILIANA grazes MARITZA's cheek tenderly as they exit.)

Scene 4

SUNDAY AFTERNOON: A motel room. MARITZA has just helped LILIANA onto the dresser as the lights are coming up. LILI's only wearing a bed sheet around her. MARITZA's in front of her, in a tank top and boy shorts.

MARITZA *(re: sheet)* More over the shoulder.

LILIANA Like this?

MARITZA Yeah. Now just stand there for me.

(LILIANA stands in her pose then feels silly.)

LILIANA *(She starts getting off the dresser.)* Mari, me siento ridicula.[73]

MARITZA No, come on, babe. Just stand for me.

(She's all hands with LILIANA and turns her around.)

Let me see your back.

LILIANA Are you arresting me?

MARITZA No, I'm imagining you with wings.

(MARITZA runs her hands all over LILIANA then she pulls off the sheet.)

LILIANA Hey!

MARITZA Lilith sprouted these amazing wings and dragon talons. All my new pieces are of wings and talons.

LILIANA I don't want dragon talons.

MARITZA Oh, but you do. Lilith was a badass with fucking dragon wings. She'd terrorize men in their sleep and incite nocturnal emissions from them.

LILIANA Her superpower was making guys have wet dreams?

MARITZA Yeah. And also killing babies. A hundred babies a day. // So some people think of her more as a demon.

LILIANA What.

LILIANA Well, yeah. If she went around killing babies.

MARITZA It's complicated. She only killed the babies because God sent his angels to kill her babies for leaving Adam.

LILIANA I never heard any of this.

MARITZA Before Eve, God made Lilith. //

(beat)

And God made her equal to Adam in every way. But Adam was kind of an asshole who got it in his head that she should lie beneath him and let him fuck her.

LILIANA Is this in the Bible?

LILIANA He liked to do it missionary style. Nothing wrong with that.

MARITZA No, he didn't want her on top. As in, he wanted her to know that she was beneath him and less than him so she was like "fuck that" and she uttered the hidden, unutterable name of God. And poof she went off flying and wouldn't come back. No matter how many angels God sent for her. She was like "fuck that, I will not lie under that douchebag."

LILIANA Adam has always sounded very boring to me. Like wouldn't be a very good dancer.

MARITZA He didn't have to try too hard, did he? Everything was handed to him. He was a daddy's boy. Why would Lilith want to stay with him?

LILIANA Well, he did come from a good family.

MARITZA Adam was a pussy. He goes and whines to daddy about the wife situation so God—being the enabler that he is—gives Adam, Eve. Made from his rib and willing to be his little wifey and lie beneath him and have dinner for him on the table when he got home from doing nothing.

LILIANA Poor Eve. Second wives always have it the worst.

(beat)

Are we going to order room service?

MARITZA There's no room service in motels, baby girl. I can go run and get you something.

LILIANA Whataburger? Toasted bun.

MARITZA You want Whataburger?

LILIANA Yes. But in a little bit.

(They stare at each other a bit.)

So this is what you're making your art about? I mean, like your paintings.

MARITZA Not just paintings. But yeah. Lilith is what I'm taking a look at next. Not just in paintings though. I'm starting to work with other materials.

LILIANA Maritza. You're so smart. You're the smartest person I know.

MARITZA I'm not smart.

LILIANA *(getting down from the dresser and onto the bed)* No, you are. // You teach me things.

MARITZA Whoa. Easy.

LILIANA Can I like, make a hole on your head and put a straw in and suck out your smarts?

MARITZA Ouch. That would hurt my head.

LILIANA I mean, I'd leave you a little bit so you could finish your art stuff.

MARITZA Well thank you.

(LILIANA sucks on her ear playfully.)

LILIANA Here, give me some smarts, right now. // *(nuzzling her ear)* …come on, don't be stingy.

MARITZA That's creepy, Lili. That's so creepy. This whole thing builds into a pretty sweet but hot make out session. I mean, you let this go on for a while, ok?

(They end up tangled, MARITZA on top of LILIANA.)

MARITZA Run away with me.

LILIANA Bite my toe. Here…bite my toe-

MARITZA I'm dead serious.

LILIANA Me too. Bite it.

MARITZA I can't just leave you down here this time. I think you're going to go putrid, here.

LILIANA Wilting flower. Me voy a churir.

MARITZA I'm serious.

LILIANA Wait, Changuita,[74] Alberto is out of town. We have a whole day left. Ah, do you know what it's been here with you for two whole fucking days? I got freakin' bed sores and I love them. When do we just get to lie around and…Mari, please. Not yet. This is the best two days I've had in five years. Please, could we wait?

MARITZA Why wait? I mean, let's just fast forward to the end right now. // Let's spare us the-

LILIANA *(starts tugging on MARI's jeans, trying to prevent her)* No no no no…what are you doing…no nono.

(she's got the jeans)

Not yet. Please. Why do you want to put these on? Why are you trying to leave me?

MARITZA Give me back my pants Liliana.

LILIANA Why are you being like this? Que mala eres.[75]

MARITZA Oh, I'm being bad?

LILIANA See? You do understand Spanish. Cuando te conviene verdad...[76]

MARITZA *(trying to get her jeans back)* Give me back my pants...

(LILIANA sticks her fingers in her panties and MARITZA stops. LILI then sticks her wet fingers in MARI's mouth.)

MARITZA Mala hierba.[77] See how bad you are?

LILIANA Don't call me that. I hate it.

MARITZA My mom was right. You're a bad seed.

(LILIANA wraps herself in the sheet again.)

LILIANA Don't call me that. Why doesn't your mom like me? I hate that she never liked me.

MARITZA Well, what do you think? Her daughter never moved on, walking around this world with a wire still stuck in your socket, // even 1,000 miles away.

LILIANA The way you say things..

MARITZA It's true. I've been on pause for what? Seventeen years?

LILIANA I don't want to talk about all this.

MARITZA No, of course not.

LILIANA Pinche choro mareador...[78]

MARITZA Fuck you, I don't know what that means.

LILIANA You always kill it. You kill the mood //. We're sitting here super nice talking about baby killers and the missionary position and you just have to go a tirarme tu pinche rollo que marea.[79]

MARITZA What is this to you? Wait, answer that. Why do I ask this every time? I ask this every fucking time and your answer breaks my heart every fucking time.

LILIANA What do you want me to do?

MARITZA You know what I want you to do.

LILIANA You think this, between these four walls, you think this is real?

MARITZA Do I think it's real or do I think it's sustainable?

LILIANA What?

MARITZA Do I think you'd come out of this room holding my hand? No.

LILIANA *(overlapping)* Oh, my God Maritza. Claro que no![80]

MARITZA But do I think this is real? Do I think you've been in love with me since we were thirteen? Do I think I've been then ONE for you no matter what dudes have come in and

out of your life? And do I think that you're too chicken shit to do anything about it cuz you're too fucking hooked on being a fucking rich girl? Do I think that? Sure.

(Silence)

LILIANA Here are your jeans. Here. We should go, both of us.

(LILIANA starts to look for her dress. She finds it and puts it on. Find her panties and puts those on too, now she looks for her shoes. MARITZA watches her do all this. Doesn't put on her jeans.)

LILIANA I can give you cash for... I can't use my card but I can give you cash.

(They stare at each other)

Mari, you think I'm here...you think this doesn't cost me. You think it's just nothing. That you're nothing to me. To me you're actually...

(beat)

But everything costs. This is something I realized very early on. Everything has a price. And these two days with you, they're going to cost me big. But I don't care, I'll pay. Because it was so worth it.

MARITZA What the fuck are you talking about?

(A moment.)

LILIANA He is a monster. He likes choking. He likes belts. // He likes sticking things in places where they shouldn't be stuck. He's not a human to me sometimes. When he's grunting on top of me, or when he's ripping out my ass with no warning—because with Alberto, the more I scream the hotter he gets. But only if I mean it. No faking that shit...

MARITZA Wait, what?

MARITZA ...Lili.

LILIANA And that's the price. I pay for everything I own, Maritza. Everything I have. That car out there? Oh, I paid for that. With interest!

MARITZA I think... you need... to stop telling me this or I'm going to go and kill this motherfucker.

LILIANA No. Just...please, stop being in a fucking Antonio Banderas movie! Just. Stop. If you say something. If you do something, what will happen? He tosses me and my father's medical bills don't get paid. My mother loses her house, her health insurance too. My little sister has to come back from college and what? Wait tables? And me. I mean, what would happen to me? I have nothing. All I have is him.

(beat)

We should go.

MARITZA You can't keep paying for your sister's tuition with your body.

LILIANA Ok, now you're calling me a hooker.

MARITZA You're calling you a hooker.

LILIANA It's so easy for you. You're free up there—

MARITZA This is free?

LILIANA You're up there, doing what you love. You can see who you want. You can go where you please. I got a family to feed, plus I'm not going to stand here and tell you that every thing's all bad. Que hipócrita sería.[81] So before you give me those googly ass eyes, don't think that I got it so bad. Let's go, I want to go.

MARITZA Why did you call me down here?

LILIANA Because I'm a fucking idiot.

MARITZA No, it's because you want to be with me. That's the truth of it.

LILIANA God, don't you know that that is the only thing I think of sometimes. Forgetting everything and running to you? Not having to worry about my dad, my mom, my sister. Everybody.

MARITZA Alright then. This time we make it happen. This time you come with me.

LILIANA In what world are you living, Maritza?

MARITZA He's out of town, we can do it before he comes back. We borrow a car from my cousin and we drive all the way up to Chicago.

LILIANA He'll find me, Mari.

MARITZA That's why we dismantle that narco truck of yours. Trade it with my cousin for parts so he can give us some hooptie that will take us north. It's not hard, Lili. He won't be able to track us. You just leave that iPhone here and take only what you need.

LILIANA What do you mean only what I need?

MARITZA Ok, you take whatever you want. Whatever we can fit in the back seat and in the trunk. Nothing electronic though, ok? No iPad. No laptop. No…whatever else you got. Just you and your drawers // and your face paint and your fancy shoes, But come on, not all of them, ok? And we go, Liliana. We just start it. Take the video out of pause and finally press play. Like it was meant to be.

LILIANA Mari.

MARITZA This is a long time coming. Every so often we keep getting pulled back for a reason.

LILIANA I know.

MARITZA That's why you called me, Lili. And we are going to be fucked up unless we finally do this, we're never going to be whole. We'll walk around with big gaping holes for the rest of our lives.

(beat)

Please baby, you have to leave with me.

LILIANA …

(LILIANA kisses MARITZA.)

MARITZA Tonight.

(a pause while she waits for an answer)

Lili?

(Then LILIANA kisses her back forcefully: It's a yes.)

Scene 5

SUNDAY EVENING: The master bedroom. LILIANA is packing. She does a little mad dance of "should I take this? No. Yes, I need it" with almost everything she considers. After a while we hear a knock.

LILIANA I'm taking a nap!

(more knocking)

Quien es?!

YUYA *(off)* Soy yo.

LILIANA I'm taking a nap te digo. I'm napping! Go away.

YUYA *(off)* Open the door.

LILIANA Yuya, respeta! I'm napping! Go away.

YUYA *(off)* Open the door!

(some furious knocking)

LILIANA Vete muchisimo a chingar a tu madre! Que no te digo que estoy tomandome…

(YUYA has opened the door with her key. Fucking YUYA.)

LILIANA Fucking Yuya. I fucking hate you.

YUYA Que haces?

LILIANA Te odio, me oyes? // I fucking detest you.

YUYA What are you doing? What are you doing?

LILIANA What does it look like I'm doing? Close the fucking door at least.

(As she says this and YUYA goes to close the door, FABIOLA enters the room in a freaking tornado of tears and Housewives of The Rio Grande Valley dramarama.)

FABIOLA ...Aaaggrr... he's a fucking asshole! Mydad'samotherfuckingasshole! Oh, my God! I can't stand him! I can't fucking stand him. I want him to fucking fall off a cliff.

(some crying. It's deep for FABI right now.)

I'm like completely... He's totally cut me off!

(She holds out 5 credit cards. Gold, platinum... BLACK.)

He cancelled them all! My Sak's card, my Macy's card. He cancelled...HE CAN-CELLED MY NORDSTROM'S CARD FOR FUCK'S SAKE. What am I going to have to shop at fucking Old Navy now?!

(slight breakdown)

My gas card. He cancelled my motherfuck-ing gas card! You know what that means right? That I can't fucking go anywhere. That means I'm trapped here.

YUYA *(to herself)* Ay no, Dios mio.

FABIOLA What the fuck am I supposed to do with my mother fucking life right now?!

LILIANA What happened? Your dad's in Guada-lajara. He's not even... calm down Fabiola. Calmadita... when did you talk to him? // Is he here?

FABIOLA Yeah, on the phone just now. And now he hung up on me and won't answer.

LILIANA Fabiola, is he here?

FABIOLA I want to kill myself right now.

LILIANA Fabiola, what happened?

FABIOLA He saw that I wasn't going to school.

LILIANA He what?

FABIOLA I haven't... I'm not in school right now. I just needed some time to figure some stuff out... Hey, I don't need the righteous shit right now, ok? I don't need judgment right now, Liliana.

LILIANA You haven't been going to school?

FABIOLA No. But that's only because I didn't enroll, ok? And the thing he doesn't see is that I made that decision with like a clear adult mind. It wasn't like my first two years where I had to drop out of classes because I wasn't going, you know? Because I overslept or because, well, most of my professors were total douche bags. They didn't know what the hell they were talking about. Whatever.

That's not even the... But why can't he see that this time, I made a conscious, respon-sible decision. To actually not waste money and time and whatever-aggravation. I con-sciously didn't enroll this semester. Alright, I didn't enroll this whole year. Ok? I didn't enroll this year and well... He got all- Oh, god he scared the fuck out of me. He was like King Kong. You know how he gets like King Kong.

LILIANA Yes.

FABIOLA Yeah, but see he never gets like that with me.

LILIANA I know.

FABIOLA And he just... took it all away. He's never done that, Liliana. I'm like really scared right now because he's never done that. Even when I went to rehab for the... I mean he was like more caring than he was mad. Oh, my God I'm going to kill myself. That's what I'm going to tell him. That I'm going to kill myself. // See how he'd like his only daughter to ...

LILIANA Shh. Calm down, calm down, Fabi.

FABIOLA Don't fucking tell me to calm down! Are you listening to me?!

LILIANA Yes, I am listening to you.

FABIOLA You have to talk to him.

(beat)

Liliana. You have to talk to him for me.

LILIANA ...ah, I think this is between you and him. Yo no me quiero meter.

FABIOLA You have to help me! // I mean, what am I going to do? Live here like a prisoner? Like a slave? Just because he got into a mood?

LILIANA Fabi, I don't want to get in the middle of...

FABIOLA I need some cash.

LILIANA If I take cash out right now, Fabiola...

FABIOLA That's true. Who's to say he didn't cancel your shit too, right?

LILIANA He wouldn't cancel my...

YUYA You should check anyway.

LILIANA Shh. Cierra el pico.

LILIANA I can't help you with actual money, Fabiola. I don't think he'd be very happy about that.

FABIOLA Right. But if you

(She heads to the jewelry boxes. Plural. There are a few.)

gave me one of your little danglies here to sell, he wouldn't ever notice. Because why would he notice? // Or no, the really fancy stuff is in your closet, I know because I looked once. You have like fucking Cartier and Harry Winston shit. Oh, you have the Tiffany brooch he gave you the first year! The one with the big ruby.

(FABIOLA has gone in the closet and hasn't stopped talking.

LILIANA What! What are you…

FABIOLA *(off)* It's in all these drawers right here, // I've seen them. I just need one of these and… Oh, my God. Is this a Chopard watch? Yes. Look at this thing! Why don't you ever wear this? Fuck me. David Yurman bracelets are worth nothing right? They won't give me shit for these. Where are your earrings?

YUYA *(the following four lines overlap with FABIOLA's closet monologue)* You're just going to let her?

LILIANA What do you want me to do?

YUYA You can't just let her.

LILIANA What do you want me to do? Little fucking bitch.

YUYA You're going to let her clean you out like that?

(FABIOLA emerges with a ton of things and the brooch.)

FABIOLA Found the brooch. This thing's huge and tacky. You don't want to wear this.

LILIANA Fabiola, mi vida, could you sit down so we can—

FABIOLA Do you have earrings?

LILIANA …you can't take those things.

FABIOLA He's not even going to notice.

LILIANA No, you can't take those things because they're mine.

FABIOLA Liliana, I like you but I don't want to say something offensive to you, ok?

(moves to go)

LILIANA You're not going anywhere with those. Those are my things.

FABIOLA Excuse me, but nothing in this house is yours, ok? You're here on lease. Don't start getting any ideas and DON'T start getting comfortable, honey. // You got a shelf life of about…

LILIANA *(She snatches the shit. FABIOLA puts up a little fight but loses.)* Well, HONEY, until he sends me away, these are my things. And you're a spoiled little bitch to come in here and think you can just take my stuff. Do you hear that? Who raised you?

FABIOLA Are you serious right now?

LILIANA Dead serious. Who fucking raised you? Wolves?

(Pause)

FABIOLA I'm calling my father and telling him exactly what kind of a gold digger he brought into our house.

LILIANA Do it. Maybe he'll answer the phone.

FABIOLA Fuck you.

LILIANA Come on. Call him. Oh, wait. Did he cut off your phone too?

FABIOLA Fuck you, you tacky bitch.

(Storming off, she bumps into YUYA.)

Get out of my fucking way you fucking idiot!

(She exits. Good riddance.)

(Door slam. YUYA and LILIANA are a little stunned. A moment. Oh, shit.)

YUYA Si se contenta con su Papa- It won't be pretty if she gets her daddy's ear again.

LILIANA I KNOW! Don't you know I know that blood is blood. It doesn't matter though. That doesn't matter anymore.

(She starts to pull herself together and resumes the packing.)

I don't give a fuck. Fuck that little bratty bitch. And fuck Alberto. I don't care anymore. What can he do to me now, huh?

(YUYA is staring at LILIANA. It's unnerving.)

WHAT? What is this face? What!

YUYA How many years and I've kept my mouth shut? Not one word. And don't think I don't know the cochinadas you do with her. Doing disgusting things with your bodies—the two of you. Sucias.

LILIANA Callate pendeja.

YUYA Liliana, you know you can't leave with her. What, you would leave your father, the way he is right now? So sick? // You would leave your pobre mamacita? That poor woman. // You think you get to run off with that puta in your happily ever after and not think about anyone but yourself? M'ija, what will happen to your family, then? You know Alberto will cut them all off.

LILIANA Shut up. //

LILIANA Callate Yuya. //

LILIANA Shutthefuckup! Shut the fuck up hija de tu puta madre! Shutthefuckup…shut up Yuya…

(LILIANA has rushed to YUYA in a fury. She is beating her back, her arms. YUYA cowers and covers her face, and takes the blows. LILIANA lets it all go. They both end up on the floor. The hitting becomes an embrace of sorts.)

LILIANA Don't say these things to me, Yuya.

YUYA You can't go anywhere. Too many of us depend on you. Who knows how long this guy will keep you around but in the mean time, you have to be a smart girl y aprovechar.

(quick beat)

Man, if I had your possibilities, I would not be fucking this up. I'd be saving every penny I could. Hiding shit. Stashing it away. You need to get smarter about this, Lili. And then, when it's done, then maybe you can think of... maybe you can think of whatever cochinadas you want to think about. When you've squeezed everything you can out of this whole thing. Es un investment. Are you listening to me?

(takes LILIANA's face, still both on the floor)

This is all an investment. But you gotta buck up. Be a mujercita. You think I don't want to go off, galivanting and...I don't know. You think I like being for your every whim? I didn't say when I was a baby girl, a mira, that's what I want to do with my life. Live at the whims of those who have more. But I got people who are counting on me and I'm the only thing they got. And your Papi and your Mami, tu hermana Cecilia, you're the only thing they got. It's not about you, it's about them. So buck up.

(She untangles herself and stands up)

You listening? You're gonna have to buck the fuck up.

(She exits.)

Scene 6

LATE SUNDAY: Outskirts of McAllen. One of those side roads off of another side road made of dirt. MARITZA is sitting on a rock, the headlights from an old car are her only light source. She's pacing. Making plans. A while before we hear the crackle of tires on the dirt. LILIANA gets out of her Expedition and MARITZA is activated; she's a galvanized girl right now. She's on GO.

MARITZA See? I told you that it would take no time at all. Nolana and then to the highway. // It's actually easy to get to, right?

LILIANA Yeah, no... it wasn't hard.

MARITZA The iPhone. You left that iPhone at home right? They can track it.

(LILIANA nods.)

MARITZA And the GPS. You didn't use the GPS right? I mean, you kind of didn't need it the way I told you to come.

LILIANA No, I didn't use the GPS.

MARITZA Good. That's good, baby.

LILIANA I hate that thing anyway. That woman always sounds like she's mocking me. "Turn Left here." Fuck you! YOU turn left here.

MARITZA Is this bag all you got? // We should switch out your bags and put them in my car.

LILIANA What? No, of course not. Do you expect me to shove the contents of my entire— This is a purse! This is a purse, Maritza.

(It's kind of big for a purse, but whatever. You could fit a head in there.)

MARITZA Yes. I'm sorry, this is a purse.

(MARITZA holds LILIANA by the arms. She stares deep into her. Checks her to see if she's alright. Kisses her maybe. LILIANA lets her.)

MARITZA Hey.

(Pause)

Hey.

(beat)

How are you doing, baby?

LILIANA I think I have to pee.

MARITZA There's a gas station. We can stop there // before...

LILIANA Do you live in a two flat?

MARITZA Do I what?

LILIANA Do you live in a two flat. And what IS a two flat, for that matter? I've heard people in big cities say they live on two flats and actually to me, that sounds very uncomfortable.

MARITZA What, like a condo? Like a split home?

LILIANA What's a split home?! A split home sounds even worse than a two flat. I don't... Maritza, do you split your home?

MARITZA Are you asking if I have a roommate? I don't have a roommate.

LILIANA What kind of a house do you have?

MARITZA I don't have a house. You know that. People in Chicago don't have houses, Lili. Well, not like the houses you're used to. I have an apartment. And not like the apartment where your sister lives that is basically a townhome. Ok. Liliana what's with the questions?

LILIANA So nobody has a house in the entire city of Chicago?

MARITZA Some people do.

LILIANA Some? Which people? How do people have kids?! Where do people put their kids?

MARITZA Where do people *put* their kids?

LILIANA O see, I find it hard to believe that a family with three kids lives in an apartment. That's something I find very hard to understand.

MARITZA *(really trying hard not to lose her patience)* Well, yes, actually, families with three kids do live in apartments but also people who need more room move to the suburbs. If space happens to be an issue.

LILIANA Would we live in the suburbs if we needed more room?

MARITZA No, I'd rather stab myself in the eye than live in the suburbs! Where the fuck is all this coming from? Why would we need more room? What, are we thinking of having kids now? Is that what we're doing?

LILIANA Well, are we? Those are questions, right?

(beat)

In your life, do you ever want kids, Maritza?

MARITZA Um, you know what I want? I want to get going. I want to get on the road, put some distance between McAllen and us and when we get to like, I don't know, Austin or Dallas then I can talk about kids, or getting a pet or whatever else you want. // Right now I want to get on the road.

LILIANA *(overlapping)* Kid are not pets.

MARITZA I know kids are not pets.

LILIANA You don't want kids either, do you? Alberto doesn't want kids. That was one of his conditions. I want kids. I want kids really bad. What's the point if there are no kids, you know? What's the point? God, I've never said that out loud.

MARITZA All of this. I mean, ALL of it, baby, we will sit down and talk about. I want to spend days and days just talking about this kind of shit. Imagining this life and that life. I can't fucking wait. But right now, I want you in that truck, I want to drop it off where my cousin told me to drop it off and I want to get the fuck out of the valley. Now can you please get your ass in that truck? Liliana?

(LILIANA's like on another planet.)

LILIANA It was like a diamond heist getting out of the house. You know what you forgot to think about? The cameras. We have a million cameras. But don't worry, I thought of the cameras. I thought about everything. I said, I'll pack my life in those suitcases and think about everything. The cold. The stairs. What kind of shoes will be good for the subway, because you're making me go on the subway, right? // That's the kind of thing I'm signing up for. Hey, I like the subway. I've been on the Underground. I rode around in that.

MARITZA The EL. Yeah, you're going to have to take the EL, Liliana. It's not a fucking tragedy that your ass will have to get on the bus once in a while.

LILIANA Wait, what? What did you say? It's not a fucking tragedy? To you maybe it's not a fucking tragedy but what am I going to do up there? Nunca he conocido a un negro, Maritza! I've never in my life had a conversation with a black person? What will I say?

MARITZA Alright, youknowwhat—

LILIANA I won't know what to say to them.

MARITZA Alright, you're going to have to not say racist shit like // that when we're up there, Liliana. We're going to have to re-train that fucking xenophobic mind of yours.

LILIANA Why is that racist? It's true!

(beat)

Retrain? Like I'm a doggie?

MARITZA I didn't mean like a dog. // Come on, Liliana. Jesus, come on.

LILIANA Because I'm a little animalito to be trained? Because I'm a little idiot who didn't go to college to learn words like xenophobic. For your information, I know what xenophobic means. Para que lo sepas. Everybody always thinking I'm so stupid.

MARITZA Who's thinking you're stupid? Baby, I don't think you're stupid. Lili, please. You're picking a fight right now. // You're afraid of this trip and you're picking a...

LILIANA Don't tell me what I'm doing! Plus we're not just taking a *trip*, Maritza. Para ti esta facilito, no? // I'm about to flip myself upside down, but to you it's just a trip.

MARITZA Alright, you're right. Not just a trip.

LILIANA This is the— no, // listen to me. Callate! Listen to me. Logistics. You and I didn't talk about the logistics. What's so bad that I want to talk about the pinche logistics, huh? What's so wrong with that?

MARITZA But baby... We have to...

MARITZA What logistics?

(an "oh fuck" beat)

Liliana. Do you have bags in that truck?

(beat)

Are there suitcases in that truck? Are you coming with me, Liliana?

LILIANA My father. In all of this never have you mentioned what we're going to do about my father. My sister. How come you haven't brought that up? You haven't talked about anything but Chicago, but here. The life I'm leaving here, you haven't mentioned that once. What the fuck am I going to do about… I don't know, my friends. I'm leaving all my friends!

MARITZA Those people aren't your friends, Lili.

LILIANA I know you don't think so but I do have friends, Mari. I have good friends here.

MARITZA Fake ass people that greet you with a kiss on the cheek and a stab in the back.

LILIANA What do you know about my life?

MARITZA What?

LILIANA What do you know about my life anymore? En serio. What do you know about what my life is now?

MARITZA You're serious?

LILIANA Look, I have a life here. // Que a ti no te guste es otra cosa.[82] But I like a lot of my life here and that's what you will never understand. I like walking into a restaurant and seeing people gasp. I like to hear them whispering. Them whispering in that good way.

MARITZA Wait, what are we talking about right now? What are you saying?

MARITZA They're not whispering in the good way. They are measuring you up and down, Liliana.

LILIANA What! I like that. You don't get that I like that. I like being recognized. I like it when Alberto and I make our appearance. I know that's stupid to you, pero a mi me gusta que me envidien.[83] For so long I had nothing. Nothing, Maritza. And now look at me. Oh, you don't get it. You don't get that it's not all so bad. That man saved our life. What would we have done? My family would be on the street. I'd be working at Sally's Beauty Supply or something. On welfare… who knows. I don't want to think about it.

MARITZA What are you saying right now, Lili?

LILIANA Nothing. I'm not saying anything. Just that it's kind of hard to be told your life is shit. My whole life is not shit. I'm not…shit…

(LILIANA breaks down. Like falls to the ground and shit.

MARITZA is on her, kissing her, trying to hold her. LILIANA pulls away but MARITZA's clasp is strong. LILIANA finally gives in.)

MARI I'm sorry if I made this sound easy. Sshhh. It's not easy. Oh, you're shaking. Nonono, no shaking Mama. You don't have to be scared anymore.

(kisses)

It's all done. Tonight, that's all over and done with. In a day we'll be in St. Louis at my brother's and then, two days, tops, we'll be in the Chi. Just you and me in Chicago. You know the first thing I'm gonna do for you when we get home? I'm going to run you a bath. You loved baths, right? Well, I have a big old bath tub.

LILIANA I'll turn into a raisin.

MARI Yeah, a big old sexy fucking raisin. And then, when you've gotten your fill of baths and sleeping and whatever the fuck. Then you go do you. You go do what you got to do for you. I mean, what you were always meant to do before the money problems and this motherfucker got a hold of you. You can just be you.

LILIANA Who the fuck is that?

MARI No. I know you. You're in there, you're somewhere in there under all this shit on your face, under this weave.

LILIANA It's not a weave. Son extensiones.[84]

MARI Denial.

LILIANA Hey, this is Indian hair. It cost me 1,200 dollars.

MARI Oh, is that right? Well, let's me and you and your Indian weave get out of here so we can get going. Plus your skirt's going to get dirty sitting there on the ground like that.

LILIANA The ground is so dry here. You know, you never think about that… You never touch the ground. So rocky…

MARITZA You don't care if you get all dirty?

LILIANA I never just sit like this.

MARITZA I know. You're going to rip your tight ass skirt. You OK?

LILIANA *(nods)* Look at this big old rock…

(She's been fingering a rock, she picks it up, it's heavy on her hand)

MARITZA You know, I like you a little dirty. When you're just you. When you don't give a fuck. I like it when you get whispies like this, these little strands. I like it when they fly away. When your makeup rubs off, when I see your real lips without all the sticky shit.

LILIANA Eres una pinche hippie.[85]

MARITZA I like the color of your lips. They don't make that color in a lipstick. I love your lips.

(Kisses and kisses and maybe, if it's not too much, more kisses.

They're both tangled on the ground. A long pause as they size each other up. MARI stands up. LILIANA is going to do something, there's a moment, a good moment there and then LILIANA's iPhone rings. MARI's mood changes. She sees that it's not her phone.)

MARITZA That's not my phone.

(beat)

Why is your iPhone ringing?

LILIANA I thought I left it at home.

MARITZA Did you?

LILIANA Es Alberto.

MARI I told you to not bring that shit with you.

LILIANA What am I going to do? Not have a phone?

MARI You're not thinking of answering that shit, are you?

LILIANA I have to answer it, Maritza.

MARITZA Don't fucking-

LILIANA *(answers that shit)* Bueno? Hola mi amor. // Que paso mi rey?[86] Already? I thought you were coming back on Tuesday—you're here now?
(to MARITZA) Fuck he's here.
(to ALBERTO) Si mi amor.[87]

MARITZA Oh God, I'm gunna hurl...you had to bring your fucking piece of shit iPhone.

LILIANA Como? Eh, si no...esque ando aqui con una amiga.[88]

(beat)

Just a friend. We're just having coffee.

(beat)

Si- Si, Nadamas termino aqui y voy directito para la casa-[89]

(MARI yanks the phone from LILIANA and hangs up)

MARITZA! Me va a matar.[90] You can't just hang up on him. Give me the phone. Maritza. Give me the phone.

(The following is a messy game of "keep away," MARITZA gets a little rough at pushing

LILIANA *away, but LILIANA keeps hurling herself at her trying to get the damn iPhone.)*

MARITZA Do you even have bags in the car?

LILIANA Of course I have bags in the car. I HAVE TWO FUCKING BAGS IN THAT TRUCK WHICH NOW HOLD EVERYTHING I HAVE IN THE WORLD.

(MARITZA's holding the phone above her head, LILIANA lunges for it again.)

LILIANA Puta madre, dame el pinche telefono![91] I have to call him back!

MARITZA Fuck you, you Mala Hierba.

LILIANA *(She's a hot mess for real now.)* Please Mari.

MARITZA Fuck you and your tears, fucking actress. You had me do this whole fucking thing-

LILIANA We'll talk in two seconds, just please... Mari, let me call him back. I'm not doing this to be... you are not understanding, he'll be so pissed. He'll get like a maniac. // OhGodOhGod. He probably came back early to deal with fucking Fabi. Maritza, please!

(She's bawling by now.)

Mari, please...

MARITZA You were never coming to Chicago. Why would you bring this phone? GOD! And I'm a fucking dumbass who runs around making this whole elaborate plan—Fuck... My mom always warns me too. "Es mala hierba. She'll break your heart or worse."

LILIANA Mari, please... // you don't know what will happen...

MARITZA She kept telling me. "She's bad news."

(The phone rings again. They freeze.)

LILIANA Maritza, he will kill us! //

(Dives for the phone)

Dame el telefono porfavor.[92]

MARITZA Get the fuck away from me...

(They start being a little too rough with each other over this fucking phone.)

LILIANA I'M NOT PLAYING, I NEED TO ANSWER! DAME EL PINCHE TELEFONO-[93]

MARITZA You know what? You're right, somebody should answer this mother fucking phone.

LILIANA Maritza...

MARITZA *(Answers it.)* Hello?

LILIANA NO!

(The following is even messier. LILIANA lunges for the phone as MARI tries to remain on it. They struggle. MARI drops the phone and dives to get it. She gives LILIANA a giant kick that sends her flying to the ground. LILIANA almost hits her head against that big ass rock she was playing with. Ugh. Why are they being a Latina Lesbian stereotype right now? MARITZA puts the stupid phone to her ear and speaks.)

MARI Hey...hey, sorry about that. Sorry, my man. What's up Alberto? How are things, my friend? Hey, I meant to tell you, nice party the other night. Loved the band. Classy stuff.

(beat)

Ah, funny you should ask that, funny story. You see, I'm a friend of your wife's. Actually, very good friend, you stupid fuck! Let me tell you a little fucking story about destiny and about

(LILIANA's gotten up in a flash and in her panic, she's picked up that rock she was playing with earlier. That fucking thing is heavy as hell but before she has a chance to think, she rushes to MARITZA and raises it over her head to hit MARI in the back of the head! But right before we see the blow:)

BLACKOUT.

Oh, shit.)

Scene 7

SUNDAY NIGHT: LILIANA, face scrubbed clean and wearing a messy ponytail, stands like a statue staring into the eerie light of the pool. From inside the house you can hear ALBERTO shouting something and FABIOLA replying with loud whimpers. We can't really understand what the fight is about, but we can tell someone is very angry. After a bit YUYA enters. She lights a cigarette and takes a drag. After a beat she notices LILIANA standing by the pool.

YUYA No asustes.[94]

(beat)

I knew you'd come back.

LILIANA *(still looking at the pool)* I came back.

YUYA I know. That's good. That's real good, Lili.

LILIANA I came back.

(A pause. We can hear the fight going on inside.)

YUYA Don't even think about going in there. Es Armaggedon up in there. Book of Revelations. Pinche huerca's in there pleading her case.

LILIANA He'll get over it.

YUYA I don't know if her tears will work this time, I watched him go in el study; red steam was coming out de sus ears.

(beat)

Whatsu matter? You sad?

LILIANA Am I sad...?

YUYA Yo sabia que you'd come back. You did the right thing, m'ija.

(Pause. Some more shouting from inside.)

YUYA What happened to your face?

LILIANA *(Suddenly a slight worry)* Why, do I have something on my face?

YUYA Well, no tienes makeup on.

LILIANA Oh.

(beat)

I had to scrub it all off.

YUYA Why are you all...looking like that? With your hair like that? Ah, yo se. A last hurrah before you sent her off? Ey, whatever you had to do. S'long as you got rid of her. However you had to say your goodbyes. Because, chulita, you got some shit to worry about in that house.

(beat)

Wait. You sent her away, right? Liliana, did you send her away?

LILIANA She's gone.

YUYA A que bueno.

LILIANA And I came back.

(beat)

Because this is what I chose, right?

YUYA Si, mi'ja.

LILIANA *(finally animating)* Yuya, do you know the story of Lilith?

YUYA De who?

LILIANA She was a wife first and then, because she didn't do what she was told, she became a demon. But I know she was no demon. It's just what people say. People like to say awful things. People call you things, when you're little, they say things because maybe your dad doesn't have money and he owes people and you show up with torn shoes and all the girls in school, they…they say mean things. They say mean things about your family. They call you names. But you're not a mala hierba. You're not. You're not a demon.

(beat)

Poor Lilith. She had to grow those talons to claw her way out. I understand her.

YUYA Te estas freakiando, Lili? You want me to get you a Tafil to calm down?

LILIANA I'm no demon, Yuya.

YUYA Stop saying demon, it's freaking me out. You want a pill?

LILIANA Tell me I'm no demon.

(beat)

YUYA Ey. Whatever you got going on, todo tus feelings, you gotta know it's worth it because this whole thing? All this? It takes work. And you puttin' in the work, m'ija. You're good at this. At this wife thing.

LILIANA Yes, I am. I can be Eve and lie beneath him.

YUYA Yeah, you do what you got to do. Convince him now for a baby and you will be golden.

LILIANA You think he would let me keep a baby this time?

YUYA There are ways. But you have to do something with that face and just, put yourself together.

LILIANA I want babies, Yuya. Lots of them.

(Abruptly and out of freakin' nowhere, FABIOLA and her puffy, wet face enter through the patio doors.)

FABIOLA Great. Fucking great.

(She starts to go back inside.)

FABIOLA Is there nowhere to go in this fucking house!

LILIANA Fabiola, wait.

FABIOLA What. Seriously, what. I really don't feel like fighting with you right now.

LILIANA I don't want to fight with you either.

FABIOLA Oh, please.

LILIANA I don't.

FABIOLA Listen, you win it all, okay? You win.

LILIANA You think somebody wins here? Nobody ever wins.

FABIOLA All I know is that ever since you came to our house dad has been completely different. He would have never, I mean never screamed at me like he just screamed at me. You totally turned him against me.

LILIANA You think I did that?

FABIOLA Of course.

(beat)

Not that you give a fuck, but he's the only person I have left in the world. You swooped in here and poisoned him. He wants nothing to do with me. He just told me. You don't know what that feels like. To have absolutely no one.

(A silence while FABIOLA cries. LILIANA slowly gets up.

YUYA's just in the corner observing.)

LILIANA What did he say to you? What exactly did he say to you?

FABIOLA What *didn't* he say to me…

LILIANA What was the last thing he said? Does he want you to leave? Is he going to help you anymore?

FABIOLA You-know-what-Liliana…!

LILIANA I'm trying to help you.

(Beat.)

LILIANA What did he say?

FABIOLA That I'm out of chances.

LILIANA You're not out of chances.

(beat)

Are you hungry?

FABIOLA What?

(It's as if LILIANA's wings expand throughout the following…)

LILIANA Fabi, you're going to go inside with Yuya. She's going to make you dinner, because I'm almost positive you haven't eaten. Yuya, you're going to make her dinner. Whatever she wants. You figure it out. And I'm going to go, I'm going to go talk to your dad. And then you're going to talk to him again. And apologize. Without all this. Like a grownup. And tomorrow you're going to go back up to Houston. With his support. And you're going to go back to school, and stay out of trouble. You will stay out of trouble, okay. And you and me, Fabi, you and me we are going to have an understanding.

(beat)

Do we have an understanding?

FABIOLA What?

LILIANA Do we have an understanding?

FABIOLA I don't even know what you're...

(beat)

FABIOLA Yeah. We have an understanding.

(LILIANA takes out a makeup compact from her purse.)

LILIANA Good. Yuya. Take her inside and make her some dinner.

(LILIANA starts applying makeup.)

LILIANA Go on. Anda, ve con Yuya. I'll be in to talk to your dad in just a minute. Don't you worry about a thing.

YUYA *(to FABIOLA)* Do you want your eggs benedict?

FABIOLA What? No. Just...whatever. Just make me whatever. Thank you.

YUYA Buena pues.

Notes

1. Yes, put those on Yuya.
2. Guess
3. Please, you think I didn't notice?
4. She is a brat.
5. beat them upside the head
6. I am going to reason with them.
7. I'm telling you
8. I feel bad for her.
9. She went
10. and she comes and tells me in the
11. Just like that,
12. she always forgets it.
13. but mine, she doesn't remember.
14. so just be grateful
15. because she'll go tattle tell to Alberto.
16. just for him and give
17. That's why we pay them what we pay them, right?
18. Dear God, what a mess.
19. I'm going to have a heart attack
20. I mean, God willing.
21. Don't be disrespectful with me.
22. HOW ARE YOU GOING TO SAY SOMETHING LIKE THAT TO ME?!
23. bitch
24. Of course
25. Viper.
26. Forgive me.
27. With that fucking viper tongue.
28. Hi. Did you get here ok?
29. Yuya, that is all. Thank you.

(YUYA goes inside and FABIOLA follows.)

LILIANA *(stopping her)* Fabiola. We're not going to worry about a thing.

(They exit.

LILIANA slowly applies blush. This is a meticulous ritual.

Something happens to her before our eyes. A hardening?

Carefully, she takes out a blood red lipstick from her purse and applies it like a neurosurgeon. She stares into the compact as if she's lost something. Nope. It's all still there. But better. Her attention turns to the bag. She contemplates it for a moment, then she grabs it and stands up. She heads towards the patio doors and right before she's going to go inside, LILIANA pulls down her gorgeous hair from that pony tail and fluffs it up. In she goes.

Mala hierba.)

30. No, of course not.
31. For real.
32. I found this package
33. No because then
34. fucking shit
35. What do you mean
36. We gave him three pieces.
37. No way
38. Oh, Yuya! Why do you traumatize me?
39. mousy little thing
40. Where did he find that little Indian?
41. Me right here like, "nice to meet you. Hi." Gross.
42. Then he'll get mad
43. It looks good on you.
44. Yes? Come in.
45. Yuya, go see if someone needs something downstairs. Go.
46. I'm not going to say it again
47. Aren't you melting/cooking in it?
48. What a potty mouth you have, eh.
49. Please don't raise your voice.
50. Who is it?
51. What are you talking about?
52. Shut up, don't remind me of it.
53. You see how you have me?
54. Then
55. tame, here comes this fucking…
56. Motherfucker
57. is not very happy with her.
58. She just sticks out her hand
59. Daddy, please.
60. Imagine if Alberto catches us. Please God don't let him wake up.
61. Fuck me…
62. Why do you worry about her?
63. What do you mean why do I worry?
64. Are you stupid?
65. Go on.
66. You're crossing the line, Yuya.
67. That's why I'm saying
68. and God knows what.
69. If not we're fucked.
70. Seriously.
71. and we're lucky because if your dad finds out that you were-
72. barfs on the
73. Mari, I feel ridiculous.
74. Little monkey
75. You are so bad.
76. Only when it's convenient, right…
77. Bad seed/weed
78. Fucking broken record…
79. with the same old fucking dizzying song.
80. Of course not!
81. I'd be a hypocrite.
82. That you don't like it is another matter altogether.

83. I like to be envied.
84. They're extensions.
85. You're a fucking hippie.
86. Hello? Hi sweetheart. What's going on, dear?
87. Yes, of course.
88. Excuse me? Eh, yes no... I'm here with a friend.
89. Yes–yes, as soon as I finish here and I'll head straight home.
90. He's going to kill me.
91. Fucking shit, give me the motherfucking phone!
92. Give me the phone please.
93. GIVE ME THE FUCKING PHONE-
94. Don't scare people.

———————————

Lynn Nottage

Biography

Lynn Nottage is a Pulitzer Prize-winning playwright and a screenwriter. Her plays have been produced widely in the United States and throughout the world. *Sweat* (Pulitzer Prize, Susan Smith Blackburn Prize) moved to Broadway after a sold out run at The Public Theater. It premiered at and was commissioned by Oregon Shakespeare Festival American Revolutions History Cycle/Arena Stage. Other productions include: *By The Way, Meet Vera Stark* (Lilly Award, Drama Desk Nomination), *Ruined* (Pulitzer Prize, OBIE, Lucille Lortel, New York Drama Critics' Circle, Audelco, Drama Desk, and Outer Critics Circle Award), *Intimate Apparel* (American Theatre Critics and New York Drama Critics' Circle Awards for Best Play), *Fabulation, or The Re-Education of Undine* (OBIE Award), *Crumbs from the Table of Joy, Las Meninas, Mud, River, Stone, Por'knockers, Antigone Project*, and *POOF!*.

She is the co-founder of the production company Market Road Films, whose most recent projects include *The Notorious Mr. Bout*, directed by Tony Gerber and Maxim Pozdorovkin (Premiere/Sundance 2014) and *First to Fall*, directed by Rachel Beth Anderson (Premiere/IDFA, 2013).

Nottage is the recipient of a PEN/Laura Pels Master Playwright Award, Literature Award from The Academy of Arts and Letters, Columbia University Provost Grant, Doris Duke Artist Award, The Joyce Foundation Commission Project & Grant, Madge Evans-Sidney Kingsley Award, MacArthur "Genius Grant" Fellowship, Steinberg "Mimi" Distinguished Playwright Award, the Dramatists Guild Hull-Warriner Award, the inaugural Horton Foote Prize, Helen Hayes Award, the Lee Reynolds Award, and the Jewish World Watch iWitness Award.

Her other honors include the National Black Theatre Festival's August Wilson Playwriting Award, a Guggenheim Grant, Lucille Lortel Fellowship, and the Visiting Research Fellowship at Princeton University. She is a graduate of Brown University and the Yale School of Drama, where she has been a faculty member since 2001. She is also an Associate Professor in the Theatre Department at Columbia School of the Arts.

Artistic statement

I write to illuminate spaces darkened by a history of omission, hunting and gathering stories about people marginalized by circumstance. In particular, I'm drawn to stories of women from the African diaspora.

N*gg* is my very personal exploration of a far too common word that has trailed me through life, at times inflicting invisible wounds and challenging me to fight against the confines of its definition.

12 *N*gg**
Lynn Nottage

LYNN A couple of months ago someone asked me when was the last time I was called nigger. I bristle even saying the word. But as it happens, it was a few summers ago and, in of all places, Africa— and as you can imagine, it came as quite a shock. I was in Kigali, Rwanda, a city known for its luscious rolling hills, pristine sidewalks and of course genocide…Another word that elicits a strong visceral response when spoken aloud. I was on an early morning walk through the hilly urban landscape with some of my theatre colleagues, a group of rag tag artists and students looking at how art could be used as a tool for healing. We were on our way to yet another lugubrious workshop on the "theatre of the oppressed."

My colleagues had established a competitively brisk pace, but you see, I was feeling a little sluggish because I had chosen to have a few too many Primus beers at the bar the night before. Studying genocide is depressing, and sometimes one must lubricate.

It was one of those God crafted mornings, where everything seemed vexingly perfect. There was the faint scent of burning wood wafting through the air, there was the sound of lively commerce awakening and of course the streets were crowded with slender handsome people who appeared to be sculpted from fine mahogany.

It had become ritual, as we rounded the top of a long winding steep hill, for a group of lanky teenaged boys congregated in front of a music shop to shout to my White colleagues "Mzungu, Mzungu," which is a Swahili word for White person or foreigner. The teenagers would burst into spontaneous laughter, point and then quickly lose interest when my colleagues refused to return the volley.

But, on this one particular morning I had fallen far behind. I was luxuriating in my slow meditative walk. I was savoring the colors and smells of Africa, marveling at the many hues of brown, from the reddish dirt roads, to the cracking facades of the mud homes to the burnished skin of merchants toting their wares to market.

As I rounded the top of the hill, I found myself face-to-face with the group of teenagers loitering around the music shop. Their posture shifted with anticipation upon seeing me and in unison they shouted, "nigga, nigga." I stopped, turned with surprise, because I wasn't sure if I had heard them correctly. Perhaps they were using some special Kinyarwanda word for good morning or hello. Surely they didn't use the N-word. Not the N-word. "Excuse me?" I said with just a touch of edge in my voice. And they repeated it more loudly this time so there was no mistake, "nigga, nigga," and then they burst out into laughter. To be honest, I didn't know how to respond. In that instant, all cleverness drained from my body, as I was confused and caught off guard by the assault. These tall ebony boys in the middle of Africa had just called me nigger.

As I walked on, mind and heart aflutter… my first impulse was to giggle at the irony, and then my second to was to feel quiet rage, because I knew they had no understanding of the historic resonance of the word. They were not part of the lengthy political debates revolving around the N-word in the United States. They were no doubt parroting the lyrics of some hip-hop hymn.

But for the rest of my stay in Kigali, I found myself contemplating their intent. Did they mean to wound or to praise? Was it shout out or shout down? Did they mean to create a barrier or bridge? Was it meant like the familiar "tu" in Spanish or was it more of a razor blade designed to make a precise incision? Believe me, I spent far too much time obsessing about the encounter. But, it launched me into thinking about all of the times in my life I was called the N-word. And since I do all of my thinking on the page, I began to write down the incidents, trying to come to terms with a word that has loomed large in my life. And what I've come to understand is that if we purge the word from our vocabulary, then part of my childhood disappears, for better or worse.

When I was growing up my father's side of the family used the word liberally. It was like garnish sprinkled on the plate to add flavor and color. I can say this now, with a kind of cock-eyed nostalgia, it was their absolute favorite vocabulary word. The political context be damned, it was their word. Two syllables of provocation. Paprika. Vinegar. Salt and pepper. Sugar.

It was an all-purpose word, used to describe someone you loved, "my nigga," someone who you revered, "the nigga," and someone you despised—"that nigga." Of course, it took on relatively different meanings depending on the inflection and context, like Mandarin. This was a given. My grandmother Dorothy, a tiny, perpetually sour woman used the word like a weapon designed to disarm and diminish. Hence, "them, Niggas." My uncle Willy, a self-styled street hustler, used nigga as a term of endearment; it was reserved for people he liked, or better yet, loved—it was familiar, like an embrace, or warm bread fresh from the oven. "Us, Niggas."

I was first introduced to the N-word by my uncle Willy. He was a world class junky, a hustler savant, who used language in the most tantalizing ways. My father used to say his brother could talk the paint off of the walls. In fact, he could do so in several languages: Spanish, Arabic, and a little bit of Chinese. My uncle once convinced a cop who was in the process of arresting him to loan him $100. Indeed, he was capable of most anything he put his mind to except keeping away from heroin. It was his Achilles heel. In fact, it landed him in prison for the greater part of his life.

And while Uncle Willy was in prison he collected international stamps and slowly had the Koran tattooed all over his entire body in blue ink. The inscriptions completely covered his arms and legs, circumventing his gaunt frame with carefully selected homilies from the holy book. The Arabic words were slightly blurred as if rendered by an unsure or hasty hand. But he was proud of his warrior markings, and liked to say he carried the words of the Prophet everywhere.

I won't get into the irony of God being with him as he shot heroin into his vein, but I always wondered which passage he favored for insertion of the needle…But anyway. Uncle Willy was that friendly and exuberant junkie at the 116th Street fair who danced drunk and shirtless to the sounds of the Ohio Players and Eddie Palmieri. But I'm off subject.

Uncle Willy was the first person to introduce me to the N-word. He used to call us, me and my cousins, "niglets." "My little niglets." It was affectionate. As we got older we grew into being full-blown niggas, but we began as niglets. I remember asking him when I was about five or six, what's a niglet? And he said it was a "little nigga" and I asked, well, what is a nigga? And he said, "We're niggas." And right then, he opened this whole world of wonder. "Were we related to the other the niggas Uncle Willy always talked about?"

I pressed him, because I didn't understand. And he took a moment and said with his raspy, authoritative voice, "Look, you'll be called nigga from time to time, sometimes by cats you know, like me, but more often by folks you don't know. Dig. White folks. They'll throw it at you, try to hurt you, for reasons I can't even explain right now, but don't let it touch you, because it's just a word, like revolution, if shouted by the wrong person it can be made to sound ugly, dangerous, dark but it don't mean it's so. So you remember, you're my nigger, even if you don't get no bigger."

I told my mother what Uncle Willy said, because everything out of his mouth had to be fact checked. She was mortified that I even knew the word; it was as though I'd shoved rotting mackerel in her face. Her lip curled, her body tensed and she wouldn't even allow it spoken in her presence, and hence gave no explanation other than that the word was like a spear used to pierce the soul and it's best to cleanse it from the mind.

And it was exactly two and half years later, 1974, that I was first called a nigger by someone outside of my immediate family. I was attending a predominately White camp in the Poconos Mountains. A riding camp. Camp Equinita. For some unknown and mysterious reason my parents had decided it would be a good idea for a clumsy urban child like myself to learn to ride a horse. I still do not entirely understand why, nor have there been many occasions for me to ride horses in my lifetime, but I guess the important thing is that I know how to post when I trot, grip my thighs when I canter, and keep a loose rein when I gallop. It is just the sort of knowledge that may one day save my life.

But anyway, I managed to pass a pleasant summer filled with campfires, canoe trips and long forest walks where I'd collect wild raspberries and red-spotted newts. It was a rather idyllic summer full of camp fires and s'mores, until one afternoon while I was standing in line at the camp canteen waiting to buy about 25 cents worth of pixie sticks and candy buttons, when this older freckle-faced White girl, a rather self-important adolescent, behind me began talking very loudly with a friend. They were discussing O.J. Simpson, which intrigued me, because you see like me, O.J. has a rather large head. This was during the height of the football player's stardom, before his darkness would be made apparent. Back then, we were just two bigheaded Black people, and many folks don't know this, but there's an unspoken kinship that exists between people with very large heads. And so I listened carefully as this teenaged girl quoted her father's half-baked notions about race and the athletic prowess of the Buffalo Bills' star running back. The line was moving at snail's pace, which allowed the girl to go into painful detail about O.J.'s massive Mandingo thighs. And then someone asked rather innocently, "Who is this O.J. Simpson?" And the freckle-faced girl slowly turned in my direction, pointed a finger at me and with the sort of disgust only an adolescent girl can conjure, she said...

"He's a nigger like her." And I drew in a deep breath, stood tall and proudly stated "I'm a not a nigger, I'm a niglet." There was laughter. I was only quoting my wise Uncle Willy. But I remember, the sting of the freckle-faced girl's tone, the touch of venom in her words and I implicitly understood that the way she wielded the word was far more potent and dangerous than my Uncle Willy had let on. And I didn't like it. The word nigger didn't sound friendly and sweet like when Uncle Willy summoned us across Sheep Meadow in Central Park.

That evening outside of my cabin I related the story to my friend Laurie Wilson. She was one of only four other African American campers at the time. At nine years old she was the first radical Black feminist I had ever met. She wore a short tatty Afro and refused to wear a t-shirt on hot days, because the boys didn't have to. She audaciously strutted around camp topless with her t-shirt shoved in her back pocket. No one could make her put it on. No one. So I told Laurie, who expressed pre-adolescent rage, and she suggested that we corner the girl in the stable ghetto-style and whip her with our riding crops. We entertained the idea of thuggery, a Brooklyn beat down, for one full day until Laurie decided it best to tell Sue, our hunch-backed camp counselor who expressed genuine Quaker shock. It should have ignited a firestorm at our seemingly liberal Pennsylvania camp, but it did not. Who knew the power of this little word? And suddenly the politics of race were injected into our bucolic summer, and everything threatened to get ugly, but then something startling happened...President Nixon resigned, distracting everyone and my little crisis evaporated into a memory. But the scar remained, and I knew that my adventures with the N-word in racist America were only just beginning.

And that summer ended. And I returned to my rough and tumble multi-culti Brooklyn neighborhood, where thankfully children had names like Di-onne, Flaco, Lateef, Pito, Tiny, Oswaldo, Shirley, Rosa and David. A place where big afros and big butts were the accoutrement of every fly girl. It was also a neighborhood of artist squats, communes, rebel community gardens, SRO's and reefa spots. It was the neighborhood between neighborhoods, where outsiders retreated for community: hippies, commies, junkies, artists, queers, angry Vietnam vets and civil servants—a place of delicious paradoxes, such as my next-door neighbor, a spicy-tongued Muslim woman who dressed in full purdah by day. She'd sit on the stoop for hours and chastise girls for wearing mini skirts, berating passersby with unthinkably foul language, and then come sundown she'd sneak out of her house in sexy pink hot pants and three inch platform shoes to walk the hooker strip a block away. This was all while her husband, a pious taxi driver, worked his all-night shift. New York City in the seventies, y'all, this sort of thing happened and no one judged her. There was a strange sense of camaraderie that bonded us, we were all outsiders and it's only when we ventured into the land of gabardines and pizza, the Italian Neighborhood, Carroll Gardens, that hurtful words like nigger, spic, faggot reached our ears. But we didn't go there often, our neighborhood was our buffer zone and refuge. And we stayed put.

And so, tucked safely away in my neighborhood, it would be exactly two years before my next full-frontal assault by the N-word, and by that time I understood the context. I hated the sound of the word even from Uncle Willy's playful mouth. I lived in fear of the word, which seemed to spill with ease and thoughtlessness from the mouths of White people. A pinprick. A puncture wound. I was warned against it by my mother, taught how to fortify and fend it off, like a karate man in training.

By now it was 1976, the bicentennial. Two hundred years of American so-called Independence. One of my best friends was Isemi; her Mom was a full-blown incense-burning omnavashivaya-chanting Scandinavian hippy and her father, George, was a radical Japanese writer, inventor and prolific alcoholic. He lived to provoke the establishment. Their home was a place where boarders levitated behind closed doors and you might find a sumo wrestler at the breakfast table.

George had an incredible sense of adventure; he's the sort of man who'd drive on the wrong side of the Brooklyn Bridge, just for the thrill of it. He was a restless, intrepid spirit. He couldn't stay still and we children were his ideal companions because we didn't know any better. He'd drink a bottle of sake, conjure a destination, load us into his orange Renault and on a whim he'd take us on mad road trips, like skiing in the remote mountains of Canada, camping in a teepee in the Poconos or a weekend retreat at a yoga camp where we'd rise at 4:30am to bake bread for our room and board. We followed him wherever he wanted to go, because we knew he'd deliver something unusual and electric. He was a rule breaker.

And in 1976, the bicentennial year, there were still many rules in America that needed to be broken. And it was in this year that George somehow got it into his mind that he wanted to ski one particular mountain in New Jersey. I believe it was called Hidden Valley. He wanted to ski there precisely because it was the one place in the Northeast where we couldn't ski. You see, it was what you call "restricted." And you know what that means? It was a "private mountain," a private club, White, which meant that those us, people of color, were officially uninvited. Which is once again one of those wonderful paradoxes of the seventies, because it wasn't like there were a whole lot of Black folks trying to break down the door to ski in New Jersey, but…they, them had established those rules just in case we wanted to.

And the fact that Hidden Valley was the forbidden fruit was of course why George wanted us to ski there so very, very badly. He talked about it all of the time, fetishizing the mountain, speculating about the quality of the slopes and the nature of the powder.

"It must be wonderful," he'd say, "why else would they keep that lily white snow from us?" He petitioned, fought, lobbied and after the threat of litigation, he was invited to join the club. And he decided, of course, that he would bring us—me, my little brother, and his daughters, us children of color—along as his first guests.

I still remember with absolute clarity the moment we walked into the ski lodge. Boots clumping. Ka-lump. Ka-lump. *"Billy Don't be a Hero"* was playing on the jukebox. *"Billy don't hero, don't be fool with your life, Billy don't be hero come back and make your wife, and as he started to go, I said Billy keep your low, low,*

low…" The song was playing, but all else was silent, hushed. All of the Mayflower white heads in the lodge turned toward us. Piercing, probing, judgmental eyes; the disdain was palpable. We froze, paralyzed, hyperaware of our otherness. We were Black people skiing; this anomaly confused, perplexed and then enraged them. George was emboldened by half a bottle of vodka, but we had nothing to make us brave. So, there we stood. Afraid. Silent. Cold as hell. Finally, George whispered, "Fuck'em, walk." Ka-lump. Ka-lump. It was the longest walk in my life. Suddenly we were the Little Rock Nine in Arkansas—we were crossing the bridge in Selma, Alabama. We were warriors in the Civil Rights Movement, fighting for the right to ski in New Jersey. We sat at the lunch counter loaded with our righteous indignation, drank down our hot chocolate, fending off the nasty stares, and waited for the inevitable, but the N-word never came. It never came. We grabbed our ski gear and hit the slopes. The white snow, reflected light, and the White faces watched our every move, and I thought, "My God, I have never been in a whiter place than a ski slope in my entire life."

We skied for most of the day, relieved that we'd survived, and around midday we stopped to take in the beautiful view of the mountains. Almost happy. We barely noticed two young men traveling up on the ski lift pointing and laughing at us, laughing. And when they were just above our heads, it came: the word, "Niggers!" They shouted and it echoed throughout the valley, Niggers, Niggers, Niggers, ricocheting off the mountainsides. It was an endless assault from all directions. Echoing. Niggers, Niggers, Niggers. And I gasped, and thrust my arms in the air giving them my mightiest gesture, my middle fingers, a powerful fuck you, and as they passed laughing I realized they couldn't see my fingers because they were hidden inside my mittens. But the gesture was liberating. It felt grand and defiant. My right arm thrust in the air like Tommie Smith giving the Black Power salute at the Mexico City Olympics. And then we skied down the slope, and got back on the chair lift and skied down again. And I realized that that word, as much as it stung, couldn't and wouldn't stop me, us, from doing what we loved. And as we drove back home, George sighed, and through his slurred speech he said, "That slope sucked, it was icy, fuck'em, let 'em have it. Next week we'll drive to Canada." And we never went back.

And then another few years passed, and a DJ put a record on a turntable, and an MC grabbed a mic buzzing with static. It was schoolyard in downtown Brooklyn, or some might say it was the Bronx, or some might say it was Queens. But nevertheless, for me it was Brooklyn on an impossibly humid day. We had scaled the schoolyard fence to get closer to the music and join a crowd of sweaty teens in the midst of boogying, as it was known back then. The bass was so assertive that the glass panes of the bodega were dancing. There was an air of danger in the atmosphere, a rumor was spreading that the Puerto Rican gang, the Crazy Homicides, might show up to shut down the party. But it didn't matter, because as we danced, the MC was about to do something we had never heard before, his head was bobbing and swaying, his voice hoarse from coaxing the crowd into motion, his arm conducting, a metronome keeping time and then all of sudden he was rhyming, chanting, no…he was rapping.

And at that moment we couldn't have known that a revolution was occurring, that music would forever be transformed by a few spontaneous words of braggadocio and celebration, and in that moment we couldn't have known that the N-word would morph and mutate, becoming something improbable, leading a whole generation of young people to reclaim it for their own. No, we were savoring our street party. It would be the last of its kind in my neighborhood, because of the inevitable violence that always followed on too-hot days. But that is an entirely different story, because my adventures with the N-word were not yet over.

Katori Hall

Biography

Katori Hall is a writer hailing from Memphis, Tennessee. Hall's plays include: *The Mountaintop* (2010 Olivier Award for Best New Play), which ran on Broadway in 2011 starring Angela Bassett and Samuel L. Jackson (for two theatrical seasons, the play has been one of the most produced plays in America), *Hurt Village* (2011 Susan Smith Blackburn Prize), *Children of Killers, Hoodoo*  *Love, Remembrance, Saturday Night/Sunday Morning, WHADDABLOODCLOT!!!, Our Lady of Kibeho, Pussy Valley*, and *The Blood Quilt*. Her plays have been presented on six continents, and she is currently under commission to write a new play for the UK's National Theatre.

Her additional awards include the Lark Play Development Center Playwrights of New York (PoNY) Fellowship, the ARENA Stage American Voices New Play Residency, the Kate Neal Kinley Fellowship, two Lecomte du Nouy Prizes from Lincoln Center, the Fellowship of Southern Writers Bryan Family Award in Drama, a NYFA Fellowship, the Lorraine Hansberry Playwriting Award, the Columbia University John Jay Award for Distinguished Professional Achievement, the Otto Rene Castillo Award for Political Theatre, and the Otis Guernsey New Voices Playwriting Award.

She was a participant of the Sundance Screenwriters' Lab, where her play *Hurt Village* was developed into a film, and also Sundance's inaugural Episodic Story Lab, where she developed her television show *The Dial*. Also in television, Hall was staffed on the first season of TNT's show *Legends*, executive produced by Howard Gordon and Alex Cary, and is currently developing Stephen L. Carter's #1 national best-seller *The Emperor of Ocean Park* into a pilot with Fox Network, executive produced by John Wells.

Hall's journalism has appeared in *The New York Times, The Boston Globe*, UK's *The Guardian, Essence*, and *The Commercial Appeal*, including contributing reporting for *Newsweek*.

The Mountaintop and *Katori Hall: Plays One* are published by Methuen Drama. Hall is an alumna of the Lark Playwrights' Workshop, where she developed *The Mountaintop* and *Our Lady of Kibeho*, and a graduate of Columbia University, the American Repertory Theater Institute at Harvard University, and the Juilliard School.

She is a proud member of the Ron Brown Scholar Program, the Coca-Cola Scholar Program, the Dramatists Guild, and the Fellowship of Southern Writers. She is currently a member of the Residency Five at Signature Theatre in New York City. Katori will make her feature directing debut with a film adaptation of *Hurt Village,* which received its world premiere at Signature in 2012.

Artistic statement

I was hit by the acting bug when I was a sophomore at Columbia University. During my first class, our teacher asked us a question, "Upon looking at you, who do you think you are? Are you young? Are you fat? What is your type? How old are you?"

I returned back to my dorm room and I looked in the mirror. I was short. I was attractive. I was 19. And I was black. These were all superficial, yes. But the casting of actors often deals with the superficial. I was an ingénue, obviously, but I was a black ingénue. And even then I had worried if there were any parts for me. The next time we returned to acting class, I was assigned a scene partner, Kelly, another young black woman, who would soon become a fast friend. "So you all know your types. This is your assignment for next week: go to the library and find a contemporary play that has a scene for you and your scene partners' types."

I and Kelly went to the library. We were sure, these two young black women were gonna find something to sink their teeth into. We spent hours in that library, pouring over plays. Asking the same question over and over again, "Where are we?"

We went back to class dejected:

> "Kelly and Katori, what scene are you doing?" she asked.
> "Well Becky, we actually couldn't find anything. We actually need your help. We can't seem to find a play that has a scene for two young black women," I said.
> "Well, of course there has to be something on the shelf," she said.
> "We couldn't find anything. Can you think of one?"

10 seconds went by. 20 seconds went by. 40 seconds went by….55 seconds went by…Our teacher could not in that moment conjure up a single play that had a scene for two twenty-year-old black women. In that moment, I said to myself, "I have to write those plays then!"

That was when I became a playwright. Though I continued on to acting school, I pursued both things simultaneously. I always say the best playwriting school was acting school. I learned about theatrical language by imprinting it on my tongue. I learned what an actor needed to bring a character to life.

A playwright is a storyteller who tells stories that demand a witnessing. I write what I want to learn more about. Gaining an actual entry point into a world I don't know anything about is the first step to writing. My journalism experience has made me very comfortable asking tough questions—the first person narrative is always the place to start so I always conduct interviews if I can. I then follow it up with at least 10 books or articles minimum that dig into the world I want to write about. Minimum. It's a jumping off point. The heart fills in the rest.

Production history

The world premiere of *Our Lady of Kibeho* was produced by Signature Theatre (James Houghton, Founding Artistic Director; Erika Mallin, Executive Director), at the Pershing Square Signature Center in New York City, on November 16, 2014. It was directed by Michael Greif. The set design was by Rachel Hauck; the costume design was by Emily Rebholz; the lighting design was by Ben Stanton; the sound design was by Matt Tierney, the original projection design was by Peter Nigrini; the original music and music direction was by Michael McElroy; and the production stage managers were Michael McGroff and Winnie Lok. The cast was as follows:

ALPHONSINE MUMUREKE	Nneka Okafor
ANATHALIE MUKAMAZIMPAKA	Mandi Masden
MARIE-CLAIRE MUKANGANGO	Joaquina Kalukango
FATHER TUYISHIME	Owiso Odera
SISTER EVANGELIQUE	Starla Benford
BISHOP GAHAMANYI	Brent Jennings
FATHER FLAVIA	T. Ryder Smith
NKANGO	Bowman Wright
EMMANUEL	Niles Fitch
GIRLS 1–4	Jade Eshete, Danaya Esperanza, Stacey Sargeant, Angel Uwamahoro
VILLAGER	Kambi Gathesha, Irungu Mutu, Jade Eshete, Danaya Esperanza, Stacey Sargeant, Angel Uwamahoro

13 *Our Lady of Kibeho*
Katori Hall

Characters

The Trinity

ALPHONSINE MUMUREKE 16 year old Rwandese girl, cultural name means "Leave her alone, she speaks the truth."
ANATHALIE MUKAMAZIMPAKA 17 year old Rwandese girl, cultural name means "one who settles arguments and brings peace."
MARIE-CLAIRE MUKANGANGO 21 year old Rwandese young woman, cultural name means "Woman."

The Church

FATHER TUYISHIME Head priest at the school.
SISTER EVANGELIQUE The head nun of the school.
BISHOP GAHAMANYI The town bishop, head of the Butare Diocese.
FATHER FLAVIA Italian, an investigative priest from the Holy See, the "miracles office" at the Vatican.

The Chorus

NKANGO Anathalie's father, a farmer.
EMMANUEL Young boy who is cured of AIDS.
GIRLS 1-4 Classmates at Kibeho College.
VILLAGERS 1-3 Kibeho villagers.

Setting

Kibeho College, an all-girls Catholic school in Kibeho, Rwanda. 1981-1982. Before.

Language notes

Rwandese accents—They would probably be speaking French and Kinyarwanda to each other, but for an English-speaking audience, a French-based Rwanda accent is ideal.

Punctuation notes

//   denotes overlapping dialogue.

--   denotes continuous dialogue.

—   denotes interrupted dialogue.

PRAYER TO OUR LADY OF KIBEHO

Blessed Virgin Mary, Mother of the Word, Mother of all those
Who believe in Him, and who keep Him in their life;
We look upon you in contemplation.
We believe that you are with us, like a mother in the midst of Her children,
    even though we do not see you with our eyes.

You, who are the infallible pathway to Jesus the Saviour.
We bless you for all the favors you gratify our life,
Especially since you humbled yourself
And chose to appear miraculously in Kibeho
At the very time our world needed it most.

Grant us always light and strength,
So that we may worthily keep in us
Your message of conversion and repentance
In order to live in accordance with your Son's Gospel.
Teach us how to pray truly, and love one another as He loved us,
So that, as you willed, we may always be beautiful flowers
That produce nice flavor to everyone and everywhere.

Virgin Mary, Our Lady of Sorrows,
Grant us to value the cross in our life,
So that we may complete in our own bodies
All that has still to be undergone by Christ
For the sake of his mystic Body, the Church.

And when we come to the end of our pilgrimage on earth,
Let us live with you for all eternity, in the heavenly Kingdom.

Amen.

Inspired by true events…

ACT ONE

Scene 1

Kibeho, Rwanda. 1981. Lush hills can be seen rolling in the distance. Passion fruit and bananas hang from towering trees. Fact: it is the most beautiful place in the world. Even God goes on vacation here. The sounds of girls singing a hymn in an exquisite four-part harmony in Kinyarwanda can be heard echoing through the corridors.

ALPHONSINE, a teenage girl, sits outside an open door. She is conservatively dressed with her hands folded in her lap looking down. She has no shoes. Her slender thigh pulses up and down making her foot pat the concrete floor. She is nervous. The CHOIR can be heard beneath the following exchange:

SISTER EVANGELIQUE She is a liar! Just a // liar!

FATHER TUYISHIME Sister Evangelique!

SISTER EVANGELIQUE I don't know who this little snot thinks // she is!

FATHER TUYISHIME Sister, why do you have to speak such // nastiness?

SISTER EVANGELIQUE I wouldn't have to say such things if she wasn't such a liar.

FATHER TUYISHIME What if she is telling the truth?

SISTER EVANGELIQUE Do you believe in tall tales now?

FATHER TUYISHIME No, of course not, // Sister!

SISTER EVANGELIQUE She could not have seen what she said she saw. She is just trying to frighten the other girls. Keep them from sleeping at night.

FATHER TUYISHIME It *is* a good story.

SISTER EVANGELIQUE It is blasphemy!

FATHER TUYISHIME Sister!

SISTER EVANGELIQUE She must be punished! We let her get away with this, the whole school will crumble under the weight of blasphemy, // ANARCHY!!

FATHER TUYISHIME Sister.

SISTER EVANGELIQUE She will cause the other girls to begin lying, too!

FATHER TUYISHIME Sister!

SISTER EVANGELIQUE If she thinks this is the way to get an A in catechism, well--

FATHER TUYISHIME SISTER! *(Beat.)* Did you punish her yet?

(The singing stops. Beat.)

SISTER EVANGELIQUE Just. A little. Bit.

FATHER TUYISHIME Sister...

SISTER EVANGELIQUE I leave the rest to you.

(Beat.)

FATHER TUYISHIME *(O.S.)* Alphonsine!

(ALPHONSINE grips the side of the chair. She does not get up.)

FATHER TUYISHIME *(O.S.)* ALPHONSINE!!

(SISTER EVANGELIQUE, a tall brown woman dressed in all of her blessed nunnery, steps out of the office.)

SISTER EVANGELIQUE Do you hear Father Tuyishime, my child? Or have you been struck deaf and dumb again?

ALPHONSINE Yes.--I--I--I mean, no...Yes, I hear--I heard him, Sister.

SISTER EVANGELIQUE Hmmmm. Well, you better go get your licks then.

(FATHER TUYISHIME walks out and leans against the door. He is a handsome man. Charming and young. The Sister waits.)

FATHER TUYISHIME You can come in, Alphonsine.

(ALPHONSINE stands up softly. She passes SISTER EVANGELIQUE who gives her a stern look. The Sister waits. Beat.)

FATHER TUYISHIME The other girls might need your...*loving* presence, Sister Evangelique.

SISTER EVANGELIQUE *(Sincerely)* You think I have a loving presence?

(Beat.)

FATHER TUYISHIME Please, Sister.

SISTER EVANGELIQUE Fine. Shall, I come by later? To help you with the--

FATHER TUYISHIME I can fill the jerricans myself, Sister.

SISTER EVANGELIQUE Well... I guess my work here is done.

FATHER TUYISHIME Yes. Sister. It is.

(The Sister walks away leaving the two alone. A picture of Jesus floats above their heads. The Father looks to it for some strength. Beat. The Father turns to ALPHONSINE. He sighs heavily. He opens a file on his desk.)

FATHER TUYISHIME Alphonsine Mumureke... Tutsi...

(He looks at her features. Nods to himself. Closes the file. Beat.)

FATHER TUYISHIME Would you like a sip of water?

ALPHONSINE Please don't send me home. My mother would be // so disappointed.

FATHER TUYISHIME First. Let us get you some water.

(He walks to a jerrican and pours ALPHONSINE a cup. She gulps it down. He pours her another. She bangs it back gladly. She finishes.)

ALPHONSINE Thank you.

FATHER TUYISHIME Must be parched. Tongue must be toasted from all those tall tales you have been telling.

ALPHONSINE No. I am. Just. Hot.

FATHER TUYISHIME Amen.

(He takes his collar off and places it on the desk. ALPHONSINE'S eyes bug out and she bursts into laughter.)

FATHER TUYISHIME Shhhhh! Don't tell.

(ALPHONSINE laughs louder. Her smile is like the sun rising above the hills in the distance.)

FATHER TUYISHIME Tutsi you are indeed. Tutsi women always have the prettiest smiles.

(ALPHONSINE stops smiling and looks down.)

FATHER TUYISHIME I'm sorry if that makes you uncomfortable.

(ALPHONSINE'S thigh begins to pulse nervously.)

FATHER TUYISHIME I didn't mean it. Like that. I mean—I am one who cannot tell a lie.

ALPHONSINE As well as I.

(Beat.)

FATHER TUYISHIME So I must "punish" you somehow. What do you think your "punishment" should be?

ALPHONSINE I can help you here in the office.

FATHER TUYISHIME *(Smiling)* Oh, that would be a punishment, eh?

ALPHONSINE Yes. No….*(giggling)* maybe.

FATHER TUYISHIME It would. I wake up in such a foul mood most mornings. Wooo watch out!

(ALPHONSINE laughs again, bringing more of the sun into the tiny cramped office.)

ALPHONSINE You are a very honest man.

FATHER TUYISHIME I try to be, Alphonsine. Are you honest?

ALPHONSINE Yes. I try to be.

FATHER TUYISHIME So are you telling the truth? About what you saw?

ALPHONSINE Yes.

FATHER TUYISHIME Alphonsine, I think you *imagined //* that.

ALPHONSINE No, no! I saw. I *saw*! Almost like I could touch Her, smell Her.

FATHER TUYISHIME Well, maybe you were just…hot. Hallucinating!

ALPHONSINE No, Father, I was not hallucinating.

FATHER TUYISHIME --With so many of you all, packed like tea leaves in a box. No air to circulate in those dormitories. I have to tell, Sister Evangelique to leave the door open --

ALPHONSINE --She was real. No, you're not listening to me. I promise you, I swear to you

that, I saw Her. I saw Her. I saw Her. NO! I SAW HER!!!--

(The Father is taken back by her ferocity. AL-PHONSINE clamps her hand over her mouth.)

ALPHONSINE I am // sorry.

FATHER TUYISHIME It is alright.

ALPHONSINE I am soo, soo sorry.

FATHER TUYISHIME It is alright.

ALPHONSINE I was not HOT. I am not lying. I promise. I only speak the truth.

(Beat.)

ALPHONSINE So what is my punishment for this?

FATHER TUYISHIME Ehhh, you will have to… ehhh…empty the dormitory buckets at night.

ALPHONSINE Anything else?

FATHER TUYISHIME And sweep the halls in the morning…

ALPHONSINE Anything else?

FATHER TUYISHIME …

ALPHONSINE *Anything else*, Father Tuyishime?

(She holds her hands out, expecting the licks of the ruler. Beat. He puts his hand over her hand and pushes it down. She looks up in surprise.)

FATHER TUYISHIME Report to my office. Every morning. 7 o'clock. Sharp.

(ALPHONSINE rises from her chair. She begins to walk out of the cramped office.)

FATHER TUYISHIME One more thing, Alphonsine.

ALPHONSINE Yes, Father.

FATHER TUYISHIME What did She look like?

ALPHONSINE Look like?

FATHER TUYISHIME Was She *muzungu*?

(He points to the picture of the white Jesus on the wall looking down at them. With the bluest of eyes and the blondest of hair…ALPHONSINE takes a pause and as if she is in a trance and sees her…)

ALPHONSINE She was not white or black. She was just….beautiful.

FATHER TUYISHIME Like you?

(The sweet sounds of the choir start back up. ALPHONSINE blushes.)

ALPHONSINE No. Much more beautiful than me.

FATHER TUYISHIME *(To himself)* Hmph. *(To her)* Hurry on. You will be late for rehearsal.

(ALPHONSINE walks out. FATHER TUYISHIME looks after her.)

Scene 2

Lights Shift.
ALPHONSINE joins the group of girls at choir rehearsal outside in the courtyard. MARIE-CLAIRE is utterly bored out of her friggin' mind and she keeps on getting the harmony wrong. ANATHALIE sings sweetly. But then it starts raining.

SISTER EVANGELIQUE See, God is crying because you all sound so horrible. We are done for today.

(The girls giggle as they run away from the rain. Everyone makes sure to steer clear of AL-PHONSINE. MARIE-CLAIRE points at ALPHONSINE'S messy hair, which makes ANATHALIE giggle. They giggle together.)

SISTER EVANGELIQUE Marie-Claire! Can I speak with you a moment?

ANATHALIE Ooooo!

MARIE-CLAIRE Hush it. Meet me in the back by the banana//beer trough.

ANATHALIE Sshhhhh! I know! I know...

(ANATHALIE giggles and walks away. MARIE-CLAIRE walks up to SISTER EVANGELIQUE. They stand beneath a partition keeping them from the rain.)

MARIE-CLAIRE Sister, I promise that I will have the harmonies memorized by tomorrow.

SISTER EVANGELIQUE Oh, will you?

MARIE-CLAIRE I just have a horrible time remembering.

SISTER EVANGELIQUE Perhaps it is because you are getting so old.

MARIE-CLAIRE But I'm only 21, Sister.

SISTER EVANGELIQUE In Kibeho, that means you practically have one foot in the grave.

(Silence. MARIE-CLAIRE is not amused.)

SISTER EVANGELIQUE Excuse me, Marie, I'm not myself lately. These recent *happenings* have put me on edge.

MARIE-CLAIRE They have put me on edge as well.

SISTER EVANGELIQUE Have they?

MARIE-CLAIRE Yes, Sister.

SISTER EVANGELIQUE What do you think of them?

MARIE-CLAIRE What is there to think of them?

SISTER EVANGELIQUE Do you believe this fool?

MARIE-CLAIRE Ennnh, my father once said "the village fool sometimes speaks the truth."

SISTER EVANGELIQUE Did he really?

MARIE-CLAIRE Yes.

SISTER EVANGELIQUE I've never heard of such a saying. *(Slight disgust)* Must be Tutsi.

(MARIE-CLAIRE stiffens.)

MARIE-CLAIRE No, it is from our people.

SISTER EVANGELIQUE Hmph *(Pause)* So do you believe her?

MARIE-CLAIRE No. I did not say that. I have my own mind.

SISTER EVANGELIQUE And what does your own mind say?

MARIE-CLAIRE She just wants attention.

SISTER EVANGELIQUE Well, she certainly knows how to get it. *(Under her breath)* She has Father Tuyishime's full attention now. She will be working in his office. As punishment.

MARIE-CLAIRE That's all she gets for punishment?

SISTER EVANGELIQUE Does she need more?

MARIE-CLAIRE If *I* were the head nun, I would have given her 20 licks with the ruler, made her clean the latrines and wash everyone's knickers for the entire month. If I can speak my mind openly--

SISTER EVANGELIQUE *(Trying to interrupt)* Go ahead.

MARIE-CLAIRE --and honestly. I would have made her do all of that and then some. *I* would have been smacked clear across the face for such blasphemy, probably even expelled! It's disturbing to think she could actually get away with, get AWAY with // it all.

SISTER EVANGELIQUE She hasn't gotten away with anything. Rather she won't.

MARIE-CLAIRE I could run this place much better than you—

(SISTER EVANGELIQUE yanks her up hard.)

SISTER EVANGELIQUE Until you are across the river, beware how you insult the mother alligator.

(Beat.)

MARIE-CLAIRE Sorry. Sister.

(SISTER EVANGELIQUE lets her down gently.)

SISTER EVANGELIQUE The next time she goes into another one of her little trances, you pinch her. You pinch her hard.

MARIE-CLAIRE I don't wanna touch her when she goes there. Her eyes...gone. No life. Almost like's she's sleeping with her eyes // wide open.

SISTER EVANGELIQUE Watch her. In the dorms. You are the eldest of the group. I'm going to need you to take control of things.

MARIE-CLAIRE Control of things?

SISTER EVANGELIQUE Yes, my darling Marie-Claire. Control.

MARIE-CLAIRE I can do that.

(*SISTER EVANGELIQUE looks into MARIE-CLAIRE'S face as if looking into a mirror.*)

SISTER EVANGELIQUE I know.

(*MARIE-CLAIRE smiles.*)

SISTER EVANGELIQUE Go along, now. Don't you have some songs to be learning?

Scene 3

The thunder rolls and lights shift. The sun has broken through the clouds. ALPHONSINE is taking the books from Father Tuyishime's office and dusting them.

ANATHALIE comes up behind her and watches her through thick glasses.

ANATHALIE How long are you on punishment?

ALPHONSINE He say a week.

ANATHALIE Ahhhh, that means you get to go to confession!

ALPHONSINE There is nothing to confess.

ANATHALIE Is it weird that I love to go to confession?

ALPHONSINE Perhaps it's that you have an unclean heart.

ANATHALIE (*Offended*) I am a virgin, Alphonsine. All virgins have unclean hearts.

(*ALPHONSINE continues to dust.*)

ANATHALIE (*Pushing up her glasses*) I'd love to be on punishment for Father Tuyishime.

ALPHONSINE Anathalie!

ANATHALIE Wha? He's extraordinarily cute. Too bad he can't get married.

(*ALPHONSINE laughs bringing more sunlight to drive away the storm.*)

ALPHONSINE You better get away, before she comes.

ANATHALIE Ah-ah! Marie-Claire doesn't rule me.

ALPHONSINE Are you sure about that?

ANATHALIE She is a lion, all roar and menace, but you? You are a flea. Quiet. Little. Almost invisible.

ALPHONSINE Well, a flea can bother a lion, but a lion cannot bother a flea.

ANATHALIE Too smart for your own good.

ALPHONSINE And too dumb for yours.

ANATHALIE You are the one who goes deaf and dumb, pretending that you're gone. But we know. We know you're just acting. You just want attention. You silly, silly girl. You just want people to see you.

ALPHONSINE See me? No, I want you to see her, Anathalie. Oh, I wish you could see what I see. Know what I know. Know Her! She wants to embrace us with the greatest love. Her arms are so wide that they wrap around the world twice over. She loves us more than our parents. She loves us even though we live in sin. She wants us to pray, Anathalie. Pray! It is the only way to stop the pain. The only way. She showed me how the world could be.

ANATHALIE She did? What did She show you?

ALPHONSINE I don't know if I can tell you.

ANATHALIE Come on! How did the world look?

(*Beat.*)

ALPHONSINE More beautiful than this land of a thousand hills, my friend. Rwanda has nothing on where she would take us. It is a land where mountains float. Where one is never hungry. It is a land where sickness is no more. Darkness is no more. Fear is no more. Hate does not hide itself in the cracks of men's hearts. It is a land of love. Everywhere love.

ANATHALIE Sounds like heaven alright, but don't we have to die to get there?

ALPHONSINE No, Anathalie, no! She said, we can have it. Here on earth. We just have to pray. Repent. Purge your unclean virgin heart, Anathalie. Pray with me. So you can see it, too…

(*ALPHONSINE'S hand is stretching to ANATHALIE'S. ANATHALIE steps closer and begins to reach out her hand, but—*)

ANATHALIE I wouldn't want to see that.

ALPHONSINE Why?

ANATHALIE Because I don't think the world could ever be that beautiful.

(*MARIE-CLAIRE enters with her gang of girls trailing. ANATHALIE quickly brings her hand up to push up her glasses. MARIE-CLAIRE pushes ALPHONSINE, who was already on her knees, making her fall spread eagle onto the ground…*)

ANATHALIE Marie-Claire!

MARIE-CLAIRE (*Drunken giggles*) What?

ANATHALIE Leave her alone.

ALPHONSINE You all reek of banana beer.

THE GIRLS So!

GIRL #1 I think I'm going to be sick.

MARIE-CLAIRE Such a light-weight. Anathalie, I thought I told you to meet us by the banana beer trough?

ANATHALIE *(Looking at ALPHONSINE)* I was. I was going to, but—

GIRL #1 Alphonsine, where did Father Tuyishime give you the licks?

MARIE-CLAIRE On the bottom?

ANATHALIE Marie-Claire!

MARIE-CLAIRE What? Bad girls usually get it on the bottom. Where did he put your welts? Let me see. Let me see!

(MARIE-CLAIRE goes to lift ALPHONSINE'S skirt. Balling up her fist—)

ALPHONSINE Do that again and I will slap you so hard your descendants will feel the sting!!

THE GIRLS Whoa....

MARIE-CLAIRE So the Virgin Mary visits mean old nasty girls like you?

GIRL #1 A Tutsi on top of that.

ALPHONSINE I'm not lying.

GIRL #2 Tutsis lie.

ALPHONSINE We do not.

GIRL #2 That's what my ma said.

ALPHONSINE Well, maybe your ma is proof that Hutus lie.

GIRL #3 Well, why don't I see Her, huh? Why doesn't She speak to me?

ALPHONSINE I do not know. How I wish She would.

ANATHALIE But wouldn't it be something? If she wasn't lying? Our Lady here in Kibeho...

MARIE-CLAIRE The day Our Lady visits Kibeho is the day the Pope comes to Africa.

ANATHALIE Stranger things have happened.

MARIE-CLAIRE Wha, Anathalie? Do you believe this liar? This blasphemer. This WITCH!!

(MARIE-CLAIRE pushes ALPHONSINE again.)

ANATHALIE Marie-Claire, stop it.

MARIE-CLAIRE Whose side are you on, Anathalie? You must walk on the side of the righteous! She is a witch.

THE GIRLS *(In unison)* A witch!

MARIE-CLAIRE We all know you come from the village of Zaza.

GIRL #1 Those people are fools. They worship statues and drink the blood of babies.

GIRL #3 I heard they cut out the hearts of chickens and dance with them above their heads.

MARIE-CLAIRE They are heathens!!!

THE GIRLS Heathens!

ANATHALIE Marie-Claire. I said // stop it! Leave her alone. You all stop!

MARIE-CLAIRE You are a witch! A witch!

THE GIRLS *(In unison)* A witch! A witch!

MARIE-CLAIRE What, you want to protect the little witch from Zaza?

(MARIE-CLAIRE snatches ANATHALIE'S glasses off of her face.)

ANATHALIE Give my spectacles back, Marie Claire.

GIRL #1 You blind fool.

(MARIE-CLAIRE tosses it to the other girl.)

GIRL #2 Here give them to me!

ANATHALIE Stop it! Stop it! I can't see!

MARIE-CLAIRE You believe what she says, huh?

ANATHALIE Give them back!

(Forgotten on the ground ALPHONSINE slowly rises up until she is on her knees. We see that she is staring into the distance. Her back arches and the winds begin to change. The pages of the books she was dusting begin to rustle like the leaves on a tree.)

MARIE-CLAIRE Look! Look! She's doing again.

GIRL #1 She's possessed.

GIRL #3 Look at that evil in her eye.

(ALPHONSINE looks utterly at peace. Exuberant even. Stars stream from her eyes. She is somewhere else.)

GIRL #1 Don't go near her!

MARIE-CLAIRE Pinch her.

ANATHALIE Marie-Claire! Stop being mean!

MARIE-CLAIRE *(Ignoring her)* Go *pinch* her.

GIRL #1 Eh-eh! She's not going to possess me.

GIRL #2 I told you! I told you! She's a witch!

GIRL #3 I think she's just possessed.

MARIE-CLAIRE I said pinch her.

THE GIRLS EH-EH!!

MARIE-CLAIRE Fine, then I'll do it.

(MARIE-CLAIRE goes up to her and pinches her. Pinches her hard. ALPHONSINE does not move, she luxuriates.)

ANATHALIE Leave her alone!

MARIE-CLAIRE You won't move, enh? You won't move? *(To the other girls)* Let's play a little game.

(MARIE-CLAIRE takes her rosary off. She goes to the far corner of the corridor. She throws her rosary. It hits ALPHONSINE in her head who doesn't flinch. She is in another world.)

MARIE-CLAIRE Damn it!

ANATHALIE Marie-Claire! I'm going to tell Sister Evangelique.

MARIE-CLAIRE Don't be such a snitch!

GIRL #1 Ooooo, I wanna try!

GIRL #2 Me, too!

(They take their rosaries off and they play their ad hoc game--similar to horse shoes or a game one plays at the carnival.)

THE GIRLS Ring around the rosary...Ring around the rosary!!

GIRL #4 *(Sings in Kinyarwanda)* Eii oooooooo Eii oooooooo Eii oooooooo!

(They continue to hit her in her head. But AL-PHONSINE is gone. Not hearing the yells of the girls. She begins to speak to someone high, high above their heads.)

ALPHONSINE I have been. I've been praying my rosary every night.

MARIE-CLAIRE What is she saying? What are you saying devil girl?

GIRL #1 Don't get too close. She's gonna bite you.

GIRL #3 Yaaaay! I scored.

ALPHONSINE Are you sure? // They make fun of me all the time. It's getting hard.

MARIE-CLAIRE Point one for you! Come, Anathalie, join us.

(ANATHALIE does not move.)

MARIE-CLAIRE I said Anathalie join us.

(MARIE-CLAIRE slaps ANATHALIE. ANATHALIE, buckling beneath the peer pressure, reluctantly takes off her rosary.)

MARIE-CLAIRE Throw it! Throw it!

(Tears stream down ALPHONSINE'S cheeks. She is looking at the Virgin Mary. ANATH-ALIE tries to throw it around ALPHON-SINE'S neck, but it hits the floor.)

MARIE-CLAIRE You throw like my grandmother.

ANATHALIE Well, I wouldn't have to throw like your grandmother if I could see! Give me back my specs--

MARIE-CLAIRE Not until you do it again. Again!

THE GIRLS Do it again! Do it again!

(ANATHALIE takes another throw, but AL-PHONSINE'S hand rises and she catches the rosary with her hand.)

THE GIRLS Oooooooo!

MARIE-CLAIRE See, she's lying! She's lying!

(ANATHALIE is staring at her.)

ANATHALIE Give it back! Give it back!

MARIE-CLAIRE Give it back to her. Give it back!

(ALPHONSINE' refuses or rather she is lost.)

ANATHALIE Give it back! Give it-- *(gasp)*

(Suddenly ANATHALIE is struck by something. Her back arches and she bends backwards onto the ground as if she is a prima ballerina.)

THE GIRLS Give it back! Give it back!

(ANATHALIE falls onto her knees. She begins to look at the same direction as ALPHONSINE.)

GIRL #1 Look! Look at Anathalie. Look at her.

(A warm light begins to dance across ALPHON-SINE and ANATHALIE'S faces. It's as if the sun is reflecting on water, and playing peek-a-boo with their lips. An intense joy ripples through their bodies. ANATHALIE is staring up something floating high above their heads. Tears begin to stream from her eyes. She is somewhere else....)

MARIE-CLAIRE Anathalie.....Anathalie? Wha-What's going on? What's happening? Anathalie, Anathalie! Come back! Come back. Come back. Come...back...

Scene 4

FATHER TUYISHIME'S office. ANATHALIE and ALPHONSINE are sitting with bags packed. SISTER EVANGELIQUE is looking over them... pleased.

SISTER EVANGELIQUE Soon these shenanigans will all be over.

ANATHALIE Why did you bring him here?

SISTER EVANGELIQUE Someone needs to knock some sense into you.

(FATHER TUYISHIME comes in followed by NKANGO, ANATHALIE'S father, a big hefty farmer.)

FATHER TUYISHIME I'm glad that you could come on such short notice, Nkango.

NKANGO Anything that concerns my child, is my business. Where is she?

SISTER EVANGELIQUE Over here.

NKANGO So this is how you treat my hard work, Anathalie? You go and get yourself in trouble.

ANATHALIE Papa, please understand.

(His hand goes to his belt.)

NKANGO Excuse me, are you speaking?

ANATHALIE No, Papa, //I'm not.

ALPHONSINE Shhhh, //Anathalie.

ANATHALIE *(To Alphonsine)* Wha?

NKANGO Is this the one you're in cahoots with?

ANATHALIE Papa, I'm not in cahoots with// anyone.

ALPHONSINE SHHHHH, Anathalie!

(NKANGO begins to take off that belt.)

NKANGO We said go to school and this is what you go and do? Follow some heathen right out of an education. *(Pointing to ALPHONSINE)* What are you going to do with her?

SISTER EVANGELIQUE She is an orphan. No father.

NKANGO What a shame. She needs someone to beat her good for this foolishness.

FATHER TUYISHIME Nkango, there is no need--

NKANGO You might be a father, Father Tuyishime, but you are not the father to Anathalie Mukamazimpaka. Come on Anathalie, get your things. I am taking you out of this school for good.

ANATHALIE No, Papa, please I promise. I promise I won't speak to her again. I promise!

FATHER TUYISHIME Nkango, I'm sure Anathalie is very sorry for her actions. For lying—

NKANGO She'd better be. Come on.

(ANATHALIE doesn't move. She continues to hold on to ALPHONSINE.)

NKANGO You don't want to listen?

(He quickly begins to remove his belt.)

FATHER TUYISHIME Maybe we can come to some kind of agreement.

SISTER EVANGELIQUE Agreement?

NKANGO No, she's coming home. I don't know why you haven't expelled her.

SISTER EVANGELIQUE That's what I said.

NKANGO Come on, Anathalie.

FATHER TUYISHIME Perhaps because it is imperative that she learn from these mistakes, she can…confess.

NKANGO *(Sarcastically)* And how many Hail Marys will get her out of this?

SISTER EVANGELIQUE A hundred and twenty-three.

FATHER TUYISHIME Sister Evangelique!

ANATHALIE I will do them. I will do them. Whatever I need to do Papa. But please just let me stay in school. Hail Mary, full of grace. The Lord is // with thee. Blessed are thou among women…*(continuing beneath the following exchange)*

FATHER TUYISHIME See, she has already started. 122 more to go—

NKANGO No, she must get out of here.

FATHER TUYISHIME But she needs her schooling.

(NKANGO slaps his belt against the desk. It makes everyone jump. Silence.)

NKANGO I am but a lowly farmer, Father. We are all just farmers. If the village thinks I have a daughter who is a witch who will buy my banana, huh? Who will buy my cassava, huh? Who will buy? The entire village rather go hungry than eat the ground nuts of a man who has fathered a witch. I cannot have it. She will come back to the field where she will not catch this-this-uh virus. You are infecting my daughter.

FATHER TUYISHIME I am not a mosquito.

NKANGO Well, I much rather her die of malaria than of lies. I should have never let you come. This was nonsense anyhow and all of this is proving me right. Your mother was always wrong. Book learning makes a girl go crazy. Come, now Anathalie, before I have to come and get you.

(But ANATHALIE is gazing off.)

ANATHALIE *(Pointing)* But Father *She* wants me to stay.

NKANGO Anathalie, get your things NOW! I don't care what your friend says—

ANATHALIE N-N-N-N-No, not Alphonsine. Her…

(ANATHALIE points to an empty space.)

NKANGO Anathalie, don't make me come and GET YOU!

(The hefty farmer punches the wall. It splinters. Everyone except for ANATHALIE jumps…)

ANATHALIE But Papa look! Look how She floats.

(ANATHALIE'S eyes start rolling into the back of her head. SISTER EVANGELIQUE bolts from her chair.)

SISTER EVANGELIQUE Ah-ah. Not again.

(ANATHALIE falls down on her knees and there is the most angelic expression on her face. She laughs. Giggles. Coos. Laughs. Giggles. Coos. Like a baby staring up at her mother.)

ALPHONSINE It's spreading. Just like She said it would….

NKANGO *She? Who is She? Wha…*

FATHER TUYISHIME What does She look like, Anathalie?

ANATHALIE So beautiful words cannot describe—

FATHER TUYISHIME What is She wearing?

ANATHALIE A long veil. White. Glowing. Like the stars on a clear night—

FATHER TUYISHIME Her skin?

ANATHALIE Smooth. No marks. Like no one I've ever seen—

NKANGO My God, Father!! Why are you egging this nonsense on? // Jesus Christ!

FATHER TUYISHIME SHHH, Nkango! And Her eyes—

(NKANGO goes to pick up the tiny ANATH-ALIE. He grabs her and--)

NKANGO Eh-eh!

(She does not budge. He tries to pull on her again, but the hefty farmer's strength cannot pick up his slim daughter. He heems and haws, but she is like a tree trunk rooted to the floor. He tries to lift her again. But can't…)

NKANGO Will somebody help me?

(SISTER EVANGELIQUE jumps up to help. But she, too, can't lift her.)

SISTER EVANGELIQUE She must have a belly full of stones.

(These adults grunt and twist, but she is like Mount Kilimanjaro. Immovable. She giggles. Coos. Laughs and coos some more. Finally, spent from their lifting. They watch ANATHALIE whose tongue is like a television changing channels. She speaks French. Then Kinyarwanda. She speaks in many many tongues. The tongues of the universe.)

NKANGO What are you saying my child? Father, Father! What is going on?

FATHER TUYISHIME *(Ignoring him)* Alphonsine what is She saying?

ALPHONSINE She needs the village people to listen. She needs them to hear the message.

NKANGO No, she needs to come home. She's sick.

ALPHONSINE She needs to be heard. It is the only way. This is Mama Mary's decree…

FATHER TUYISHIME What is Anathalie seeing now?

ALPHONSINE She is seeing the goodness…The beauty…The light…

FATHER TUYISHIME What light, Alphonsine?

(Just then ALPHONSINE drifts off and they are looking at the same space. Both of the girls cooing like little babies.)

NKANGO My child! My poor child! She has been struck dumb. She is dumb. My child.

(ANATHALIE'S father holds her, softly. Suddenly the young women draw in seven quick breaths. As if they are gasping for air underwater.)

NKANGO Anathalie, Anathalie…

(They take in one big breath and both ANATH-ALIE and ALPHONSINE collapse to the floor.)

NKANGO Is she…

SISTER EVANGELIQUE Are they?

(Lights shift.)

Scene 5

A candlelit room.
ALPHONSINE and ANATHALIE are lying side by side in two beds. SISTER EVANGELIQUE looks over ALPHONSINE. She does the sign of the cross over her. Puts a dab of holy water over her head. She turns her back to ALPHONSINE to the bed ANATHALIE is lying in. She pulls out her pocket watch. She checks the time. She is about to put the watch back into her pocket until she gets an idea. SISTER EVANGELIQUE stares at ANATHALIE, who lies there stiff as a board. The Sister puts the pocket watch beneath her nose. She waits for the fog, but—

SISTER EVANGELIQUE No breath.

(SISTER EVANGELIQUE lifts her arm. Checks it.)

SISTER EVANGELIQUE Barely a pulse?

(Behind SISTER EVANGELIQUE, AL-PHONSINE slowly rises not making a sound. The candle light pushes her shadow around the room. SISTER EVANGELIQUE puts her ear to ANATHALIE'S chest. She waits and waits and waits. She hears….nothing. Concerned, SISTER EVANGELIQUE takes ANATH-ALIE'S face lovingly into her hands. She makes the sign of the cross and—)

ALPHONSINE Don't worry. She will not succumb.

(SISTER EVANGELIQUE practically jumps out of her skin and lunges at ALPHONSINE in the darkness!)

SISTER EVANGELIQUE Jesus!!!

ALPHONSINE Oh.

SISTER EVANGELIQUE Jesus!!!

ALPHONSINE Didn't mean to scare you.

SISTER EVANGELIQUE I thought you were asleep.

ALPHONSINE Seems like you are hell-bent on making that permanent.

(Beat. SISTER EVANGELIQUE eyes' bore holes through ALPHONSINE. Not caring, ALPHONSINE stretches as if she's had the best nap in her life. She takes her time. An extensive yawn that lasts eons. Finally, she swings her leg around the side of the bed. She smiles at SISTER EVANGELIQUE. Beat.)

SISTER EVANGELIQUE Oh, so you think this is funny?

ALPHONSINE I am not laughing, Sister.

SISTER EVANGELIQUE Well, get that silly little smirk off your face, before I slap it off.

ALPHONSINE I cannot help but have a bit of Easter in my heart. I shall come back to Earth now and be in despair like all you others.

(ALPHONSINE mocks the Sister's deep frown lines. SISTER EVANGELIQUE is not pleased. Then ALPHONSINE bursts into laughter.)

ALPHONSINE Oh, Sister. Frowns make a woman look so ugly. Always remember a Rwandan woman's beauty is in her--

(SISTER EVANGELIQUE sharply smacks ALPHONSINE. Weak from her trip to the other side, ALPHONSINE falls onto the bed.)

SISTER EVANGELIQUE How dare you? How. Dare. You? You little ingrate, you little *(searching for the word)*....witch! Yes...Is that what you are? A witch. A shitty little witch? I think so. I think that's exactly what you are. I know you. I know your kind. You shake hands with the devil and use the same hand to make the sign of the cross. You've been conjuring your little spells and everyone is falling beneath the spell you are casting. The Father and now Anathalie. But I will cast you out. I will cast you OUT!

(ALPHONSINE has brought her gaze back to SISTER EVANGELIQUE'S. ALPHONSINE, though she is smaller and more slight than Sister, seems to grow taller and wider. Her presence expanding. Swallowing up all the space in the tiny room. The Sister begins to shake in fear. Actually. Visibly quake. There is a fire in ALPHONSINE'S eyes that has not been there before. A blinding light...)

ALPHONSINE You do not scare me anymore.

(SISTER EVANGELIQUE takes a step back. She turns her head away. She gathers herself. The shaking soon subsides. ALPHONSINE turns sweet.)

ALPHONSINE She will be heard. Whether you like it or not.

SISTER EVANGELIQUE Is that so?

ALPHONSINE Yes.

(Beat. SISTER EVANGELIQUE'S glare melts. Asking from the deep end of her heart:)

SISTER EVANGELIQUE Why can you hear Her, and I cannot?

ALPHONSINE You can hear Her through me. If you are ready to listen....Are you ready?

(Silence from SISTER EVANGELIQUE.)

ALPHONSINE May I go now?

SISTER EVANGELIQUE *(Breathless)* Please.

(ALPHONSINE hops off the bed. She does the sign of the cross over ANATHALIE. She looks at her friend and smiles. Satisfied.)

ALPHONSINE She'll be coming out of it soon. Very soon.

(ALPHONSINE exits. Incredulous, SISTER EVANGELIQUE stares after her.)

(Lights shift.)

Scene 6

Day. The Father's office. FATHER TUYISHIME has a visitor, BISHOP GAHAMANYI. They are very relaxed. In man-mode, cracking up:

BISHOP GAHAMANYI And Mama Rusibanga chased Dada Rusibanga down the hill with her hoe. I tell you it was a sight to see.

FATHER TUYISHIME *(Wiping tears from his eyes)* I wish I would have been there.

BISHOP GAHAMANYI *(Shaking his fist)* Dada Rusibanga should have given Mama a piece of his mind.

FATHER TUYISHIME *(Laughing uncomfortably)* Well....he was supposed to be turning the field not playing futbol.

BISHOP GAHAMANYI It was Saturday!

FATHER TUYISHIME Still he should have—

BISHOP GAHAMANYI *(Interrupting)* Eh-Eh! Two lions cannot rule one valley.

SISTER EVANGELIQUE Your Excellency, that is very true.

(They stop and turn and look at the door. SISTER EVANGELIQUE genuflects upon seeing the Bishop.)

BISHOP GAHAMANYI Sister Evangelique, so you agree with me?

SISTER EVANGELIQUE To a certain extent.

BISHOP GAHAMANYI Good. Good.

(Uncomfortable silence.)

FATHER TUYISHIME Are the girls—

SISTER EVANGELIQUE Fine. They are both fine.

BISHOP GAHAMANYI Young girls will do anything for attention these days.

FATHER TUYISHIME *(Smiling)* Indeed, they will.

BISHOP GAHAMANYI Sometimes I don't mind it. We all need to be listened to--be heard. But this might all be going a bit too far—

SISTER EVANGELIQUE Yes, usually all one needs is a pretty face and nice waist to get your attention. Your Excellency, sooooo nice of you to bless us with your presence today. Last time we saw each other, I think it was dry season.

(The men stop smiling. FATHER TUYISHIME shoots SISTER EVANGELIQUE a "shut the fuck up" glare.)

BISHOP GAHAMANYI *(Tightly smiling at Sister's audacity)* It is true that I don't get a chance to come to Kibeho very often.

FATHER TUYISHIME Well, those seven hills can be as big as mountains. Wheew!

BISHOP GAHAMANYI Eh-Eh! Did I tell you Dada Rusibanga banged me in the knee at the last futbol game?

FATHER TUYISHIME Sorry, sorry.

SISTER EVANGELIQUE I suppose if you are out of shape with a flabby stomach and a banged up knee, yes those hills can be hard. But most of my girls can run up them with jerricans full of water balanced on their heads. All of this, of course, before they get their lesson at 7:30 in the morning.

(Bishop ain't got time to play with no SISTER EVANGELIQUE so:)

BISHOP GAHAMANYI Well, I'm here at 6:30 this morning because there is a rustle down in the valley. It's making the banana trees shake

with a whisper that might soon grow into an uncontrollable roar.

FATHER TUYISHIME I am trying my best to control it, Your Excellency.

SISTER EVANGELIQUE *You* are?

FATHER TUYISHIME Yes…I am.

BISHOP GAHAMANYI Well, one of the girls' father has been spreading rumors about how he saw his daughter…ehhhh…catch the spirit so to speak. That his daughter is a prophet.

SISTER EVANGELIQUE I bet his bananas are selling like Primus beers now.

BISHOP GAHAMANYI This is not a time for joking, Sister. There's worse news.

FATHER TUYISHIME Worse news?

BISHOP GAHAMANYI A reporter from Radio Rwanda wants to interview me about these two girls. Radio Rwanda. *(Pause)* Have they been punished?

SISTER EVANGELIQUE No.

FATHER TUYUSHIME Yes.

BISHOP GAHAMANYI Well, which one is it?

SISTER EVANGELIQUE *(Lying)* Yes.

FATHER TUYUSHIME *(Admitting)* No.

FATHER TUYISHIME Well, no and yes.

BISHOP GAHAMANYI No and yes?

SISTER EVANGELIQUE Yes and No.

FATHER TUYUSHIME No and Yes.

BISHOP GAHAMANYI You know how our country folk can be. They believe. They believe so easily. It warms my heart that they believe. It makes our jobs easier for us, eh?

FATHER TUYISHIME Yes, Your Excellency.

BISHOP GAHAMANYI Yes. The country folk will believe anything you tell them. But we cannot, we absolutely cannot have them believing in this.

FATHER TUYISHIME But you didn't see it. Them. The girls.

BISHOP GAHAMANYI I don't need to see in order to—.

(Pause. Wait a minute…)

BISHOP GAHAMANYI Don't tell me you believe these shenanigans, Father?

(Pause. The Father and Sister look at each other.)

SISTER EVANGELIQUE Someone from the diocese needs to investigate these girls. Give them psychological evaluations. For young girls to do this they are not right in the head.

BISHOP GAHAMANYI There are no psychologists in Rwanda.

SISTER EVANGELIQUE Well, we should fly one in! Eh-if I were the head of the diocese, I would order an investigation so fast that it would have started yesterday.

BISHOP GAHAMANYI But you are not the head of the diocese, neither will you ever be, *Sister* Evangelique. As I said, I know what young girls will do to get attention. To get the Father's attention. Isn't that right, Father?

(The Bishop hits Father in the arm.)

FATHER TUYISHIME *(Blushing)* Oh, stop it.

BISHOP GAHAMANYI It is only natural. I understand. I understand it all. Look at him. That skin. Those chestnut eyes.

SISTER EVANGELIQUE Yes, yes, yes. I know I see them every day.

BISHOP GAHAMANYI Well, then you know. Maybe if you meted out some well-needed discipline, more often, Sister Evangelique, maybe this situation would be under control.

SISTER EVANGELIQUE Are you blaming // me?

BISHOP GAHAMANYI *(Overlapping)* You must lead by example, Sister. You are like their mother. Please, act like one. Let them know that these lies will only lead them down the path of perdition. It cannot be tolerated.

SISTER EVANGELIQUE But—

BISHOP GAHAMANYI Father Tuyishime needs your help. I know how you women can be, coddling them, letting them get away with things, but—

SISTER EVANGELIQUE *(Interrupting)* Me?

BISHOP GAHAMANYI *(Continuing)*—with Father's Tuyishime's recent appointment as head chaplain, he cannot deal with these shenanigans. It's your responsibility now.

SISTER EVANGELIQUE Now? It's *always* been mine.

BISHOP GAHAMANYI Sister, please. The diocese is none too happy with the recent happenings of bullshit.

SISTER EVANGELIQUE And neither am I.

BISHOP GAHAMANYI But it seems like you're allowing these girls to run amuck and take control of the school.

SISTER EVANGELIQUE Perhaps if *he* were not goading them on.

FATHER TUYISHIME Sister Evangelique, I have not been goading them on!

SISTER EVANGELIQUE You have too!

BISHOP GAHAMANYI *(To FATHER TUYISHIME)* You've been goading them on?

SISTER EVANGELIQUE Yes!

FATHER TUYISHIME No!

SISTER EVANGELIQUE He has!!! Asking them what She looks like, what kind of veil She has on.

FATHER TUYISHIME Sister!

SISTER EVANGELIQUE Yes, it's been you the whole time.

BISHOP GAHAMANYI I don't care who is goading who and what and where and why. Get it under control or I will SHUT. IT. DOWN. This school will be closed. Do you understand me? Do you both understand me?

SISTER EVANGELIQUE *(A whisper)* Yes.

FATHER TUYISHIME *(A whisper)* Yes.

BISHOP GAHAMANYI Finally, something you both can agree on.

(Bishop walks out of the door with a wobbly knee. The Sister glares at the Father.)

SISTER EVANGELIQUE Your Excellency, next time you choose to grace us with your lovely presence it will all be settled. Kibeho will soon be quiet.

BISHOP GAHAMANYI Good. Because the roar in the valley is getting rather loud.

Scene 7

Night time. All is quiet. SISTER EVANGELIQUE is walking the corridor with a candle in one hand and her rosary in the other.

SISTER EVANGELIQUE Hail Mary, full of grace, the Lord is with thee; blessed are thou among women, and blessed is the fruit--

(She stops. She tries again.)

SISTER EVANGELIQUE Hail Mary, full of grace, the Lord is with thee; blessed are thou among women--

(She stops. She brings her rosary and puts it on her lap. She cannot pray her rosary. She begins to cry. The door to the girls' dormitory opens. SISTER EVANGELIQUE hurriedly wipes away her tears. A figure appears in the shadows.)

SISTER EVANGELIQUE Who's there?

(The figure does not answer.)

SISTER EVANGELIQUE I said who's there?

MARIE-CLAIRE It is me.

(MARIE-CLAIRE in bare feet walks into the corridor.)

SISTER EVANGELIQUE Why are you not asleep?

MARIE-CLAIRE I need to use the latrines.

SISTER EVANGELIQUE There are buckets in the dormitory.

MARIE-CLAIRE I need my privacy.

SISTER EVANGELIQUE Don't we all.

(They stare at each other. SISTER EVAN-GELIQUE gestures for MARIE-CLAIRE to go ahead. But she doesn't.)

MARIE-CLAIRE You are upset.

SISTER EVANGELIQUE No. Dear child, why would you--

MARIE-CLAIRE Your eyes are blood-red.

SISTER EVANGELIQUE It is just the dust. The red Rwandan dust. Go on. Go ahead.

(Silence.)

SISTER EVANGELIQUE You don't need to use the latrines, do you?

MARIE-CLAIRE No, Sister.

(MARIE-CLAIRE takes SISTER EVAN-GELIQUE'S hand into her own.)

SISTER EVANGELIQUE If only those silly girls knew the consequence of their actions. Bishop Gahamanyi wants to close down Kibeho College because of them.

MARIE-CLAIRE No!

SISTER EVANGELIQUE Yes! Yes, all because of their little stunts.

MARIE-CLAIRE He cannot close the school just because of a few spoiled ground nuts. They cannot stop all of us from going to school. They cannot.

SISTER EVANGELIQUE But they are, Marie. Un-less they stop, they will ruin the dreams of every young girl sleeping in that dormitory. And every mothers', too. I have watched many young girls plucking potatoes from their field, fetching water from the well with many a baby on their back. I have seen many young girls start life with bright eyes only to have them swollen shut by the hand of a man. If only they knew that there was much more to life than being a man's wife. My mother carried me on her back. Never learned to read. Never learned much. Well. I promised myself that I would never be like my mother. Fetching water, sewing, babies...

MARIE-CLAIRE That will not be me, either.

SISTER EVANGELIQUE No, Marie-Claire. Not you. That will not be your life. You are too feisty for that. A man would kill you with that mouth of yours.

(SISTER EVANGELIQUE pinches MARIE-CLAIRE on her cheek.)

SISTER EVANGELIQUE You should go into the nunnery. You'd be a good nun.

MARIE-CLAIRE Like you?

SISTER EVANGELIQUE Like me.

(They sit in silence drinking in the darkness.)

SISTER EVANGELIQUE Next time they want to play their little games. You burn them. *(She smiles to herself.)* That should awaken them from their spell.

MARIE-CLAIRE Burn them?

SISTER EVANGELIQUE Yes, you have my permis-sion. Truth and morning become light with time.

(She blows out the candle.)

(Lights shift.)

Scene 8

Day. MARIE-CLAIRE and her mean-girls are holding court outside in their "cafeteria"-- a tree.

GIRL #1 Today's eggs are soooo horrible.

GIRL #2 I miss my Ma-maa's bitoki.

MARIE-CLAIRE You may not have to miss it for long.

GIRL #2 I will surely be missing it. Holiday isn't for another...wha?...three months until Easter...

GIRL #3 Ugh.

MARIE-CLAIRE Well, those little witches keep on spinning their tales we'll have a holiday sooner than later.

THE GIRLS What do you mean?

MARIE-CLAIRE The Diocese is going to close Kibeho College.

THE GIRLS Nooooo!

MARIE-CLAIRE Yes!!

GIRL #1 But I like it here.

MARIE-CLAIRE I thought you hated the eggs.

GIRL #1 I rather eat these runny eggs than cook a batch for my ugly brothers any day.

GIRL #2 You ever thought it was true?

MARIE-CLAIRE Of course not!

GIRL #3 But it's Anathalie. If it was just weirdo Alphonsine maybe not, but Anathalie, too? Anathalie prays her rosary seven times a day.

MARIE-CLAIRE So?

GIRL #2 She's the most devout of us all...

GIRL #1 If I had her ugly Tutsi teeth I'd be pray-ing the rosary a million times a day.

GIRL #3 Eh-Eh! She Hutu.

GIRL #1 *(Jeering)* Well, she must be mixed then.

GIRL #2 It's Alphonsine who started it all. Tutsi Lying Through Her Teeth Alphonsine. My mother was right. They are all liars. They think the whole world revolves around them. They don't care what they do to hurt other people--

GIRL #3 Yeah...they are...selfish!

GIRL #1 So selfish!

GIRL #3 Yeah...that's what my Da-da said. They think they are better than everyone.

GIRL #1 Smarter.

GIRL #2 Taller!

GIRL #1 Wiser!

GIRL #2 Prettier.

(GIRL #1 and GIRL #3, sucking their teeth, looking at GIRL #2)

GIRL #2 Well...they are.

GIRL #1 No, they're not.

GIRL #2 Eh-eh!! My Da-da said that Tutsi women always have such a pretty face.

GIRL #3 Well, Marie-Claire has a pretty face.

(The girls look at Marie-Claire's face.)

MARIE-CLAIRE What are you saying?

THE GIRLS *(Very quickly)* Nothing.

MARIE-CLAIRE Go get me another plate of eggs. NOOOOWWW!!!

(The worker bees hurriedly fly away to bring back honey for their queen. MARIE-CLAIRE pushes away the food. Actually, she is not very hungry. She eyes ALPHONSINE eating her breakfast quietly beneath another tree. MARIE-CLAIRE walks over to her. ALPHONSINE does not look up.)

ALPHONSINE You can have my eggs if you want.

MARIE-CLAIRE Where is Anathalie?

ALPHONSINE Resting. The first few trips are always very tiring. But she will get used to them--

MARIE-CLAIRE You know not what you do.

ALPHONSINE I am a human being. We never know what we are doing.

MARIE-CLAIRE I hate you and all your "mysterious" talk. You're not so mysterious, Alphonsine. I know you. I know your kind.

ALPHONSINE I bet you do.

MARIE-CLAIRE If I was your father, I'd beat you black and blue--eh-eh, wait, you don't have a father. I heard he divorced your Mama and left you to fend for yourselves. Must have

been a rotten household. She didn't know how to take care of a man. Maybe that's what you're after. A father. A Father Tuyishime.

ALPHONSINE I do not need a father--

MARIE-CLAIRE You crave his attention, don't you?

ALPHONSINE His attention is not the one I crave.

MARIE-CLAIRE Whose attention *do* you crave?

ALPHONSINE Marie-Claire...yours. Do I have it?

(Beat.)

MARIE-CLAIRE You just want everyone to hate you.

ALPHONSINE *(She shrugs)* The speaker of truth has no friends.

MARIE-CLAIRE And the teller of lies is an unfortunate fool. You are hell-bent on dying. If the people from the village hear about this....well....en, henh...

ALPHONSINE *(Chuckles to herself)* I have already been made aware of this. She has told me that and it is fine. I am fine with it. With it all. Truth is not afraid of the machete.

MARIE-CLAIRE So....You want to die?

ALPHONSINE If you had seen the world She's shown me. That could be ours? Well...you'd die for it, too, Marie-Claire.

MARIE-CLAIRE No, I will live out my days and grow old here. In Kibeho. A nun.

ALPHONSINE You? A nun?

MARIE-CLAIRE Yes, I'd make a good one.

ALPHONSINE That you would.

MARIE-CLAIRE Shut up! I've been called!

(MARIE-CLAIRE goes to strike ALPHONSINE, who does not move, does not flinch.)

MARIE-CLAIRE You are not afraid of me? Why?

ALPHONSINE *(She looks at her softly)* Cause we are sisters of the same tribe.

(MARIE-CLAIRE stands stunned. Caught. Does she know?)

MARIE-CLAIRE I am not, and will never be your *sister*.

(ALPHONSINE looks after MARIE-CLAIRE as she stomps away.)

ALPHONSINE *(Watching)* She who leaves truth behind, soon returns to it.

Scene 9

Confession. Dusk makes the light flowing through the stained glass window dance across the red dirt floor. FATHER TUYISHIME is in the confession booth nodding off, slightly snoring. ALPHONSINE enters.

ALPHONSINE Father...Father....FATHER

(*He wakes up with a jolt.*)

ALPHONSINE Father—

FATHER TUYISHIME Alphonsine?

ALPHONSINE Yes, Father it's me.

FATHER TUYISHIME Oh, sorry, my dear child. This coffin has become a bit warm.

ALPHONSINE Don't worry. All the girls say this is the best place for a nap. All warm and cozy.

(*He laughs then takes a deep breath. He stares at her through the scrim.*)

ALPHONSINE Yes, Father?

FATHER TUYISHIME Nothing.

ALPHONSINE I thought you were staring at me because I have not been to confession in so long. How long has it been?

FATHER TUYISHIME About...one month, six days, give or take, more or less, around thereabouts. You've been // busy.

ALPHONSINE Oh, that long.

FATHER TUYISHIME Yes, that long.

ALPHONSINE I'm sorry.

FATHER TUYISHIME As I've said you've been busy....What is on your heart today child?

ALPHONSINE I have much I must // confess.

FATHER TUYISHIME Mmmm.

ALPHONSINE Much I need to say.

FATHER TUYISHIME Mmmmmmmmm.

ALPHONSINE Much I need to release.

FATHER TUYISHIME What has made your heart so heavy, dear child?

ALPHONSINE I am trying to understand this, Father. This mantle that has been placed upon my head. I don't understand it, Father.

FATHER TUYISHIME Neither do I.

ALPHONSINE I am just a dirt poor girl with no shoes, no friends, no father who has not read every word in that Bible and yet She chose me.

FATHER TUYISHIME There are things beyond our control, my dear child.

ALPHONSINE Why did she choose me? I mean, why didn't she choose, Sister Evangelique?

FATHER TUYISHIME We all know why She didn't choose Sister Evangelique.

ALPHONSINE But at least I feel as though people would have listened to her. She is a grown up. She's...(*deepening her voice*) loud...

FATHER TUYISHIME It is much better to be burned by the sun, than by a raging fire, Alphonsine.

ALPHONSINE She tells me things, Father. She wants me to do things. Things a girl is not supposed to do. Things I don't now how to do.

FATHER TUYISHIME What does she tell you Alphonsine?

ALPHONSINE I don't know if I can say.

FATHER TUYISHIME Alphonsine, let your tongue confess.

(*Beat.*)

ALPHONSINE Do you know the President?

FATHER TUYISHIME President Habyarimana?

ALPHONSINE Yes. Do you know him?

FATHER TUYISHIME No, I don't know him I know *of* him.

ALPHONSINE *Of* him?

FATHER TUYISHIME Yes, like every other Rwandan I suppose.

ALPHONSINE Well, She needs me to give him a message.

FATHER TUYISHIME A message? To the President?

ALPHONSINE Yes, I need to give him a message. She says it's important.

FATHER TUYISHIME The Virgin Mary has a message for the President of Rwanda?

ALPHONSINE I know it sounds weird, but--

FATHER TUYISHIME Maybe this booth is indeed a bit too hot. Would you like to step out for a moment, catch a whiff of sanity and then we could // continue?

ALPHONSINE You think I'm lying, again.

FATHER TUYISHIME No, I don't think, you're lying. I think you are...crazy.

ALPHONSINE Father, please--

FATHER TUYISHIME Really Alphonsine, this is all getting to be a bit—

ALPHONSINE She says it's urgent and that if I need to, I should walk from Kibeho to Kigali to get it to him.

FATHER TUYISHIME That's a pretty far walk for a young woman with no shoes.

ALPHONSINE He must know—

FATHER TUYISHIME Know what, Alphonsine?

ALPHONSINE That there is evil lurking in men's hearts. More evil than he has ever known. It is close to him.

FATHER TUYISHIME Alphonsine, this is preposterous.

ALPHONSINE He must, purge it. Purge the madness from men's hearts, Purge it from his own. She says I must get to Kigali and tell him this.

FATHER TUYISHIME But as you say you're but a dirt-poor girl, a Tutsi no less. Do you think a man of his stature would listen to you?

ALPHONSINE *You* listen to me.

FATHER TUYISHIME That is my job.

ALPHONSINE Is that not his, to listen to his people?

FATHER TUYISHIME Depends if it is a message he wants to listen to.

ALPHONSINE But he's the President, he must listen to everything.

FATHER TUYISHIME Which means he tends to listen to nothing at all.

ALPHONSINE Then he is a fool.

FATHER TUYISHIME I concur.

ALPHONSINE She needs him to pray, like She needs *you* to pray.

(ALPHONSINE clamps her hand over her mouth.)

FATHER TUYISHIME Like what, dear child, what?

ALPHONSINE You have not prayed for yourself in eight years, eight months, and 2 days. Ever since--

FATHER TUYISHIME How do you know that Alphonsine?

(Silence.)

FATHER TUYISHIME HOW DO YOU KNOW?

ALPHONSINE She told me.

(ALPHONSINE reaches her hand across the divide. FATHER TUYISHIME does not touch her.)

ALPHONSINE I'm sorry for your sorrow.

FATHER TUYISHIME Has it been that long since….

ALPHONSINE Our Lady says your mother was beautiful.

FATHER TUYISHIME Oh, Alphonsine she was. Mama used to wear purple flowers in her hair. She would never let me have all the porridge in the pot. She would say say, "always leave something at the bottom for the ancestors." Such a giving woman, beautiful woman. Slaughtered. Like a goat. 1973. When your president, President Habyarimana overthrew President Kayibanda. When the world changed…

ALPHONSINE Was your mama like me?

FATHER TUYISHIME Yes, she was Tutsi like you.

ALPHONSINE Have you cried lately, Father Tuyishime?

FATHER TUYISHIME No, Alphonsine…I cannot cry…

ALPHONSINE Well…a man's tears fall into his stomach.

FATHER TUYISHIME Ah, so that is why I'm always sooo full.

ALPHONSINE You must get out of this coffin. Come into the sunlight.

FATHER TUYISHIME Alphonsine your laugh is all the sunlight I need.

(She laughs.)

ALPHONSINE Come outside. The Son awaits you.

(Lights shift.)

Scene 10

Soon after.

SISTER EVANGELIQUE goes to the well to fill her jerrican with water. EMMANUEL, a young boy, has a baby tied to his back He has on ragged clothing. No shoes.

SISTER EVANGELIQUE You do not belong here. Get off the premises. No vagabonds allowed.

EMMANUEL How come you're here?

SISTER EVANGELIQUE Sa, you little runt!

EMMANUEL Sorry, sorry.

SISTER EVANGELIQUE No begging. This is a school not a bank. We have no francs for you.

EMMANUEL Please, Sister. My little sister and I have the "sickness."

SISTER EVANGELIQUE The sickness, eh?

EMMANUEL My parents. Both died of the "sickness."

SISTER EVANGELIQUE *(Softening)* Eeehhhhhh.

(She looks around then digs into her pocket and presents some coins.)

EMMANUEL This is all you have?

SISTER EVANGELIQUE Sisterhood doesn't pay very much.

(The sounds of singing can be heard coming in the distance.)

SISTER EVANGELIQUE What? What is that sound?

EMMANUEL Sounds sweet doesn't it?

SISTER EVANGELIQUE I've never heard that song before…

EMMANUEL The village made it up. For the girls.

SISTER EVANGELIQUE For the girls?

EMMANUEL The girls who have favor with the Virgin.

SISTER EVANGELIQUE Who told you that?

EMMANUEL The village is vibrating with the good news. Isn't it good news? Mama Mary. Here. In Kibeho? We've come to see the miracle.

SISTER EVANGELIQUE There are no miracles here.

(There is singing coming far from the hills in Kinyarwanda.)

EMMANUEL We've all come to see the girls who see.

(The singing is growing louder and louder and louder.)

EMMANUEL Is that one of them?

SISTER EVANGELIQUE Yes...

(He looks to ALPHONSINE who is standing beneath a tree. She waves to him.)

EMMANUEL Look at that light around her.

SISTER EVANGELIQUE Yes, there is a light.

EMMANUEL Look at her glowing. Just look at her.

(ALPHONSINE actually does begin to glow. It begins to blind her. The tree that ALPHONSINE was standing beneath begins to move and sway as if a great wind is moving in, but ALPHONSINE stands there unmoved.)

EMMANUEL I need to touch her.

(Her light grows brighter.)

SISTER EVANGELIQUE I...I...can't see...my eyes are burning....

(The sound coming up the hill sounds beautiful, rising like a wave coming to break over the school. ALPHONSINE is bathed in a beautiful light. She looks upward.)

VILLAGER 1 Where are they?

VILLAGER 2 (A BLIND MAN) My feet hurt.

VILLAGER 3 Quit complaining.

VILLAGER 1 The girls better be here.

VILLAGER 2 (A BLIND MAN) These girls are just lying.

VILLAGER 3 I should have left you home in bed. This man of mine. Always so negative.

VILLAGER 2 (A BLIND MAN) Woman, just hold my hand.

VILLAGER 3 You are!

VILLAGER 2 (A BLIND MAN) I'm here just in case.

VILLAGER 1 Just in case?

VILLAGER 2 Just in case this is real---

EMMANUEL I want to touch her. She's glowing.

SISTER EVANGELIQUE Don't! Don't go over there! She might burn you!!

(The singing is getting louder and louder.)

VILLAGER 1 Who is that girl talking to?

VILLAGER 3 Where?

VILLAGER 1 See her! See her over there!

EMMANUEL Look at that light around her. I need to touch her. Me and my baby sister. We got the "sickness."

(The singing gets louder and louder. A crowd is coming closer.)

EMMANUEL Please let me touch your light.

(The noon sun, hanging high in the sky begins to dance across the aqua blue of the day. ALPHONSINE raises her hands to the sun. It splits in half and starts dancing around her finger tips. Rainbows stream from her finger tips. The crowd has stopped singing, stunned into silence. Another sun pops out from behind the first. And it too splits in half, it is a sky with four suns spinning round and round. A sky with four suns has the light of 4 universes, but the light is not blinding, it's warm. A cloud parts and there is a face. A slight face. Something. Lips moving. EMMANUEL starts crying.)

EMMANUEL See it! In the sky!!

(The cloud suddenly begins to swirl like a tornado. The winds start blowing again.)

SISTER EVANGELIQUE Where?

EMMANUEL In the sky. Mama Mary's in the sky!!!

(There is a swirl of clouds. A faint figure can be seen. But as soon as it appears it is disappeared by the sky.)

Scene 11

Night. The girls' dorm. SISTER EVANGELIQUE is walking past. The girls are all abuzz discussing what happened just hours before.

SISTER EVANGELIQUE If you do not go to bed now every bottom in here will be feeling the licks of Father Tuyishime's cane.

(The girls look at each other in even more excitement.)

GIRL #3 But Sister Evangelique—

SISTER EVANGELIQUE But nothing. Finish up. Then Go. To. BED.

GIRL #3 But we just can't get it out of our minds.

GIRL #4 Speak for yourself...

(GIRL #3 imitating the sun.)

GIRL #3 The sun danced with us. It split in half again and again and then it danced with us. Sister, didn't you see it?

SISTER EVANGELIQUE *(Totes lying)* See what?

GIRL #4 I didn't see it either.

GIRL #3 It is because you are a heathen.

GIRL #4 Are you calling Sister Evangelique a heathen, too?

(SISTER EVANGELIQUE gives GIRL #3 the I'ma-beat-yo-ass- right-now look.)

GIRL #3 *(Stammering)* No-no-no-no that-that is not what I meant.

SISTER EVANGELIQUE Everyone finish your wash up. Then get to bed. I don't want to say it again

(Just then ALPHONSINE and ANATH-ALIE enter with the other girls. Everyone ignores SISTER EVANGELIQUE. They are drying their hair off, fresh from their showers. The other girls tend to them. Taking away their towels, their basins, their soaps. SISTER EVANGELIQUE glowers then goes....)

GIRL #1 Oh. My. Goodness. You made the sun spin.

GIRL #3 You are so cool. Kwela

GIRL #1 I mean, WOW! You made the sun spin.

GIRL #2 That was just--WHOA.

ALPHONSINE I didn't make the sun spin. It was She.

GIRL #1 Whatever you did it was the most amazing thing ever. Oh, my God.

GIRL #2 Ah-ah! You are breaking a commandment—

GIRL #1 Eeeeh.

(GIRL #1 makes the sign of the cross and does a Hail Mary.)

GIRL #2 Tell us, tell us what She said again.

THE GIRLS Yes, tell us! Tell us!

ANATHALIE And She says that young women must be chaste in spirit and chaste of heart.

GIRL #1 I don't know how much longer I can do that with Father Tuyishime around.

GIRL #2 Me neither...

(The girls do a little handshake.)

ANATHALIE She says that we should not use our bodies as instruments of pleasure. True love comes from God. Instead of being at the service of God, we have been at the service of men, but we must make of our bodies instruments destined to the glory of God.

GIRL #3 Speak plainly, Anathalie.

ANATHALIE Keep your legs closed!

THE GIRLS Ooooooooo!

(MARIE-CLAIRE walks in with a soccer ball. She is athletic and lithe, kicking the ball with her slender leg. She catches it on the back of her head.)

MARIE-CLAIRE Anyone wanna play futbol with me?

GIRL #1 Sister Evangelique doesn't like it when we play inside.

GIRL #2 Yes, Marie-Claire.

MARIE-CLAIRE What, you two don't wanna play with me, now?

GIRL #2 *(Ignoring her)* And then she said we should be pious, right?

ANATHALIE She says we must be pious.

MARIE-CLAIRE No one wants to play a quick game?

THE GIRLS NOOO!

GIRL #3 Marie-Claire, did you see Alphonsine make the sun spin?

MARIE-CLAIRE I heard about it.

GIRL #3 *(Sighing)* It was soooooooooo amazing.

GIRL #4 Ah-ah! I don't believe it.

MARIE-CLAIRE Me neither. It is rainy season ya know.

GIRL #4 For true!

MARIE-CLAIRE For true!

(MARIE-CLAIRE kicks the ball around. She sees the entire dorm kowtowing to her enemies. She sets up the ball as if she's about to kick it into to play. She sends it flying right into the crowd of the girls. It hits somebody—probably ANATHALIE—in the head.)

GIRL #2 Marie-Claire!

MARIE-CLAIRE Ooops!

(MARIE-CLAIRE and GIRL #4 laugh.)

(MARIE-CLAIRE retrieves the ball from the corner and comes back to the middle of the dorm, bouncing it on her foot and then bouncing it on her knee.)

GIRL #1 Why do you play around so much?

ALPHONSINE Are you okay, Anathalie?

(ANATHALIE picks up her glasses that have fallen off.)

ANATHALIE Marie-Claire, you do not have to resort to such nastiness. I am still your friend--

MARIE-CLAIRE Friend? No friend of mine would link arms with the likes of her. What, you could not stand for Alphonsine to have all the attention?

ANATHALIE No, Marie-Claire I think that is you.

MARIE-CLAIRE Ah! Attention garnered in the wake of lying is attention I do not need. You are insane, following this knappy-headed heathen through the gates of hell. You both are going to rot for these lies.

ANATHALIE You just go ahead and sit high and mighty on your pedestal of judgment Marie-Claire. You may be my best friend, but Mother Mary is not a friend worth losing for a nonbeliever.

MARIE-CLAIRE Nonbeliever?

(MARIE-CLAIRE comes up to ANATH-ALIE to rough her up, but ANATHALIE this time decides to fight back. The girls are utterly shocked at ANATHALIE'S ferocity. Almost like she's become a new woman.)

ANATHALIE Look, Marie-Claire, I'm tired of your shit!

THE GIRLS Oooooooooo! She said shit! Shit! She's tired of your shit!

ALPHONSINE Anathalie, do not be pulled into her despair.

ANATHALIE As long as she doesn't pull another one of her pranks out of her dirty knickers.

MARIE-CLAIRE I don't have dirty knickers.

ANATHALIE That's right, you don't have any!

THE GIRLS Oooooooooooooo!

(An embarrassed MARIE-CLAIRE, feeling her power dwindling, takes aim and sends the ball flying into the group of girls yet again. MARIE-CLAIRE doubles over laughing. SISTER EVANGELIQUE appears at the door of the girls' dormitory.)

SISTER EVANGELIQUE That is enough Marie-Claire!!! What did I tell you about playing with that ball in here!!!!

(All the girls scatter-scatter and run to their beds.)

SISTER EVANGELIQUE Lights out! And put that damn ball up before I burn it!

(SISTER EVANGELIQUE slams the door. And the girls giggle and giggle. They are giggling.)

SISTER EVANGELIQUE *(Off stage.)* What. Did. I. Say?

(Silence.)

(MARIE-CLAIRE once again throws her ball at the girls, but the ball becomes frozen in air as if caught by an invisible hand. ANATHALIE and ALPHONSINE'S beds are bathed in the most gorgeous light, like a supernova, like the light of every star God ever made. Their bodies writhe as they are bathed in the brilliance.)

GIRL #1 Oh my God!

GIRL #2 What is going on?

GIRL #3 They are doing it again.

MARIE-CLAIRE I'm so sick and tired of this!

(MARIE-CLAIRE pushes a girl off the bed.)

MARIE-CLAIRE Hand me that candle!

GIRL #4 Where?

MARIE-CLAIRE Right there! Right there!!

(The girl runs and retrieves the candle.)

GIRL #1 Marie-Claire! Why are you doing this? Why?

(MARIE-CLAIRE takes the candle and places it beneath ALPHONSINE'S right arm. Smoke emits as fire meets flesh, but ALPHONSINE is so entranced she doesn't feel the burn...)

MARIE-CLAIRE What in the hell's name...

ALPHONSINE *(To the Virgin Mary)* I'm being burned?

(ALPHONSINE moves her left arm out of the way. MARIE-CLAIRE stands there stunned as ALPHONSINE refuses to move her right arm-- the one that is being burned. ALPHONSINE finally removes the other arm. MARIE-CLAIRE drops the candle in fear.)

MARIE-CLAIRE Sister Evangelique! Sister Evangelique they are doing it again.

GIRL #1 Oh, my god!! Look at their eyes. They are rolling into the back of their heads.

GIRL #3 It is a possession!

GIRL #4 I want to go home! This school is overrun by demons. I want to go home, I need to go home, I want to go home--

ALPHONSINE I care not about this world. I only want to speak your truth.

MARIE-CLAIRE Sister Evangelique!!

GIRL #3 Oh, my God! Look at their eyes.

MARIE-CLAIRE Sister Evangelique!!!

(SISTER EVANGELIQUE bursts in.)

SISTER EVANGELIQUE What did I tell all of you? Go. To—

MARIE-CLAIRE Sister Evangelique look at them!

ALPHONSINE She says we must pray.

(Those girls who believe get their rosaries out and begin to pray…)

THE GIRLS Our Father which are // in heaven….

GIRL #3 I'm scared. I'm scared. // They're scaring me.

GIRL #1 Shhh and just pray. Do as she says!!

ALPHONSINE AND ANATHALIE We must pray.

MARIE-CLAIRE Sister Evangelique! Look at them.

SISTER EVANGELIQUE No no no no no no no, my dear children. Don't be fooled.

(The dormitory is filled with prayer.)

ALPHONSINE AND ANATHALIE She said we must pray for the sins of man.

(A soft voice comes riding in on the wind. Buttery and sweet. It slides through the chaos like smoke and embraces the biggest unbeliever of them all…)

MARIE-CLAIRE What? Who is this?

(MARIE-CLAIRE looks up to see ANATHALIE and ALPHONSINE.)

MARIE-CLAIRE Anathalie! Alphonsine! You are playing tricks on me! You are playing tricks.

(But they are too busy looking up into the sky. Their mouths are not moving. MARIE-CLAIRE buckles over as if she's about to vomit.)

MARIE-CLAIRE I am feeling faint—

SISTER EVANGELIQUE Marie-Claire—

(MARIE-CLAIRE turns around and takes a swing. She almost punches SISTER EVANGELIQUE straight in the jaw. SISTER EVANGELIQUE lurches back.)

SISTER EVANGELIQUE Marie-Claire!

MARIE-CLAIRE Stop calling my name! Stop calling my name!

(She continues to swing.)

MARIE-CLAIRE No, I'm not. I'm NOT!!

(MARIE-CLAIRE frantically looks about the room.)

MARIE-CLAIRE *(Under her breath)* I'm…I'm going crazy. I'm going crazy. Noooo. This is all a dream a dream a dream a dream a dream a dream a dream a dream a dream a dream. *(Screaming at the top of her lungs)* GET OUT OF ME!! GET OUT OF MY HEAD!! I AM NOT CRAZY. I AM NOT CRAZY. NOT LIKE THEM. NOT LIKE THEM. PLEASE, GOD! I DON'T WANT TO BE LIKE THEM. NOT LIKE THEM!!

(She starts beating herself in the head. Punching at the air, trying to knock Our Lady out. Our Lady slaps her in the face. MARIE-CLAIRE doubles over.)

MARIE-CLAIRE *(Orgasmic)* It feels like butter melting in my belly.

(MARIE-CLAIRE is taken over by the rapture. Her toes curl and her body shakes and quakes.)

SISTER EVANGELIQUE You are having a seizure! She is having a seizure! Father Tuyishime! Help! Help!!

(SISTER EVANGELIQUE runs out into the hallway.)

MARIE-CLAIRE What is this? What is happening to me?

(She continues to quake. And pulse. Then suddenly. ALPHONSINE and ANATHALIE rise into the air! The girls start screaming at the two flying above their heads!)

MARIE-CLAIRE *(Moaning)* Yessssss-- I can feel you.

(SISTER EVANGELIQUE runs back in from the hallway. She screams!)

MARIE-CLAIRE Yessssss-- I can touch you.

(MARIE-CLAIRE reaches her hands out! SISTER EVANGELIQUE stands stunned at the scene…)

SISTER EVANGELIQUE Marie-Claire! You, too?

MARIE-CLAIRE YES!!!!

(MARIE-CLAIRE looks up and she is bathed in Our Lady's light. Her body slackens. And she is hoisted far above the heads of everyone, joining ANATHALIE and ALPHONSINE in the sky. The trinity is now complete. The girls are screaming. They are scrambling. But someone or something has locked the door. They cannot get out. There is nowhere to run. Nowhere to hide. They hang like clouds. Three big bangs occur. The bed ALPHONSINE floats above breaks in half. The bed ANATHALIE floats above breaks in half. The bed MARIE-CLAIRE floats above breaks in half.)

(Blackout.)

End of Act One

★

ACT TWO

Scene 1

Six months later.
FATHER TUYISHIME'S office.

FATHER TUYISHIME sits at his desk.
FATHER FLAVIA, an Italian priest, sits opposite.
A group of girls are outside the door whispering:

THE GIRLS *(Sotto voce)* It's Jesus! Jesus…Come here. Look! It's Jesus! Jesus!

FATHER TUYISHIME Father Flavia, I'm so glad you could make it.

THE GIRLS *(Getting louder)* It's Jesus! It's Jesus! Muzungu! Muzungu Jesus!

FATHER TUYISHIME Sa!

(FATHER TUYISHIME shooes them away. The girls run, but their excited whispers can still be heard down the corridor.)

THE GIRLS *(Sotto voce)* It's Jesus! It's Jesus!

FATHER FLAVIA They are very excitable.

FATHER TUYISHIME They act like they're never seen a white man before. Forgive them, please.

FATHER FLAVIA They are forgiven.

FATHER TUYISHIME Would you like some water?

FATHER FLAVIA Would love.

FATHER TUYISHIME It's not holy, but it'll have to do.

(FATHER TUYISHIME fills a can of water. FATHER FLAVIA accepts, but does not drink. Beat. Looking deep into the cup inspecting it…)

FATHER FLAVIA If only I could turn water into wine.

(He knocks it back.)

FATHER TUYISHIME Father Flavia, I hope the trip has not been too rough for you.

FATHER FLAVIA Ah, the plane ride was fine. Rome to Addis Ababa then Kigali. But the road to Kibeho…

FATHER TUYISHIME *(Laughing)*…is not a road.

(Fanning himself:)

FATHER FLAVIA --It's a bumpy spiral staircase up a very huge hill.

FATHER TUYISHIME A hill that stops at Heaven's doorstep.

(FATHER TUYISHIME points out the window.)

FATHER TUYISHIME Look at that view. They call it the Switzerland of Africa.

FATHER FLAVIA Who says that?

FATHER TUYISHIME There is a saying in our country, Rwanda is so beautiful that even God goes on vacation here.

FATHER FLAVIA He might vacation in Rwanda, but always remember He lives in Rome.

FATHER TUYISHIME I see…We are glad that someone from the Vatican has taken the time to grace Kibeho with a papal presence.

FATHER FLAVIA Eh, Well, the Pope was too busy soo…

(They burst into laughter.)

FATHER TUYISHIME It is a joy to see these young women confirmed. Validated—

FATHER FLAVIA Validated?

FATHER TUYISHIME Why, yes, is not your role here but to validate?

FATHER FLAVIA I am only here to be the Church's eyes and ears. I could never validate, just gather the evidence.

FATHER TUYISHIME Surely we must be valid enough if you've come this far. We must be important if you are here to be the Church's eyes and ears as you say.

FATHER FLAVIA Surely you are not so naive as to think that. The validations of apparitions must carry with them the weight of remarkable evidence and three broken beds in a girls' dormitory in Rwanda does not remarkable evidence make.

FATHER TUYISHIME So you are not here to prove them right but rather to prove them wrong?

FATHER FLAVIA I should have been a lawyer.

FATHER TUYISHIME But it happened.

FATHER FLAVIA Were you there? Were you a witness?

FATHER TUYISHIME No, but were you there when Jesus was crucified?

FATHER FLAVIA I'm not that old, Father.

FATHER TUYISHIME Well, some things do not need to be seen in order to believed.

(SISTER EVANGELIQUE appears at the door.)

SISTER EVANGELIQUE And yet some do. I had to see for myself if the Son had come down from Heaven *(chuckling to herself)* Jesus, indeed.

(The two men look towards the door to see SISTER EVANGELIQUE towering.)

FATHER TUYISHIME Rumors spread fast here.

SISTER EVANGELIQUE If only I could say the same for truth.

FATHER TUYISHIME Father Flavia is on special assignment from the Holy See.

SISTER EVANGELIQUE First time I am hearing about this special visit from our friends at the Vatican. Wish the deputy head nun would have been informed of such a special visitor to Kibeho College.

(FATHER FLAVIA holds out his hand to SISTER EVANGELIQUE.)

FATHER FLAVIA And you must be that deputy head nun.

SISTER EVANGELIQUE Let us not concern ourselves with such silly little titles, just call me *Sister* Evangelique. I am just glad that per my suggestion someone is here to investigate these girls.

FATHER FLAVIA What do you think of these… occurrences?

(SISTER EVANGELIQUE looks to FATHER TUYISHIME for approval to speak. He gives it.)

SISTER EVANGELIQUE Me? I am not of the same mind as my superior here.

FATHER FLAVIA *(To FATHER TUYISHIME)* So you believe the visions are real?

FATHER TUYISHIME I don't know if I believe they are real…I just…I just hope they are.

FATHER FLAVIA Hoping and believing are two different things, Father Tuyishime.

FATHER TUYISHIME Cannot have belief without hope that what you are believing is true.

FATHER FLAVIA *(Smiling)* I'll drink to that. When was the last "vision" as you call it?

FATHER TUYISHIME The Virgin Mary has been coming frequently, visiting with the girls since the dorm incident six months ago. But that incident was perhaps the most expressive of them. The girls flew into the sky like crested cranes. After which their beds rose and buckled mid-flight. Sister Evangelique saw it even though she will not admit….

SISTER EVANGELIQUE 'Til this day I know not the heathens who hoisted them into the sky.

FATHER FLAVIA So you were the only witness?

FATHER TUYISHIME Other girls saw it, too –

(With a wave of her hand--)

SISTER EVANGELIQUE They were suffering from hysteria.

FATHER FLAVIA As young girls are wont to do.

FATHER TUYISHIME *(To SISTER EVANGELIQUE)* And what about you? Where you suffering from hysteria?

SISTER EVANGELIQUE I was suffering from trickery. If I could go back to that night and smoke out the culprit who helped them work their magic trick, I would.

FATHER TUYISHIME I know your girls are strong and all, lifting and balancing jerricans atop their heads for hours at a time, but certainly they cannot have lifted themselves and their beds with their minds.

SISTER EVANGELIQUE Would you rather they have been possessed by the devil? If they are not lying, which let us hope to God they are, then surely it was the devil himself that entered those girls.

FATHER FLAVIA *(Agreeing)* Truth be told, it sounds more like a possession.

FATHER TUYISHIME I have performed an exorcism before. This was no such thing. The room smelled like jasmine on a misty morning for weeks. In fact, the girls have turned the dormitory into a chapel, eh--a shrine! Stacked the broken beds and surrounded it with fruits for the Virgin to eat. No, no, no… The devil did not enter these gates of Kibeho.

SISTER EVANGELIQUE But you were not there. *I* was there. Me. And what I saw were three girls shaking hands with the devil. Father Flavia, I hope you find what you have come here for, which are three lying little blaspheming snots--

FATHER TUYISHIME Sister--

SISTER EVANGELIQUE Excuse me, I must go pray. You will find me in the chapel if you need me.

(SISTER EVANGELIQUE swiftly excuses herself.)

FATHER FLAVIA Oh, my. She would fit in splendidly at the Holy See.

FATHER TUYISHIME Yes, her habit is steeped in the perfume of skepticism.

FATHER FLAVIA Smells divine.

FATHER TUYISHIME No, what is divine is that there have been continuing occurrences … miracles happening.

FATHER FLAVIA Miracles? Here?

FATHER TUYISHIME Yes, there seems to be such a thing. The girls say *Nyina wa Jambo* wants them--

FATHER FLAVIA Nina-who-wha?

FATHER TUYISHIME (Enunciating loudly and slowly) *Nyina wa Jambo.* That is what the girls say She calls herself. "Mother of the Word."

FATHER FLAVIA So the Virgin Mary speaks--

FATHER TUYISHIME Kinyarwanda.

FATHER FLAVIA Well, she certainly knows how to get to all of her children.

FATHER TUYISHIME Indeed. In fact, She wants the girls to start having weekly presentations with the people of the village. Spread her message "like seeds on a flower bed," She says.

(Beat. FATHER FLAVIA *takes this all in.*)

FATHER FLAVIA Do you know what a precession is, Father?

FATHER TUYISHIME When someone dies we have one.

FATHER FLAVIA No, Father that is a procession, I said *precession.*

FATHER TUYISHIME Is this something I should know about it?

FATHER FLAVIA The world is round, correct?

FATHER TUYISHIME That is what I've been told.

FATHER FLAVIA The world revolves on an axis and every 25,800 years supposedly the earth wobbles on it axis. It's called precession. When it happens the constellations in the night sky change. The North Star is no longer the North Star. True north points to some other star. We are due for another wobble in about, oh, 18,274 years.

FATHER TUYISHIME I do not understand why this of importance to the girls, // Father Flavia.

FATHER FLAVIA Do you believe in God, Father Tuyishime?

(Pause.)

FATHER TUYISHIME Of course. Don't you?

FATHER FLAVIA Of course, of course….but sometimes I wonder if God made the stars or if the stars made Him.

FATHER TUYISHIME Are you man of the cloth or a man of scientist?

FATHER FLAVIA (Smiling) Both. I have traveled all over the world to suss out the truth of

these happenings. Our Lady has shown Her face in Portugal. In Italy, quite naturally, even in the mountains of India, but never, ever in the jungles of Africa.

FATHER TUYISHIME Well, this is not a jungle, Father.

FATHER FLAVIA I beg your pardon, Father?

FATHER TUYISHIME Rwanda is not the jungle.

FATHER FLAVIA Could have fooled me. We are about to embark on a long journey, my dear friend. Confirmations are indeed a long and arduous process….Where can I wash my hands? I hope you don't mind, but I would like to start the tests as soon as possible.

FATHER TUYISHIME Tests what tests?

FATHER FLAVIA Liturgical, psychological, medical- that is all. It is what we at the Holy See re- quire for the Congregation's archive. Mini- mum. Where are the girls?

FATHER TUYISHIME Follow me.

(FATHER FLAVIA *stands up from his chair.* FATHER TUYISHIME *begins to lead him out of the office, but then he stops* FATHER FLAVIA.)

FATHER TUYISHIME I must warn you. She said something to them. To one girl espe- cially. She has a message. A message for the president.

FATHER FLAVIA A message for the President? Of Rwanda? Does she have a message for the Pope as well?

FATHER TUYISHIME Well, actually—

(FATHER TUYISHIME *passes him a sheet of paper.* FATHER FLAVIA *reads it.*)

FATHER FLAVIA Oh, my.

FATHER TUYISHIME Of course she'd like to tell you herself.

FATHER FLAVIA Of course, of course…let's see if the world is indeed wobbling.

Scene 2

The girls sit in the courtyard cafeteria, eating lunch. ALPHONSINE, ANATHALIE, and now MARIE-CLAIRE sit at a table all their own. The other girls look at them in awe.

MARIE-CLAIRE I hope Father Tuyishime's ser- mon is better than last week.

ANATHALIE His face is sermon enough. Takes me to heaven for the hour. His tongue just ruins it.

MARIE-CLAIRE Anathalie, you are going to hell. Straight to hell.

ANATHALIE *(With a smirk on her lips)* Well, see you there.

(GIRL #1 walks, up the Trinity.)

GIRL #1 Marie-Claire, can you bless my rosary?

MARIE-CLAIRE Of course, dear child.

(MARIE-CLAIRE commences to blessing…. Suddenly FATHER TUYISHIME and FATHER FLAVIA come into the courtyard.)

THE GIRLS *(Giggling sotto voce)* Jesus. It's Jesus…

MARIE-CLAIRE Well, if it isn't the *muzungu*…

ANATHALIE She said the trials will come

ALPHONSINE Well, let them start. This is all par for the course.

ANATHALIE *I'm* ready, Alphonsine, but something tells me he may grade more harshly than even Sister Evangelique…

FATHER TUYISHIME And there they are. The fighter, Marie-Claire Mukangango. Name means "Woman." To her right Anathalie Mukamazimpaka--

FATHER FLAVIA Mukamizima--whaaaa?

FATHER TUYISHIME Mukamazimpaka-- means "One who brings peace," and the first one, the genesis, Alphonsine Mumureke, "Leave her alone, she speaks the truth."

(Looking at them is like staring directly at the sun and not being blinded. FATHER FLAVIA cannot break his gaze.)

FATHER FLAVIA A trinity. Gotta love God. Always works in threes.

FATHER TUYISHIME That is what the villagers have begun to call them! They have been slaughtering goats daily for the girls. Please, come and have some.

FATHER FLAVIA Would love.

(FATHER FLAVIA walks past the school girls who part to make way for the white man.)

THE GIRLS *(Flirting)* Jesus. Hey, Jesus!

FATHER TUYISHIME *(To the other girls in Kinyarwanda)* How many times do I have to tell you! *Ni kangaha ngomba kubabgira!* *(To the Trinity)* Girls, please meet—

THE TRINITY Father Flavia

FATHER FLAVIA Well, the wind certainly has wings here.

FATHER TUYISHIME He's here to—

THE TRINITY We know

ALPHONSINE *She* has told us.

FATHER FLAVIA *She*? Father, can I speak with the girls, privately?

(They look around to see everyone staring.)

FATHER TUYISHIME There are no walls here.

FATHER FLAVIA I just think it would be better, if I got acquainted with the girls. A bit. By myself.

FATHER TUYISHIME Surely, anything you need to ask can be--

ALPHONSINE Father Tuyishime, it is fine.

(Pause)

FATHER TUYISHIME Fine, but please make it quick. The girls have mass soon.

(FATHER TUYISHIME haltingly walks away and joins SISTER EVANGELIQUE standing on the other side of the courtyard.)

MARIE-CLAIRE *(To Flavia)* Please ask as many questions you want.

ANATHALIE We can answer a million if need be. Anything to miss ma--

ALPHONSINE Anathalie!

FATHER FLAVIA *(Surprised)* Mmph. How splendid that I can understand you. Your French is *magnifique*.

MARIE-CLAIRE *(In Kinyarwanda)* Unfortunately, yours sounds like a pig giving birth. *Icayawe cyumvikana nk' ingurube ibyara.*

FATHER FLAVIA What did she say?

ALPHONSINE Only that we all should be thankful for your compliment.

FATHER FLAVIA *(Mmmmhmmm)* May I sit?

MARIE-CLAIRE *(All smiles now)* Well, what are you two waiting for? Make room for the man. Anathalie, Alphonsine.

(MARIE-CLAIRE, forever the Queen Bee, swats at them to make room. She instantly turns into the cultural ambassador of the group.)

MARIE-CLAIRE We heard that you have come here to test us.

ALPHONSINE Marie-Claire, you really do not have any, manners about, yourself?

FATHER FLAVIA You, indeed, get right to the point.

MARIE-CLAIRE Well, the day after tomorrow belongs to the fool. Mother Mary told us you were coming.

FATHER FLAVIA Did *She*? And what else did *She* say?

(The girls giggle amongst themselves.)

MARIE-CLAIRE *(Coy)* Wouldn't you like to know. What questions can we answer for you?

(Taking out his pad of paper.)

FATHER FLAVIA The Holy See requires that a visionary's spiritual knowledge be in compliance with Church doctrine.

(ALPHONSINE looks to her counterparts to translate.)

MARIE- CLAIRE Alphonsine, what he means is that he wants to know if we are good little Catholic school girls. Isn't that right, Father Flavia?

FATHER FLAVIA Indeed.

(He brings out his notebook.)

FATHER FLAVIA Where is Mary buried?

MARIE-CLAIRE She was not buried. She was *assumed,* body and soul into heaven.

FATHER FLAVIA Good. Anathalie, is God the Holy Spirit?

ANATHALIE Yes, Father.

FATHER FLAVIA The Son?

ANATHALIE Yes.

FATHER FLAVIA Is the Father the Son?

ANATHALIE No, Father.

FATHER FLAVIA Alphonsine…Alphonsine

ALPHONSINE Yes. Yes…My answer is yes.

FATHER FLAVIA But I haven't even asked the question yet?

MARIE-CLAIRE *(Barking in Kinyarwanda)* Alphonsine, you idiot. Get it together. *Alphonsine gichuchu itonde.*

ALPHONSINE *(In Kinyarwanda)* Sorry. Sorry. *Mbabarira. Mbabarira. (In English)* What is the question?

FATHER FLAVIA Are God, the Son, and the Holy Spirit one?

(Pause.)

ALPHONSINE Nooooo.

MARIE-CLAIRE *(In Kinyarwanda)* Alphonsine, the answer is yes. *Alponsine, igisubizo ni yego.*

ALPHONSINE *(In Kinyarwanda)* What? This white man is confusing me. *Iki? Uyu muzungu ari kun vanga.*

MARIE-CLAIRE *(In Kinyarwanda)* That is what he's supposed to do. Do you want to be a visionary or not? *Nibyo agomba gukora, ushaka kuba umu visioneri cyangwa?*

ALPHONSINE *(In Kinyarwanda)* I don't want it as bad as you do. *Simbi shaka nkawe.*

ANATHALIE *(In Kinyarwanda)* Shut up, both you, right now! *Mwebi muziba nonaha!*

(MARIE-CLAIRE jeers towards ANATHALIE. She then sharply turns to FATHER FLAVIA.)

MARIE-CLAIRE Knowing the answers to your little questions is not what makes us visionaries. It is She. We do not need your approval.

FATHER FLAVIA If you want to be a visionary, my approval is what you need most.

MARIE-CLAIRE These other girls might joke that you are Jesus, but you are not Him, so do no walk around as such.

FATHER FLAVIA Indeed that is very true, Marie. But I can't help but wonder why Mother Mary would pick young girls who do not know simple basic liturgy. Furthermore, why she would choose someone with such a nasty disposition…

MARIE-CLAIRE Well, God works in mysterious ways.

ALPHONSINE Please give me another question. Let me answer another—

(FATHER FLAVIA slaps his notebook closed.)

FATHER FLAVIA No, no no we are done…for now…

(FATHER FLAVIA gets up just as the bell rings. The bell rings. FATHER FLAVIA walks away.)

SISTER EVANGELIQUE Everyone, time to head to the chapel. Now.

ANATHALIE Why did you have to chase the *muzungu* away? Now we have to go to mass.

MARIE-CLAIRE I wouldn't have had to, if Alphonsine didn't have the brain of a gecko.

ALPHONSINE Sorry, sorry…

ANATHALIE Oh well, if I fall asleep no one will know. *(Indicating her glasses)* That's the great thing about these thick things, don't you think so, Alphonsine? Alphonsine…

(But ALPHONSINE is oblivious, looking far into the distance as the winds begin to blow. A warmth fills the space, like dinner rolls baking in an oven.)

MARIE-CLAIRE She's here. *Nyina wa Jambo--*

(The TRINITY are suddenly brought to their knees staring in the same direction as before. High above their heads. A mad hush envelopes the air. All the other girls grow quiet and surround them.)

GIRL #2 Look how they stare at the sun as if they are staring into darkness.

GIRL #3 Move over. I want to be closer.

(They are steadfast and rapt, their unblinking eyes seared to a vision upward. MARIE-CLAIRE in trance mode is pitch perfect. They sing in melodic harmony.)

THE TRINITY *(In Kinyarwanda)* Mary, Mother of Peace. It is you who all Christians cherish *Mariya mubyeyi mwiza w' amahoro. Ni wow'ab-akristu bose bakunda* We pray to you mother of God intercede for us before Jesus *Tu rak-wambaza mutoni w'imana du haki rw'iteka kuri Yezu*

(More and more girls place their rosary into MARIE-CLAIRE'S hands until she has a mountain dangling from her arms. FATHER FLAVIA slowly walks up to ALPHONSINE staring at the heavens.)

FATHER TUYISHIME Finally, these girls will be confirmed.

SISTER EVANGELIQUE Enh-henh.

(FATHER FLAVIA stands in front of AL-PHONSINE for a beat. He then pulls out a long needle from his robe. It catches the light of the sun.)

FATHER TUYISHIME Wait, what are you doing? What are you doing?

(FATHER FLAVIA stands in front of AL-PHONSINE for a beat. He then pulls out a long needle from his robe. It catches the light of the sun.)

FATHER TUYISHIME Wait, what are you doing? What are you doing?

(FATHER FLAVIA quickly plunges the needle into ALPHONSINE'S eye!)

FATHER TUYISHIME Stop it!

(FATHER FLAVIA pulls it out. ALPHON-SINE just keeps looking up into the sky. FA-THER TUYISHIME runs and grabs FATHER FLAVIA.)

FATHER FLAVIA Let go of me.

FATHER TUYISHIME What do you think you're doing? You cannot hurt these girls.

FATHER FLAVIA I am not hurting them: I am testing them.

FATHER TUYISHIME You are torturing them!

FATHER FLAVIA Sister Evangelique, I need your help. If Father Tuyishime won't help me, surely you will? Hold her still, please.

SISTER EVANGELIQUE Certainly.

(SISTER EVANGELIQUE doesn't even have to think about it. She's over there beside him in a hurry.)

FATHER TUYISHIME *(To SISTER EVANGELI-QUE)* Don't. Don't do this.

FATHER FLAVIA Hold her tightly.

(FATHER TUYISHIME grabs SISTER EVANGELIQUE)

FATHER TUYISHIME Must you be a persecutor as well?

SISTER EVANGELIQUE They must be outed. They must be outed at once.

(SISTER EVANGELIQUE yanks herself from FATHER FLAVIA'S grip who is now in front of ALPHONSINE, posed to plunge the needle through her sternum. She takes her place behind ALPHONSINE.)

FATHER TUYISHIME You can plainly see that she is lost. Alphonsine is lost in the rapture--

FATHER FLAVIA The Congregation for the Doc-trine of the Faith demands this for consider-ation. They must pass the medical tests.

FATHER TUYISHIME This is what the Vatican calls a medical test?

FATHER FLAVIA This is only the beginning.

FATHER TUYISHIME This is BARBARIC!

FATHER FLAVIA Those who see Her, I mean *really* see Her can't feel a thing. You can twist their heads to the point where they are looking backwards, or try to rip their legs from their sockets and still, still they can't feel a--

(FATHER TUYISHIME grabs the needle from FATHER FLAVIA who has its point to plunge into her sternum.)

FATHER TUYISHIME GIVE ME THIS!

BISHOP GAHAMANYI *(Interrupting)* Father Tuy-ishime, let Father Flavia do what he has come here to do.

(They look to see that the Bishop has found his way up the hill. He looks over the proceedings with a somber look.)

BISHOP GAHAMANYA These girls have to prove themselves. Let them. Let them in the eyes of God.

(Beat. FATHER TUYISHIME can do noth-ing. FATHER FLAVIA nods then plunges the needle deep into ALPHONSINE'S sternum, which trickles blood like the body of Christ on a Cross. She should be in terrible pain. But she does not move. She does not flinch, for she is swept up in the rapture. The girls continue to sing as blood runs a river into the brown ground.)

Scene 3

FATHER TUYISHIME'S office. En media res--

BISHOP GAHAMANYI But Father Tuyishime--

FATHER TUYISHIME That's enough for his *evidence*--

FATHER FLAVIA I need more--

FATHER TUYISHIME That is enough--

FATHER FLAVIA The medical commission will need a full vetting of medical and psychological history. For all I know, these girls have a high tolerance for pain.

FATHER TUYISHIME A high tolerance for pain? Contrary to popular belief we Africans are too made of blood and bone. Indeed if we stay in the sun too long, we faint.

FATHER FLAVIA Hmph.

FATHER TUYISHIME We bleed when you slice our dark flesh. And that is what you did. You sliced into dark innocent flesh. We are on a hill, but this is not Calvary, Father.

FATHER FLAVIA Your Excellency, please make him listen.

FATHER TUYISHIME I am the head of this school. Kibeho College is *my* hill. *My* responsibility.

BISHOP GAHAMANYI No one is saying that Father Tuyishime--

FATHER TUYISHIME You no longer have my permission to continue with these tests.

FATHER FLAVIA I do not need *your* permission.

FATHER TUYISHIME Oh, yes, you do.

BISHOP GAHAMANYI Father Tuyi--

FATHER FLAVIA I do not need *your* permission as I have been sent by the Pope, let me re-peat *the Pope* to be the eyes and ears of the Church. The Church you supposedly vowed a lifetime of obedience and supplication. Now, if you do not let me do my job then I will leave. I will pack my bags and --

BISHOP GAHAMANYI Father Flavia please let us not get ahead of ourselves--

FATHER TUYISHIME We have to protect these girls. We cannot let blood pool in these halls just to prove a point.

BISHOP GAHAMANYI But you do admit that it is point that needs to be proven by any means necessary.

FATHER TUYISHIME By any means necessary? Tsk!

BISHOP GAHAMANYI We are embarking on a confirmation process. Apparitions require great evidence.

FATHER TUYISHIME You saw how the girls bleed with no feeling. You saw everything. That is enough.

FATHER FLAVIA That is *not* enough.

FATHER TUYISHIME What about the beds?

(FATHER FLAVIA snorts his disapproval)

FATHER FLAVIA This guy.

FATHER TUYISHIME You need to leave. You need to leave the premises at once.

BISHOP GAHAMANYI Father Tuyishime--

FATHER TUYISHIME I am the head of the school. I demand that he leaves.

FATHER FLAVIA You have a weak stomach for faith I see. If you have seen the things I've seen. Seen the lengths parishioners will go to manipulate the Church for their own benefit. Belief in the impossible trumps even the power of believing in God, which is in itself quite impossible. If what they are claiming is indeed happening here, if God has touched their hem, they will be cloaked in the sun, which on this earth, would make. Them. God. They have to earn that cloak, my dear boy. *That* power must be earned.

(No, he didn't. Mmm, yes he did. The Fathers have reached an impasse.)

BISHOP GAHAMANYI Sister Evangelique…Sister Evangelique…

(Though she was listening in the corridor she pretends that she was far away.)

BISHOP GAHAMANYI SISTER EVANGELIQUE!

SISTER EVANGELIQUE Yes, your Excellency, sorry I was down the hallway. Far-far down the hallway--

BISHOP GAHAMANYI Can you please show Father Flavia to the visitors' quarters? Father Flavia, perhaps you would like to take a nap before supper?

(BISHOP GAHAMANYI says this more like a command than anything else.)

FATHER FLAVIA Yes, I would like that very much, Your Excellency.

(FATHER FLAVIA genuflects then follows SISTER EVNGELIQUE out. BISHOP GA-HAMANYI turns his attention back to FATHER TUYISHIME.)

BISHOP GAHAMANYI When two elephants fight, it is the grass that suffers.

FATHER TUYISHIME Who is the head of this school?

BISHOP GAHAMANYI Who is, or who should be?

FATHER TUYISHIME Either.

BISHOP GAHAMANYI Sister Evangelique.

FATHER TUYISHIME Really?

BISHOP GAHAMANYI Yes, she should. But you dear Father Tuyishime were chosen for a reason. You are Tutsi, correct?

(Uncomfortable beat.)

FATHER TUYISHIME Yes. Yes, I am.

BISHOP GAHAMANYI As has every King of our land has been Tutsi.

FATHER TUYISHIME We are a royal tribe.

BISHOP GAHAMANYI Correction, we are a *chosen* tribe.

FATHER TUYISHIME I would say by Belgian corroboration.

BISHOP GAHAMANYI Corroboration indeed, but support nonetheless. You are chosen. You, Father Tuyishime have been chosen…by me.

FATHER TUYISHIME Am I but a figurehead?

BISHOP GAHAMANYI You are truly a figure, but being a head? I'm not so sure. There is always someone above the head, above the tree, and dare I say above the sky. You must remember butter cannot fight against the sun. I understand your concern. I truly do, but if we do not allow him the space and time for an investigation we will regret it. Horribly.

FATHER TUYISHIME And why is that?

(Pause)

BISHOP GAHAMANYI Since this all started happening there have been seven youths who claim to have visions of the Virgin Mary.

FATHER TUYISHIME Seven?

BISHOP GAHAMANYI Seven so-called visionaries. You remember that little boy, Emmanuel who had the sickness? Claimed that he was cured that day the sun danced? Well now Emmanuel is saying he saw Jesus in a corn field. Can you believe? Jesus. In a corn field?

FATHER TUYISHIME Who is to say this boy did not in fact see what he said he saw?

BISHOP GAHAMANYI Jesus? In a corn field?

FATHER TUYISHIME Seems like the perfect place---

BISHOP GAHAMANYI Said he had hair of knotty ropes that fell around his shoulders like a lion. And that he was a tall, wiry man wrapped in a *kitenge*. A *kitenge*? Well, Emmanuel was soon stripped naked in the streets, his clothes shredded like banana leaves before a feast. They say he has gone mad staring at the sun looking for this Jesus. He and the others are all just crazy children who have caught the religious fever, but

these girls, *these* girls could make the sun shine forever on this small little village no one knows about, cares about.

FATHER TUYISHIME This is a change of heart from your previous position.

BISHOP GAHAMANYI Do you know how many people visited Fatima after those three little children saw the Virgin Mary?

FATHER TUYISHIME No, but--

BISHOP GAHAMANYI A million a year. Can you imagine a million a year descending upon Kibeho? The villagers could sell rosaries, shirts, tapes of the girls' lovely messages--

FATHER TUYISHIME Our faith cannot be commodified, Bishop.

BISHOP GAHAMANYI I'm not talking about commodification, I'm talking about confirmation. These girls are our only chance and we need to help them any way we can. They are already passing the medical tests, but the liturgical ones, EN-HENH…

FATHER TUYISHIME Alphonsine gets nervous sometimes--

(BISHOP GAHAMANYI leans in. Pulls out a paper from his robe and sets it on FATHER TUYISHIME'S desk.)

BISHOP GAHAMANYI Well, sometimes even us chosen ones need some help. Make sure Alphonsine knows these answers backwards and forward. She must pass the next test--

FATHER TUYISHIME If she gets everything right, he will be suspicious.

BISHOP GAHAMANYI Say the Virgin Mary told her the answers.

FATHER TUYISHIME That would be cheating.

BISHOP GAHAMANY It would be studying.

FATHER TUYISHIME So you want me to lie?

BISHOP GAHAMANYI I want you to *help* goddamn it! I have seen Alphonsine's grades. You would think that a Tutsi woman would have passed on better smarts to her child. You'd think she was Hutu with how stupid--

FATHER TUYISHIME *(Barking)* BISHOP GAHAMANYI, *(softening)* Your Excellency, *(even softer)* please.

(Beat.)

BISHOP GAHAMANYI This will be good for Kibeho. Good for the future of Rwanda.

FATHER TUYISHIME The future of Rwanda?

BISHOP GAHAMANYI If these girls are confirmed, and they *will* be confirmed Father Tuyishime, with or without your help, they will make a name for Rwanda, a name for this village. In the future I see a shrine, taller than any tree with a steeple that scratches the belly of the clouds...we shall call it Our Lady of Kibeho, a church surrounded by millions, *millions* dancing with love.

FATHER TUYISHIME Is that what you see, Bishop?

BISHOP GAHAMANYI Why, yes, my dear, don't you?

(Beat.)

BISHOP GAHAMANYI We descend from kings, Father. We are the chosen...As it goes for these girls. These girls...are meant to be confirmed. Let them be.

FATHER TUYISHIME I understand, Your Excellency.

BISHOP GAHAMANYI I knew you would. Well, I have to get home in time for supper. She's making G-nut sauce tonight.

(BISHOP GAHAMANYI starts wobbling out of the door.)

FATHER TUYISHIME Let me help you down the hill. I see, your knee's still paining you.

BISHOP GAHAMANYI Oh, I'm fine. I've been moving up and down a bit better. The wife makes a tea leaf bandage for it every night. Made the swelling go down.

FATHER TUYISHIME Your Excellency, I've been meaning to ask...Your wife?

(The Bishop winks at the Father.)

BISHOP GAHAMANYI Only in Rwanda can a Bishop take a wife.

(They do their man-mode crack up thing, but then they are interrupted by the sound of a wave of voices cresting over the hill. Dusk is turning into night. Along the horizon gas lanterns light the way for a group of villagers. It seems like the space where the skies meet the earth are dotted with hundreds and hundreds making their way to high point on the hill.)

FATHER TUYISHIME My, God...

BISHOP GAHAMANYI See, Father Tuyishime. Looks like the people have chosen them, too.

Scene 4

Nighttime.
FATHER TUYISHIME'S office. FATHER TUYISHIME and ALPHONSINE are studying by candlelight.

FATHER TUYISHIME Is the Eucharist Christ's body and blood?

ALPHONSINE No. It is not his flesh--

FATHER TUYISHIME Alphonsine!

ALPHONSINE The answer is yes?!?!!

FATHER TUYISHIME Yesssss...

ALPHONSINE But Father, we are not cannibals.

FATHER TUYISHIME Catholics are. The answer is yes.

ALPHONSINE The wafer turns into the body of Christ? Eh-eh, I don't believe.

FATHER TUYISHIME You must. "Unless you eat the flesh of the Son of man and drink his blood, you have no life in you; he who eats my flesh and drinks my blood has eternal life, and I will raise him up at the last day."

ALPHONSINE Who makes such rules?

FATHER TUYISHIME Jesus.

(ALPHONSINE slams her hands on the desk.)

ALPHONSINE Sorry, Father, I am just not good at this--

FATHER TUYISHIME Calm down--

ALPHONSINE I am never going to get this right. I am going to look stupid in front of Father Flavia, yet again.

FATHER TUYISHIME No, you won't. I'll make sure you won't.

ALPHONSINE I mean, how am I supposed to know all of this? I haven't read the Bible. In its entirety....

FATHER TUYISHIME *(So disappointed)* Oh, Alphonsine...neither have I.

(They both break into laughter.)

ALPHONSINE Father!

FATHER TUYISHIME I know.

ALPHONSINE How can you call yourself a priest?

FATHER TUYISHIME I have the collar. Isn't that enough for you Mademoiselle Alphonsine?

ALPHONSINE To tell you the truth. I'm not that big of a fan of the Old Testament. The New Testament has a bit more...action.

FATHER TUYISHIME What about the tale of Sodom and Gomorrah?

ALPHONSINE Ah-ah

FATHER TUYISHIME Samson and Delilah?

ALPHONSINE AH-ah.

FATHER TUYISHIME Ruth?

ALPHONSINE Boring.

FATHER TUYISHIME Fine. What about, Cain and Abel? That's one of my favorites..."And the Lord said to Cain...'What have you done? Your brother's blood cries out to Me from the ground! So now you are cursed from the ground that opened its mouth to receive your brother's blood you have shed.'"

ALPHONSINE I don't like that story

FATHER TUYISHIME Why not?

ALPHONSINE Cain just gets away with it.

FATHER TUYISHIME No, he was left to wander the world without home. Without family. With an aching heart.

ALPHONSINE No, he gets to walk around with his life. It's not fair. It is not fair.

FATHER TUYISHIME *(More to himself)* God never is.

(Beat.)

ALPHONSINE Should we be doing this, Father? Should you be helping me?

FATHER TUYISHIME No.

ALPHONSINE You are too sweet to me. Too sweet.

(She perches herself elegantly on his chair. FATHER TUYISHIME indicates her bandages.)

FATHER TUYISHIME Are you alright?

ALPHONSINE Yes.

FATHER TUYISHIME He did not have to do that to you girls.

ALPHONSINE It is fine. We know that we are to be tested. She has prepared us for it all.

(FATHER TUYISHIME nods.)

FATHER TUYISHIME Did Sister change your bandages?

ALPHONSINE No, I did not need her to.

(FATHER TUYISHIME knows what that means.)

FATHER TUYISHIME Here, let me look.

(He touches ALPHONSINE's sternum.)

ALPHONSINE Tsssssss!

FATHER TUYISHIME Sorry, sorry. It must hurt.

ALPHONSINE Yes.

(He goes into his desk drawer and pulls out some more bandages. He pours some water from the jerrican into a bowl on his desk. He slowly peels the bandage from her sternum. He wipes the coagulated blood away from her chest. It hurts. She flinches in pain.)

FATHER TUYISHIME Sorry. Sorry.

(She lets him treat her.)

ALPHONSINE You still haven't prayed.

FATHER TUYISHIME How do you know?

ALPHONSINE She told me.

FATHER TUYISHIME She tells you a lot.

ALPHONSINE She only tells me what I need to know.

FATHER TUYISHIME Sometimes, that is all we need.

(He has bandaged her. They stare into each other's faces.)

ALPHONSINE Father.

FATHER TUYISHIME Yes, Alphonsine--

(ALPHONSINE leans in to kiss the Father. FATHER TUYISHIME sits there still, his lips entertaining the possibility of her touch. But just as ALPHONSINE leans in he abruptly pushes her away.)

FATHER TUYISHIME Alphonsine!

(ALPHONSINE reacts in pain.)

FATHER TUYISHIME Are you alright? Did I hurt you?

ALPHONSINE I'm sorry, Father Tuyishime. I'm sorry.

FATHER TUYISHIME What were you doing, Alphonsine?

ALPHONSINE I do not know, Father.

FATHER TUYISHIME Why did you do that?

ALPHONSINE I do not know Father. Please forgive me.

FATHER TUYISHIME Alphonsine--

ALPHONSINE I want it to stop. I thought that maybe if I did something wrong, then maybe, She would stop. She would stop talking to me. Stop making me feel…feel like…the way you make me feel sometimes.

FATHER TUYISHIME And what is that Alphonsine?

ALPHONSINE Loved.

FATHER TUYISHIME Alphonsine. I can't imagine the burden that you must have to bear right now. The emotions that you are dealing with. I do not envy you. But always remember that God does not give us more than we can bear.

ALPHONSINE Yes, He does. You know He does.

FATHER TUYISHIME I wish I could help you somehow. Carry your boulder for a day, Alphonsine. But you are stronger than me. You could carry two boulders if necessary. Some of us are made for this life.

ALPHONSINE Why me?

FATHER TUYISHIME Why not, you, Alphonsine?

ALPHONSINE But I am so dumb, Father. I do not know all the answers.

FATHER TUYISHIME But you know all the questions and you will spend a lifetime asking them.

ALPHONSINE I do not want to be like you. I want my prayers to be answered.

FATHER TUYISHIME Well, you must keep asking the questions. I stopped a long time ago.

Scene 5

The girls' dormitory. The Trinity's three broken beds lay carefully in the corner, cracked and caving in on their sides. The other young girls have surrounded the beds with wildflowers gathered from the countryside, fruits for the Virgin Mary to eat. Candles stand scintillating around the shrine. Some girls tending to it. Others praying in front. The entire space is abuzz with excitement. A radio balances on a GIRL #2's lap.

GIRL #1 Do you have some varnish?

GIRL #3 Do you have some water and flour? I need to press my uniform.

GIRL #2 Get off of my bed. You are wrinkling my sheets.

GIRL #1 You are in bed anyway, why does it matter?

GIRL #4 I have some.

(GIRL#4 passes over the nail polish.)

GIRL #2 Pink will look good with your skin.

GIRL #1 It's not for me. It's for the Virgin Mary.

GIRL #4 *Ewe!* Give it back. If She's so beautiful she doesn't need my help.

GIRL #3 Shhh! *Ziba!* All of you.

RADIO RWANDA Thousands are making the pilgrimage tomorrow to see the girls, dubbed the Trinity...

MARIE-CLAIRE *(In faux shock)* I will not be equated with God, the Son and the Holy Spirit.

ANATHALIE Oh, take your protest out there to the crowds.

MARIE-CLAIRE You woman! *Wa mugore weh!*

ALPHONSINE Shhhh!

RADIO RWANDA In preparation for the Feast of the Assumption, parish priests from southwestern Gikongoro to the capital of Kigali have been sharing tapes of the girls' messages:

(The voice of Marie-Claire streams through the radio. It is sweeter. Distant. A different timbre.)

MARIE-CLAIRE *(IN A TRANCE)* "In every garden there will be dry flowers, flowers that are slightly wilted, and flowers that are in full bloom. People are like flowers. Some are good, some are bad, but most are in the in between---

GIRL #1 Can you believe that's you?

(The girls scream and clap as if the girls are playing a new song.)

MARIE-CLAIRE Shhhhhh!! I can't hear myself.

MARIE-CLAIRE *(IN A TRANCE)* --Wilting. Almost dying. And almost living. But each and every person no matter where they are in the garden is deserving of our water, our love. Some say it's a waste to water a dying flower. But as we know life can be resurrected and continue on. My beautiful little flowers. Our love is never wasted. Never wasted on kindness....."

ANATHALIE Why does Marie-Claire always gets the good messages?

ALPHONSINE It doesn't matter. The only thing that matters is that it is spreading. Spreading like She said it would.

GIRL #1 What time is She coming tomorrow?

ALPHONSINE We will gather with the villagers and She will come when She wants.

ANATHALIE *(Under her breath)* No, tell them 10, so they will be there by noon.

ALPHONSINE Ten. I meant, Ten am sharp! Do not be late or you will miss your blessing.

GIRL #4 Tomorrow is for the fool.

GIRL #1 Such a bitter nut.

GIRL #2 *(Smdh)* Shame, she is still the only one left.

GIRL #4 No, Sister Evangelique still has some sense about her. The only one sane in this place...

GIRL #1 So how do you explain the Virgin Mary speaking to Marie-Claire now? How do you explain?

GIRL #4 Maybe old gal wanted to stay around here in school because she couldn't find anyone to marry her.

THE GIRLS Ehhhhh...

MARIE-CLAIRE Watch the ground you tread upon my dear child.

GIRL #4 What will you demand that the earth open up and swallow me whole?

(MARIE-CLAIRE starts inching towards GIRL #4.)

MARIE-CLAIRE I am warning you.

GIRL #4 Or what? What, Marie-Claire? What will you do? Where is She? Where is your Virgin Mary, now? Huh? Where was She when my mother was riddled with bullets? Her body left on the side of the road? Where was She? Where was her Son? Where was everybody? *Everybody?* Where were they? WHERE WERE THEY????

(All the girls are stunned by GIRL #4's admission. Even the girl herself is stunned by what has fallen from her mouth. Silence descends upon the girls.)

MARIE-CLAIRE If you would just allow me to pray for you, maybe the pain will—

(MARIE-CLAIRE reaches out to the GIRL #4 who snatches her hand away.)

GIRL #4 I do not need *your* prayer, Marie-Claire. Where is *She?*

(GIRL #4 runs out of the dormitory in the tears.)

ANATHALIE She is right, Marie-Claire. You are not Jesus.

MARIE-CLAIRE Believe me. I know that I am not a healer. If I were, I wouldn't be walking around looking like somebody's pincushion.

(Indicating her bandages.)

MARIE-CLAIRE Poked and prodded and prodded and poked every time we have a vision? *Tsk.* But, there is pleasure in the pain of proving...

(MARIE-CLAIRE begins to climb into bed.)

ANATHALIE Oh, "bad girl, gone good." *Ziba....*

MAIRE-CLAIRE Eh-eh, these months have transformed me. I have repented just like Mama Mary told me to do. She does not ask us to be perfect, but she does ask us to be devout...

(ALPHONSINE laughs, annoying MARIE-CLAIRE.)

MARIE-CLAIRE We are temples, Alphonsine. Soil the palace gates and She may refuse to come back.

ANATHALIE What in the world are you talking about, Marie-Claire?

MARIE-CLAIRE I have seen her. Sneaking, Alphonsine. You do not belong to Man. You belong to God.

ALPHONSINE You have not seen me do anything.

MARIE-CLAIRE Don't make me say--

(ALPHONSINE, embarrassed by MARIE-CLAIRE'S warning, jumps onto her like a lioness.)

ALPHONSINE You are lying!

(This time ALPHONSINE is getting the better of her.)

MARIE-CLAIRE I am not! YOU KNOW I'M NOT!!

ALPHONSINE You are! YOU ARE!!

(ANATHALIE tries to break them apart.)

ANATHALIE We cannot let it come to this. Listen to me! Listen!!!!

THE GIRLS Sister Evangelique! Sister Evangelique!

ANATHALIE Mama Mary will be so disappointed in us.

(SISTER EVANGELIQUE runs in with a vengeance.)

SISTER EVANGELIQUE Do you all want to cry?

GIRL #1 Sister Evangelique they are fighting. They are fighting again.

(ANATHALIE cannot pull them apart.)

ANATHALIE Stop it, both of you! Stop It—

GIRL #1 Marie-Claire, calm down! Calm down!

GIRL #4 Sister Evangelique, do you want me to go get Father Tuyishime?

SISTER EVANGELIQUE Yes, dear child –

(Suddenly ANATHALIE sinks to her knees in convulsions. ALPHONSINE and MARIE-CLAIRE turn to fallen ANATHALIE. She has been possessed by Our Lady. She has begun to speak in tongues.)

SISTER EVANGELIQUE On second thought, go get Father Flavia down the hall as well.

(Vines start growing along the walls. Flowers start blooming out of the cracks and crevices of the dorm...)

GIRL #3 Oh my!

SISTER EVANGELIQUE Wha-what-what is this--happening--here--what--is, my--my---goodness.

GIRL #1 She is watering us. Just like She said She would.

GIRL #2 Her little flowers.

GIRL #3 Look! Look!

(All of the girls stare are in awe of the jungle growing inside of their dorm. GIRL #4 re-enters with FATHER TUYISHIME.)

GIRL #4 I found--BABAWE....

(GIRL #4 is taken by what is growing at her feet.)

FATHER TUYISHIME The girls are—goodness

SISTER EVANGELIQUE The room. The room smells like—

FATHER TUYISHIME Jasmine and hugs.

GIRL #4 She is here...

(GIRL #4, the last convert, falls on her face in supplication. FATHER FLAVIA out of breath comes into the door.)

FATHER FLAVIA Do not be persuaded. This is possession. A sweet possession...

(He takes a step towards ANATHALIE with his tools poised to prod. ANATHALIE looks at him with enormous serenity. When she opens her mouth, perfect Italian flows out.)

ANATHALIE (OUR LADY) *(In perfect Italian)* Luis, so we meet again. *Luis, ci incontriamo di nuovo.*

FATHER FLAVIA Where is that coming from?

ANATHALIE (OUR LADY) Here. Luis! Right. Here. *Qui. Luis! Proprio. Qui.*

SISTER EVANGELIQUE What is she saying? Girl, what are you saying?

ANATHALIE (OUR LADY) *(In perfect Italian)* Tell that wench to shut her mouth. I've about had enough of her conniving ways. *Digli a quella sgualdrina di chiudersi la bocca. Ho avuto abbastanza dei suoi modi conniventi.*

FATHER FLAVIA *(In perfect Italian)* Mother Mary? *Madre Maria?*

ANATHALIE (OUR LADY) *(In perfect Italian)* What, you don't recognize me? You don't believe my words would fall out of the lips of a little black girl? Her lips suit me well. *Che? Tu non mi conosci? Non puoi credere che le mie parole cadono fuori dalla bocca di una ragazzina nera? Le sue labbra me vanno bene.*

FATHER FLAVIA *(In perfect Italian)* I am stunned, I am stunned speechless. *Sono stordito, sono impietrito.*

ANATHALIE (OUR LADY) *(In perfect Italian)* Yes, I see you with your mouth standing agape. Fish faced-Luis. Remember that's what they used to call you in primary? *Sì, ti vedo con la bocca spalancata. "Faccia di pesce" Luis. Ti ricordi quando ti chiamavano così alla scuola?*

FATHER FLAVIA (In perfect Italian) How do--- Come tu può--

ANATHALIE (OUR LADY) *(In perfect Italian)* I know all about my children. Especially the ones that walk in faith with me. My little flowers as I like to say. *Conosco tutt'i miei figli. Specialmente quelli che camminano nella fede con me. Mi piace dire "mio piccolo fiore.*

(FATHER FLAVIA'S feet are consumed by flowers and vines.)

FATHER FLAVIA *(In perfect Italian)* But why here? Why Rwanda, Mother Mary? *Ma perché qui? Perché Ruanda, Madre Maria?*

ANATHALIE (OUR LADY) *(In perfect Italian)* You weren't complaining when I flew you to Brazil, I tell you that! *Non ti sei lamentato quando ti ho volato in Brasile, ti dico che!*

FATHER FLAVIA *(In perfect Italian)* Forgive me. Forgive me. *Perdonami, perdonami.*

ANATHALIE (OUR LADY) *(In perfect Italian)* Luis, I have a message that is bigger than Rwanda. It is meant for the entire world. There is a sickness in the hearts of men. And these girls. They know it well. You know it well, too... *Luis, cio un messaggio molto più grande di Ruanda. È per il mondo intero. C'è una malattia nel cuore degli uomini. E anche nelle ragazzine. Lo conoscono bene. Anche tu lo conosci bene...*

FATHER FLAVIA *(In Italian)* What do you mean? *Ma che mi stai dicendo?*

ANATHALIE (OUR LADY) *(In perfect Italian)* I know what happened to you, Luis. Forgive him, Luis, you are not alone in the belly of the whale. *Io so cosa ti e successo, Luis. Perdona, Luis, non sei solo nella pancia della balena.*

(FATHER FLAVIA falls to his knees with tears in his eyes. The others stand back and see that little room has become the most perfect garden.)

ANATHALIE (OUR LADY) *(In perfect Italian)* Luis, I need you to pass along this message to my little flowers. My little flowers I say... *Luis, ho bisogno di passare questo messaggio ai miei piccoli fiori. I miei piccoli fiori, io dico...*

MARIE-CLAIRE Beloved Mother Mary, whose Heart suffered beyond bearing because of us, teach us to suffer with you and with love, and to accept all the suffering God deems it necessary to send our way. Let us suffer—

(MARIE-CLAIRE during the ecstasy has fallen to her knees. She raises her rosary. It glows and changes colors.)

Scene 6

FATHER TUYISHIME'S office.

FATHER TUYISHIME and SISTER EVANGELIQUE are staring at a visibly shaken FATHEvR FLAVIA.

FATHER TUYISHIME Are you alright, Father Flavia?

FATHER FLAVIA Are you? Do you have something to drink, Father?

FATHER TUYISHIME Give him some water--

FATHER FLAVIA Do you happen to have something…a wee bit stronger.

FATHER TUYISHIME *Urgwagwa.*

FATHER FLAVIA What is that?

FATHER TUYISHIME Banana beer.

FATHER FLAVIA I'll take it.

(FATHER TUYISHIME takes a flask out of his desk drawer. He unscrews it and FATHER FLAVIA takes a swig, then two, then three.)

FATHER FLAVIA I have seen some rather complex hoaxes. Traveled all around the world. I have seen many, many things, Father, but this, this one is a striking, *striking* hoax!

FATHER TUYISHIME Flowers grow fast in Africa, but not that fast, Father.

FATHER FLAVIA Well, maybe it was mass hallucination. We wanted to see something there. We wanted to see--garden. We wanted it to be real. *(More to himself)* Yes, it had to be a hallucination that we all saw.

FATHER TUYISHIME Why can't you see the miracle that is staring you right in front of your face.

FATHER FLAVIA Because those girls have been primed.

FATHER TUYISHIME Primed. Primed to do what?

FATHER FLAVIA They know things that they are not supposed to know. Especially the Anathalie girl. She knew about…about…

SISTER EVANGELIQUE What did she know?

(FATHER FLAVIA takes another swig.)

FATHER FLAVIA Who taught them Italian?

FATHER TUYISHIME The girls speak French and Kinyarwanda. That's it.

FATHER FLAVIA So no one knows Italian? They've had absolutely, no access to the language?

SISTER EVANGELIQUE If only the Italians would have colonized us instead of the Belgians.

FATHER TUYISHIME What did Anathalie say to you? What did she say to you to make you so….so…

FATHER FLAVIA The rosary. That Marie-Claire prayed. It's a special one. It originated in the Middle Ages by the Friar Servants of Mary, a sect based in England. It's called The Rosary of the Seven Sorrows.

FATHER TUYISHIME Seven Sorrows. Never heard of it.

FATHER FLAVIA Are you sure?

FATHER TUYISHIME If you are insinuating that we taught these girls these things.

(FATHER FLAVIA looks to SISTER EVANGELIQUE)

FATHER FLAVIA I'm assuming you do not know either.

SISTER EVANGELIQUE How I wish I did, so I could wipe that smirk off of your lips.

FATHER FLAVIA Sorry. Sorry. I know. You couldn't have. There's no way the girls would have known it. It died out centuries ago.

FATHER TUYISHIME So now do you believe?

FATHER FLAVIA It doesn't matter if I believe, Father Tuyishime. They in the Vatican have to believe—

FATHER TUYISHIME But do you believe?

FATHER FLAVIA It's not my job not to –

FATHER TUYISHIME But do you believe?

(FATHER FLAVIA looks at FATHER TUYISHIME. He will not answer this question, though his eyes say otherwise…)

FATHER FLAVIA The girls say Our Lady has something to share tomorrow, during the Assumption. A secret to tell the villagers. If they are devout, if these girls are truly seeing Her, then they will know the true secrets of the Church only those She chooses can know.

FATHER TUYISHIME And then they will be confirmed?

FATHER FLAVIA They will be *considered.*

(FATHER FLAVIA looks back at the photos on the desk.)

FATHER TUYISHIME Well, that's all we can ask for.

FATHER FLAVIA Goodnight, Father.

(FATHER FLAVIA looks at FATHER TUYISHIME. A beat of understanding passes between them. SISTER EVANGELIQUE stands at the door with a flashlight in hand. He walks slowly to the door. He turns back.)

FATHER FLAVIA Can I have the uh---

(FATHER TUYISHIME hands him the bottle of the banana beer.)

SISTER EVANGELIQUE I will walk you to your room. I know the darkness of these halls well.

(FATHER FLAVIA nods a thanks and walks out before her.)

Scene 7

Moments later. SISTER EVANGELIQUE is walking through the halls doing her usual patrolling. MARIE-CLAIRE comes out of the dormitory. She walks right up to SISTER EVANGELIQUE who does not acknowledge her presence.

MARIE-CLAIRE Why are you still not speaking to me? After all that has happened?

(SISTER EVANGELIQUE begins to walk away.)

MARIE-CLAIRE Answer me.

SISTER EVANGELIQUE You must think you are hanging in the sky with the sweetest bananas if you think I am supposed to answer to you. Be careful, my dear Marie-Claire. All fruit must fall to the ground.

MARIE-CLAIRE Sooner, if there is someone there to cut them down.

SISTER EVANGELIQUE *(Eyes welling at the admission)* I could kill you. Kill you for being so blessed. By *Her* presence. By *Her* light. By *Her*... But now I know...I am not worthy of God's grace, for evil thoughts have taken over my mind like vicious vines, breaking through the bricks of my faith. I cannot see the goodness, the garden--

MARIE-CLAIRE Tonight, you saw it tonight.

SISTER EVANGELIQUE Yes, I saw it with my eyes, but my heart? I am spiritually blind, my heart dumb. How could I have been so wrong? The same hands I lifted up in prayer are the same hands I used to nail you all to a cross. How easily in the name of God we are turned into monsters. Marie-Claire, can you forgive me? Can you all forgive me--

MARIE-CLAIRE Of course--

SISTER EVANGELIQUE But will He? Can my God forgive me? Will He hear my wretched prayers?

MARIE-CLAIRE Only if you ask for His mercy...

(MARIE-CLAIRE goes to her knees and tries to bring SISTER EVANGELIQUE down to her knees in prayer. SISTER EVANGELIQUE, pulls her hands back.)

SISTER EVANGELIQUE No, I am not worthy. These hands are better for plucking the petals than tilling the soil...

(A door opens. ANATHALIE steps outside the dormitory with a candle.)

ANATHALIE Marie-Claire. Marie-Claire, are you alright?

MARIE-CLAIRE Yes, Anathalie. I am. Alright. I was just going on a short call.

ANATHALIE Long call seems more like it... Come back to bed. We must rest we have a big day tomorrow.

(MARIE-CLAIRE softly walks away.)

SISTER EVANGELIQUE At least I can rejoice that the Virgin Mary does not only favor the Tutsi. She has chosen another Hutu to spread her message. At least I can share in that victory.

(MARIE-CLAIRE stops and she turns back to SISTER EVANGELIQUE.)

MARIE-CLAIRE She speaks to us all, Sister. Those who are Hutus, like you....and those who are Tutsi...like me.

(SISTER EVANGELIQUE stands stunned.)

SISTER EVANGELIQUE You?

MARIE-CLAIRE Good night. As you have said before, truth and the morning become light with time.

Scene 8

The sun pokes its head out from the bottom of the hill. Climbing ever upwards to find its rightful place in the morning sky. Thousands of villagers blow out their candles. The murmur is infectious. A VILLAGER has made a t-shirt with pictures of the girls' faces and is selling cassettes.

VILLAGER 1 Trinity tapes. Get them now. Almost sold out.

VILLAGER 2 How much?

VILLAGER 1 Two thousand francs, but if you buy two, I'll let you have them both for three thousand.

VILLAGER 2 Give me three.

(ANATHALIE stands on her tiptoes looking out into the crowd from the dormitory window.)

ANATHALIE They are too-too early.

MARIE-CLAIRE You said ten.

ANATHALIE And it is seven!

ALPHONSINE I suppose they want to get a good seat.

ANATHALIE I wonder if my Papa is out there.

ALPHONSINE I'm sure he wouldn't miss this for the world.

(MARIE-CLAIRE swoops in and takes a comb out of her pocket and starts fluffing the girls' afros.)

ANATHALIE Ouch!

MARIE-CLAIRE If you combed your hair more often it wouldn't hurt!

ALPHONSINE *(Laughing)* You two.

(She fluffs up ALPHONSINE'S afro, too.)

MARIE-CLAIRE There. We don't want them to think they are raising a group of jungle bunnies up here now do we.

ANATHALIE Who cares what they think?

MARIE-CLAIRE Eh-eh! I do. Do you see all those cameras out there? You don't want to go down in history as the knappy-headed trinity now do you?

(MARIE-CLAIRE looks over her sisters. She settles on ALPHONSINE. Beat.)

MARIE-CLAIRE Here, put these shoes on, Alphonsine.

ALPHONSINE But they are yours.

ALPHONSINE Giving to your sister who has given you much is not giving but paying.

(ALPHONSINE brings the pair of shoes to her chest. Her eyes well with tears.)

ALPHONSINE Thank you.

MARIE-CLAIRE *(Snapping)* They are meant to be worn on your feet not your chest. Hurry, hurry. Finish getting ready. Today is a big day.

(The courtyard. A reporter stands with a crew in front of the makeshift stage.)

REPORTER We are here at Kibeho College where, the three girls, known through the village as the Trinity, say that the Virgin Mary is set to visit this morning. As many as 20,000 have climbed the seven hills up to Kibeho to celebrate the Assumption of Mary. *(To a villager)* And where have you come from?

VILLAGER 1 All the way from Nyamata in the east.

REPORTER Do you believe?

VILLAGER 1 Ennnnnnnh. If She comes, I will believe. If She does not come, I think these young girls will have a problem on their hands.

VILLAGER 2 (FORMER BLIND MAN) Well, I believe. I was here that day the sun danced.

REPORTER You saw the sun dance?

VILLAGER 2 (FORMER BLIND MAN) I had been blind to my wife for years. But that day

Mama Mary ripped me from the darkness and brought me into the light I saw Her face and then my wife's…Thank God a woman is more than her breasts.

VILLAGER 3 Don't listen to him. He's out of his mind. Just like that little boy over there.

VILLAGER 1 Oh, shame. He was cured of the sickness! Now he has gone crazy!

(Little EMMANUEL, who had been healed from AIDS, stands disheveled, with barely any clothes on, and welts all over his body. His eyes roll into the back of his head as he repeats his mantra.)

EMMANUEL *(In Kinyarwanda)* The rivers will run red with blood…the rivers will run red with blood. The rivers will run red with blood. *Inzuzi ziza tembgamo amarago… Inzuzi ziza tembgamo amarago… Inzuzi ziza tembgamo amarago…*

VILLAGER 1 Look at him poor thing. *Iyoooo, urababje disi.*

EMMANUEL *(In Kinyarwanda)* The end of days are near. They are near… *Imperuka, turi kuba mu'mperuka.*

VILLAGER 3 Shut up you fool! You know not what you say.

EMMANUEL *(In Kinyarwanda)* Brothers will rape their sisters. Mothers will kill their sons. The river. Oh the river. The end of days. We are living in the end of days… *Abahungu baza fata kungupu babo ababyeyl bazi' cya abana babo mzuzi oh inzuzi, imperuka turi kuba mumperuka.*

(EMMANUEL is pushed aside as the crowd surges to make way for--)

VILLAGER 1 There is the father of the seer Anathalie!!!

(NKANGO, who once wore garments holey from working in the fields, now wears a sorta new Chicago Bulls t-shirt and sneakers bought straight from the market.)

REPORTER *(Barking in Kinyarwanda to one of the pilgrims)* Get out of my way. Get out of my way! *Igirayo. Igirayo!* *(Back to her BBC lilt)* Is it true you are the one whose daughter has favor with, the virgin?

NKANGO Indeed, it is me.

REPORTER How does it feel to know your daughter Anathalie is a visionary?

NKANGO It is not a surprise to me. Something told me that when she went to Kibeho

College she was destined for greatness. That is why her mother and I worked so hard in the fields. To give her the good Catholic education that has lead to this opportunity. Like I said, no surprise. She is a good girl.

REPORTER The passion fruit must not fall too far from the tree?

NKANGO No-no-no, I'm but a small man. A small man.

(Other villagers are taking pictures with Nkango.)

VILLAGER 1 Nkango! Nkango! Can you get Anathalie to bless my rosary?

NKANGO Sure, sure, sure.

VILLAGER 2 (FORMER BLIND MAN) Mine, too!

(And Nkango is swept away by the singing, surging crowd.)

REPORTER And there you have it. The village is awaiting. Waving their rosaries, praying, singing. You hear it? The crowd is calling for them. Waiting on the girls who call the Virgin Mary *Nyina wa Jambo*, Mother of the Word. Stay turned. Reporting August 15, 1982 for the BBC.

Lights shift.

The dormitory. The noise of the crowd wafts in through the open windows. Before the glistening shrine the girls stand in front of Father Flavia in prayer. Poised. Pressed. He does the sign over them. Father Flavia looks out of the window.

FATHER FLAVIA You girls draw a bigger crowd than The Supremes.

THE TRINITY Who?

FATHER FLAVIA You don't know about The Supremes? My goodness, what are they teaching you at this school?

(FATHER TUYISHIME joins them.)

FATHER TUYISHIME Are you all ready?

(The girls stay put.)

FATHER FLAVIA I will be there—

FATHER TUYISHIME Doing your usual torturing?

FATHER FLAVIA No, Father, there is no need. But they at the Vatican will need me to record the proceedings. Make sure the young girls are in line with doctrine.

FATHER TUYISHIME Very well. After you, ladies.

(The threesome walk from the dormitory into the courtyard where they are met with love and adoration from a crowd serenading them. Bowing down to them.)

VILLAGER 1 Trinity Tapes. Get your Trinity tapes!

VILLAGER 2 (FORMER BLIND MAN) Let me touch your robes.

VILLAGER 1 Trinity Tapes. Get them now.

VILLAGER 3 Please pray for me.

NKANGO Anathalie, your Papa is here! Your mother is here, too, over there! Over there!

VILLAGER 1 Two for one. Get your Trinity tapes right here.

EMMANUEL *(In Kinyarwanda)* The end of days is near…The end of days is near… *Imperuka, turi kuba imperuka.*

(The girls pass EMMANUEL and he touches their clothing. A shiver passes through them. The sky begins to darken… The three girls go step by step, climbing the makeshift podium in the middle of the courtyard. They join BISHOP GAHA-MANYI, who stands before the microphone in a blinding white robe.)

BISHOP GAHAMANYI Parishioners welcome! We know that you have come from near and far-- some very far-- *(indicating FATHER FLAVIA)* to be part of this momentous day. This is the first time we are celebrating our annual Assumption of Mary feast here on the school grounds. As many of you know there have been rumblings of Our Lady's presence here in Kibeho. Well, I'd like to be the first to—

VILLAGER 2 (FORMER BLIND MAN) Where are the visionaries?!!?

VILLAGER 3 *(So friggin' embarassed)* Sweetie, please!

VILLAGER 1 *(In Kinyarwanda)* Nobody want to see Bishop. *Nta muntu ushakakureba Bishop.*

VILLAGER 2 (FORMER BLIND MAN) I want to hear the visionaries.

BISHOP GAHAMANYI Please, be patient. Our Lady I'm sure would be saddened by your blatant disrespect of --

VILLAGER 2 (FORMER BLIND MAN) Give them the microphone!

VILLAGER 3 Sweetie, PLEASE!!

VILLAGER 2 (FORMER BLIND MAN) I want to hear the one from the radio. The one from the radio I say!!!

BISHOP GAHAMANYI Fine. Fine… *(In Kinyar-wanda, under his breath)* I tell you these village folk! *Aba baturage! (Indicating Marie-Claire)* Marie-Claire.

(BISHOP GAHAMANYI shuffles off. MARIE-CLAIRE steps up to the microphone.)

MARIE-CLAIRE Thank you all for coming. We are happy that despite the heavy clouds you are here to listen to receive Our Lady's message. It says a lot about your commitment to the teachings of the Church. About your commitment to the Word. The words of *Nyina wa Jambo*.

ANATHALIE In order for you to hear them. We must prepare the grounds for her. She only comes when there is kindness.

ALPHONSINE Join us. Join us in prayer. Lift your hands to the sky.

(They look up and the sky has shifted from being sunlit to hanging heavy with darkened clouds. The girls begin singing a hymn for Mother Mary and the ENTIRE village joins them. The voice of the girls merge into the villagers, creating a sweet fusion. The air vibrates as thousands of voices are lifted into the sky.)

ANATHALIE *(Under her breath)* Where is She?

MARIE-CLAIRE *(Under her breath)* She is coming. She is coming.

(FATHER FLAVIA is near the platform recording. The sky is darkening more.)

VILLAGER 1 We want Mother Mary! Where is Mother Mary?

MARIE-CLAIRE Why is it taking Her so long?

VILLAGER 2 (FORMER BLIND MAN) Look in the sky.

(Clouds are swirling. Faster and faster.)

ALPHONSINE Keep singing. Everyone keep singing.

(Finally there is a rustle on the wind…. The sky changes. It now seems as though the brightest sun is in the sky, but there is rain. The heavens open up… She is here… They stare above the crowds heads. Lovingly transfixed… The crowd surges forward shaking the platform, but the girls stand unmoved. But suddenly, a gush of tears start flowing from the girls faces.)

ANATHALIE Mama Mary, why are you crying?

ALPHONSINE She's crying.

MARIE-CLAIRE Please don't cry.

ANATHALIE Please.

ALPHONSINE Mama Mary, what is it?

MARIE-CLAIRE But you must.

ANATHALIE You must.

ALPHONSINE Show us.

ALPHONSINE and MARIE-CLAIRE Show us!

ANATHALIE Please show us, why you are crying.

VILLAGER 1 What are the girls saying?

VILLAGER 2 (FORMER BLIND MAN) Press closer. Closer.

(The crowd surges trying to hear what the Virgin Mary has to say. But suddenly the girls start shaking, convulsing, quivering. Shaking. BISHOP GAHAMANYI who is sitting beside the other clergy suddenly stands.)

BISHOP GAHAMANYI What, what, is going on?

(The girls begin to vomit.)

BISHOP GAHAMANYI What is She showing them? What is She—

THE TRINITY The hills of Rwanda will run red with blood. The hills of Rwanda Will Run Red With Blood. THE HILLS OF RWANDA WILL RUN RED WITH BLOOD. THE HILLS OF RWANDA WILL RUN RED.

Light shift. Time is stretched and echoey in this space.

In the black, there are moans and screams. The crackle of burning of fire. The electric slice of a machete being drug across asphalt. Echoes. Echoes. A light pulses and we see shards of a vision. Visions of the unthinkable. The unseeable. The unvoiceable. Marie-Claire is running, running, running, running, red ribbons streaming from her feet. Until she is felled.

SISTER EVANGELIQUE *(V.O.)* Marie-Claire speak to me sweet child.

NKANGO *(V.O.)* Anathalie, please wake up. She is dead!

SISTER EVANGELIQUE *(V.O.)* She is not dead. This has happened before. She can't be--

NKANGO *(V.O.)* Then what is she? What has She done to my daughter?

ALPHONSINE *(V.O.) (Whispering)* The end of days are near.

MARIE-CLAIRE *(V.O.) (Whispering)* The end of days are here.

SISTER EVANGELIQUE *(V.O.)* The fever. The fever is spreading to the other girls.

Lights shift.

Scene 9

FATHER TUYISHIME'S office.

MARIE-CLAIRE sits staring into space, rocking herself. ANATHALIE'S body lays across the desk. ALPHONSINE is in the same hot chair she started in at the beginning of the play.

SISTER EVANGELIQUE MARIE-CLAIRE speak to me! *(Aloud but more to herself)* I have never seen her so still. So quiet.

FATHER TUYISHIME She's been that way since the vision. Struck dumb.

SISTER EVANGELIQUE Eh! She is struck dumb and all the girls are struck with a fever. There aren't enough buckets. It's a mess. I tell you a mess. These poor girls.

FATHER TUYISHIME Why did you all say those things, Alphonsine?

ALPHONSINE She showed us. Showed us what they needed to see.

SISTER EVANGELIQUE They were mumbling utter nonsense. Utter nonsense I say.

(FATHER FLAVIA stands over ANATHALIE.)

FATHER FLAVIA Ten hours and still no pulse.

SISTER EVANGELIQUE No breath.

FATHER FLAVIA What she saw must have frightened her.

FATHER TUYISHIME Well, it absolutely frightened me.

BISHOP GAHAMANYI The other girls seems to be suffering from some mass hysteria.

FATHER TUYISHIME What about the other villagers?

BISHOP GAHAMANYI They heard it. Heard it all.

FATHER TUYISHIME Tell them the girls made it up.

FATHER FLAVIA Made it up?

BISHOP GAHAMANYI Yes, Father Flavia. They have made this nonsense up. Or they have gone crazy. Just like that little boy Emmanuel.

FATHER FLAVIA But why would they lie?

(FATHER FLAVIA plays the tape. The girls' disembodied voices fill the room.)

THE TRINITY *(V.O.)* "The hills of Rwanda will be littered with graves. The rivers will run red with the blood of babies. Sons will slaughter their fathers, husbands will rape their wives, babies will have their brains dashed out by mothers. We are in the end days…"

FATHER TUYISHIME Turn it off.

FATHER FLAVIA Listen…

FATHER TUYISHIME I said turn. It. Off.

TRINITY *(V.O.)* "Sorrow will sink Rwanda and the passion fruit that grows from our trees will bleed with the blood of the fallen. The hills of Rwanda will run red blood.

THE HILLS OF RWANDA WILL RUN RED WITH BLOOD. THE HILLS OF RWANDA WILL RUN RED WITH--"

(FATHER TUYISHIME takes the radio and throws it against the wall. It smashes into a million little pieces.)

FATHER TUYISHIME This is not real. They made it up.

FATHER FLAVIA We need you to settle yourself--

FATHER TUYISHIME They have made it up.

(FATHER TUYISHIME shakes the motionless ANATHALIE.)

FATHER TUYISHIME Tell them that you made, that you ALL made it up--

(BISHOP GAHAMANYI tries to grab FATHER TUYISHIME.)

FATHER TUYISHIME Tell them that you are lying.

BISHOP GAHAMANYI Father Tuyishime--

FATHER TUYISHIME Please, Anathalie.

FATHER FLAVIA If you believed the initial visions why can't you believe this one.

(FATHER TUYISHIME turns around to FATHER FLAVIA.)

FATHER TUYISHIME You SHUT UP! YOU SHUT UP!!!

FATHER FLAVIA Calm down Father.

FATHER TUYISHIME No, there is not evil here in Rwanda. THIS is where God goes on vacation. THIS is the land of love, of milk and honey. Where I was born--

FATHER FLAVIA Calm down, Father--

FATHER TUYISHIME Fix them! We have to fix them! Stop them for seeing these--these-- these horrible things--

FATHER FLAVIA This is something we can't fix, Father--

FATHER TUYISHIME Cure them! Things need to go back to normal, before, before,

FATHER FLAVIA Before what?

FATHER TUYISHIME --They are disrupting the order of things. Making the everyone afraid--

FATHER FLAVIA They should be--

FATHER TUYISHIME --Getting things out of order here--

FATHER FLAVIA --But, Father--

FATHER TUYISHIME --The world is buckling, buckling beneath my-

FATHER FLAVIA But why wouldn't you want to hear what Mother Mary has to say?

FATHER TUYISHIME BECAUSE I DON'T WANT TO BELIEVE FATHER! I DON'T WANT TO BELIEVE THIS!!

(FATHER TUYISHIME has covered his eyes like a little boy hiding from the boogeyman...)

FATHER TUYISHIME The world. The world is wobbling.

(FATHER TUYISHIME crouches down on the floor of his office torn asunder.)

MARIE-CLAIRE I saw a girl. Running down a hill. She had legs so long they could take her into tomorrow. She had feet so quick they could cut down blades of grass. She ran up those seven hills of Kibeho to the tippy top, to heaven's doorstep. She knocked hoping that God would let her in, but she could not knock fast enough. It came down. A slice. Her head rolled down those seven hills in search of a grave.

ALPHONSINE It is a sign.

MARIE-CLAIRE It was not a sign; it was me.

SISTER EVANGELIQUE Where is God? Where is God here?

ALPHONSINE God has nothing to do with this. Only man. *She* says we need to--

BISHOP GAHAMANYI Enough of this nonsense. ENOUGH. It is only hell that they are talking about. And we all know that exists.

FATHER FLAVIA But they are talking very specifically about a hell on Earth—

BISHOP GAHAMANYI The world is always ending. Has been ending for years—

FATHER FLAVIA Not like this. There is something dangerously specific about this vision, and if I were you I'd listen.

BISHOP GAHAMANYI Is it so easy to believe visions of violence when they fall from African lips—

FATHER FLAVIA No, Your Excellency, it is easy only when they fall from a visionary's lips, which these three girls undoubtedly are.

(Beat.)

FATHER TUYISHIME So they will be confirmed?

FATHER FLAVIA They have passed every test. Every physical test. Every mental test. Every psychological evaluation--everything they have said has been in line with doctrine. From the light to the dark....

(FATHER FLAVIA gathers the tape from the broken recorder. FATHER FLAVIA'S silence says it all)

BISHOP GAHAMANYI *(Switching gears one last time.)* But Father Flavia, this is not the kind of vision that engenders the increase of faith.

FATHER FLAVIA It is the kind of vision that produces fear, which, knowing the God I know, is a good thing.

(All Bishop can do is watch as FATHER FLAVIA seals the tape in a velvet pouch and leaves. BISHOP GAHAMANYI stands there staring into the void.)

FATHER TUYISHIME Well, Your Excellency, you got what you wanted.

BISHOP GAHAMANYI Indeed. God help us. God help us all.

Scene 10

Next day.

FATHER FLAVIA walks down the corridor with his bags packed. He passes the girls' dorm. Since the night, the lush garden has turned to a rotting brown. The flowers are wilted from their spring, and now leaves plunge from the vines committing a million little suicides onto the floor.

FATHER FLAVIA puts his bags down and walks up to the death and destruction.

FATHER TUYISHIME What will your final report be?

(FATHER FLAVIA whirls around to find FATHER TUYISHIME has snuck up behind him.)

FATHER FLAVIA Wheew! You scared me.

FATHER TUYISHIME I said, "what will your final report be?"

FATHER FLAVIA It sometimes takes 100 years for the Church to approve apparitions.

FATHER TUYISHIME Well, hopefully, we have that long.

FATHER FLAVIA But it only took the Fatima visions 13 years to be approved., So you never know...

FATHER TUYISHIME *(More to himself)* Thirteen years...

FATHER FLAVIA That particular "trinity" were mere children when they saw Her in 1917. Lucia, the eldest, said that Mother Mary had given her three secrets. The first secret was that there was a hell. The second was that World War II would come. But she held onto the third secret for 23 years until one day in 1944 at the height of the very war She predicted, Lucia wrote it down on one sheet of paper. That sheet traveled by train from Portugal to Rome and was locked away in a special vault in the Vatican. Every Pope who has read it has refused to let the secret be known to the public.

FATHER TUYISHIME Do you know the secret?

FATHER FLAVIA Of course, of course.

FATHER TUYISHIME And did it come to fruition?

FATHER FLAVIA Remember that letter for the Pope you gave me?

(FATHER FLAVIA gives FATHER TUY-ISHIME the piece of paper he gave him earlier in the 2nd act.)

FATHER TUYISHIME Alphonsine's?

(FATHER TUYISHIME looks at the paper.)

FATHER FLAVIA She even makes a circle over her "I"s. Just like Lucia...

(FATHER FLAVIA returns ALPHON-SINE'S letter gingerly into his inner breast pocket.)

FATHER TUYISHIME I am leaving my post here, Father Flavia. The Bishop says that my appointment was a mistake.

FATHER FLAVIA Perhaps it was.

FATHER TUYISHIME Where are you off to next?

FATHER FLAVIA A place called Medjugorje.

FATHER TUYISHIME Medju-ju-who-who-wha-wha?

FATHER FLAVIA Father, you can say Mukamzim-paka but you can't say Medjugorje?

FATHER TUYISHIME Never heard of it.

FATHER FLAVIA It's in Yugoslavia.

FATHER TUYISHIME Wheew! Our Lady has been busy this year.

FATHER FLAVIA Or maybe it is the Devil?

FATHER TUYISHIME Well, He is often busy, as well.

FATHER FLAVIA And you? Where are you going?

FATHER TUYISHIME Where a lot of *us* are going—

FATHER FLAVIA "Us?"

FATHER TUYISHIME Us Tutsis. We are heading to Uganda. It is not where God goes on vacation. But it will have to do.

(FATHER FLAVIA sadly understands.)

FATHER FALVIA Good day, Father.

(FATHER FLAVIA takes his bags and starts his way down the hill.)

Scene 11

FATHER TUYISHIME walks back to his office to find ALPHONSINE waiting for him. The sounds of the girls singing songs can be heard outside.

FATHER TUYISHIME You are not on punishment anymore.

ALPHONSINE I know.

FATHER TUYISHIME Then what are you doing here so early in the morning?

ALPHONSINE I thought I would help you clean.

(She is sweeping the bits of broken radio into the trash bin.)

ALPHONSINE It seems we made a mess of your office last night.

FATHER TUYISHIME Indeed.

(She begins to pick up books that are scattered on the floor. She tries to put one of the books away high on the shelf. She cannot reach it.)

FATHER TUYISHIME Here, let me help you.

(He takes the book from ALPHONSINE and looks deeply into her smile. He breaks their gaze and looks down at the book. He blinks and opens it, inside a worn rosary.)

ALPHONSINE Your mama's.

FATHER TUYISHIME I've been looking for it.

ALPHONSINE Well, now it is found. You prayed last night. She told me.

FATHER TUYISHIME My goodness, She tells you everything.

ALPHONSINE Well, She has become my best friend.

FATHER TUYISHIME I'm still trying her out.

ALPHONSINE Please, keep praying. She needs you to do this.

FATHER TUYISHIME I know.

ALPHONSINE And please, please stay. The girls don't want you to leave.

FATHER TUYISHIME The gods I think have decided for me, my dear Alphonsine.

ALPHONSINE Who will take your place?

FATHER TUYISHIME Sister Evangelique. She is being promoted from deputy head nun to head mistress. It will soon be a place run by women. And, personally, I think that is good.

(ALPHONSINE eyes begin to well, but she nods her head in understanding. FATHER TUYISHIME brings a hand to her face and begins to wipe her tears away. Suddenly,

ANATHALIE *shows up at the door. The two jump apart.)*

ANATHALIE Come on Alphonsine, they're singing the new song! Marie-Claire with her horrible voice is absolutely ruining it.

ALPHONSINE I'll be there in a minute--

(ANATHALIE runs off.)

FATHER TUYISHIME You should go, now. Join the other girls.

(Beat.)

ALPHONSINE Good day, Father Tuyishime. "One who we are thankful for."

FATHER TUYISHIME Good day, Alphonsine Mumereke. "Leave her alone, she speaks the truth."

(She smiles bringing light into that tiny office. And then she leaves him. FATHER TUYISHIME goes and stands at the doorway of his office. They are singing a new song, "Our Lady of Sorrows." FATHER TUYISHIME looks out across his country, his land, his people, his heaven on earth, the land of a thousand hills, the land of Rwanda, before.)

(Blackout.)

Vera Starbard

Biography

Her clan is L'eeneidí, and her Tlingit name is T'set Kwei. But she is known to most as Vera Marlene Starbard, born on Prince of Wales Island in Southeast Alaska. She moved frequently around the state of Alaska as a child, following her father's position as an Alaska State Trooper, and often turned to her Tlingit and Dena'ina Athabascan heritage for artistic inspiration.

Writing was part of Vera's story from the beginning. One of her most treasured accolades is "Best Story-teller in Ms. Stichik's First Grade Class," and she forged ahead in editing various Alaskan school newspapers all through high school. Her first professional editing job came at age 18, and she has made writing and editing part of her work since.

After completing a Tlingit novel with an award from the Rasmuson Foundation, and receiving numerous state and national awards for editing and writing, she became editor of First Alaskans Magazine. A fellow of both Stanford University's First Nations Futures Program, and the Healthy Native Communities Fellowship, Vera has long been an activist in issues impacting her culture and community. She is a cofounder of Alaska Native theatre company Dark Winter Productions, and owner of Writing Raven Communications.

After premiering *Our Voices Will Be Heard* at Perseverance Theatre in January of 2016, Vera became writer-in-residence at Perseverance through the Andrew W. Mellon Foundation's National Playwright Residency, a three-year, three-play commitment.

She married Joe Bedard in 2015, and lives with him in Anchorage amongst friends, family, and too many cats.

Artistic statement

Our Voices Will Be Heard began as a short story called *The Eyes of Love* that I wrote when I was 18. It was an allegory about the sexual abuse I experienced at the hands of my uncle as a child, and my family's reaction to the secret coming out. I wrote it in one long night at a diner, and I put it away.

Over a decade later, I dusted it off and submitted the short story as a play idea to the Alaska Native Playwright Project. The project's goal was to take experienced Alaska Native writers and teach them about playwriting. But one difference became apparent in the first few days of the project – the perspective of the abuse had changed from that of a child, to that of an adult. This time around, I explored the story through my mother's point of view.

Details changed from the "real" story to the imagined world of the play. For instance, my own father was very supportive, but the father of *Our Voices Will Be Heard* is portrayed quite differently. But I wanted to create how the secret and revelation of my abuse felt, not a historically accurate biography.

Sexual abuse is too often portrayed in my community as a uniquely Native experience. But it is unfortunately a cross-cultural experience, and while I relied on my culture, and my personal experience, to tell a single story of abuse, my hope was it would speak to everyone. And while the "literal" story of the family is about what happened to me, and how we got through it, the interwoven Storyteller character speaks to my hope: a future where sexual abuse and incest is so unbelievable and nonexistent, a person must rely on the telling of a myth to impart the truth of it.

Production history

In 2012, *Our Voices Will Be Heard* was commissioned as part of the year-long Alaska Native Playwright Project, an effort of the Alaska Native Heritage Center in Anchorage, Alaska. It was completed in 2013, and after its first public reading in Anchorage, it was submitted to the Native Voices at the Autry Festival of New Plays and Playwright Retreat.

Once accepted, it was workshopped in Los Angeles in 2014, followed by a public reading at The Autry, and a reading at the La Jolla Playhouse in San Diego. Perseverance Theatre then brought the play to Juneau, Alaska for a reading before deciding to produce it, and then to New York City for a reading at the Lark Play Development Center.

Our Voices Will Be Heard was developed and premiered in January 2016 at Perseverance Theatre, Juneau, Alaska, with Art Rotch, Executive Artistic Director. Directed by Larissa FastHorse (Lakota), the World Premiere was a three-community production, premiering in Hoonah in late February, and Anchorage in mid-February.

Cast

LITAA	Erika Stone (Iroquois)
KUTAAN	Erin Tripp (Tlingit)
TA	Robert Vestal (Cherokee)

JINIHAA	Frank Kaash Katasse (Tlingit) – Juneau Premiere
	Dylan Carusona (Ojibway/Turtle Clan Oneida) –
	Hoonah and Anchorage Premiere
SAGU	Deanndre King (Tlingit)
SHANAA	Jane Lind (Aleut)
WANADOO	Leeta Grey (Tlingit)
STORYTELLER	Jack Dalton (Yup'ik)

Designers and production staff

Stage Manager: Anne Szeliski
Asst. Stage Manager: Zebadiah Bodine
Sound Designer: Ed Littlefield (Tlingit)
Northwest Coast Visual Artist: Rico Worl (Tlingit)
Set Design: Akiko Nishijima Rotch
Lighting Design: Art Rotch
Dramaturge: Luan Schooler
Costume Designer: Meg Zeder

14 *Our Voices Will Be Heard*
Vera Starbard

Characters

LITAA Tlingit, Wolverine Clan, mother of Kutaan, wife of Ta, clan leader. Older sister to Jinihaa and Wanadoo. Begins in early 20s, ages to mid–30s and early 40s.

KUTAAN Tlingit, Wolverine Clan, daughter of Litaa, Wanadoo, and Ta. Begins as infant, ages from 13 to about 18.

SHANAA Tlingit, Wolverine Clan, mid 40s, mother of Litaa, Jinahaa, and Wanadoo. Begins in 40s, ages from 50s to early 60s.

TA Tlingit, Lynx Clan Leader (ga̲ak), husband of Litaa. Begins in 30s, ages from mid 40s to early 50s.

WANADOO Tlingit, Wolverine Clan, daughter of Shanaa, mother of Sagu. Younger sister of Jinihaa and Litaa. Begins in early 20s, ages from mid 30s to early 40s.

SAGU Tlingit, Wolverine Clan, infant, son of Wanadoo. Begins as infant, age 13.

JINAHAA Tlingit, Wolverine Clan, son of Shanaa. Younger brother of Litaa and older brother of Wanadoo. Begins in 20s, ages from late 30s to mid 40s.

STORYTELLER Tlingit, Wolverine Clan, man, late 20s to 40s
Note: Wolverine Clan is "Nooskw", Gold Clan is "Góon" with a Lynx crest

Setting

We begin as an abstract, exaggerated late–19th-century Tlingit village (Southeast Alaska deciduous rainforest.) The world is transitioning from a traditional clan-house system to that of the white cannery towns. The first movement of the play is set in the traditional village, and most of the second movement is set in a cannery town.

The beginning set is vibrantly colored, with a "too-perfect" feel, representing the image the family is putting up to hide the darkness.

The cannery town is angular and black and white, representing this new world with new rules the mother and daughter finds themselves in.

The final set is the village again, but with much dim, more worn coloring and scenery. Their real house is showing.

Note on Tlingit people

Originating in Southeast Alaska, the Tlingit people knew a forest as their home, and a rich and colorful coastal culture. At this time in their history, they were known for being warriors and a tough people. They put a premium on honor, prestige and wealth, and took the matrilineal (based on the mother's side) clan system to a high level of political complexity. Public shame or embarrassment could literally start wars. Painted, sewn or woven crests (usually an animal) would display to the world just who that individual was, and what clan they represented.

FIRST MOVEMENT

Scene 1

JINIHAA *begins singing Ka Haa Satu in Tlingit off stage.*

ALL *(Singing.)* Naa liyéidi duwa.áxch

Ḵa haa ḵusteeyí

Naa liyéidi duwa.áxch

Ḵa haa satú[1] *(Song repeats.)*

(A cedar box drum begins playing loudly and curtain goes up on the stage. It is the inside of a large cedar house in late 19th century Southeast Alaska, bright and lit with many traditional oil lamps. Food for a feast is piled high around, and the colors of the home, the props are all vibrant. It is Spring. The voice calls out and singing begins in tempo with skin drums that begin playing. People dance in through the oval doorway, dancing with energy and excitement. They are all wearing brightly colored button blankets with gold, silver and copper embellishments, all spotless. Beneath their robes they wear clothing representative of late 19th century Tlingit village people, mostly deerskin with a few pieces of clothing showing 19th century Western influence. Soon the stage is filled with people, including TA, LITAA, SHANAA, JINIHAA, WANADOO, and two babies, KUTAAN (girl infant) and SAGU (boy infant) held by LITAA and WANADOO. Singing stops with a "whee!" from all and laughter. Lights go down immediately as the dancers turn around and stop singing.)

Scene 2

STORYTELLER enters wearing jeans, sneakers and a modern Tlingit-design t-shirt beneath his button blanket.

STORYTELLER Oh my goodness! *(rubs shoulder)* You'd think I'd learn not to ask a Tlingit grandmother when the fry bread will be done. Just so you know – the answer is, "When it's done."

But I promise you it will be worth it! I know this is your first koo.eex, but don't be nervous. We of the Nooskw clan want to honor you with our best food at this party, and the ladies back there are certainly close to perfection! Fry bread with some Nagoon berry jam! Oh yes… *(looks longingly to the back)* So good…

Well, we're in this together! I'll tell a story while we're waiting.

Let me think… what would be the best story to tell.? Maybe of Bear and Beaver… Or a story of Raven is always popular…

Ah ha! I know just the right story, and I bet you haven't heard it before. It is exactly the story for today's koo.eex.

This is one of my favorite stories - it is one of the first stories I remember my grandmother telling me. I warn you - some people don't like it because it doesn't seem to have a happy ending. But grandma always used to say, "You should listen anyways, you may find something you weren't looking for." *(Settles in.)*

This is the story of a woman who lived long, long ago, back before my grandmother lived, back before my grandmother's grandmother lived. She seemed like a regular young lady who wouldn't hide things from those she loved. But she had a big secret she kept from just about everyone in the village.

Do you know the secret the woman in the story was keeping?

She was one of the Wolverine People! *(Pause – expecting recognition)*

What – don't you know who the wolverine people are?

Well, now I HAVE to tell this story! Not knowing the wolverine people…

Anyways, back so long ago, back during the time when the creatures of the land still talked to us, some of them, like the wolverine people, lived with the human beings, side-by-side, every day.

I know! How could such a thing happen? How could humans live with such a fierce animal and not know? Those claws! That attitude!

But the wolverine people did not always look and act like wolverines we know today. And this woman – she is known as Wolverine Woman – hunted with her wolverine family at night. They were such a close pack. And in the day, they looked like human beings and lived amongst regular people.

Only Wolverine Woman didn't want to hide from the human beings in the village any longer. So one day, she told her secret to her friend – only her friend didn't believe her! So Wolverine Woman transformed right in front of her, and showed her friend who she really was. But her friend was terribly frightened, and ran to tell everyone in the village. The humans made Wolverine Woman leave her home, and her family was too scared to speak up, so they let her go. And so now all wolverines live away from other wolverines. They are very solitary creatures.

(long pause) Uh… that's it. That's the end of the story. She was alone.

I told you it didn't have a happy ending! Well, as my grandmother used to say, "If you're looking for happiness in a story – stop. That is not where happiness is."

(A loud, pointed cough from behind.)

OH! *(Looks at audience.)* FRYBREAD! I'll be right back to serve you the best fry bread you've ever tasted. Only *(looks around him)* maybe set aside a piece or two for me for later? *(STORYTELLER exits.)*

(Cross-fade to dancers who entered the brightly lit room, JINIHAA, SHANAA, LITAA, WANADOO and TA. LITAA and WANADOO are holding infants.)

Scene 3

JINIHAA *(Speaking to audience)* Gunalchéesh, gunalchéesh!

You have done us much honor these past days for being our guests at this koo.eex. We hope you have found wisdom in our stories, joy in our dancing, and full bellies from our food.

And any day is an especially good day when we get to eat my sister Wanadoo's deer stew, no? Wanadoo, come up and tell us what you put in that delicious concoction!

WANADOO Jinihaa – you promised, little brother! *(slaps him playfully on the arm)*

JINIHAA I must know! What is it? Special herbs you gather at midnight? Do you twirl around the fire backward when no one is looking? Come now – there should be no secrets here!

(A raven calls outside the house. JINIHAA laughs.) You see? Even cousin raven agrees – tell us!

WANADOO Huh. My secret is you have very bad taste and are easy to please.

JINIHAA *(laughs)* True enough, true enough.

LITAA *(aside to JINIHAA)* Little brother – our guests…?

JINIHAA Oh yes, thank you sister. *(speaks to audience)* Today we truly celebrate much. After so many months of sadness, we put an end to our grieving. While we remember those we lost by remembering what they gave us, it is now a time of joy and life and song.

Why – I think now is a good time for just that! Ta – come here! *(TA moves closer.)* Ta, my good friend, and husband to my sister. You have held us up in our sorrow for so many months.

TA It was all done with love for my wife's family, and respect for the great Nooskw clan.

JINIHAA Your gifts were received with equal love. And now I have a song I want to give you – *(LITAA pinches him.)* OW! What–? *(LITAA tries to whisper to him so the audience doesn't hear.)* I cannot hear – order? OH… *(looks at audience, embarrassed)*

Yes, well. It is a good thing my big sister looks out for me. In my – uh – eagerness to present Ta with this gift, I have skipped ahead in the order of things a bit…

SHANAA Oh leave him be, daughter! It is my Jinihaa's first time leading a koo.eex. He is doing so well for someone who had to take responsibility so young. And you did not mind, did you Ta?

TA I –

LITAA There is a reason for the proper order in which our clan has always done things, and adhering to it is a sign of respect, is it not Ta?

TA I think... I think no smart man ever disagrees with either his wife, or his wife's mother!

JINIHAA He is a man who has learned the wisdom that has escaped lesser beings for ages! *(back to audience)* We will now turn back to our path! We are celebrating two more reasons for joy. First – Wanadoo?

Wanadoo's dear husband did not live to see his handsome son born, and we will miss him, but I am proud to take on the responsibility of an uncle for this boy. Today, Wanadoo's son will receive a name. My mother will speak on this.

SHANAA Gunalcheesh, gunalcheesh! What an exciting day! This is almost as exciting as the day Jinahaa here got his name, no? Everyone just told me all the time how cute he was.

JINIHAA Mother –

SHANAA Oh son, do not be embarrassed Jinahaa. You *were* so cute!

But I remember, just the day before we named you was that time you stopped breathing. It was so frightening, and I was nearly hysterical. Many people thought he was dead. But just when everyone was ready to give up, he breathed again, and my mother said he must have some big purpose. My goodness, I know he does.

(LITAA clears her throat loudly.)

What – oh yes, yes! Now, we have talked much about these names, and have chosen them carefully.

Now, my first grandson! Bring him over here Wanadoo.

Daughter, I know you do not like to talk in front of people, but tell everyone here what funny thing your baby boy did just yesterday. *(WANADOO is embarrassed and shakes her head.)* Go on now Wanadoo.

WANADOO Well... he... my son... was on the bench while I was cooking and... and the dogs came... the dogs... *(WANADOO is flustered and looks for rescue.)*

JINIHAA Oh sister – let me tell it!

The baby is sitting on the bench while Wanadoo is cooking nearby. One of the dogs comes by and suddenly tugs the blanket right off him! The boy comes tumbling out and I go running for him, thinking he's hurt. But – we hear him laugh! I shoo the dog away and the mutt drops the blanket over my nephew's head. When I finally get to him and take the blanket off, why, he laughs again! My sister and I are worried this poor baby is badly hurt, and he just thinks he's playing peek-a-boo with the dog! *(JINIHAA laughs and gives WANADOO a side-hug. She smiles.)*

SHANAA Ah! The sweet boy is so smiling and happy! Those of you old ones, you remember my uncle Sagu? What a good man he was, and how he could make anyone laugh with his stories? Oh yes, and my boy Jinahaa certainly takes after him a bit too. You heard him - he tells the best stories!

(LITAA clears her throat.)

Yes, yes daughter... well, once we saw this happy baby boy, it only seemed natural that this boy should be named Sagu.

(Speaks to baby SAGU, and holds a small piece of cedar bough across his forehead.) Your name is Sagu. Now everyone will repeat your name, so it will be yours.

EVERYONE Sagu-a, Sagu-a, Sagu-a.

SHANAA And here is this button robe, which he will wear when he is older. I made sure to use our clan crest when making this blanket, so everyone could see that Sagu comes from the mighty Nooskw Clan.

(JINIHAA and WANADOO unfold and hold up the blanket, made with lots of gold embellishments. There is a gold wolverine design. SAGU is handed back to WANADOO.)

SHANAA And now, my first granddaughter. Born less than a day after my Sagu. For her, well, everyone can see how beautiful she is. She came out with almost as much hair, and with almost as good a skin as Jinahaa did when he was born.

Now Ta, even though you are the leader of the honorable Goon clan, are you not proud of the beautiful baby girl my clan has given you?

TA *(laughs)* I certainly must agree with you about her, Shanaa. She is perfect.

LITAA *(playfully)* Perfect! You are just so smitten! It does not seem to matter to you that she wakes up crying five times a night. You jump up like she's the most beautiful singer you've ever heard.

SHANAA Litaa, you should be grateful you have such an attentive father for a husband.

LITAA I was just teasing-

SHANAA Now maybe you will finally understand everything I went through, raising such a bossy daughter. When she cries you cannot just boss her into being quiet.

JINIHAA Oh, I think my big sister will do all right. She has the "mother look" down already.

LITAA What "mother look?"

JINIHAA That one.

(KUTAAN cries. TA immediately picks her up and she stops crying.)

LITAA I will say, Ta is the only one that can get her to stop crying so quickly. She is already her father's child!

TA Of course she is!

SHANAA And do you not think she will make a beautiful bride one day, and she will marry someone very important?

LITAA Mother, Ta and I were thinking we would make sure she could walk and speak before you married her off!

JINIHAA Have a care, sister, mother brings up a good point. You should probably start the marriage rounds now. Potential infant suitors have already heard tell of her.

Why, mothers across the land are probably in tears as they try and cover up their more unfortunate looking daughters.

Mother made sure of that. *(TA, LITAA, JINIHA and WANADOO laugh.)*

SHANAA Oh tush! I never did such a thing.

Now, for this pretty girl's name, it was only natural that she be named for my beautiful auntie Kutaan. Now let me see that sweet thing. *(Speaks to baby KUTAAN, and holds a small piece of cedar bough across her forehead.)*

Your name is Kutaan. Everyone repeat her name now, so it will be hers.

EVERYONE Kutaan-a, Kutaan-a, Kutaan-a.

SHANAA And here, here is a special robe made for Kutaan. It took me a long time to make, but I knew she needed something extra beautiful. *(JINIHAA and LITAA hold up the blanket, made with lots of silver embellishments. There is a silver wolverine design.)*

(Baby KUTAAN starts to cry. JINIHAA immediately takes her.)

JINIHAA Eeshaan, little niece. You just come here. I will not let that noisy old woman talk about you anymore. *(makes cooing noise and rocks her)*

(Baby KUTAAN stops crying. LITAA and TA look surprised.)

TA It looks like Kutaan sure likes her Uncle Jinihaa!

JINIHAA Well little Kutaan, I have my own gift I made for you. Here's a pretty little doll for a pretty little girl.

LITAA Be careful, brother, or I will be waking you in the middle of the night to settle her down when she cries!

JINIHAA I would not mind watching after this sweet girl a bit.

WANADOO It looks like Kutaan has *two* leaders looking after her. And a cousin to grow up with, and a mother who will teach her all the correct clan ways, and a grandmother who will make her pretty things, and an auntie who adores her. Her feet will never touch the ground.

JINIHAA That is how it should be. With her cousin Sagu, and her father, and her big, strong, brave, mean old uncle looking after her, she will be spoiled like she should be and nothing bad will ever, ever happen to her. Will it little one?

Now let me tell you some stories, Kutaan...

(JINIHAA walks away, cooing at baby KUTAAN, waving a little doll above her as others look on.)

Scene 4

STORYTELLER enters.

STORYTELLER Oh, man! Who knew these Tlingit grandmothers could boogie so long? You know, that reminds me of this joke about Tlingit women! What do you get when a Tlingit women comes across – uh... No. No, I probably shouldn't tell that joke right now...

I still can't believe you didn't know about the wolverine people. I know our stories seem so harsh sometimes, but my grandmother used to say the stories that are hardest to hear are the most important ones to listen to. You can't be too gentle when you tell a tale worth hearing.

You know, wolverines used to be very gentle creatures. No really! I know - I wouldn't want to come across one now!

But they also used to hunt in large family packs. Working together, they brought down huge animals. Only now, Wolverine

Woman was alone, and being so gentle, she was reduced to following other animals around for their scraps.

One day Wolverine Woman went to eat the leftovers of some animal, and there was Bear still trying to eat. Bear usually tossed Wolverine Woman scraps, but Bear was just taking his time. And Wolverine Woman started to get angry. Angry she had to wait. Angry that Bear was only giving her the scraps and keeping all the best bits to himself. Angry that he was so big and strong, and she was so small.

At first she snapped at Bear. Then she started to fight with him. Soon, Wolverine Woman's rage was so great, she scared Bear away! It didn't take Wolverine Woman long to learn her fierce anger meant she could hunt her own food. Not only did she scare Bear, but this little creature could kill animals as big as a deer now all by herself.

And that is how wolverines turned from being so gentle into such fierce fighters. And why even the great Bear looks over his shoulder for a wolverine.

Speaking of… I better get back to all those grandmothers. Getting Tlingit protocol wrong is one thing, but heaven help me if I mess up these dances! *(STORYTELLER exits.)*

(Lights cross-fade to cedar home.)

Scene 5

It is the same cedar home, but not laid out for a feast. It is summer. You can hear drums in the distance. SAGU, 13, runs in the door, wearing the gold-emblazoned button blanket he was given at his naming 13 years earlier.

SAGU Kutaan? Kutaan! Come on, you are already late and Sigeidi is ready to spit! Augh! Kutaan?

(KUTAAN, 13, enters from the side, fastening her silver-emblazoned button blanket around her. She runs around finding and putting on her regalia as she talks.)

KUTAAN Oh, I am on my way. We have sung this song a thousand times – I hardly think we will be forgetting it in the next few moments.

SAGU Yes, but you know we need to be extra prepared for this feast tonight. I mean, if we forget a line in the song today, Sigeidi will eat us alive. Her big, strong son is getting

married, and you know that means she will want everything sooo perfect. *(Imitating an old woman's voice)* That means practice, practice, practice!

KUTAAN *(laughs)* Uch. As if her son marrying that deer-faced thing is so special!

SAGU Oh, just you wait. They will likely be marrying us off in a few years, and I wager you are going to be all sappy over some little dark man with big calf muscles!

KUTAAN Huh! You are just so smug. I bet when you are old enough to marry, you are going to fall for some really smelly old woman you will have to help around the village.

SAGU Ah – I would not mind a smelly old woman as long as she was very rich, and I could sit around and eat those dleit kaa cakes all day.

KUTAAN Oh – did I tell you? One of the men who came to the feast told me more about the dleit kaa town. He said it is getting bigger and bigger. And more dleit kaa people come every day. He said they have places in the town where all they do is sell things like those cakes, and–

(LITAA enters.)

LITAA Who said that?

KUTAAN Oh, mother. Uh… just one of the men that came for the feast.

LITAA I should not have to tell you, daughter, that a good Nooskw clan girl does not talk to strange men.

(TA and JINIHAA enter.)

TA Who is talking to strange men?

KUTAAN I did not mean to, the trader just started telling stories and I was nearby.

LITAA That should not matter. You have been taught better manners.

TA Oh, do not be too hard on her, Litaa. Jinihaa and I heard him and it was pretty interesting. It has been a while since I have seen that dleit kaa town, and to hear him tell, it must be twice the size it was when I last was there.

LITAA All right, but you really need to get to practice Kutaan. Find your headdress and get moving.

(KUTAAN hurriedly tries to open boxes, while also trying not to let others see in the boxes she is looking. As she looks, she leaves more things out of the boxes.)

SAGU Sorry auntie… but you have to admit Sigeidi is on a bit of a rampage.

LITAA Even so, you children need to respect that she is your elder. *(mutters to JINIHAA)* Even if she is being impossible.

Kutaan, why are you not out practicing?

KUTAAN I am nearly ready, but I cannot find my headdress.

(LITAA sits and begins to prepare food for the feast.)

LITAA I should just sew things onto you for how much you lose them. A nooskw woman is responsible for all the household items, you know. You must learn to take better care of things.

SAGU I will help you look Kutaan!

(SAGU moves toward KUTAAN.)

KUTAAN *(quickly)* No, thank you cousin, I will find it.

(WANADOO and SHANAA enter.)

SHANAA Well I never! That Sigeidi just ordered me to bring out the berry dishes. *Ordered* me.

WANADOO I do not think she means ill. On a normal day she likes everything just so. Today is so important for her, she must be feeling so much pressure to get it right.

SHANAA Hmph. Well she will get my dish when it is good and ready.

(SHANAA and WANADOO settle in to prepare dishes with LITAA. KUTAAN'S searching gets more hurried.)

WANADOO Do you need help, Litaa?

LITAA Oh, thank you sister. *(more loudly so KUTAAN can hear)* But the biggest help may be to get my daughter out the door.

KUTAAN *(hiding tears)* I am sorry mother – I just…

LITAA Kutaan, you cannot really be crying over this? A nooskw woman should not cry like you do.

TA What's the matter, daughter?

KUTAAN *(continues looking through large cedar boxes)* My head piece is missing!

TA Do not cry daughter, we will all help you look.

(TA and JINIHAA start to open boxes. KUTAAN jumps forward and closes the box TA was trying to open.)

KUTAAN It is okay, I do not need help. I will find it.

SHANAA You men should be out there with all the guests, anyways. Leave us to our work.

TA Do not worry little deer. You have a beautiful robe – no one will notice your headdress is missing.

KUTAAN Sigeidi will.

JINIHAA I will go with you to Sigeidi. I will tell her I did not finish repairing the headdress and so it is not ready to wear.

SAGU You are taking your life in your hands, uncle…

(JINIHAA takes KUTAAN by the elbow and leads her out, TA and SAGU also exit. LITAA moves over to all the boxes KUTAAN was looking through, with items strewn about.)

LITAA What a mess this is!

SHANAA My, it looks like an ooxjaa blew through here!

LITAA Yes, and that ooxjaa's name is Kutaan. *(Begins to tidy the mess.)* She has been acting so strange lately. I am beginning to think something is wrong.

SHANAA Oh, you always think everyone is doing something wrong. She is just at that age. Although, people in the village think Ta spoils her too much. I told them you do your best to make her a respectable Nooskw woman.

LITAA *(sighs)* Yes, mother. *(picks up a toy that is clearly not Tlingit)* But I do think her fascination with that dleit kaa town is too much. Every time there is a trader in the village she is down talking to him, wanting to know what they are building. I do not like her always trying to be around them. I do not like it.

WANADOO I would not worry. How much harm can she get into just talking to them?

LITAA I suppose.

(LITAA tries to straighten up KUTAAN'S mess. The drums play as they work in silence. SHANAA stops to listen.)

SHANAA Oh, just listen – the young things are getting good are they not? Well, my Jinahaa has been assisting them so much, it is not terribly surprising. Do you remember Litaa, he used to sing all the time when he was little?

LITAA I remember my brother banging on cedar boxes until my head hurt. And cleaning up after him just like this.

SHANAA *(laughs)* Well, he is so creative he has more trouble keeping tidy. It's how very intelligent people's minds work, you know.

LITAA *(mutters)* Well he must be a genius.

(WANADOO chuckles.)

SHANAA What?

LITAA Hmm?

SHANAA He teaches those children everything he knows, and the children say they just love him. Do you know he has even been teaching Kutaan extra lately?

LITAA No, I did not know that.

SHANAA Oh, your daughter just never tells you anything, does she? My son tells me he has been helping her extra, during her sewing time.

LITAA While she is with the other girls and Sigeidi?

SHANAA Oh, I think they go someplace else so they do not bother everyone.

LITAA That is not proper. A nooskw woman should learn the women's roles, not the men's. Why is she being taught extra, in any case?

SHANAA From what Jinihaa says, it is because she is not remembering the songs very well. And he knows all the roles. He always had such a good memory like that.

(Drums stop.)

LITAA I just do not understand Kutaan lately. She has been so forgetful and secretive, and all the aunties who teach her say she does not pay attention. She has always been sensitive, now she cries if I say anything at all.

WANADOO Oh, we all acted like that at one time, did we not? She is at such a hard time in life.

SHANAA And you really should go easier on her, Litaa. I was never so tough on you.

(SAGU and KUTAAN enter.)

SAGU Whew! Well, after about a million hours of practice just this week, Sigeidi says we *might* not embarrass the clan today. But she does not seem certain.

KUTAAN If she told me to sing that line one more time –

LITAA Kutaan? I hope I am not hearing you talking about your elders disrespectfully?

KUTAAN No...

LITAA And what is this I hear about extra practice with your Uncle Jinihaa? He should not have to take the time to do that. You should be remembering the songs.

(KUTAAN is silent.)

Well?

SHANAA Leave her be, Litaa! Come here grandchild. Have some of my special berry sauce.

LITAA Please, mother. She needs to answer me.

SHANAA Oh, tush. Here, have a taste.

SAGU You know, there's a secret admirer who would not mind your messy ways at all, Kutaan.

KUTAAN Huh. Some boy with big calf muscles?

SAGU No, really! You know that Eech clan boy that was hanging around while we practiced? He was making moony eyes at you the whole time!

KUTAAN I do not wish to talk about things like that, cousin.

SAGU He is not so bad –

SHANAA The Eech clan boy... Do you mean the son of the Eech clan leader? That is very interesting...

SAGU Mm hmm. He told one of the other boys he thought Kutaan was the most wonderful singer he had ever heard. So we know he *must* be love blind.

KUTAAN Sagu – stop.

SAGU *(beat)* I am sorry. I did not mean to upset you.

(TA and JINIHAA enter.)

TA Well, everything is nearly ready out there. And who did you upset?

SHANAA Kutaan. But there is no reason for her to be upset. She has a young boy from the very prestigious Eech clan interested in her. Would it not be interesting if they were to marry?

JINIHAA Hmm, I don't know if I approve of this. What do you say, Ta? Sounds like it's time to play "Chase the Frightened Deer"...

TA *(chuckles)* I do not know if I would go that far, but I do think she is a bit young to be thinking of marrying important clan leader's sons.

(JINIHAA starts to sneak food from what the women are preparing.)

KUTAAN *(quietly)* I will not be marrying him.

SHANAA I might remind you, Ta, that this is the same age you started following Litaa around. *(chuckles)* Why, do you remember that little Lynx you carved her? I think she carried that around with her for months!

(TA moves to LITAA and puts his arm around her.)

TA Ah yes. I worked so long on that. I wanted to create a lynx so that any time she thought of looking at some other boy, she would look at it and think of me instead!

LITAA Huh. Already trying to bribe me!

JINIHAA Well, it worked!

(Moves toward KUTAAN.)

But that kind of thing won't work on my clever niece, will it?

KUTAAN *(crying)* I am not getting married!

(Everyone stops to look at her.)

JINIHAA I am sorry, Kutaan. I was only teasing.

SHANAA Oh, you men keep getting in our way. This is all women's talk and women's work! Get, get! You too Sagu!

(TA and JINIHAA exit. SAGU stops by KU-TAAN before leaving.)

SAGU I am sorry, cousin. I did not mean to upset you. I just…

Not all men are like him, Kutaan… I won't be like him.

(KUTAAN doesn't answer. SAGU exits.)

SHANAA Grandchild – fix your robe. And now that those men are gone – what do you mean you will not marry, grandchild? And someone from a prestigious clan! Your own grandfather's clan!

(KUTAAN wipes away tears.)

WANADOO Mother, please. She does not have to think about this now. We all are picking on her.

(WANADOO gets up and hugs KUTAAN.)

Will you go get me some more salmon strips, niece? And look – I have a little sweet just for you.

(KUTAAN exits. LITAA watches her exit.)

LITAA Did all that seem quite odd?

WANADOO What? Kutaan?

LITAA Yes… She has never wanted to be around boys at all. Not like some of the other girls.

SHANAA Well, that just shows how well you brought her up, daughter. She is not one of those silly, low-class girls who run after any boy that comes their way. My grandchild will wait for an appropriate boy.

WANADOO And *then* she will run after him?

SHANAA Of course not. He will see how beautiful she is and run after her!

LITAA But – girls her age should want to be around boys. She doesn't like being around any of the boys, or the men. Except…

WANADOO Except what?

LITAA Except those traders. The ones from the dleit ḵaa town.

SHANAA *(sound of disgust)* Oh I do not like those traders. You never know what family they came from.

LITAA If she will not listen to me, I am going to speak to Ta and Jinihaa. Maybe they can at least make sure the traders do not talk to her anymore.

SHANAA Yes – Jinihaa will fix it. They like to deal with him best, you know. He makes such good bargains with them. He is just like my brother used to be. You remember your Uncle Lushke?

(LITAA and WANADOO look quickly at each other.)

Your Uncle Lushke could talk them into anything!

LITAA Yes – Uncle Lushke certainly could…

(KUTAAN enters with salmon strips and gives them to WANADOO.)

Kutaan, come here. Now – I have been thinking and – I am very serious about you not being around those traders anymore.

KUTAAN But –

LITAA Do not argue. I have told you before not to go around them and you do not listen. I will be speaking to your Uncle Jinihaa later and he is going to fix this problem.

(KUTAAN moves quickly away, trying to hide her tears. She starts fiddling with the boxes, and something falls to the floor.)

It is no use trying to cry with me, Kutaan. It will not change my mind.

And do not make a mess with your things again – I just cleaned those up.

(LITAA grabs the item that fell and opens a box to put it back in.)

KUTAAN No! Not -

LITAA What on earth-

(LITAA holds up multiple dolls, filthy and in tatters. Some barely have limbs hanging on them.)

Kutaan! What is the meaning of this?

(KUTAAN is frozen.)

This is mad – all these beautiful dolls… just… in tatters. These were gifts Kutaan!

SHANAA *(tsking noise)* Children her age are just so careless.

LITAA Careless? Mother – this is not just careless. She clearly destroyed these dolls!

SHANAA I remember when Jinihaa would play like that. He would make a whole village out of mud and then destroy it like he was a monster.

LITAA This is quite different! Something is the matter. Kutaan, what is wrong with you?

SHANAA Nothing that is not perfectly normal. Frustrating, but normal.

WANADOO I am sure you will not do it again, will you?

(KUTAAN shakes her head.)

LITAA No. No – this is not normal! Come here.

SHANAA Leave her be.

LITAA You tell me right now. Did – *(long pause)* Did someone hurt you?

SHANAA Litaa! What is this?

LITAA I want to know, daughter. I have been watching you and – I think someone hurt you.

KUTAAN No!

LITAA Tell me -

SHANAA I do not know what has gotten into you. You are being such a bully. She said no. What made you think such a thing?

(TA and SAGU enter.)

TA It's just about time! Why don't-

LITAA Someone is hurting Kutaan, mother. I know it.

TA What is this? Hurting Kutaan?

SHANAA Ah – your wife is making up things in her head. You better talk to her.

TA Litaa – what is going on? Our daughter looks terrified.

LITAA Ta, I found this *(hands him doll)*. Something is very wrong with her, and I know – I just know – that someone is hurting her.

TA What makes you think that?

LITAA Children do not destroy things they treasure for no reason.

TA That does not mean someone is hurting her.

LITAA Daughter – tell them.

KUTAAN I-

TA Stop. Stop this Litaa. I dealt with this already.

LITAA What do you mean you dealt with this?

TA *(sighs, considering his next words)* If you must know, yes. There was a situation. But it was long ago and nothing happened, right Kutaan? She was just scared. I am sure these dolls are just a part of that scare she had. But she was much younger then and – my darling, can we not talk about this at a better time?

LITAA Why did you not tell me?

SHANAA Just look at how you are behaving! Of course he was right not to tell you. Scaring my poor grandchild and going on about some dolls.

LITAA You knew about this too?

TA You are just so hard on her. When she came to me, I knew it would upset you and would make things even worse between you. It was not any terrible thing. I promise we will talk about this later.

LITAA *(long pause)* You still should have told me sooner, husband.

TA I know… I know. I am sorry. It was not right of me. I will not make the same mistake again.

(Kisses LITAA'S forehead. LITAA puts the dolls back in the box and picks up a bowl, but does not continue working, and stands to the side in thought.)

(JINIHAA enters.)

JINIHAA What a bunch of mopey faces! We are all ready to start out there.

WANADOO Sister, can I help you with something?

LITAA Oh… oh no.

(LITAA fiddles with a small cedar box.)

JINIHAA Ta – can I help *you* with anything?

TA You might want to pry up your sister there.

(JINIHAA moves over to LITAA and playfully elbows her.)

JINAHAA What is the matter, sister? *(pokes her in the side)* Are you afraid of Sigeidi too?

(TA, SAGU and WANADOO all laugh.

KUTAAN *does not laugh, but moves forward on the stage with her blanket wrapped tightly around her.*

LITAA *begins to slowly stir a bowl, watching KUTAAN from across the room.)*

TA Ahh – even *I* would be afraid of Sigeidi today! I tell you, if we fail to marry off that boy of hers just so, we will have no peace in this village for winters to come!

(As the others talk amongst themselves and get ready, she watches as JINIHAA slowly moves closer to KUTAAN.)

SAGU I cannot see why anyone is letting Sigeidi get away with her temper today. She can be strict, but today she is downright rude!

TA (*chuckling*) So I suppose you were brave enough to tell her what is what today, huh Sagu?

SAGU Certainly not! My battle strategy has been carefully thought out.

You see, when I see Sigeidi coming – I turn and run as fast as I can in the opposite direction.

TA I think that is wise nephew. Just last night, I heard Sigeidi's husband tell her to stop being so rude to him. I have not seen hide nor hair of that man since!

(*TA, SAGU and WANADOO laugh. Across the room, JINIHAA reaches up to intimately stroke KUTAAN'S cheek as she tries to step away, but she is backed into a corner. She starts to cry.*)

Maybe we ought to start a search party for Sigeidi's husband before –

(*LITAA drops the box loudly on the floor, its contents spilling out. Everyone stops what they are doing and saying to look at her, including JINIHAA and KUTAAN.*)

WANADOO Litaa! Are you okay? (*scrambles to help clean it up*) What is it?

LITAA (*Looking at KUTAAN*) Oh no! No!

(*Everyone looks at LITAA. JINIHAA drops his hand and moves away from KUTAAN.*)

LITAA The way Jinihaa touched her cheek just now... and the way she moved back. How could I not see it?

JINIHAA It was an innocent gesture.

SHANAA All this fuss because he touched her cheek – are you going mad, daughter?

LITAA I know what I saw. It was the same way Uncle Lushke touched me!

(*WANADOO puts her hand to her mouth.*)

WANADOO Oh mother – you said he stopped...

SHANAA Shush!

LITAA What do you mean stopped? You mean – Jinihaa has done this to others?

SHANAA Done what? Touched someone's cheek? This is ridiculous and we must get out to our guests.

(*SHANAA tries to walk forward, expecting LITAA to get out of her way, but LITAA will not move.*)

You cannot bully me like this!

LITAA Did Jinihaa hurt someone else, mother?

SHANAA No he certainly –

SAGU Yes. Yes he has.

(*SHANAA and LITAA both stop and look at SAGU.*)

LITAA You know of someone nephew? Who?

SAGU It was... when I was little...

LITAA Sagu – did Jinihaa hurt you too?

JINIHAA Why would I hurt my only nephew?

SAGU (*does not look at JINIHAA*) Yes, auntie –

SHANAA Wanadoo – speak to your son!

WANADOO Sagu... please. This is not helping...

LITAA (*turns to look at WANADOO*) You knew this?

(*WANADOO hides her face.*)

Wanadoo... How could you not speak up when you know – you KNOW – what it is like to be hurt by your uncle?

WANADOO Mother promised... I did not think...

LITAA You did not think of protecting your son?

WANADOO I did! It stopped – and it was not so bad. It was nothing very bad...

SHANAA There was nothing wrong at all, just Sagu confusing things. He never had a father. He doesn't know any better.

LITAA Ta – why do you stand there and say nothing? You must do something!

TA Maybe we should –

SHANAA He must stop his wife before she embarrasses us all, that is what he must do. The guests can hear your screeching.

JINIHAA I told you, I would never –

LITAA You shut your mouth–

SHANAA You bully your husband, you try and get this child to tell lies, you pick on your brother. What more will you do to hurt me? Why do you hate me?

(*LITAA considers SHANAA and then turns to KUTAAN.*)

LITAA Kutaan, tell them this instant. Tell them what he did.

(*KUTAAN looks terrified. SAGU goes and puts his arm around her. KUTAAN begins to speak.*)

TA Kutaan, remember your promise!

LITAA Promise..?.. This – *this* is what you failed to tell me?

TA I dealt with it last winter. Nothing is going on. Kutaan will even tell you herself.

LITAA No... no. This is not right... Who are you people?

You must tell them Kutaan.

(KUTAAN does not speak. LITAA takes KU-TAAN by the shoulders and speaks slowly.)

I was once a girl whose uncle liked to take her to dark places and touch her. My mother did not believe me. But if my daughter told me that happened to her – I would believe her.

But you have to tell them what is happening. I cannot help if I do not know.

(KUTAAN looks to TA.)

SHANAA Grandchild, you don't listen to her. Go to your father.

(TA moves as if to take KUTAAN'S arm. KU-TAAN moves as if to go with TA but LITAA yanks KUTAAN away.)

LITAA All right - if you want things to stay as they are –

(LITAA turns KUTAAN to face the others, in-cluding JINIHAA.)

(raises voice) If you want what is happening to stop, you have to tell them right now. You have to tell them I'm not crazy – that Jinihaa is hurting you.

(SHANAA is shaking her head at KUTAAN. She still does not speak.)

Kutaan. If you do not speak now I will know you *like* it.

(KUTAAN does not speak. SAGU walks over to her and takes her hand.)

KUTAAN *(long pause – looks at SAGU)* I do not like it. I... I want it to stop. Yes... Uncle Jinihaa... does things...

(Everyone looks at JINIHAA. He does not speak at first, then buries his head.)

JINIHAA I never hurt her. Things just...I just love her so much and... I got carried away with how much I love her.

(LITAA starts to move toward JINIHAA and he jumps behind his mother. SHANAA grabs LITAA'S arm.)

TA Litaa please - This is something that is be-tween your brother and me. I will deal with this later.

LITAA Just like you dealt with it last winter? I have spent a lifetime watching this village put this sort of thing off until "later."

(Nobody speaks. LITAA starts to remove KUTAAN's robe.)

SHANAA No! Don't do that Litaa!

LITAA *(pauses – but does not look at SHANAA)* That's right mother. You know what we are hiding, don't you?

(LITAA completely removes KUTAAN'S robe. Underneath her colorful robe is a dingy, dirty robe of faded color. The wolverine crest is a barely dis-cernible face with bared teeth. There are gasps. KUTAAN turns away from everyone, hiding her face.)

Yes, this is what we hide. We hide it beneath these perfect robes, but this is what you have done to my Kutaan. This is what Jinihaa has turned my daughter into.

SHANAA Litaa, this is shameful!

LITAA This *is* shameful. *I* am ashamed she had to hide it from me...

(LITAA removes her robe as well. Beneath is an even dirtier robe, with the same wolverine crest.)

You see daughter, I have been hiding this, too. I too have been hurt by people in this village. I too have been made dirty and ashamed.

SHANAA *(trying to speak quietly)* For shame! The guests will all hear you!

LITAA Let them hear. *(turns to speak to family, audience)* This is who I am. You know me as Litaa, from the proud Nooskw Clan, the wife of Ta. But this is who I truly am. This is my real clan.

(Nobody speaks. LITAA turns to WANA-DOO, who looks startled.)

Wanadoo - sister... now is the time. We must stop this disease.

(WANADOO starts to slowly take her robe off, but SHANAA reaches out and pulls WANA-DOO toward her, holding her robe on. WANA-DOO bundles her blanket around her and moves to stand behind SHANAA, not looking at LITAA. LITAA says nothing more to her, but speaks to everyone.)

My daughter and I will leave this place.

TA Do not go, Litaa.

LITAA We will stay if you make that monster leave. Will you do that for your daughter?

TA I just want a peaceful village... Surely what you are asking does not restore peace in this place.

LITAA I never did think I would see the day in which my husband would choose "peace" in the village over the safety of a child. *His* child. This is no husband of mine. This is no father to his daughter. This is no *man*.

(LITAA and KUTAAN begin to leave. TA starts to move toward LITAA and KUTAAN, but SHANAA puts her hand out to stop him.)

SHANAA Ta, let her go. She won't last long out there alone.

(LITAA and KUTAAN continue to leave. SAGU runs out to them before they get to the door, ignoring SHANAA trying to keep him back.)

SAGU Kutaan! Wait...

(SAGU embraces KUTAAN. He looks to LITAA.)

I – I am sorry, Auntie.

(LITAA holds SAGU'S face in her hand.)

LITAA There is nothing you should be sorry for, nephew. You can come with us.

(SHANAA and WANADOO quickly jump out and pull SAGU back.)

I am so sorry Sagu...

(KUTAAN and LITAA exit.)

Scene 6

(STORYTELLER enters slowly.)

STORYTELLER Wolverine Woman was born in a time when the world was much warmer than it is now. And there were many strange creatures we don't see anymore. Can you imagine a big lizard crawling around these lands now? Weird. But it used to be true.

But the land was growing colder, the winters longer. And Wolverine Woman was not doing well in the cold.

One day, Otter saw her huddled and trying to keep warm, and he was not very nice.

He showed off his long, luxurious coat, and made fun of her short, brittle hair. "Your pitiful fur can't compare to MY luxurious locks, he said. Your hair is just sad! No wonder you're so – cold."

Wolverine Woman grew angry. And her anger was hot.

Otter showed off, as otters do. And the more he showed off, the more Wolverine Woman felt herself grow angrier and angrier. And in this anger, she found she no longer had to huddle in the cold. Soon, she was so angry, the snow felt like nothing to her. In fact, her anger kept her so warm, she started to make her home right in the white snow itself.

But she also found that only her anger kept her warm. She could not let up for a second, or the winter would take her over. If she started to feel happy again, she would find another creature, another reason – anything that would keep her feeling angry.

And this is how wolverines still are – angry at everything. Wolverine Woman was brave enough to want to live as she was created... but then the coldness of a bitter winter changed her heart.

I know that seems sad. What kind of a life must Wolverine Woman have had? But I want to remind you, while so many other creatures didn't make it through the cold– *she* was still alive.

Oh my – we've talked the night away! Just a dance of lights on the horizon. But that's why I love this land... Even at its darkest, there is always a little bit of light.

(STORYTELLER exits.)

★

SECOND MOVEMENT

Scene 1

LITAA and KUTAAN enter a 19ᵗʰ century Alaskan hotel and saloon bedroom. The colors are gray and monotone, and everything is very sharp and angular. They are wearing their dirty button robes and put down their, sacks.

LITAA Here it is, Kutaan. The man we met said we might stay here if we work.

KUTAAN What kind of work will you have to do, mother?

LITAA Cleaning floors and such.

KUTAAN But that is lower class work!

LITAA What do you think we are now, Kutaan? After three months in that nasty cannery camp, you should appreciate how much better this is. Now come. Our room is just here under these stairs. Wait – *(stops and puts down the sacks)* – It's time to take off your robe.

KUTAAN *(gripping robe)* Mother –

LITAA Kutaan, do not argue. You will take this robe off. You do not need it in this place.

KUTAAN *(still gripping robe)* But how will they know what clan I am from? How will the dleit kaa know who I am?

LITAA *(beat)* Kutaan, we are nobody here. The dleit kaa do not have clans. Now take off your robe. You cannot wear it at the school anymore either.

(KUTAAN slowly takes off her robe and hands it to her LITAA. LITAA also takes off her robe. They are both wearing very plain, monotone clothing, more Western than Tlingit. LITAA puts away their belongings, takes out sewing supplies.)

KUTAAN Mother... I do not want to go back to that school anymore!

(LITAA sits and begins to sew and barely glances up.)

LITAA It is shameful to listen to you sometimes, Kutaan. Barely three months at this school and you have already given up.

KUTAAN But you do not understand mother! This woman – this teacher – she does not like us! I am trying to learn this dleit kaa language, but she does not teach it well – she just gets mad when we do not understand fast enough.

LITAA *(not stopping)* Then you must learn the dleit kaa language faster.

KUTAAN Mother... she *hits* children who speak our language.

LITAA *(stops sewing and starts to turn around, but pauses and slowly goes back to sewing)* Then you must learn how to not be hit, Kutaan.

KUTAAN Mother! *(hides her face, starting to cry)*

LITAA Kutaan, stop your crying this instant. You were let off too easy in the village but you cannot cry here as you did before.
Do you think it will be easy here, cleaning up after people like a low-class person? All you have to do is learn some words.

(LITAA hands her a shirt.)

Here now – do not think on people like that teacher. Think on things that will get us through the winter, like mending this shirt for the people who pay us. Keep your hands busy.

(KUTAAN reluctantly takes the shirt and sits down to sew beside LITAA. There is a silence in which KUTAAN seems to want to say something.)

(Cross-fade.)

Scene 2

LITAA is noticeably older, and a little slower. She pauses in her scrubbing to stretch and rub her back. KUTAAN sits beside her, sewing a nightgown, her hair up in the bun of a young lady. Both work in silence, and LITAA stands slowly, holding her back.

LITAA Daughter, let us sing the nooskw song.

KUTAAN Oh mother! Why that one again? It is a child's song.

LITAA You still miss the last parts. You only learn the parts you like, and you do not bother to learn the difficult parts.

KUTAAN But I do not understand why we even sing the old clan songs mother. You said yourself our clan does us no good out here.

LITAA We sing them because they teach us things. Our ancestors put their wisdom in the songs so we can still learn from them. It is not like those silly dleit kaa songs.

KUTAAN What dleit kaa songs?

LITAA Oh, that one about those three mice and they could not see and they cut their tails or some such thing! Silly! They teach nothing. But these songs, these clan songs come from those with wisdom. So we will learn them, and maybe one day we will understand better.

KUTAAN *(sighs)* Yes, mother. But, may I tell you something that happened in school first?

LITAA *(not looking up)* I hope you have been behaving.

KUTAAN *(getting excited)* Yes, but listen!
We were learning about science and animals. But the teacher was going so fast, and some of the little ones, like this girl Ganook, could not understand her and what she was saying. So the teacher asked Ganook to describe the behavior of a deer.
She left her village when she was a baby, and did not know how a deer behaves.

LITAA But you knew the answer, did you not? Did you tell the teacher?

KUTAAN No! I mean, yes, I knew the answer, but I did not tell the teacher.

LITAA *(sighs)* Kutaan, we have been over this year after year. No matter how the teacher treats you, you must learn what she is teaching and make sure she knows you know it.

KUTAAN But this is even better – I helped Ganook!

LITAA *(sits back)* All right Kutaan – tell me.

KUTAAN Well, when we stopped for lunch, I started to tell her a story. You remember the story of the deer and the bear that Sigeidi used to tell? I told Ganook that story, and how deer was a strong creature at first, but then he is scared, and spooks at everything, especially bear, who wants to eat him.

LITAA Ah – I always liked that one.

KUTAAN And the story helped her! When the teacher started picking on Ganook in class again, she just started reciting the behavior of a deer, just like that! All right from the story!

(KUTAAN throws up her hands with a flourish, waiting for her mother's reaction.)

LITAA *(smiles)* Well of course, that is good clan knowledge and you listened well to –

(LITAA recoils from what she was about to say.)

No – no Kutaan. This is no good.
If this teaching interferes with your own studies you must stop.

KUTAAN Mother, that is not how a Nooskw clan woman would help others back at home. She would help the other first and –

LITAA Well we are not home, are we?

(KUTAAN begins to sew. After a long moment, LITAA begins to sing.)

(LITAA begins to sing.)

LITAA K'isáani aawasháat
K'isáani aawasháat
Lgayeik̠ tsá we nóosk!²

(Song repeats.)

(KUTAAN smiles as she recognizes the song, and begins to sing. Soon they are singing the song in a round, and are more cheerful as they sing. They laugh as the tempo goes faster. But then LITAA glances at KUTAAN's work.)

LITAA Ach – Kutaan. You have let the stitches go uneven again.

(LITAA takes the nightgown from her and starts examining it.)

I told you again and again.

KUTAAN They are not that bad...

LITAA Hmph! *(shows her the stitches)* Look at that - all different spaces.

KUTAAN It is just a stupid old nightgown. They are not even paying us the regular price for it.

LITAA *(shakes her head in dismay)* I used to weave beautiful robes that the greatest clan leaders prized, and now I work on smelly old rags. But do you think I work with less attention to these? Your father may have let you get away with being lazy, but if you are supposed to do it, you treat this nightgown like it is the most valuable dancing robe you have ever seen. Now – do it over.

KUTAAN *(flustered)* Okay, but I need to do it later. I want to go to that evening social I told you about.

LITAA *(not looking at her)* Of course you do.

KUTAAN *(warily)* Are – are you angry, mother?

LITAA Would you be angry if your daughter ran off to have fun and failed to do what she promised?

KUTAAN What did I fail to do?

LITAA You promised to do our laundry.

KUTAAN *(confused)* But I did –

LITAA Why are you talking back to me? I told you to do all the laundry, and there, look, laundry all over the place. Such a mess.

KUTAAN *(walks over to where she is pointing in the hamper)* Yes... but... but these two dresses need that different kind of soap, and I thought since they were our Sunday dresses I would just do them later.

LITAA Always later, always later. You are so selfish sometimes, Kutaan. Just go to your party, and I will do all the work.

KUTAAN No, mother... I do not have to go. I can stay home from the social. I am sorry...

LITAA And now you stay home and mope and make me feel like a bully for not letting you go? No – go to your ridiculous social.

(KUTAAN stands uncertainly, clearly not sure what to do. She finally moves toward the laundry basket, and grabs a dress.)

KUTAAN I will wash them now and they will be hanging up in no time, and I will just go a little late to the social.

LITAA *(stops her cleaning completely)* And so we look like these low-class Indians who cannot show up to a gathering on time! You will just shame us Kutaan! Get out, of here!

KUTAAN *(begins to cry)* I am sorry, mother... I just... I just do not understand what I can do now to make it better...

LITAA You cannot make it better, Kutaan! That is the point! You cannot make any of this better!

KUTAAN *(sobs)* What can I do to –

(LITAA quickly approaches KUTAAN and throws the laundry at her.

As KUTAAN cries out and then falls to the floor crying, LITAA stands over her.)

LITAA STOP! CRYING! All you do is make a mess and have me clean it up for you!
I will tell you what you can do! Clean up your own goddam mess!

(KUTAAN runs from the room. LITAA slowly catches her breath.

LITAA surveys the room. She turns and brings a trash can to the back door, emptying it into a large bin. Near the trash is a crate she sits on, burying her face in her hands. A raven hops nearer to her, searching for food. He squawks loudly, startling LITAA.)

LITAA Oh, you surprised me cousin Raven! Are you looking for some mischief, or some food, little yeil?

(LITAA grabs a crust of bread from the garbage and tosses it at the raven.)

Ahh... you do not trust me? Well... I suppose that is wise. Never know what kind of harm can come from us humans, eh?
Maybe you saw that scene my daughter made in there? She is just so frustrating, raven. She can be a good girl... but oh, when she does things like that, when she makes a mess and cannot clean it up properly herself!
I see your big, black eyes glaring at me, raven. I see you think I am too hard on her. But do you know what I gave up for her? You know nothing of it, wandering the earth as you do. You cannot know what it means to be a part of a family one day, and alone the next.
Oh, and they could be a good family, cousin! They could make me laugh, so...
I know! How could I not have known?
These people, these are the same people who left me alone with Kutaan, who would rather a little girl — MY little girl...
They all turned their backs...

(LITAA buries face in hands.)

Oh how I miss them! I miss them, I miss them, I miss them!
And I love them, raven! Even still, even after they hurt me so much, even after all these years, I love them, and wish I could be there. Wanadoo helping me to cook... kissing my handsome husband's face. Even my mother, brushing my hair...

I know he was her son... but wasn't she my mother too?
You cannot know how lonely this feeling is, raven, because you never lost so much.
I am as hollow as this trash can inside *(angrily kicks trash can.)* I stink of emptiness, and everyone can smell it on me.

(RAVEN is startled, and LITAA turns to it.)

Yes — I am angry, cousin! I am angry that I had so much, and now it is gone, and I am here alone, and Kutaan cannot even be grateful for it and if it were not for her-

(LITAA stops and looks at RAVEN.)

I hate her sometimes, Raven.
How can a mother feel this way? It was not her fault, what happened. She was just a child... but without her, I would be home right now...
I know I should not feel this way! But all I see when I look at Kutaan is the face of my sister, my mother, people to help me and love me! Not cleaning up the garbage of these dleit kaa people! *(kicks trash can)*
Ah! Raven! Stop staring at me with those eyes!

(LITAA runs back inside.)
(Cross-fade.)

Scene 3

LITAA is sewing clothes, seated. KUTAAN enters, looking concerned.

LITAA *(briefly looks up)* You are late, daughter.
KUTAAN I am sorry, mother. I just... something happened.
LITAA *(distractedly, as she turns to sew a different piece of clothing)* Oh?
KUTAAN It is Mr. James.
LITAA The new school teacher?
KUTAAN Yes. Yes, he...
LITAA *(stops to look at her daughter)* Kutaan — what?
KUTAAN Mr. James is hurting some of the girls. Hurting them...
LITAA *(stands up and takes a sharp breath)* Is he hurting you?
KUTAAN *(quickly)* No!
LITAA Kutaan!
KUTAAN No - He... he tried.
LITAA *(begins to pace)* Well, I am going to go down there and -
KUTAAN He did not touch me. He tried — but I told him no.
LITAA *(pause)* You told him no?

KUTAAN Yes, and he told me he knows how to "fix" girls that tell.

LITAA *(still pacing)* Have you told anyone about this?

KUTAAN No, I came right home to tell you.

LITAA *(stops pacing and looks directly at KUTAAN)* You must tell someone. Immediately. You must tell the town's night police.

KUTAAN The police – but, the police are all dleit kaa! They will not help us.

LITAA They have stopped some of the men at the bars from hurting women before. They might help.

KUTAAN They only helped because those women were dleit kaa, I am sure.

LITAA It does not matter. You must tell someone.

KUTAAN But he didn't do anything to me. He just tried.

LITAA But you know he is hurting other girls, do you not?

KUTAAN Well, I suspect… but I did not see anything.

LITAA Then you must tell them what happened to you. Tell them what he said.

KUTAAN Do you want them to kick me out of school?

LITAA Do not be foolish. Of course not. But if they do not believe you, if they push you out, if they treat you even worse – Kutaan, if they throw *rocks* at you – You. Must. Tell. *(brings KUTAAN's chin up to face her own)* If you do not wish these girls to be harmed any more, this is what you must do.

KUTAAN *(turns away)* I cannot do that!

LITAA What do you mean you cannot? Do you have a voice, or did you lose it?

(pause)

It is very simple. If you have a voice, that is all it is. It is speaking and speaking until someone hears you. And you do not stop until someone does. A child learns to use her voice before she is a winter old. But you are not a child anymore. As a woman, you must learn *when* to use it. This is one of those times.

KUTAAN But what if they do not believe me? What if it does no good?

LITAA I tell you, Kutaan, it does not matter. You must use your voice to let someone know. And if nobody listens, you must at least show those girls that you are using your voice for them. You must show them that someone is going to say, 'This is wrong.' You must let them hear you.

KUTAAN No – no mother! –It will be so terrible again and they won't believe–

LITAA *(sharply)* Ah – Kutaan. This is shameful talk! If you do not use your voice right now, you may as well be hurting those girls yourself.

KUTAAN Mother! That is terrible! I am not hurting those girls!

LITAA But you are allowing it to happen when you have the ability to make it stop. You bear responsibility now. If you choose not to speak – you are letting it happen.

No daughter of mine will stand by and let children be hurt. Now – turn around right now. Go down to the night police, and tell them what you know.

KUTAAN I cannot do that again!

LITAA What do you mean, again?

KUTAAN To stand there again like when you made me– when I had to tell about Jinihaa. The way they all looked at me…

LITAA *(long pause)* Oh daughter… I… Maybe that is not how I should have…

If I had that moment over again, I may have – handled it differently.

But even so – even if the police have the same reaction, you still need to tell.

KUTAAN *(beat)* Mother?

LITAA That's enough! Now –

KUTAAN I am! I am… I just…

LITAA You just what?

KUTAAN Mother… will you please come with me?

LITAA *(beat - awkwardly)* Of course, daughter.

(LITAA and KUTAAN exit.)
(Cross-fade to STORYTELLER.)

Scene 4

(STORYTELLER enters.)

STORYTELLER May I tell you the saddest Wolverine Woman story I heard? Well, Wolverine Woman had a child.
(laughs softly) Oh no, that's not the sad part! The sad part is Wolverine Woman discovered she could no longer shape shift.
You see, she was out one day with her daughter when they met Deer Woman, who knew Wolverine Woman as a human being. But now Deer Woman did not recognize her old friend. Wolverine Woman tried to change back to her human form, but discovered she could not. Deer Woman left, not knowing who this angry looking creature was.

It seems Wolverine Woman had lived in the cold so long, and covered herself in the protection of her claws and her fight, that she had lost that other ability she had been born with to change back to her human side.

But she did want that ability for her child. While Wolverine Woman had been prepared to live out her long life in bitter cold, she wanted her child to know what the embrace of human arms felt like. And Wolverine Woman realized, of all the gifts she gave her daughter, she could not give her this gift.

So instead, Wolverine Woman gave her child different gifts. She taught her child anger. But also her fierce will to live. And she decided that if she could not teach her child to be a human, she would give her better gifts. Wolverine Woman gave her child huge paws so she could run through the heavy snow with ease, and the ability to run and run without having to stop.

And with these gifts, Wolverine Woman's child never let a mountain stand in between where she was, and where she knew she needed to be.

(Slow drumbeat in the distance.)

Ah – you hear that? They are about to begin an honor song. We should listen.

(Drumbeat fades as STORYTELLER exits.)

Scene 5

LITAA is sitting with bundles around her, slowly putting items in a travel bag. KUTAAN enters.

KUTAAN You wouldn't believe what happened today…

(KUTAAN slows as she sees what LITAA is doing.)

Are we going somewhere?

LITAA We are going back to the village.

KUTAAN Why would we do that?

LITAA It is about Sagu. He… Sagu died.

KUTAAN *(puts her hand up to her mouth)* What? What do you mean? How do you know?

LITAA Your Father sent for us. A man came… he knew Sagu by name. Your cousin… Your cousin… threw himself off a cliff.

KUTAAN No! Why? Why would he do such a thing?

LITAA The man said… He said Sagu was caught with… he was caught with a little girl.

KUTAAN …You mean?…

LITAA Yes. Yes. My nephew started hurting children too.

(There is a long pause. Neither LITAA nor KUTAAN speak.)

We will go home in the morning.

(LITAA and KUTAAN start to pack together. KUTAAN stops.)

KUTAAN Mother… If we are going back to the village… We must have robes to wear at the funeral.

LITAA Yes, I suppose so. Here, you can wear the one I was making for your graduation. It is nearly done. I will just wear my old robe.

(LITAA hands KUTAAN a folded blanket.)

KUTAAN You cannot wear that mother. It is old and falling apart.

LITAA *(tries to smile)* Well, it should suit me just fine, shouldn't it? Come, let us get ready.

KUTAAN *(turns to drawers)* I have something for you.

(KUTAAN takes a folded blanket from the drawer and brings it to LITAA.)

LITAA What is this?

KUTAAN Ever since you started working on my graduation blanket… I did not think it was right for me to be the only Nooskw clan woman here that had a new robe. So I worked on it after school. The children helped sometimes.

(LITAA takes the bundle.)

LITAA You made me a new button robe?

KUTAAN It is not so much. It is not as beautiful as grandmother would have made, or as well done as you usually do. But I am still learning.

(LITAA looks at the edges for a long moment.)

LITAA The stitches are quite even. *(looks at KUTAAN)* It is a good robe, daughter. *(pause)* Now, come. We will say our farewell to Sagu.

(Cross-fade to cedar house.)

★

THIRD MOVEMENT

Scene 1

The cedar house, with a scene set for a funeral. It is the same cedar house, but the colors are all muted, faded. SAGU lay on a table, ready for burial. WANADOO, JINIHAA, TA, and SHANAA stand around the body, singing softly. WANADOO and TA are crying. TA begins to sing a Tlingit cry song, and the rest of the group slowly joins, one by one, a slow, sad song.

ALL A<u>x</u> téi<u>x</u>'
    Kadagáax
    A<u>x</u> téi<u>x</u>'
    Choon wudichún[3]

(Song repeats)

(LITAA and KUTAAN enter, at first unnoticed. As they stand unnoticed, LITAA pulls her robes out of the bag she is carrying, and puts it back on. KUTAAN does not put her robe on. When the song ends, LITAA sings another verse, clearly and loudly, and everyone turns to her.)

LITAA *(softly, stopping her singing)* We are here.

(WANADOO runs to LITAA immediately with a sob, embracing her. TA begins to move toward them, but stops. JINIHAA and SHANAA move closer to each other, watching the scene.)

TA Oh Litaa, I knew you would come!

LITAA Of course. I loved Sagu... I loved him like a son.

WANADOO Come – come sister! *(gestures to TA)* Here, here is your husband Litaa. He will comfort you.

(LITAA moves toward TA uncertainly. TA pauses, then catches LITAA in an embrace.)

TA My darling wife... how I missed you.

LITAA I missed you too, husband.

(TA releases LITAA and holds out his arms to KUTAAN. KUTAAN moves awkwardly into his arms. TA then holds KUTAAN's face in his hands.)

TA My little deer - you are a beautiful young woman now. You look so like your mother.

WANADOO You see? I knew she would come. She would come for Sagu, and it will all be as it was.

(WANADOO moves to catch JINIHAA'S hand while LITAA and TA are embracing. She brings JINIHAA over while LITAA does not notice, to stand beside her.)

Now, Litaa, everything will be fine. Embrace Jinihaa and...

LITAA *(pulling back)* No! No – do not touch me!

WANADOO But sister, surely at a time like this –

LITAA Never, Wanadoo! There is no time that he will be anything to me again!

SHANAA You see? You see now? She will always be that stubborn, ungrateful child with no respect. I wanted to think the best of her, but they were right. She won't change.

TA Do you not see we can be a family again? With Sagu laying there you will *still* say your way is right?

(LITAA looks at SAGU and her head bows.)

SHANAA You have always been that way, Litaa, always your way. Well I ask you what being so right brought you? My Jinihaa did nothing wrong, yet you moved away and people think it is his fault. It is just not fair to him!

JINIHAA Life is so difficult for me now, Litaa. Everyone looks at me different. Surely that is enough revenge for you?

TA Be reasonable Litaa... just be reasonable...

WANADOO Oh sister, if you could just stop trying to stir things up, we could all be together. Sagu would have wanted this, I know it. He missed you...

KUTAAN What is this?

(turning to TA, SHANAA, JINIHAA and WANADOO)

How dare you all!

SHANAA Kutaan - respect!

KUTAAN You do not get my respect, grandmother!

TA Kutaan –

KUTAAN No, father. You do not get it either. You do not get my respect, you do not get my obedience, you do not get my silence! You do not get anything because you threw me away with both hands!
What are you people?

SHANAA You are the most disrespectful grandchild –

KUTAAN You will not silence us ever again, old woman! Our voices will be heard.

You think Sagu would have wanted us to all embrace and be happy together? No – no he would not.

My cousin wanted away from this place so badly he threw himself off a cliff to escape it. You know why.

My cousin – my brother – got caught with a little girl. Not a day later he couldn't live with who he was, could he?

(WANADOO turns away, covering her ears.)

You dare hide away from it, Wanadoo! Sagu told you about what happened to him when we were little and you did nothing! You carry part of the blame for turning him into what he hated.

(turns to TA) And you too father. You knew. *(TA shakes his head)* You knew about him, and you knew about me, but you wanted it all put away, for the sake of "peace." Was your "peace" worth it?

SHANAA This is terrible, young lady. Terrible things to say about sweet Sagu. Do not blame us. Your mother left of her own accord!

KUTAAN Do you think making it impossible to stay is so different from making a person go away? It is no secret who pulls the strings in this village. I blame you most of all.

SHANAA This behavior is what comes of *that* woman raising you alone!

KUTAAN *That* woman?

That woman was on her hands and knees for years because the people that were supposed to be there for her abandoned her.

That woman was the only one brave enough to look that monster in the face – and tell him no!

You do not talk about her. *That* woman is a good mother! You never were.

(KUTAAN moves toward JINIHAA and SHANAA, who turn their backs. She grabs the back of their robes, and tears them off as JINIHAA and SHANAA cry out, huddling together. Underneath their shiny robes are tattered blankets barely hanging onto them, filthy scraps. They try and hide themselves behind them but cannot.)

KUTAAN I see who you really are! I see inside you – and it is hollow and ugly and filthy! No one here is clean.

(She tosses the robes aside and turns toward LITAA.)

You were right to take me from this place, mother. There is only sickness here.

(LITAA and KUTAAN exit.)

Scene 2

STORYTELLER *enters, holding a newborn baby.*

STORYTELLER And now it is finally time to give my niece her name. Gosh – look at all that curly hair!

Do you remember I said Wolverine Woman used to have thin, brittle hair? Her anger was all that kept her warm.

But while Wolverine Woman had grown angry because of what meager scraps she had to fight for, her child knew only a mother who fought to keep her alive. The child grew healthy and strong, with long, thick hair. And on the day she was turned from the den, the child cut off all her beautiful hair, and gave it to her mother. The hair provided some warmth, so Wolverine Woman did not have to be quite so angry to survive. And because of this last gift, all wolverines have fur so thick that the snow can't penetrate it, and the bitterest winds can't pull it apart.

Well, that is how I heard the story from my grandmother, anyway.

Now, this little girl will receive her own gift. The gift and responsibility of a Nooskw Wolverine clan name. This name was given to my grandmother, who received it from her grandmother.

Since you've heard these stories now, I hope you will help me with this last bit. Don't worry – you can't get it wrong! Well – we're all Tlingit here, so let's just assume there's no way you can get it totally right, so you may as well try a few wrong ways. But there's a kind of freedom in that too.

When I hold this bit of cedar bough over her forehead, she will take the name of Kutaan. It is a name rich with respect and history and love. With this name, Kutaan will have her feet on the ground, and her ancestor's strength to push her forward.

(Holds cedar bough on infant's forehead.)

Your name is Kutaan, little one. And now we will repeat your name, so it will be yours. Kutaan-a. Kutaan-a. Kutaan-a.

(STORYTELLER exits.)
(Cross-fade to KUTAAN and LITAA)

Scene 3

KUTAAN and LITAA *are outside the cedar house, beside a docked canoe. There is no other scenery around, the backdrop is only black, and a spotlight highlights only KUTAAN, LITAA and the tip of the canoe. KUTAAN is busily preparing things to leave as LITAA seems thoughtful.*

LITAA Kutaan, wait. Things are different…

KUTAAN What do you mean?

LITAA I must stay here.

KUTAAN How they spoke to you just now – how little they have changed…

LITAA But I love them, Kutaan. I love them still, and they live in blindness. They are worse now than when we left. When I left them. They need help out of it.

KUTAAN They do not deserve help. They are happy in their blindness.

LITAA You still have much to learn. They are not happy. Not at all.

KUTAAN But they do not deserve help!

LITAA They need help, and I love them. So I will stay. There is nothing for me in the town, and there is much for me to do here. A lifetime of –

KUTAAN I cannot do it, mother!

LITAA Cannot do what?

KUTAAN Stay here! Let us go back to the town and we will make a life there. A good life – better than what we can have here.

LITAA Oh daughter, I am not making a decision for you.

KUTAAN Of course you are! I know you miss them, but I do not think we should stay. And I did not get a chance to tell you! They want me to teach! They offered me a place teaching little girls at the new school. Let us go and make this new life together.

LITAA Kutaan – you do not have to stay.

KUTAAN *(pause)* So… you want me to leave?

LITAA Daughter –

KUTAAN No, that is it! You want me to leave! Of course. Of course you do.

You want to stay with the people you really want to be with, have always wanted to be with, and you do not want the person who started all this trouble to stay with you and make it more difficult.

LITAA I haven't said a word about wanting you to leave.

KUTAAN Yes you have…

LITAA No, you silly girl. I have not. But I understand that it is difficult for you here. It is difficult for me too… Your words in there… You used your voice, Kutaan. And I was so proud.

I realized in that moment that your voice will carry very far, daughter, much farther than mine ever could.

My voice was meant for this place. I will use my voice to help the people I love. And you will use yours to help children in the dleit kaa world. You have a life there, and it can be a good one.

KUTAAN I cannot leave you alone here.

LITAA *(pause as she considers something)* Do you remember the song I used to sing to you when you could not sleep at night?

KUTAAN The lullaby?

LITAA Do you remember the words, daughter?

KUTAAN Yes… I do not understand…

LITAA Just listen.

(LITAA sings a Tlingit lullaby as KUTAAN listens. There are no drums or other noises, just LITAA's voice.)

Eesháan, eesháan
Geet awagéet
Eesháan, eesháan
Geet awagéet
Aas seiyí áa wudlisáa

Ax yádi, ax yádi
I tseen wulitseen
Ax yádi, ax yádi
I tseen wulitseen
A tuwáa dáx

Ax yées wáat, ax yées wáat
Xoot' aawaxút
Ax yées wáat, ax yées wáat
Xoot' aawaxút
Gaan awdigaan[4]

It just sounds like a song about a storm. But it is really a song about what a mother's job is. You may not believe me, because even though I tried to be a good mother, I failed at my most important job.

KUTAAN You didn't fail! You –

LITAA No – I failed to protect you when you were little, and then I failed to protect you again and again. Many mothers fail at this. So when a mother fails to protect, then a mother's job is to hold on. When there is a storm your child is in, you hold on with all your might and cover your child with your arms. Because a child believes they have done something wrong to deserve the storm. But a mother – a mother knows if you hold on long enough, the child will know the rain falls on everyone. Do you understand?

KUTAAN I think so…

LITAA A child believes the storm is their fault, but a woman – a woman knows it was just something she had to get through. A woman cannot have someone holding onto her forever, or she will always be a child.

KUTAAN I think you are telling me to leave!

LITAA That is a child's thinking, Kutaan.

A mother is *never* the one to let go in a storm.

(*KUTAAN stops to look out at the canoe, and turns to her mother. She embraces her for a long time, then turns and pushes the canoe out.*

LITAA walks back toward the house as a spotlight comes up on SHANAA, sitting alone. SHANAA is huddling against the cold, trying to cover herself with the scraps of filthy rags around her shoulders. *LITAA walks by her without looking.*

A raven calls out.

LITAA stops and turns around, looking at SHANAA trying to cover herself. LITAA turns and brings out a plain, woolen blanket from a cedar box beside the house, and goes to her mother. Without speaking, LITAA wraps the blanket around her mother's shoulders. She begins to hum the lullaby she sang to KUTAAN earlier.)

(*Lights fade.*)

Notes

1. "Ka Haa Satu (Our Voices)" – Pronunciation & English Translation
   Naa lee-yay-dee doo-wah actch (You can hear it from far away)
   Kah hah koos-tee-yee (Our culture)
   Naa lee-yay-dee doo-wah-actch (You can hear it from far away)
   Kah hah sah-too (Our voices)
2. "Nóosk (Wolverine)" – Pronunciation and English translation
   Ki-sah-nee ahh-wah-shawt (The young boys, they trapped it)
   Ki-sah-nee ahh-wah-shawt (The young boys, they trapped it)
   Legah-yay-ck tsah weh noosk (Don't let the wolverine bite you!)
3. "*Ax Téix'* (My Heart)" – Pronunciation and English translation
   Ach tayke (My heart)
   Kah-dah-gah-ck (It is crying out)
   Ach tayke (My heart)
   Choon woo-dee-choon (It is wounded)
4. "Geet Awagéet (It's Pouring Rain)" – Pronunciation and English translation
   ee-shawn, ee-shawn (My poor baby, my poor baby)
   geet ah-wah-geet (The rain is pouring down)
   ee-shawn, ee-shawn (My poor baby, my poor baby)
   geet ah-wah-geet (The rain is pouring down)
   ahs say-yee ah woo-dlee-sah (Come rest in the shelter of the tree)
   Ach yah-dee, ach yah-dee (My child, my child)
   ih tseen woo-lee-tseen (You became strong)
   Ach yah-dee, ach yah-dee (My child, my child)
   ih tseen woo-lee-tseen (You became strong)
   ah too-wah dahck (Because of the rain)
   Ach yees what, ach yees what (My grown child, my grown child)
   xhoot ah-wah-xhoot (You chopped it down)
   Ach yees what, ach yees what (My grown child, my grown child)
   xhoot ah-wah-xhoot (You chopped it down)
   gahn aw-dee-gahn (Now the sun is shining)

Hannah Khalil

Biography

An award-winning Palestinian-Irish writer, Hannah's stage plays include *Ring* (Soho Theatre London's Westminster Prize), *Leaving Home* (The King's Head), *Plan D* (Tristan Bates Theatre, nominated for the Meyer Whitworth Award), *Bitterenders* (winner Sandpit Arts' Bulbul 2013, performed at Golden Thread Theatre's ReOrient Festival in San Francisco, 2015), *The Worst Cook in the West Bank* (Liverpool Arabic Arts Festival), and *Scenes from 68★ Years* (Arcola Theatre, London, 2016).

Hannah's radio plays include *Last of the Pearl Fishers* and *The Deportation Room*, both for BBC Radio 4. Plan D is published in the United States as part of *Inside/Outside: Six plays from Palestine and the Diaspora* edited by Naomi Wallace and Ismail Khalidi; *and Bitterenders* will be part *of Double Exposure: Plays of the Jewish and Palestinian Diasporas*, published in 2016 by Playwrights Canada Press. Hannah's first short film *The Record* won the Tommy Vine Screenwriting awards and is in pre-production due to be shot summer 2016.

Artistic statement

I always enjoyed writing but didn't start penning drama until I was at university. Once I did, the stories that always interested me were human ones; I have a keen sense of injustice and like to explore this unfair world through my writing. But there was a topic that I was avoiding in my early plays, a topic that should have been at the top of my list of injustices to address, a topic I was afraid of: Palestine.

Although I had visited my family in the West Bank and knew a (very) little about my father's homeland, I had never studied it. My British secondary school history assignments did not cover the Palestinian side of 1948. And by the time I was 20, I'd been so busy assimilating that I was terrified by the weight, the responsibility of discovering, researching, and understanding what had occurred on that piece of coveted ground east of the Mediterranean.

But then I attended a seminar at SOAS (School of Oriental and African studies) set up by their Palestinian society around Oral Histories of Palestine. It was incredibly inspiring and led me to write my first play about Palestine: *Plan D*.

When that play was produced in 2010 I was surprised and delighted by the amount of people who approached me afterwards – Palestinians in the diaspora – to tell me their story: what happened to them, their family, what happens to them now, every day, living under oppression.

And what stories they were, full of pathos and drama and dark, dark, wry humour. What a resource I'd been gifted. But how to tell all these stories? So many… If I were to write each into a play that would be my life's work. I decided to try a patchwork approach, including many references, and the dates of each scene. I did however make a script note for any would-be director of the piece that in staging it the dates are not vital. They are more for the reference of director and actors in rehearsal, because the overall feeling of the play should be that whatever the date, 1948 or 2008, the situation for Palestinians remains the same.

So I undertook the joyous task of writing each of these stories as a scene. That was the easy part. More complicated was the assembly job that followed; placing the scenes in a structure that would give the sense of journey to an audience despite not having one central character and objective to follow. This shaping was a long and detailed job, the work of five years of development, workshops, and readings. I owe a debt to my long-term collaborator, and husband, Chris White who was there to help me every step of the way. And to visionary producer Alia Alzougbi, whose dedication and work eventually brought the play to the stage, at the Arcola Theatre in East London in April 2016. I'm thrilled and honoured that the play is published as a part of this volume of *Contemporary Plays by Women of Color*.

For everyone who shared their stories with me, it's my privilege to pass them on in this play.

Production history

Scenes from 68★ Years was first produced at the Arcola Theatre, London in a co-production with Sandpit Arts from April 6-30, 2016.

Cast

Maisa Abd Elhadi
Yasen Atour
Taghrid Choucair-Vizoso
Janine Harouni
Pinar Ogun
Mateo Oxley
Peter Polycarpou

Crew

Writer: Hannah Khalil
Director: Chris White
Designer: Paul Burgess
Lighting Designer: Martin Langthorne
Sound Designer: Jo Walker
Producer: Alia Alzougbi
Production Manager: Grace Craven
Stage Manager: Maia Alvarez Stratford
Assistant Costume Designer: Hollie Everill-Taylor
PR: Liz Hyder
Publicity image: Mohammed Joha

15 *Scenes From 68* Years*
Hannah Khalil

Author's note

The * in the title of this play denotes the number of years since the creation of the State of Israel in 1948. This version of the play was produced in 2016, hence 68 Years, so if you intend to produce the piece please update the number accordingly.

Please note, the dates in the stage directions are for the performers' information and it's possible but not necessary to include them in performance, at the discretion of the director. Please also note that although the scenes are not numbered they are intended to be performed in the order in which they are published.

Scene: 2010

The stage is in complete darkness, everything is still. Perhaps we hear a gentle sigh or the sound of a body turning in a bed.
Pause.
Suddenly everything changes.
The sound of a door being broken down with one hard smash.
The sound of feet moving and voices – but the stage should still be in complete darkness throughout this scene.

VOICE 1 *(Shouting)* Get up, get up now, where is he, where is he?

VOICE 2 *(Shouting)* Move!

(We hear a child scream and begin to cry, it's not clear if this is from this house or next door.)

VOICE 3 My wife is not dressed

VOICE 6 I have no clothes on –

VOICE 2 HE SAID GET UP GET UP NOW GET UP GET UP GET UP

VOICE 4 We are civilians –

(The sound of a door opening and a gun being cocked then a child screaming and crying in fear, the child continues to cry throughout the rest of the scene.)

VOICE 4 Don't point that at him he is a child

VOICE 5 Get him out then

VOICE 1 Where is he? Tell us!

VOICE 2 Move, we want to talk to your husband

VOICE 6 I'm not leaving him alone with you

VOICE 2 Get the fuck out and take your –

VOICE 3 We don't know anything

(The sound of someone falling over, the soldier has kicked the man to the floor.)

VOICE 6 Leave him!

VOICE 4 I'm filming this

VOICE 5 What?

VOICE 4 I have a camera and I'm going to show the world

VOICE 5 PUT THAT DOWN IMMEDIATELY

VOICE 3 Please calm down

VOICE 5 STOP FILMING

VOICE 3 I'll come with you – let my wife and child –

VOICE 2 GET THEM OUT

VOICE 5 IS HE STILL FILMING?

VOICE 1 Where is he?

VOICE 2 WHO? WHO's filming

VOICE 5 Him

VOICE 2 WHO THE FUCK IS FILMING!
VOICE 5 Him

(Suddenly a film projection appears of what the cameraman sees as his night vision comes into focus, a soldier in full army fatigues right in front of him, pointing a gun at him)

VOICE 2 SOLDIER PUT THAT FUCKING CAMERA DOWN OR I'LL SHOOT YOU

Scene: 1948

In the middle of the space there is a body – it is a boy. His face and hands are both bandaged, as is one of his legs. One arm is in a sling.
Pause.

BOY Mama!

(A beat)

BOY Mama! Come here! I need you!

(A beat
The BOY's FATHER rushes in.)

FATHER What is it?
BOY Where's Mama?
FATHER She's hanging the washing – why are you shouting – be quiet!
BOY I need her, I can't breath – you did it too tight
FATHER Let me see

(He examines the bandages on the BOY's face and moves them around his nose area.)

FATHER Is that better?
BOY Not really.
FATHER Breath through your mouth
BOY I'm hot. When are they coming?
FATHER Any minute
BOY You said that half an hour ago.
FATHER They will be here. They said they would and they will. You know it's not easy for them to move around.

(A beat)

FATHER Now please stop shouting, be a good boy. They will be here. Be good.
BOY What can I do? I want to play but I can't like this
FATHER Then think. Think about how lucky you are. To have both your parents here with you, about what you want to do with your life, what you will study at university. I think you should be a doctor, don't you?
BOY Because you are a doctor, right?
FATHER Not only because of that, but because you have an instinct for it. Remember the bird you found, made the bed for him, kept him warm
BOY It died
FATHER Comfortably. And dignified. Thanks to you
BOY But a doctor should make people better, not help them die
FATHER If things are beyond help then it is better to make it easy to go.
BOY Like Sayed?
FATHER Yes

(A beat)

FATHER Now be good and quiet, I'll bring them here when they come. Ok?
BOY Ok
FATHER And don't call your mother, she has a lot to do
BOY She doesn't know they are coming does she?

Scene: 2003

A pavement. A man sits outside his shop on a folding chair. He is smoking a cigarette. Either side of him is a tank.
He shifts his chair a little to the left to move out of the shadow cast by one of them.
He sees the SOLDIER looking at him and smiles.

SHOPKEEPER Hello my friend. I'm just getting the sun. Very good for you, you know. Healthy. Vitamin D.

(He sits finishes his cigarette and enjoys the sun a little more. Then he takes out his mobile. He dials a number.)

SHOPKEEPER Where are you? I've got nothing to do here. I'm sitting in the sun. I know but a shop with no food is like a blunt pencil – pointless. *(A beat.)* Come on have a sense of humour! I know. I know. How long have you been there? No. You can't have been.

That's bad even for Huwara. Are there lots of people? Really. I hope you locked the car. People could steal the things. They're desperate. And you know what the soldiers are like.

(As he says this he looks up at the tank, wary they may have heard him, they haven't.)

I know it's not your fault, I'm not blaming you – but I don't want it all to go bad in the heat, why don't you try another way – how about you turn around and try Awarta checkpoint? I know it's meant to be for trucks but your car is full isn't it? So tell them it's a mini truck... try it – you may as well. What have you got to lose? I need those things – maybe I should ask Fouad next time eh? He'd manage to sweet talk his way through, Yulla Awarta, try it –. Ok ok bye

(He hangs up the phone and leans back in the chair again.)

FRIENDLY SOLDIER *(From top of tank)* Well?
SHOPKEEPER He's stuck at Huwara checkpoint. So no Coca Cola for a few hours... you should call one of your friends down there – he's the one with the blue hatchback.
FRIENDLY SOLDIER Sorry mate, I'd help if I could – but I'm just a lowly Turai – a Private

(A beat)

FRIENDLY SOLDIER Shame, I could kill a coke...
SHOPKEEPER I know – these checkpoints hurt everyone eh? I tell you what, how about a nice shay bin nana? That will refresh us?
FRIENDLY SOLDIER Well – I wouldn't say no
SHOPKEEPER I make it really good – I have a pot of mint on the back step and it tastes so fresh. You wait – you have to try it to believe it. We'll all have a cup. It will make us feel refreshed and revived. The best. Trust me.
FRIENDLY SOLDIER Ok, thanks

(He gets up and goes into the shop to make the tea.)

Scene: 2005

We are outside a house, it is old but well kept. There is a small gate and front garden, outside which stand two men.

TRANSLATOR Are you sure about this?

(A beat
The MAN nods.
A beat)

TRANSLATOR And it's definitely this one?

(The MAN nods.)

TRANSLATOR Ok. But I'll warn you again – you must be prepared for – well you know

(The MAN nods)

TRANSLATOR Right then – you stay here. I'll go.

(The MAN stands by the gate, the translator walks up to the door and knocks. He looks back at the man and smiles weakly. Eventually the door is opened by the RESIDENT.)

RESIDENT Hello
TRANSLATOR Hi, I'm sorry to bother you, I'm a translator, I'm working with the Orchestra, you know the
RESIDENT Oh yes, they are wonderful – I have tickets for tomorrow night

TRANSLATOR Oh, that's good. Well this man here

(He points to the MAN.)

TRANSLATOR is one of the musicians and, be-lieve it or not, his mother used to live here
RESIDENT In Jerusalem
TRANSLATOR In this very house
RESIDENT Oh. I see.
TRANSLATOR And well, he wondered if he could have a quick look inside,

(Pause
The RESIDENT looks at the MAN who stares back – he doesn't smile, nor does he frown. He wears a blank expression on his face. The RESIDENT considers this face.)

RESIDENT And he's a musician?
TRANSLATOR Yes. A very good one. The best.
RESIDENT Of course he can come and have a look, come on,

(Gesturing to the MAN)

RESIDENT Come in

(The TRANSLATOR gestures to the MAN who tentatively approaches the front door. They all go in and the door closes behind them.)

Scene: 2016

A girl in Palestine has left a message on Skype.

RULA Ya Nadia – not there? Shoo? It's 10.20 with me, we agreed... oh right – the time difference... yes you're two hours behind me. Imagine Palestine being ahead of the West in something. I'll try you later. I'm waiting for you cousin...

(She blows a kiss to the screen.)

Scene: 2003

Huwara checkpoint. A huge group of people stand waiting in the heat. People with cars have got out and are milling about. They are all looking at one female soldier, standing there.
A man approaches her.

BLUEHATCHBACK MAN What's the situation?

SOLDIER Step back please

BLUEHATCHBACK MAN How long will we have to wait here?

SOLDIER Step back please. I'm waiting for orders.

BLUEHATCHBACK MAN I have a car full of food, it's going to go bad in this heat. That's my one there – see? The blue hatchback? I've got Coca Cola – want one?

(The SOLDIER doesn't reply)

BLUEHATCHBACK MAN I just want to know if you think it's worth me waiting. I don't want to leave if it's going to be 15 minutes, but I don't want to wait if it's going to be closed all day. I need to get to Ramallah. With my supplies. I'm de-livering them. It would be a shame if they went bad.

(A beat)

BLUEHATCHBACK MAN So what do you think? I know all this isn't your fault – should I stick it out a bit longer or go?

(No answer
The MAN looks despondent, he's not sure what to do. He takes out his mobile and moves away from the SOLDIER – he makes a call.
A young WOMAN in a hijab walks forward and hands her papers to the SOLDIER.)

SOLDIER What's this?

WOMAN My papers

SOLDIER The checkpoint is closed.

WOMAN But it's 3 o'clock

SOLDIER and?

WOMAN You told me yesterday

(A beat)

WOMAN To come back – remember? I'm the student. I study here and my parents live over there – 10 minutes walk. I haven't seen them for a month because this check-point is always closed on the days I'm not studying.

(A beat)

WOMAN You told me to come back here with my papers today at 3 and you would let me go and see my parents

(A beat)

WOMAN They're old

(A beat)

WOMAN I miss them.

SOLDIER I think you have me mixed up with someone else. You probably think we all look the same.

WOMAN No, I know it was you. I remember

SOLDIER You must be mistaken.

(A beat)

WOMAN Please.

SOLDIER Step back. This checkpoint is closed.

WOMAN But –

SOLDIER Step back

(The MAN has finished his phone conversation and approached again.

BLUEHATCHBACK MAN Is it worth trying Awarta? I know it's usually for trucks but – ?

(No answer)

BLUEHATCHBACK MAN We don't want to bother you – really just let us know if it's worth us waiting or not.

(The SOLDIER turns her back on them. The two rejoin the throng of people, watching and waiting to see if the checkpoint will open.)

Scene: 1948

A group of male soldiers are inside a house. The house is empty but there are signs that it has only recently been vacated, the table is laid for dinner. The SOLDIERS look at the things in the house.

SOLDIER 1 Look at this picture

SOLDIER 2 It's very nice isn't it?

SOLDIER 1 It is. Colourful. Do you want it?

SOLDIER 2 No – no you saw it first – you can have it

SOLDIER 1 Are you sure? Do you think it will get ruined in the jeep – that would be a shame.

SOLDIER 2 I tell you what – lets take it out of the frame and roll it up – then you can get it reframed when you get home.

SOLDIER 1 Good idea

(The two men very carefully take the picture down and proceed to remove it from the frame and roll it up.)

SOLDIER 3 *(From offstage)* They've got a gramophone! I haven't seen one of these for ages! Listen!

*(Umm Kulthum's "Fakarouni" plays
The soldiers stop and listen.
The sound of the needle sliding off the record.)*

SOLDIER 3 *(Still offstage)* Sorry about that

SOLDIER 2 What a racket!

SOLDIER 3 Try this

(On comes Eric Satie's "Gymnopodie No. 3")

SOLDIER 1 That's more like it.

(SOLDIER 3 comes on.)

SOLDIER 3 It's in really good condition. We should bring it with us, give it to the captain for the mess

SOLDIER 2 Good idea.

SOLDIER 3 And the kitchen is fully stocked – try this jam – it's delicious

SOLDIER 1 What kind?

SOLDIER 3 Quince – it's lovely

SOLDIER 1 It's heaven – is there much there?

SOLDIER 3 I'll collect up the jars, I've never tasted anything like it

(He goes back next door.)

SOLDIER 2 There's some lovely embroidered bedding next door as well, I'll pile it up to bring.

SOLDIER 1 See if you can get something to wrap it in, we've got to be careful with this stuff on the Jeep. It could get ruined,

SOLDIER 3 *(From offstage)* Chaps, there's a whole cake in the larder – get in here!

Scene: 2002

We are in a small studio flat, a woman is there, with a dressing gown on. She sits on the bed applying makeup. The radio is on, it is the world service and the news.

NEWS READER Things are looking bleaker than ever for the Middle East peace process as the siege at the church of the nativity in Bethlehem continues, where the IDF claims that Palestinian militants are holed up in the church. Meanwhile, in Ramallah, Palestinian leader Yasser Arafat's compound is still blockaded by tanks, which prevent anyone from entering or leaving the buildings. Elsewhere, the IDF have cordoned off the Jenin Refugee camps and brought in bulldozers in their hunt for Palestinian terrorists. Human rights organisations claim a civilian massacre is taking place as water and electricity have been cut off from the camp. No international

media or humanitarian aid are permitted into the area. At least a dozen Israeli soldiers have been killed and it is feared that several hundred Palestinian civilians may have died as the bulldozers razed the camp.

(The sound of a buzzer. The WOMAN gets up, hurriedly puts away her make up and turns off the radio and answers the entry phone.)

WOMAN Hello? Come up

*(She checks her hair and face in the mirror.
She takes off her dressing gown to reveal a modest, but sexy negligee.
There's a knock at the door
She opens it, there is a man there. He is the FRIENDLY SOLDIER from the tanks outside the shop scene.)*

FRIENDLY SOLDIER Hi.

WOMAN Hi, come in. How are you?

FRIENDLY SOLDIER Oh, fine, a bit better

WOMAN And your mother?

FRIENDLY SOLDIER Getting worse

WOMAN I'm sorry to hear that… Would you like something to drink?

FRIENDLY SOLDIER No, thank you

WOMAN What's the matter?

FRIENDLY SOLDIER Nothing, I'm sorry I'm late. The traffic was a nightmare. Almost a standstill on Ayalon. There was a bomb scare. Then I had a run in with this taxi driver

WOMAN Arab?

FRIENDLY SOLDIER No, Israeli

WOMAN What happened?

FRIENDLY SOLDIER I clipped his tail light – it was an accident – you could hardly see it – but he went crazy asking me where I was going. He wanted my number

WOMAN What did you do?

FRIENDLY SOLDIER Drove off. I couldn't give it to him. You know I'm signed off for stress – I have to avoid anything like that…

(A beat)

FRIENDLY SOLDIER Did you get my message?

WOMAN No I didn't – but it's ok. When you are coming I normally clear my afternoon.

FRIENDLY SOLDIER I didn't know that. You didn't get my message?

WOMAN No. But I don't mind. You're here now.

(A beat)

WOMAN You seem really shaken. You're not yourself.

(A beat)

WOMAN Did the taxi driver bother you that much?

FRIENDLY SOLDIER Check the message I left you

WOMAN Why?

FRIENDLY SOLDIER I asked you something in it. Check it.

WOMAN Why don't you just –

FRIENDLY SOLDIER Check it.

WOMAN Ok, ok

(She gets up and finds her mobile.)

WOMAN Are you sure you won't have a drink?

(He shakes his head.
She listens to her voicemail. She hangs up.)

WOMAN I see.

FRIENDLY SOLDIER Is it ok?

WOMAN What do you mean?

FRIENDLY SOLDIER Do you mind?

WOMAN Why would I mind? If it's what you want

FRIENDLY SOLDIER It is. Very much

WOMAN I'm a little surprised.

FRIENDLY SOLDIER So am I – but I thought I should be honest with you. If I can't be with you then –

WOMAN Yes. But I'll need you to be more specific.

FRIENDLY SOLDIER What?

WOMAN You need to tell me what you want.

FRIENDLY SOLDIER Oh. Well. Perhaps I – hold on.

(He takes a jotter and pen from his pocket and writes for a moment or two.
He then hands the paper to the woman.
She reads, nods.)

WOMAN What does that say?

FRIENDLY SOLDIER Wall.

WOMAN Oh.

(She continues to read.)

WOMAN Ok. Well it's not exactly – I mean it's unusual.

FRIENDLY SOLDIER If you are uncomfortable –

WOMAN No, no it's ok. But it's going to be double.

FRIENDLY SOLDIER I'll pay you triple.

WOMAN Do you want me to change?

FRIENDLY SOLDIER Would you mind?

WOMAN What shall I wear?

(He goes to her drawers and looks at the clothes.
He takes out a pair of dark tracksuit bottoms and denim shirt with a faint military air.)

WOMAN Really?

(He nods.
She takes off the negligee and puts on the tracksuit bottoms and shirt and faces him.)

FRIENDLY SOLDIER Good. Do you have any boots?

(She takes out a pair of heeled boots)

FRIENDLY SOLDIER They're a bit trendy

WOMAN It's all I have

(She puts them on.)

FRIENDLY SOLDIER Can you tie your hair back, and take off your make up.

(She shrugs and does so. He looks around the space for the props he wants. He brings a chair

centre stage and takes some of her tights out of the drawer. He's warming to the task, getting into it. He takes a pillow off the bed.)

WOMAN Ready

FRIENDLY SOLDIER Great. Now here's what I'm thinking.

(He whispers into her ear, she raises an eyebrow but nods.)

FRIENDLY SOLDIER Understand?

WOMAN Understand.

(He takes off all his clothes except for his underpants.)

FRIENDLY SOLDIER No talking.

WOMAN Understand.

(A beat)

FRIENDLY SOLDIER Go!

(She pushes him into the chair and ties his hands to it with a pair of tights. He is acting scared. She then takes another pair of tights and stuffs them into his mouth so he can't talk. Finally, she takes a pair of black tights and blindfolds him.
A beat.
She stands on his foot. He moans loudly.
She then pushes the chair so it falls backwards – he cries out.

She gets a small table and throws it upside down on his chest, he yelps in surprise. She sits on it crushing his torso, again he makes a noise.
She bounces up and down a little, knocking the wind out of him.
Finally she hesitantly picks up the pillow from the bed and holds it above his face for a moment. Then she presses it down hard.
He moans and struggles a little.
She silently counts to four, then lifts it up.
A beat.
He is breathing hard and moaning.
She presses the pillow down on to his face again, more moaning and gentle struggling ensues. Again, she silently counts, this time to five, then lifts the pillow up.
A beat. More hard breathing and moaning from the man.
She gets the pillow and presses it harder still on his face – she's getting a taste for this.
He moans and struggles.
She silently counts to 4, 5, 6, 7 – the moaning and struggling has stopped. She is frightened. She casts the pillow aside.)

WOMAN Are you alright?

(She pulls the gag out of his mouth.)

FRIENDLY SOLDIER I told you NO TALKING.

Scene: 1992

A group of women sit on a rug outside, they have a bag with food in it and are sharing a picnic.

WOMAN 1 Right has everyone got a glass of tea? I want to say congratulations to Fatima, we wish you a very happy healthy married life

WOMAN 2 Here here

WOMAN 1 With lots of children

(Laughing)

WOMAN 1 Boys!

WOMAN 2 Why boys?

WOMAN 3 Thank you. This is such a nice idea.

WOMAN 1 Did you see the house yet?

WOMAN 3 No, not yet. Why?

WOMAN 1 Everyone's saying that Fouad has gone to soo much trouble to make it perfect for you.

WOMAN 3 Really?

WOMAN 1 I heard he got a new mattress, imported from Italy

(The women laugh, WOMAN 3 looks embarrassed)

WOMAN 2 You mean from Abu Riyad's warehouse!

WOMAN 3 I feel very special

WOMAN 1 You even got to choose your own husband – lucky girl

WOMAN 2 And such a handsome one eh?

(Two soldiers who are passing stop.)

SOLDIER 1 Good afternoon, ladies

WOMAN 1 Good afternoon.

SOLDIER 1 What are you doing here?

WOMAN 3 We're having a picnic

SOLDIER 2 Nice day for it.

SOLDIER 1 On your own?

WOMAN 1 Yes. As you see.

SOLDIER 2 What's in the bag?

WOMAN 3 Just some pastries and mezza,

SOLDIER 1 And the flask?

WOMAN 2 Tea. With mint.

SOLDIER 1 Would you mind opening the bag?

(WOMAN 1 opens it.
SOLDIER 1 peers in.)

SOLDIER 1 Looks nice eh?

SOLDIER 2 Wish my wife could cook like that

(A beat)

SOLDIER 1 Enjoy your afternoon

(They move off.)

WOMAN 2 Pass me the tea.

Scene: 2003

Inside the shop, it looks pretty empty. The FRIENDLY SOLDIER and the SHOPKEEPER sit drinking tea, the soldier is on the folding chair the shopkeeper on an empty olive oil can.

FRIENDLY SOLDIER Then my father died

SHOPKEEPER Yaboyay, what bad luck. How did he die?

FRIENDLY SOLDIER He had a heart attack, in his sleep, so it would have been completely painless they said.

SHOPKEEPER And your mother? How did she take it?

FRIENDLY SOLDIER That's the worst part, she was devastated, crying and crying. But when I went back the next day she was fine, then I realised she'd forgotten – that's the disease you see, so I had to tell her again, and her reaction was exactly the same, awful. This happened every day for a week until the nurse said 'Don't tell her anymore, it's not worth it'.

SHOPKEEPER Poor woman

FRIENDLY SOLDIER And now I have to lie to her, she says why hasn't that bastard come to see me, tell him I'm getting a divorce. And I say he's busy with work, or he's at the dentist or anything that comes into my head. It makes me feel really bad. I got signed off work for stress last year you know

SHOPKEEPER That's bad, how old is your mother?

FRIENDLY SOLDIER 70

SHOPKEEPER And to think my old mum is 87 and still climbing olive trees, I am blessed…

FRIENDLY SOLDIER You are mate, you are.

(A beat)

FRIENDLY SOLDIER Does she really climb –

(An Arab man comes into the shop then sees the soldier and turns to go.)

SHOPKEEPER Yusef, hello! How are you my friend, yulla come and try don't be shy!

NERVOUS MAN I'm in a hurry

SHOPKEEPER What are you after?

NERVOUS MAN Nothing. *(Looking pointedly at the soldier.)* Nothing.

FRIENDLY SOLDIER I better be going, thank you for the shay

SHOPKEEPER It's ok, you don't have to go

FRIENDLY SOLDIER I better – don't want anyone to steal my tank.

(SOLDIER goes.)

NERVOUS MAN What was he doing here?

SHOPKEEPER Drinking tea, probably going to buy something until you came in like a ticking bomb

NERVOUS MAN What do you mean?

SHOPKEEPER Look at yourself Yusef you are a twitching mess. A bundle of nerves

NERVOUS MAN What the hell do you expect there's bloody tanks parked in the streets!

SHOPKEEPER We've all got our problems my friend, my supplies are stuck at Huwara! What's the matter?

NERVOUS MAN I've only got a few hours before they re-impose curfew but how will I know when they do it?

SHOPKEEPER You'll know

NERVOUS MAN How?

SHOPKEEPER When everyone else disappears

NERVOUS MAN Every other Palestinian in Ramallah seems to have an inbuilt clock – they instinctively know when the curfew is starting – except me

SHOPKEEPER Just look around to see who's about

NERVOUS MAN I do that but then by the time I've realised, I'm the only one left, it's too late and those sons of bitches start taking pot shots at me

(SHOPKEEPER is laughing)

NERVOUS MAN It's not funny – look

(He pulls up his shirt to show a bandage on his stomach.)

SHOPKEEPER Shit – you were shot?

NERVOUS MAN Yes I was shot. Why are you surprised! There are men with guns, tanks!

SHOPKEEPER You should be careful – get inside when there's a curfew

NERVOUS MAN I KNOW ! That's what I try to do but I never know when it is.

SHOPKEEPER Relax, what can I get you? Tea?

NERVOUS MAN I'm in a hurry – but I need …

SHOPKEEPER Yes?

NERVOUS MAN You know –

SHOPKEEPER Oh. I don't have any

NERVOUS MAN Don't lie! Before all this they were as common as olives, now you can't find them anywhere. Please

SHOPKEEPER What do you want it for?

NERVOUS MAN Why does it matter? Do you have any or not?

SHOPKEEPER I have but it depends what you want it for

NERVOUS MAN Do you have any or not? Stop wasting my time

SHOPKEEPER How many do you want?

NERVOUS MAN One, two

SHOPKEEPER Well it can't be for cooking then

NERVOUS MAN What difference? Is there one kind for cooking and another kind for –?

SHOPKEEPER No they are all the same but the price is different. I'll get them

(He goes to the back of the shop and comes back with two onions.)

NERVOUS MAN Thank you

(He hands over a note, the SHOPKEEPER gives him change.)

NERVOUS MAN What's this?

SHOPKEEPER Your change

NERVOUS MAN Where's the rest?

SHOPKEEPER Prices fluctuate my friend – it's the economy

NERVOUS MAN Two onions!

SHOPKEEPER They're in demand at the moment

NERVOUS MAN You've charged me 3 times the regular price

SHOPKEEPER Because I know you – anyone else would have to pay 5 times. Do you want them or not?

NERVOUS MAN It's a lot of money

SHOPKEEPER I'm the shopkeeper I can charge what I like

(The man gives him a cross look.)

SHOPKEEPER If you don't want give them back

NERVOUS MAN Let me think

SHOPKEEPER You better hurry up, the curfew is not far away

NERVOUS MAN What? How do you know?

SHOPKEEPER Can't you tell? The street sounds different

NERVOUS MAN Oh my God. I'll take them, this time.

SHOPKEEPER Send my regards to your wife – tell her she'll get a better price if she comes in

NERVOUS MAN Why?

SHOPKEEPER Because she uses them for cooking… Get home safely
(The man exits.)

Scene: 1948

The BOY covered in bandages sits centre stage. There is a group of young men around him, and his father stands behind him.

FATHER Mohammed, what is that?

MAN 1 My gun.

FATHER I told you I didn't want guns in my house

MAN 1 But I might need –

MAN 2 No – go and put it by the door with the others

(MAN 1 goes off to dispose of his gun.)

FATHER If my wife saw that, with the boy,

MAN 2 I'm so sorry. It won't happen again.

*(A beat
MAN 1 returns.)*

MAN 2 You were saying?

(As the FATHER speaks he undoes the bandages from the BOY's head and then his hands and leg.)

FATHER I was finished actually. I just hope you were all listening. I know some of you will think that this is women's work, but it's 1948, not 1928. This is the modern world. A new era for us and it is vitally important for all of you to understand the principles of first aid, it may make the difference between life and death. You need to practise so why don't you pair up, as there's an odd number one of you can use my son here, the rest of you work on each other, just pick one part of the body to bandage and have a go, I'll come back in 10 minutes and let you know how you've done. There's more supplies in this box here.

*(The FATHER leaves the room.
The men get in pairs, MAN 1 goes to the BOY.)*

MAN 1 Do you mind if I bandage you up again?

BOY No just so long as it's not my head.

MAN 1 How about I do your arm and sling it?

BOY Ok.

(The MAN starts.
The BOY watches him critically
The MAN notices.)

MAN 1 What is it? Too tight?

BOY No, not nearly tight enough. Remember what he said, it has to stop the swelling and the flow of blood so it needs to be really tight. Start again.

MAN 1 Right

(He does.)

BOY That's better

(The MAN continues to work.)

MAN 1 So I suppose you are going to be a doctor like your father?

BOY Why do you say that?

MAN 1 You seem to know what you are doing.

BOY Only because he always uses me as the test dummy

(A beat)

BOY I don't want to be a doctor.

MAN 1 No?

BOY No. Ask me what I want to be

MAN 1 No.

BOY Why?

MAN 1 Because I already know. And it's a bad idea

BOY Why?

MAN 1 It's too dangerous. And you are too smart.

BOY I'm not. I want to help. Let me hold your gun

MAN 1 No.

BOY Please! Why?

MAN 1 Because you are a boy. But according to them you are a man.

BOY What do you mean?

MAN 1 Their law says any one of us over the age of 10 with a weapon will be treated as an adult

BOY So?

MAN 1 So maybe you aren't as smart as I thought. You'd go to prison, maybe even be executed. Just for being caught holding a gun. Understand?

(The MAN has finished and looks at his handi-work. It's a bit messy but does the job.)

BOY I'm not afraid.

MAN 1 You should be.

BOY I want to help.

MAN 1 How's your counting?

BOY I can do it

MAN 1 How many can you count to?

BOY As many as you like

MAN 1 Well if you want to help maybe you could count some bullets for me

(The BOY smiles.)

BOY What happens if they catch me with bullets?

MAN 1 What use are bullets without a gun?

(The FATHER re-enters the room.)

FATHER Right let's see how you are doing.

(He goes to two men, one of whom has a bandage on his head.)

FATHER What's this?

MAN 2 He has a head wound,

FATHER He'd be dead by now if that's the best you can do. Come on, all of you, I keep telling you, this is life and death. You need to pay attention. Right Wallad, come here, I need your head

BOY Oh!

FATHER You're saving these men's lives. Now everyone watch

(He begins to bandage up his son's head again.)

Scene: 2005

We are now inside the house where the MAN and TRANSLATOR are being shown round by the RESIDENT.

RESIDENT And finally this is the kitchen, which is pretty much as it would have been in 1948, in your mother's time.

TRANSLATOR This is the kitchen, similar to how it would have been in 1948,

RESIDENT The windows have been re-done obviously. And I think there used to be a wall here which was demolished to give the place more space, open it up and make it lighter

TRANSLATOR There are new windows and a wall may have been removed here

RESIDENT Oh he's looking at those tiles? They have been here as long as the house, I think that wall was covered in them once. Most of them fell off, but those four clung on somehow, refused to fall off, my wife hates them, wanted me to remove them but I insisted we keep them. They are authentic.

TRANSLATOR He saw you looking at the tiles and says that they are originals, most have fallen off

RESIDENT Would you like a glass of wine?

TRANSLATOR We wouldn't want to impose on you any more – you've been extremely kind.

RESIDENT Nonsense, come on, have a glass with me.

(The RESIDENT takes out three wine glasses and a bottle from the fridge, pours wine and ushers them to sit at the table. The three drink for a moment in silence.)

TRANSLATOR I'm very surprised you let us in. Do you mind me asking how long you have lived here?

RESIDENT 7 years, we came from the Loire Valley, in France.

TRANSLATOR Oh it's beautiful there – all the vineyards

RESIDENT That's right. But my family were only there for a generation, they were originally from Krakow in Poland.

TRANSLATOR I see

RESIDENT So you know what happened to them. Except my grandmother, she got out. Hid in a suitcase. Only got as far as Paris and then the war ended.

(A beat)

I still have that suitcase, it's an heirloom. You wouldn't believe someone could fit in it. She must have been so small. Desperate.

TRANSLATOR Yes.

RESIDENT My grandmother always wanted to come here, but she didn't make it. So my wife and I brought the suitcase here, a kind of pilgrimage and fell in love with it. You know when you feel you belong somewhere? We decided we should move here. To Jerusalem. My mother was furious, she said, "Don't you want a quiet life?"

(A beat)

RESIDENT I'd like him to know that we love this house. We loved the place as soon as we saw it. We stood outside and put our arms around one another and thought, this is it, ok maybe my father, or grandfather or great grandfather didn't live here, but my ancestors did and that's in the bones, you know. This is the end of the journey started by my

grandmother. And now we, she, can have peace. It's like it was built for us. Home.

(A beat)

RESIDENT Maybe don't translate that – it might seem insensitive.

(Pause)

TRANSLATOR You feel at peace? Even with everything that's going on?

RESIDENT Peace comes from inside you. If I didn't feel peace I wouldn't have let him in would I? But I'm not surprised, that he came. I knew he would

TRANSLATOR How?

RESIDENT It's like the final bit of the puzzle: this house has always had a feeling, a presence

TRANSLATOR A ghost?

RESIDENT No not that – it's like it has a memory. Sometimes you feel it in some of the rooms – a breeze like the echo of someone who was once there. It sounds stupid I know. My wife says I'm crazy, but I'm not. I knew it. I knew someone would come, sometime,

TRANSLATOR And he did.

RESIDENT I've looked forward to it actually, knowing that would be the full stop. The end, he'd see we belong here, and he could move on with his life and us ours, be at peace.

(Pause)

RESIDENT Do you want to translate that?

(The TRANSLATOR drains his glass awkwardly.)

TRANSLATOR Perhaps later, thank you so much for your hospitality, we really should go, there's a rehearsal in a while and he can't be late

RESIDENT Ok, well I hope that he's – you know he could have taken photos if he'd wanted

(They get up and move towards the door. The MAN and the TRANSLATOR step outside.)

RESIDENT Good bye then, I hope the concerts go well, I'm really looking forward to them

TRANSLATOR *(to MAN)* He hopes the concerts go well. *(to RESIDENT)* Thank you

RESIDENT Oh hold on, wait a minute. Just wait there.

(The RESIDENT closes the door on the men and goes inside)

TRANSLATOR He told us to wait for a moment

(Pause

The RESIDENT opens the door beaming.)

RESIDENT I found it – look, it's one of the tiles from the wall. I threw most of them away but I remembered I kept one. Maybe he'd like to have it. *(Directly to the MAN)* Here – take this – it would have been on the wall when your mother was here

(The RESIDENT looks directly at the MAN and hands him the tile which the MAN takes and stares at.)

TRANSLATOR Thank you.

RESIDENT I thought he'd like it. Goodbye then,

TRANSLATOR Goodbye, thanks

(The RESIDENT shuts the door.
The MAN stares at the tile, then looks at the house. He continues to stare at the house until the TRANSLATOR gently takes him by the arm and leads him away.)

Scene: 1960

There is a long queue of people from one side of the stage to the other, waiting, smoking looking bored.

Scene: 2010

Inside an office. A male Western CHARITY WORKER is talking to an Israeli female OFFICIAL. Both hold lists in their hands which they consult periodically.

OFFICIAL What else?

CHARITY WORKER Toilet cleaner

OFFICIAL Ok

CHARITY WORKER Baby wipes

OFFICIAL Ok

CHARITY WORKER Female hygiene products

(She looks at him he's a little embarrassed, she smiles a little.)

OFFICIAL Tampons?

CHARITY WORKER And sanitary towels

OFFICIAL Ok

CHARITY WORKER Toothpaste

OFFICIAL Ok

CHARITY WORKER Toothbrushes

OFFICIAL Ok

CHARITY WORKER Bath sponges

OFFICIAL Ok

CHARITY WORKER Candles

OFFICIAL Ok

CHARITY WORKER Blankets

OFFICIAL Ok

CHARITY WORKER Mineral water

OFFICIAL Ok

CHARITY WORKER Plastic combs

OFFICIAL Ok

CHARITY WORKER Sticks for brooms

OFFICIAL Ok

CHARITY WORKER Tea

OFFICIAL Ok

CHARITY WORKER Coffee

OFFICIAL ummmm oh yes here – Ok

CHARITY WORKER Canned tuna

OFFICIAL Ok

CHARITY WORKER Canned beans

OFFICIAL Ok

CHARITY WORKER Canned pineapple

OFFICIAL No sorry

CHARITY WORKER What?

OFFICIAL You can't bring that in

CHARITY WORKER Why?

OFFICIAL It says so here

CHARITY WORKER I can't bring in canned pineapple?

OFFICIAL Nope

CHARITY WORKER What about canned peaches

OFFICIAL No sorry – no canned fruit

CHARITY WORKER Oh. Right. Ok. So the canned tuna and beans is ok, but not the canned fruit

OFFICIAL You got it. No canned fruit.

CHARITY WORKER Right. Ok so I'll –

OFFICIAL You'll have to off load it. Anything else

CHARITY WORKER A few other things yes

OFFICIAL Go on then

CHARITY WORKER Tahini

OFFICIAL Yes

CHARITY WORKER Zaatar

OFFICIAL Yes

CHARITY WORKER Olives

OFFICIAL Yes

CHARITY WORKER Pasta

OFFICIAL Yes

CHARITY WORKER Sesame seeds

OFFICIAL Yes

CHARITY WORKER Black pepper

OFFICIAL Yes

CHARITY WORKER Salt

OFFICIAL Oh – wait – I can't – no I can't see that here

CHARITY WORKER No salt?

OFFICIAL I don't think so – hm odd one – I can check on that if you like

CHARITY WORKER Please. What about chicken stock powder?

OFFICIAL Yes that's ok

CHARITY WORKER And I've got some clothes

OFFICIAL Of course

CHARITY WORKER Shoes

OFFICIAL Fine

CHARITY WORKER And some chocolate and toys and that's it

OFFICIAL No

CHARITY WORKER No?

OFFICIAL No. You can't bring those last two things in. I'll check on the salt

CHARITY WORKER I can't bring in chocolate or toys, why?

OFFICIAL Not on the list, I'm afraid

CHARITY WORKER Why?

OFFICIAL I didn't write it friend, I'm sorry

CHARITY WORKER But why – in your opinion – why would the state want the children of Gaza to be denied toys?

OFFICIAL Good place to smuggle guns I guess

CHARITY WORKER What about chocolate?

OFFICIAL I understand your frustration but please, I'm just doing my job

CHARITY WORKER You realise that there are 1.5 million people who are effectively imprisoned in Gaza and half of them are children – it's going to be your problem when they all come of age don't you think?

OFFICIAL Don't take that fucking tone with me – you Westerners, you're so fucking self righteous. Wake up! We're just doing your dirty work – the shit you don't have the courage to do yourselves.

(Pause)

CHARITY WORKER I'm sorry. I – it's hot and it was a long drive. I'll, I'll off load the toys, chocolate and canned fruit. Would you check the salt situation for me?

OFFICIAL I've just remembered – salt's off the list too. So you better off load that as well. Then you can be on your way.

Scene: 2016

A girl in Palestine waits in front of a computer.

RULA *(quietly)* Bastana el daw el akhdar … Waiting – for the green light, for the little noise it makes. To show she's there. Waiting. Everyone here is watching me so I'm pretending I'm already talking to her. But there's no one there yet. She's not online. No one is listening. There's no audience. Or is there? Maybe I'm being watched… by those Anonymous guys… or the secret service… or someone else. Well I don't care. I'm going to talk anyway. And my English is better than any of the hameers in this library so they don't understand what I'm saying. Yalla Nadia! Weinik inti? I hate waiting. I will never get used to waiting. Waiting. Don't you make me wait too. Come on! I'm getting nervous. For the question I need to ask you. Nervous! Silly isn't it! To talk to my cousin, on the other side of the world.

England. While I'm here in Palestine. I shouldn't be nervous of her. There's nothing to be scared of. Just a little question – she can say yes, she can say no – I hope she says yes… but it can't hurt me. There are more dangerous things. There are more dangerous things to be scared of. I should be scared of the dark. That would be smart. At night. Outside. It's dangerous. But I go out anyway. Wait until everyone else is in bed. And then I sneak out. In my black hoodie. Armed. Sneak down the backstreets. My hair is hidden, so is my face. I want them to think I'm a boy. A ghost. A phantom. I go looking for my spot. My target. I always know where it will be. I plan in advance. I'm organised. Decide the best way to get there without being spotted. And once I arrive and make sure no one is around I take out my weapon and start. Spraying. Red. Green.

Black. White. Those are my colours. You can guess why. I have one picture – logo – tag. Not like Handala the barefoot Palestinian boy – mine is a tree. I use a stencil. It was sent to me by a woman in Syria. She used it there. This tree's branches spell out words – whatever I want them to say – so this way it's an original and a copy at the same time. I like that. Sometimes I write "tahrir". Freedom. Sometimes I write the names of people in prison – people who everyone thinks are forgotten, sometimes the names of the dead. It depends. On what's happening. But the most exciting part is the next day when someone discovers this new drawing on the wall. They all start talking and wondering who is the new Palestinian Banksy! Khally wally Banksy... His pictures are considered art. No one would dare touch them... but mine are gone by the end of the day. Painted over. Gone but not forgotten. I need to make sure they're not forgotten. So, I'm waiting for my cousin Nadia to call me... to ask her...

(She turns to someone nearby who has said something to her.)

No I'm still using it – sorry this is an important call – from London.

Scene: 2002

An attractive WOMAN stands outside Tel Aviv airport, she is waiting for a taxi. She sees the TAXI DRIVER in his car and approaches him.

WOMAN Are you free?

TAXI DRIVER Depends – where you going?

WOMAN Home

TAXI DRIVER Where's that?

WOMAN Ramat Aviv

TAXI DRIVER Oh – Ok, I should warn you the traffic's a nightmare today – there was a bomb scare in town and everyone's acting crazy

WOMAN I don't care how long it takes – I just want to get back to my house

TAXI DRIVER Let me help you with your bag

(He lifts it into the boot.)

WOMAN What happened to your taillight?

TAXI DRIVER Like I said there are crazy people out today.

(They get in the car – she in the front seat. He starts the engine and they drive a little while in silence.)

TAXI DRIVER So you been on holiday? Lucky you

WOMAN Sort of

TAXI DRIVER Where were you?

WOMAN Poland

TAXI DRIVER No wonder you don't have a tan

WOMAN It was cold.

TAXI DRIVER Should have gone to the Red Sea – that's where I always go

WOMAN It wasn't just a holiday

TAXI DRIVER No?

WOMAN I had to go – for my service

TAXI DRIVER Oh, oh right. I did that – years ago – I remember they took my fingerprints on the first day and pictures of my teeth – I though – hey I'm not the prisoner here!

WOMAN Where did you serve?

TAXI DRIVER Ended up a driver! All over. Chauffeuring Generals – all sorts. What I'm good at... Poland – so did they make you go to?

WOMAN Auschwitz

TAXI DRIVER Ah. Have you been before?

WOMAN No

TAXI DRIVER That's a tough one eh? Seeing the actual place... what happened there... Really gets you. Never affected my family – they came here in the 1920s, but it's a terrible place. Eerie... you can feel the presence of all those poor people, don't you think?

(A beat)

TAXI DRIVER I kind of also always wondered why? You know why send us there? It's a terrible thing and it's important to remember, but it's too late to change that now. I mean did you feel it was relevant to you?

WOMAN What do you mean? Of course it's relevant

TAXI DRIVER Excuse me, I mean to your day-to-day work – on the front. I mean it's important to remember like you say, that people want to destroy us and all that, but when you are in the service you are reminded of that

every day aren't you? When you live here
you are reminded of that every day. Why
send the young people to Auschwitz, or
Belsen, it's depressing.

WOMAN That's offensive.

TAXI DRIVER Oh I don't mean to offend you –
I'm just trying to say it's a shame a nice young
girl like you has to go and experience all
that. See it. I dreamt about it for months
afterwards.

(A beat)

WOMAN So what happened with your taillight?

TAXI DRIVER Oh nothing much – some guy
was in a real hurry – you'd think his pants
were on fire, and he clipped it. But when
I got out and asked for his number he just
drove off… what's the world coming to eh?

WOMAN Arab?

TAXI DRIVER No Israeli. People are so disap-
pointing aren't they? Israeli and Arab, there

are good ones and bad ones and this one was
a bad one,

(The WOMAN begins to sob.)

WOMAN Stop the car

TAXI DRIVER We're in the middle of traffic – do
you feel sick?

WOMAN I need to get out, I can't breath.

TAXI DRIVER What is it? You're white

WOMAN Just STOP

TAXI DRIVER I think you're having a panic
attack

WOMAN STOP THE CAR

*(He stops the car and she gets out. We hear other
drivers beeping at him)*

TAXI DRIVER HEY HEY Easy pal! She's not
well! Same to you!

*(While the TAXI DRIVER waits for the
WOMAN to sort herself out this scene bleeds into
the next and we simultaneously see—)*

Scene: 2002/2007

*A MAN is shown into a room where he sits down
on a chair to wait. He is the man who had the blue
hatchback in the checkpoint scene. He is alone. He
goes to light a cigarette but sees a no smoking sign. He
puts away the packet and waits. He hums a few bars
of Umm Kulthum "Fakarouni."*

*As both TAXI DRIVER and BLUE HATCH-
BACK MAN wait they say in sync:*

TAXI DRIVER/BLUEHATCHBACK MAN What a
day. All I want is drive around but there's

always something in the way. Imagine to
be in America. The open road, route 66,
miles and miles of clear road as far as the eye
can see. No traffic jams, check points, road
blocks, diversions, nothing. Just a straight
clear road all the way to the horizon. Not
even another car. You could fall asleep at
the wheel and nothing bad would happen.
Imagine. Driving off into the sunset…
A dream.

Scene: 2010

*A WOMAN with a camera and a bag stands outside
another house, she knocks on the door.*

WOMAN Haitham, come on – it's time. Are you
ready?

VOICE FROM INSIDE No – I can't I can't come
today

WOMAN What do you mean? Open the door
are you ok?

VOICE FROM INSIDE I'm busy – not well

WOMAN But it's Friday – and it was your idea –
it's great come on open the door

VOICE FROM INSIDE I think it's a bad idea

WOMAN It's not it's brilliant – open it –
everyone else is waiting for you. They all
look fantastic honestly

VOICE FROM INSIDE Really?

WOMAN Really. Open up.

*(The door opens a little then more and a MAN
stands there looking sheepish. He is dressed up as
one of the characters from Avatar and his skin is
painted blue. He has false pointy ears and a long
black wig in plaits.
WOMAN looks at him and nods encouragingly
then starts to laugh.)*

MAN I knew you would laugh

WOMAN It's just – you look – great. Come
on. It's a great idea – it'll definitely get the
world's attention

MAN You think so?

WOMAN Of course, come on they're waiting.

MAN I'm not the only one dressed like this, am I?

WOMAN No – Mohammed, Kamila and Hameed – loads of people.

MAN Ok – hold on a minute

(He gets his Palestinian flag from inside the door.)

MAN Let's go then.

(They begin to walk to the bottom of the street, as they do more people join them, some dressed as Avatar characters, some with their faces covered with scarves, others in more traditional western clothes. WOMAN with her camera begins to take photos. NERVOUS MAN appears.)

MAN Yusef! What are you doing here?

WOMAN You said you weren't coming again

MAN What did the doctor say?

NERVOUS MAN That my stomach ulcer is worse than the bullet wound,

WOMAN That's the third time you've been shot in as many years – you are so unlucky

NERVOUS MAN What do you mean unlucky – I'm alive aren't I?

MAN You shouldn't be here, you aren't even from Bel'in

WOMAN You're like a dog with a bone, always back for more

NERVOUS MAN I have to stand in solidarity with you

MAN What did Hanan say?

NERVOUS MAN She thinks I'm visiting my mother, if she knew I was here she'd really kill me, seriously – Hanan is scarier that the whole of the IDF, so no photos please? Eh?

(They approach a barrier where there is a partition marked by barbed wire and metal girders. Several people put on gas masks including WOMAN with camera. We do not see the soldiers but they are on the other side of the partition. The villagers of Bel'in begin their peaceful protest chanting: "No wall in Bel'in"
They wave their Palestinian flags and a couple of men begin to shake the barrier with their hands
Suddenly a tear gas grenade is fired at them it lands at the feet of WOMAN with camera.)

MAN Shit! I knew I forgot something –

(NERVOUS MAN takes an onion from his pocket and a small penknife and cut it in half.)

NERVOUS MAN Here

(The two men hold the onions to their noses. Avatar MAN picks up the canister and throws it back in the direction it came from.

WOMAN begins to take photographs.

More tear gas canisters are thrown as someone shouts from the crowd, "Shame on you! This is a peaceful protest!"

The protestors scatter to avoid the tear gas.

The stage is now empty but covered in smoke.)

Scene: 2011

A little BOY is in bed sleeping, it is dark, the early hours of the morning. He is young. His MOTHER enters the room and gently tries to wake him up.

MOTHER Majeed, Majeed – wake up. It's time.

BOY Huh? He's mine…

MOTHER Darling

BOY I'm taking him home

MOTHER Majeed, wake up darling…

(The BOY stirs.)

BOY Oh, Maama. I was dreaming.

MOTHER Not bad ones again?

BOY Is it time for me to get up?

MOTHER It is, my boy it is.

BOY But it's too early.

MOTHER The bus is coming soon, now come on, up you get.

(She encourages him to get up and fetches his clothes. He talks as she does this, and begins to dress himself, she helps him a little now and then.)

BOY It was such a nice dream. There was a cat. A kitten. He was tiny, I could pick him up in my hand. He was a tabby and he liked to be grabbed by the back of the neck because that's what mummy cats do isn't it? But his wasn't there. His mummy. She was gone somewhere else and I found him in the car park, just wondering about. And I put him inside my jacket and he was all warm, and I could feel him moving as he breathed next to my heart. And I showed Sami and Lamia and they were jealous, they tried to take him away but I said you can't because he's mine. He's my cat now.

MOTHER Did you give him a name?

BOY No, you woke me up, I didn't get that far.

(The MOTHER is now beginning to brush his hair.)

MOTHER Now you remember what you have to say today?

BOY Yes. Are you coming Maama?

MOTHER Darling we've been over this. You know I'm not allowed. You have to go. Be a brave boy. You've done it before.

BOY I know.

(A beat)

MOTHER There – you look all smart, now go and brush your teeth

(The BOY goes to brush his teeth. The MOTHER brings out several bags for him to take with him.)

MOTHER So in this one is your breakfast, try and have a little sleep on the bus first, then when you wake up at the first checkpoint eat something ok?

(A beat)

MOTHER Aren't you excited?

BOY I want you to come.

(A beat)

BOY Sami says Daddy is in Israel

MOTHER What – when?

BOY He said the bus takes so long because I have to travel to a whole nother country

MOTHER Did he?

(A beat)

MOTHER I can't come. You know they don't let me. That's why you have to go. You are the man of the family now, what are you going to say?

BOY "Mother sends her love and devotion, we both think of you every day and before we eat a meal we say a silent prayer."

MOTHER Good, what else?

BOY Sitti is healthy, the olive oil is nearly ready, Farouk is engaged and I got 10 in my English test

MOTHER Bravo – clever boy

BOY But why can't you come. I don't like the check points alone

MOTHER You are with the other children and Mr. Red Cross. Come on now – you have to be brave. What would your father do if you didn't visit?

BOY What will happen when I'm 16?

MOTHER That's a long way off – why?

BOY Sami says when I'm 16 I can't go and see him any more – who will see him then?

MOTHER Oh, don't worry about that you silly billy – Daddy will be home long before that. Now come on I think the bus is here.

Scene: 1960

The long queue of people reappears from one side of the stage to the other it has moved slightly. People *continue to wait, smoke, looking bored. A man whistles Umm Kulthum's "Fakarouni."*

Scene: 2002

A traveller stands outside Tel Aviv airport he has a couple of suitcases and is waiting for a taxi. The TAXI DRIVER approaches him.

TAXI DRIVER Looking for a taxi?

MAN Yes please

TAXI DRIVER Over here, that's my car, let me take your bag

MAN That's kind thank you

TAXI DRIVER No problem, where you going to?

MAN It's a bit of a journey

TAXI DRIVER Where you headed?

MAN Nazareth

(The TAXI DRIVER stops and puts down the bag)

TAXI DRIVER Are you kidding me? I can't believe this day

MAN No. Nazareth, it's where I'm from

TAXI DRIVER It's another country

MAN Its only 100 Kilometres

TAXI DRIVER 102

MAN I'll pay you whatever you like

TAXI DRIVER I don't go there.

MAN Please – there are no other drivers around – I'm in a hurry

TAXI DRIVER I'll need protection money

(A beat)

MAN I need to get home to see my father. He's not well.

(A beat)

TAXI DRIVER I think you need an Arab driver. I just don't know that area at all. I never get fares out of Tel Aviv. Besides the traffic's bad today and there are loads of crazies about

MAN Please. I need to get there.

TAXI DRIVER But I told you I don't know the way

MAN I do, I'll show you

TAXI DRIVER I don't have a map that goes that far

MAN I have it all up here *(gesturing his head)*

TAXI DRIVER How can I trust that? When was the last time you were in Israel?

MAN 1988

TAXI DRIVER Well it has changed a lot since then. You won't remember

MAN I can't forget – honestly, it's etched on my memory, this is my home

(A beat)

TAXI DRIVER I really think you should wait for an Arab driver. You know what's been going on – there was almost a bomb today. Nazareth isn't safe for me.

MAN You'll be with me

TAXI DRIVER How can you protect me? What if we are pulled over by gunmen?

MAN You keep quiet and I'll talk. In Arabic, to them. I'll tell them who I am, that my Father is unwell. We will be fine.

(A beat)

MAN It'll probably never happen anyway

TAXI DRIVER That's the trouble with you Arabs, you always look on the bright side – don't see the bad things that could happen

(A beat)

MAN I'll pay you double what it says on the meter

TAXI DRIVER Danger money

MAN Danger money

(A beat)

TAXI DRIVER And you are sure you know the way?

MAN Like the back of my hand. Don't be afraid.

(A beat)

MAN Trust me

TAXI DRIVER Oh all right then, come on, before I change my mind.

MAN What happened to your taillight?

TAXI DRIVER Don't ask

(The two men move to the car, and we hear the engine starting, then a radio comes on with a news report which we hear as the car drives away.)

BBC NEWS READER Tomorrow is Israeli Independence day and the one day a year when the Israel government allows Palestinians to visit the sites of their former homes, Israel says it will put the IDF on alert for any terrorist activity that may occur…

(Static as the DRIVER retunes the channel.)

TAXI DRIVER Is that the real reason you're back then? To visit the site of your former home? Cause trouble?

MAN No, I told you I'm from Nazareth, my father's sick

(More static as the TAXI DRIVER tries to tune it.)

TAXI DRIVER And now I can't find any music… come on you piece of crap
(More static)

Scene: 1978

Inside a very very basic house, almost a shack. An OLD MAN holds a radio, it is battered and the batteries are taped to the back. He is trying to get a reception to hear the news.

He keeps trying.
Nothing but static.
It begins to get something – it is a recording Umm Kulthum's "Fakarouni." he smiles, and begins to slowly sway and mouth the words. He gets into it, and puts down the radio to dance more, but as he does so it loses the signal and becomes static noise again.
He tuts, annoyed, and turns it off. He then moves to a stool and sits down. He takes out a cigarette and begins to smoke it. Suddenly he moves his hand to his head, something has dripped on it. He looks to the

ceiling, there's another drip. He moves his chair to one side and looks at the floor to see if he's right – if there's a drip from the roof. He watches, he waits, he's right, there is. He watches one, two, three drips. He gets up and takes a cooking pot and puts it under the drip. He sits smoking and watching it.
Pause
Suddenly his young grandson runs into the room.

BOY Seedi Seedi did you hear the news? They've liberated our lands!

GRANDFATHER What?

BOY We are free we can go home! Anytime we like! They've liberated //

GRANDFATHER Thanks be to God *(He jumps up and grabs the radio.)* when did you hear that?

BOY Just now – come on – we can go back

GRANDFATHER I knew it was coming – patience – that's what I said *(He gets a bag and begins to fill it with his clothes and things)* Didn't I tell you all, I knew it. It couldn't last forever, liberated… free at last

(The BOY begins to laugh.)

GRANDFATHER What?

(The BOY is laughing hysterically now.)

BOY You believed it!

GRANDFATHER What! You little bastard… come here

(The MAN picks up the stick and chases the BOY – he hasn't a hope in hell of catching him.)

GRANDFATHER You little bastard

(The BOY runs away from his grandfather still laughing and then runs out of the room. The OLD MAN stands, out of puff.)

GRANDFATHER You little bastard.

(He lowers himself back into his chair and lights another cigarette. He watches the drip again as his breathing gradually returns to normal. Pause A MAN walks in.)

MAN You didn't fall for that again?

GRANDFATHER He's a little bastard

MAN He knows you will always go for it.

GRANDFATHER The next time it'll be true and I won't believe him

MAN You will.

(A beat)

MAN There's a drip?

GRANDFATHER I know – that's why I put the pot

MAN You can't continue to live like this it's been 30 years – I'm going to get some iron from Mohammed, lay it on the roof and

GRANDFATHER No. Leave it

MAN You need a proper roof dad

GRANDFATHER No.

MAN Please – let me – I worry about your health…

GRANDFATHER No.

MAN Having a proper roof doesn't mean anything –

GRANDFATHER This is not where I live. It's temporary.

MAN But it's been temporary for –

GRANDFATHER What would your mother think eh? Defeat? Not yet

MAN It's just a roof dad.

(A beat)

GRANDFATHER Tell that boy of yours next time he pulls that stunt I'll be ready – and if I catch him he won't be able to sit down for a week

(A beat)

GRANDFATHER Nothing better to do…

Scene: 1960

The long queue of people from one side of the stage to the other reappears. The order has changed slightly – it has moved a little. More waiting, smoking, looking bored.

Suddenly a man jumps forward and breaks into a loud and fevered rendition of "Fakarouni." His wife clips him round the ear to shut him up. More bored waiting in line.

Scene: 1992

The women sit on their rug outside, continuing their picnic.

WOMAN 2 Can you believe Hanan has been married 10 years

WOMAN 3 Really?

WOMAN 1 It's true, I have.

WOMAN 2 What a wedding!

WOMAN 1 It wasn't a wedding

WOMAN 3 Why?

WOMAN 2 Curfew.

WOMAN 3 Oh yes

WOMAN 1 You were just a girl so you wouldn't remember, but we had to be indoors

WOMAN 2 And the bastards cut the electricity too.

WOMAN 1 That's right

WOMAN 2 Well at least your first time was in the dark – just like you!

(They laugh, WOMAN 3 looks embarrassed.)

WOMAN 1 And my mean mother-in-law was pleased because she didn't have to feed the guests all night!

(The soldiers are passing again and stop.)

SOLDIER 1 Good afternoon ladies

WOMAN 1 Good afternoon.

SOLDIER 1 Still here?

WOMAN 3 We're having a picnic

SOLDIER 2 Nice day for it.

SOLDIER 1 What's in the bag?

WOMAN 1 Just some pastries and mezza,

WOMAN 2 Just like before

SOLDIER 1 And the flask?

WOMAN 2 Still tea.

SOLDIER 1 Would you mind opening the bag?

(WOMAN 1 opens it.
SOLDIER 1 peers in.)

SOLDIER 1 Nearly finished it all

SOLDIER 2 Didn't leave any for us

(A beat)

SOLDIER 1 Enjoy your afternoon

(They move on.)

WOMAN 3 Shall we go?

WOMAN 2 No

WOMAN 1 Fadia

WOMAN 2 What? I haven't finished my tea.

Scene: 2010

A kitchen where a WOMAN puts the finishing touches to dinner and puts it on the table. Her SON is watching TV in the next room, there is a news story about the protests in Bel'in and images of the men dressed as the characters from Avatar.

MOTHER Come on everyone – dinner is ready!

(The family come into the kitchen, there's a young SON, a FATHER and MOTHER and a teenage DAUGHTER.
They all sit and the table and begin to pour glasses of water.)

FATHER Shall I serve Tabbouleh?

DAUGHTER Not much for me.

MOTHER If you aren't eating meat anymore you need to eat vegetables

DAUGHTER I've changed my mind

MOTHER What do you mean you've changed you mind? I bought some really expensive vegetarian cheese for you

DAUGHTER It doesn't seem right

MOTHER That's what you said – and we respected that but Raquel if you want us to take you seriously as an adult you have to – *(to her husband)* speak to her

FATHER Your mother's right. We respect your choices, you are nearly an adult, but –

DAUGHTER I'm sorry it just seems wrong to choose not to eat meat when there are people not a million miles away who don't get any choice about what they eat

(Pause)

FATHER That's fine. You must do what you think is right – but try and take your time to make a decision – particularly when it affects the rest of the family.

DAUGHTER How does me being a vegetarian affect –

MOTHER If you cooked occasionally you'd understand.

(A beat)

DAUGHTER Ok. Sorry Mum.

SON So you're not a veggie any more?

DAUGHTER No

SON Oh. Did you see the news dad?

FATHER What news?

SON There were some crazy people dressed up as that movie

FATHER Which one?

SON The 3-D one?

DAUGHTER *Avatar*

MOTHER What's that?

SON They painted themselves blue – isn't that funny!

MOTHER Mm. Do you want more chicken?

SON And they were all sniffing onions but that's not in the film

MOTHER Eat your food

DAUGHTER The onions help with the tear gas

SON How?

FATHER Anyone want water?

DAUGHTER Tear gas makes you feel like you can't breath but the onion helps

SON Awesome I'm going to do that for Yoav's party! It'll be really funny

MOTHER Do what?

SON Dress up as one of those blue guys

FATHER I think it's best to stick with your cowboy outfit

SON But –

FATHER It's already up there in the cupboard, otherwise your mother will have to find blue paint

(Pause)

FATHER I noticed the envelope's still there on the counter

MOTHER I can post it for you if you like?

DAUGHTER No – I'll do it.

FATHER Just remember there is a deadline.

DAUGHTER I know

FATHER Don't imagine you are the only girl in the world who wants to go to Oxford

DAUGHTER I don't

(A beat)

DAUGHTER I don't want to go to Oxford

SON Uh oh

(A beat)

SON I've finished – can I go to my room

MOTHER Don't you want more Tabbouleh?

SON No

MOTHER Dessert?

SON What is it?

MOTHER Ice cream

FATHER What do you mean you don't want to go? We spent a month on your personal statement

MOTHER Let's talk about this later

FATHER Did you know about this?

MOTHER I had a feeling…

FATHER But if you stay you'll have to do military service.

MOTHER You are not doing that.

DAUGHTER I don't want to leave

FATHER What are you saying? You want to stay here, go to university here, over my dead body

MOTHER It's not safe.

DAUGHTER Yes it is

MOTHER What about the rockets?

DAUGHTER How many people have died from the Hamas rockets mum?

SON Can I go upstairs?

DAUGHTER How many? You don't know do you? I tried to find out – I looked on the IDF website I know how many rockets have fallen here – but there's no record of how many people have died

SON Why?

FATHER Go upstairs

SON Why?

DAUGHTER Because they didn't kill anyone

MOTHER What about Mrs Silverman's niece?

DAUGHTER She's alive

MOTHER Thank God – but she was in hospital for 2 days

DAUGHTER That's because she threw herself down in the middle of the road when she heard a car backfiring

FATHER We live in a climate of fear – they've made that. That's why we want something better for you.

MOTHER Where is she getting all of this from? Who have you been talking to?

DAUGHTER No one. There's a thing called the internet

SON Can I take some ice cream upstairs?

FATHER So what exactly is your plan for your life?

DAUGHTER I don't know. I just don't want to go to Oxford.

FATHER I dreamed of going to Oxford, but we couldn't afford it, I've saved all my life so –

DAUGHTER Let him go

SON Me – no! I don't want to go to England

MOTHER No one's going to send you there

DAUGHTER Yet – you better watch out

FATHER Go upstairs

(The BOY goes from the room.)

DAUGHTER I haven't even got in yet. It'll probably never happen

FATHER Is that what this is about? Of course you will get in

(A beat)

DAUGHTER I'm not going to Oxford, I'm going to the West Bank to see for myself

FATHER The West Bank?

DAUGHTER Maybe Gaza too – you can't stop me. I'm nearly 18. I need to know what is going on.

MOTHER Don't go there look on the internet… watch TV. It's too far

DAUGHTER Further than Oxford?

MOTHER Yes.

FATHER Go upstairs

DAUGHTER I'm not a child you can order around.

FATHER You are still my daughter. And you are still underage.

(She goes.
A beat.
The FATHER stands up and picks up the envelope.)

FATHER I'm going to post this.

Scene: 2007

BLUE HATCHBACK MAN who has been wait-ing all this time on the chair is met by an OFFICIAL.

OFFICIAL Ah, hello – I'm Captain Harami, from the GSS

BLUEHATCHBACK MAN GSS?

OFFICIAL General Security Services

BLUEHATCHBACK MAN Oh, yes of course, I see.

OFFICIAL Your ID card

(The MAN hands it over.)

OFFICIAL Mr Farouky? I understand you are a driver?

BLUEHATCHBACK MAN Yes, I transport things around the West Bank

OFFICIAL What sort of things?

BLUEHATCHBACK MAN Fruit, vegetables, sup-plies, whatever my boss tells me to

OFFICIAL And how is that?

BLUEHATCHBACK MAN Fine, mostly

OFFICIAL You never have any problems?

BLUEHATCHBACK MAN Of course. That's why I'm here. There seems to be some issue with my permit. I keep being stopped

OFFICIAL Oh dear. That must be inconvenient

BLUEHATCHBACK MAN It is.

OFFICIAL So you want a permit for the West Bank?

BLUEHATCHBACK MAN I have one, but I want it renewed – it doesn't seem to be working

OFFICIAL What about a permit for Israel?

BLUEHATCHBACK MAN Oh no, I don't need that. Just for the West Bank.

OFFICIAL But would you like a permit to en-ter Israel – it would mean you could move around freely. Think what your boss would say about that – I bet there aren't many of his employees who've got one of those.

BLUEHATCHBACK MAN No, there aren't. But I don't need one – just for the West Bank – honestly

OFFICIAL Think about it for a moment. The freedom to come and go.

(A beat)

OFFICIAL I could organise that for you no problem.

BLUEHATCHBACK MAN Really?

OFFICIAL Yes – very easy. I just fill out this form and you'd get your permit in a few days along with a free mobile phone

BLUEHATCHBACK MAN A phone? Really?

OFFICIAL Yes, all you'd have to do is give me the odd call when you drive around and tell me what you see on the roads.

BLUEHATCHBACK MAN What? No. No, it's ok. I'll just take the West Bank permit please.

OFFICIAL Think about it, I'm not so hard to talk to am I?

BLUEHATCHBACK MAN I'm just a driver – I drive, reporting is for reporters – or the po-lice, not me.

OFFICIAL Think it over //

BLUEHATCHBACK MAN No no really – it's not for me

OFFICIAL You know these computers are not like a filing cabinet – things never get lost. If someone is rejected for a permit on security grounds that rejection is recorded for ever. You should think about that.

A beat

OFFICIAL Think about it and take my number,

BLUEHATCHBACK MAN No, no honestly, thank you. Just a West Bank permit will be //

OFFICIAL *(Handing him back his ID card)* If you want me to help you, you have to help me.

(The OFFICIAL exits leaving the MAN con-fused. He sits back down again.)

Scene: 2016

We hear a Skype ring tone then see two faces on the screen. They are cousins. RULA is a 20-year-old Palestinian woman living in the West Bank and NADIA is a 30-year-old mixed-race Palestinian British woman living in the UK.

When the picture comes up both women scream and wave madly at each other.

RULA Marhaba Nadia

NADIA HI hi! Oh my God I can't believe we managed to Skype, yay we did it!

(More maniacal waving)

NADIA Where are you?

RULA At University! What about you?

NADIA In my house – do you want to see it?

RULA Sure

NADIA Ok, I'll just pick up the laptop and show you around. Don't get excited it's a tiny flat! So here's the kitchen area, you see, all my herbs and things, the fridge,

RULA You have a washing machine in the kitchen?

NADIA That's a dishwasher actually. Then this is the sitting room, TV, sofa and the sofa opens into a bed, it's where I sleep. And then through here is the bathroom, that's it! Tiny isn't it?

RULA It looks so clean and lovely. Everything is so new and shiny. Modern

NADIA Enough about me, how are you doing? How's your studying going?

RULA Good, although I hate Shakespeare

NADIA What? Say that again I can't hear you properly

RULA I can't speak too loudly I'm in the library – I said I hate Shakespeare

NADIA WHY? He's amazing

RULA Very hard to understand

NADIA It's easier when you see it on stage.

RULA Did you lose weight? Your face looks so thin

NADIA Not at all. What about you – how are you? *(low voice)* why are you covering your head? I didn't know you did that? Your mother doesn't does she?

(RULA types a message at the bottom of the screen which her cousin can see it says: My father thinks it's safer for me to cover when I'm out.)

NADIA I understand.

(A beat)

NADIA It's so nice to see you ! To speak to you!

RULA You too!

NADIA It was such a good idea of yours! I didn't even know you had access to Skype!

(A beat)

RULA Actually there's something I wanted to ask you, that's why I wanted to do this, it's nicer face-to-face than the phone isn't it?

NADIA Much nicer, what did you want to ask?

RULA I'm shy – but my mother told me I should ask…

NADIA You can ask me, come on what is it?

(Pause)

RULA I don't want you to feel like you have to – oh I'm embarrassed to ask

(A beat)

RULA Oh I wish you could speak Arabic…

NADIA I think I know what you are going to say … Is it about coming here Rula? Because I don't have the space really or any money it's just really really hard for me. I want to help but you know its-

RULA No no it's not that. Uncle Hameed said you had a new iPhone 6 and I wondered if I could have your old one –

NADIA Oh. Oh god.

RULA But maybe you still need it

NADIA No, no, I'm sorry. I'm embarrassed of course you can have it –

RULA Only if you don't need it

NADIA I'd love you to have it - shall I post it?

RULA No, a friend of my fathers is in London in 2 weeks can I give him your number? Then he will meet you and bring it for me, it's much faster. You remember when we used to write to each other and it would take months

NADIA And we had to write in our special code

RULA Exactly. Is it ok?

NADIA Of course. It's a bit scratched

RULA But the camera works?

NADIA Perfectly

RULA Oh my God I'm so excited! Mahmoud is going to go crazy with jealousy

(A beat)

NADIA I'm sorry I thought you –

RULA Don't worry – when will you come to visit? We would love to have you here

NADIA I want to – but my mum says it's too danger – *(she stops herself)*

RULA What did you say? You cut out

NADIA It's too expensive

RULA Too what I can't hear you? Hello

(The image of NADIA has frozen, RULA's internet connection has gone.)

RULA Hello? Hello? Nadia? *(to someone who is waiting)* No I'm not finished, I got cut off… you have to wait

Scene: 1960

The long queue of people from one side of the stage to the other reappears. But now we can see the front of the line. There is a MAN at a desk.
    Pause
    Eventually the man at the front has been dealt with and the second MAN moves to the desk.

OFFICIAL Just a minute

(Pause)

OFFICIAL Ok, give me your form

(The MAN hands it over)

OFFICIAL You want a passport?
MAN Yes. This is the right line?
OFFICIAL Yes.

(He looks over the form.)

OFFICIAL Your name?
MAN Saeed.
OFFICIAL Full name
MAN It's on the form
OFFICIAL Full name
MAN Saeed bin Hameed Al Hassan bin Ibrahim al Faisal Walleedi
OFFICIAL Too long

MAN Sorry?
OFFICIAL Too long.

(He draws a line across the paper.)

MAN Why did you do that?
OFFICIAL I just told you – it's too long. So I've cut the last few words – your passport will be in the name Saeed bin Hameed al Hassan,

(A beat)

MAN But that's not my name
OFFICIAL Listen son, five names are enough for anybody
MAN But it's not my name

(The OFFICIAL eye balls him.)

OFFICIAL You've been waiting 5 hours. 1 name per hour. I thought you wanted a passport
MAN I do.

(A beat)

OFFICIAL So what's your name?
MAN Saeed bin Hameed … al Hassan …

(A beat)

OFFICIAL Good. NEXT

Scene: 2007

The interior of a house, IDF soldiers destroy everything (there should be male and female soldiers here), overturning tables, scattering things from drawers, breaking crockery may be even putting a bullet or two into the cushions so feathers fly everywhere. It should feel like wanton, deliberate destruction, not an act of rage.

Scene: 1992

The women sit on their rug outside, packing up from their picnic. WOMAN 1 sees some feathers on the ground.

WOMAN 1 Did you see these feathers – looks like a couple of pigeons had a fight.. there's even blood
WOMAN 2 More likely one was eaten by a fox

(A beat)

WOMAN 3 You went to so much trouble – thank you I've had a lovely time.
WOMAN 1 Good. Well it's too important an occasion to miss – engagement, a wedding… babies

WOMAN 3 Stop talking about babies! You make me embarrassed. You know Saleh's mother put her hand here and said she thought I would be very fertile
WOMAN 2 She didn't! Old witch
WOMAN 1 Mothers-in-law!

(The women laugh, WOMAN 3 looks embarrassed.)

WOMAN 2 How dare she, god they just think we are baby machines don't they? It makes me sick
WOMAN 1 I quite like it
WOMAN 3 What?
WOMAN 1 Making babies!

WOMAN 2 Stop it, you're embarrassing Fatima again

WOMAN 3 Stop raising your voices

(The soldiers are passing again and stop. The women stop packing up.)

SOLDIER 1 Good afternoon, ladies

WOMAN 1 Good afternoon.

SOLDIER 1 Still here?

WOMAN 2 Still here

SOLDIER 2 Nice day for it.

SOLDIER 1 Bag empty yet?

WOMAN 1 More or less

SOLDIER 1 And the flask?

WOMAN 2 Empty

SOLDIER 1 Would you mind opening the bag?

(WOMAN 1 opens it.

SOLDIER 1 *peers in.)*

SOLDIER 1 Nearly all gone

SOLDIER 2 Didn't leave any for us

(A beat)

SOLDIER 1 Are you going soon?

WOMAN 2 Why, shouldn't we be here?

SOLDIER 2 It's a free country. We're just asking.

WOMAN 1 We are just talking.

SOLDIER 1 Well you've finished your picnic so you must be going home soon… enjoy your afternoon

(They move on.)

WOMAN 3 Shall we go then?

WOMAN 2 Sit back down. We'll go when we are ready.

Scene: 2007

BLUE HATCHBACK MAN from before is back waiting in the chair, he has been here for some time. The same OFFICIAL enters.

OFFICIAL Ah, hello – Farouky isn't it?

BLUEHATCHBACK MAN Yes General Harami

OFFICIAL Permit? So did you think about it?

BLUEHATCHBACK MAN Now I can't move around at all – they told me I have a security block on my file and that I have to see you if I need to have it removed

OFFICIAL Did you think about my suggestion?

BLUEHATCHBACK MAN Yes but really I only want to travel in the West Bank – I don't want any trouble.

OFFICIAL Do you know a Wahid Al Faisal?

BLUEHATCHBACK MAN What?

OFFICIAL He is in prison in Israel – do you know him?

BLUEHATCHBACK MAN Yes.

OFFICIAL How?

BLUEHATCHBACK MAN He is my sister's husband – my brother-in-law.

OFFICIAL He's a dangerous man. Hamas. We can't give you a permit because of him.

BLUEHATCHBACK MAN But he's not even a blood relative. I've never visited him in prison –

OFFICIAL That doesn't matter. There is a risk. We need proof that you are not in league with this man.

BLUEHATCHBACK MAN Why should I be punished because he is in prison?

OFFICIAL Are you Fatah?

BLUEHATCHBACK MAN I'm just a driver, I don't know anything about politics, really.

OFFICIAL We are both Palestinians, our lives are all politics

BLUEHATCHBACK MAN I just want to be able to drive where I need

(A beat)

BLUEHATCHBACK MAN But you want me to collaborate

OFFICIAL Cooperate

BLUEHATCHBACK MAN I don't want to cooperate

OFFICIAL You are stubborn aren't you? Do you think you are special? I have hundreds of your friends calling me. You aren't the first and you won't be the last. Now come on. Make life easy for yourself.

(A beat)

OFFICIAL I understand from your file you have six children, that's a lot of mouths to feed…

BLUEHATCHBACK MAN No. This is not right. I have four

OFFICIAL But on your file //

BLUEHATCHBACK MAN Two died. Twins.

OFFICIAL Oh. Sorry

BLUEHATCHBACK MAN They were young. But Samia, Hannah, Janine and Nasir are doing well

OFFICIAL Four is still expensive

BLUEHATCHBACK MAN They're not here. Samia, Hannah and Janine in London – Nasir in Belgium. Doesn't your computer tell you that?

OFFICIAL Universities cost money. Visas, accommodation.

BLUEHATCHBACK MAN They're all working Mashallah, Samia runs a refuge for women in Acton, Hannah is at BBC Arabic, Samia sprays perfume at Selfridges and Nasir is a chef. They all send money.

OFFICIAL Then why – if you don't mind me asking – why do you need this permit? You clearly don't need to work

BLUEHATCHBACK MAN General – I have been married for a long time. And that is because of my job. You understand? I need that permit.

OFFICIAL I see... well

(The OFFICIAL holds out the phone for BLUE HATCHBACK MAN who looks at it. He is trying to decide whether to take it or not. He wavers. He is about to move as the scene ends (we should not know whether he is moving to take the phone or to leave.)

Scene: 2013

A kitchen where a woman puts the finishing touches to dinner and puts it on the table. Her 19-year-old and 13-year-old sons sit at the table.

MOTHER Ok. It's ready. Go ahead.

SON 2 (13) Tabbouleh again? I'm sick of tabbouleh

SON 1 (19) *(hits him across the back of the head)* Eat it.

(They sit in silence eating tabbouleh with bread.)

SON 1 Is there Zaatar?

(The MOTHER gets up and fetches some, putting it on the table.)

MOTHER I was thinking of making Mousakkan on Friday, Umm Mazin said we can have a chicken in return for some of my soap

SON 2 Brilliant!

SON 1 I won't be here.

MOTHER Why?

SON 1 I've got Uni

SON 2 On a Friday?

SON 1 Yes.

MOTHER We'll wait till the following week then

SON 2 Oh! Can't we do it without him. Leave him leftovers?

MOTHER No. A family meal needs to be the whole family

SON 2 It's never the whole family though is it?

(SON 1 clips SON 2 across the back of the head again.)

SON 2 You better stop that you know!

SON 1 Or what?

SON 2 I'll pay you back

SON 1 What you going to do shortie?

SON 2 You wait.

(A beat)

SON 2 I've put you in hospital before

MOTHER STOP you know you're not to bring that up

SON 1 Be careful.

(A beat)

SON 2 Are you scared?

MOTHER Stop it!

SON 1 Of a few grape seeds?

SON 2 The doctor said if I'd pushed them in any further you'd have been permanently deaf

SON 1 At least I wouldn't have to listen to your singing

SON 2 I'm good. Everyone says I'm good. I'm good aren't I Mum?

(SON 1 starts a rendition of Mohammed Assaf's "Al Keffiyeh." It's a mocking imitation of his brother singing it and when he has finished he puts his hand out like he is begging for money.)

SON 2 MUM!

MOTHER *(She's trying not to laugh)* Stop – Wallah stop! He's good

SON 2 Umm Mazin said I'm even better than Mohammed Assaf

SON 1 Did she.

(Pause)

MOTHER So. University on a Friday?

SON 2 He's lying, look at his eyes! I bet he's seeing a girl – is it Samira – with the big/

MOTHER Shut up or I'll tell your brother what happened yesterday

(A beat)

SON 1 What happened yesterday?

SON 2 You promised

(A beat)

SON 1 What happened? Huh?

MOTHER Your brother was brought home by the police

SON 1 What?

SON 2 Don't tell him, you said you wouldn't

(A beat. The younger SON appeals to his MOTHER with a look.)

SON 1 What happened?

MOTHER He was selling things

SON 1 What things? Not guns – I told you to stay away from Hussein

MOTHER Guns? In God's name, guns! Who said anything about guns? What do you know about guns?

SON 2 There were no guns – tell her Khalid

SON 1 It's ok mum, but what was it then? Bootleg booze? Records? Cigarettes?

MOTHER Flowers

SON 1 *(laughing)* Flowers?

SON 2 Shut up! I told you not to tell him mum!

SON 1 Where did you get them? Where did he get them?

MOTHER He persuaded Saleh and Jamal to collect wild flowers with him – he said they were for Sitti – and then he sold them at the side of the road

SON 1 Flowers?

(A beat)

SON 1 Quite the little entrepreneur! ASDA price

SON 2 Fuck off!

MOTHER Raheem – watch your mouth!

SON 2 I told you not to tell him, I told you he'd just laugh at me.

(A beat)

SON 1 No – it's inventive

MOTHER But he had no permit so the police brought him home.

(A beat)

MOTHER I told him in this day and age it's not safe to go walking in fields that don't belong to you

SON 1 It's true. No more scavenging eh?

SON 2 Well what else am I supposed to do – I can't live on Tabbouleh forever!

(He storms out of the room.)

SON 1 He'll cool off. Always had a hot head.

MOTHER I do worry about him though. What will he do?

SON 1 Think up another scam to make money

MOTHER In future I mean. I can't see him getting a scholarship and going to Birzeit University like you.

(A beat)

SON 1 Birzeit isn't everything

MOTHER It's a huge achievement. The first person in our family to go to University, and with no father to support you

SON 1 I know you are proud

MOTHER Proud! You have no idea. You always make me proud and happy I don't know what we would do without you,

SON 1 You'd be fine.

(A beat)

MOTHER Are you really going to University on Friday?

SON 1 Of course

MOTHER Your brother's not right about Samira?

SON 1 Don't be silly! She's a child!

(A beat)

MOTHER What is it then... what's the lecture?

SON 1 Oh it's something about international law

MOTHER You're lying, oh my God, what are you doing? Talk of guns at my table and now you are lying to me, yaboyay! What have I done to deserve this!

SON 1 Stop mother

MOTHER My son lying to me,

SON 1 I'm not lying

MOTHER You are, you are, oh what will I do if something happens to you, I can't bear to think of it

SON 1 Nothing's going to –

MOTHER My own son, lying to his mother – who has made you do this? Yes, you have been sneaking around – I pretended it wasn't happening? Ya Allah! I can't bear any more tragedy in my -

SON 1 Stop stop I'll tell you – I'm not lying I am going to Uni but it's not a lecture... It's an interview. On Skype. The internet. With UCL

MOTHER UCL?

SON 1 University college London. I've applied for a transfer to do my final year there.

MOTHER London?

SON 1 Yes. If I can go and study there then //

MOTHER But it's so far away... for a whole year

SON 1 Well I was thinking once I'd finished my course I could get a job there – the pay is really good – then I could –

MOTHER Move there?

SON 1 Yes. My English is pretty good

MOTHER But you are Palestinian –

SON 1 There are plenty of //

MOTHER Don't you know what that means?

SON 1 Of course. I've lived here all my life...

MOTHER So you understand you have to be here. What if everyone left? They'd win

(A beat)

SON 1 Mum there are more Palestinians living outside of Palestine than in it – it's not our fault – this happened to us, there's nothing we can do

MOTHER What are we doing then? Come on, let's go – all of us, let's tell everyone in the street, it's too late we've lost, all the years of hardship, being murdered, imprisoned, having our homes taken, our jobs, our fields, our olives, our ability to move from one place to another – everything we have endured has been for nothing. They've won. So let's just leave it to them, disappear. It's what they want. You are doing what they

want. You are an educated young Palestinian man. We need you here. Stay.

SON 1 I can't. I can't bear it any more. I need to go.

(A beat)

SON 1 I'll come back – to visit

MOTHER They won't let you. It's a one-way door.

SON 1 They will. They'll have to. I'm Palestinian.

MOTHER If you leave you won't be.

SON 1 Yes I will. I'll achieve more out there for us than I can in here – this is suffocating me.

(A beat)

SON 1 Do you understand?

MOTHER No.

SON 1 I have to go

MOTHER No you don't, you want to.

SON 1 It's impossible

(A beat)

SON 1 I shouldn't have told you... anyway I've got to pass the interview first. It'll probably never happen.

Scene: 2002 and now

A group of people approach a clearing. They position themselves in a formal grouping facing one point in the space, like a congregation in a church.

LITTLE BOY How do you know this is the right place?

MOTHER We just know – it's in our hearts

LITTLE BOY But there's nothing here

TEENAGE GIRL That's what they want you to think – they destroyed it all but they can't destroy those

(She indicates a cactus.)

LITTLE BOY A cactus?

MOTHER She's right – that's the proof we were here – they don't grow naturally, they have to be cultivated. They were used around the village to keep wild dogs and predators out,

LITTLE BOY They're still here

TEENAGE GIRL Proof

(Everyone has taken their positions.)

MOTHER Are you ready?

LITTLE BOY Yes

TEENAGE GIRL Don't be scared

LITTLE BOY I'm not.

(A formal pre-theatre hush goes over the crowd and a middle-aged MAN stands up to address the crowd. He is the MAN who was trying to get home in the taxi scene.)

MAN Welcome everyone on this, the sad occasion of Nakba Day. Take a good look around at what once was our village and retain every sight, smell and detail of our home, because, as Israeli law states, we will not be permitted to re-enter this place until Nakba Day next year. This is our one day to reflect and remember our past, what happened in this place. The things we must none of us, ever forget. I'd like to welcome Abu Zaman, who is the oldest living member of our community. Abu Zaman.

(An OLD MAN gets up and stands in front of the crowd.)

OLD MAN Our village. Stood here. We had a simple but prosperous life, four main farming families for whom everyone worked or was associated. There was no records office – we didn't need one, everyone knew who owned what where the borders of land lay these things were ingrained, in the blood and the hearts of every man woman and child from this place. Over here in the centre of the village was the communal taboon oven. Each house would take turns to make the bread for the village. We all shared.

(A beat)

I was born in 1925, in June. My mother was working in the fields, she came back to the house which stood over there, gave birth, handed me to my grandmother and returned to the fields.

(A beat)

When I was 23 everything changed. Of course there had been rumblings beforehand, suggestions, the wind was changing… But here, so close to the border we felt safe and protected. Then on the 25th of April 1948 soldiers entered this village. They went from house to house and ordered everyone out, into this central square. Where you are standing now, that is where we all stood. Waiting. We were not afraid. We had nothing to hide. They could turn our houses upside down, they would only find oil, blankets, bread and chickens, we had no guns or bullets. We waited. Here.

(A beat)

Once everyone was gathered they took men of age to one side, over there, the women and children were on the other side, there. They were told to go. Walk. Everyone looked confused. When this woman's grandmother – Umm Hameed tried to go back to the house to get another blanket for her baby daughter the solder hit her in the face with the butt of his gun. She had a scar for the rest of her life, God rest her.

(A beat)

So the women and children began to walk, the men were taken to a field to the west – over there – and left to sit in the sun, with no water or food. We sat and sat. Then we began to get angry. We were hungry and thirsty and worried about our women. One of the village elders tried to speak to the soldiers. They were all going into the houses, we couldn't see what they were doing. The soldiers wouldn't listen to him. Then Fareed Khalili stood up – he was 18. He went to

the soldier who was guarding us by the gate. He said this is enough. Fine you are in our village, do what you want but let us go – we have families, mothers and children who need us. The soldier took out a gun and shot him in the head. They wouldn't let us bury him, they threw his body into the well by the fourth field.

(A beat)

Two days later we were all put into a van and taken south – the opposite direction from our families. We were driven for seven hours and then let out. We did not know where we were. We did not know how to contact our families. We began the walk home.

(A beat.
He is overcome.
The MAN who introduced him gets up to help him.)

Sorry – no I'm ok.

(beat)

We began the walk home.

(A beat)

We are still walking.

(He sits down, there is a silence and a pause.)

MAN Thank you Abu Zaman. Thank you very much. Now I need Kamil al Samuh

(A beat)

MAN Where are you Kamil?
MOTHER *(whispering)* Go on, do you want me to come with you?
LITTLE BOY No

(He gets up and moves to the front.)

MAN Ok Kamil?
LITTLE BOY Yes.
MAN Do you want your Mother?
LITTLE BOY No
MAN This, as you all know, is Kamil Al Samuh – the youngest speaking member of our community. Now Kamil you understood everything Abu Zaman said didn't you?
LITTLE BOY Yes.
MAN Well we need you to tell us what he said so we know that you remember – so you don't forget – so you can tell everyone
LITTLE BOY Ok.

(A beat)

LITTLE BOY Mum – does he want me to do it now

MOTHER Yes Kamil – go on, like we practised

(The MAN steps back to give the boy the floor.)

LITTLE BOY This is where our villages was before the Nakba. There were lots of farmers. And here in the middle was the oven, which everyone shared to make the bread. In 1948 the catastrophe happened. On the 25th of April 1948 soldiers came and made everyone go out of their houses and stand in the middle – like you all. All the boys went over there. All the ladies had to leave or the soldiers would shoot them – her granny was hurt by a soldier. She's dead now. But not cause of that.

(Pause)

The soldiers shot a man for asking to go to his family. He was put in the deep well. Then all the boys were put on a truck and driven far away from here and their families.

(Pause

The BOY looks like he is about to cry.)

MAN Are you ok – don't get upset

LITTLE BOY They were driven far away from their …

(A beat)

LITTLE BOY They were driven away from their …

(A beat)

LITTLE BOY They …

(He begins to sob.)

LITTLE BOY I can't remember any more! Mum – sorry I can't

MAN It's ok

(The MOTHER begins to get up but the OLD MAN gets up first and goes to the BOY and whispers in his ear.)

LITTLE BOY Shall I say that?

(The OLD MAN continues to whisper.)

LITTLE BOY They began the walk home. (he listens) We are still walking. (he listens) And so will our children, and our children's children, until we are back in this place, our home, for good.

(A beat.

The OLD MAN has stopped whispering to him.

The BOY looks at the OLD MAN.)

LITTLE BOY Is it finished?

(The OLD MAN smiles at him sadly and shakes his head.)

Vickie Ramirez

Biography

Vickie Ramirez (Tuscarora) is an alumnus of The Public Theater's Emerging Writer's Group of 2009 and a
founding member of Chukalokoli Native Theater Ensemble and Amerinda Theater. Her work has been
previously developed and/or presented at Labyrinth
Theater Company, Native Voices at the Autry, The
Public Theater, The Flea, Missoula Writer's Colony,
Roundabout Theater's Different Voices Program, and
The 52nd Street Project. Recent productions include
Glenburn 12 WP for Summer Shorts at 59E59 Theaters,
and *Standoff at Hwy#37* for Native Voices at the Autry
in Los Angeles and South Dakota. Ramirez has received the 2009/2010 NYC
Urban Artists Fellowship and the NYSCA Individual Artist Award in 2010.

Artistic statement

Standoff at Hwy#37 began as a one-act commission for Ohio Northern University's 9th Annual Theater Festival. I got the commission but had no real plan –
maybe a comedy. Then, New York City passed a bill demanding a cigarette tax be
imposed on all cigarettes generated by Indian Reservations, despite the fact that it
was in direct violation of several treaties and tribal sovereignty. It was upsetting,
but much more upsetting was Mayor Bloomberg telling the Governor to "get a
cowboy hat and a shotgun" because "this is the law of the land and we will enforce
the law." It was such an over-the-top statement, I didn't understand why there was
no general outrage. Here was the Mayor of New York City advocating violence
against the Senecas, despite the fact that the dispute in question was a treaty issue
and, up until that moment, ABSOLUTELY no violence was involved. This wasn't
the first time. In May 1997, Governor Pataki sent heavily armed State Troopers
backed up by the National Guard to block the borders of Seneca Territory over
the same issue.

I tried to stir up outrage amongst my friends, but surprisingly, they shrugged it off. They didn't understand what the "big deal" was. And so...*Standoff at Hwy#37* was born.

Production history

Standoff at Hwy#37 was developed by Native Voices at the Autry at the Native Voices 2013 Annual Retreat and Festival of New Plays. The play was first commissioned as a one-act by Ohio Northern University for the 2011 Annual Theater Festival. The world premiere was produced by Native Voices at the Autry in Los Angeles, California and ran from February 26 to March 16, 2014.

Production staff included director Jon Lawrence Rivera and executive producers Jean Bruce Scott and Randy Reinholz. The world premiere cast included Eagle Young, LaVonne Rae Andrews, Kalani Queypo, Delanna Studi, Tinasha LaRayé, Matt Kirkwood, and Fran DeLeon.

16 *Standoff at Hwy#37*
Vickie Ramirez

Characters

THE GUARDSMEN:

THOMAS LEE DOXDATER (Tuscarora) 24, PFC – Accomplished, confident, a perfect soldier

LINDA BALDWIN (African American) 19, PFC – Ambitious, small but scrappy, competitive

CAPTAIN DONALD HEWITT (Caucasian) 34, Military lifer with disappointed ambitions

THE PROTESTORS:

DARRIN JAMIESON (Cayuga) 30, No settled home or reservation, gets by on his looks and his charm

SANDRA HENHAWK (Mohawk) 32, Raised in the city, officious

AUNT BEV (Mohawk) 62, Charming and flirtatious, a slightly glam version of the Grandma/Auntie type. Always has snacks

Setting

Upstate New York. The border of a small town and the local Haudenosaunee reservation (the protest site). Aunt Bev's house on the rez.

The back-drop is a multi-media display where photos and slides can be projected. (Or solid, selected photos.) At different times, the slides will be of untouched reservation lands, and photos of land claim protests.

During the protest, STAGE LEFT there is picnic table with a large flat of the Haudenosaunee wampum belt (the Iroquois flag) hung on its side. CENTERSTAGE is a sign…*WELCOME TO THE SITE OF THE NEW HIGHWAY #37 BYPASS.*

For Aunt Bev's house, a traditional quilt hangs center stage. There is a small sofa, the armchair and a dinner table with chairs.

Pronounciation notes

Haudenosaunee (Ho-danno-SHOW-knee) – The People of the Longhouse
Ongewehonwe (UNG-gweh-hone-WEH) – The One People

Iroquois (Ear-oh-QUOYSE)

Wampum (whom-pum)

Onondaga (Aw-non-DAH-gah)

Seneca (Sen-eh-KAH)

Mohawk (MOW-hawk)

Cayuga (Kah-YOO-gah)

Oneida (Oh-NIGH-dah)

Tuscarora (TUSK-ah-ROAR-ah)

Sago (SAY-goh) – Hello (Mohawk)

NDN (In-DIN)

Chi'wen (Chey-WEN') Hello (Tuscarora)

Satnyeh (Sat –n-YEH) Sit down (Tuscarora)

Punctuation note

// : indicates dialogue entry of the following character

PROLOGUE

Lights up on the stage. Dawn. CONCURRENT RESOLUTION 331 (1) is projected on video screens.
As AUNT BEV enters there is a recording playing the sounds of recent land claim protests. Pictures from OKA Caledonia, Wounded Knee and other land claims flicker past on the screens.
Over the cacophony, we hear New York Mayor Michael Bloomberg's statement from his August 13th, 2010 radio show (this can be the original or an actor reading the statement).

BLOOMBERG'S VOICE *"I've said this to Governor Paterson, I said, you know; Get yourself a cowboy hat and a shotgun. If there's ever a great video, it's you standing in the middle of the New York State Thruway saying, you know, Read my lips – the law of the land is this, and we're going to enforce the law."*

(AUNT BEV listens as the protest sounds get louder waits a beat then smiles.)

AUNT BEV *(To audience.)* Seems like somebody doesn't really know the Law of the Land. The original law. The Great Law. The law before New York was New York and before America was America. Our law. *(A spotlight goes up on AUNT BEV. She is in storyteller mode.)* Many, many years ago the Haudenosaunee - that's us, The Ongwehonwe, The One People. We have a lot of names but the one everybody knows is

"Iroquois." It's WRONG. It's taken from an insult by some smart-ass Algonquins. Means "little snakes" - "little snakes" they're ones to talk, I've dated Algonquins - *(She makes a measuring gesture with her thumb and forefinger.)* - But I'm getting sidetracked. Haudenosaunee. The People of the Longhouse. Now, way, waaaaaay back (long before the Invaders came) there was a time of terrible conflict and bloodshed amongst the Five Nations. Brother was killing brother. It all seemed hopeless until the Creator sent someone to restore peace, love, and harmony amongst the people. He was the Peacemaker and his Great Law not only brought Peace, but brought us all together as the Ongwehonwe, the One-People. That law still governs the now Six Nations of the Haudenosaunee.

AUNT BEV *(Cont'd, gestures to the Haudenosaunee Flag.)* This wampum was made to commemorate that coming together. It represents the original Five Nations. In the center is the Tree of Peace, where the Nations buried their weapons. The tree represents the Onondaga (the keepers of the Central Fire); the two outside squares are the warrior nations - the Senecas (the keepers of the Western Door) and the Mohawks (the keepers of the Eastern Door). The Cayuga and the Oneida,(the two Younger Brothers) are the squares in between and the Tuscaroras, well – they're the little bit of that white line that extends off the edge. That's what happens sometimes, when people don't find their path. They can go off the edge.

Scene 1

P.F.C. THOMAS LEE DOXDATER, 24, enters. He circles the stage, checking the perimeter. He spots AUNT BEV.

AUNT BEV Sago, dear –

THOMAS Hello Ma'am. Protest starting already?

AUNT BEV Gotta get here early to beat those bulldozers – ennit? *(Beat.)* Ennit?

THOMAS I'm not here for the protest.

AUNT BEV Oh. Okay then. I thought –

THOMAS Yes?

AUNT BEV You're NDN, right?

THOMAS Yep.

AUNT BEV You look Haudenosaunee –

THOMAS Yes, ma'am.

AUNT BEV You're not here for the protest?

THOMAS Not how you think.

(CAPTAIN HEWITT, 34, enters with PFC LINDA BALDWIN, 19. AUNT BEV exits unseen.)

CAPTAIN HEWITT Doxdater! Report?

THOMAS Perimeter clear. Except for the Elder, Sir.

BALDWIN "Elder?" You're so weird.

THOMAS It's respect. What would you call her?

BALDWIN *(Looks around.)* Nothing. No one's there.

CAPTAIN HEWITT Cut the chatter. Eyes on me! Follow the line.

(CAPTAIN HEWITT takes position in front of the sign. He carefully walks a straight line from the sign to center upstage. BALDWIN and THOMAS watch attentively.)

CAPTAIN HEWITT *(Gestures stage left.)* This area is undisputed reservation territory, a safe zone for the protestors. As long as they stay on their side of the line, they're fine. That same rule applies to us.

BALDWIN Sir – what if things start getting out of control? If people start getting violent or something –

THOMAS Not happening.

BALDWIN This is a protest. Could happen.

THOMAS Why? Because we're a pack of Wild Indians?

BALDWIN I didn't mean that.

THOMAS *(To CAPTAIN HEWITT.)* Trust me sir. This isn't gonna be violent.

CAPTAIN HEWITT I do. You're in charge. I have to check the other sites up the line.

BALDWIN Wait –

CAPTAIN HEWITT Problem, Baldwin? Doxdater is qualified. Do you know why we can't cross the line?

BALDWIN No – but –

CAPTAIN HEWITT Doxdater, explain.

THOMAS Sovereign territory, sir!

CAPTAIN HEWITT It's Indian land.

BALDWIN But Doxdater // is Indian.

CAPTAIN HEWITT Doxdater is representing the interests of the United States of America. While he's on duty and in uniform, he's one of us.

THOMAS Yes, sir!

BALDWIN But, sir –

CAPTAIN HEWITT Our job is to make sure the protesters are safe, but also to ensure they do not cross into the disputed territory. *(He gestures stage right.)* This is the area in contention.

THOMAS Yes, sir!

CAPTAIN HEWITT This should be an easy one, probably will be just a bunch of old folks. Sometimes there are a few troublemakers – but nothing that we need worry about.

THOMAS // Right, sir!

BALDWIN Sir, I don't think –

CAPTAIN HEWITT The rule is – they keep it civil, we keep it civil. There are rumors that they may try to blockade the bridge and the railway, but that's only if things get out of hand. We're not gonna let that happen.

THOMAS No, sir!

BALDWIN Not gonna happen, sir.

CAPTAIN HEWITT Doxdater?

THOMAS Yes, sir?

CAPTAIN HEWITT I'm off to make the rounds – It's your game here.

BALDWIN SIR!

(Beat. HEWITT and DOXDATER finally notice her.)

CAPTAIN HEWITT What NOW, Baldwin? It better be lady problems because I've answered your concern.

THOMAS *(Aside to CAPTAIN HEWITT.)* Woah, look at that face! Definitely...lady problems face.

(CAPTAIN HEWITT finds this hilarious. BALDWIN doesn't.)

BALDWIN It seems like a conflict of interest.

CAPTAIN HEWITT Doxdater!

THOMAS Yes, sir?

CAPTAIN HEWITT Anything changed since our earlier conversation?

THOMAS No. Like I said – it's not my rez.

CAPTAIN HEWITT Good enough.

(CAPTAIN HEWITT exits. DOXDATER and BALDWIN post up.)

THOMAS *(Calls after him.)* Thank you Sir!

BALDWIN You're a deadman.

THOMAS It was a joke.

BALDWIN It wasn't funny.

THOMAS You're too sensitive.

BALDWIN "Sovereign territory, sir!" – so that's how to get ahead. Pimp your background.

THOMAS I earned this.

BALDWIN Right. The fact that you're an Indian and we're here to control a protest by a bunch of Indians is just a coincidence.

THOMAS It's why they pay us.

BALDWIN "It's not my rez" – what does that even mean?

THOMAS Just what I said – it's not my rez.

BALDWIN But it is your people.

(DARRIN JAMIESON, 30, enters. He carries an overstuffed armchair and a large colorful tote bag.)

DARRIN *(Calling offstage)* Hey Aunt Bev, where do you want your chair?

(AUNT BEV enters.)

AUNT BEV Oh, I don't know, somewhere cozy…I want a view of everything.

(They survey the stage and DARRIN spots BALDWIN.)

DARRIN Hey, how YOU doin?

BALDWIN Forget it.

(AUNT BEV grabs the chair and pulls it into place while DARRIN bothers BALDWIN.)

DARRIN I never thought I'd say this – on you, that outfit looks good.

BALDWIN Nice…purse. Pretty colors –

DARRIN Aunt Bev, please tell this lovely lady I'm holding your bag for you. Because, I'm a gentleman.

AUNT BEV You are a good boy, now give it back to me, I'm hungry.

(AUNT BEV sits in her chair, directly under the Highway Expansion sign.)

BALDWIN She can't sit there.

DARRIN C'mon sweetheart – be nice.

BALDWIN Ma'am? We're gonna need you to move your chair.

AUNT BEV Don't worry dear, I just want to be able to see everything, that's all.

(THOMAS spots AUNT BEV and moves toward her.)

THOMAS Ma'am, you're on disputed territory.

DARRIN Hey, Tommy! Long time no see! Look at you, all official and everything. How you doin', man?

THOMAS Ma'am, can you please move your chair?

AUNT BEV Sago again, officer.

THOMAS I'm not a policeman.

AUNT BEV Sago, soldier –

DARRIN He's National Guard, Aunt Bev –

AUNT BEV Sago, guardsman.

(CAPTAIN HEWITT enters.)

THOMAS Ma'am – you can't sit here.

DARRIN Hey, Tommy, back off. She can sit where she wants.

(CAPTAIN HEWITT joins them.)

CAPTAIN HEWITT Correction. She can't sit here.

AUNT BEV Chair too big?

CAPTAIN HEWITT When she's on Indian Land, she can sit wherever she wants.

AUNT BEV She wants to remind you, it's all Indian land. Isn't it, guardsman?

CAPTAIN HEWITT Not according to the government, ma'am.

AUNT BEV Which one?

THOMAS The U.S. government, ma'am.

(CAPTAIN HEWITT stalks over to stage right.)

CAPTAIN HEWITT DOXDATER! Front and center!

DARRIN Uh-oh!

AUNT BEV Are you in trouble, hon?

CAPTAIN HEWITT Doxdater!

(THOMAS steps over to CAPTAIN HEWITT, BALDWIN follows.)

BALDWIN The Indian thing isn't helping, is it?

CAPTAIN HEWITT Baldwin, were you called?

BALDWIN I'm as well-certified as Doxdater, in fact in some categories I'm rated higher –

THOMAS Hah! You beat me in spit and polish, Baldwin, that's it.

CAPTAIN HEWITT I'm well aware of your qualifications.

BALDWIN Is this a gender thing, sir? Because I think she might be more receptive to another woman.

CAPTAIN HEWITT *(Cuts her off.)* Do you speak Mohawk?

BALDWIN Pardon me?

CAPTAIN HEWITT Doxdater can speak to these people.

THOMAS I'm Tuscarora. And they all speak English.

BALDWIN It's his Tribe, sir –

THOMAS The word is nation, Baldwin and yeah, we're all Haudenosaunee - but they're Mohawks.

BALDWIN Which means?

DARRIN It means, secretly, Tommy would love to tell some Mohawks to suck it, but never would in front of white people.

THOMAS Pipe down, Darrin!

BALDWIN Hah, so you do know him!

CAPTAIN HEWITT Baldwin, Doxdater!

THOMAS *(Salutes.)* // Sir!

BALDWIN *(Salutes.)* Sir!

CAPTAIN HEWITT Doxdater, I don't understand the difference between tribes and nations and all that - my question is…are you good?

THOMAS Yes, sir!

CAPTAIN HEWITT I can put in a good word. Reassignment doesn't guarantee demerit. We tried something, it didn't work - that's all. No issue.

BALDWIN *(Mutters.)* Boy's club strikes again.

CAPTAIN HEWITT Pardon me, Baldwin?

BALDWIN Nothing, sir!

THOMAS I can handle it, sir.

CAPTAIN HEWITT Done. Now go be nice to the little old lady –

(He gestures towards AUNT BEV, who gives him a friendly wave. CAPTAIN HEWITT nods back at her.)

CAPTAIN HEWITT She's positioned herself right on top of the contested portion of the land. I'm sure that's no mistake.

THOMAS No, sir.

CAPTAIN HEWITT You have an "in" here. I'm sure she'll listen to a nice young Tuscarora man.

THOMAS Yes, sir.

BALDWIN Sir, I was very close to my Granny and //

THOMAS Thank you for your trust, Sir.

CAPTAIN HEWITT Of course. Don't fuck up.

(He EXITS. As soon as he is gone, BALDWIN rolls her eyes.)

BALDWIN Wow. He's the dad you didn't know you had.

THOMAS Jealous?

BALDWIN I do not need to prove anything to some old white dude.

THOMAS Hah, says you!

BALDWIN You can "handle it", huh? What if one of them jumps you?

THOMAS *(Points at AUNT BEV.)* One of them?

BALDWIN They may look harmless. Doesn't mean they are. Are you really prepared to do whatever's necessary? That's your people over there.

THOMAS That's the job.

BALDWIN You should've gone for reassignment.

THOMAS Right. *"Those Indians always need special treatment."*

BALDWIN Oh, poor baby. You don't need to worry, not when he's gonna "put in a good word for you."

THOMAS Wouldn't make a difference.

BALDWIN Yeah it does. What are you gonna do? You have friends here…even if they are Mohawk.

(She gestures toward DARRIN.)

DARRIN Hey sweetheart I see you looking at me! Tommy! Help a brother out, will ya?

THOMAS He's not Mohawk. He's Cayuga.

BALDWIN Whatever - he's your friend.

THOMAS Everyone knows Darrin. That doesn't make him a friend.

BALDWIN Wow. Real asshole today, aren't you?

THOMAS Look, I've got a job to do. That's it.

(DARRIN comes up between them.)

DARRIN *(Flirting shamelessly.)* Hey, tell her about the time I pulled you outta the old well. You should've seen it, gorgeous. It was the hunts for the Midwinter Feast - first one I'd ever been on. I was excited, but the kid here, he practically had ants in his pants.

THOMAS Why are you talking, Darrin?

DARRIN I'd never been to one before. Never seen a proper deer hunt - the right kind of hunt, the traditional one? Tommy's Dad said that since I was almost a man, I needed to learn how to do it right. With respect.

THOMAS *(Mutters.)* Respect, that's a good one.

DARRIN Since it was my first hunt and Tommy was just six, we both had the same job. Calling the deer with the antlers. *(He mimes clicking the antlers together.)* The first chance he could, Tommy ran off. No one else noticed, so I took off after him. Stupid kid ran over an old well and practically fell through. He was halfway down when I found him. I pulled him out, but he dropped the antlers. Cried like I'd killed his puppy. Well, that's me - saving babies. I'm heroic like that.

BALDWIN *(To DARRIN.)* You need to get back behind the line.

DARRIN Awwww, come on, let's keep it friendly.

THOMAS Back behind the line, Darrin!

DARRIN Man....

(DARRIN goes.)

BALDWIN So - not a friend? How does he know everybody?

THOMAS He's got no rez, no family, so he has nowhere to go. He just stays with people until people get sick of him.

BALDWIN He lived with you?

THOMAS For a while. Then we were done, too. That's how he lives - He moves to the next house and the next rez and wears everybody out.

BALDWIN And people just let him…

THOMAS What else are they gonna do? Let him starve? I know, it's tempting.

(DARRIN whispers with AUNT BEV. She waves THOMAS over.)

BALDWIN You're getting summoned.

(He unslings his rifle and hands it to BALDWIN.)

THOMAS Take my gun -

BALDWIN Why?

THOMAS Respect goes a long way, Baldwin.

(THOMAS strides over to AUNT BEV, keeping carefully on his side of the "boundary.")

THOMAS Did you need assistance, ma'am?

AUNT BEV So you're Essie Doxdater's grandson!

THOMAS Yes, ma'am.

AUNT BEV Let me look at you. Take after that good-looking father of yours, don't you? She said you were gonna be a soldier —

THOMAS Just a guardsman, ma'am.

DARRIN Whatever happened to medical school?

THOMAS What? Nothing.

AUNT BEV You're gonna be a doctor?

THOMAS No, ma'am. I don't know what he's talking about.

DARRIN You used to always say you were going to be a doctor.

THOMAS Yeah? I used to wanna be an astronaut, too.

AUNT BEV Astronaut Indian…that far above the Mother? Well, why not -maybe you'll run into the Sky People.

THOMAS I was eight, ma'am.

DARRIN Aunt Bev - everyone just calls her Aunt Bev.

THOMAS Aunt Bev.

AUNT BEV Either way…You're planning for your future. Essie must be so proud.

DARRIN I bet your parents are.

THOMAS When did you get out?

DARRIN A few months ago -

THOMAS You crashing here now?

AUNT BEV Darrin's staying with me for a bit.

THOMAS Some things never change.

DARRIN I'm just working some things out.

AUNT BEV We know, Darrin.

THOMAS Been working things out for a long time, huh?

DARRIN I've got plans —

THOMAS Right.

AUNT BEV Don't be so doubtful. As long as someone's living - they've got potential.

THOMAS Yes ma'am.

AUNT BEV What about you? When you're done with this?

THOMAS I'm happy in the Guard, ma'am.

AUNT BEV Protector of the land.

BALDWIN Doxdater wants to transfer to regular army.

(She hands him back his rifle.)

AUNT BEV Want to save the world too, huh, Thomas?

DARRIN I knew it man, pretty soon you'll be a general or some shit.

BALDWIN Hah!

THOMAS You can't see me in stars, Baldwin?

AUNT BEV Well, why not? If he's good at this?

BALDWIN I know Hewitt likes you - but that's not how it works. Started a little late.

AUNT BEV Age doesn't mean incapable, it just means it's easier to get people to move your chair for you -

THOMAS Speaking of which -

AUNT BEV Hmmm?

THOMAS Aunt Bev, would you mind if I moved your chair just a little to the left –

AUNT BEV Oh, but I won't be able to see as well over there - I like it here.

(THOMAS leans in closer to her.)

THOMAS Ma'am, I hate to insist, but -

(SANDRA HENHAWK, 32, enters. She spots THOMAS and rushes over to join AUNT BEV.)

SANDRA Back off, Storm-troopers!

DARRIN Oh here we go, now –

THOMAS You need to relax, ma'am.

SANDRA RELAX! It looks like you and Murder-Drone Barbie //

BALDWIN // Barbie? Seriously? //

SANDRA are trying to intimidate an old woman.

AUNT BEV Hey! Middle-aged.

THOMAS Okay, everybody calm down. NOW.

DARRIN I'm completely calm.

THOMAS We're just asking her to move her chair, that's all.

SANDRA You condescending asshole.

DARRIN Geez Sandra, it's still early. Eat something.

BALDWIN *(To AUNT BEV.)* Ma'am - we're gonna have to make you move, anyway.

AUNT BEV What's your name, dear?

BALDWIN Private Baldwin…Linda Baldwin –

AUNT BEV Linda Baldwin…it makes me so proud to see you in uniform. Women were only allowed to be nurses and secretaries in the military when I was growing up.

BALDWIN Thank you, ma'am -

AUNT BEV The Haudenosaunee have a long-standing tradition of women warriors, did you know that?

BALDWIN I didn't.

SANDRA You're looking at one right now, sister!

AUNT BEV In our society women are recognized for their power. The men may be chiefs, but we choose them.

BALDWIN Really? Does Doxdater know that? Because I think he missed that lesson.

THOMAS Very funny.

SANDRA What is she talking about?

DARRIN Relax - there will be plenty of time to fight everybody.

AUNT BEV Of course we would send the men out for an offensive attack - but we would fight side by side when it came to defense.

BALDWIN Really? I like that!

SANDRA - As evidenced by the Oka crisis in 1990 – when the Quebec government came in with teargas and blocked food to the reservation. Women and children linked hands and stood against well-armed government forces –

DARRIN You've set her off, now.

SANDRA As evidenced by the Seaway Bridge dispute in 2009, when government officials tried to stop a funeral procession from going across the bridge - from one side of the reservation to the other - to the burial ground –

THOMAS Or some people might say, tried to cross the American/Canadian border without going through customs.

SANDRA I recognize no such border.

AUNT BEV Its reservation land, dear - no border there.

THOMAS Maybe once upon a time, but that was before we had terrorists to worry about.

SANDRA You calling us terrorists?

DARRIN No - Tommy's one of us.

SANDRA What?

AUNT BEV Thomas Lee Doxdater, banded member of the Tuscarora Nation, Eel Clan.

SANDRA *(To THOMAS.)* Traitor!

THOMAS Do I know you?

SANDRA You should know me as one of your people.

THOMAS I'm not Mohawk.

AUNT BEV But you are Haudenosaunee.

DARRIN Naw, you don't know her - Sandra is Marjorie Henhawk's daughter. She got adopted, lived in the city most of her life.

SANDRA Shut up, Darrin!

THOMAS Why are you here now?

SANDRA Excuse me?

DARRIN You know how it is. She boomeranged. What's your name now? I forget.

SANDRA I changed it back to Henhawk.

THOMAS But you're still from the city.

SANDRA So, tell me where you're from? Turning against your own people?!

THOMAS I'm maintaining the peace.

DARRIN That's right! We're all peaceful because Thomas is here.

SANDRA You're in the uniform of an occupying power and you're NOT turning against your own people?

BALDWIN Occupying! We're not occupying anything!

SANDRA Sorry, honey, you're an invader -

BALDWIN My people didn't invade.

SANDRA Well, you are now. Until last year, our reservation extended another mile and a half to the east of this boundary. Been like that for over three hundred years, then all of a sudden, a developer builds a new complex just north of here, and decides he doesn't want his fancy new folks having to drive around the rez to get to the highway. Then surprise, surprise! Somebody finds a document that claims we ceded all rights to the property in 1926.

BALDWIN Maybe they found the document because they finally had reason to look for it.

SANDRA What?! Wow - I thought you might understand, being a member of a fellow oppressed culture -

BALDWIN Right. Sure.

SANDRA But obviously you're pretty comfortable in your place in the hierarchy -

BALDWIN What?! Do you know what black people go through in this country?

THOMAS Baldwin - don't engage.

SANDRA Yeah.

BALDWIN No you don't - don't even.

SANDRA I know more about you than you know about us! But that's what happens when you get colonized. Genocide - literally and spiritually.

THOMAS Nice speech. Indian 101?

BALDWIN At least your society respects women.

DARRIN You tell her, sweetheart!

SANDRA Patronizing jerk. She's not gonna sleep with you.

DARRIN Why not? You did.

SANDRA Not relevant!

THOMAS ALRIGHT! Shut it down! We're getting off track here.

SANDRA You don't get to tell me what to do -

BALDWIN Or me either!

THOMAS I'm in charge, Baldwin.

BALDWIN Yes SIR.

THOMAS Look, we're not saying you can't be here - I'm just trying to stop things from getting out of hand.

(DARRIN lets out a war whoop.)

AUNT BEV It's a protest, Thomas - people are upset. It's gonna get out of hand.

(THOMAS crouches down beside AUNT BEV.)

THOMAS Aunt Bev, you could really, really help -

AUNT BEV Are you hungry?

THOMAS No, I'm fine, thank you.

AUNT BEV I have corn soup and scones *(pronounced scawns).*

THOMAS Delicious, I'm sure - Aunt Bev -

AUNT BEV Yes, dear?

THOMAS Could I please move your chair?

(AUNT BEV pats his cheek, fondly.)

AUNT BEV No dear.

(Lights down.)

Scene 2

Lights up. Spotlight on the wrong side of the boundary. SANDRA angles her phone to get good reception. BALDWIN spots her and heads over.

SANDRA *(On cell phone.)* Come on Evie, you owe me one! This protest is important.

BALDWIN Hey, you know you're not supposed to be over here -

(SANDRA waves her off, the proceeds to ignore her as BALDWIN tries to draw her attention.)

SANDRA Yeah, you'll be sorry you didn't send a reporter – Johnny Depp supports us!

BALDWIN *(Skeptical.)* Johnny Depp? Really?

SANDRA *(Waves her off again.)* He may even turn up - well, no I didn't get a commitment –

(She flinches and stares at the phone.)

BALDWIN Hung up on you, huh?

SANDRA Doesn't matter - don't think you're off the hook! My next call is to the New York Times!

BALDWIN And they're gonna come here?

SANDRA This protest means something to a lot of people!

BALDWIN I can see that - I can see it means a lot to all three of you. Or four? Johnny Depp is coming? Because I want an autograph.

SANDRA I said we have his support. His assistant said that Mr. Depp is very supportive of Native issues and that she would be happy to relay the invitation to him.

BALDWIN I'm sure he is and you might even get a check at some point but right now - there's just the three of you and right now, you are trespassing.

SANDRA There's better reception over here.

BALDWIN I can detain you for this. If the Captain or Thomas saw you - they would.

SANDRA And you're not gonna?

BALDWIN Get back behind the line. From one oppressed culture to the other.

(SANDRA steps back as BALDWIN exits and SANDRA rejoins AUNT BEV and DARRIN. Lights up on full stage. AUNT BEV enjoys her corn soup. DARRIN is stretched out on the picnic table, dozing. SANDRA pokes him. He tries to wave her off. She pokes him again. All GUARDSMEN are offstage.)

SANDRA Get up!

DARRIN Can't you sit peaceful for five minutes?

SANDRA I don't like how quiet it is. Bet they're gathering reinforcements.

DARRIN Okay, wake me when the tanks come.

SANDRA Why are you here?

DARRIN What?

SANDRA Is this a joke to you? You're all friendly with the guardsmen - you're stretched out on the picnic table instead of flipping it over to use as a barricade - why are you here?

DARRIN I do things my way, you do things your way -

SANDRA When are you gonna take this seriously?

DARRIN *(Sits up.)* I am serious. They announce they're taking land again, like it doesn't matter. Like we can't do anything about it. Well, I am doing something about it. Just don't see the need to be in everybody's faces yet, that's all.

SANDRA I'm trying to get through to these people.

DARRIN Won't happen.

SANDRA If we can get them to understand -

DARRIN Don't waste your time. They don't care. They never do.

SANDRA If you think that then why even come?

AUNT BEV We're not here to get them to change their minds about us. They've already decided. Indians are fine as a sad memory. Easy to express regret about history as long as it stays in the past.

DARRIN *"Oh those poor Indians, we did so many terrible things to them." "That was 200 years ago, don't you have casinos now?"*

AUNT BEV They've already heard what we've had to say and they're not interested.

SANDRA That's why I organized this protest!

AUNT BEV No, you organized it so we can prevent the outsiders from taking more land from us.

SANDRA *(Points to DARRIN.)* He's protecting the rez?

DARRIN Just don't see the need to be all bitched out about it. While they're friendly we can be friendly -

SANDRA This isn't supposed to be friendly.

AUNT BEV Right now, we're just talking. Save your energy for the real fight.

SANDRA Are you sure this isn't because of the Apple?

DARRIN Apple ennit? *(Mocking.)* What do you know about Apples, you're not even rez?

SANDRA I know more than you.

DARRIN From the internet.

AUNT BEV Shhh, Darrin! *(To SANDRA.)* Sandra why does Thomas bug you so much?

SANDRA Why are you giving him a pass? He's raising arms against us.

AUNT BEV I'm not giving him a pass.

SANDRA He's an Indian siding with the invaders!

AUNT BEV They are also our allies, dear -

SANDRA What?

AUNT BEV Treaties -

SANDRA They don't respect treaties - how does that make them allies?

AUNT BEV Yep. They're bad allies.

(THOMAS enters. He listens as AUNT BEV talks.)

AUNT BEV We honor the treaties. We're Haudenosaunee - we are not victims. We're here to protect the land as is our duty. We don't need them to acknowledge the past or admit any wrongs. That's not this fight. We just need them to move their highway bypass.

(BALDWIN enters. Sees AUNT BEV still in the same place. She makes a face at THOMAS and he nods. They both head for AUNT BEV.)

THOMAS Aunt Bev - I really need you to move now.

AUNT BEV Oh, I know. Likewise, dear.

THOMAS I have to follow orders. Even here.

AUNT BEV That's okay, I know you'd do the right thing, if you could.

BALDWIN There's rules, ma'am. Everyone has to follow them.

AUNT BEV Well, of course. That's how it works in the military, right? You take orders and do what you're told. Input from the troops is not needed.

THOMAS Right.

AUNT BEV So different from Longhouse, huh Thomas? There everybody gets to voice their opinion.

THOMAS If the Captain decides to use force, I won't be able to stop him.

BALDWIN We'll probably have to help him.

(DARRIN hops off the table and steps up to face-off against THOMAS.)

DARRIN You know what's gonna happen if you do, right Tommy boy?

AUNT BEV So sweet but I can take care of myself, Darrin. I'm sure Linda and Thomas both know that.

BALDWIN But, ma'am –

THOMAS Yes, ma'am.

AUNT BEV Good.

(Beat. CAPTAIN HEWITT enters. He stops when he sees AUNT BEV, who gives him a friendly wave.)

CAPTAIN HEWITT DOXDATER! BALDWIN! Fall in!

THOMAS Sir!

BALDWIN Yes, sir!

(THOMAS and BALDWIN fall into formation in front of CAPTAIN HEWITT.)

CAPTAIN HEWITT Doxdater, I asked you to get that woman to move, did I not?

THOMAS Yes, sir.

BALDWIN She won't move, sir.

CAPTAIN HEWITT Oh yeah?

(He stalks over to AUNT BEV. DARRIN and SANDRA hover but she waves them off. She gives CAPTAIN HEWITT a bright smile. He doesn't return the gesture. They face off for a moment in silence.)

CAPTAIN HEWITT Ma'am, we need you to move your chair.

AUNT BEV Sago! Aren't you something, with all those badges – what is your title exactly?

CAPTAIN HEWITT Captain.

AUNT BEV Captain. That's impressive!

CAPTAIN HEWITT Thank you, ma'am.

AUNT BEV Such a handsome man, and such fancy badges! You must have to beat the girls away with a stick.

CAPTAIN HEWITT I admire your strategic abilities, but you've played that harmless little old lady card a bit too much, now.

AUNT BEV Not so old –

CAPTAIN HEWITT And not so harmless – Do you know where I just came from, ma'am.

AUNT BEV The john?

CAPTAIN HEWITT No. The town. Folks had some interesting things to say.

AUNT BEV Oh, I don't go to town much. The rez has everything I need.

CAPTAIN HEWITT I bet it does. I spoke with the local police chief – you know to make sure they had what they needed. Let them know we're here –

AUNT BEV That's very considerate of you.

CAPTAIN HEWITT Yeah. I happened to mention you.

(HEWITT puts a hand on Aunt Bev's armrest. It's a power play – THOMAS doesn't like it.)

THOMAS Sir –

CAPTAIN HEWITT It's our side of the border, we're good.

THOMAS Let me handle it.

CAPTAIN HEWITT So far you haven't. I don't think you know who you're dealing with.

BALDWIN Sir?

CAPTAIN HEWITT This is YOUR protest, isn't it? "Aunt" Bev.

SANDRA This is MY initiative.

CAPTAIN HEWITT *(To AUNT BEV.)* You let her think it was her idea? That was kind of you.

AUNT BEV I am kind, captain.

THOMAS What's going on?

CAPTAIN HEWITT Doxdater, AUNT BEV is famous.

(As CAPTAIN HEWITT talks, the backdrop flashes with photos from different land disputes - photos with soldiers and police, protests, fires, and fighting from each of the uprisings mentioned by CAPTAIN HEWITT.)

CAPTAIN HEWITT Caledonia/Six Nations land dispute in 2008, Akwesasne/Cornwall Bridge dispute in 2009, The Oka crisis in 1990 – *(AUNT BEV just smiles.)* But it doesn't stop there – it goes back to Wounded Knee in '73 and Alcatraz in '69…

(Slides of the land conflicts flicker across the backdrop.)

AUNT BEV Keep going, captain.

CAPTAIN HEWITT There's more? I shouldn't be surprised. It seems, ma'am, wherever you go, MAJOR crises follow - sometimes even resulting in bloodshed –

AUNT BEV Understandable when one is fighting off occupying forces…

CAPTAIN HEWITT Occupying? It's my country too. I've spent the better part of my life fighting to protect it. I'm not saying there isn't a lot of bad - you and I both know our history has had its moments - but there's a lot that's great too. One of the greatest things in this country is that the people have the right to protest, peacefully.

AUNT BEV They do, don't they.

CAPTAIN HEWITT Yes.

AUNT BEV You're welcome.

CAPTAIN HEWITT Pardon me, ma'am?

AUNT BEV Ever heard of the Haudenosaunee Confederacy and the Great Law, captain?

CAPTAIN HEWITT I'm speaking about the Constitution.

AUNT BEV So am I -

CAPTAIN HEWITT The CONSTITUTION, ma'am. The SUPREME LAW of this land.

AUNT BEV Oh I know, captain. Thomas knows too -

CAPTAIN HEWITT Oh yes he does. He swore allegiance to it.

(Beat. THOMAS stares forward, ignoring AUNT BEV as she tries to catch his eye.)

AUNT BEV Just say what you need to say.

CAPTAIN HEWITT I believe that you know exactly what you are doing. I believe you are deliberately trying to provoke an incident.

AUNT BEV Maybe.

CAPTAIN HEWITT I have a lot of respect for you, but I don't underestimate you. You can play games with the rest of them, but I'm not afraid to be the bad guy if the situation requires it. You understand?

AUNT BEV Yes, captain.

CAPTAIN HEWITT Doxdater! Baldwin! You understand?

THOMAS Yes, sir.

BALDWIN Yes, sir, captain sir!

CAPTAIN HEWITT Move your chair, ma'am or we'll move it for you.

(AUNT BEV starts to pack up her totebag, putting all the snacks away – and then she pulls out a war club, and sets it in her lap.)

CAPTAIN HEWITT Right that's it! Baldwin! Doxdater! With me.

(He stalks over to stage right. BALDWIN and THOMAS follow.)

CAPTAIN HEWITT We're taking her in.

THOMAS What? It's a peaceful protest! Sir.

CAPTAIN HEWITT What's that thing she pulled out of her bag? Doesn't look peaceful to me.

THOMAS It's an old war club. It's symbolic.

CAPTAIN HEWITT War club? Yeah, I don't think I'm misreading the situation. You were supposed to charm her, Doxdater.

THOMAS Well, if you didn't come in and threaten her -

CAPTAIN HEWITT Excuse me?

BALDWIN Captain! I agree with Doxdater - She's not dangerous. She just wants you to know she won't be intimidated, that's all.

CAPTAIN HEWITT Oh yeah, Baldwin? You can handle her?

BALDWIN It's her pride, sir. She's a warrior - she told me the women of her tribe //

THOMAS Nation //

BALDWIN have always been warriors.

CAPTAIN HEWITT So you two are friendly -

BALDWIN I think we understand each other -

CAPTAIN HEWITT Fine, Baldwin. See if you can get through to her or at the very least, disarm her - Doxdater -

THOMAS Yes, sir?

CAPTAIN HEWITT Not impressed.

(He exits. BALDWIN unslings her rifle and hands it to THOMAS.)

BALWIN Respect goes a long way, Doxdater.

(She goes over to AUNT BEV.)

AUNT BEV Hello dear -

BALDWIN I admire you so much - strong women like you are my role models. Every time they get angry because I ask too many questions, I picture all the women in the past who've come before me - women who were annoying and pushed too hard and persevered. Meeting you in person - it's a revelation! A culture that takes it for granted that women are leaders and warriors and are capable of anything. I want to know more!

AUNT BEV I'm happy to teach you - come visit anytime.

BALDWIN Thank you!

AUNT BEV I'll be right here.

DARRIN Haudenosaunee Women…leaders, warriors and stubborn as hell.

BALDWIN Admirable - truly, but this kind of effort deserves to be about a bigger cause.

SANDRA Our home isn't worth the effort? Is that what you're saying?

THOMAS Baldwin, don't start this conversation.

SANDRA Right, Apple - run away scared -

BALDWIN Apple?

THOMAS Red on the outside, white on the inside.

BALDWIN Oh. Like Oreo? Not nice.

THOMAS Nope.

DARRIN *(To SANDRA.)* You're one to talk.

SANDRA Because I'm not rez? I'm as Indian as you are. I belong here with the rest of you. I don't know what else you want me to do.

DARRIN Geez Sandra! Say, So what? I'm a city NDN, get over it.

THOMAS Just be who you are.

SANDRA *(To THOMAS.)* Who are you, exactly? You're here - in that uniform, trying to control us.

THOMAS I know my language, I know my clan. I go to Longhouse regularly. When's the last time you went?

BALDWIN Aunt Bev, moving the chair isn't giving up anything. We can still have the conversation.

AUNT BEV True, but we're having a conversation now, aren't we?

DARRIN *(To SANDRA.)* He's the real deal, Sandra. He's traditional.

SANDRA It's traditional to turn against your people?

THOMAS I gave my word. When I signed up, when I put on this uniform, I made a commitment - I swore on my honor. A warrior's honor is everything. My dad taught me that.

DARRIN Your dad's the most honorable man I've ever known.

THOMAS Yeah, well that's how he raised me. Captain Hewitt understands honor. Dad tried to teach you, too bad it didn't take.

(Beat. DARRIN reacts.)

SANDRA The way of the warrior - very New Age of you.

AUNT BEV It's not a joke, Sandra.

THOMAS It's okay, Aunt Bev, I've been mocked before. *"Hey Kemosabe, get out of the way and I'll give you some nice shiny beads."*

BALDWIN There's a lot of jerks in our unit.

THOMAS First time I've heard it from another NDN.

SANDRA Must be your first time being a traitor.

THOMAS I'm not a traitor. I'm honoring my family. I'm following a path that was my father's and my grandfather's -

SANDRA And you're living the traditional way -

THOMAS Every day.

SANDRA As a National Guardsman.

AUNT BEV The two aren't incompatible, dear.

SANDRA *(To AUNT BEV.)* Bullshit!

THOMAS See that? You don't speak to elders that way.

SANDRA I didn't - I didn't mean -

AUNT BEV It's fine. It's a tough situation. It's hard for our young people these days. How much do you compromise? How much do you give up to get along?

SANDRA He is standing here holding a gun on his own people -

THOMAS I'm not the first one here to do that.

SANDRA What?

DARRIN Wow, man. Right under the bus - I was wondering when it was coming.

THOMAS You talk about my dad. How honorable he is and how much you respect him - how much respect did you feel when you pulled a gun on him and my mom?

DARRIN It was a shitty thing to do.

THOMAS Yeah, you're gonna tell me? You robbed my family.

DARRIN I was messed up. I'm clean now.

THOMAS So that makes a difference?

DARRIN Well, that's what happens when you got nowhere to go and no way out, all right? You do stupid shit. You screw over the people who matter. And you spend the rest of your time regretting it and trying to find a way to make it right.

THOMAS You can't make it right.

DARRIN I get that, okay?

THOMAS I found a way to fit.

DARRIN Yeah, you did. It's good to see, man.

THOMAS Oh, we're good now? Is that what you're trying to get me to say? Because we're not.

(Beat. DARRIN is silent.)

AUNT BEV *(To THOMAS.)* People make mistakes, big ones sometimes. But that doesn't stop Darrin from caring about you - or being the same guy who saved you from that well.

DARRIN Don't bother Aunt Bev. It's okay.

AUNT BEV He was punished, he paid for it.

THOMAS Yes, ma'am.

SANDRA You know something - you might be traditional and know everything there is to know about our culture //

THOMAS I didn't say that. //

SANDRA but that doesn't stop you from being a complete asshole.

THOMAS You don't know me.

SANDRA I don't think I want to, thanks.

BALDWIN More going on here than just a little land dispute, huh?

SANDRA Little land dispute?!

BALDWIN I don't see why it's such a big fuss. They're just running a road - there's still lots of land here for you all.

DARRIN Lots, huh?

THOMAS Does this look like a lot of land to you, Baldwin?

BALDWIN I meant for the size of the population. You're not even using this land - it's just overgrown.

AUNT BEV You mean it's growing - the way the Creator intended it to?

DARRIN Why does everybody gotta cut up a piece of land when they see it?

BALDWIN The plants could be replanted -

AUNT BEV To other land that's already over-cultivated?

SANDRA That's the government solution for everything, huh? Move anything that gets in the way. Plants, people...

BALDWIN The highway expansion will help a lot of people.

AUNT BEV Not our people.

SANDRA This is how genocide works!

BALDWIN Don't be so dramatic, genocide?

THOMAS Yeah, genocide. What do you know about it, Baldwin?

BALDWIN You're still here - and you have your culture -

SANDRA Because we fight for it every day.

BALDWIN It's not like you were slaves, you know?

SANDRA Yes, we were - read a history book some time.

BALDWIN I did and I remember you were slave-OWNERS -

DARRIN We were not.

BALDWIN On the Trail of Tears I heard you all had slaves carrying your stuff for you -

AUNT BEV A third of the nations that were driven onto the Trail of Tears, died during that walk.

DARRIN Right - we didn't believe in owning land - but we believed in owning people - RIGHT.

AUNT BEV Some nations did own slaves. Not the best part of our history.

BALDWIN Ha! How do you like them - apples?

AUNT BEV The nations lost everything when the government tore them out of their homes and pushed them onto a new land. They adapted - not always in the best way.

BALDWIN Ma'am, I know it's been bad for Indians. I'm not trying to say you haven't had it rough, but at least you've still got your culture and your language - we don't even have that.

AUNT BEV It's not a competition, dear.

BALDWIN No offense - most of you aren't even really Indians, you know// - you're all so... mixed...

DARRIN Whoa, what?

THOMAS Sorry if we're not Indian enough for YOU, Baldwin //

SANDRA We're 1 percent of the population, what do you expect?

AUNT BEV Be careful dear, they like it when we fight each other. When the poor and the oppressed start seeing each other as the competition, they win. Don't play along, Linda.

BALDWIN I'm not!

SANDRA Yes, you are. *(To Thomas.)* And you are too!

(CAPTAIN HEWITT enters.)

CAPTAIN HEWITT No success, Baldwin?

BALDWIN We're talking, sir.

CAPTAIN HEWITT Right. Doxdater, get on the reservation side, Baldwin, get ready - on three we grab the chair.

THOMAS Wait - I can't go on the rez.

CAPTAIN HEWITT If I relieve you of duty, you can. Get over there and grab the chair.

THOMAS Wait - what?

SANDRA Well, there it is. You heard him, Thomas.

THOMAS Sir -

CAPTAIN HEWITT *(To THOMAS.)* Strategy. A good soldier exploits every advantage he has.

SANDRA Exploits - yeah.

CAPTAIN HEWITT Grab the chair!

BALDWIN Come ON Thomas!

CAPTAIN HEWITT That was a direct order, kid.

THOMAS You relieved me of duty, didn't you?

CAPTAIN HEWITT Are you giving me attitude? You forget your place, private!

THOMAS She's an elder. You can't just drag her away when she hasn't done anything.

CAPTAIN HEWITT We're just moving the damn chair!

AUNT BEV Over my dead body.

CAPTAIN HEWITT Can be arranged!

THOMAS Sir!

CAPTAIN HEWITT I told you, ma'am. Push me to the point where I HAVE TO take action - I will do so. Doxdater!

(Beat. THOMAS doesn't move. BALDWIN crouches down beside AUNT BEV's chair.)

BALDWIN I'm sorry, Aunt Bev -

CAPTAIN HEWITT Move, Doxdater!

SANDRA So what are you gonna do Thomas? You feel so good about who you are now?

CAPTAIN HEWITT Doxdater - ARE YOU GONNA GRAB THAT CHAIR OR NOT?

THOMAS No Sir - and neither are you.

CAPTAIN HEWITT Private Doxdater, you're insubordinate.

(CAPTAIN HEWITT grabs AUNT BEV's chair and pulls. A loud click as THOMAS arms his rifle and raises it, aims at HEWITT.)

THOMAS Sir - you need to step back. Now!

CAPTAIN HEWITT Drop that weapon, Private!

(CAPTAIN HEWITT steps forward, ready to disarm THOMAS.)

THOMAS Don't, sir! You're trespassing on the Sovereign Territories of the Haudenosaunee Confederacy. I'm within my rights to shoot if I so chose -

CAPTAIN HEWITT And I'm within my rights to beat you with that rifle, if I so choose.

(AUNT BEV jumps behind her chair and holds up her hand.)

AUNT BEV Um, not really, captain - as you've so clearly pointed out, there's a border here. Thomas is on Indian land. But you can still have the chair if you want it.

DARRIN Fuck that!

(DARRIN grabs the back legs of the chair and drags it back over the border.)

AUNT BEV So, as you see Captain, you are not legally allowed to touch any of us. No chair, no custody, no knocking guns around. Nothing.

CAPTAIN HEWITT Right. Of course, ma'am, you know that your security will only last until I get the okay from Albany, right?

BALDWIN You raised your gun against your CO. Are you crazy?

DARRIN One craaaazyyy NDN!

AUNT BEV You can put that down now, Thomas - you made your point.

THOMAS I don't think so -

AUNT BEV We don't like guns.

THOMAS Grandma always says we're adaptive. Me, I like my gun -

CAPTAIN HEWITT This means Leavenworth - you realize that?

THOMAS Yes. If my government decides to give me up to yours.

(THOMAS tears off his insignia, throws it on the ground beside HEWITT. CAPTAIN HEWITT steps forward to face THOMAS.)

CAPTAIN HEWITT You're gonna regret that.

AUNT BEV Now, now, captain - no need to be a sore loser.

CAPTAIN HEWITT I hope you're satisfied. He just destroyed his life. He's done.

THOMAS Or maybe I'm finally figuring things out.

(SANDRA grabs THOMAS and drags him offstage DARRIN exits next, waving the chair in triumph. AUNT BEV is left alone, facing the guardsmen.)

CAPTAIN HEWITT We'll be back. Be ready.

(CAPTAIN HEWITT and BALDWIN exit. Lights down on AUNT BEV watching them leave.)

★

ACT II

MONOLOGUE

AUNT BEV stands in front of a large projection of the Two-Row Wampum.

AUNT BEV One of our first treaties was with the Dutch. They wanted to do business with us. Trade. They consulted with their governor and came back with an offer and just like on T.V., the offer started with the phrase "the Great White Father." We had to stop them right there and then. You say that you are our father and I am your son. We say, we will not be like father and son, but like brothers. This wampum belt confirms our words. These two rows will symbolize two paths or two vessels, traveling down the same river together. One, a birch bark canoe, will be for the Indian people, their laws, their customs and their ways. The other, a ship, will be for the other people and their laws, their customs and their ways. We shall each travel the river together, side by side, but each in our own boats. Neither of us will make compulsory laws nor interfere in the internal affairs of the other. Neither of us will try to steer the other's vessel.

Scene 1

AUNT BEV's house. Immediately after the act break. There is a sofa covered in a Hudson's Bay Blanket, and quilt work pillows and a coffee table. A wooden dining chair is stage left. DARRIN, SANDRA and THOMAS all rush in first - AUNT BEV follows. DARRIN rushes in with the chair, he puts it in place like a trophy.

THOMAS Shit!

AUNT BEV Language, Thomas!

SANDRA What happened to "you don't speak that way to elders?"

THOMAS Sorry, Aunt Bev.

DARRIN That was AWESOME, man!

AUNT BEV Shhh! Everyone - *satnyeh!* Calm down and let me think.

THOMAS I turned my gun on my CO.

AUNT BEV I was there, hon - I saw.

DARRIN That was classic - that was OUTLAW!

SANDRA That was insane.

THOMAS Oh yeah? Because I thought you wanted me to stand with you?

SANDRA Of course I did but //

THOMAS because for me to do that I had to stop Captain Hewitt and Baldwin from advancing! *(To AUNT BEV.)* Because that's what they were doing. You get that, don't you?

AUNT BEV I don't like guns.

THOMAS Aunt Bev?

DARRIN No worries, Tommy - Aunt Bev will handle it.

AUNT BEV What's gonna happen next, Thomas?

THOMAS Probably - call it in - contact the governor.

SANDRA Why?

THOMAS They need to get permission to come in and get me.

SANDRA They're gonna invade!

DARRIN No way!

THOMAS I'm AWOL, I broke rank and disobeyed a direct order - they're coming alright.

SANDRA They can't just do that!

AUNT BEV Yeah, they can.

SANDRA What do we do?

DARRIN What would A.I.M do! *(He raises a "red power" fist.)*

AUNT BEV Quiet, Darrin. *(To THOMAS.)* I'll go to the council. If they're gonna come - they'll have to go through them first.

SANDRA Right. Let them face the council! Tribal people protect each other - it's what we do!

AUNT BEV Sandra - why don't you head back to the protest site? Keep an eye open for any updates.

SANDRA Got it!

(SANDRA exits.)

AUNT BEV Darrin - Keep Thomas company. Watch his back.

DARRIN Yes, ma'am!

THOMAS Ma'am, it would be better if I went with you. They could move on me at any time.

AUNT BEV Better to keep your head down. If you hear anything, see anything, you head to Sandra's. It's only a mile and a half away. Darrin knows where it is.

DARRIN Oh, yeah, I do. *(He nods at THOMAS - guy code for "yeah, I nailed that.")* Not forgetting that one.

THOMAS Great.

AUNT BEV I'll see you soon.

(AUNT BEV exits. THOMAS and DARRIN are alone.)

DARRIN Have no fear, Darrin is here! It's you and me against the world, buddy!

THOMAS Shit.

Scene 2

Spotlight, The Protest Site —a press conference. SANDRA is front and center. There are clicks and flashes of cameras as she reads a prepared statement. (Can be in the black or with photos on video display)

SANDRA *(Reading.)* "Whereas the confederation of the original Thirteen Colonies into one Republic was influenced by the political system developed by the Iroquois Confederacy as were many of the democratic principles which were incorporated into the Constitution itself……the original framers of the Constitution, including, most notably, George Washington and Benjamin Franklin, are known to have greatly admired the concepts of the Six Nations of the Iroquois Confederacy…The Congress also hereby reaffirms the constitutionally recognized government-to-government relationship with Indian tribes which has been the cornerstone of this Nation's official Indian policy;" This is from the Concurrent Resolution 331*, which was passed by the 100th Congress, second session in 1988. It confirms our existence and status as a sovereign government. Therefore Eminent Domain does not apply. This time it's some greedy developers who want our land, and we say NO MORE! *(Pauses for a "question.")* I'm not saying that is why Private Doxdater did what he did, but you have to understand - the provocation is extreme. *(Pauses for another "question.")* He won't be coming forward at this time, no. We are waiting to meet with tribal leaders first. *(Pauses for another "question.")* No... I don't really know - but that's his commanding officer, feel free to ask him.

(Spotlight up on CAPTAIN HEWITT, flanked by BALDWIN. Cameras flash.)

CAPTAIN HEWITT No comment.

(Lights up on protest site. SANDRA is on the rez side of the border. HEWITT faces off against her, still flanked by BALDWIN.)

CAPTAIN HEWITT That was a bad move.

SANDRA I don't know, so far, I'm pretty happy with the result.

CAPTAIN HEWITT Where is he?

SANDRA I'm sorry - am I in uniform? I don't have to answer your questions.

CAPTAIN HEWITT Look Sweetheart, I don't think you understand the seriousness of this situation. I'm trying to help you all out, here.

SANDRA Well, sweetheart - I appreciate it, but I think we've got it covered.

(BALDWIN snorts a laugh, but covers it with a cough when HEWITT glares.)

CAPTAIN HEWITT Thanks to you, the whole world knows that Private Doxdater is AWOL and insubordinate!

SANDRA You mean he finally remembered who he was and where his true loyalty lies?

CAPTAIN HEWITT His loyalty, just like YOURS, should be to this country and its constitution.

SANDRA Our loyalty is to our people.

CAPTAIN HEWITT We all live in the United States, which makes me your people.

SANDRA Your people break treaties like toothpicks and Thomas — he really believed you chose him for this mission on merit.

CAPTAIN HEWITT I did.

SANDRA Right. And it was just convenient that you could "relieve him of duty" when you needed to bend the rules.

CAPTAIN HEWITT A good officer -

SANDRA Exploits opportunities. You were threatening and manhandling an elder. Are you really surprised this happened? Don't be surprised if it starts happening more.

CAPTAIN HEWITT Fine words, darlin' - do you really want me to escalate this?

SANDRA Ooooh! The big bad military machine taking on the Indians. That's okay, we're used to it! Do your worst.

CAPTAIN HEWITT Right. Baldwin!

BALDWIN Yes, sir!

CAPTAIN HEWITT Take point!

BALDWIN Yes, sir!

(HEWITT exits.)

BALDWIN That was really stupid.

SANDRA Thanks G.I. Jane, but I'm good.

BALDWIN Hewitt is trying to protect Thomas.

SANDRA Right.

BALDWIN He's Hewitt's protégée. He practically adopted him the moment he showed up.

SANDRA *(Sarcastic.)* Right - the little NDN kid?

BALDWIN The little warrior kid. Thomas is all about honor and serving people and so is Hewitt.

SANDRA That guy?

BALDWIN He did two tours in Afghanistan before he was switched to the guard. Thomas respects the hell out of him.

SANDRA You don't?

BALDWIN I have ovaries.

SANDRA So, I'm not wrong, Hewitt is an asshole.

BALDWIN I don't think you realize how serious this is. Thomas just bought himself ten years in Leavenworth //

SANDRA Ten years? //

BALDWIN if he's lucky. AWOL isn't good but turning your gun against your CO, that's major. The powers that be won't forgive — but if Thomas turns himself in, Hewitt could claim it was an emotional breakdown.

SANDRA He wants Thomas to say he's crazy? No way.

BALDWIN I know you don't trust me or Hewitt, but this is the only way.

SANDRA Why do you care?

BALDWIN He's my friend.

SANDRA Sure he is.

BALDWIN Yeah he is. He's a pain in my, well you know - but we are friends. I wouldn't have made it through basic without him. And this is major.

SANDRA You really think it will work?

BALDWIN It's the only option.

Scene 3

AUNT BEV'S house. DARRIN sits on the sofa as THOMAS paces.

DARRIN Tommy, sit down! Relax. You're stressing me out.

THOMAS Yeah? They could be knocking down the door at any minute. Go ahead and stress out.

DARRIN Eat something. Have some tea. Don't worry about anything until there's something to worry about.

THOMAS Yeah, that's you isn't it? *"Don't worry – it's all fine!"* Well, people who take responsibility - worry.

DARRIN It's a waste – Everything always works out in the end. You never get more than you can handle.

THOMAS You think that because someone always steps in to solve it for you. Well not me. I save me - I don't wait for other people to do it.

DARRIN Yeah? - Aunt Bev's off saving you right now, ain't she?

THOMAS *(To himself.)* What am I doing?

DARRIN Being an asshole –

THOMAS Hewitt believed in me.

DARRIN The guy who brought you here to stand against us?

THOMAS We weren't. We were here to keep the peace.

DARRIN If that's what you say.

(AUNT BEV enters.)

THOMAS Hey Aunt Bev, what's the news?

AUNT BEV I saw Bertha Silversmith, one of the clan mothers. They're pretty upset. There's already been trouble. People are being harassed when they buy groceries, when they try to see the doctor and three cars were set on fire.

THOMAS How did they find out? It just happened.

AUNT BEV Moccasin Telegraph. And it's twice as fast now with Facebook. Heck, some of the clan mothers even do the Twitter.

THOMAS That's it, isn't it? They're not gonna support me.

AUNT BEV We don't know for sure.

THOMAS Can't you speak for me, Aunt Bev? Make my case? *(Beat.)* I'm on my own.

DARRIN Naw - tell him, Aunt Bev.

AUNT BEV You got yourself into this situation.

THOMAS I was protecting you.

AUNT BEV Thomas –

THOMAS If someone put their hands on my grandmother the way the captain was gonna - I'd lose it. I started thinking of all the grandmothers, all the elders and the children who'd been pushed aside and dragged away and my gun was up and it felt right.

AUNT BEV You can't get so swept up in the past, Thomas. It will never stop.

THOMAS I thought you wanted me to join your protest?

AUNT BEV I wanted you to put down your gun and refuse to take any further action. A peaceful protest.

THOMAS Right. Because that's worked so well before.

AUNT BEV Peace is how our nations came together in the first place.

THOMAS That may have been how we came together, but that's not how it works now. You've been peacefully fighting this bypass for how long? What's it got you?

AUNT BEV I'm trying my best to help you.

THOMAS The captain was trying to help me. He said I was a natural soldier.

AUNT BEV You might've been a good soldier this morning but when you turned your gun on your captain, you became the redskin who can't be trusted.

THOMAS What am I gonna do?

AUNT BEV Well, you can stick it out here, on the rez - and wait for official word from the council.

THOMAS Or?

AUNT BEV You could go north. Our reservations run straight up through Canada.

THOMAS Like a coward.

AUNT BEV Who cares? It doesn't matter.

THOMAS Yes, it does.

DARRIN Everyone will understand.

AUNT BEV What else can you do? Your captain is probably gathering reinforcements while we speak. Darrin's still on parole. What will happen if you fight it out here?

DARRIN Doesn't matter - I got your back kid.

AUNT BEV And Sandra - she's in charge of this protest, will she be arrested for helping you?

THOMAS There's gotta be other options –

AUNT BEV Well, the council hasn't met - Bertha is gonna try and intervene with the clan mothers. We can wait if you really want to –

THOMAS I want to.

AUNT BEV Fine, but I think we should prepare, just in case.

THOMAS Okay, Aunt Bev.

AUNT BEV We've done it before. We can run you from rez to rez, like we did for A.I.M. It's not that hard.

(AUNT BEV exits.)

THOMAS I don't want to go to Canada.

(SANDRA enters.)

SANDRA Hey.

THOMAS Chi'wen Sandra.

SANDRA Is Aunt Bev here?

DARRIN Yeah.

SANDRA How's it looking?

THOMAS Not good. The clan mothers are worried. All sorts of stuff is happening in town. Bad stuff.

DARRIN Aunt Bev wants us to A.I.M. him up into Canada.

SANDRA They're not gonna support you?

THOMAS We don't know but - she thinks we need to prepare.

SANDRA What if I said I had another possibility?

DARRIN Well, speak up for crap's sake.

SANDRA You need to go.

DARRIN That's nice.

(DARRINS heads for exit. SANDRA grabs his arm.)

SANDRA Wait - *(She whispers in his ear.)*

THOMAS Do you guys need a moment alone? Because it's no problem -

SANDRA The short answer would be NO. No way in hell.

DARRIN See? Every day she breaks my heart. *(SANDRA rolls her eyes.)* I'm gonna head over to the protest site. You two talk.

(He exits.)

THOMAS What were you two whispering about?

SANDRA So…Baldwin…is she trustworthy?

THOMAS Yeah.

SANDRA Well, we may have a solution.

(SANDRA leads THOMAS as they exit.)

Scene 4

Midnight. The protest site. CAPTAIN HEWITT is waiting. DARRIN enters.

DARRIN Just you, right, Sarge?

CAPTAIN HEWITT Captain.

DARRIN Whatever, bud.

CAPTAIN HEWITT Is he here?

DARRIN *(Signaling THOMAS.)* Ca-Caw! Ca-Caw!

(THOMAS enters cautiously.)

THOMAS Hey, cap. *(He salutes. HEWITT doesn't react.)* No, huh?

CAPTAIN HEWITT Your idiot friend asked me to come.

DARRIN That's not cool, man —

(THOMAS drags DARRIN over to the side, DARRIN takes a "lookout" position.)

THOMAS Thanks for coming.

CAPTAIN HEWITT What the hell do you want, Doxdater? Because right now, I'm thinking that if I stand here and raise my gun and shoot - I'm not breaking any law.

THOMAS Sir -

CAPTAIN HEWITT You drew on me, you little shit!

THOMAS I know! I'm sorry.

CAPTAIN HEWITT After everything I've done for you! What the hell, kid?

THOMAS Cap //

CAPTAIN HEWITT We were on the same team.

THOMAS I'm sorry.

CAPTAIN HEWITT I thought we saw eye to eye. I thought you were somebody I could trust. You know - Torres asked me why I was pushing you for O.C.S. and I told him - Doxdater's solid. He's the one guy who'd go to hell and back //

THOMAS I am!

CAPTAIN HEWITT Not today. I asked you if you were okay, didn't I?

THOMAS Yes.

CAPTAIN HEWITT You were all *"I'm fine - it's fine, it's not my rez."*

THOMAS I know.

CAPTAIN HEWITT I trusted you! On your word. I gave you that respect. And then when you were struggling, I gave you an out.

THOMAS I know you did.

CAPTAIN HEWITT So why didn't you take it?

THOMAS I didn't want to disappoint you.

CAPTAIN HEWITT Well, good job, kid.

THOMAS I love the job. You know I do. I finally found a place where I fit or at least I thought I did. It shouldn't have gone down the way it did. I know you would've shot anyone else who did that to you. It was just today -

CAPTAIN HEWITT What the hell did I do? I wasn't gonna take the old lady in.

THOMAS No. But you were gonna pick her up and toss her aside like she was a sack of garbage.

CAPTAIN HEWITT So that's it? That's all? You threw away your career – both our careers - for that?

THOMAS Why'd you have to go and put your hands on her? After I told you? I WARNED you. You brought me here because I know NDN people, well did you forget I was one? Shit, captain - do you even know what you did? We've been pushed and grabbed and dragged away from our families and then you were gonna grab her too, like she was nothing. An ELDER. Right in front of me.

CAPTAIN HEWITT She was trying to provoke an incident!

THOMAS No, you provoked the incident. I was fine. They all questioned me – judged me for following orders and I was fine – because I knew you were a man of your word, a man of honor.

CAPTAIN HEWITT I am.

THOMAS Not today! You weren't honorable today.

CAPTAIN HEWITT Well, I'm the asshole.

DARRIN Yeah, you are.

THOMAS Shut up, Darrin!

CAPTAIN HEWITT Why am I here?

THOMAS I guess I'm not that honorable either. Baldwin said you wanted me to turn myself in.

CAPTAIN HEWITT She did, huh?

THOMAS She said it was your idea. That you could make a case for emotional distress or something.

CAPTAIN HEWITT Were you distressed, Thomas?

THOMAS Yes.

CAPTAIN HEWITT She's right it could work. I could say that the shock of standing against your own people was too much and you couldn't take it anymore.

THOMAS I couldn't take it anymore.

CAPTAIN HEWITT So all you have to do is agree that you snapped and we can take you in. I think the press will lose interest once they hear it's psychological.

THOMAS The press?

CAPTAIN HEWITT Your friend didn't tell you? She called a huge press conference right over there. Seems like I wasn't the only one who wasn't honorable today.

THOMAS Aunt Bev?

CAPTAIN HEWITT No, the mouthy one. The one who was in your face as much as she was mine.

THOMAS Sandra.

DARRIN Bullshit.

CAPTAIN HEWITT Are you gonna turn yourself in?

THOMAS Would you?

CAPTAIN HEWITT Probably not, but I wouldn't use me a role model. We wouldn't be here if it wasn't for me, after all. If you're gonna turn yourself in, you should do it now. No one's around – easier to keep it low profile.

THOMAS I don't want a cover-up!

CAPTAIN HEWITT You just embarrassed the National Guard and the U.S. Army. Yeah, we cover it up. You get a medical discharge and we all calm down. Business as usual.

THOMAS I don't want business as usual.

CAPTAIN HEWITT Don't let one mistake blow up your life.

THOMAS And everything that happened today will be for nothing.

CAPTAIN HEWITT They got some press for their protest. It's not all lost.

THOMAS I'm not crazy.

CAPTAIN HEWITT I know.

THOMAS What you did was wrong - and what you were about to do was even worse.

CAPTAIN HEWITT You overreacted.

THOMAS No. I didn't.

(THOMAS stands at attention.)

CAPTAIN HEWITT Don't listen to me kid, I'm tired. I'm not thinking clearly. We can work it out in morning. *(THOMAS doesn't move.)* You stupid shit.

(CAPTAIN HEWITT exits.)

DARRIN *(Shouts after him.)* Dick!

THOMAS Canada, here I come.

Scene 5

Later. AUNT BEV'S house. THOMAS packs up. SANDRA is curled up in the armchair, searching the web.

SANDRA I don't understand. What happened with Baldwin's plan?

THOMAS Done.

SANDRA We still haven't heard from the council -

THOMAS Do me a favor - don't call the press until I've actually left the rez, okay?

SANDRA What are you talking about?

THOMAS The captain told me - you had a nice turnout.

SANDRA I'm sorry.

THOMAS Sure.

SANDRA I thought it would benefit you and the protest. I thought - if people could hear your side -

THOMAS You didn't ask my side.

SANDRA Didn't have time. It was too good of an opportunity.

THOMAS To make sure everyone knew what happened.

SANDRA Well yeah, isn't that what you wanted?

THOMAS They were advancing on Aunt Bev. I wasn't making a stand.

SANDRA Yes you were. They were about to do something wrong and you said "no." That is taking a stand.

THOMAS People are calling me a traitor.

SANDRA To this government? So, what?

THOMAS I'm not a traitor.

SANDRA You were protecting your people.

THOMAS I gave my word as a warrior and I broke it.

SANDRA More of the "Warrior Code."

THOMAS It's not a joke. Bet you had a nice cushy job in the city.

SANDRA I came back here, okay?

(DARRIN enters with some road maps. THOMAS and SANDRA don't notice.)

THOMAS Did you ever hear that an Indian man is three times more likely to go to jail than to college? We heard it every day. "Watch out, you don't wanna end up in jail." Because every family has one - guys like Darrin, who screw up over and over again. So they numb themselves and derail because they can't find a way to fit. Because everything in this world we live in now is set up to crush who we are. But I found my place - or I thought I did.

(DARRIN exits upset.)

SANDRA Hey, at least you know who you are. For the longest time, I tried to forget I was Indian. I was tired of explaining myself. Tired of the stupid questions. Do you speak Indian? What's a sweat lodge like? Tired of being judged by TV standards, and movie standards - to these douche-bags, you're not Indian if you don't act like an extra from *Dances With Wolves*. Well, hello - that's Western people. We were 500 different nations - NATIONS - as in different languages and traditions - and no, I don't know what happens in a Hopi sundance because, I'm Haudenosaunee, Mohawk specifically and sorry if I like to wear high heels occasionally. I got so tired of validating who I was to them, and tired of their presumption that their opinion mattered. Like they had the right to question us about who we are. So I stopped being Indian. I got so tired of it, I finally decided to learn Spanish, just to shut everybody up.

THOMAS Well, you solved it, then.

SANDRA I thought so - then, one day the mayor said something incredibly stupid and, I thought - racist and I couldn't get anyone to care. It felt like a punch - like a slap out of nowhere, and I didn't - even realize it, but I'd started crying. So I told "my people" in the city - my friends, my ex - and they all laughed. Like it was a joke. I guess it was my fault because I'd always made jokes and laughed along in the past, because hey, "I have a sense of humor".

THOMAS You do?

SANDRA I did then - until I realized that nobody cared what was happening with us. I had a good job, a job that was all about selling things, making people believe things and I couldn't get anyone to buy the idea that what he said was wrong. I realized then that my job was pretty useless - who I was, was pretty useless. So I came here, and dammit if I wasn't gonna find a way to be useful. That's why I came back and that's why I started this protest - because I've played the game and ignored shit and have gone along to get along and I ended up pretty screwed. I'm allowed to be angry here. People know what I'm talking about here.

THOMAS I'll be honest - I'm kinda 50/50.

SANDRA Jerk!

THOMAS Hey, it's the rez. We tease because we care.

SANDRA Well, thanks.

(AUNT BEV enters with DARRIN.)

AUNT BEV Sandra.

SANDRA Yes, Aunt Bev?

AUNT BEV Get out of my chair.

(SANDRA jumps up as AUNT BEV sits down.)

AUNT BEV So, Darrin, what's the rundown?

DARRIN We've got a huge crowd down at the site! There's a long lineup, Powlesses are there, Maracles, and the Longboats brought six hundred and forty-three of their closest cousins.

AUNT BEV We're a success.

THOMAS Congratulations.

DARRIN People have heard about Tommy and what he did. They figure the least they can do is show up.

THOMAS Good. I'm glad it wasn't for nothing.

DARRIN It wasn't.

(AUNT BEV'S phone rings.)

AUNT BEV *(Answers the phone.)* Hello. Yes? Okay…right…I'll be there…I don't know Bertha, give me a break, okay? Okay - we'll be there soon.

THOMAS What's happening?

AUNT BEV I'm gonna speak at the council.

SANDRA Can I come? I want to explain about the -

AUNT BEV Press conference? *(SANDRA reacts.)* Yeah, you should come.

THOMAS That's alright. You go ahead. I'll finish preparing for the trip.

AUNT BEV Darrin, watch out for Thomas.

THOMAS Thomas will watch out for Thomas.

DARRIN Relax kid, I'm just back-up.

SANDRA Well, okay - let's go to the council.

(AUNT BEV and SANDRA exit.)

DARRIN I know you're still pissed at me.

THOMAS I don't wanna talk about it.

DARRIN I heard what you said about me.

THOMAS Lurking? Why am I surprised.

DARRIN I didn't plan to, but then I heard your mouth.

THOMAS I didn't lie. You derail, it's what you do.

DARRIN It's not because I don't fit, kid. It's because I didn't trust myself. You grew up with people believing in you, relying on you. I didn't have that.

THOMAS My parents trusted you. I did too. Until you broke it.

DARRIN Yeah, but that was only two years. Two years can't undo fourteen years of scrambling to survive by any means necessary.

THOMAS Okay. You had a hard life. I accept your apology. You're forgiven. Is that what you want, because I'm busy.

DARRIN You know your captain is right - you are a little shit.

THOMAS Well, what do you want, Darrin?

DARRIN Don't ever again say that this world is designed to crush us. The Creator made us and we are what we're supposed to be. Yeah, sure dumbasses like me screw up sometimes, but that doesn't condemn all our people. We fit.

THOMAS I know.

DARRIN You just forgot is that it? That's how they beat you, Tommy.

THOMAS Yeah? I have no idea what I'm doing, Darrin. I'm out of my depth.

DARRIN It's okay.

THOMAS No, it's not. I dragged all of you into this with me and I have no idea. No plan. No strategy.

DARRIN That's everyone, most of the time. It's FINE.

Scene 6

Aunt Bev's house. AUNT BEV and SANDRA are outside.

AUNT BEV He was too impulsive.

SANDRA He's young and emotional - he got carried away. Why can't they cut him some slack for that.

AUNT BEV He didn't need to react like that.

SANDRA So you're with them?

AUNT BEV Thomas is one of us - ONE. The council and the clan mothers have to think of everyone.

SANDRA So we just throw him to the wolves.

AUNT BEV And you didn't?

SANDRA I called them for the protest -

AUNT BEV And you didn't mention Thomas at all, huh?

SANDRA I wanted to get us a little more publicity. These things usually fall by the wayside. I wanted us to have an impact.

AUNT BEV You managed that, alright.

SANDRA I was trying to help the community.

AUNT BEV You wanted to be the hero. You should've asked. We could've told you that the press is a tricky thing — it can be a friend and it can bite you on your butt.

SANDRA I know that - I was prepared for that.

AUNT BEV But it didn't bite you, did it? It bit Thomas.

SANDRA I'm sorry.

AUNT BEV Tell Thomas, don't tell me.

SANDRA You know it's not your fault, right?

AUNT BEV Pardon?

SANDRA You didn't do this. Thomas has a mind of his own.

AUNT BEV He did it to protect me.

SANDRA He reacted the only way he could. He was raised as a warrior, isn't he? It's part of his job.

AUNT BEV I suppose. Well, what's done is done.

SANDRA Canada, here we come. I hope Thomas likes maple syrup.

AUNT BEV We'll need to distract those guardsmen.

(They enter Aunt Bev's. THOMAS and DARRIN enter from the bedroom.)

AUNT BEV Okay Thomas. I think it's time you went on a trip.

THOMAS I'm all set.

DARRIN *(Pulls keys out of his pocket.)* I'm ready – the Charger just had a tune-up.

AUNT BEV That's great – Bertha can be a little heavy on the pedal.

SANDRA Bertha Silversmith? The clan mother?

DARRIN Whoa – no, you don't. I'm driving.

SANDRA Noooo, you're not.

AUNT BEV You're still on parole, Darrin - why don't you guard the house?

DARRIN It's my car!

SANDRA You need to keep your nose clean. You should probably stay away from the site, too. Lots of press there. I can handle distraction.

(She exits.)

THOMAS I appreciate it, buddy - I really do. But Aunt Bev's right - I gotta go. Take care of yourself.

AUNT BEV Wait, Thomas!

(AUNT BEV helps Thomas remove his gun and jacket.)

AUNT BEV You've got to leave all this stuff behind - especially the gun. Don't argue with me - we don't wanna draw attention to ourselves. *(To DARRIN.)* We'll call you. As soon as Bertha and I get him across the border.

DARRIN Come on - you've gotta let me help!

THOMAS Get rid of that stuff, D. If they come on the rez, I don't want you to get into trouble for helping me.

DARRIN I'm a good driver - we won't get caught.

THOMAS We're cool. Don't worry. Take care of yourself.

(AUNT BEV exits – THOMAS follows close behind, stopping to wave at DARRIN on their way out.)

DARRIN Shit.

Scene 7

A photo of a rez gas station with an elaborately "tricked out" DODGE CHARGER is projected on the screens. THOMAS paces as AUNT BEV enters, triumphantly brandishing the keys over her head.

AUNT BEV Bertha's almost done paying for the gas. Ready for our adventure?

THOMAS She likes cars, doesn't she?

AUNT BEV Once a wheel girl, always a wheel girl!

THOMAS I thought she was gonna do a cartwheel when she saw this one.

AUNT BEV Her first car was a Charger, I knew she wouldn't be able to resist it.

THOMAS She going to be able to drive with the walker?

AUNT BEV Her legs are a little wobbly but her feet are fine. She'll get you where you're going.

THOMAS Aunt Bev - did you just hear yourself?

AUNT BEV We're old Thomas, we're not dead.

THOMAS What kind of warrior puts clan mothers - grandmothers at risk, just to cover his six.

AUNT BEV Hey, we're happy to help. We've done this many times for many people.

THOMAS How recently?

AUNT BEV It's really not a big deal.

THOMAS How recently?

AUNT BEV About twenty-five years ago but //

THOMAS Give me the keys. //

AUNT BEV You can't.

THOMAS Yes, I can. I'm finally thinking clearly.

AUNT BEV This was my fault – you wanted to protect me and instead //

THOMAS I did what I was trained to do. It's my duty to protect you. I'm not gonna put you at risk now.

AUNT BEV You have to let me help you.

THOMAS You have. You helped me clear my head. What they were doing was wrong. I still believe that. If I run - all this is for nothing.

AUNT BEV I enjoyed pushing you - pushing your captain. I wanted to win. I told myself it was to protect you but I didn't realize -

THOMAS You're an elder. You're supposed to speak up. I'm a warrior. I'm supposed to be looking out for you. Right now, I do that by turning myself in.

AUNT BEV They're gonna arrest you.

THOMAS Well, good - I bet there's still reporters there. Let them arrest me. I have a story to tell and now they'll listen.

AUNT BEV Thomas, I really don't think this is a good idea.

THOMAS Tell Bertha sorry, but I get to drive. I'm not gonna be driving for a while and this is one sweet ride. She can take it for a spin when I'm gone.

AUNT BEV Thomas -

THOMAS Give me the keys, Aunt Bev.

Scene 8

The protest site. The backdrop flickers with pictures of protesters, from all over. Cameras flash. SANDRA stands on the picnic table with her bullhorn. HEWITT is on point upstage. Right, BALDWIN patrols the border, weapon drawn.

SANDRA *(Through the bullhorn.)* Honor your treaties! Honor the Mother! Move the highway bypass! *(To BALDWIN.)* A rifle? Seriously?

BALDWIN *(Patrolling past SANDRA.)* We are on alert, ma'am. The powers that be are concerned about trouble, since someone leaked Thomas' story.

SANDRA We're not alone anymore.

BALDWIN No you're not. Hope Thomas is fine with that.

CAPTAIN HEWITT BALDWIN!

BALDWIN *(Salutes.)* Yes, sir!

CAPTAIN HEWITT Lock it down!

BALDWIN Roger that, sir!

CAPTAIN HEWITT *(To SANDRA.)* Is there a reason you're harassing my people?

SANDRA So much for trying to help Thomas.

CAPTAIN HEWITT I gave him a chance. He passed. He'd rather sink us all.

SANDRA Yeah? Good for him.

(He shrugs. DARRIN enters. He is wearing Thomas' uniform jacket and his cap is pulled down low, and the rifle is raised over his head.)

BALDWIN Weapon!

CAPTAIN HEWITT Drop your weapon!

(HEWITT pulls out a pistol and aims, BALDWIN drops into place behind him rifle shouldered, ready to fire.)

SANDRA Oh DON'T! Don't shoot!

(DARRIN raises the rifle higher over his head and steps closer.)

CAPTAIN HEWITT Stop the advance or I will shoot!

SANDRA Darrin! Stop it!

(DARRIN stops. He drops to his knees beside the border, in front of HEWITT.)

DARRIN I'd like to offer you my unconditional surrender, sir.

SANDRA Are you out of your mind?

CAPTAIN HEWITT You're kidding me.

DARRIN I, Private First Class Thomas Lee Doxdater -

(Flashbulbs go off.)

BALDWIN It's not gonna work.

SANDRA Stop it, Darrin!

DARRIN *(To SANDRA.)* Quiet!

(THOMAS and AUNT BEV enter. THOMAS runs forward.)

THOMAS Are you out of your mind?!

SANDRA Yes, he's insane!

DARRIN *(To the Guardsmen.)* I, Thomas Lee Doxdater, Private First Class –

(THOMAS walks over to DARRIN and grabs the rifle.)

DARRIN *(Stage whisper.)* Get outta here, man, you're gonna wreck it!

THOMAS This is my old unit, Darrin. They all know what I look like.

(Beat. DARRIN lowers his arms and nods at HEWITT.)

DARRIN I figured - they're your friends, they'd go for it and these reporters would have their story.

THOMAS They could've shot you, you dumbass. Why would you do something so stupid?

DARRIN Because you don't know where you fit - I do.

THOMAS Darrin -

DARRIN You got a future - a real future. You can't be rotting in a jail cell.

THOMAS This is the only way anything means anything. I could've let captain Hewitt save me, but no one would know anything happened. Same if I run to Canada. If I turn myself in, I can fight back in with their laws and prove that I'm not a criminal - that it's not a crime for an Indian to stand up for his people. I'm gonna fight the beast from the inside out - and I can't do that from Canada.

DARRIN Why can't you just live your life? That's fighting too.

THOMAS Someone's gotta take a stand first.

(Moving with purpose he grabs the cap from DARRIN'S head and stretches out his hand for the jacket. DARRIN removes it and hands it to him. THOMAS is back in full uniform.)

THOMAS Aunt Bev, it was a real honor.

AUNT BEV Was it?

THOMAS I made the choice. It's okay. Sandra –

SANDRA You've got a lot of guts, Apple.

THOMAS Thanks, City NDN.

SANDRA I'm sorry.

THOMAS Naw, it's good. I'm famous now! No cover ups.

BALDWIN Come on, Thomas.

CAPTAIN HEWITT Give him a minute.

(THOMAS nods to the captain –turns back to the protestors.)

THOMAS I really appreciate what you did –

DARRIN Did nothing but fail.

THOMAS No. It was honorable. Thank you.

(He hugs DARRIN.)

AUNT BEV What am I gonna say to Essie?

THOMAS A warrior faces his fears.

(THOMAS spins in a military quarter turn, arms raised, gun above his head.)

THOMAS Private Thomas Lee Doxdater requesting permission to surrender.

CAPTAIN HEWITT Permission granted. Step forward Doxdater.

(THOMAS steps forward and HEWITT steps over to meet him. Flashbulbs pop as the HEWITT snaps the cuffs on his wrists. The protesters all watch in silence. lights down except for a spotlight on AUNT BEV.)

EPILOGUE

AUNT BEV "In all of your deliberations…self-interest shall be cast into oblivion. Look and listen for the welfare of the whole people and have always in view not only the present but also the coming generations, even those whose faces are yet beneath the surface of the ground - the unborn of the future Nation." - The Great Law

APPENDIX

Concurrent Resolution 331(★)

100th Congress 2nd Session, Concurrent Resolution 331 Passed October 21, 1988 RECOGNIZING CONTRIBUTIONS TO THE UNITED STATES by the IROQUOIS CONFEDERACY AND OTHER INDIAN NATIONS –

Whereas the original framers of the Constitution, including, most notably, George Washington and Benjamin Franklin, are known to have greatly admired the concepts of the Six Nations of the Iroquois Confederacy;

Whereas the confederation of the original Thirteen Colonies into one republic was influenced by the political system developed by the Iroquois Confederacy as were many of the democratic principles which were incorporated into the Constitution itself; and –

Whereas, since the formation of the United States, the Congress has recognized the sovereign status of Indian tribes and has dealt with Indian tribes on a government–to–government basis and has entered into three hundred and seventy treaties with Indian tribal Nations; …

Now, therefore, be it Resolved by the House of Representatives (the Senate concurring), That—

1. the Congress, on the occasion of the two hundredth anniversary of the signing of the United States Constitution, acknowledges the contribution made by the Iroquois Confederacy and other Indian Nations to the formation and development of the United States;

2. the Congress also hereby reaffirms the constitutionally recognized government-to-government relationship with Indian tribes which has been the cornerstone of this Nation's official Indian policy;

3. the Congress also acknowledges the need to exercise the utmost good faith in upholding its treaties with the various tribes, as the tribes understood them to be, and the duty of a great Nation to uphold its legal and moral obligations for the benefit of all of its citizens so that they and their posterity may also continue to enjoy the rights they have enshrined in the United States Constitution for time immemorial.

    Agreed to October 21, 1988.

Vasanti Saxena

Biography

Vasanti Saxena is a playwright of Chinese and Indian descent, who currently lives in Los Angeles. Her plays have been produced and developed in New York at Ensemble Studio Theatre and New York Theatre Workshop; Chicago at Chicago Dramatists with Silk Road; and Los Angeles at Chalk Rep, Company of Angels, and Santa Monica Rep.

Sun Sisters was the winner of East West Players Pacific Century Playwriting Competition, a finalist for Chicago Dramatists Many Voices Project, and a semi-finalist for both the O'Neill National Playwrights Conference and the Princess Grace Award. Vasanti's short play *Closing Time* was published in *The Best Ten-Minute Plays 2011* (Smith and Kraus). Other plays include *Tar Pits and Wounds, Weekend Getaway, Shift,* and *Even the Stone.*

Vasanti has received an NYTW Emerging Artist of Color Fellowship, an ARC grant from CCI, and an EST/Sloan commission. A graduate of Brown University, she holds an MFA in Playwriting from Columbia University. Vasanti is a founding member of The Temblors, a collective of Los Angeles-based playwrights.

Artistic statement

Theater is a realm where all things are possible. And, for me, the magic lies in the language of a play. The challenge is to work with it, to play with it, to craft it – to reveal the meaning between and under and beside what is spoken. Between and under and beside what is taking place on stage. Through language, including visual language, a play can conjure something realer than reality, offering a way to see what lies beneath the polite maneuverings on the surface.

In my plays, I strive to give voice to those who are typically unheard – or not heard enough – in theater. In *Sun Sisters,* this includes a Chinese mother telling her daughter things she would never reveal in everyday circumstances. Some characters are limited by their race, gender, sexuality, or an intersectionality of identities, while others are not. Instead, their unique identities give them a foundation from which to fly.

Sun Sisters was born from a question: Do we ever really know our parents? It's hard to say. We came into their lives after they had already lived much of their own. Perhaps a mother's scolding when her daughter wears a skirt that's too short comes from the shame she was taught by her own parents. Perhaps a father's rage when he hears his adult child missed a credit card payment comes from his memory of being denied a home loan when he first arrived in this country with a young family and a job, but *no* credit. And perhaps these experiences were too personal to share – because to do so would show weakness to their children, for whom they had to be strong. They had to be strong when you were born. When you lost your first tooth. When your heart broke for the first time. A parent's strength can come at the cost of a parent's truth.

Sun Sisters is dedicated to my mother, who loved beautiful things.

Production history

Sun Sisters premiered on July 29, 2011, at Company of Angels in Los Angeles. It was directed by Lui Sanchez; the set design was by Luis Delgado; lighting design was by Sarah Templeton; sound design was by Howard Ho; and costume design was by Karla Contreras. The cast featured Jennifer Chang, Robert Hardin, Elaine Kao, Peter Kwong, Jully Lee, Andrea Lwin, and Momo Yashima.

17 *Sun Sisters*
Vasanti Saxena

Characters

EDWARD   A Chinese man in his early 60s. An accomplished architect and professor. Charming and charismatic.

ANGIE   A Chinese woman in her late 50s. In the last stages of a terminal cancer. Somewhat dictatorial. With flashes of playfulness.

JESS   Angie's daughter. Biracial. 30s. Successful budding architect. Strong, except when she's around Angie.

YOUNG ANGIE   Angie at 21. Exuberant and wanting to embrace life. Always dressed fashionably, with a preference for miniskirts when appropriate.

LINDA   A Chinese woman in her early 20s. Young Angie's best friend. Traditional. A bit overwhelmed by Angie. Somewhat secretarial.

CARLTON   A Caucasian man in his early 20s. Unimaginative but well-intentioned. Future investment banker sans polish.

EVELYN   A Chinese woman in her mid–20s. Charming. Serious. Elegantly butch. She wears slacks when none of the other women of that time do. Hair almost in a men's cut, but not quite.

NURSE   Played by the actors who play LINDA, CARLTON, and EVELYN

Setting

The present and the past of Angie's memory.

Young Angie, Carlton, Linda, and Evelyn are all from Angie's college days. They sometimes exist as memories and sometimes enter the action of the play like ghosts haunting the present world of Angie and Jess. They enter the action of the play more aggressively as it progresses and, by the middle of the second act, the past exists side-by-side with the present.

Scenes in the present take place in Angie's house; living room, attic, and bedrooms. Scenes in the past take place on and around Young Angie's college campus and in her apartment. The places in the past should overlap those of the present. For example, Young Angie's apartment of the past occupies the same space as Angie's living room of the present.

Note

The poems "Wild Nights!" and "The props assist the House" are by Emily Dickinson.

Prologue

Lights up on EDWARD, a Chinese man in his 60s. He wears a jacket and tie, and has the air of an accomplished professor. He lectures the audience as though they are a group of graduating architecture students. Slides of each of the buildings he describes appear behind him as he mentions them.

EDWARD An architectural creation that serves a purpose perpetually holds our interest. *(Slide of the Pyramids.)* The Pyramids were built for a purpose. *(Slide of the Colosseum.)* As was the Colosseum. *(Slide of the Forbidden City.)* The Forbidden City. *(Slide of the Taj Mahal.)* The Taj Mahal. The very fact that they were created to fulfill a human need...to thank the gods, to provide shelter, a meeting place, to give safe passage to the dead...gives them a dignity that so many of our modern buildings lack. Their beauty lies in this very pureness of intention. As you embark on your careers, be it as architects, interior designers, what have you... Whatever you design...never lose sight of this purpose. Free yourself of the urge to create art. To create something aesthetically pleasing. Create an edifice that serves. Believe me, when others enter, they will know what you intended. They may not be able to give voice to it. But they will feel it.

★

ACT I

Scene 1

ANGIE's living room. A sofa by the window, two armchairs, end tables, and a coffee table piled high with magazines and newspapers in the middle of the room. ANGIE, a Chinese woman in her late 50s, holds a rolled up section of a newspaper and consults with JESSICA, a Chinese-Caucasian woman in her 30s.

ANGIE *(Gesturing with the newspaper)* I want one big open space. You understand? Big. Open.

JESS An open space.

ANGIE Yes.

JESS No walls.

ANGIE None.

JESS I'll have to think about this.

ANGIE What is there to think about? It's very simple.

JESS Whether it's possible.

ANGIE Of course it's possible. Money isn't an issue. And time...

JESS I have time.

ANGIE You do.

JESS I want to do whatever's best for you. What you want.

ANGIE This is what I want.

JESS I know. But are you thinking about resale value? A house without rooms isn't going to attract many buyers.

ANGIE I could not care less about resale value. You know...I think it could be marketed as an artist's loft. *(She unrolls the newspaper she's holding and shows it to JESS.)* See? I was reading the "Home" section. Artist's lofts are very in right now. People pay a lot of money.

JESS It's a house.

ANGIE A loft-like house.

JESS I don't know...

ANGIE I'll pay you well.

JESS That's not the issue.

ANGIE Just because you're my daughter doesn't mean your work is free.

JESS I don't know if I can do it.

ANGIE How long did you go to school?

JESS What?

ANGIE For how many years?

JESS A lot.

ANGIE Was that time and money wasted?

JESS Of course not.

ANGIE Good. Then you will find a way.

JESS Couldn't we just move furniture around or something?

ANGIE What would that accomplish? Would it give me the big, open space feeling?

JESS It might. I mean, we could try moving some things out of the way now.

ANGIE I know what I want. And that's not the answer. I want to feel more open here. Like there is nothing in my way.

JESS If we get rid of some of the furniture...

ANGIE No, no. You're not listening to me. I want to get rid of the walls themselves.

JESS Do you know what goes into an architect's training? Knowledge of structure.

ANGIE This structure is ugly.

JESS This structure is fine. You don't like the design. The interior design. We can fix that by rearranging...

ANGIE I don't like the walls.

JESS These walls are load bearing.

ANGIE So?

JESS So...Get rid of the walls and the ceiling will fall down.

ANGIE No!

JESS They hold the weight of the ceiling.

ANGIE The ceiling will fall down?

JESS Without the walls.

ANGIE *(Laughs)* On our heads!

JESS Yes. On our heads.

ANGIE That would not be so good. Not what I want.

JESS No big open space feeling then.

ANGIE Only a crushed head feeling.

(They both laugh. ANGIE starts to cough. Holds her stomach. She's obviously not well. JESS doesn't know what to do. Waits for it to subside.)

JESS Why didn't you tell me on the phone?

ANGIE What?

JESS You could have told me on the phone. Before I got here.

ANGIE You know better. The phone is not for bad news.

JESS It would've been nice to be prepared.

ANGIE What do you need to prepare for? You come home. You help.

JESS Just to get a sense of...expectations.

ANGIE Expectations?

JESS Time.

ANGIE That is something I don't have a sense of. But I should thank you for taking time from your busy schedule.

JESS That's not what I mean. I told you I'd fly out to look everything over. Meet with contractors. Whatever you need me to do. I just didn't expect...

ANGIE You didn't expect me to need more.

JESS You've lost weight.

ANGIE Yes. *(Beat.)* I'm not even on a diet. I am not so strong as I used to be. There's a lot that needs to be done.

JESS Are you getting treatment?

ANGIE For what? I've seen the women with no hair. Scarves around their head and they think they look exotic. No. Everyone knows they are dying. They are sick. It isn't fashion.

JESS It's hope.

ANGIE It's denial. A lie. I will not be a woman who lies.

JESS Tell you what. Why don't we just focus on this room for now? It's your favorite room in the house, right?

ANGIE It's my favorite window.

JESS Your favorite view?

ANGIE No. My favorite window. I can look outside but no one can look in. There is something to be said for privacy. Some things are not meant for an outsider's eyes.

JESS Like what?

ANGIE *(Gestures to herself)* This.

(JESS starts to move some smaller pieces of furniture...chairs, end tables...to one corner of the room. She picks up a crystal bowl from the coffee table with the intention to clear it off and move it, then sits down with the bowl in her hands. Bereft. ANGIE sits next to her.)

ANGIE That is the kind of thing you should take with you when you go. You don't have something like this, do you?

JESS No.

ANGIE I don't think you buy nice things. The last apartment you had, nothing on the walls. So boring. How can you design houses when you can't even decorate?

JESS I decorate.

ANGIE Nothing on the walls.

JESS It's minimalist.

ANGIE Boring.

JESS Zen.

ANGIE *(Laughs)* You don't even know what Zen means. So American. Zen does not mean boring.

JESS Ok, mom.

ANGIE You should have some pretty things. Take this.

JESS That's OK.

ANGIE Really. Take it.

JESS You should keep it. I don't want to take anything you like so much.

ANGIE There are things that should be handed down. Generation to generation. Many of these things Bobby has. He has a family. A wife. And you know how she is. No appreciation.

JESS She's not so bad.

ANGIE You know the town her family comes from? The southern part of China. You know what they say about that town? They say the people are so mean even the birds are scared to fly over it.

JESS What?

ANGIE The birds are too scared to fly over. The people are so mean.

JESS She makes Bobby happy.

ANGIE She has no taste. At least you appreciate. It's good for you to take some things. Maybe make your apartment look nicer.

JESS We like our apartment.

ANGIE My daughter should have pretty things.

JESS Katie doesn't like clutter.

ANGIE That person doesn't know what you should have.

JESS She has great taste.

ANGIE That person doesn't like pretty things. She should find her own apartment.

JESS *(Not wanting to get into it)* You know what?

ANGIE What?

JESS I was thinking. There are some things I might like.

ANGIE Good. Good. You take anything you like. It's good that you show interest.

JESS Anything?

ANGIE Of course. You want paintings? *(AN-GIE gets up and takes a painting off the wall.)* This one is very cheerful. It will make you happy.

JESS Maybe just some of my old clothes.

ANGIE What clothes? *(She looks JESS up and down.)* Nothing here will fit you.

JESS I was thinking of my baby clothes.

ANGIE So sentimental.

JESS Baby things.

ANGIE Ai-yah. Jessica. There is sentimental and there is silly. Now you are being silly.

JESS Maybe I could just take a look…

ANGIE You don't even know where your things are.

JESS The attic.

ANGIE You won't know where to look.

JESS I'll just poke around.

ANGIE Poke around? You think you can find things just by poking around?

JESS I can try.

ANGIE We'll look together.

JESS What?

ANGIE This is something mother and daughter do together.

(ANGIE goes to the door to the attic. Opens it. Peers in. JESS joins her.)

JESS You don't have to.

ANGIE It can be an adventure. Let's see if we can find something worth taking.

Scene 2

Slide of a modest house is behind EDWARD.

EDWARD This was one of my early projects. Still charming, I think. And then came the bigger projects. Bigger houses. Buildings. But it was the small homes…homes like this one… that were my favorite. For such a structure, purpose is paramount. The most basic? Shelter. But after that, the challenge. Higher purposes, if you will. Before the design comes the discovery. How do the occupants…the people…want to live? Which is more important? Entertaining or small family dinners? Openness or a sense of privacy? Light and air? Or cozy corners? The wonder of it… the magic…is that all of it is possible with the right basic structure. With good bones, anything is possible. *(He holds out an arm and grasps the forearm, indicating the bone.)* Good. Bones.

Scene 3

The attic. ANGIE sits on a trunk covered with cushions. JESS sorts through boxes. Boxes and piles of clothes surround them.

ANGIE So many old things. So many opportunities to get rid of them. Donate to Goodwill. To the church. People who need them. But then who would remember everything? Strangers would not feel the same way in our clothes as we do. Our bodies remember.

Feeling of the fabric. Familiar. Fitted to our form. Pushing our mind to remember the last time we were so beautiful. So happy. A stranger couldn't feel the same. A stranger wouldn't appreciate.

JESS Selfish.

ANGIE What?

JESS Selfish to keep everything when it could be put to better use by someone else. What good is it to keep all this tucked away up here? In boxes. Suitcases. Trunks. Plastic. It stinks. Mothballs. Stinks up here.

(ANGIE opens a window.)

ANGIE Even the past needs to breathe.

JESS I guess.

ANGIE "I guess." How you talk. So uncaring.

JESS I care.

ANGIE Not the way you talk.

JESS I'm sorry. My head just hurts.

ANGIE Mothballs.

JESS I think so.

ANGIE Fresh air now.

JESS Yes.

ANGIE I feel better too.

JESS Do you?

ANGIE Fresh air.

JESS Really? Because we can go back downstairs.

ANGIE I'm fine.

JESS Take a break.

ANGIE No.

JESS Just for a little while.

ANGIE Jessica. I don't want to go downstairs. *(Beat.)* Funny.

JESS What?

ANGIE Now you come home. You cook for me. Help me. But you still don't listen.

JESS I do…

ANGIE It's ok though. Now we do things mother and daughter do together.

JESS We'll do whatever you want.

ANGIE We don't do enough together. You never come home. Never visit. Such a busy life. Always go go go. Too busy to see your mother.

JESS I didn't know you wanted me to.

ANGIE Of course I wanted you to. How can you even say…?

JESS Never mind.

ANGIE When was the last time you visited me?

JESS Not long ago.

ANGIE When?

JESS I don't know. It wasn't that long… It wasn't…oh.

ANGIE Yes?

JESS I'm sorry. Really, mom.

ANGIE Only for the big things my daughter comes home. It has to be a very big thing. When Bobby graduated. That was a big thing. When your daddy was…sick… that was a big thing. When Bobby got married, also a big thing. I can't make big things just to get you home. But Jessica does not come home unless there is a big thing.

JESS I'm here now.

ANGIE A big thing.

JESS All you had to do was ask.

ANGIE I should not have to ask all the time.

JESS How am I supposed to know?

ANGIE You are a sensitive girl.

JESS But if you don't tell me…

ANGIE You are like me.

JESS It's not like there's a psychic connection.

ANGIE There is always a connection. *(Beat.)* I'm guilty too, you know.

JESS Guilty?

ANGIE There was a time I wanted you to go.

JESS You did?

ANGIE Don't misunderstand. You are everything to me. But when you left for college, I thought, Finally. Peace. No more listening for you to come home. No more worrying. At least not in the same way. It's a different kind of worrying when your children leave home. Not the everyday worry. It's more… general. And the general worry is not so bad. Not the missing you. The missing you hurt me every day. But I did not miss the worrying.

JESS I didn't know.

ANGIE I hurt your feelings.

JESS I didn't know you worried so much.

ANGIE A mother's love is something you will never understand.

JESS Don't say that.

ANGIE It's the truth. You will never know what it feels like.

JESS Actually, it's not out of the question.

ANGIE Of course it is.

JESS Katie and I have been talking.

ANGIE Do not ever have children. Not with your lifestyle.

JESS What are you thinking? That I'd hurt the child? That she'd suffer because of me?

ANGIE You don't understand.

JESS You don't think I'd be a good mother?

ANGIE Promise me you won't hurt yourself.

JESS What?

ANGIE That you won't do anything...artificial. That you won't do something...unnatural... just to have a baby. Don't abuse your body that way. I'm not thinking about your child. I'm thinking about you. My child.

JESS Of course you are.

ANGIE Just promise me.

JESS I can't.

ANGIE Even now?

JESS That's not fair.

ANGIE Even now.

JESS I don't want to talk about this anymore.

ANGIE We have to. I know you don't like it, but I have to make myself clear. I am asking you for a promise.

JESS I'm asking you for some understanding.

ANGIE That's not what it's called. You don't even know what you're asking for, do you?

JESS Peace?

ANGIE My blessing.

JESS Is it really too much to hope for?

ANGIE For that? Yes.

JESS Then just forgive me.

ANGIE Forgive you? For what?

JESS For hurting you.

ANGIE Oh, Jessica. You can't worry about hurting me. You worry about yourself. Your life. We were once the same body. You came from me. And now. Still. Your body is my body. Your hurt is my hurt. You don't want me to hurt anymore? You stop hurting yourself.

JESS I shouldn't be here.

ANGIE This is your home.

JESS Doesn't feel like it.

ANGIE How can you say that? Look at all this. You see this pile right here? Do you know what's in these boxes? Your things.

JESS In boxes.

ANGIE All yours.

JESS If they're packed away like that. In boxes. Taped shut. They don't exist.

ANGIE Then open them. *(JESS doesn't move.)* Open. *(JESS still doesn't move.)* You think just because things are packed away, that you can't see them...they don't exist? Look. They take up space.

JESS I don't even know what's in them.

ANGIE Here. This one. Girl scouts. Uniforms. Badges. Camping equipment. This one? Clothes from elementary school. This one? Your baby things.

JESS Baby things?

ANGIE Blankets, bibs, cloth diapers, the mobile that was over your crib.

JESS The moon and stars.

(ANGIE opens the box and pulls out the mobile. Hangs it up. Triumphant.)

JESS How do you remember all that?

ANGIE I packed. I should remember.

JESS But after all these years?

ANGIE I have memory like...what is the saying?

JESS Like an elephant.

ANGIE Elephant? No. I don't like that. I have memory like...

JESS That's the saying.

ANGIE My memory is good enough.

Scene 4

The past. LINDA, a college student, peers in a store window.

LINDA Angie! Angie, kan dze ge. Come look at this.

(YOUNG ANGIE enters. She takes her time looking in windows along the way.)

LINDA Kwai dyen! Hurry up!

YOUNG ANGIE Why are you always shouting?

LINDA Why are you always walking so slowly?

YOUNG ANGIE I was looking at something.

LINDA Well look at this. Isn't it adorable?

YOUNG ANGIE Why are you looking at baby clothes?

LINDA I'm not just looking. I'm planning. I think a girl would be better than a boy, don't you? The clothes are so much cuter. Yes. I have to have a girl.

YOUNG ANGIE You have to get married first.

LINDA Of course I'll get married first. Jim will ask. When we have our degrees. He will ask. I'll say yes. We'll get married. Then I'll have a baby.

YOUNG ANGIE You have been planning.

LINDA Of course. But I'm worried about you.

YOUNG ANGIE About me? Why?

LINDA You don't seem to be planning very well. You know. Your future.

YOUNG ANGIE Carlton will ask. When we get our degrees.

LINDA You're not going to marry Carlton.

YOUNG ANGIE Why not?

LINDA He's American.

YOUNG ANGIE So what? We're in America.

LINDA What will your parents think?

YOUNG ANGIE They sent me here to get a good education. I'm in America. I'm meeting Americans.

LINDA But to marry one!

YOUNG ANGIE Come on, Linda. It's the sixties. They know I'm a modern woman.

LINDA But what kind of baby will you have?

YOUNG ANGIE A strong, beautiful one. You know what they say. It's better if the parents come from far away from each other.

LINDA But different countries!

YOUNG ANGIE The farther away the parents are from, the more attractive the baby will be.

LINDA That's an old wives tale. What happened to being a modern woman?

YOUNG ANGIE It makes sense. If people from the same family have children, aren't those children weaker? Not so healthy?

LINDA Yes.

YOUNG ANGIE Same logic. One day, I'm going to have beautiful babies. *(She sees the mobile in the store window and points to it.)* And that will be perfect for them.

LINDA What?

YOUNG ANGIE That. Hanging there. With the moon and stars. What is it called?

LINDA A mobile.

YOUNG ANGIE Yes. That mobile will be perfect. The moon and stars. Perfect for a boy or a girl. Blue and yellow. Perfect for both.

LINDA I guess you're not so bad at planning.

YOUNG ANGIE When my baby looks up, she'll see the sky and know that all her dreams can come true.

Scene 5

The attic. ANGIE and JESS as before.

JESS How do you remember all that?

ANGIE I packed. I should remember.

JESS But after all these years?

ANGIE I have memory like …

JESS An elephant?

ANGIE Elephant? No.

JESS That's the saying.

ANGIE I don't like that.

JESS But that's…

ANGIE I change it.

JESS What?

ANGIE I change it. Let me think. I have memory like…like…help me. What has a long memory?

JESS I don't know.

ANGIE Imagination.

JESS An elephant.

ANGIE Imagination. Not repetition.

JESS A turtle?

ANGIE No. No. A turtle is a very bad thing.

JESS Why?

ANGIE You just know never to call someone a turtle. Now think. What has a long memory?

JESS I don't know.

ANGIE A lion!

JESS No they don't.

ANGIE Of course they do! Why else are they king of the animals? You have to have good memory so you don't make the same mistakes twice. To survive. You know. Darwin.

JESS A lion.

ANGIE Your mommy has memory like a lion. See? Here. Intermediate and high school. This one. Your dolls.

JESS What about this one?

ANGIE Stuffed animals.

JESS And in here?

ANGIE Hmm. I don't know.

JESS You don't?

ANGIE I'm thinking.

JESS Should we open it?

ANGIE Wait. Wait. I packed it. I should know what's inside.

(JESS opens the box and pulls out a cocktail dress, fashionable for the 1960s. ANGIE claps her hands and laughs.)

JESS This isn't mine.

ANGIE No!

JESSICA It's kind of ugly.

ANGIE It's mine.

JESSICA You wore this?

ANGIE Twice.

JESSICA Oh my god.

ANGIE Is there more? *(JESS pulls out more dresses, one by one. They are all from the 60's. Some tailored and tasteful. Some gaudy.)* They're beautiful! Let me see. *(JESS holds one up.)* I remember. *(JESS holds up another one.)* Awful. Just awful. *(JESS holds up a red cocktail dress.)* Let me see. *(JESS gives the dress to ANGIE. ANGIE holds it up to herself. Considers it. Looks at JESS.)*

ANGIE I think I could fit into this now.

JESS Do you want to try?

ANGIE I think I could. Your mother is skinny now. That's one advantage.

JESS I'll help you.

(JESS helps ANGIE get into the dress.)

ANGIE I might even be the size I was then. What do you think?

JESS I don't know.

ANGIE Of course you don't. But I am skinny. I can feel my hipbones. I can feel my ribs. *(JESS zips up the dress.)* I have a figure again.

JESS How do you feel?

ANGIE How do I look?

JESS Beautiful.

ANGIE I look beautiful?

JESS Yes.

ANGIE Like a movie star?

JESS A glamorous movie star.

ANGIE You know…when I wore this dress. I was younger than you are now.

JESSICA You were?

ANGIE I had first come to this country. And I was so excited by all the fashions. Things we couldn't get in Taiwan. Things the movie stars would wear. So glamorous.

JESS How could you afford them?

ANGIE It was important. Remember this. You can always afford beautiful things. Remember. *(Beat.)* Oh, I had so many beautiful things. And so many young men to invite me places. Let me see. Let me see myself.

JESS We have to go downstairs.

ANGIE Downstairs?

JESS To the mirror.

ANGIE We can do that. We can go downstairs.

(JESS leans over to help ANGIE up.)

JESS Put your arm around my neck.

(ANGIE puts her arm around JESS's neck and they slowly stand together. They walk to the top of the stairs. Look down.)

ANGIE Do you know how many steps there are?

JESS What?

ANGIE Have you counted? You used to. When you were a baby. Toddler. Counted all the steps in the house.

JESS I don't remember.

ANGIE You were showing off. That's what I thought. Such a little girl and showing off her counting.

JESS Hold on to me.

ANGIE Now I know why you counted. So careful. So serious. Every one. You counted them because every step took all your concentration. All your effort. Any step could be the one that makes you fall.

(YOUNG ANGIE and CARLTON appear at the bottom of the stairs. The end of a date. JESS and ANGIE don't see them. YOUNG ANGIE

wears the same red dress ANGIE is wearing. CARLTON eyes the stairway in disbelief.)

CARLTON You must be kidding.

YOUNG ANGIE No.

CARLTON And you do this every day?

YOUNG ANGIE If I want to leave the apartment.

CARLTON There's no way I could do that. Walk up and down. Just to get home. Or leave.

YOUNG ANGIE You would do it for the opera. Yes?

CARLTON I don't like opera.

YOUNG ANGIE A museum?

CARLTON Maybe.

YOUNG ANGIE You see? Places like that are made to inspire a willingness to do the unusual. Physical effort for the sake of … *(She doesn't know the right word and gestures to imply "grandeur.")*

CARLTON Grandeur?

YOUNG ANGIE Yes! Grandeur!

CARLTON But for home?

YOUNG ANGIE You have never seen my home.

CARLTON It's an apartment.

YOUNG ANGIE With grandeur.

CARLTON University housing.

YOUNG ANGIE Technically.

CARLTON In reality.

YOUNG ANGIE No. In reality, it is the opera. A museum.

CARLTON You're crazy.

YOUNG ANGIE A cathedral. No. The Vatican.

CARLTON The Vatican?

YOUNG ANGIE Or the Met. Depending on if I feel decadent or pious. Then again, the Vatican is both, is it not?

CARLTON Don't joke like that.

YOUNG ANGIE Well it is.

CARLTON It's a holy place.

YOUNG ANGIE Ok. Ok. Then the Met. We can keep it…secular. Ok? Carlton?

CARLTON How decadent is it?

YOUNG ANGIE What?

CARLTON This home of yours? I think I should see it.

YOUNG ANGIE Do you?

CARLTON I will if you invite me up.

YOUNG ANGIE *(Backpedaling.)* You do not like stairs.

CARLTON But for grandeur…

YOUNG ANGIE Carlton.

CARLTON *(Disappointed.)* You have to study.

YOUNG ANGIE My poetry paper.

CARLTON Dickens?

YOUNG ANGIE Dickinson.

CARLTON A rain check then?

YOUNG ANGIE A rain check?

CARLTON Another time?

YOUNG ANGIE Oh! Yes. A rain check.

(YOUNG ANGIE runs up the stairs past AN-GIE and JESS and disappears into the attic. As YOUNG ANGIE passes her, ANGIE slips, cries out. JESS has to keep her from falling. They hold each other.)

ANGIE Ow ow ow ow ow.

JESS Sorry.

ANGIE You're hurting me.

JESS Where?

ANGIE My leg.

JESS Just hold on.

ANGIE It twisted.

JESS Just try to sit down.

ANGIE There's no chair.

JESS I know, mom. Right here. Just for now, ok? Just to catch our breath. *(They sit on the steps.)* We're closer to the top than the bottom. So I think the best thing to do is go back up.

(ANGIE looks fearfully up at where YOUNG ANGIE ran.)

ANGIE No.

JESS You can sit more comfortably there.

ANGIE We were going to the mirror. I want to see myself.

JESS But for now…

ANGIE Are you ready?

JESS Are you? *(ANGIE holds her arms up to JESS, like a child wanting to be picked up.)* Mom?

ANGIE You help.

JESS You want me to help you walk?

ANGIE I already fell down one time. I don't want to fall again.

(JESS struggles to pick ANGIE up. She starts to carry ANGIE down the stairs.)

ANGIE Be careful, Jessica. This is not a baby you're holding. This is your mother.

Scene 6

EDWARD Now think for a moment of the spaces in between. Stairways. Escalators. Elevators. Those parts of a structure that enable movement from one level to another. Whether it's from one floor of a house to the next or the lobby of a skyscraper to the ninety-sixth floor. Spaces that, by the magic of human ingenuity, manage to defy gravity. Nature. Resistance to nature in order for us to feel more human. The time we spend in one of these in-between places may seem like time lost. Time that doesn't matter because it's neither a place we came from nor the place we need to be. And what of the in-between places that link buildings? Think for a moment of the walk from your last class to this one. Did it take five minutes? Ten? Was that time lost to you? Or did it serve a purpose? Did something…happen?

Scene 7

YOUNG ANGIE and LINDA on campus. Laughing like schoolgirls even though they're in college. YOUNG ANGIE strikes a pose and LINDA snaps her picture.

YOUNG ANGIE Another one! Another one!

LINDA Come on, Angie. Enough. We're going to be late for class.

YOUNG ANGIE Just one more. It's such a beautiful day.

LINDA OK. One more.

YOUNG ANGIE Let's go up there.

LINDA Where?

YOUNG ANGIE That rock. We can stand there and be on top of the world.

LINDA It's not that big.

YOUNG ANGIE Let me see you climb it then.

LINDA We don't have time.

YOUNG ANGIE Let's see, Linda. I'll bet you can't.

LINDA I'm not the one who wants to be on top of the world.

YOUNG ANGIE What's wrong with that?

LINDA That you're all talk.

YOUNG ANGIE Oh really?

LINDA No. Angie, don't. It doesn't look safe.

(ANGIE climbs onto the rock. Stands with her arms outstretched.)

YOUNG ANGIE Like this. Take one like this. *(She kicks one leg up. Can-can.)* Hurry up. I can't hold it. *(LINDA snaps a picture.)* Hey. There she is again.

LINDA Who?

YOUNG ANGIE Turn around. Over there.

LINDA Look at her with all those boys.

YOUNG ANGIE She's so…confident.

LINDA Can you imagine? Being the only girl with all those boys?

YOUNG ANGIE What department is she in?

LINDA I'm not sure. Oh. I think that's Peter. He's pre-med.

YOUNG ANGIE She's pre-med?

LINDA I don't know. I don't think so.

YOUNG ANGIE She's not liberal arts though.

LINDA That's for sure.

YOUNG ANGIE I wonder which one's her boyfriend.

LINDA Stop it!

YOUNG ANGIE Do you think she has more than one?

LINDA Maybe.

YOUNG ANGIE She's really confident.

LINDA No shyness there.

YOUNG ANGIE Linda?

LINDA What?

YOUNG ANGIE Let's go talk to them.

LINDA What are we going to say?

YOUNG ANGIE You can think of something. It's not fair for her to have all the attention.

LINDA I don't think that's a good…

YOUNG ANGIE She's coming this way. Don't stare at her! She probably knows we're talking about her.

LINDA Well everyone talks about her. It isn't respectable to socialize with so many boys.

YOUNG ANGIE Shh!

(EVELYN enters. Walking toward YOUNG ANGIE and LINDA, and writing seriously in her notebook. YOUNG ANGIE and LINDA watch with interest. YOUNG ANGIE takes the camera from LINDA and runs to EVELYN.)

YOUNG ANGIE Excuse me. *(EVELYN stops.)* My friend and I were wondering. We want a picture together. Could you…? *(YOUNG ANGIE holds out the camera.)* If you're not in a hurry, of course. Are you in a hurry?

EVELYN I have class.

YOUNG ANGIE Oh.

(EVELYN looks at her watch, then looks up at YOUNG ANGIE.)

EVELYN But no. I'm not in a hurry.

(YOUNG ANGIE runs to LINDA. They put their arms around each other and smile. EVELYN snaps a picture. Blackout.)

Scene 8

The living room. ANGIE sits in an armchair, reading the newspaper. JESS is taking magazines off the coffee table and piling them in a corner.

ANGIE *(Reading from the newspaper.)* "More than a hundred people gathered last night at the Museum of Contemporary Art to discuss their concerns about the newest exhibit, which they are calling pornographic. Rising-star photographer Alexa Mars's work features images of nude limbs intertwined to suggest acts of…" Oh! This is too much.

JESS That bad, huh?

ANGIE Do these people have nothing better to do?

JESS What?

ANGIE Who are they to judge someone else's art? I mean, look at this, Jessie. Is this photo so bad? *(Notices that JESS is moving the magazines and papers.)* What are you doing?

JESS You're not going to read these.

ANGIE How do you know?

JESS They're magazines.

ANGIE I can see that. What are you doing with them?

JESS You don't read magazines.

ANGIE I do.

JESS You don't. Dad did. *(Beat.)* There are just so many of them. We should throw them away.

ANGIE Let me see.

(JESS hands her a magazine.)

ANGIE Oh! It has an article about Princess Diana. I like her. So tragic! We should keep it.

JESS Are you going to read it?

ANGIE Later.

JESS Fine.

(JESS takes the last of the magazines off the coffee table and starts to drag the table out of the room.)

ANGIE Now what are you doing?

JESS Giving you some open space. Isn't that what you want?

ANGIE Bring it back.

JESS You don't use it, do you? I mean, it isn't really serving a purpose.

ANGIE It holds the magazines.

JESS Not anymore.

ANGIE But it's pretty.

JESS It's in the way.

ANGIE I walk around it.

JESS You shouldn't have to.

(JESS drags the coffee table all the way out. ANGIE gets up and walks to the center of the room. Considers the empty space, then lies down in the space where the coffee table was. Closes her eyes. JESS enters, sees ANGIE. Worried, she goes to her.)

JESS Mom? Mom? Are you ok?

ANGIE Shh. I'm listening.

JESS To what?

ANGIE The floor.

JESS What?

ANGIE I'm listening. Feeling. Wondering. (*She opens her eyes.*) Do you think the floor feels better without having to bear the weight of that table, those papers, all those years of stories?

JESS The floor doesn't have feelings.

ANGIE How do you know?

JESS It's a floor.

ANGIE Will you feel better when you don't have to bear the weight of me?

JESS Don't talk like that.

ANGIE You're right. Depressing. (*She sits up.*) Help me.

(*JESS helps ANGIE up and to the sofa.*)

ANGIE It's better to talk of happy things. Tell me something happy. (*JESS is silent.*) OK. I will find something happy to tell you. You know this is my favorite place in the whole house. Right here. When you and Bobby were little, you played on the floor. Right there where the coffee table was. Where I was lying. I can look at that space and see little you and little him. Legos scattered all around. No. His were scattered. Yours were organized by color and size. You had some kind of organization. Some kind of…what is the word?

JESS System?

ANGIE Taxonomy.

JESS So I was organized and he was messy.

ANGIE He's still messy.

JESS He should be here.

ANGIE He doesn't need any more clutter in his life. He already has to worry about his job. His family. He doesn't need to worry about me, too.

JESS I think he'd want to know what's going on though. And maybe he could share the…

ANGIE The burden?

JESS The time with you.

ANGIE Since when do you want to share with your brother?

(*JESS gives up. ANGIE parts the curtains and looks out the window.*)

ANGIE Look at that.

JESS What?

ANGIE Such a shame.

JESS They look fine to me.

ANGIE Do you know who that is?

JESS No.

ANGIE That girl. You used to play with her.

JESS We were friends?

ANGIE Not in the house. When I took you to the park. You would run around and make so much noise. Such a headache.

JESS I don't remember.

ANGIE She pushed you on the swings and you went so high. So high and screaming and screaming "Stop! Stop!" But she kept pushing you higher and higher.

JESS (*Remembers.*) Then I threw up.

ANGIE Such a mess.

JESS I remember. You were really mad.

ANGIE Yes. How could she do such a thing?

JESS At me. You were really mad at me.

ANGIE I was not.

JESS You said I embarrassed you. Made a mess for everyone to see. Grabbed my arm and dragged me home.

ANGIE I was mad at her.

JESS Doesn't matter now.

ANGIE I was mad at her. Not you. Listen to me. I was never mad at you. (*Beat…ANGIE looks back out the window.*) Look at her now. With that toddler of hers. You know she has no husband. It's only her and that little one.

JESS Must be hard.

ANGIE For her parents. How ashamed they must be. For their daughter to end up like that.

JESS She looks happy.

ANGIE She isn't. Believe me. She can't be. (*ANGIE and JESS look out the window in silence.*) It's getting dark. Close the curtains. Close the curtains before you turn on the light. We don't want people to be able to see inside.

Scene 9

YOUNG ANGIE, dressed for a night out. She has parted the curtains and is peering out the window. LINDA enters. She's also dressed to go out, but more conservatively.

LINDA Is that what you're going to wear?

YOUNG ANGIE What's wrong with it?

LINDA It's a bit much, don't you think? For a faculty party?

YOUNG ANGIE I wore it to Professor Haring's party last semester.

LINDA He's a poetry professor. I don't think engineers are quite so bohemian.

YOUNG ANGIE Architects.

LINDA Same thing. They're not the types to appreciate your… (*Gestures to YOUNG ANGIE'S outfit.*)

YOUNG ANGIE *(Laughs.)* Tonight they'll just have to be.

(The doorbell rings.)

YOUNG ANGIE Which one do you think that is?

LINDA It isn't Jim. He's never on time.

(YOUNG ANGIE goes to the window and looks out.)

YOUNG ANGIE You're right. *(She shouts out the window.)* It's open. Come on up.

LINDA It's just not fair. You get to go to a faculty party and I have to go to Jim's place and cook dinner.

YOUNG ANGIE I still don't see why you can't just cook dinner here.

LINDA I told you, Angie. It isn't proper for a young woman to entertain a man in her home.

YOUNG ANGIE But it's ok for you to go to his place.

LINDA That's different. I can leave when it's time. And besides, I don't want him to see my…

YOUNG ANGIE Your what?

LINDA My bed. It might give him ideas.

(A knock on the door. YOUNG ANGIE opens it to EVELYN, dressed in a tailored suit and holding a bouquet of flowers. YOUNG ANGIE and LINDA try to hide their shock at her appearance.)

EVELYN I didn't realize there would be two beautiful young ladies here.

(EVELYN takes a single flower from the bouquet and gives it to LINDA, who hesitantly accepts. She hands the bouquet to YOUNG ANGIE.)

EVELYN For you.

YOUNG ANGIE They're lovely.

EVELYN For a lovely…night.

(YOUNG ANGIE and LINDA are both charmed, but try to hide it.)

YOUNG ANGIE So. Evelyn. How did you like the Steps to the Vatican?

EVELYN Excuse me?

LINDA The stairs. Angie's been calling them the Steps to the Vatican for the last week.

EVELYN And why's that?

YOUNG ANGIE Good for if I'm feeling decadent or pious.

EVELYN The Vatican is both though, isn't it?

YOUNG ANGIE *(Laughs.)* So am I.

EVELYN Is that so?

LINDA She's bohemian. Poetry majors are like that.

EVELYN I'm afraid I lack experience in the ways of poetry majors. You'll have to forgive me if I overstep.

YOUNG ANGIE I forgive you in advance.

EVELYN Careful. Sounds like carte blanche.

(EVELYN helps YOUNG ANGIE on with her coat and offers her arm. YOUNG ANGIE hesitates, then slides her arm into EVELYN's.)

LINDA Angie!

EVELYN Linda, it was nice to see you again.

YOUNG ANGIE Have fun at Jim's.

(EVELYN and YOUNG ANGIE exit.)

LINDA *(Calls after them.)* Don't stay out too late.

Scene 10

Night. The living room, almost bare. All that remains is one armchair, the sofa against the window and an end table next to it. ANGIE walks around the room with her arms outstretched, enjoying the space. JESS lies on the floor, exhausted.

ANGIE *(Admiring.)* This is much better.

JESS You like it?

ANGIE There is room to walk around. To breathe.

JESS Is this the feeling you wanted?

ANGIE To move.

JESS One big open space?

ANGIE To fly!

JESS So it's ok?

ANGIE It's better than ok. You did a good job. You must have many happy customers.

JESS Clients.

ANGIE Clients. Yes. They are lucky to have you.

JESS You know this isn't what I do for a living. Just move furniture around.

ANGIE I should hope not! We didn't pay all that money for our daughter to become a furniture mover.

JESS I don't even do this at home. Katie usually moves the heavy stuff.

ANGIE She sounds like a butch girl.

JESS What did you say? How do you know that word?

ANGIE What word?

JESS "Butch."

ANGIE Oh, Jessica. Your mommy is not so ignorant as you think. I know that there are those

kinds. The butch girls. They can move furniture. And the other kind. The regular girls.

JESS What kind am I?

ANGIE You are not one of those. You are my
daughter. My beautiful, talented daughter.
You went to a good school. You have a good
job. You have happy clients. None of this
is a surprise. I always knew you would be
successful. You were always so logical. Such
a clear mind. Like your daddy. You think in
a straight line. Steps. One. Two. Three. But
you were sensitive, too. Not many people
have that combination, you know? Maybe
that's why you... (*Shakes away the thought.*)

JESS Why I what?

ANGIE That's why you are so good at your job.

JESS You think?

ANGIE You gave me the open space feeling.

JESS And the ceiling didn't come crashing
down.

ANGIE (*Laughs.*) It didn't. We should celebrate.
Did you bring the cookies I asked for?

JESS Sure did.

ANGIE I think I could have one. And tea?

JESS Anything you want.

(*JESS kisses ANGIE's cheek and exits as
YOUNG ANGIE and EVELYN enter. Sneaking
into YOUNG ANGIE's apartment after their
night out.*)

YOUNG ANGIE Shh.

EVELYN Do you think Linda's home?

YOUNG ANGIE Shh! (*Looks around.*)

EVELYN I don't want to intrude.

YOUNG ANGIE It's ok. She's still at Jim's. Can I
get you anything?

EVELYN Like what?

YOUNG ANGIE (*Slightly suggestive.*) What do you
want?

(*EVELYN considers the offer, then plays it safe.*)

EVELYN Perhaps some tea.

YOUNG ANGIE Tea?

EVELYN If it isn't too much trouble.

YOUNG ANGIE Tea.

EVELYN And some biscuits. Savory. Not sweet.

YOUNG ANGIE Crackers?

EVELYN Yes. Crackers. If it isn't too much
trouble.

YOUNG ANGIE No trouble at all.

(*YOUNG ANGIE exits. JESS enters with
fresh tea and a plate of cookies. ANGIE is staring
at EVELYN.*)

JESS Here you go, mom. These look delicious.
Took everything I had not to open the box
in the car. (*Takes a bite.*) Mmm.

(*EVELYN takes a cookie, takes a bite. Exits in
the direction YOUNG ANGIE did. ANGIE
watches her go.*)

JESS Are you going to taste yours? Mom?

(*ANGIE takes a bite. Chews. Makes a face.*)

JESS What's wrong?

ANGIE Salty.

JESS What?

ANGIE Savory. Not sweet.

JESS Maybe you got a bad one. Try mine.

(*ANGIE tries it.*)

ANGIE Bitter.

JESS Maybe that's what they're talking about.

ANGIE Who?

JESS It's just. I read that your sense of taste
could change. Some foods could taste...
different.

ANGIE That's not fair.

JESS Have you noticed anything like this before?

ANGIE Nothing is the same now.

JESS Tea should be ok. Mild.

ANGIE Mild.

JESS You want to drink some?

ANGIE That's all I can have now? Mild?

JESS It'll be less offensive.

ANGIE All of this is offensive. I don't want
bland. I don't want bitter. I want sweet.
(*Sadly.*) Sweet. Sleep. Is it time to sleep?

JESS It's been a long day.

ANGIE Yes.

JESS Can I help you to bed?

(*ANGIE doesn't respond. JESS goes to her,
helps her up and they walk slowly offstage as lights
fade.*)

Scene 11

*In the almost-black, we hear voices, like two young
girls afraid of the dark, but it isn't clear who is
speaking.*

YOUNG ANGIE Are you awake? Are you? Are
you awake?

EVELYN Hmm?

YOUNG ANGIE Are you awake?

EVELYN I'm sleeping.

YOUNG ANGIE I can't.

EVELYN You can't?

YOUNG ANGIE Sleep.

EVELYN Oh.

YOUNG ANGIE Can you?

EVELYN What do you want?

YOUNG ANGIE I'm just asking.

EVELYN What's wrong?

YOUNG ANGIE I can't.

EVELYN You can't?

YOUNG ANGIE What do you want?

EVELYN What are you doing?

YOUNG ANGIE Doing?

EVELYN Yes. What are you…

YOUNG ANGIE I can't sleep.

EVELYN Shh.

YOUNG ANGIE You're awake.

EVELYN So are you.

YOUNG ANGIE What?

EVELYN You're awake.

YOUNG ANGIE I can't sleep. What are you…?

EVELYN Try.

YOUNG ANGIE I can't.

EVELYN Close your eyes.

YOUNG ANGIE I…

EVELYN Your mouth.

YOUNG ANGIE What?

EVELYN Close your mouth.

(Separate spotlights on ANGIE and JESS. They sit up suddenly in bed. Scared. They listen. JESS stands up and goes to the window. Peeks out. Nothing. She goes back to her bed and tries to sleep. She can't. She gets up again and goes to check on ANGIE.)

JESS Mom?

ANGIE What? What is it?

JESS Shh. Nothing. Just checking on you.

ANGIE Jessica. I'm fine. It is not your job to check on me. I should be checking you.

JESS I couldn't sleep.

ANGIE Ai-yah. You had a snack too late. Gave you nightmares again.

JESS No. No nightmares.

ANGIE A bad feeling?

JESS No. I'm fine. Are you sure you're sleeping ok? Nothing bothering you? Noises maybe?

ANGIE Did you hear something? You scared of ghosts like when you were little?

JESS I never believed in ghosts.

ANGIE When you were a little girl you did. So many nights you came into my room. Woke up me and your daddy. You heard footsteps.

JESS Footsteps?

ANGIE Yes. You said someone was walking outside the house. You thought it was a ghost.

JESS Did we ever check?

ANGIE Check what? It was only a squirrel or stray cat. Nothing to check.

JESS You didn't hear anything?

ANGIE No. Now lie down here with me. It's time to sleep.

JESS Ok.

ANGIE And Jessica? One thing to remember.

JESS Yes?

ANGIE No more snacks so late.

Scene 12

The living room. CARLTON and EVELYN are drinking beer. LINDA approaches them with a plate of hors d'oeuvres.

LINDA You have to try these!

CARLTON What is it?

LINDA Just try one.

CARLTON Is it sweet or salty?

EVELYN Salty. Thousand-year-old egg.

LINDA Don't tell him that.

EVELYN That's what they are.

LINDA *(Faux patience.)* Eggs marinated in special sauce.

CARLTON Really?

EVELYN You don't have to.

CARLTON No. No. I like to try new things. *(Unsure.)* With my fingers?

EVELYN Sure. I'll have one too.

CARLTON *(Taking a bite.)* Oh.

LINDA Good, huh?

EVELYN Not bad.

CARLTON No. Not bad.

EVELYN I think you need a fresh beer. Linda?

LINDA Sure.

EVELYN I'll have one too.

(LINDA exits in a huff.)

CARLTON So which school are you in?

EVELYN Architecture.

CARLTON You mean art?

EVELYN No. Architecture.

CARLTON Oh. You're going to be a teacher.

EVELYN Why would you say that?

CARLTON Well, you're studying buildings and everything, so I just thought…

EVELYN I'm going to build them.

CARLTON Really? I didn't think…Well that's unusual, isn't it?

EVELYN How so?

CARLTON It's not exactly expected.

EVELYN Expected?

CARLTON You know. Traditional.

EVELYN I see. No. I tend to shy away from the traditional. Rather boring. Don't you think?

CARLTON Boring? Yes. Actually, it seems we have that in common. Not that we're boring. At least, I don't think we are. Buildings can be interesting I guess. And I'm in business, you see. Which is very exciting. Small world, isn't it?

EVELYN And we have what in common?

CARLTON You said you shy away from the traditional.

EVELYN And you?

CARLTON I do too! I'm open to different experiences. Different cultures. I'm glad to be getting to know more Orientals. I think it will make my relationship stronger.

EVELYN Really?

CARLTON My girlfriend. She's Chinese. We get along great. She's supposed to be here, but knowing her she went out and bought a new dress or something.

(LINDA returns with 3 beers.)

LINDA What did I miss?

EVELYN Carlton was just telling me how much we have in common.

LINDA Who?

EVELYN Him and me.

CARLTON That's right.

EVELYN Us.

(ANGIE of the present—enters in her robe and slippers. She walks with the cane. LINDA, CARLTON, and EVELYN see her as she was when she was young.)

LINDA Angie! You made it! Carlton's been wondering where you were.

CARLTON You look great. Definitely worth the wait.

EVELYN Hello, Angie.

CARLTON You two know each other?

EVELYN We've met.

CARLTON Angie?

EVELYN I'm glad to see you again.

LINDA Angie. Are you OK?

(Blackout. End of ACT I.)

★

ACT II

Scene 1

The living room. JESS consults with the NURSE, played by actors playing LINDA, CARLTON, and EVELYN.

JESS Are you sure nothing's broken?

NURSE (LINDA) Nothing's broken.

JESS You're sure?

NURSE (CARLTON/EVELYN) I'm sure./She was lucky this time.

JESS This time?

NURSE (CARLTON/LINDA) It could happen again./She shouldn't be left alone.

JESS No. Of course not. If I'd known she was that weak... I can't believe I found her like that. On the floor.

NURSE (CARLTON) Are you having trouble caring for her?

JESS She's my mother.

NURSE (LINDA) You know what I mean.

JESS I just didn't realize she could just fall like that. Faint.

NURSE (EVELYN) She hadn't mentioned feeling dizzy?

JESS No. But she got tired easily. I should have known.

NURSE (CARLTON/LINDA) She'll be ok now./You just can't let her out of your sight.

JESS But sometimes I have to. What if I'm working?

NURSE (EVELYN) Is your work so important?

JESS I have clients.

NURSE (CARLTON/EVELYN) Do they know what you're doing?/Here?

JESS There's no need for them to know.

NURSE (LINDA) You might be right.

JESS You think?

NURSE (LINDA) What I mean is...you might not need to be here much longer.

JESS I just got here.

NURSE (CARLTON/EVELYN/LINDA) Maybe she didn't want to bother you before./Maybe she didn't want you to have to take time away from your job./Your life.

JESS She doesn't care about my life.

NURSE (CARLTON) She's your mother.

(He exits.)

JESS You know what I mean.

NURSE (Evelyn) If you really believe that, why are you here?

(She exits.)

JESS Do I have a choice?

NURSE (LINDA) You could check her into the hospital. Or a hospice. I'm sorry. But I've seen this before. I know how it goes. I can send you some reading materials. Or have a hospice worker come by.

JESS She won't like that.

NURSE (LINDA) It's up to you. Here's my card. Give me a call if you change your mind.

Scene 2

Lights up on EDWARD. He lectures.

EDWARD It's always nice to have options, isn't it? A vital part of being human. But what if your options are limited? If external forces remove some of your options because, say, they don't trust that you'll choose the right one? *(He clicks to a slide of the Seagram Building.)* Consider for a moment the Seagram Building. Mies van der Rohe's tribute to the Dutch and German art compounds. But in New York. A thirty-eight story vertical box made of glass and steel. So great was the architect's desire for uniformity. For sameness. Even the curtains had limitations. Privacy was one thing. Individuality another. These curtains could be only one color. White. And they would stay in one of only three positions. Open. Closed. Or halfway. Imagine living in such a place. Night falls and there are no decisions to be made. Open, closed, halfway. At such a time, in such a place, the decision is out of your hands.

Scene 3

(Lights up on YOUNG ANGIE, holding a small red book of poetry. Exuberant.)

YOUNG ANGIE Wild nights! Wild nights!/ Were I with thee,/Wild nights should be/ Our luxury!/Futile the winds/To a heart in port,/Done with the compass,/Done with the chart./Rowing in Eden!/Ah! The sea!/ Might I but moor/To-night in thee!

(EVELYN enters and goes to YOUNG ANGIE. There is an intimacy between them now. YOUNG ANGIE gives EVELYN the book of poetry. EVELYN opens the book and reads as she exits and lights come up on CARLTON.)

CARLTON I'm trying to be patient, Angie. I really am. But you don't meet me after class like you used to. And when you do, it's like you can't wait to run off again. You've been, I don't know. Moody. And it isn't like you. Not the Angie I know. Is it your term paper? For that damn Professor Haring? Is that what's made you so tense? You know it's only poetry. It isn't like a real class. Fine. Fine. Maybe I don't understand. What is it? Dickens? Sorry. Dickinson. Whatever.

(Lights bump up on the living room. ANGIE dozes on the sofa. A mug of tea on the end table next to her. EVELYN stands behind her.)

EVELYN So beautiful. Your face. Head tilted back. Eyes closed. Your face upside down and you look like a different person. A person I never met. A person who doesn't dream of running and running. A person who doesn't dream. What is it you're so afraid of in your dreams? What are you running from?

(ANGIE jerks awake and YOUNG ANGIE, CARLTON, and EVELYN disappear. ANGIE reaches for the mug. Knocks it over.)

ANGIE No. Oh, no. No. No. No.

(JESS enters.)

JESS What's wrong?

ANGIE Tea spilled.

JESS Don't worry. I'll get it.

ANGIE My stomach.

JESS Oh…

ANGIE It hurts.

JESS I know.

ANGIE You don't know anything. You left me alone.

JESS You were sleeping.

ANGIE You can't leave me alone. You see what happens? Who will protect me if you're not here?

JESS Protect you?

ANGIE They bother me. They talk too loud. When you go, anyone can come and say whatever they want to me.

JESS Mom. There's no one here. It's just you and me.

ANGIE They talk too loud.

JESS You must have been dreaming.

ANGIE You are supposed to stay with me. All the time. You can't leave me alone.

JESS I'm right here.

ANGIE You never stay.

JESS Shh. Don't worry about that now.

ANGIE You will worry for me?

JESS Sure.

ANGIE It won't be too much?

JESS I'll do everything for you.

ANGIE I worry this is too much for you.

JESS It's a lot for both of us. But I was thinking. Maybe I could use some help. I talked to Katie. She said she could take some time off work.

ANGIE We don't need her help.

JESS I might.

ANGIE You don't.

JESS If you got to know her. I think you'd like her.

ANGIE I know enough.

JESS You've never met her.

ANGIE I know enough not to like her.

JESS What happened to being worried about me?

ANGIE All my worry is for you. Now you talk about a baby. See? I pay attention.

JESS I see.

ANGIE If you did, you would not think to create a life.

JESS We want one.

ANGIE Ai-yah. So selfish.

JESS It's my choice.

ANGIE The choices you make will cause you pain.

JESS I'm not suffering.

ANGIE You will.

JESS You don't know.

ANGIE I have lived longer than you. I know things you will never know.

JESS Not about this.

ANGIE I've had enough of your agenda.

JESS It isn't an agenda. It's a wish.

ANGIE If I had known I'd have such a selfish child …

JESS You wouldn't have had me?

(ANGIE stands up slowly, leaning on her cane for support.)

ANGIE *(Quietly.)* If you have a child, you deserve a selfish one. One that doesn't listen. Doesn't visit. One that puts her life ahead of yours even when her actions make you so sad. So sad the sad gets stuck inside you. And when it's stuck inside, it grows and grows until it gets so big it eats your insides…pancreas, stomach, liver…until it kills you.

(ANGIE is shocked by what she has just said. She starts to shake and seems like she may fall.

JESS helps ANGIE sit back down. They sit quietly for a moment.)

JESS I'll make you some tea.

ANGIE I don't want tea.

JESS Are you hungry?

ANGIE I don't want to eat.

JESS How about another nap? I can go and do some work while you rest.

(ANGIE ignores JESS. JESS picks up a section of the newspaper.)

ANGIE What are you doing?

JESS Travel section.

ANGIE Are you going away?

JESS Maybe we can plan a trip. For when you get better. *(She starts flipping through the pages.)* Italy would be nice. All those gorgeous old buildings.

ANGIE Ruins.

JESS Or maybe New Zealand. Lots of open space there.

ANGIE Sheep.

JESS What?

ANGIE Too many sheep. Oh! Stop. Turn back a page. There.

JESS India?

ANGIE There. I want to go there.

Scene 4

Lights up on EVELYN and YOUNG ANGIE sitting in the Quad looking at one of Evelyn's architecture books.

YOUNG ANGIE Oh! Stop. Turn back a page. What's that?

EVELYN This one? It's the Taj Mahal.

YOUNG ANGIE It's beautiful.

EVELYN I should have known you'd like it. It's one of the most romantic buildings in the world.

YOUNG ANGIE Really?

EVELYN You don't know the story behind it?

YOUNG ANGIE All I know is that it's beautiful. It looks so pure even with all that ornate decoration and the…?

EVELYN The spires.

YOUNG ANGIE Yes. The spires. It's like they're reaching to the heavens.

EVELYN Maybe that's what he was hoping they'd do.

YOUNG ANGIE Who?

EVELYN The emperor. He built it for his wife.

YOUNG ANGIE Did she like it?

EVELYN She was dead. He built it as a tribute to his love for her.

YOUNG ANGIE That's so tragic.

EVELYN Can you imagine?

YOUNG ANGIE What?

EVELYN That kind of love?

YOUNG ANGIE I don't have to.

EVELYN I wonder…

YOUNG ANGIE What?

EVELYN If you'd let me build something for you.

YOUNG ANGIE Before or after I'm dead?

EVELYN You've been reading too much Dickinson.

YOUNG ANGIE So before?

EVELYN To start. A house. *(She opens her sketchbook and starts drawing.)* What's important to you?

YOUNG ANGIE Love.

EVELYN In your home.

YOUNG ANGIE Beauty.

EVELYN It will be beautiful. But in thinking of a house, purpose is paramount. Which is more important? Entertaining or small family dinners?

YOUNG ANGIE Entertaining.

EVELYN Openness or a sense of privacy?

YOUNG ANGIE Openness.

EVELYN Light and air? Or cozy corners?

YOUNG ANGIE Can't I have both?

EVELYN You can have anything you want.

(YOUNG ANGIE tries to see what EVELYN is drawing. They struggle over it. YOUNG AN-GIE snatches the sketchbook away. She loves what she sees.)

YOUNG ANGIE For me?

EVELYN For us.

YOUNG ANGIE This is much too grand for us.

EVELYN Not if everything goes well next week.

YOUNG ANGIE What's happening next week?

EVELYN I've been asked to speak at a conference.

YOUNG ANGIE A conference?

EVELYN It could lead to big things. An interview. A position. A salary. We could start a life.

YOUNG ANGIE We could?

EVELYN I'm so excited, Angie. It's almost too good to be…

YOUNG ANGIE Don't say it. Bad luck.

EVELYN Don't be so superstitious. It's really almost too good to be…

YOUNG ANGIE *(She puts her hand on EVELYN's mouth.)* Shhh.

Scene 5

The living room. ANGIE reads a section of the newspaper. JESS reads another.

ANGIE This is too good to be true!

JESS Hm?

ANGIE The world has taken an interest. Finally. Someone is doing something.

JESS About what?

ANGIE Look. *(She shows the article to JESS.)* I was reading. See? And there is an article. It has the answer.

JESS *(Skims the page.)* I don't understand.

ANGIE Use your eyes. No, no. This story. This side. They are having a conference.

JESS *(reads)* "International leaders will gather to discuss potential solutions…"

ANGIE Yes. Yes. They will gather to help me.

JESS This conference is political, mom.

ANGIE They have made a special conference. All for me.

JESS Mom…

ANGIE The next paragraph. See? They mention my name. "Angie Wilson is our first priority." See? Here.

JESS This article is about a political…

ANGIE They mention my name. This part here. "We are working around the clock to resolve Mrs. Wilson's crisis. In time, we will ensure that there is no such thing as death."

JESS *(Understanding ANGIE's mental state.)* God.

ANGIE Yes! Isn't it wonderful?

JESS *(resigned)* It is.

ANGIE But they can't get here. You understand? They need your help.

JESS What do they want me to do?

ANGIE You have to make arrangements. Make arrangements so they can fly here.

JESS Here?

ANGIE You have the Travel section. Find good flights. They will fly here. From all over the world. The leaders. And when they come, there will be no such thing as death.

JESS I see.

ANGIE Then you will make arrangements?

JESS When do you want to see them?

ANGIE Oh, Jessica. You just make phone calls. Here. Take this. *(ANGIE gives JESS the newspaper. JESS exits.)* They will fly.

Scene 6

YOUNG ANGIE and LINDA in their apartment. Getting ready to go out on their respective dates.

LINDA Where are you going tonight?

YOUNG ANGIE I don't know. I think she's planning a surprise.

LINDA Who?

YOUNG ANGIE Evie.

LINDA I thought you were going out with Carlton tonight.

YOUNG ANGIE Nope.

LINDA When's the last time you saw him?

YOUNG ANGIE I don't know. Last week. The week before? Why? Are you in love with him?

LINDA I'm in love with Jim.

YOUNG ANGIE Oh stop being so serious. I'm only joking.

LINDA Angie…

YOUNG ANGIE What?

LINDA You've been spending a lot of time with Evelyn.

YOUNG ANGIE Mm-hm.

LINDA You should be careful.

YOUNG ANGIE What are you talking about?

LINDA I'm not stupid. And neither is Carlton. Or the rest of campus. People have been talking.

YOUNG ANGIE They have?

LINDA She's not like the other girls.

YOUNG ANGIE I know she isn't.

LINDA Then you should know what they're talking about. And what they're saying about you.

YOUNG ANGIE I don't care what they say about me!

LINDA You should see Carlton.

YOUNG ANGIE Why?

LINDA He loves you. You don't want to miss your chance at happiness.

YOUNG ANGIE I'm happy now. Doesn't that count for something?

LINDA What about your babies?

YOUNG ANGIE What?

LINDA Remember when we were walking in town the other night? And we saw that mobile? And you said it would be perfect for your babies?

YOUNG ANGIE That's for later. The future.

LINDA And how do you think you'll reach that future with the choices you're making now?

YOUNG ANGIE *(Quiet.)* What about my heart?

LINDA Think carefully about your heart. Its shape. The human heart is shaped like this. *(She demonstrates.)* Wider at the top, then narrowing. Like an arrow pointing to the next generation. That's why the human

heart grows downward. So all the love at this higher level can…concentrate…and in this concentrated form flow down to our children. You can have that, Angie. You said yourself that you know he'll ask you to marry him. But he's been asking me why you haven't returned his phone calls. Why you don't want to talk to him. I let him know how important marriage and family are to you. I'm trying to look out for you. He will only ask so many times.

Scene 7

ANGIE Jess? Jessica?

JESS What's wrong? What's the matter?

ANGIE Did you call them? Did you arrange everything?

JESS Yes, mom. Everything's taken care of.

ANGIE They're coming?

JESS They're coming.

ANGIE When will they be here?

JESS Soon?

ANGIE *(She looks critically at JESS.)* I need my purse.

JESS Why?

ANGIE Do you have to ask so many questions? Just get it.

(JESSICA brings ANGIE her purse and ANGIE takes out foundation, lipstick, powder, hairbrush, etc. Puts on makeup as she talks.)

ANGIE These are international leaders. Important people. They are coming to see me so we should look nice.

JESS I think they'll understand.

ANGIE There is nothing to understand. We can look nice, so we should.

JESS You look fine.

ANGIE *(ANGIE checks her appearance in the mirror.)* Now I do. Your turn. *(She gestures for JESSICA to sit next to her.)*

JESS I don't need any…

ANGIE Come, Jessica. I will fix you. *(JESS sighs and submits to ANGIE's makeover.)* Such a pretty face. Such a shame. You know… It would have been so easy for you to find a tall, handsome husband. Then you could have a baby like you want.

JESS We're not talking about that now.

ANGIE You're right. Let's just enjoy this. We are spending time together like we should. And soon the people who can help us will be here. And we will have nothing to worry about. Aren't you excited?

JESS I need help.

ANGIE They will be here soon.

JESS I need Katie.

ANGIE You need only yourself.

JESS I don't know...

ANGIE Jessica. Think of what's important. People are coming from all over the world. They want to help me and my daughter thinks only of what she needs.

JESS You're right. This isn't the time.

ANGIE You should listen to me while you can.

JESS Don't say things like that.

ANGIE Like what?

JESS Just. I want to listen to you. I do. But could you listen to me too?

ANGIE I listen.

JESS Mom.

ANGIE What?

JESS Do you even see me?

ANGIE What are you talking about? I see you. You're right here. What else is there to see?

JESS If you could just open your mind. Really open your mind.

ANGIE Open your eyes.

JESS They're wide open.

ANGIE And still. Still. You will never see what I see.

Scene 8

YOUNG ANGIE's apartment. YOUNG ANGIE and EVELYN enter after a night out.

YOUNG ANGIE How could you embarrass me that way?

EVELYN I thought you creative types are open minded. I didn't think it would matter.

YOUNG ANGIE Well it does. It does matter. You can't throw around words like "husband" and "wife" that way.

EVELYN It was a joke.

YOUNG ANGIE Some people took it seriously. You have a reputation, you know.

EVELYN *(Acknowledging.)* I do.

YOUNG ANGIE People look at you differently.

EVELYN They do.

YOUNG ANGIE Your actions reflect on me.

EVELYN Always so concerned about what others think.

YOUNG ANGIE If you'd just make an effort. Must you always wear slacks? Wear your hair that way? Can't you just look like a normal girl once in a while?

EVELYN Is that what you want?

YOUNG ANGIE *(Hesitating. It isn't what she'd want.)* Yes.

EVELYN Perhaps you should see Carlton. He's been calling quite often.

YOUNG ANGIE Perhaps I should.

EVELYN You are in high demand. I'm afraid I've been taking too much of your time.

YOUNG ANGIE Energy.

EVELYN What?

YOUNG ANGIE I don't have the energy for this. This... "love that dare not speak its name."

EVELYN You and your literary references. But this isn't a story.

YOUNG ANGIE I wish it were. Then we could be like the ladies of the sun.

EVELYN They were sisters.

YOUNG ANGIE Who says so?

EVELYN I know the folk tale. They were the sun sisters.

YOUNG ANGIE And who were the people who wrote the folk tales?

EVELYN Scholars.

YOUNG ANGIE Men.

(Lights up on JESS. She speaks to ANGIE, who is asleep.)

JESS Remember the story you used to tell me when I was little? You told me it was about how girls need to be strong.

YOUNG ANGIE Once upon a time, there was a young god who lived in the sun and whose sisters lived in the moon. The young god was handsome, but his sisters were ravishing. Once you looked at them, you couldn't turn your eyes away, and all the young poets spent all night staring at the moon instead of writing poetry.

JESS The two goddesses had been very carefully brought up. Their mother had often told them that it wasn't nice for young maidens to let themselves be stared at. So they got very upset when the young poets not only stared at them but even shouted up at them hoping they would hear.

YOUNG ANGIE Sister. I'm afraid we cannot remain here any longer.

JESS Said the first of the two moon goddesses.

EVELYN No. We cannot.

JESS Replied the other.

YOUNG ANGIE But where in heaven can we go?

EVELYN Let's change places with our brother in the sun!

JESS The next day, they visited their brother in the sun. When they told him of the many poets who stared up at them at night, he said

EVELYN That is not right or proper.

JESS The sisters asked him if he would change places with them and he agreed. That night, all the poets who looked up at the moon were disappointed. But by sunrise word had spread that the sisters were now in the sun. When the poets rushed to the windows to look at the sun, they felt tiny pricking pains in their eyes.

EVELYN Some said it was the strong rays of the sun.

YOUNG ANGIE But others said it was the sharp embroidery needles of the two goddesses, who pricked the eyes of anyone who dared stare at them.

JESS Now I know what you were really telling me. Not to be strong. But to protect myself from prying eyes. It's always been about appearances, hasn't it?

(Lights down on JESS and ANGIE.)

YOUNG ANGIE If only it could be that simple.

EVELYN It could be.

YOUNG ANGIE Don't you understand? I want a place. To be someone's wife.

EVELYN You could be my wife.

YOUNG ANGIE Don't be ridiculous.

EVELYN Am I? Is that what you think of me?

YOUNG ANGIE The things you say.

EVELYN What about the things I do?

YOUNG ANGIE Never. You're too sensible.

(EVELYN gets down on one knee.)

EVELYN Am I being sensible now?

YOUNG ANGIE What are you doing?

EVELYN Do you think I look ridiculous?

YOUNG ANGIE You look beautiful.

EVELYN You could be my wife.

YOUNG ANGIE No. No, Evie. I need to be able to....belong. To feel right. That things are right. You understand, don't you? You have to.

EVELYN I've never felt like I belong.

YOUNG ANGIE I guess you haven't.

EVELYN But you know what? I've always felt right.

Scene 9

EDWARD Symbolism is meant for stories. Poems. Drama. Where architecture is pragmatic. That is the problem in trying to interpret a building. Yes. There is meaning to it, but inside. In the commonest houses. The greatest skyscrapers. The holiest churches and temples. That is where the meaning lies. In how livable or workable the structure is. As I've said, the life within. And if a structure doesn't serve its purpose, it must be redesigned. Changed. And sometimes. No. Most times. The change is far more difficult than the construction.

Scene 10

ANGIE sleeps on the sofa. CARLTON perches beside her. JESS sleeps on the floor near them.

CARLTON Angie. Honey. I wish you'd talk to me. Linda let me in. I hope you don't mind. I didn't know what else to do. I call and call and you never pick up the phone. I've been thinking. You know how you always make fun of those girls who get married right after college? Well, maybe they're not that bad. I mean, they seem happy, right? Like I said, I've been thinking and maybe it's more important than either of us think. I know you're more important than I thought. I miss you, Angie. I want. I want us to be together. You know? As man and wife. Will you just think about it? Think about being my wife?

(CARLTON goes to exit. ANGIE sits up. Awake.)

ANGIE Carlton?

(JESS wakes up.)

JESS Mom?

ANGIE I will, Carlton. Come back. Please come back.

JESS Shh.

ANGIE Carl?

JESS He's gone, Mom. Dad's gone. You were dreaming.

ANGIE I'm all alone.

JESS I'm here. See? It's me. Jessica.

ANGIE Jessica.

JESS Yes.

ANGIE There's so much you don't know.

JESS It's ok.

ANGIE I loved your daddy so much.

CARLTON Did you?

ANGIE Of course.

CARLTON Did you really?

JESS I know you did. He loved you too.

ANGIE He did, didn't he?

CARLTON More than anything.

JESS You ok now?

ANGIE I will be.

(CARLTON exits.)

ANGIE You made all the phone calls?

JESS Phone calls?

ANGIE You said you'd make arrangements. Did you?

JESS Yes.

ANGIE So they're coming?

JESS Don't worry.

ANGIE That's your job now.

JESS They're on their way.

ANGIE Good girl. (Beat.) Good daughter.

(The doorbell rings.)

ANGIE What are you waiting for? Let them in.

(JESS exits to answer the door. EVELYN slips past her and enters the living room, unseen by JESS. EVELYN holds a box of chocolate, which she sets down as she takes in her surroundings. She sees a framed photograph, picks it up, considers it. ANGIE sees her. Past and present blend.)

ANGIE Put that down. *(EVELYN doesn't hear her.)* This is not what I wanted. Jessica!

JESS *(O.S.)* Just a minute!

ANGIE This is not who I wanted to come.

(Lights up on EDWARD. He is talking about the photograph that EVELYN is looking at.)

EDWARD Amazing what cameras can do nowadays. Now we can relive our memories in color. Takes away from the imagination though. How much nicer it was to see a blackand-white image. Fill it in with the colors we want. Are the trees still green or have the leaves turned color? Oranges fighting with reds. Yellows. Is her wedding dress white or red? Is she glowing with happiness? Or is the strain along the edges of her smile confirmed by the pallor of her face? Now. Now the color seems imposed. I don't want to see this copy of reality. I want to see what I remember.

(EDWARD watches the following scene.)

YOUNG ANGIE *(O.S.)* Ice or no ice?

EVELYN No ice.

ANGIE Why is she here?

YOUNG ANGIE I'm so happy you're here.

(JESS enters.)

JESS Who? Who's here?

YOUNG ANGIE Are you ok in there?

JESS Are you ok?

EVELYN Fine. Entertaining myself. Looking at photos and seeing that your past only extends so far. Your history is new.

ANGIE Jessica.

JESS What is it?

EVELYN Its newness is everywhere. On the walls. The shelves. Unfamiliar.

ANGIE Make her go away.

JESS Shh. It's just me, Mom. It's me.

EVELYN I don't recognize a thing.

(YOUNG ANGIE enters with a plate of hors d'oeuvres. She is obviously pregnant.)

YOUNG ANGIE You've never been here before.

EVELYN I don't recognize you.

YOUNG ANGIE I've put on a few pounds.

ANGIE That's not…

EVELYN That's not what I'm talking about.

ANGIE Evie.

YOUNG ANGIE I'm the same.

JESS Who?

YOUNG ANGIE Here.

ANGIE You don't see her?

JESS Maybe you should close your eyes.

YOUNG ANGIE Eat.

JESS Rest.

(JESS puts her hands over ANGIE's eyes. ANGIE moves them and watches EVELYN and YOUNG ANGIE.)

EVELYN Impressive.

YOUNG ANGIE It's nothing.

EVELYN You are quite the hostess.

YOUNG ANGIE You're a guest.

EVELYN A guest.

YOUNG ANGIE It's been some time.

EVELYN Such a fine way to entertain a guest. A guest in your beautiful home.

YOUNG ANGIE Please.

EVELYN *(Considers the plate of food.)* And what might this be?

YOUNG ANGIE For the vegetables.

EVELYN A dip?

YOUNG ANGIE Spinach and sour cream.

EVELYN I see.

YOUNG ANGIE For the vegetables.

EVELYN And so many…how many? One, two, three… four kinds of biscuits.

YOUNG ANGIE Crackers.

EVELYN Crackers. And all these cheeses. What is this? Camembert?

YOUNG ANGIE Yes.

EVELYN Brie. And this ugly one?

YOUNG ANGIE Port wine.

EVELYN A paragon among hostesses. But of course, that is what is expected of the wife of a businessman.

YOUNG ANGIE Your call surprised me.

EVELYN *(Scornfully.)* An American businessman.

YOUNG ANGIE I didn't expect to see you again.

EVELYN How is life with the businessman?

YOUNG ANGIE He is a good man.

EVELYN And your family? What do they think?

YOUNG ANGIE They came to the wedding.

EVELYN How nice of them. And they don't mind that he deals with money?

YOUNG ANGIE As opposed to?

EVELYN Things that matter.

YOUNG ANGIE Like what, Evie? Art? Literature? Music?

EVELYN Perhaps.

YOUNG ANGIE You have very specific ideas about how other people should live their lives. Just because you have this idea of who you think I am…

EVELYN Is that all it is?

YOUNG ANGIE What?

EVELYN An idea of you?

YOUNG ANGIE I don't really mean…

EVELYN You mean I don't know you.

YOUNG ANGIE I'm not that girl anymore.

EVELYN I don't know if you were ever that girl.

YOUNG ANGIE What does that mean?

EVELYN I mean… I thought you were born for better things. Higher things. You come from a good family.

YOUNG ANGIE You know…

EVELYN It's in your blood.

YOUNG ANGIE For all your revolutionary feminism…

EVELYN You were born for higher things.

YOUNG ANGIE Your traditionalism can be really overwhelming.

EVELYN A life of the mind.

YOUNG ANGIE We are in America now. I have made my decisions because I come from a good family.

EVELYN And I?

YOUNG ANGIE *(disparaging.)* You have managed to get a good education.

EVELYN As you say, we are in America now. Your good family means nothing here. And you don't even have your family name anymore. Americans have no good names. "Wilson." Does that have meaning? They are all the same. *(Beat.)* Does he read?

YOUNG ANGIE Of course.

EVELYN Turgenev?

YOUNG ANGIE He's American.

EVELYN Steinbeck then.

YOUNG ANGIE I don't know.

EVELYN Faulkner.

YOUNG ANGIE The newspaper.

EVELYN A businessman.

YOUNG ANGIE Yes.

EVELYN And have you, too, forgotten how to read? Lack of insight is contagious.

YOUNG ANGIE I still read.

EVELYN Do you?

YOUNG ANGIE Your face.

EVELYN Maybe you do.

YOUNG ANGIE Still open.

EVELYN I can't change my face.

YOUNG ANGIE Broad forehead. Nose. Eyes. Clear and wide.

EVELYN I was never one to lie.

YOUNG ANGIE You will always have an open face.

EVELYN What do you see?

(YOUNG ANGIE looks at EVELYN. Suddenly uncomfortable, she gets up. Starts watering a plant.)

YOUNG ANGIE This plant looks better already.

EVELYN Angie.

YOUNG ANGIE See? I noticed the edges of the leaves turning brown. Sometimes I forget to water. Every other day. Twice a week, at the very least. I forget sometimes. Brown leaves. Water.

EVELYN Angie…

YOUNG ANGIE Perhaps not as green as they should be. But greener now.

EVELYN Have you thought of me?

YOUNG ANGIE I think of everything else.

EVELYN You can control your thoughts?

YOUNG ANGIE I'm very busy. We entertain a lot. Variation is important. And everyone expects Chinese food when they come here. So exciting. So exotic. Parties every week. Menu has to change. Dress has to be different. Different food. Different dress. Same house. Same people. His friends. Same talk.

EVELYN And you?

YOUNG ANGIE What?

EVELYN You. What do you talk about?

YOUNG ANGIE *(Smiles.)* The baby.

EVELYN You are respectable now.

YOUNG ANGIE Yes.

EVELYN A married woman. A woman who will no longer be a woman but a mother. Look at you. If you smiled, you would look like a happy Buddha.

YOUNG ANGIE *(Defensive.)* I am happy.

EVELYN You're not smiling.

YOUNG ANGIE A mother does not smile when she's happy. She just feels content.

EVELYN And you are content?

YOUNG ANGIE Of course.

EVELYN Do you love him?

YOUNG ANGIE Of course I do.

EVELYN He's your husband.

ANGIE *(angrily to EVELYN.)* Did you come here to make fun of me?

JESS Of course not. How can you ask me that?

ANGIE *(To JESS.)* Not you. Her. You leave me alone. You stay with me. It makes no difference. You let anyone say what they want to me.

JESS What is she saying?

ANGIE You want to know?

JESS I've always wanted to know.

YOUNG ANGIE *(to ANGIE.)* It's time.

ANGIE I can't.

JESS Tell me.

EVELYN *(to ANGIE.)* Tell her.

ANGIE Please.

YOUNG ANGIE Open her eyes.

ANGIE You won't understand.

YOUNG ANGIE She will.

JESS I will.

EVELYN Open her eyes.

ANGIE There was a woman. A strong, beautiful woman.

YOUNG ANGIE Yes.

ANGIE Her name was Evelyn.

JESS Evie?

EVELYN Yes.

ANGIE She was a friend.

EVELYN No.

ANGIE She had all the strength of a man. And all the sensitivity of a woman.

JESS And she was your friend.

EVELYN *(Emphatic.)* No.

ANGIE More than a friend.

JESS More?

EVELYN Yes.

ANGIE She visited me after your daddy and I were married. She asked me so many questions. Too many questions.

EVELYN Do you love him?

YOUNG ANGIE Of course I do.

EVELYN Of course. He is your husband.

YOUNG ANGIE Did you come here to make fun of me?

EVELYN To make fun of…? Oh, no. I just wanted…

YOUNG ANGIE To make fun of my life.

EVELYN To visit an old friend.

YOUNG ANGIE An old friend?

EVELYN I did not want to talk about the present. To see it, yes. But not talk about it. I wanted… I want…

YOUNG ANGIE To see if I like married life.

EVELYN To see you. And to ask if you…

YOUNG ANGIE What?

EVELYN Do you ever think about me?

YOUNG ANGIE I don't want to. I can't think about you. I'm going to have a baby. I have to be careful.

EVELYN Is a thought so dangerous?

YOUNG ANGIE Now it is. You should know that.

EVELYN Tell me.

YOUNG ANGIE What?

EVELYN Tell me what I should know.

YOUNG ANGIE When a woman is pregnant, whoever she thinks about most during the pregnancy…

EVELYN Is who the child will resemble.

YOUNG ANGIE Yes.

EVELYN *(She has the answer she wanted.)* Your traditionalism is overwhelming.

YOUNG ANGIE Don't joke. I don't want this baby to end up like you.

EVELYN Am I so terrible?

YOUNG ANGIE It's a hard life.

EVELYN It wasn't so hard with you. Angie… Do you remember when we found those chocolates? From that fancy shop near campus. Remember?

YOUNG ANGIE You had just got your first paycheck. You were so proud.

EVELYN So were you.

YOUNG ANGIE "Anything you want," you said. "Don't even look at the price."

EVELYN And you didn't.

YOUNG ANGIE We found those lovely chocolates.

(EVELYN gives YOUNG ANGIE the chocolates she brought.)

EVELYN With the brandy in the middle.

YOUNG ANGIE It burned my lips. The brandy.

EVELYN And do you remember what you told me?

YOUNG ANGIE Evie…

EVELYN What you told me it made you think of?

YOUNG ANGIE Don't.

EVELYN Tell me.

YOUNG ANGIE Your kiss.

EVELYN Yes?

YOUNG ANGIE How it burned my mouth. And how no one had ever kissed me the way you did.

EVELYN And you asked me…

YOUNG ANGIE Is this how it is between women?

EVELYN What do you mean?

YOUNG ANGIE Is this…is this the difference between kissing a woman and kissing a man?

EVELYN The difference is in kissing someone you love.

(EVELYN opens the box and holds a chocolate out to YOUNG ANGIE.)

YOUNG ANGIE I'm afraid.

EVELYN Don't be. I see that you belong here now.

(YOUNG ANGIE bites into the chocolate.)

EVELYN Remember. Remember and think of me from time to time.

ANGIE I remember.

EVELYN *(to ANGIE)* I know you do.

ANGIE Evie?

EVELYN Do you think of me?

ANGIE I try not to. Especially after…

EVELYN After what?

ANGIE Your letter.

EVELYN We're not there yet.

ANGIE But I…

EDWARD We're not there yet.

ANGIE I'm afraid.

YOUNG ANGIE I'm afraid.

EVELYN *(to YOUNG ANGIE)* Don't be. I see that you belong here now.

(YOUNG ANGIE bites into the chocolate again.)

EVELYN Remember. Remember and think of me from time to time.

YOUNG ANGIE I will.

EVELYN I know you will.

YOUNG ANGIE Is that what you wanted?

EVELYN You know what I wanted. But I see now that it's not possible. Not like this. But steps will be taken just the same. Not for you, Angie. Not for us. They have a life of their own.

YOUNG ANGIE What does? You're scaring me.

EVELYN I was going to offer you a place. As a wife.

YOUNG ANGIE I have a…

EVELYN My wife.

YOUNG ANGIE You know I don't want that.

EVELYN As this man's wife.

YOUNG ANGIE I don't understand.

EVELYN Look at me, Angie. What do you see?

(YOUNG ANGIE takes EVELYN's face in her hands. Looks. Sees.)

ANGIE She looked at me with a man's eyes.

(EDWARD takes the small, red book of poetry out of his pocket. He reads.)

EDWARD The props assist the house/Until the house is built,/And then the props withdraw—/And adequate, erect/The house supports itself;/Ceasing to recollect/The auger and the carpenter./Just such a retrospect/Hath the perfected life, A past of plank and nail,/And slowness— then the scaffolds drop—

ANGIE Affirming it a soul.

YOUNG ANGIE Why couldn't you have told me before?

EVELYN I wanted to be more than just a suitable man for you to marry.

JESS You wanted to marry her.

ANGIE She was everything I could have wanted.

JESS If she was everything you wanted, how could you let her go?

ANGIE The choices you make can cause you pain.

JESS Then why didn't you choose her?

(Beat.)

ANGIE I wanted you.

JESS You didn't know if I'd be a boy or a girl. If I'd look like you or Dad. If I'd be pretty or smart.

ANGIE I knew you'd be perfect. Except…

JESS Oh, mom.

ANGIE I suppose I knew that too. Really. You are not to blame. It was me. My actions. You came from my body. I just didn't think you'd absorb my thoughts. My weakness is to blame.

JESS You can't really believe that.

ANGIE I thought about her every day you were inside me.

EVELYN You did?

ANGIE Every single day.

JESS Did you ever see her again?

EVELYN No.

ANGIE I got a letter.

EDWARD Yes. The letter.

ANGIE Your daddy and I. Addressed to Mr. and Mrs. Wilson. "Your college friend wrote us," he said. He recognized her name. I took it to the bathroom and opened it. She had changed. Become something different. Not Evelyn.

EVELYN No.

ANGIE Edward.

EDWARD Me.

ANGIE She had changed for me.

EDWARD No.

ANGIE You did. You changed because you loved me.

EDWARD Oh, Angie. You were always so vain.

ANGIE And you were such a beautiful, beautiful woman.

EVELYN Thank you.

JESS You loved her.

YOUNG ANGIE I did.

JESS Didn't you?

ANGIE I did.

EVELYN Thank you.

EDWARD But then I became myself. I found a home in my body.

ANGIE I knew then that I had lost. Like you had died.

EDWARD The life behind the structure. Beneath the skin. It had emerged.

ANGIE It wasn't fair.

EDWARD Life had broken through.

JESS But I don't understand. How can you be so against me and…?

ANGIE You have changed the rules.

JESS Can't you be happy for me?

ANGIE It isn't fair.

JESS No, mom. I guess it isn't.

EVELYN *(to YOUNG ANGIE)* Have you thought of a name?

YOUNG ANGIE I haven't decided yet. What do you think?

EVELYN and EDWARD Jessica.

YOUNG ANGIE I like that. Jessica.

(JESS looks up, as though she's heard her name called. She sees YOUNG ANGIE. They look at each other. YOUNG ANGIE puts her hand on her stomach. JESS does the same. Mirror image. Lights fade.)

———————————

Marcie R. Rendon

Biography

Marcie R. Rendon is enrolled in White Earth Anishinabe, a playwright, poet, performance artist, and freelance writer. She has four published plays, two non-fiction children's books, with poems and short stories in numerous anthologies. Her first novel, *Murder on the Red River*, was published in 2017 with Cinco Puntos Press. Her plays have been published in *Performing Worlds into Being: Native American Women's Theater, Footpaths & Bridges: Voices from the Native American Women Playwrights Archive,* and *Keepers of the Morning Star: An Anthology of Native Women's Theater.*

As creator, producer, and director of the grassroots Raving Native Productions, she produces plays for the Minnesota Fringe Festival, curates all-Native cabarets at venues in Minneapolis/St. Paul, and has worked nationally since 1994 with tribal communities and colleges to create site-specific theater. Rendon received the Playwright Center's Many Voices Residency Award, has twice been a recipient of the Many Voices Multi-cultural Collaboration Grant, and is a former Jerome Foundation Fellow. In 1998, Rendon received the St. Paul Company's Leadership In Neighborhoods Award to "create a viable Native presence in the Twin Cities theater community."

Rendon writes to create a mirror to see ourselves as Native people. The lives, past-present-future, of Native women and their families are a recurring theme in Rendon's plays. She also uses her work to explore the simultaneous existence of beings in both the physical and spiritual world exploring the interdependent nature their existence has across time and space in this holographic universe. Rendon's work has been described as funny and meaningful, with a humanity that doesn't shy away from the many textures of life, from the mundane to the spiritual to the unpleasant, hilarious and tragic.

Artistic statement

We were kept in their mindset as "vanished peoples." Or as workers, not creators. And what does this erasing of individual identity do to us? Can you believe you exist if you look in a mirror and see no reflection? And what happens when one group controls the mirror market?

As Native people, we have known that in order to survive we had to create, re-create, produce, re-produce. The effect of denial on our existence is that many of us have become invisible. The systematic disruption of our families, the removal of our children, was effective for silencing our voices.

However, not everyone can still that desire, that up-welling inside that says sing, write, draw, move, be. We can sing our hearts out, tell our stories, paint our visions. We are in a position to create a more human reality. In order to live, we have to make our own mirrors.

Production history

The creation of *The Adventures at Camp KaKeeKwaSha and the Magic Musky Casino!* is the end result of a series of conversations with international Mohican composer Brent Michael Davids, his partner Ann Millikan, another internationally known composer and myself when we were lamenting the lack of opportunities for Native playwrights and composers. We were talking about old Hollywood films that featured native actors, somehow got to animation and radio plays and then there was an "aha" moment of "let's write a podcast, like a radio play but we can put it on the internet" – We brainstormed the concept, characters, and storyline and also researched how to write for radio and podcast – and the writing commenced. Davids composed the opening song and Millikan reads for Nurse Chappelle and Veronica on the podcast. The original podcast can be heard at: http://ravingnativeradio. blogspot.com.

18 *The Adventures at Camp KaKeeKwaSha and the Magic Musky Casino!*
Marcie R. Rendon

Setting

Scene I: Bandshell and Woods

Scene II: Nurse Guinneviere Chappell's Cabin

Scene III: Swimming raft at Bass Lake, Band Camp beach

Scene IV: Conversation between Tribal Police and KB-ops Operatives

Scene V: Campfire at Night

Scene VI: Back at Tribal Police Headquarters

Scene VII: At the exit road by the burial grounds

Scene VIII: At the exit road by the burial grounds

Scene IX: At the exit road by the burial grounds

Episode 1

THEME MUSIC (0:30)   opens each episode

> Buses coming, here we go!
> Tacky duds from head to toe. Machine washah over flow,
> On to Camp KaKeeKwaSha.
> Big Casino past the train!
> Toot the horn and pull the chain.
> T.V. watchah don't complain, Rustic Camp KaKeeKwaSha.
> Don't stand up in your canoe!
> Or the lifeguard speak to you.
> Agree witcha the sky is blue, Play at Camp KaKeeKwaSha Baaaaand Caaaaamp!

Scene 1

Bandshell and Woods

CHILD's voice outdoors yells: kuh-KEE-kwuh-shah!!

(Sound of a belly flop hitting the water)

CHILD's watery voice: Uuh!!! That hurt.

(We hear muskrats chittering in almost intelligible sounds; birds screech and take off in a flutter. Hear

the movement of band instruments, folding chair screeches.)

DIRECTOR *(Tapping the metal music stand)* Campers, welcome back to Camp KaKeeKwaSha. All of you have familiar faces so you should know; except when it is raining, we will meet here in the band shell. If it does rain, we'll move to the dining hall. Let's work together to make this a good year.

BOYS' and GIRLS' VOICES: Yes. Sure. Great. Yabetcha.

DIRECTOR B-flat, can I please get a B-flat – a simple B-flat, girls and boys?

(Instruments play a B-flat.)

DIRECTOR OK good – with a little life now. We're going to play the, uh the... – play the...

LAKEISHA Camp Song?

DIRECTOR That's right, The Camp Song. We are going to play the camp song. You should remember it from last year. With a little life, I say.... With a one, anda two anda.....

(The song gets off to a rousing start – there is heard an additional flute and a drum playing a tom-tom beat coming from a distance. Off in the bushes at the lake's edge SQUIRREL and JIGGS are hidden and playing flute and drum along with the band camp kids.)

DIRECTOR STOP!!!

(All is silent.)

DIRECTOR Again, from the top.... Four.... Three....

(Again, the song gets off to a rousing start. Again there is heard an additional flute and a drum playing a tom-tom beat.)

DIRECTOR STOP!!

BRINDLE What's the matter, Ms. Bach?

DIRECTOR RJ!!?? Stop making that god-awful noise!! And Brindle O'Dingle...

POGO O'Dingle?

DIRECTOR ...my name is Batch! Wallis Batch! Not Bach! RJ!! – I do not care who your parents are, STOP fooling around. I am the director. Follow my direction!

RJ I didn't doing anything.

(Under his breath)

Who bunched her undies?

DIRECTOR AGAIN! No fooling around this time.

VERONICA What's she talking about?

LAKEISHA Dunno.

DIRECTOR Or I will keep you here 'til suppertime! Four... Three....

(Again, the song gets off to a rousing start – again there is heard an additional flute and a drum playing a tom-tom beat.)

DIRECTOR Stop!!! Get out!! Stop!!! Get out of here, ALL of YOU!!! GO!!! Why do I submit myself to this torture??!! GO!!!!

(Sounds of instruments being put away, chairs screeching, footsteps. And then we hear a rustle of leaves in the woods and two Indian guys' voices.)

SQUIRREL Our director sounds upset.

JIGGS *(Slapping sounds)* The mosquitoes are rough out here in the bush. I thought we were keeping pretty good time.

(Bandshell sounds and talk continue to alternate with the rustle of leaves in the bush.)

RJ Veronica, you wearing your bi-ki-ni to swim??!!! Please say yes.

SQUIRREL *(Slapping face)* Got-em! This is only our third practice. I thought we were doing pretty good.

LAKEISHA I don't know why you have to be so lame – grow up.

RJ What do you want to see grow?

LAKEISHA Disgusting.

JIGGS You sure you put a B-flat on that flute when you carved it?

SQUIRREL How was I to know each hole on the flute had a name? I was just trying to copy the birds outside my house.

(Plays the full scales)

Guess the birds sing in B-flat, no? You think? Three days with a band and I'm playing like the birds sing.

VERONICA You're sick, RJ. Ms. Bach – would you show me the fingering for the song one more time?

RJ Wanna see what my fingers can do with my sax?

LAKEISHA Shuttup.

DIRECTOR Sure Veronica, start here – pointer, middle....

RJ 'ronica, look at my middle finger. It has tree fungus growing on it.

VERONICA Get away from me. Aiii! Go! Ms. Bach...

DIRECTOR Batch.

VERONICA ...make him stop.

(VERONICA and LAKEISHA run away.)

Pogo, wait for us.

DIRECTOR RJ, let me see that hand. Have you been in poison ivy?

RJ I don't think so.

DIRECTOR That looks awful. I think you need to go see the nurse.

RJ I think I should call my dad. He knows a skin specialist in Eden Prairie.

DIRECTOR Your father isn't here. Do not even start that this year. I don't care whose dad is a rich rock star and can pay for new buildings for the camp each year. We get a brand new dining hall just so someone's son can go here free - a legacy camper so we have to babysit him, so his parents can jetset all over the world.

And I don't think it's one bit funny, the way you were playing the drum today, making fun of the fine Indian people who…

RJ Whattaya mean? That wasn't me.

DIRECTOR …who have granted us the land for this camp. This is a great opportunity, and you the legacy camper you just want to blow it, make fun of the Indians. You think you can get away with being a jerk cause your dad has teenyboppers screaming at his feet, making millions….

RJ And besides, my father says we're part Cherokee. My hand.

DIRECTOR Go to Nurse Chappell.

RJ Aw, man, not Nurse Hachette—

DIRECTOR Guinneviere Chappell works all winter at the Mayo Clinic. You should be grateful she even agrees to come here each summer. She does not have to come here…

RJ Yeah, right. We all know she uses summer camp as her opportunity to hone her hinkey torture skills.

DIRECTOR That is just not true. You kids….

RJ My hand.

DIRECTOR Come on, I'll walk you over there.

(Sounds of them walking away turn into sounds of JIGGS and SQUIRREL crawling through brush.)

JIGGS Watch that branch.

SQUIRREL You tryin to take my eye out?

(We hear kids playing in water, other kids trying to canoe, the sounds of JIGGS and SQUIRREL still moving through the bush.)

JIGGS Lookit them kids try to canoe. It's going take them all afternoon just to get away from the dock. Maybe they'll scare the Magic Musky right to us.

SQUIRREL I think our director was upset about the drum….

JIGGS Maybe I shoulda played a traditional song?

SQUIRREL Traditional. I been on this rez your whole life and I ain't never seen you do anything traditional. You sure you're even Indian?

JIGGS Takes more than braids and a flute to make an Indian bro.

(Sound of a branch hitting a body)

JIGGS Ow, man, now why'd you do that? I am traditional.

(Starts singing and dancing)

Hey-ya-hey ya aiiii iia aye!
See my ankle bracelet here? Courtesy of the B-I-A
Tribal cops wanna follow me
No more shining deer for me Aye ya hey
Put some bells on my ankle here Dance the pow-wow trail you see Hey-ya-hey ya aiiii iia aye!

SQUIRREL *(laughing)* Knock it off. Come on. I'll push the canoe out. Jump in; don't want to get your ankle wet. Let's go catch Magic Musky. Maybe then they'll let you off rez arrest.

(Sounds of them putting canoe in water and pushing off shore)

Scene II

Nurse Guinneviere Chappell's cabin

DIRECTOR Go on in to the nurse's station. Nurse Chappell will fix you right up.

(Door opens and closes. Sounds of metal instruments being moved around.)

NURSE CHAPPELL Get undressed and up on the table.

RJ I am not taking off anything. It's my hand I need something for. *(Hollering)*
Director Batch – don't leave me here alone!

DIRECTOR *(Heard walking away)* Let her take care of you now. I'll be right in my office.

NURSE CHAPPELL Let me see that hand.

RJ I think we should call my dad.

NURSE CHAPPELL No need to bother your dad with a little jock itch. Why don't you drop your pants and bend over here.

RJ Bend over?!! It's my hand.

NURSE CHAPPELL Standard procedure. Have to take every camper's temp that I see.

RJ Well then, stick that thing under my tongue. That bend-over torture trick may have worked two years ago when I was just a kid but uh-uh, not this year.

(The rest is mumbled as if he has a thermometer under his tongue.)

All you have to do is look at my hand here and let me know…

(Back to normal voice although he squeaks with fear.)

What are you doing with those wires?

NURSE CHAPPELL Standard procedure. A little electric current kills the bacteria….

RJ NO – I have an R-FID in my hand. You'll fry the frequency and my father will kill you! The KB-Ops will be here so fast you won't know what hit you!

NURSE CHAPPELL R-FID? KB-Ops? What new toys did Daddy send you with this year?

RJ It's not a toy. It's an imbedded tracking device.

NURSE CHAPPELL A tracking device? In your hand?

RJ Someone threatened to kidnap me…

NURSE CHAPPELL Your dad never ceases to amaze me.

RJ …take me from my dad…for my father's money.

NURSE CHAPPELL Ah a metal chip in your hand.

RJ Yes

NURSE CHAPPELL So the RFID knows where you are at all times.

RJ Roger. They know I am in Nurse Guinneviere Chappell's cabin.

NURSE CHAPPELL *(There is the sound of electric static)* Can they hear me?

RJ GET those wires away from my hand. YES, they can hear you. Put the wires away and give me something for this rash.

NURSE CHAPPELL Standard procedure. Standard procedure. I don't know why you all balk at standard procedure. Here, put this anti-bacterial cortisone cream mixed with a touch of zinc on your hand. Should cover anything that crawls.

(Screen door slams)

NURSE CHAPPELL *(to herself as we hear water being poured, metal clinking together)* I wonder if I should have told him to stay out of the water. Metal, water, zinc – human body conducts electricity. What is the standard procedure here?

(A sizzling sound, followed by an evil sounding oooh from NURSE CHAPPELL.)

Scene III

Swimming raft at Bass Lake, Band Camp beach

(Sounds of water play and a whirring sound like an electric mixer.)

LAKEISHA *(Seeing SQUIRREL and JIGGS across the lake)* I could lay on this raft all day. Veronica, check out them Indian guys fishing.

VERONICA Hey – look what Pogo's gone and done.

LAKEISHA The guy with braids is cute.

VERONICA Pogo's got a fan hooked up to that canoe.

LAKEISHA Pogo!! Give us a ride.

(Whirring sound is closer.)

POGO Can't. Haven't figured out how to stop and go yet. Where's Brindle?

VERONICA Swimming.

LAKEISHA He keeps diving under the raft, playing with the muskrats.

BRINDLE *(Coming up out of the water)* Sweet. There's about eight of them. Mom, dad, and babies.

(Muskrat chittering increases; whirring sound continues; they talk loudly over the whirring as POGO continues to circle the raft.)

LAKEISHA Cool. How'd you make it?

POGO Well, I started with the intake fan from over the…

BRINDLE I'm going back, the muskrats are upset.

POGO What?

BRINDLE *(Before he dives back down)* Nothing

POGO I'm going to go see if those guys caught anything.

(Whirring sound and boat going through water, POGO circles their canoe.)

JIGGS Ahneen

POGO Boo-zhoo, Pogo indizhinakaz.

SQUIRREL What'd he say, Mr. Tradish? Look at that rig.

JIGGS You from the camp?

POGO Yep. Catch anything?

(Voice fades away)

I have to go, haven't finetuned the stop and go mechanics yet.

JIGGS *(Yelling)* You play in the band?

POGO *(Hollers)* What band you say? Osage/ Pequot and Mdwekatan Sioux. You? Have to catch you on the go-round.

SQUIRREL You see that crazy Indian? Jerry-rigged that fan and got himself a sailboat.

JIGGS Bet he plays in the band.

RJ *(Heard from a distance, a dive and then hollering)* Pogo, come and get me.

SQUIRREL Hey Jiggs! Get your feet out of the water. Want to kill us both with that ankle bracelet?

JIGGS Man, I forgot. Good thing I didn't 'lectrocute myself.

SQUIRREL Hope you didn't fry Magic Musky on the lake bottom. *(Back at the raft)*

LAKEISHA Aiiiiiiiii!!!

VERONICA Oww

LAKEISHA What the heck was that?

VERONICA I got a shock. Did you?

(We hear an increase in muskrat chittering sound.)

BRINDLE *(Sputtering and pulling self up on raft)* What the sweet jesus was that?

LAKEISHA Felt like an electric current. There ain't a cloud in sight

(Hollering)

Pogo –

POGO What?

LAKEISHA Are you sure that thing is safe in water?

POGO I can't hear you. Let go RJ, I have to keep going.

RJ *(Pulling self up on raft)* Crazy Pogo. Look at that thing he made.

LAKEISHA Did you get a shock?

RJ Touch me baby I'll let you know.

VERONICA Sick.

(Splash of someone going over side of raft)

RJ What got into Brindle?

LAKEISHA He's obsessed with muskrats.

BRINDLE *(coming back up through water)* You guys, these muskrats are talking to me!

VERONICA Oh my god, his brain was fried.

BRINDLE Serious.

LAKEISHA Sure, Brindle.

(Serious increase in muskrat chitter that sounds like they are talking in sentences.)

BRINDLE Listen!

(Camp dinner bell rings.)

RJ Race you back!

(Sounds of three splashes in, whirring sound moves to shore)

BRINDLE It's ok guys, talk to me.

(Soft chittering of muskrats that sound increasingly like intelligent talk.)

Scene IV

Conversation between Tribal Police and KB-Ops Operatives

(Sounds of static, electronic equipment)

KB-OPS KB-Ops from Ely, Minnesota headquarters. Magic Musky Tribal Headquarters come in please.

SUE MOCCASIN 'lo.

KB-OPS Chief of police please.

SUE MOCCASIN Who?

KB-OPS Your chief. Who's in charge?

SUE MOCCASIN Me.

KB-OPS Where's your police chief? This is **KB-Ops.**

.SUE MOCCASIN Bingo palace catching coverall. What's your problem and I'll tell you if it's worth your trouble for me to get him.

KB-OPS We had a blip on our radar showing mixed activity on our guy Purple Haze just about a half hour ago. Nothing since. Anything show up on your radar?

SUE MOCCASIN Uh-uh.

KB-OPS Well, can you double check with the chief? The blip was questionable. Do you have a weather anomaly or something else going on over there?

SUE MOCCASIN Jiggs.

KB-OPS Jiggs? What kind of weather formation is that?

SUE MOCCASIN Deer shiner.

KB-OPS Our job is to protect a child's life. Either talk English to me or get the Tribal Chief of Police.

SUE MOCCASIN When the Chief of Police, my husband, gets back, he'll tell you the same thing. Jiggs got caught shining deer last month. He went fishing today and stuck his electronic ankle bracelet in Magic Musky Lake. Short-circuited the Monopoly Game over at the casino just when someone thought they had a hit. Big fight. My husband, the Chief of Police, had to break it up. Jiggs, the deer shiner, saw your Purple Haze, being dragged behind a canoe that some little rich Indian kid had a fan hooked up to. He was blowing himself around the lake dragging the other guy behind him.

KB-OPS What rich kid?

SUE MOCCASIN The one with all the oil and casino money. I'll tell my husband, the Tribal Chief of Police, sir, that you called.

(Click. More static and electronic sounds)

KB-OPS Anyone know who Shining Deer is? Sounds like we got a competing company tracking youth over there. Purple Haze appears to be fine for the moment. Not to worry about any competition. We ARE the highest paid babysitters in the industry. We peep so parents can sleep.

Scene V

Campfire at Night

(Night sounds in the woods: crickets, frogs, sound of campfire.)

BRINDLE This fire is toasty.

(A snap of a branch is heard.) What was that?

RJ Muskrats.

VERONICA *(Hushed scary voice)* The Woman Who Never Exits.

BRINDLE I'm telling you, the muskrats are trying to talk to me.

LAKEISHA What do they say, feed me, feed me?

RJ That's the mosquitoes.

BRINDLE The babies can't talk yet of course, but the mom and dad are trying to tell me something.

LAKEISHA Who, Veronica?

VERONICA The Woman Who Never Exits. She stands up there on the highway by the old burial grounds.

RJ That's only about a quarter mile from here.

VERONICA They say that everyone around here has seen her. Sometimes folks will pick her up and she'll go dancing with them at the casino. Except no one else ever sees her with them. Some guys try to take her home. She's really beautiful everyone says. But she disappears right out of the cars up there by the burial mounds.

LAKEISHA Does not.

BRINDLE Does she talk?

VERONICA Ms. Bach said that one time, not during the summer, she was driving limo for the casino. Just making some extra money. And she saw this lady standing up there at the exit. She stopped to offer her a ride. She got in.

LAKEISHA Indian?

VERONICA Yeah. She got in and when she drove by the burial grounds she disappeared right out of her car.

BRINDLE Did not!

VERONICA That's what she said.

RJ So you think she's there now?

POGO According to the logic of string theory, everything is connected along wavy strings. The strings connect like a circle. She is probably buried in the cemetery but her spirit travels as far as the strings will let her. When she gets in a car the electrical…

BRINDLE I hope they're not mad at me. I can just make out the tone of what they are saying. When that jolt of electricity…

VERONICA Yeah, what was that?

POGO The current threatens the waviness of the string and she is popped back into the ground. That would be my theory on why she disappears from the vehicles that pick her up. Check this out. I put the marshmallow here, push this button and it telescopes the marshmallow right over the fire. This wire conducts heat and lets me know…

LAKEISHA Something from Pogo's canoe.

POGO No. Not my canoe. I know what I'm doing.

LAKEISHA Let's go see if she's there.

RJ It's only a quarter of a mile.

VERONICA We're supposed to be in our cabins at 9:30.

LAKEISHA The counselors are still meeting. They won't even know we're gone. We'll be back long before cabin check.

RJ We have a half hour, plus. Come on.

LAKEISHA Come on.

VERONICA I need a flashlight.

RJ It's a full moon.

POGO My hands are sticky.

LAKEISHA Stay in single file. If we see a car coming, hit the ditch. Lay flat until they're gone.

BRINDLE There might be snakes.

RJ Muskrats are water RATS, and you're afraid of snakes?

VERONICA Be quiet.

(Sound of a car driving on a gravel road)

LAKEISHA *(Loud whisper)* Lay down!

(Bodies hitting the ground, laying in weeds, muffled sounds of "eiw! what's that; it's muddy; shhhh; lay still")

Scene VI

Back at Tribal Police Headquarters

(Police scanner sounds, electronic sounds and a beep, beep, beep before a magazine is slammed on a table)

SUE MOCCASIN That gol'darned Jiggs. Out in the woods again! Cover-all ain't over for another half hour. Chief will be mad as hell if I drag him out of there now. Some people's children never learn. Taser? Mace? Flashlight? I'm gonna deal with this underage, punk juvenile delinquent myself this time. Tired of these no good rez punks trying to ruin my marriage.

(Door slams, car engine starts)

Scene VII

At the exit road by the burial grounds

VERONICA Ms. Bach said she stands right here at the north corner of the exit road.

LAKEISHA Hey, Woman Who Never Exits, are you here?

VERONICA Knock it off.

BRINDLE She's not here. Let's go.

RJ Another eBay hoax.

(Sound of car)

VERONICA Car!

(Sound of kids laying down in ditch – shh; quiet)

RJ Hey Keister, your warm hand on my leg feels so good.

LAKEISHA That's not me you pervert, shuttup!

VERONICA I don't see any lights.

BRINDLE Oh, great, we got a ghost car.

POGO There's a woman standing up there.

LAKEISHA No way.

POGO Serious. I'll be back.

BRINDLE Don't leave us.

SUE MOCCASIN *(Yelling)* Jiggs, your gig is up. Get your flat-ass, Indian butt up here *(Sound of kids jumping up, running into each other, stumbling, running away)*

RJ Help, she's got me!!

(Sound of Mace being sprayed)

RJ My eyes!

RJ *(Crying)* You guys, come back.

LAKEISHA *(Muffled whisper)* He's hurt.

VERONICA Is that a cop?

SUE MOCCASIN Shuttup Jiggs. I've had it up to here with your fooling around. Just cause

your uncle sits on the tribal council doesn't give you free reign on the rez.

VERONICA *(in a scared voice)* Rain on the rez?

RJ I'm not Jiggs.

SUE MOCCASIN I'm taking you in for resisting arrest, attacking a police officer.

VERONICA Where are the guys?

LAKEISHA *(Standing up hollering)* Let him go now!

SUE MOCCASIN An accomplice. Not Squirrel. Where you hiding him? Come here girlie; let me see your face.

(LAKEISHA walking from ditch to gravel road; sound of electricity. LAKEISHA moans in pain and a thud of her falling to the ground.)

SUE MOCCASIN Taser Crazer! Your little girlfriend can't help you now Jiggs.

RJ I am NOT Jiggs. Are you out of your mind you over-sized fascist witch.

(Electrical zap; RJ moans and thuds to ground.)

SUE MOCCASIN I like this Taser.

(Turning body over)

Uh! You're not Jiggs.

(Sound of car door slamming, and car taking off, throwing gravel. We hear a whirring sound approaching.)

Scene VIII

At the exit road by the burial grounds

VERONICA *(Scared whisper)* Pogo?

(Whirring sound and sound of leaves blowing helicopter sounds)

POGO What did she do?

VERONICA Zapped them.

POGO Where's Brindle?

VERONICA What is that thing?

POGO Helicopter that I just sort of threw together from parts. Help me get these straps around them. We need to get them out of here before the KB-Ops show up.

VERONICA KB-Ops?

POGO RJ's protectors. It'll be a federal case if they find him like this on tribal land. Buckle her up in that other strap, then I'm gone. Meet you back at camp. You're going to have to run. Listen.

(Sound of big helicopters in the far distance)

POGO Run.

(Whirring sound of POGO's small helicopter)

Scene IX

At the exit road by the burial grounds

WOMAN WHO NEVER EXITS *(in a distinctive rez voice)* They never learn. There are things you can never explain. Things happen on this reservation that never happen anywhere else. Sue Moccasin would make a better Chief than her gambling husband. She is a better Chief. They had their first kid when she was sixteen. His uncle got him the Chief's job. He had to fill the chairman's freezer with musky all one winter. But Sue Moccasin's old man has been Chief of Police ever since. Sue does a fine job in the position.

Each year our reservation provides space for these misfit youth. They come and play music. Not the kind of music I want to hear, but music. I like country, or good old rock and roll. Pow-wow music is good too. You know, it's not their fault. Their parents are all too busy. Their parents don't know how to slow down and see the kids grow. So, they ship them here.

To breathe the fresh air. Swim in our magic waters. Roam the woods and hear the trees talk. Although most of them don't hear that good. That Brindle kid knows something the rest of them don't. Pogo, he's a different story. All that Indian wealth. Might just be the first Indian Einstein. And RJ. Is he Cherokee? Is he one of ours? Who am I to judge? I wonder what that Taser did to the R.F.I.D. chip in his hand? Did it fry the circuit or just the skin covering it? And the girls. I have a fondness for good strong Indian women. Most will say LaKeisha isn't one of ours cause her daddy's black. But you saw how she stood up unafraid to protect her friend. Even though RJ doesn't know how to be a girl's friend. We need strong women at home like her. Will she get lost in the other world out there? Veronica, she just needs some time to grow. Lost children are lost children no matter how you look at it.

(Car comes along the road.)

Here's my ride. Ahneen nii-jii. Going to the casino? *(Car door slams. Car drives off.)*

Cusi Cram

Biography

Cusi Cram is a playwright, screenwriter, filmmaker, and occasional performer. Her plays have been produced by: Primary Stages, LAByrinth Theater Company, The Denver Center, Princeton's Lewis Center for the Arts, The Echo Theater, The Williamstown Theater Festival, South Coast Repertory, New Georges, and on stages large and small all over this fine country. Her theater work has been generously supported with residencies and prizes from The Bogliasco Foundation, the Camargo Foundation, The Herrick Foundation, Ford Foundation, Space on Ryder Farm, and the Stillpoint Fund. Her  plays are published by: Samuel French, Broadway Publishing, and Playscripts.

She's also written many teleplays and pilots for both kids and adults and worked as a writer on Showtime's *The Big C*, starring Laura Linney, for several seasons. She is a long-time writer on WGBH's children's program *Arthur* for which she has received three Emmy nominations. Cusi recently directed her first film, *Wild and Precious*, through AFI's Directing Workshop for Women where it won The Adrienne Shelly and Nancy Mallone Awards and played at over twenty festivals nationwide.

She teaches playwriting and screenwriting in the Fordham/Primary Stages Playwriting program and in NYU's Dramatic Writing Department. She is a graduate of Brown University and the Lila Acheson American Playwright's Program at Juilliard. She lives in Greenwich Village with her husband, the award-winning writer/actor Peter Hirsh, and their two champagne tabbies.

Artistic statement

The Wild Inside was the first play that I wrote for specific actors. LAByrinth Theater Company in New York had proposed that I write something for members of the company, so I asked some of the actors I wanted to work with if there were things they were aching to do on stage that they had never done before. One actor (quite macho, I might add) said he wanted to really "be a woman", not "play a woman" but rather inhabit a woman's essence. Hence, Bob and Paloma were born. Another actor wanted to play someone who wasn't nice, he got Benito. And another actor wanted to really be in love on stage, I concocted the part of Isabel for her. Lonesome George was inspired by the physical presence and vibe of an actor in the company. There was something about the way he moved through life that reminded me of a very wise tortoise.

I also had written a few plays that took place in living rooms and apartments, so I wanted to set something in a more fluid and magical world. I had been to the Galapagos (I was the guest of someone on a celebrity cruise) and I felt it could be a fun and unexpected place to set a play. I think what might be different about this play from some of my other work is its more overtly playful tone. *Midsummer Night's Dream* is one of my favorite plays and I wanted to bring some of that farcical romping into this world. The stakes are high but one senses things will work out in the end. I also loved the idea of a TV family stuck on a deserted island, they are so exposed and they can't hide behind their celebrity, so as the play progresses everyone has to ultimately face who they really are and what they want. In a quasi-Darwinian way, all the characters have to adapt to their new circumstances and their new selves.

Many of the themes of the play, the possibility/impossibility of change, the complicated nature of love, the weirdness of being on television and the complexity of Latino identity and identity in general are themes I return to again and again in my work. I think being a mutt—I am half Bolivian and half Scottish—has poised me for better or worse, to always feel like a bit of an outsider wherever I am, so identity, both cultural and personal are subjects that I am always questioning. What does it mean to be Latino? What does it mean to be Latino but not feel particularly Latino? What does it mean to be American and half Latino? And because from a very young age I was a professional actor, I think I am also questioning what it means to perform complicated identities on stage. There are often characters who are actors in my work, perhaps because at a very fundamental level, I feel like I am an actor first. I love actors. I write for actors. I am so grateful for their bravery and bareness on stage. This play was written for some of my favorite actors in the world. It wouldn't exist without them.

Production history

The Wild Inside was written for LAByrinth Theater Company and was a part of the 2009 Barn Series at the Public Theater and was subsequently developed at the Lark Playwright's Development Center, Primary Stages and with students in the Department of Theater at Fordham University in a production directed by Jackson Gay.

It was written for: Carlo Alban, Julian Acosta, Yetta Gottesman, Florencia Lozano, Sal Inzerillo, Paula Pizzi, and is dedicated to their inspired artistry.

19 *The Wild Inside*
Cusi Cram

Characters

LONESOME GEORGE   A Tortoise. Ancient. Tired. A poet with a shell.

CORAZON   Latina, 30–45. Unexpected, glamorous, and full of longing. A tour guide. English is not her first language.

BOB   Latino, 35–45. A TV actor. Does not seem quite real, until he does.

CARLA   Latina, 35–45. A TV actress. Does not seem quite real until she does.

ISABEL   Latina, 25–30. Not an actress. Always seems real.

BENITO   Latino, 18–24. A TV actor. Spoiled with very hidden depths.

Setting

An island in the Eastern Pacific.
One of the Galapagos Islands.
An Island that still has tortoises.

PART 1

Lights fade up slowly to reveal Lonesome George—the oldest living tortoise in the entire world and the last of his kind. He sits. He looks. He has been around for centuries, literally.

LONESOME GEORGE Endurance.
Overrated.
Misunderstood.
One good year is better than many mediocre ones.
Time teaches you things but then you get so old you forget what you have learnt.
Then, there's the body.
It lets you down.
I was never vigorous.
My species is slow and steady, steady and slow. But we get things done.
I eat leaves, grass, lots of grass, day after day, grass.
I mated. Watched eggs hatch. Raised little ones that grew and grew for forty years.

Then one day, there was no one left to mate with, no more little ones
to raise.
Just me.
I outlived everyone. Not by choice but by chance.
I still do tortoise things. Slowly. But I do them.
I have aches.
Century old aches.
And I'm not always steady.
I miss the steadiness.
I miss not knowing what lies ahead.
I know now.
I know.

(Lights up on CORAZON, BENITO, ISABEL, CARLA and BOB. CORAZON leads them over rocky terrain very quickly and skillfully in three-inch heels and a short skirt.)

CORAZON Everyone be careful. People tend to twist their ankles on the rocks.

CARLA Did you hear that Bob?

BOB My shoes have extra ankle support.

(BOB holds up his leg and displays his shoe. CARLA barely glances at his shoe.)

CARLA Look at that! Shame they're so HIDEOUS.

(ISABEL wears flip flops.)

ISABEL My ankles are killing me.

BOB What you need is extra ankle support, Isabel.

(Pointing to CORAZON who is far ahead of them.)

ISABEL She seems to do OK without ankle support. *(whispering to Carla)* Do you think there's something off about her?

BOB Golf?

CARLA She said OFF.

BOB I love golf. But you can't play golf here.

ISABEL It's useless.

BENITO What I wanna know is why she's wearing fuck-me-cross-eyed pumps on a hike?

ISABEL Inappropriate language and thoughts, Benito.

CARLA I don't think Corazon is cross-eyed.

BOB Who's cross-eyed?

BENITO I said...her pumps could make you cross-eyed.

CARLA Did someone say humps?

BOB Now just who is cross-eyed?

CORAZON Is something wrong?

ISABEL *I* said silly me, my shoes are untied.

BOB and CARLA Silly you. Tie your shoe.

(ISABEL lamely pretends to tie her flip flop.)

CORAZON Gather round, gather round. I have a question for you.

BOB Corazon has a question.

CARLA Imagine that!

ISABEL Imagine what?

CARLA What?

BOB What?

ISABEL Why do I bother?

CORAZON It's more of riddle than a question.

BENITO BO-RING.

CORAZON Here is my question: Is an amoeba as well adapted to their environment as a New Yorker is to their small and expensive apartment?

BENITO Who cares about some amoeba?

CORAZON I do. I care.

BENITO Well, I don't.

ISABEL Tone, Benito.

BENITO What tone?

CARLA I like the word amoeba.

BOB Evocative.

ISABEL What does it evoke, exactly?

BOB Good question.

CARLA Bob can't really answer questions.

CORAZON Can anyone else answer *my* question?

ISABEL I would say, an amoeba is the same as a Native New Yorker...in relation to their apartments, I mean... environments.

CORAZON They are equally adapted, that is correct. Darwin believed there was no higher or lower form of evolution.

BOB I did not know that.

CARLA I don't know anything about Darwin.

BOB Me neither. Not a thing.

CARLA We should get a book Bob. Maybe a Darwin for Dummies?

CORAZON Imagine. It could have been on this very rock, looking at this very expanse of horizon where Darwin realized evolution is merely a combination of chance and necessity.

CARLA This very rock he thought, chance.

BOB Necessity, looking at these waves.

CARLA and BOB Beautiful.

CORAZON And now...

BENITO Lunch?

CORAZON Something better than lunch. Follow me.

(CORAZON begins to skillfully climb a hill in her heels. Everyone follows her.)

ISABEL How do you do it? In those heels?

CORAZON I've adapted to my environment.

ISABEL But in heels?

CORAZON I've done far more dangerous things in heels.

ISABEL Did you study science....somewhere?

CORAZON I am a student of nature, human and mother.

ISABEL And is there a place, a university where you got a degree in that? Mother Nature U?

CORAZON You ask a lot of questions.

ISABEL You avoid answering them.

CORAZON Science is not organized common sense.

ISABEL Was that an answer?

(The group arrives in front of LONESOME GEORGE.)

CORAZON Ladies and Gentleman, it gives me great pleasure to introduce you to Lonesome George.

BENITO That is one big motherfucking turtle.

CORAZON Tortoise. George is a tortoise and a magnificent specimen of his species—the Geochelone Elephnatopus Abingdoni.

LONESOME GEORGE *(to CORAZON)* You are quite a specimen, yourself.
Also magnificent.

CORAZON Notice his unusually long neck—adapted to reach for leaves from higher branches native to this island.

LONESOME GEORGE Whatever you do, don't stop looking at me.
I'm not sure I exist without your gaze.

CORAZON George is two hundred years old.

LONESOME GEORGE 192. I'm 192. Not two hundred. Not yet.

BOB 200, now that's a lot of years.

CARLA Very astute, Bob.

CORAZON Imagine what he's seen. Imagine what he's endured.

ISABEL He must be exhausted.

GEORGE Not near you, near you I feel spry and manly.
I feel alive.
ALIVE!

BENITO I'm exhausted. Is the tour done soon?

ISABEL Focus, Benito. Focus.

BENITO On what? The old turtle?

CORAZON Tortoise. There is speculation that George may very well have encountered Darwin when the Beagle explored these islands.

CARLA Thrilling.

BOB Thrilling AND fascinating.

CARLA And historical.

BENITO Who was Darwin again?

ISABEL Benito have you not listened to a single thing Corazon said?

BENITO I was looking at those birds...hee hee. They got such a funny name. Hee hee. And they got those blue feet.

CORAZON There's always someone, who can't quite get over the fact that there's a bird called the blue footed booby.

BENITO Hee hee. She said booby.

ISABEL I'm sorry.

BENITO Iz, she said booby.

CARLA He's young.

BOB Ah, youth.

CARLA Still amused at life.

BOB He's lucky.

ISABEL He's an idiot.

BENITO Don't call me an idiot in front of other people.

CORAZON Benito, do remember that bird I showed you earlier?

BENITO The booby. Hee. Hee.

CORAZON The other one?

BENITO The one that wasn't the booby. Hee. Hee.

ISABEL It's a waste of time, Corazon.

CORAZON Remember, there's no higher or lower form of evolution.

ISABEL Darwin never met Benito.

BENITO What's up your ass today?

(ISABEL glares at BENITO.)

BOB Now kids, pipe down. Let's listen to Corazon.

ISABEL I'm not a kid.

CARLA Normally, I'm not interested in birds. But today, today I am.

BOB Tell us all about birds, Corazon.

CORAZON I showed you a finch, Benito.

BENITO I don't remember.

ISABEL See. Some "species" are incapable of evolving.

CORAZON Until they have to. There is a moment, a moment when evolution is inevitable, a species must change; a moment of punctuated equilibrium.

CARLA I am lost. But I don't mind. Not one bit.

BOB Me neither. I'm absorbing something.

CARLA I'm a sponge.

BOB A sponge, soaking it all up.

CARLA That is what sponges do, Bob.

CORAZON The bird I showed you was a finch; it had a broad, wide beak for cracking seeds. Remember?

BENITO All birds look alike.

CORAZON Now, this island has tons of seeds. But Marchena, the next island over, is covered in cactuses and finches there have long, down-curved beaks, perfect for reaching into cactus flowers.

BENITO I get it.

ISABEL No you don't.

BENITO The birds have the right kinda beaks for where they live.

CARLA He is so quick.

BOB Clever, almost.

CORAZON Over time the finches have developed physical traits that enable them to survive.

GEORGE Sometimes, I feel as if I may not be able to survive without you.
But all I do is survive.

CORAZON Just think, the theory of evolution by means of natural selection was born from a finch's beak.

CARLA I wish I'd been born from a beak.

CORAZON Come a little closer.

(Everyone gets closer to LONESOME GEORGE.)

LONESOME GEORGE What can I do to make you see me, the way I see you?

CORAZON Notice George's stunning shell or carapace.

GEORGE If I give you my profile?

(GEORGE turns his head in profile.)

CORAZON Observe its elegant dome shape.

GEORGE Or look deep into your eyes?

(GEORGE stares at CORAZON.)

CORAZON What a cathedral of a shell!

GEORGE Or look away from you in a mysterious manner.

(GEORGE looks out at the sea.)

Will you see me, the way I see you.

(CORAZON turns away from GEORGE.)

CORAZON I like to think of him as the Notre Dame of the Galapagos.

BENITO Can he do anything?

CORAZON He can eat. George is over five hundred pounds.

LONESOME GEORGE 487 pounds.
I've recently slimmed down.
Slimmed down for you.
Do you see what I've done.
Done for you?
See me. Please.

CORAZON Everyone knows that "galapago" means saddle in Spanish?

CARLA I feel like I knew once.

BOB It rings a bell. I do have, some, some Spanish.

ISABEL I don't speak much.

CARLA I speak a little.

BENITO I don't speak Spanish.

CORAZON But how is that possible?

BENITO We're American, that's how. You got a problem with that?

CORAZON I have no problem with Americans speaking English. But on TV you play Latinos.

BENITO Latinos in LA. In America. I think you have a problem with America.

ISABEL Easy, Benito.

CORAZON But throughout North and South America you are the symbol of a happy Latino family.

CARLA The Family Garcia is a happy family, on and off the set.

BOB HAPPY. Happy.

CORAZON Ah ha! You don't speak Spanish because it's not necessary to your environment.

ISABEL Plenty of people speak Spanish in LA.

CORAZON But you don't NEED to speak Spanish. Natural selection at work in the world of sitcoms.

BENITO Lay off about the Spanish.

LONESOME GEORGE You keep talking to her like that and I'll bite into you as if you were a cactus flower.
I speak Spanish. Yo hablo Espanol, Corazon.

CORAZON Alright then, in Spanish, "GALAPAGO" means…

BENITO Saddle. You said that already.

ISABEL Interrupting, Benito. No interrupting.

LONESOME GEORGE Keep on interrupting so I can stare.

Stare at her legs.

She is such a long-legged mammal.

None of my wives had long legs.

They all had legs like football players.

BENITO Can I ride the turtle?

CORAZON He's a tortoise and DO NOT, I repeat, DO NOT on any account touch him. He has no immunity to your germs. You could kill him.

LONESOME GEORGE I would be happy to be killed by your touch.

Kill me with your touch.

Kill me.

Kill me.

CORAZON Now, if you'll just follow me. We can go and see the sea lions!

LONESOME GEORGE But the sea lions don't notice,

Notice your perfect parts.

CARLA Didn't we swim with sea lions somewhere, Bob?

BOB Somewhere we swam with dolphins. And it was wonderful.

CARLA Magical. Almost.

BENITO I don't swim.

ISABEL Come on, Benito. You've never even seen a sea lion.

BENITO I like it here with Lonesome Joe.

CORAZON His name is George.

BENITO Well, I call him Joe.

CORAZON You're not at all like the character you play on the show. He has that funny laugh.

BOB People love the laugh.

CARLA They stop him everywhere.

BOB And want him to do the laugh.

BENITO I DON'T WANT TO TALK ABOUT THE LAUGH!!

ISABEL We don't talk about the laugh. REMEMBER???

CARLA I forgot.

BOB Oopsy.

CORAZON *(to ISABEL)* I don't remember you from the show.

ISABEL I'm not on the show.

BENITO *(to CORAZON)* No more questions, Cora-zone.

(CORAZON begins to leave. She turns around.)

CORAZON Don't touch George. He's the last of his kind.

LONESOME GEORGE The very last.

(GEORGE retreats into his shell.)

CORAZON This way to the sea lions. They're mating.

CARLA Exciting.

BOB Something new. New and kinky. Such fun!

CARLA Naughty sea lions here we come!

(CARLA, CORAZON and BOB exit. BENITO takes out his phone and starts playing with it.)

ISABEL "Punctuated equilibrium" blah, blah, blah. Darwin THIS and THAT nah nah nah. In high school, I was good at science. Really good. *(beat)* I wanted to see the sea lions.

BENITO Go.

(ISABEL looks out at the blue, blue Pacific. BENITO looks intently at his phone.)

ISABEL I was wondering…

BENITO How I get reception? Good phone.

ISABEL I never wonder about phones.

(A moment, while BENITO looks at something crushing on his phone.)

BENITO Give me a fucking break.

(BENITO looks for something to punch. He looks at GEORGE. He walks away. He kicks a rock. That hurts, so he punches it. That hurts even more.)

ISABEL You shouldn't punch rocks. I mean, what's the point?

(BENITO looks at his phone again.)

BENITO Fuck there's a video. Aw, she she REALLY pisses me off.

ISABEL If you have three girlfriends one of them is bound to piss you off. Is it Cindy?

BENITO I just never get a moment, a single moment of calm. I mean, where the fuck is my Zen down time?

(BENITO's phone rings. It's the tune to a really raunchy rap song. He looks at the number. He does not pick up.)

ISABEL I wanna watch the sea lions get it on.

(ISABEL begins to go.)

BENITO Don't go, Iz.

ISABEL *(half heartedly)* Wanna visualize white light or golden clouds or snow? Or Cindy being eaten alive?

BENITO This isn't about Cindy.

ISABEL Ok then, Avocado.

BENITO Her name is Avo-CANDA.

ISABEL That's not a name, it's something you don't wanna catch.

BENITO Avocanda's hot.

(BENITO looks at his phone.)

This is just…just…like OBSCENE. Does anyone on this planet have fucking manners anymore?

ISABEL Nope. Nobody has fucking manners anymore.

(BENITO goes back to his phone.)

BENITO This is just, mind fucking blowing, Izzy.

ISABEL I am Isabel. Not Iz. Or Izzy. Isabel. I'm gonna go see the sea lions.

(ISABEL begins to leave. BENITO looks up from his phone.)

BENITO But I need your take.

ISABEL I won't have one.

BENITO You always gotta a take.

ISABEL It feels wrong…it feels wrong…after last night.

BENITO Riiight. Last night. *(beat)* You're something else, Isabel, you know that?

ISABEL I do. *(beat)* Like good something else?

BENITO Like wildly something else. And…and…

ISABEL Use your words.

BENITO If I hadn't felt so queasy from being on the boat…

ISABEL What? What would have been different?

BENITO You know…*(whispering)* It woulda been longer. I never done it on a boat before. Messed with my rhythm and shit.

(BENITO plays with his phone some more.)

ISABEL There are things…countless things you don't know about me Benito.

BENITO I know stuff about you. After last night…I know you like it a little rough. HA.

ISABEL Besides that titillating new factoid, what you really know is that I am here to mind you. I'm your minder. That's my actual job title. I'm here to talk you down from your huge, sometimes dangerous, mostly annoying rages.

BENITO And you are good at that shit. Like you should have a show.

ISABEL I suck at it. I learnt some stuff from a tape.

(BENITO goes back to his phone.)

BENITO So she starts: "I never wanted to hurt you, baby boy." Then stop doing it. Again and again.

ISABEL Yeah. HUH. Right. Ever think maybe Avocado's TEXTS are of absolutely no consequence to me WHATSOEVER!

(BENITO looks up from his phone.)

BENITO Wassup, Iz?

ISABEL It's ISABEL. Say my name you FUCK-ING FUCK. SAY MY GOD DAMN NAME!

(ISABEL takes BENITO's phone and tosses it into the Pacific. A long moment.)

ISABEL I'm not sorry.

BENITO But that's my…PHONE.

ISABEL Still not sorry.

BENITO It wasn't Avocando, fuck-wad.

ISABEL Don't call me fuck-wad.

BENITO It was my Mom. She got arrested for possession. Again. And some ass hole taped the bust. There's a meme. My mom's a fucking meme!

(Pause.)

ISABEL I'm a fuck-wad.

(BENITO paces around.)

BENITO I feel naked without my phone.

ISABEL We were naked last night.

BENITO I know. It's not like I forgot.

ISABEL You were acting like you had.

BENITO It's my way.

ISABEL You need a better way.

BENITO That's why you tossed my phone?

ISABEL I'm just trying to survive here, Benito.

BENITO Was my phone killing you, or something?

ISABEL Yes. Yes it was.

(A pause.)

Something happened. We anchored on this island and BAM, I wanted to shove my tongue in your mouth. Indefinitely. I still do.

BENITO Can we do some breathing or downward doggy and not THIS, please.

ISABEL It's strange because in the past, in the past, I was physically repelled by you.

BENITO Harsh.

ISABEL But now, now I just wanna push you against a wall, or a…or a beach and force you to feel me. Which is puzzling when you pause to think about it.

BENITO Why, why is it puzzling?

ISABEL Because last night was terrible. Like the worst, almost ever. I really want to fuck you but it has to get better.

BENITO I was queasy. The boat. First time, first time is always…

ISABEL It MUST get better.

BENITO I got a lot going on here. My Mom. Ounce of cocaine mostly on her face. It's the number one video on YouTube!

ISABEL There is always a catastrophe with you. But somehow you always manage to come out on top. I want…I want to BE like you. The world is made for angry, small-minded people just like you.

BENITO This how you flirt?

ISABEL Teach me to take life in my mouth as if it were a bone and gnaw at it. I want to gnaw at life the way you do.

BENITO What you need to do is some of that breathing. Like that deep Buddah belly crap.

ISABEL I don't want to breathe. I want to live.

BENITO Look at view. Breathe it in.

ISABEL Fuck the view. What I need you is you, Benito.

(BENITO *tries to find something to do with his hands.*)

ISABEL What are you doing?

BENITO Air texting. Fuck!

(BENITO *runs off-stage. ISABEL watches him for a second and runs after him and exits.*)

ISABEL (*yelling*) We were having a conversation! Do you even know what that is!!!

(BOB *and* CARLA *enter wearing sunglasses and swim suits. They look very glamorous. Almost too glamorous.*)

BOB But she wants to visit again. Maybe stay.

CARLA Stay?

BOB She's aching for another visit. Give her a teensy one.

CARLA There is nothing "teensy" about her!

BOB It'll be fun.

CARLA Fun for you, Bob.

BOB She's fun.

CARLA I find her boring.

BOB Not boring, caring.

CARLA Right, boring.

BOB Caring is boring?

CARLA I married you, Bob.

BOB Just an itsy bitsy visit?

CARLA I married YOU for better or worse.

BOB Exactly!

CARLA This… is WORSE THAN WORSE.

BOB What are you saying, Carla?

CARLA What do think I am saying, Bob?

BOB Say it if you are going to say it, Carla.

(*A beat*)

CARLA She's dull.

BOB Gentle.

CARLA Weak.

BOB You. You are being unreasonable.

CARLA Please! I've been a saint. I've been a martyr.

BOB How have you been a martyr? I want dates and times of your martyrdom.

CARLA I'm done with martyring. Done.

BOB You can't be done.

CARLA I can be whatever I like. I'm on TV.

(CORAZON *appears at the top of a hill.*)

CORAZON Come quickly! Two sea lions are mating! And a flock of flamingos are watching.

(CARLA *waves dramatically and raises her voice;* CORAZON *isn't that far away.*)

CARLA COMING! WE LOVE TO WATCH!

BOB (*waving*) CAN'T GET ENOUGH OF IT! (*to* CARLA) Just let it percolate, Carla.

(BOB *and* CARLA *begin to scramble up the rocks.* CORAZON *disappears behind a rock.*)

CARLA (*whispering*) Discussion over, Bob.

BOB (*whispering fiercely*) This discussion is not over and you know it.

CARLA (*a fiercer whisper*) I never want to hear her name uttered in my presence, that's how over it is, Bob.

BOB (*so fierce it's almost a spit*) Paloma!

CARLA (*another spit whisper*) Traitor!

BOB (*harsher still*) Abandoner!

CARLA (*victoriously harsh*) That's not even a word.

CORAZON (*offstage*) You've got to see this! The male has a VERY pronounced hump on his forehead.

(CARLA *and* BOB *exit.*)

CARLA and BOB (*offstage*) We LOVE humps!

(ISABEL *runs on stage.*)

ISABEL Benito!!! Let's just talk through this.

(ISABEL *looks around. She shakes her head.*)

I hope he doesn't do something stupid like punch an iguana.

(*She plops herself on a rock next to* GEORGE. *He looks at her. She looks at him.* GEORGE *cranes his neck more toward* ISABEL.)

Maybe I should just stay here? They could call me "Lonesome Iz". We could be alone together.

(BENITO's *cell phone washes up on the shore.* GEORGE *picks up the phone in his mouth.*)

Typical. I can't even make a grand gesture.

(ISABEL begins to cry. She starts to sob. GEORGE begins to bat the phone with his paws.)

What was I thinking? I wasn't thinking.

(ISABEL reaches for the phone. GEORGE puts his paw over it.)

Planning on calling someone?

(GEORGE pounds on the keys with his paws. He shakes his head and then begins to press keys with his nose. ISABEL stares out. GEORGE drops the phone in front of her.)

Can you please just eat it.

(GEORGE pushes it in front of her. She picks it up.)

I'll give it back. It's the only thing he has real feelings for.

(GEORGE shakes his head. He makes a strange noise.)

Did you just burp? Gross.

(GEORGE raises one of his paws very slowly and points to the phone.)

What?

(He keeps pointing toward the phone. ISABEL finally looks at it. She reads off the phone.)

Doubt thou the stars are fire;
Doubt that the sun doth move;
Doubt truth to be a liar;
But never doubt I love.

(ISABEL looks confused.)

Whatthefuck! You didn't write this… because… because tortoises don't text Shakespeare.

(GEORGE shakes his head.)

FUCK! I don't have enough money to have a nervous breakdown.

(GEORGE points to the phone. ISABEL looks at the message. ISABEL drops the phone as if it were on fire.)

I'm not in love. I'm not.

(GEORGE looks at ISABEL.)

Don't give me that look.

(CARLA, BOB and BENITO scramble over the rocks. GEORGE picks up the cell phone in his mouth and then hides in his shell.)

CARLA Yoo hoo! *(pointing to BENITO)* Look who we found throwing stones at pigeons.
BOB Naughty, naughty.

BENITO They were finches.
CARLA What's wrong with my little TV son?
BENITO I hate those finches and their stupid beaks.
CARLA TV Mommy wants to know why your little perfect face looks so glum glum glum.
BENITO I lost my phone.
ISABEL You didn't lose it.
BOB It'll turn up.
ISABEL I tossed it into the ocean.
BOB Well then, probably not. There are tides. Complicated tides on islands.
CARLA Don't you worry pumpkin. I'll get you another phone when we get to somewhere where TV Mommy can buy one.
BENITO Really?
ISABEL The thing is, we won't be anywhere but islands like this one for a week.
CARLA TV Mommy will think of something. I always think of something. Right, TV Daddy?
ISABEL On the show, on the show, your character Conchata is very good at getting the family Garcia out of scrapes, but this isn't the show. I don't want Benito to get his hopes up. When his hopes get dashed, he has tantrums.
ISABEL Benito, you won't be able to get a phone for a week.
BENITO Carla'll figure something out.
ISABEL She won't. In real life, she's not capable of coherent thoughts.

(A pause. Everyone looks out to sea.)

BOB We watched sea lions have sex.
CARLA It was strange but beautiful in the way strange things are.
BOB Strange things can be so beautiful.
CARLA I already said that, Bob.
BOB We swam with the sea lions.
CARLA *I* swam with them. Bob waded.
BOB Waded is a strong word, Carla.
CARLA Waded is the right word.
BOB You're not telling the whole story.
CARLA That's because there is no story. Bob was afraid of the baby sea lions. So he waded. I swam and it was delicious. I did a summersault and they did a summersault. I felt like Brooke Shields in *The Blue Lagoon*. Only, I didn't have that blond Adonis with me, I had Bob. At least I think it was Bob. Maybe it was someone ELSE, who I saw wading like a teenage girl inches from the shore.
BOB Carla. Easy. Now, about the wading…

CARLA No one wants to hear about the wading, Bob. It's not the kind of thing people are interested in.

BOB I waded because I saw a very large mother sea lion cresting a nearby cliff and Corazon told us to be careful of mother sea lions. In her lecture she said, a Swedish tourist had been nearly drowned by a mother sea lion.

CARLA But the Swedish tourist didn't actually drown, did she Bob?

BOB Well, I don't want to nearly drown, nearly drowning can't be fun. Hence the wading. I just want to be clear, clear about the wading.

(Everyone looks out to sea. GEORGE peeks out of his shell and holds the cell phone in his mouth; he does his version of waving it in the air. ISABEL sees him. No else does. ISABEL takes a deep breath in.)

ISABEL Benito and I fucked last night.

CARLA Hands over my ears. *(putting her hands over her ears)* La la la. I don't want to hear it. He is my son, at least on TV.

BENITO *(to ISABEL)* Whathefuck?

ISABEL It wasn't very good. The fucking. Like south of so, so.

BENITO Shut the fuck up.

ISABEL Why can't we talk to Bob and Carla about what happened last night?

BENITO I didn't have my SEA…legs.

ISABEL Even so, I was moved, unexpectedly moved by Benito.

(ISABEL looks at GEORGE. He has hidden the cell phone under one of his paws.)

This must seem strange, very strange to the both of you, maybe it doesn't because you're both so strange.

BOB We're strange?

CARLA How are we strange?

BENITO I don't think they're strange.

ISABEL They're like shadow people. You can't really see them.

CARLA Bob, we're shadow people.

BOB Shadow people, I like that. Mysterious.

CARLA Sexy.

ISABEL Anyway, other people, who are not shadow people might find my…feelings for Benito peculiar.

BOB Is attraction ever really peculiar? It's mysterious.

CARLA Sexy.

ISABEL OK. So let's just say, this attraction is unexpected.

BOB The best kind. The very best.

ISABEL I always thought I would feel the way I am feeling for someone who had something to offer me, some…wisdom.

CARLA Is wisdom sexy, Bob?

BOB Not my particular cup of tea but who am I to judge?

CARLA Quite right. Who are you to judge anything?

ISABEL So Carla and Bob do you think it's possible to have a satisfying and transformative emotional and sexual relationship with someone you disdain?

CARLA and BOB Yes.

BENITO I am so outta of here.

(BENITO begins to leave.)

ISABEL I wrote a poem for you this morning.

BENITO A poem?

ISABEL Yes.

CARLA There's something nice happening here. TV Mom approves.

BOB So does TV Dad. Something genuine.

CARLA Don't ruin it, Bob.

BOB I'm just describing.

CARLA Ruining.

BENITO You really wrote me a poem Isabel?

ISABEL It's not like it's good or anything.

BENITO Read it.

CARLA and BOB Read it, Isabel.

ISABEL I need to make something very clear…

BOB Let the poem do it. Poetry is clarity.

CARLA *(surprised)* Well said, Bob.

ISABEL Even though last night, was a grave, grave disappointment.

BENITO It wasn't that bad.

ISABEL He's very ALIVE.

CARLA So alive.

BOB Vital, even.

ISABEL I think he's the only person in the world who can make me feel alive again. I want to feel alive.

CARLA Me too.

BOB It's all I ever wanted. It's so hard. Why is it so hard?

BENITO What's everyone's talking about? Aren't we all alive? Read the poem, Isabel.

ISABEL Promise not to laugh.

BENITO Promise.

(ISABEL takes the poem out of her pocket.)

ISABEL Why not?
   Split me open with your lower lip?
   With a finger make me lose language.
   Turn me into another kind of animal

With your tongue's tip.
Turn me.
Turn me.
Turn me into all I have lost.
All I fear
Turn me into you.

Becoming you,
I could become all I ever was,
All I will be
And centuries more
I could be infinite
Wordless.
Yours.
I could be made simple by you.
I could be made simple.
Make me simple.

(ISABEL and BENITO look at each other for a long moment. GEORGE looks from one to the other. There is something electric in the air.)

ISABEL Say something.
CARLA and BOB Say what you're thinking.

(A beat)

BENITO I... really miss my phone!

(He runs off stage. ISABEL looks at GEORGE.)

ISABEL What the fuck am I doing?
CARLA and BOB Feeling.
ISABEL How do you do that? Spooky!
CARLA I think this could be good for Benito. Good or very bad. But something.
BOB Definitely something.
ISABEL Who have I become?
CARLA Don't ask.
BOB Too depressing.
ISABEL I'm not the kind of person to read love poems I WROTE. ALOUD.
BOB Interesting word choice.
ISABEL What word?
CARLA and BOB Love.
ISABEL I didn't mean love.

(ISABEL looks at GEORGE.)

I need him.
CARLA Desire and love, hard to differentiate.
BOB Impossible, even.
ISABEL I'm his employee.
BOB We call you his couch buddy.
CARLA You take such good care of our TV son. Sit on the couch next to him. Before you...
BOB He was pesky.
CARLA A little bit dangerous, even. And then you came along and you did things with him. What does she do with him, Bob?

BOB Yoga stretches.
CARLA Sometimes we wish you would be our couch buddy.
BOB Stretch with us.
CARLA We don't stretch enough.
BOB We don't do yoga.
CARLA and BOB We should.
ISABEL I... wish... I wish a sea lion would eat me.

(ISABEL begins to run.)

Benito, wait up! Benito!

(ISABEL exits. GEORGE goes back in his shell.)

CARLA I miss that.
BOB What?
CARLA The impulse to run after someone.
BOB I would still run after you, wherever you went.
CARLA There are no cameras here, we're on hiatus, Bob.
BOB I would run just like her.
CARLA As if your life depended on it?
BOB Every morning I wake up, scared to death you won't be there. I think, what if you ran away but didn't let me know you were running.
CARLA Only point of running is to be chased.
BOB Is that what you want, to be chased?
CARLA Yes.
BOB Then that's what I'll have to keep doing.

(They stare at each other for a moment.)

CARLA When you look at me that way, the years of little slights and HUGE disappointments, melt away.

(BOB takes CARLA in his arms and kisses her.)

CARLA Enough.

(They kiss again.)

You are enough, Bob.

(BOB pulls away.)

BOB You've never said that before.
CARLA You've never kissed so well.
BOB Interesting.
CARLA Only if you do it again.
BOB Fascinating, really.
CARLA Stop talking and keep kissing.
BOB I can't.
CARLA Make me simple. Do that. Like what Isabel said.
BOB I can't. *I* didn't kiss you. *She* did. When I kiss, I take. When she kisses, she gives.

(CARLA pulls away.)

CARLA Fuck you, Bob.

BOB *She* isn't so boring after all, is she Carla?

CARLA Go and wade with the baby sea lions! Go and wade, Bob.

BOB The truth always makes you angry.

CARLA I think we're done. Really done this time.

BOB You say that. But you always stay.

CARLA Not this time.

(*CARLA begins to leave.*)

BOB I'll chase you. She'll chase you.

CARLA I'll run so fast, you'll die trying to catch me.

BOB We'll find you and make you want her again.

CARLA Why is it always it so complicated with you?

BOB It isn't.

CARLA (*Pointing where BENITO and ISABEL have run*) It's not like them. Not anymore. Once, you were all I thought about. You were so handsome and tall and just a little unexpected. A tree of a man. I want to climb THAT tree again.

BOB Let me be a different tree.

CARLA I'm tired of this, Bob.

BOB Then let me hold you up.

CARLA You can't.

BOB But SHE can. SHE can hold you up.

(*CARLA goes to BOB. BOB strokes her hair gently. He transforms into PALOMA. He is gentler, more feminine, not campy. A woman.*)

PALOMA Shhh. Tranquila. Hush. The world cannot touch you here. When I hold you, you are safe. There is no fear. Tranquila. Don't worry. In my arms there is only comfort. I am comfort. Quiet comfort. Give me your mouth. I'll start with your mouth. So gently you will barely feel the air of my lips. Simple. So simple Shhh.

(*CORAZON enters and watches.*)

PALOMA Hay solamente amor aquí, amor y un gran abandon.

(*PALOMA kisses CARLA. PALOMA pulls away. In a deep masculine voice CARLA responds. She is now CHARLES. She speaks with an upper class British accent.*)

CHARLES What a strange specimen you are, rare, delicate and MINE.

(*They kiss. LONESOME GEORGE peeks out from his shell.*)

LONESOME GEORGE Something is changing. Moving forward because it must.

It has been so long. But today is different from every other day I've known.

It's time, time for change.

PART 2

Another part of the island. On a rock: A starfish, a rat's skull, and a large palm leaf, they are arranged artfully. CORAZON sits nearby and sketches them in a notebook. GEORGE stares. He stares long. He stares hard.

GEORGE Your neck, stretched as you draw,
Is a planet I want to discover,
Every ivory inch of it.

CORAZON I observe. I note. I calculate. And still NADA!

GEORGE If you saw me,
You would discover, discover just what you are looking for.

(*CORAZON gets up and throws down her notebook.*)

CORAZON It's never gonna happen.

LONESOME GEORGE What is it you want, Corazon?
Tell me,
Tell me,
I will do my best, my very best

To give it to you.

CORAZON One good idea. One theory. One thought that reinvents the world. Is that too much to ask for?

LONESOME GEORGE It's not a little thing.

CORAZON Because if you don't leave something HUGE and TRANSFORMATIVE behind, what's the point?

LONESOME GEORGE I was like you once, full of optimism and longing.

It took centuries for me to become a pessimist.

CORAZON Sometimes, I hate Darwin.

(*CORAZON returns to her notebook.*)

LONESOME GEORGE Then I hate him too.

CORAZON Who am I kidding? History won't remember me for anything in particular. "I wasted time and now time doth waste me."

LONESOME GEORGE "For now hath time made me his numbering clock:

My thoughts are minutes; and with sighs they jar
Their watches on unto mine eyes"
I know the poem, Corazon. I know the poem.

(ISABEL runs on, holding her poem.)

ISABEL Oh. Hey. Where is everybody?

CORAZON George and I were just catching up.

ISABEL *(cautiously)* And…what did he have to say?

CORAZON It was more of a monologue. He's a good listener.

ISABEL And a good texter.

(CORAZON looks puzzled.)

Joke. Where's the boat?

CORAZON Nearby, I'm sure. The wind does all sorts unexpected things here.

ISABEL Have you seen Benito?

CORAZON You seem to look for him quite a lot.

ISABEL It's my job. OK?

(CORAZON continues to sketch. ISABEL looks at the objects.)

I like the starfish. *(beat)* You must think I'm totally ridiculous.

CORAZON I just observe.

(GEORGE opens his mouth and makes a strange sound. CORAZON and ISABEL look at him.)

ISABEL Does he have indigestion, or something?

CORAZON This may sound crazy, but sometimes I think he's trying to talk to me.

(ISABEL looks at GEORGE.)

ISABEL Is that so impossible?

CORAZON In terms of evolution it is.

GEORGE Love is stronger than evolution.

(ISABEL looks at GEORGE. She has heard him. She is terrified.)

CORAZON He has such soulful eyes.

LONESOME GEORGE Only around you.

ISABEL *(to GEORGE)* Me?

CORAZON Who?

LONESOME GEORGE Her.

ISABEL Of course not me.

CORAZON I'm not following you.

ISABEL *(covering)* Of course not me… you're not drawing me, you're drawing some animal skull.

CORAZON *(little confused)* I don't really draw people. This is my notebook of scientific observations.

ISABEL Made any big discoveries? Like Darwin and his finches?

CORAZON *(curtly)* No I HAVEN'T.

ISABEL I didn't mean to diss Darwin. I mean the dude figured a lot of shit out.

CORAZON I am not a real scientist.

ISABEL But you know a lot about science.

CORAZON But I haven't discovered anything.

ISABEL Well…that can take a lifetime, right?

CORAZON I'm tired of waiting.

ISABEL Me too.

LONESOME GEORGE Me too!

CORAZON I have thoughts, though, big thoughts.

LONESOME GEORGE All my thoughts are about you, Corazon. Tell her.

ISABEL All my thoughts are about you, Corazon… *(covering)* and… and Darwin… uh… tell me a big thought, please.

LONESOME GEORGE I want to know your thoughts as if they were my own. Say it.

ISABEL I want to know your thoughts as if they were my own.

CORAZON That's a very kind thing to say, Isabel.

ISABEL Thanks?

CORAZON So, the more I look at nature closely—trace the veins of a palm leaf or draw the perfect geometry of a tortoise's belly, the more certain I am that there is no barrier between animal and man.

LONESOME GEORGE "O speak again, bright angel!"

(ISABEL gasps.)

CORAZON Totally dumb?

ISABEL No, it's just… does the wind by any chance sound like Shakespeare to you?

CORAZON Shakespeare?

ISABEL Uh… whenever it's windy, I hear Shakespeare.

(BOB/PALOMA and CARLA/CHARLES crest a hill and wave at ISABEL and PALOMA. PALOMA wears a sarong. CHARLES wears boxers.)

PALOMA Yoo-hoo!

ISABEL Hey, Bob, Carla.

PALOMA Maybe… just maybe I'm not Bob today.

CHARLES And perhaps today I am Charles and maybe, just maybe I am British.

(CHARLES and PALOMA kiss. GEORGE watches. It's a long, passionate kiss.)

ISABEL Yoo-hoo! Hellooo! You're not alone.

CHARLES Excuse us.

PALOMA Nothing to be ashamed of, mi amor. It's as natural as him.

(*PALOMA points to GEORGE.*)

CORAZON Where would our species be if it weren't for inexplicable moments of passion?

CHARLES Extinct.

LONESOME GEORGE Like me. Almost gone forever. Will anyone remember me?

ISABEL (*to GEORGE*) I'll remember you.

PALOMA Who?

CORAZON Me?

CHARLES I'm a tad bit confused.

ISABEL Um… if anyone, any of you become extinct, I'll remember you. I mean, if I'm not extinct too.

CHARLES Sad to think we could all be evolving toward extinction. All these centuries of work and change for naught.

CORAZON What does naught mean?

ISABEL and GEORGE Nothing.

(*Everyone takes in the thought of nothingness or naught.*)

PALOMA I know just what we need.

ISABEL A cave to crawl into?

CORAZON A lightning flash of inspiration?

LONESOME GEORGE To be remembered, no matter what?

CHARLES A stiff gin and tonic?

ISABEL That sounds really good.

PALOMA What we all need is a FIESTA.

LONESOME GEORGE People come and go from this island but they never stay and dance.

PALOMA We're not extinct yet. And THAT is cause for celebration.

CHARLES You, my dear Paloma, have a mind most singular and fine. A fiesta is just what we need.

ISABEL Why are you calling him Paloma?

LONESOME GEORGE What's in a name?

ISABEL I feel dizzy.

(*PALOMA waves and begins to exit.*)

PALOMA We'll meet you on the beach. Bring champagne and lanterns. Come as your wildest dream.

CHARLES (*to PALOMA*) You are my wildest dream, my little poppet.

PALOMA No YOU are mine.

CHARLES No you are MINE.

PALOMA I said it first.

CHARLES No I did, my dove.

(*CHARLES/CARLA and BOB/PALOMA coo off stage.*)

CORAZON Carla sounded very different.

ISABEL Sometimes, she likes to practice her English accent, though today it sounded much better than usual. Was Bob wearing a skirt?

LONESOME GEORGE A sarong.

CORAZON I have a crate of champagne buried in the mangroves on the west side of the island. I'll go and get it.

(*CORAZON gets her things together.*)

LONESOME GEORGE Say, "I love you, Corazon."

ISABEL I love you, Corazon.

CORAZON (*startled*) Thank you, Isabel. I'm touched. Deeply touched. People on my tours don't usually say that sort of thing to me. I… think you seem… nice too.

ISABEL I meant… love in the BROAD sense of the word—like in a Jesus/Buddah way.

CORAZON Oh, good. I'm so relieved. Not that…

ISABEL Yeah… No. It's just this island makes you love people and plants and TORTOISES. TORTOISES seem capable of GREAT love.

CORAZON Sometimes, I think George is the only true friend I've ever had.

LONESOME GEORGE Say, "I want more than friendship."

ISABEL He wants more than friendship.

CORAZON Who?

ISABEL I do. I mean, not with you. (*to GEORGE*) I can't do this.

CORAZON Can't do what?

ISABEL Uh… uh… what I've been doing. It's gotta stop… This thing with Benito. I love him. And he keeps running away from me, which is wildly… humiliating.

LONESOME GEORGE But I love her with all my heart.

ISABEL (*to GEORGE*) Then tell her.

CORAZON Her?

ISABEL HIM. I have to find HIM and tell HIM things, big things.

CORAZON I wish I knew what to say, unfortunately the human heart is not my area of expertise.

LONESOME GEORGE Let me teach you the geography of a tortoise's heart.

ISABEL (*to GEORGE*) Aw, that's really beautiful.

PALOMA What's beautiful?

ISABEL Love. Love is beautiful and devastating. (*to GEORGE*) I wish I could help you.

CORAZON Thank you, Isabel. I'm fine

ISABEL Good. You seem fine. Fine but alone.

CORAZON I've always been alone or felt like I was.

LONESOME GEORGE Me too.

ISABEL Me too. Corazon, you should think about your theory…

(ISABEL begins to leave.)

Animals. Humans. No difference.

(ISABEL bends down and peers around toward GEORGE.)

ISABEL *(to GEORGE)* Forgive me.

(GEORGE nods.)

CORAZON Isabel, are you alright?

ISABEL Yeah this is how I say I'm sorry, I bend down… yeah… ever since I was a little girl. 'Bye. bye.

(ISABEL exits. The wind gusts.)

CORAZON Did the wind just change directions? That's never happened before.

(GEORGE and CORAZON turn their heads toward each other at the exact same moment. CORAZON leaves. GEORGE cranes his neck around to watch her leave.
He then bends down and picks up BENITO's cell phone in his mouth. He drops it and begins to text with his paws. BENITO enters and sees GEORGE.)

BENITO Hey Lonesome Joe. Wassup? Feelin lonely?

(GEORGE is startled and knocks the phone over. BENITO sees his phone and rushes to it and picks it up. There is a text message on the phone. He reads it.)

BENITO Who wrote this?

(GEORGE looks in another direction. BEN-ITO looks at the phone.)

I don't give two shits if "Cupid is painted blind." And whoever wrote this is a shitty texter.

(GEORGE looks at BENITO.)

BENITO What? You're giving me the look. Even old man tortoises give it to me.
I know what you want.
Everyone wants one thing from me.

(GEORGE looks confused.)

Funny thing is, I started doing it for her.
She would just be so down all the time, lying in bed, not doing the dishes or laundry.
Sometimes, she'd forget to pick me up from school. You know, before. Before the show. I wanted to make her smile, so I made up a funny laugh. I thought if I laughed, maybe she would too. Everyone laughed. But her.

(BENITO is about to put the phone in his pocket. GEORGE makes a noise. Is it a laugh, or a wail?)

Something wrong?

(GEORGE laugh/wails in a different way.)

Are you doing the laugh? It's waaay more nasal than but also a little high.

(GEORGE does his version of nasal and a little high.)

More car alarm, than horn.

(GEORGE does his version of a car alarm. BENITO laughs and laughs. GEORGE does too. BENITO is about to put his phone in his pocket. He puts it in front of GEORGE.)

Know what? You keep it.

(Lights up on another part of the island. BOB/PALOMA adjusts a lantern. GEORGE watches them. CARLA/CHARLES reads a guide book entitled The Galapagos.)

PALOMA What is better than candlelight through color?

(CHARLES looks up.)

CHARLES Scientists often refer to tortoises as chelonians because they are in the taxonomic order called Chelonia.

PALOMA Babylonia?

CHARLES CHELONIA.

PALOMA More Sunburst? Or Red Current?

CHARLES Red Current.

(PALOMA finishes stringing the lanterns.)

PALOMA What do you think?

(GEORGE peeks out to look at the lanterns. CHARLES looks at his book.)

CHARLES I think the anatomical differences between reptiles in the taxonomic order Chelonia display with a clarity most certain, adaptation by means of natural selection.

PALOMA About the LANTERNS. Don't they look pretty?

CHARLES You look lovely as ever, my butterfly.

PALOMA You're useless. Where is Corazon? She said she'd bring champagne. We have champagne and power bars. Is that a weird combo? I wish I could just toss together a salad of shoots and berries. But I don't see any shoots or berries.

(CHARLES strides over to GEORGE.)

CHARLES For example, George's feet are decidedly un-webbed.

(GEORGE stretches his feet out and takes a look at them.)

PALOMA My first girlfriend, I mean, love, let's just call her my first love, had webbed feet; there was very little space between her toes. I was always encouraging her to wear socks to bed.

CHARLES George's feet are round and stumpy for walking on land.

PALOMA I have no idea why my first love had such weird feet.

CHARLES George's feet are different because they have to be.

PALOMA It's like the beaks. Remember all that beak talk?

CHARLES I heard the beak talk but I didn't fully comprehend its MAGNITUDE.

PALOMA You always do this.

CHARLES What, pray, tell do I do with such certainty?

PALOMA You think you understand the world in an instant because of some little thing. It's NOT about George's big fat feet.

(GEORGE examines his feet.)

CHARLES If is not about George's big fat feet, then what is about?

PALOMA Ayy you make so angry. Hijo de puta, you see nothing.

CHARLES Dear Paloma, I beg to differ, before this moment it felt as if I was looking at life through painted glass, the kind of glass they have in public lavatories—you can see light and make out shadows—but really it's all just a never-ending blur.

PALOMA Because you don't want someone to see you making a pee-pee, is why.

CHARLES I am not sure you are fully grasping the metaphor, my love.

PALOMA Oh, I grasp it, I'm just not interested in it.

CHARLES What, pray tell, is so boring about my metaphor?

PALOMA All this tortoise talk is not why the bathroom glass over your eyes got clean.

CHARLES I am not quite following your logic, if I dare be so bold as to call it that.

PALOMA Paloma is the Windex of your soul.

CHARLES But the glass was not dirty—it was painted. You are mixing metaphors.

PALOMA Only thing mixed up is you. I am changing you as we speak but you refuse to see it.

CHARLES But Paloma darling, is it really possible for one person to exact change upon another?

PALOMA And that is why I hate your guts. You won't see me.

CHARLES But I do.

PALOMA Not the way I want you to.

LONESOME GEORGE What force of nature? Or seismic shift?

Could make that happen?

It must.

Happen.

Or all is naught.

(GEORGE retreats into his shell.
Lights up on the fiesta in full swing. Everyone has glasses of champagne.)

PALOMA Smiles, everyone. Smiles. Where are your fiesta faces?

(BENITO drinks his own bottle of champagne alone. ISABEL tries not to watch him. She walks toward BENITO and then turns away; when ISABEL turns away, BENITO turns toward her. GEORGE watches the festivities with a keen interest. CHARLES and CORAZON are in a heated conversation. GEORGE listens.)

CHARLES *(to CORAZON)* So in your opinion Corazon, what is the essential question of evolutionary theory in the post-Darwinian universe?

ISABEL Top me off, Paloma.

(BENITO scowls.)

BENITO For fuck's sake his name is Bob. Can't just one person not go wacko on me.

ISABEL Lay it on us, Corazon. The BIG question.

PALOMA Then can we play charades?

CORAZON The essential question is: what exactly does it take to get a species to change?

(A moment of pondering the immensity of the question.)

ISABEL I feel bummed.

PALOMA Have a power bar, honey.

(PALOMA opens a power bar for ISABEL, who begins to it eat it voraciously.)

ISABEL What do you think, Benito?

BENITO I wasn't listening.

ISABEL Of course you weren't.

BENITO Where the fuck is the boat?

ISABEL People can't change.

PALOMA You are wrong there, Isabelita.

ISABEL I'm not talking about a sarong or an accent. I'm talking starting with soup and ending up with a three layer cake.

BENITO Maybe some people feel fine being soup. I love soup.

CORAZON In the natural world significant change can take centuries.

ISABEL Man, that just overwhelms me.

CORAZON I was speaking in terms of evolution. "Natura non facit saltum".

BENITO We are American. We speak ENGLISH and we would prefer you to do the same.

ISABEL She's speaking Latin.

BENITO Well I don't speak Latin.

CHARLES She said: nature never makes leaps.

LONESOME GEORGE I want to leap but I can't.

PALOMA I didn't know you spoke Latin.

CHARLES I don't.

PALOMA See, Charles is changing before our very eyes.

BENITO His name is BOB. Your name is CARLA. You live in the Valley. And neither of you have accents.

(BENITO smashes his champagne bottle against a rock. He holds the shattered bottle in his hands.)

ISABEL It's official. I quit!

BENITO You can't quit because I already fired you in my mind.

ISABEL That's the best you can do?

BENITO Ever think that maybe you should take that really judgmental mind of yours and let it go ape shit all over YOU! For example: I wouldn't be standing here with a broken bottle yelling if YOU DIDN'T SUCK AT YOUR JOB!

(BENITO waves the broken bottle in the air.)

ISABEL What??? You wanna rumble? Bring it!

(PALOMA stands between BENITO and ISABEL claps her hands.)

PALOMA La musica por favor!

(No one moves.)

La musica!!!!

BENITO There is no music!!!

(GEORGE begins to sway a little.)

LONESOME GEORGE I hear music.

PALOMA It isn't a party unless people dance.

(PALOMA holds out her hand to CHARLES. He looks at her hand for a long moment and takes it. CARLA and PALOMA dance.
They dance simply and well. Sometimes, CHARLES leads, sometimes PALOMA leads. There is something right in this dance. GEORGE, CORAZON, and ISABEL watch and begin to sway. Music begins to play. It is the music of the night, full of the sound of wind, surf and island creatures.)

ISABEL I hear music!

CORAZON Isn't it perfect?

BENITO There is no music.

ISABEL It sounds like a string quartet.

CORAZON A nature symphony.

PALOMA Dance with Isabel, Benito.

LONESOME GEORGE Dance with her!

(ISABEL looks at BENITO. BENITO looks at ISABEL. ISABEL offers her hand to BENITO. BENITO looks at ISABEL for a long moment. GEORGE stretches himself in every direction. He becomes expansive, enormous, like the world. CORAZON notices.)

CORAZON Look! George is dancing too.

CHARLES He can't help himself.

PALOMA No one is immune.

(BENITO picks up the broken champagne bottle and lunges toward GEORGE with it.)

BENITO STUPID, fucking, dancing turtle! You can't just be a turtle. You got be crazy like everyone else. Why can't you just be a turtle?

(He taunts GEORGE with the glass. GEORGE barely misses his swipes. CORAZON jumps in front of GEORGE.)

CORAZON You mean little man!

(BENITO swipes the broken bottle at CORAZON. She ducks.)

ISABEL Jesus fucking christ!

CHARLES Careful Corazon.

BENITO I am SICK to death of tortoises and tortoise talk and the world spinning so fast and changing the second I understand a single thing!

(BENITO lunges at GEORGE again. GEORGE bares his teeth at BENITO. BENITO is a little frightened but lunges at GEORGE, anyway.)

PALOMA NOT AT MY FIESTA!!!!!!

(BOB/PALOMA lunges toward BENITO and in a balletic yet forceful way brings BENITO to his knees. He holds the broken glass to BENITO's throat.)

PALOMA What on God's earth is wrong with you?

(CORAZON runs to GEORGE.)

CORAZON Did he hurt you, George?

(GEORGE basks in the glow of CORAZON's attention.)

LONESOME GEORGE No one can hurt me, if you are near.

ISABEL *(to BENITO)* You are such an… embarrassment.

CHARLES Isn't it about time you became a man?

BENITO I don't know what that means coming from you, Carla.

ISABEL When he gets confused he hurts people. Not that I'm excusing him.

BENITO I've never tried to hurt an animal be-fore, I swear.

(PALOMA takes the glass away from BENI-TO's throat. He is now BOB.)

BOB That was so uncool, man. Seriously.

(CHARLES runs over to BOB. She is now CARLA.)

CARLA Wow. Just wow.

BOB What?

CARLA The way you wrestled Benito to the floor. It was manly yet balletic.

CORAZON Forceful yet graceful.

ISABEL It was totally hot.

BOB Thanks.

CARLA It was masculine AND feminine. It was Ying and Yang. Sweet and sour. God and the Devil at once. It was everything. I love you, whoever you are.

(CARLA jumps on BOB. He twirls her around. BENITO stands.)

BENITO I'm really sorry.

(CARLA and BOB turn their heads away from him. CORAZON turns her head away, as does ISABEL. BENITO runs over to GEORGE; GEORGE slowly turns his head away too. BEN-ITO runs offstage. The sound of a cell phone ringing by GEORGE's foot. It rings and rings. Everyone looks terrified. CORAZON finally picks it up.)

CORAZON Hello? Si. Si. Claro que si. Si. Si. Si. Gracias. Si.

(CORAZON puts the phone back down by GEORGE's foot.)

The boat is on the west side of the island waiting.

ISABEL I'll go try and find him. Unless anyone else wants to.

(No one does. ISABEL runs off stage.)

BOB I don't feel like going back to LA.

CARLA I know what you mean. I wanna read Bob. I wanna read about science, and phi-losophy and…other stuff. Remind me that I wanna read. Promise?

BOB Promise. I wanna cook more and work on my Spanish and take Latin dancing lessons.

CARLA I love dancing with you.

BOB Me too. I like it when you lead.

CARLA I always did, anyway.

BOB Sometimes will you speak in that British accent?

CARLA Sure. If you promise to do some of that ballet Kung Fu.

CORAZON Sounds like fun.

BOB You should come and stay with us in LA, Corazon.

CARLA In the guest house.

BOB We have never have guests.

CARLA You could give lectures, scientific lectures.

BOB By the pool. Pool lectures. And we could dance…after the lectures.

CARLA Pool lectures and dancing. I like the sound of that.

BOB Very Ying. Very Yang.

BOB and CARLA Come to LA.

CORAZON Maybe I will. Who knows?

(BOB begins to run.)

BOB If I run to the beach will you chase me?

CARLA Of course!

BOB You sure?

CARLA Positive.

(Squeals of laughter as BOB runs and CARLA chases him off-stage. GEORGE and CORA-ZON look after them. GEORGE looks at CORAZON and says.)

LONESOME GEORGE Nothing gets lost
Nothing is created
Everything is transformed by love.

(Another part of the island. ISABEL takes a swig of champagne from her bottle. BENITO stands on a rock over the sea and also takes a swig from his bottle of champagne. He peers down into the water. He inches very close to the edge of the cliff.)

ISABEL Oh please!

(BENITO is startled.)

BENITO You scared me.

ISABEL Not very original. "Young actor leaps to his death on celebrity cruise in the Galapa-gos after terrorizing a tortoise."

(ISABEL joins him on the rock and peers over.)

Besides the water's shallow.

(BENITO stomps away and sits on a rock.)

BENITO Can you just… like… let me be.

ISABEL Just wanted to let you know, boat's here.

(ISABEL begins to leave.)

BENITO Don't.

ISABEL What?

BENITO Go. I said let me be. I didn't say go.

(ISABEL sits down on a rock.)

Can I ask you something?

ISABEL I think so.

BENITO Did you really think it was… you know… that bad last night?

ISABEL Um…

BENITO It's not the kind of question you ponder.

ISABEL It was sweet.

BENITO That makes me feel like a million bucks.

ISABEL It confused me. You confuse me.

BENITO I confuse you? Like today, you told me I'm repellant and a sucky lay but if there was a wall you would shove me against it and jam your tongue in my mouth. And you just said I was an "embarrassment."

ISABEL You are but I love you anyway.

BENITO How can you possibly love someone like me Isabel?

(ISABEL gets up and looks out to sea. She doesn't look at BENITO.)

ISABEL I hate it when people make you do "the laugh." I could punch the people who ask. And when you get disappointed I feel it. It tears me up inside. I… want to protect you from the people who hurt you—your Mom mostly, but also the Cindys and the Avocados of this world, but mostly I want to protect you from yourself and the havoc you wreak on a daily basis.

I think I can make you feel safe. I want to make you feel safe, Benito.

I've glimpsed parts of you that are magnificent and lovely I want to show you my parts and hope you see something that moves you, even just a little.

I also think you're fucking hot.

(BENITO stands up. ISABEL still looks out.)

If you run, I'm done.

(BENITO takes ISABEL's hand.
He sings a love song in perfect Spanish.

They slowly hold hands and look out at the Pacific.
Lights up on CORAZON spinning around, around, she looks up at the sky. GEORGE watches her spin.
CORAZON plops on the ground, very near GEORGE.)

CORAZON Hey Georgie. *(beat)* Actors are strange specimens… but… also beautiful and unexpected.

(CORAZON takes a swig of champagne.)

I may leave the island. Try living with humans again. Bob and Carla have invited me to LA. But I'd miss you, George. Would you miss me?

(CORAZON looks at GEORGE.)

Probably not. I'll never know, so many things I'll never know.

(beat) I'm going to buy some comfortable shoes and move to LA.

(CORAZON begins to stumble to her feet. GEORGE looks after her.)

LONESOME GEORGE Kill me.

(CORAZON spins around toward GEORGE. And looks at him.)

LONESOME GEORGE Kill me, Corazon.

(CORAZON can hear GEORGE.)

CORAZON I'm never drinking champagne with actors again.

LONESOME GEORGE "All that lives must die, passing through nature to eternity"

(CORAZON backs away.)

CORAZON Tortoises don't quote Romeo and Juliet.

LONESOME GEORGE Hamlet. Act I, Sc.2

(CORAZON crosses herself.)

CORAZON Padre nuestro que estás en los cielos Santificado sea tu Nombre

What am I doing? I believe in science. I can't remember the last time I prayed.

LONESOME GEORGE When I'm gone.

Say a prayer over me.

Say it in Spanish.

I like the ways prayers sound in Spanish.

CORAZON But George…you're not dying.

LONESOME GEORGE I'm tired. So tired, Corazon. The only thing that makes me lift my eyelids in the morning is you.

CORAZON Me?

LONESOME GEORGE I have loved you as best as I know how.
  You made life possible again, after I had lost hope in living.

CORAZON I wish I'd known. All these years… could you always talk?

LONESOME GEORGE I could always understand.
  But today my heart was so full,
  I had to talk.

CORAZON Unbelievable!

(A moment of profound realization.)

I have witnessed a moment of emotional punctuated equilibrium.

LONESOME GEORGE What you have witnessed is a moment of great love.
  Now let me sleep, Corazon.
  Let me sleep forever.

CORAZON But George, I am a scientist.

LONESOME GEORGE No you're not.

CORAZON I can't kill my greatest discovery.

LONESOME GEORGE I'm not a discovery.
  I'm George who loves you.

CORAZON But this is HUGE.

LONESOME GEORGE I thought you knew me.

(CORAZON takes in GEORGE. A long moment.)

CORAZON I'm sorry. I didn't need words to know you. You are my dearest friend. You are the wisest soul I know. You are time and memory and all that is right with the word.

LONESOME GEORGE I'm ready.

CORAZON Are you absolutely sure about this?

LONESOME GEORGE I'm not afraid, not with you by my side.
  At last, I'll know what I have been aching to know,
  Your touch.

(They look at each other.)

I am ready for everything that may or may not be.

(CORAZON gently strokes GEORGE's head. A silence.)

CORAZON This isn't a prayer but Darwin wrote it and many people think scientists are great poets and I think good poems are like prayers.
  Este planeta ha estado girando sobre su eje y orbita de acuerdo a invariables leyes de gravedad,

THE VOICE OF DARWIN This planet has gone cycling on according to fixed laws of gravity.

CORAZON y desde un principio tan simple,

THE VOICE OF DARWIN and from so simple a beginning,

CORAZON interminables formas tan bellas como maravillosas han y seguiran evolucionando.

THE VOICE OF DARWIN endless forms most beautiful and most wonderful have been, and are being evolved.

(GEORGE closes his eyes.)

———————

Kristina Wong

Biography

Kristina Wong is a performance artist, comedian, and writer who has created five solo shows and one ensemble play that have toured throughout the United States, Canada, and the UK. Her most notable touring show – *Wong Flew Over the Cuckoo's Nest* looked at the high rates of depression and suicide among Asian American women and toured countless performing art centers and universities. It's now a broadcast quality film distributed by Cinema Libre Studios. She's been a commentator for American Public Media's *Marketplace*, PBS, Jezebel, xoJane, Playgirl Magazine, Huffington Post, and a guest on Comedy Central's *The Nightly*  *Show with Larry Wilmore*, FXX's *Totally Biased with W. Kamau Bell*, Al Jazeera's *The Stream*, and *AM Tonight* on Fusion TV. Her work has been awarded grants from Creative Capital, the MAP Fund, the Center for Cultural Innovation, the Durfee Foundation, the National Performance Network, five Artist-in-Residence grants from the Los Angeles Department of Cultural Affairs, and residencies from the MacDowell Colony, Montalvo, and the Atlantic Center for the Arts and Hermitage. Kristina has twice given the commencement speech at UCLA, her alma mater. On television, she's been on *General Hospital*, Nickelodeon's *Nicky Ricky Dicky and Dawn*, and Myx TV's *I'm Asian American and Want Reparations for Yellow Fever*. More information is available at www.kristinawong.com.

Artistic statement

Before I started researching this project in 2013, I was having an existential crisis every day. Make that every hour. Making live theater for a living in a YouTubed world felt exhausting and empty. My identity, Asian American women's mental health, cats, living without a car in LA (all the topics of my past shows) had long since felt like myopic subject matter. But so did chasing retweets and likes. I knew that something about my artistic practice had to shift because I was incredibly unhappy.

So I went ahead and made another theater show. Hooray!

This so far is one of my favorite works I've made. I've used every ounce of me to make this and have had to do an incredible amount of reading, writing, dialogue, and consideration with every single word of this text. My director Emily Mendelsohn sat with me for hundreds of hours literally stitching this piece together, sometimes to the point that I would fall asleep on her! I also had a great deal of support from my managers Elisabeth Beaird and Nola Mariano at Circuit Network who catalyzed key support from the Hewlett and Gerbode Foundations, and were also National Performance Network Creation Fund commissioners on this project. They hosted Bukenya Muusa's San Francisco visit from Gulu, giving critical feedback at the many previews of this work across the country, and supporting *The Wong Street Journal* from my informal "work-in-process" showings on through the full production of the world premiere.

The Wong Street Journal continues in the tradition of my work—taking an offbeat approach to intense social issues to illuminate the strangeness of our times. And always, reporting from my life as the starting point of experimentation. When I proposed making *The Wong Street Journal* before even knowing where in Africa I was going to research the play, I would have never imagined that I'd end up with a set sewn out of felt and a hit rap album (at least in Northern Uganda). I love the artistic process when it surprises me like this.

On the internet, there is no room for failure, and vocalizing political opinions can quickly devolve into a public witch hunt (believe me, I'm the one with the match). I have so much love for everyone who has been part of this piece in some way and did not burn me at the stake for trying out ideas that didn't work, for allowing me the space to both explore and fail in this process. I am especially grateful to the friends I've met in Uganda, who shared their time and energy with me. It is an honor to share a snippet of their lives in this show.

It's one thing to spout academic rhetoric and create hashtag campaigns demanding social justice, it's another to interrogate our own privileges, be vulnerable and admit where we are wrong, and move through (and not around) uncomfortable situations. My hope is that this show offers space for audiences to feel OK in expressing our contradictions, because navigating these contradictions is part of the process of being a better ally for social justice and the patterning of a more equitable world.

Production history

The Wong Street Journal was commissioned by San Francisco's Circuit Network with support from a 2012 Playwright Commissioning Award funded by the Wallace Alexander Gerbode Foundation and the William and Flora Hewlett Foundation. *The Wong Street Journal* is a National Performance Network Creation Fund Project made possible from a joint commission through Flynn Center for the Performing Arts in Burlington, VT, Circuit Network in San Francisco, Miami Light Project, and REDCAT. *The Wong Street Journal* was created with the support of the Sally and Don Lucas Artists Program at Montalvo Arts Center. It is also made possible through a matching gift grant through the Center for Cultural Innovation's ARC Matching Gifts Program.

The production was presented at an in-progress preview in January 2015 at the Segerstrom Center for the Arts in Costa Mesa, California, a nearly finished work-in-process premiere in February 2015 at the Flynn in Burlington, Vermont, and a preview at Subculture NYC.

The world premiere of *The Wong Street Journal* took place at Z Below in San Francisco on June 17, 2015, presented by Circuit Network. The Los Angeles premiere took place in November 2015 at REDCAT. Additional performances have taken place at the Miami Light Project (January 2016), Intermedia Arts in Minneapolis, Minnesota (March 2016), The Kimmel Center in Philadelphia, Pennsylvania (April 2016), the National Asian American Theater Festival and Oregon Shakespeare Festival in Ashland, Oregon (October 2016), and Boom Arts in Portland, Oregon (October 2016).

The Wong Street Journal was performed by Kristina Wong and directed by Emily Mendelsohn. Set design is by Kristina Wong with sound design by Jessica Paz and additional music by Nerio Badman.

20 *The Wong Street Journal*
Kristina Wong

Time

The Present (circa 2013–2014).

Place

This play traverses Los Angeles, then Uganda (where the internet connection gets spotty), then Los Angeles again.

Playwright's notes

This solo play has been broken down into "scenes" with each moment flowing into the next without any hard breaks. The marking of "scenes" in this playscript is mostly to help the reader distinguish visually where the play is moving to and from. In the productions of this play, there are a dozens of archival photos and videos that are projected in a screen behind downstage. There are also videos that have been edited specifically for the production. I've only marked the videos and photos in the script that are imperative for a reader to better understand the narrative and the visual cues in the story. There are many video and photos used in production that I have not cited in this script. This story is a theatricized journey that the character of Kristina Wong narrates using actual documentation from a trip I took to Northern Uganda in October 2013. It is not purely documentary though most of the details from the play are drawn from actual events I experienced.

Pre-show

As the audience takes their seats in the house, popular songs about money, making money, and being made of money play. These songs include ABBA's "Money Money Money," Donna Summer's "She Works Hard for the Money," and Macklemore and Ryan Lewis' "Make the Money."
KRISTINA WONG, 37, a third generation Chinese American woman, sits at her sewing machine, silently sewing money sized rectangles out of a bolt of money printed fabric. Behind her is a tapestry of the New York Stock Exchange, each number and letter hand-cut and sewn from felt, presumably from the very machine we see her at.

Except instead of names of corporations whose values have gone up and down, there are names of civil rights leaders whose cultural capital have been measured like commodities on the stock exchange.

Sound cue: Recording of Kristina's voice plays as she sews at machine:

"Welcome to the (name of space)! Hi. I'm Kristina Wong, and this is my inner monologue. Speaking of pre-show announcements, I, the inner monologue am going to do the pre-show announcement. By the way, do you like my pre-show right now? I'm just like sewing. It's like my Marina Abramovic pre-show. I think I could get a grant for this. It's very durational. Anyway, a few things. One, your cell phones, go ahead and take a photo of me right now, ok, now put your phone away. Awesome. Two, if soft goods from the show just come by and get on you during the show, just leave them here in the theater after the show because you do not know where they have been. I cannot wait to see you in the lobby after the show. I am freaking out right now because my show starts in 5, 4, 3, 2—"

Cut off by sound: Stock Market Bell

PART I: LOS ANGELES WELCOME TO THE WORLD OF INTERNET WARFARE

Scene 1: Kristina's home in Los Angeles

KRISTINA turns off sewing machine and greets the audience.

KRISTINA Hi Everyone! My name is Kristina Wong and I'm SEW…. SEW…. SEWING happy that you've come to my show… THE WONG STREET JOURNAL!

(Song: O'Jay's "MONEY, MONEY, MONEY" plays. KRISTINA dances.)

A confession everyone… I'm Asian. Surprise! To my parent's grave disappointment, I'm not a Wall Street Trader. Nor captain of industry. I am a performance artist who fights for the marginalized!

(Indicates her office chair and felt iPad.)

And here's where I do my best work. The armchair. And this is what I use to take them down… the iPad.

And this is a chart of how I invest my time….

(Flips a handmade felt chart to reveal a pie chart.)

91% of the time I'm challenging other social media users on their racism, sexism, and privilege. I call out their patriarchal semantics, debate their entitled assumptions, call them out for their use of culturally biased language. I fire off social theory until I have the last tweet.

AND if those bigots do not publicly admit faulty thinking, 27% of the time is spent shaming them, putting them on blast, rebranding their image into the sexist, racist, cowards that they are. They will live in fear of me popping up in their comments section. 13% of the time I share memes in solidarity with others fighting for the marginalized in a capitalist world.

56. The number of times I humblebrag while the entire internet watches me in awe!

(Rides the office chair DS.)

And finally, 2% of the time I unplug. I leave the house and engage with the live world that I critique on social media. But I make sure that while out in the world, I check-in on social media from my tablet!

For years, I slugged it out with something called nuance, dialogue, live face-to-face human interactions in theater like this. But these were my measurable returns:

(Flips up chart to reveal bar chart with a long bar and short bar.)

(Indicates short bar.)

This is the approximate audience for when I toured *Wong Flew Over the Cuckoo's Nest*. It was a live 80 minute theater show that explored with humor and poignancy, the high rates of depression and suicide among Asian American women. Heavy stuff right? And that was my audience across seven years.

(Indicates long bar.)

And *this* is how many likes and shares I got for a blog I wrote for xoJane.com in one night called "9 whack things white guys say to deny their Asian fetish." It's a blog that people didn't read all the way, as evidenced by all the hate mail I got from people who thought that I was somehow advocating against interracial dating... but look how much traction it got on the internet because of that crazy title!!

Nuance. *(Indicates short bar.)*
Clickbait. *(Indicates long bar.)*
Nuance. *(Indicates short bar.)*
Clickbait. *(Indicates long bar.)*

Wanna know the two words I can shout out on the internet and instantly increase my value in LIKES, SHARES, and COMMENTS?

White Privilege.

(KRISTINA pulls out a TNT bomb marked "Market Volatility" and sets off detonator... Video: a bomb with text "WHITE PRIVILEGE" explodes on screen, then a half dozen clips from popular movies of white people screaming and running in a panic. KRISTINA screams at the audience, pointing at the audience like it's a witch hunt.)

White Privilege! White Privilege! White Privilege!

(Video fades out on Janet Leigh from Psycho screaming in the shower. KRISTINA calms the audience down.)

I know "White Privilege" is a polarizing term that freaks white people out and makes them run as fast as they can towards some of their best friends in the world, many of whom just happen to be black people. I know. Because when you can't find them, you come looking for me next. I know.

To be clear... White privilege is not about blaming white people for something they didn't do. It's not me trying to win the Gold Medal in the Oppression Olympics for the 200 meter stop and frisk. White privilege does not mean you are a bad person just because you are white.

(Pointing to a random white guy in the audience.)

Except for you sir. You look like a horrible person.

But let me give you a nuanced description of white privilege.

(A chart flip to reveal an all white sheet.)

Your differences are invisible. No one will ever question where you came from "originally" because they assume you always had the right to be here. If not named, White is assumed to be the default character in every novel or script. Dominant culture, the American history we study, has been shaped by white men with perms and ponytails and puffy pants with heels and tights, and their descendants... and for those of us who don't look like those shapers, we've have had to learn to adapt, to assimilate and learn to pass by the rules set up by these people. Even though my family has been here in this country for three generations.

I'm going to take a wild guess that we're not here in this theater because the (Name of Neighborhood theater is in) KKK meeting was canceled. I'm assuming we're interested in things like equity and civil rights. So I bring up this issue of white privilege because it is about acknowledging the legacy of white supremacy that white people continue to benefit from in ways that people like me don't. And it is the first step in dismantling systemic, institutionalized racism and creating a more equitable world that we all should strive for.

But this more nuanced explanation of white privilege takes so much time and plays to such a small audience and I much prefer the instant gratification of likes. And when you are a slave to likes, you do whatever it takes to get more.

(Rolls out the stock ticker scroll which instead of corporate symbols track social media traction: Twitter, Facebook, YouTube, are revealed and their numbers go up and down along three strips.)

Kristina Wong may not be a big brand name like Google, Apple, or Jesus Christ. Kristina

Wong may actually still be sleeping on a futon into her 30s, but if Kristina Wong reduces complex social justice dialogue into a spectator sport... and keeps talking about herself in third person, Kristina Wong can build her anti-imperialist anti-capitalist mega empire with these... Hashtags! Or for the old folks in the audience, the symbol formerly known as POUND sign.

(KRISTINA reveals a camouflage bag filled with a hundred hand sewn felt hashtags.)

This is how this works. I attach a word or phrase to a hashtag like #revolution or #notyourstereotype then I send it out on social media.

(Flings hashtags towards the audience.)

#Ban White male privilege! #Down with Cisgender privilege. #Stop Priority boarding status privilege. With so many words in the English Language, the possibilities are endless....
#no #stop #cancel #ban #boo
Then people begin to notice my hashtags, and they throw them back at me. Go ahead, throw it back at me.

(Audience member tosses hashtag back to the stage.)

See? That's a retweet! It's like a digital congregation applauding my every thought.
This is how change is made in this world. Ideological civilian warfare! Every tweeter for themselves! Come on. Make some change. Don't you want to change the world?

(Feverishly throws more and more hashtags into the audience as a literal hashtag war erupts among the audience.)

I can do this all day. Clickbait! Clickbait! Clickbait! And this is the legacy that I will leave when I die!

(KRISTINA stops throwing hashtags.)

Wait! This is the legacy that I will leave when I die? Hashtags? Twitter followers? YouTube Views?
There has to be more to life than this!

(KRISTINA talks back and forth to herself in the armchair.)

Kristina! You can't have an existential crisis, existential crises are for those women who read *Eat Pray Love.* You are tougher than those privileged disillusioned white women! But I spend so much time critiquing from this armchair, I don't actually even know what world I'm retweeting about anymore.
Kristina! If you actually engage the world instead of spending all your time calling others out for how they engage the world, someone is bound to call you out!
But I miss nuance! I miss really exploring the depth of an idea and not just shouting shocking things so that people look in my direction. I just want to go out in the world, engage it, and leave a legacy!
Oh yeah? Where would you go?!
I'll go to the default symbol for the world's most extreme problems and suffering... I'll go to HASHTAG Africa!

(Sound: Toto's "Africa.")

Scene 2: KRISTINA reveals a MAP OF AFRICA

But Ladies, Gentlemen, and nongender conforming people... How much do we really know about Africa?
(KRISTINA flips the sheet of a felt chart to reveals a felt applique cut-out of Africa with "Africa, The Country" cut and stitched out of felt letters. She places a felt TV set on the armchair. For the following she pulls small faces of celebrities and other props out of the TV.)

For me, all I know of Africa is what I've seen on TV. I know Egypt is at the top. And South Africa is at the bottom.
I know Ethiopia, because that's where Angelina Jolie adopted Zahara from.

(Slaps Angelina's face where Ethiopia is on the map.)

I know Sierra Leone because that's where the Beckhams—Victoria and David—almost adopted a child from.

(Slaps down the Beckhams on Sierra Leone.)

I know about Somalia because that's where the pirates attacked Tom Hanks in that movie *Captain Phillips*!

(Slaps down Tom Hanks on Somalia.)

I know about Uganda because of the Broadway musical *The Book of Mormon*—written by the *South Park* guys Matt and Trey—where the evil warlords threatened the AIDS infected villagers!

(Slaps down a white Bible image on Uganda.)

I know about South Africa, because of Nelson Mandela…

(Slaps Nelson image on South Africa.)

But it's also where Charlize Theron adopted a baby!

(Slaps Charlize Theron over Nelson's face.)

Africa is where kids are running around with no shoes….

(Slaps down image of Toms shoes founder putting shoes on third world kids.)

They are just waiting for their next shipment of Toms shoes to arrive.

(Slaps white shoe over the children in the Tom's photo.)

Africa is where girls can't go to school if they are on their periods, unless Procter and Gamble send them disposable pads!

(Slaps down maxi pad over Madagascar.)

And then everywhere else is Bono!

(Slaps down small Bono.)

Bono!

(Medium Bono.)

Bono!

(Large Bono.)

AIDS!
AIDS!
AIDS!

(Slap down three AIDS ribbons.)

GUNFIRE!   STRIFE!   VIOLENCE! EBOLA!

(Throws red felt confetti at the map.)

Ladies and Gentlemen! The dark continent! Brought to you by white people!

(Takes in the map of faces and AIDS ribbons.)

So how does someone who's not black, not white, but (surprise!) is an Asian American performance artist show up in this situation and leave a legacy without being a colonial asshole?

And where do I go exactly? It's three times the size of the United States. If America is Dropbox, Africa will always be Dropbox Pro.

And then I find it. A microloan organization in Northern Uganda, that only gives microloans to women.

The idea behind a microloan is that because some people are so poor they do not have the collateral to qualify for a bank loan, and a microloan is a teeny amount, I'm talking as low as $50 and it carries a low interest rate. And this teeny loan allows the borrower to start a business project so they can better self-determine their lives. And I am going to dramatically improve the effectiveness of a microloan by going to Northern Uganda to volunteer with this organization… for 3 weeks.

And how much must I crowdfund, i.e., cyberbeg, i.e., shake my friends down to witness the power of a $50 loan?

A $2000 participation fee made payable to their American partner in Denver.

Not including meals and incidentals.

Then $1400 on a flight to Uganda.

Then $300 in vaccinations for typhoid, yellow fever.

Then $150 for 35 day prescription for malaria pills.

Then I could have bought a meningitis vaccination for $300 then rabies for another $100 but, I just didn't have the savings.

My packing recommendation list recommends I bring—Cipro Rx—Doctor prescribed diarrhea medicine, iodine tablets, energy bars—I can only infer from this list that there is no protein in Uganda! Only a gruel-like paste that I will eat out of a rock fashioned into the shape of a bowl.

All my friends are like:

"Oh, Africa, Kristina? You're so brave! Isn't there a civil war in Africa?"

I'm actually going to Northern Uganda. The civil war ended there around 2006.

"Ooh! Africa is so sad. All those starving Ethiopians."

I'm actually going to Uganda. It's another country. There are 54 countries in Africa.

"Be careful. Just be careful. Seriously. Be careful. You are so brave… Be careful!"

All these warnings came from people who had never been to the Africa before. Don't like a billion people live there? Why are they the ones who are sad? But I'm brave for going over there?

I can only take this as a sign that I am supposed to pack with total minimalism.

(Picks up little clothes out of television and other packing supplies.)

I will pack only my filthiest khakis and dirtiest cotton tunic. Items I'd be willing to forfeit in a bus robbery/hotel robbery/armed robbery. I will wear no make-up! I will not get my eyelash extensions refilled! I will keep my money close to me in my money belt at all times! I will leave behind my iPhone, my MacBook Pro, my hard drives of data, my thumbdrives, my only connection to the outside world will be my iPad!

(Shoves money into waist, puts iPad into her camouflage bag, and flies across the room, lands.)

PART II: UGANDA

Scene 3: ENTEBBE AIRPORT, LATE NIGHT

I fly across the world and I land at the Entebbe airport at 3am. Who will be the first person to greet me on the African continent? A starving child with a distended belly? A warlord covered in flies? None of those. In the parking lot, I am greeted by Bukenya Musa, a 29-year-old articulate man who runs VAC-NET the microloan organization I will work with in Gulu. Bukenya drops me off for the night at the Kampala Hilton.

Scene 4: RIDE TO GULU, UGANDA, DAY

The next morning, we begin our rickety bus ride to Gulu, Northern Uganda. A passenger stands up at the front of the bus and starts to deliver a sermon.

"Snakes of evil and trees and light and hope and Abraham and Jesus holding snakes and holding Abraham and the lights of God and the blood of Jesus his savior…"

Wow! It's like a sermon ghost written by Gary Busey.

(Photo of Pepsi shop logo: "God Given Retail Shop.")

I've only been in this country for a few hours, but judging from the countryside I'm guessing the national motto is: "Uganda: Sponsored by Pepsi, Blessed by God".

(KRISTINA turns the handle on the scroll, we see the social media stock ticker move out of the way and in its place, a colorful African rural landscape, also sewn out of felt.)

The landscape is so lush.

(Photo of salon logo appears on the screen: "Blood of Jesus Christ Hair Salon.")

I even see a sign for "The Blood of Jesus Christ" Hair Salon. Do they do blowouts with a crown of thorns?

I was told this bus ride would take 4 hours. It's been 8.

It's pitch black night in Gulu when I check into Hotel Nok.

But in the morning, out my window. Huts!

(Video of activity outside Hotel Nok.)

There's a woman washing laundry. Is that a UCLA polo team shirt on the clothesline? One woman combs another woman's hair. A child running with a stick wearing a shirt that says "World's Best Dad"…

(Pulling out the iPad.)

I must record their every move—if not with video, then with photos, if not photos, then with tweets… Ah no internet! My head is filled with 24 hours of backlogged tweets! I need Facebook right now to applaud me for accomplishing such profound tasks as flying in an airplane, sleeping in nice hotels, and staring at people. Must record the natives! Must record the natives!

Kristina! What are you right now? The human zookeeper at the 1878 World's Fair?!?

(KRISTINA walks to the office chair and flips felt TV to reveal a mini replica of the VAC-NET Office.)

Scene 5: EXT. VAC-NET OFFICE, DAY

Bukenya takes me to the office where the work of my legacy will begin… VAC-NET, short for Volunteer Action Network. Here, I'll be working towards the end of poverty, women's empowerment, and restoring justice in post conflict zones—in just three weeks. Northern Uganda was the site of a very brutal civil war between the Ugandan government and the Lord's Resistance Army, led by warlord Joseph Kony as made infamous by a viral video campaign called Kony 2012. In the Kony 2012 viral campaign, Joseph Kony is elevated from run of the mill rape and village warlord to super evil celebrity warlord. The Kony 2012 video describes how Joseph Kony attempted to build a government here based on the 10 commandments. And because that was such a shit-tastic idea, Joseph Kony recruited children to be his soldiers, AKA kidnapped children to be his soldiers. I would find out later that during the Civil War, that this building was used to shelter Night Children. Night Children were children who would walk to Gulu Town, sometimes from as far as 12 kilometers every day to sleep in group safety so as not to be kidnapped by the Joseph Kony and his men. Today this is an office that offers microloans. "You are most welcome!"

I get a one minute whirlwind of introductions and titles.

(KRISTINA shakes hands with everyone.)

First is Monica, the Loan Program Coordinator.

Then Abuu Denis, Transportation Coordinator.

Then Emma, the Finance Coordinator.

There are two Kevins, both women, both coordinators. They tell me I can call one Big Kevin, the other Little Kevin.

Wait! Who was who? All I know is there are a lot of coordinators.

And I feel a sudden sympathy for every white person whose head I've bitten off for telling me that I remind them of Margaret Cho or Sandra Oh or Amy Tan or Lucy Liu—or any other famous Asian woman who I do not

look like because now I am having a "they all look the same" moment.

I try to project a calm, a confidence. Like "trust me I'm your new friend." But I feel so big and obtrusive. Like every neuron in my head is shooting out signals of fear that is paralyzing the ability of everyone to do the work they were already doing before I got here.

Bukenya gives me my first task.

"You will pick the woman to get the AWAHDS."

The what?

"The AWAHDS."

I'm sorry Bukenya. I don't—

"You do not understand me through my Ugandan accent.... that by the way, she is performing very poorly now"

(The dickey on the armchair is flipped to reveal word "Awards.")

Oh! Awards! Yes. Wait, what are these awards? "Every year, we give this important honor to two grassroots women who have made significant peacebuilding and development efforts in Northern Uganda."

And you want someone who just got here to decide on the winners with no context?

"You will judge and announce the winner of the Women4Peace Award because you are an outsider and have no bias."

My first gig in Uganda and it's to be their Simon Cowell.

(Graphic in: UGANDA'S GOT TRAUMA logo in the style of "American Idol" with sound: "American Idol" theme music.)
(KRISTINA as Simon Cowell.)

KRISTINA Ladies, I know some of you were once abducted by the Lord's Resistance Army, but until one of you rescues an orphan baby from a burning hut and then raises it, none of you have the winning edge!

(Graphic out: UGANDA'S GOT TRAUMA)

Scene 6: EXT. RESTAURANT PATIO AT HOTEL NOK, EARLY EVENING

(KRISTINA rehearses Acholi phrases.)

IBUTININI How did you sleep?
ICHOMABE I woke up well.
I'm learning some basic phrases in Acholi - one of 44 languages spoken in Uganda - over dinner from Jackson, a Ugandan man who is staying at my hotel.

KOPANO How are you?
NINI KRISTINA I am Kristina.

(KRISTINA in a back and forth conversation with Jackson.)

"You know, here we call you Mzungu. That is Swahili for white person."
But I'm not a white person.

"Yes, but you are a Mzungu."

You don't have a Swahili word for third generation Chinese American? Or radical woman of color?

"When people see your white skin, they will think the whites have money. So they charge you more."

Even though I got here on a playwrights commission that I spent three years applying for? And I'm not white?

"They know the whites have the money. Can I offer you a beer?"

No thank you, Jackson. I don't drink beer.

"Now why you don't drink beer?"

Well, I'm sober. I'm now two years sober.

"With everything in life. There is a start and an end."

Oh! But sobriety is good for me, Jackson. It allows me to be present and to understand myself and my decision betters. I can re-evaluate my emotional connections to people in my sobriety—

"You know. You remind me of this Mzungu woman I once met, a white woman. She was very stubborn and very ungrateful."

(Whispers of "White Privilege" echo throughout the theater and KRISTINA panics.)

Not white privilege! Some of my best friends are black! No!!

(Finally, a photo of KRISTINA drinking at a table with Jackson laughing appears on the screen.)

And this is me folks after two years of sobriety succumbing to white guilt and falling off the wagon.

Scene 7: SAME NIGHT, INT. KRISTINA'S HOTEL ROOM AT HOTEL NOK

My fingers itch to upload to scroll to refresh to retweet. Without wifi I am nothing! I am just a head full of snarky yet politically insightful thoughts!

I'm no ungrateful Mzungu! I came to leave a legacy, not to be sheltered in this hotel for Westerners! I'm going outside! I'm going into the street with the people! But I'm keeping my valuables on me in case of a hotel robbery.

Scene 8: SAME NIGHT, EXT. PITCH BLACK STREET OF GULU TOWN

KRISTINA moves cautiously into the street.

I see a woman crouched in front of her hut roasting something on a charcoal grill. I'm going to negotiate a price. But what if she is cooking dinner for her family and now I'm trying to buy her family's dinner? I can't tell what is someone's home or what's a restaurant. I can't tell what's a vendor and someone just standing in the street.

(Notices an umbrella on a mic stand.)

Look! A big umbrella, lit by candles, with the international signal for unsanctioned street food—a food cart made out of things that a food cart should not be made out of. Yes! This looks like a legitimately illegitimate vendor! There is a crowd of seven teenagers. All boys. I can take them on.

(KRISTINA in dialog with a boy at the food stand.)

So what you got here?

"Is Rolex. Chapati with eggs"

How much?

"2000 Schillings."

That's 80 cents. I don't know if this is the price. I assume it's not the right price.

Don't charge me the Mzungu price!

The boys start laughing.

I said don't charge me the Mzungu price!

"Ok. One thousand schillings."

Victory! The price dropped in half! No Groupon app required!

Now that I've shown the locals that this white girl can haggle, time to brave another interaction.

Can I take a picture of you?

They agree!

(KRISTINA pulls out iPad and takes a picture of the boys that appears onscreen. The boys are posing for the camera, throwing hand signals.)

These guys have the "ironic baller" photo thing on lockdown.

(Photo: KRISTINA posing with one of the boys. They are flashing Ugandan shillings for the camera.)

Their leader, Nerio, smiles and points at what looks like a dark shack behind him. "You! Come see our music studio! Come to our music studio."

I assess the situation. Huh! One boy in a trucker hat is holding hands with another boy, spooning him from behind, their fingers laced in a sweet lingering hand hold.

Oh!! This is the underground gay community of Gulu! I've heard how the LGBTQI community in Uganda must organize in secret, and they are doing it right here in the street by this food stand! I have to support them! This is my fight too! And so I follow multiple strange men into a dark room!

Scene 9: SAME NIGHT, INT. MUSIC STUDIO

(Lights go dark and then a music video plays on the screen. It features Nerio, the boy we met earlier, and another rapper singing R&B style in Luganda, dancing with a woman.)

As it turns out this was not the underground gay community of Gulu. But there is a music studio back here, thank God.

Nerio is playing me his music video on his computer. Holy crap this is Northern Uganda's version of K-Ci and JoJo!!!!!!!

It turns out Nerio doesn't have the internet here in this studio that he works for. The video is saved on his computer and he plays it for people that walk by. So I offer to put it on YouTube for him when I get online and he burns me a copy on a disk solidifying my role as #internationalhiphoppromoter.

(Photo of KRISTINA and Nerio in the music studio appears on the screen.)

Then Nerio says to me, "Ok Kristina, I put the music on, you rap."

(The food stand umbrella is lifted away to reveal a mic stand.)

I RAP? I rap.

(Mzungu instrumental plays as KRISTINA approaches the mic to rap.)

> Cope An No!
> Copay!
> Ninnee Kristina!
> Wongzunga!
> Mzungu!

I'm basically just shouting out everything I've learned in the last few days.

> Boda Boda!
> Two Thousand Shillings!
> Boda Boda!

> Mzungu Price!
> Boda Boda!
> Three Thousand Shillings!
> Boda Boda!
> Rolex!

(Video of Nerio playing back the recording with sound.)

Then Nerio plays back what I recorded.

Is this how bad it is in Northern Uganda that I sound good to them?

Then… Local rappers get in the booth and do response raps.

(Video of Festo Wine rapping in the booth with sound.)

First is Festo Wine lays it down in Swahili.

(Video of LMG rapping in the booth with sound.)

Then LMG Silver spits mad rhymes in Luganda.

Check out his lyrics….

(Karaoke lyrics of LMG's lyrics appear on the screen as we hear his lyrics.)

> "ana maro in kristina wong
> wan luo kany wamalo in nta pe luo
> **representing the europeans kristina wong**

KRISTINA   What?

> *(Lyrics repeat.)* **representing the europeans kristina wong**

KRISTINA   I'm not European!

> **representing the europeans kristina wong**

KRISTINA   I'm Chinese American!!

> lmg representing niletics in uganda
> amazima ono mwana lero mutwala
> anzalile kubana kristina wong,
> amazima ono lero mutwala anzalile kubana kristina wong
> amaro kimyeri kede amito myeri kedi bina awoti kedd

amaro kimyeri kede amito myeri kedi bina awoti kedd Kristina Wong"
(End LMG's lyrics.)

I imagine LMG is rapping an anthem for people to decolonize our minds, and fight together for social justice. An international global moment of solidarity for people of color.

I find out later that what LMG is singing is: "I want to get you pregnant and give you babies Kristina Wong. Lots and lots of babies." Then Nerio says: "Ok Kristina...Now you rap. More."

Rap more? What is this, a hip hop Gulag?

(KRISTINA approaches the mic again. Start karaoke lyrics. KRISTINA spits:)

At the top of Uganda,
A place called Gulu,
People are friendly,
Don't let history fool you.
At Diana Gardens,
Party's going down,
Last Friday of the Night
Tusker Pilsner passed round.
Roosters will awake you
Cock-a-doodle-doo!
At night we eat pork
It's roasted not stewed.
Boys making Chapas under the stars
Producer Nerio Make Music Always Going Hard!
(Photo: KRISTINA and rappers in the music studio.)

Scene 10: NEXT MORNING, VACNET OFFICE

Good morning, Big Kevin, Little Kevin, Bukenya! You'll never guess what happened last night. Last night I was in the hotel and I was like "I'm not an ungrateful Mzungu, I'm going out into the street!" And then I met these boys and I was like "don't charge me the Mzungu price!" And then I followed them into a dark room and we started recording a song called "Mzungu Price!" And then Nerio, the producer, he said we're going to do a whole rap album and he can get me played on the radio and in nightclubs. It's like we are the Patti Smith and Robert Mapplethorpe of international hip-hop collaboration. You guys should come with me! It's right down the street. We could go tonight! What do you think?

(As Little Kevin:)

"That is nice Kristina. Oh! The power is on and we must get back to work because the Women4Peace Award ceremony is tonight."

Oh Power is back on! I can check my social media—Oh! Nerio just messaged me.

(Graphic: Nerio's text message.)

"You know what i have Liked you, are you single like me?"

Uh oh. Hold on.

(KRISTINA types message out to Nerio on iPad.)

"Sorry Nerio, I am married and in love with my husband at home—

(KRISTINA nods "no" to the audience. She is clearly doctoring the truth.)

In fact we are working on having a baby when i get back because i am getting too old to have babies. See you later. Let's keep making this album."

Hey. Can I blame any up and coming rap producer for wanting a piece of the Wongzunga?

Scene 11: THAT EVENING, INT. BANQUET HALL OF ACHOLI INN, THE WOMEN4PEACE AWARDS

Have you noticed my voice has a natural sarcasm to it? It's like irony and cynicism had a baby in my throat. You can hear it right? I'm told it serves me well as a comedian.

But even people who know me say they can't tell when I'm actually giving a compliment.

(KRISTINA indicates video of the crowd at the Women4Peace Award Ceremony.)

For example... Wow. What a beautiful room for tonight's Women4Peace Awards Ceremony!

What a rousing opening performance from the drum and dance group!

Such a huge turnout of elected officials, NGO workers, clergy, and the women from the rural villages...

See! You don't even know if I'm being sincere and I am. It's the fucking cadence in my voice that's been weaned on a lifetime of slow claps, witty asides, and clever tweets.

Tonight is not the time for this natural dry cadence because tonight I announce the women nominated for the Women4Peace Award—the winners of which I picked the day I got here, with no help from Google. These women were forced from their homes, watched their families be kidnapped or killed. And then despite all those horrors, the women honored tonight didn't give up but instead stepped up as leaders to advocate for widows and survivors of gender based violence.

There is no satire in this moment!

This is not the "Ironic Women for Peace Awards!"

This is the time for my sincerity to emerge through the 24/7 defense mechanism that is the natural intonation of my voice!

Sincere. Honest. Earnest.

Luckily, I have some time to get in the zone because there's a quite a line-up before my announcement.

Sincere. Honest. Earnest.

We start with the Ugandan National Anthem.

(Sound: Ugandan National Anthem.)

Sincere. Honest. Earnest.

Then an opening prayer led by the American Mormon pastor—Good God they get around!

Sincere. Honest. Earnest.

There are speeches from Bukenya, local politicians, local scholars.

Sincere. Honest. Earnest.

And then it's the crowning finale.

The moment when the big honorable Mzungu in the $5 dress that Bukenya made her buy at the Main Market since she had only packed dirty camping clothes for this trip and no make up, this mzungu with her hair pulled into a messy ponytail, who just showed up last week, will announce who she picked, knowing almost nothing about Northern Uganda's long history of colonial oppression, abject poverty, and war crimes of both Uganda's government and a rebel army that forcefully recruits children... I, Kristina Wong, honorable mzungu, will announce my pick for the woman working hardest for peace in Northern Uganda.

(KRISTINA takes the mic and speaks into in, in a voice that is remarkably and unnaturally high pitched.)

Hello, my name is Kristina Wong, and I am VAC-NET's volunteer for two more weeks, and I will announce the nominees and winners of the Women4Peace Awards. Ladies, I know that I do not speak Acholi, but hope you can understand how much I respect you through the intonation of my voice. First our nominees.

(Indicates to slides of nominee names, still in high pitched voice.)

I attempt no ad-libs, in fear that any attempt to personally editorialize the lives of each woman would just come across as patronizing mockery.

And those were our amazing nominees. And now our winners. The first winner is the Chairlady for the Women's Action Network and the other woman runs "Poverty Taught Me," a group made of 104 widows. Please help me in honoring the winners of the Women for Peace Awards..., Evelyn Amony Naima and Aol Josephine.

(Wrong name slide appears. There is another nominee KRISTINA forgot.)

Oh, this was another nominee I forgot to name. Also amazing. And now, the winners of the Women for Peace Awards. The actual winners. Please congratulate Evelyn Amony Naima and Aol Josephine!

(Sound cue of women celebrating with a LALA-LALA and drumming and cheering/slide with Evelyn and Aol's names shows.)

The room fills with the energy that my presentation had sucked out.

(Photo of Evelyn and Aol Josephine wearing gold dresses and holding their trophies.)

Evelyn Amony Naima and Aol Josephine, walk slowly toward the stage wearing bright gold Gomahs, they give composed speeches in Acholi.

(Photo of the winners with the women of their villages together at the table.)

When they return to their tables, the women of their community receive them. Bring their arms around them in one group circle, leaning their heads in silently. Wow, the women of their community are truly proud of these two women and the legacy they are leaving.

There is no satire in this moment. #thereisnosatireinthismoment…. Oooh… That's a good tweet! I should tweet that. Oh! I just got wifi! I'm gonna tweet that.

(*KRISTINA motions to tweet but a message on Facebook has popped up on her iPad.*)

What? Someone named Catherine Liang has messaged me on Facebook. "How much longer are you in Africa? I've got a lot of used clothing. Can you help get them to someone there in NEED? I have a Purse too! LOL." Who are you? LOL? Excuse me Catherine Liang! I came here to leave a legacy, not to help you declutter your house! #NoPity! I'm taking you down in a hashtag war!

(*KRISTINA tweets furiously on the iPad but stops abruptly.*)

God I just lost the wifi signal!

(*Puts iPad away and speaks to audience.*)

Hey! All of Africa! Are you dealing with structural racism, corruption enabled by international aid, and exploitation of natural resources! No problem! This bag of used clothes will make it better!

Scene 12: INT. MUSIC STUDIO, THAT NIGHT

Hey Nerio, #no pity. Let's trend it!
Invest in classrooms not begging behavior
No more false gods let people be their own saviors
Nobody wants to be the subject of your pity
Believe in power to change that's this ditty
Give a man a fish and you feed him for a night
Teach him how to fish and you feed him for life
Handouts are a short term solution
Education leads to long term evolution

You see a war torn poor crumbling nation
I see a country on the brink of innovation
(Repeat Chorus, Nerio singing in Acholi)
Drop your privilege not your bombs
Drop your fears and not your psalms
Trust potential and keep calm
Cause who sent you, yo! Kristina Wong
KRISTINA Ad lib: *Sing it Nerio!*
(Chorus, Nerio singing in Acholi)

Scene 13: SATURDAY DAY, FIELD IN GULU OUTSIDE VAC–NET OFFICE, THEATER FESTIVAL

Today is Saturday, the day of Kikopo Pa Mon Gulu, VAC–NET's 6th Annual Music, Dance, and Drama festival. We're "Creating a Voice for Women!" There's over one hundred women here from villages around Gulu Town who've come to perform at this day long festival. And I've raised $4,500 to be part of this legacy - by doing what?
By moving chairs for the festival goers. Even though local people have been paid to move chairs. Yep, looking good.
I know! I'll help them at the pop-up medical clinic. We have turned VAC–NET's office into a temporary one day medical clinic where the women from the rural areas can be tested for HIV, screened for cervical cancer, they can even get IUD implants—
Except I don't speak Acholi—and I'm not a medical professional which is important if you are going to do medical things to people…
What do I do? I feel like if I do nothing, I'm just staring at people. And if I try to help people I'm in the way. What would other people, specifically my family members do if they are unable to face the awkwardness or to sit inside the depth of a situation?
I know! I will take pictures! I am sure that Kato Joseph who they hired to document this, could use additional footage. I will be the white woman filming the natives. Great.

(*KRISTINA holds iPad over her face.*)

(*KRISTINA steps out and look at the footage with us. Video: Footage of Evelyn's testimony.*)

All of these performances are done all by women, all in Acholi.
This is Evelyn Amony Naima, the women for peace award winner, giving her testimony.

(*Slide: An image from a slapstick play.*)

This particular drama has a lot of slapstick elements. That woman has created a goat costume by wrapping a red shirt around her head. She's cracking everybody up.

(Video: Women performing a choral dance with axes.)

A choral dance. It's all so organic, no clear leaders or followers.

This is the work of grassroots feminism. This feminism was not bred in classrooms between warring academics arguing about what wave of feminism we are on. SHE IS SO FIRST WAVE, YOU'RE SO FIFTH WAVE, NO I'M SIXTH WAVE! There was no graduate student on Theater of Oppressed who came down here to show these women how to perform. They have long standing performance traditions that are part of the fabric of their lives.

What traditions have I carried from past generations? I know how to sew. I carry Wong, my last name. And I can hoard hotel toiletries like the women in my family before me....

But these songs and dances have resisted colonialism. They have survived before war, inside displacement camps, and now are part of the recovery from war. If the women today do not continue these songs and dances, this connection to history will die out.

You are waiting for a punchline? I have no idea how to reduce this into a punchy 140 character tweet, except, um, #whatdoIthinkImDoingHere?

(As a Ugandan man calling to KRISTINA in the street)

"Miss! Miss! You having an existential crisis while watching the Drama Festival. Yes you! I want to get a Chinese tattoo. Can you write for me a word in Chinese to get tattoo'd?"

Well we have a punchline folks.

I'm sorry sir. Listen, one - I get you are the one person in Gulu who got the memo that I'm Asian, and not white. Two - I'm third generation Chinese American, I don't really speak Chinese... You'd actually be much better off using the internet.

"I don't know what is this internet. You are Chinese, and I want for you to translate for me." The man scribbles two words on his hand: The Great." As in "Alexander, the Great!"

Here's the thing. Chinese grammar is completely different from English. There is no "The Great" in Chinese as there is in English.

This man wants a stranger off the street with admitted incompetency in her Chinese language skills, to make an impossible translation, that he will get forever tattoo'd into his skin in the spirit of America's most idiotic of cultural appropriation, AND guess what? I'm going to translate this for him because of white guilt.

(KRISTINA relinquishes to the Ugandan man's request. Taking his hand and a pen.)

Ok, Ok. Let's see. "The Great." Let me try this.

(Slide: The man's hand reading "The Great" in ballpoint pen with KRISTINA's "大 好" scribbled below. KRISTINA translates these two characters for the audience.)

"Big. Good."

The man waves goodbye with the ink fresh on his hand.

"Next time, I want you to bring for me every word you know in Chinese."

It's an identity shit test! In America, I am just another hashtag warrior. But here, I could be anyone, a rap star, an American ambassador handing out awards, and now, the oracle of all Chinese people. My linguistic failures redeemed in the skin of Ugandan people.

(Projection: A scrap of notebook paper with every stray Chinese character KRISTINA knows with English translation scribbled alongside. Basic words like "girl," "small," "boy.")

What would happened if I met his request, writing what stray characters I remembered from Chinese school 25 years ago?

(Projection: A scrap of that notebook paper now pinned on the walls of a Ugandan tattoo parlor.)

Maybe... The scrawl of my ballpoint would be held sacred photocopied and hung in tattoo parlors in Uganda, like the original handwritten pages of the Quran all over Uganda.

(Slide: Tattoo of "出口" on a black bicep in bad ballpoint scrawl. KRISTINA illustrates to audience.)

出口 "Exit"

(Slide: Tattoo of "黄 月 男 肉" on a black chest. KRISTINA illustrates to audience.)

黄 月 男 肉 "Yellow Moon Man Meat"

(Slide: Tattoo of "水 山 大 王" on a black back. KRISTINA illustrates to audience.)

水 山 大 王 "Character that I thought was water, but wrote wrong, mountain, big, king".

(Slide: "黃君儀" scribbled on paper.)

My Chinese name 黃君儀 was given to me by my grandparents, and I've always regretted that it's not part of my legal American name. That it will die with me, but I can tell people here that 黃君儀 is like Jehovah or Yahweh—words so divine they can only be sacredly uttered in a tramp stamp.

(Slide: "黃君儀" scribbled as a tattoo on a black lower back.)

The larger you tattoo my Chinese name across the top of your ass, the closer you are to God.

Scene 14: EXT. RURAL VILLAGE IN NORTHERN UGANDA, MORNING

(KRISTINA moves to rural scene tapestry. Video: Rural area outside of Gulu Town.)

Maybe I've lived in LA too long, but I have to keep telling myself this rural village just outside of Gulu is not the backlot of Paramount Studios.

How is it that just 7 miles from this mushroom farm made with a microloan, this banana field, this g-nut garden—that there is an NGO Boom town - a hip hop studio, an internet cafe, and an all you can flush hotel toilet?

Today, we're going to visit the microloan clients. With us is Joyce Ojala, a peer counselor who mentors the microloan clients, so that when they receive loans, they know how to best use them.

(KRISTINA indicates to slide of Christine, a local woman.)

This woman in the green shirt tells me her name is Christine.

"Ninghee Kristina!" I am Kristina.

Christine takes my hand and cheers! Two Christine/ Kristinas have found each other in the middle of a rural village in Northern Uganda! Or rather, two women born in very different spectrums of the world both share a Christian name, not indigenous to our ancestors, nor the religions they worshipped. But we share the same colonial, assimilationist markers when identifying ourselves to the rest of the world!!!

(KRISTINA turns around "Market Volatility" TNT prop to reveal a hand sewn replica of a house in a field.)

Christine and the other microloan clients are part of a literacy class held in this bombed out building that used to belong to Joyce Ojala and her family. During the 20 year Civil War, the Ugandan government and the rebels could not come to an agreement on anything, but somehow they could agree that Joyce's husband, who was a peace mediator between them, was somehow the real problem and both sides attacked their house. The government arrested Joyce's husband, and as shit got really crazy, Joyce's family had to abandon this house and moved into town for protection. And now that the war is over, Joyce's family has donated this home to be used as an education center for the post war returnees.

(Video of inside literacy class.)

I'm watching women young and old whose lives have been walking headlines that were never published enough. 10s of Thousands of Ugandan Civilians dead. 20,000 Children abducted. 1.9 million people, nearly the entire population of Acholiland, was displaced. And now they have returned. Now they were sitting together, some with babies on their laps, learning to read and write for the first time. Now that they don't have to run, they have to face the long task of building their lives.

This isn't just about learning the Acholi alphabet. They are singing together, and working together. It's about building a shared confidence that their lives matter.

And here we are, the guests of honor, the mzungus they are putting a show on for so we keep pumping money into their program. Bukenya asks me if I have some encouraging words for the women that he will translate for them.

(KRISTINA stands up to address the class of women.)

Hello, Joyce, ladies. Thank you for having me here today. I just want to say, you are all incredibly—

And then tear after tear starts rolling down my face.

Oh no. Oh no Kristina. Don't be that American that cries when she sees African people. Don't do it!

I just think are all so brave. Really moving.

And there it is. Snot. Running. Sniffles. Broken voice….

Don't cry. I swear I'm not crying because I feel sorry for you. Your resilience is just so moving. Your choice to thrive is so moving. I know, it's not a choice.

I turn my face away from the women while Bukenya translates. And the women *who are not crying* listen attentively to his translation while I continue to freeze my face into a neutral position as if I'm not fucking crying. As if I am not an American cliche *Like oh my god, my life has changed after seeing Africa. Like I had no idea. Like you just realize how brave people are like like like.*

If only I had some way to tell you about how much respect I had for the power of the women in that classroom.

(Sound: Opening instrumental hook for "Boss Lady" Lyrics also appear on screen. KRISTINA takes to mic.)

Scene 15: BOSS LADY

(Chorus)
Ooooh… Boss lady.
Ooooh… Boss lady.
Ooooh… Boss lady.
I'm a lady not a bitch not a trick not a ho,
Hit a woman, call her names? Misogyny has gotta go!
Rise up. Speak Up. Stand up for your mothers.
Walk beside us, step back, that's how to be our brothers.
She knows how to manage money cuz she knows what's missing.
She can hold down a family despite all his dissing.
Rocks a baby on her back and feed the homefront
Keep humility in check when no one asks what she wants.
Keeps walking head high, when you cat call.
Won't ever give in when everyone else hits the wall.
She doesn't clown your ass when you can't get it up
But she's willing to please when you can't get enough
Breastfeeding and Cleaning, she's the silent force of life
She's ain't your slave nor your property just because she's a wife.
Holds it in when it matters
and empathizes in strife
She feels the pain of a village and leads it back to alright.
(Repeat Chorus)

(Ad lib) Let's see the 50 Gun Boss Lady Salute! Where my boss ladies at?

See the world through her eyes like Dustin Hoffman in Tootsie
You gotta earn her consent if you wanna go near her pussy.
Every woman's Wonder Woman. Superheroes without capes.
I wish she had the power to stop gender violence and rape.
Short skirt cleavage a hint of perfume.
She may look meek and girly but she controls the room.
Feminism Activism Justice Equality
All women connect in solidarity
(Repeat Chorus)
Boys the time has come to drop down to your knees!
Dethrone yourselves and crown the matriarchy.
No more reign of your terror. A new queen has come.
Castrating sexism will be the first order done.
Respect for all people that's the new national song,
if you don't know the lyrics, call me, Kristina Wong
(Chorus)
That's why the lady is the boss. Everyone woman is the queen of her queendom.
That's why the lady is the boss. Everyone woman is the queen of her queendom.
That's why the lady is the boss. Everyone woman is the queen of her queendom.

Scene 16: NEW LIFE RESTAURANT IN GULU TOWN

Who's the boss? Now in all this talk about boss ladies, there is a boss man I haven't talked enough about. Bukenya Musa!

(KRISTINA pulls off a felt fish from the felt rural landscape on the scroll and motions to eat it.)

We're having one final dinner at New Life, his favorite restaurant. It serves up local cuisine like Matoke, pasted fish and they also sell pants.

(Slide: Picture of a retail tag for pants reading "Obama 2nd Fashion Quality Pants.")

Obama the 2nd, Fashion Quality Pants.

Bukenya is not from this region. A lot of people, like Nerio, and the rappers, and the staff at VAC-NET. Many of them are not from Northern Uganda. And a lot of the people who've moved here after the war, a lot of NGOs set up shop here, and Ugandans from all over have moved here to take advantage of that trickle down Mzungu money. But not Bukenya, he started VAC-NET, on his own, without any Western NGO money and initially, no paid staff.

"So Bukenya, you have no family here? What joke made you decide to move up here and start an organization?"

Bukenya takes this pause and a breath. As a performance artist who toured a show about depression and suicide for eight years, I know this pause. It's that pause where you collect your soul and then get ready to spit it out at an audience.

(Takes the pause.)

He says, "Kristina, you know this word "destitute?" That's what I was."

(KRISTINA stands behind the moving scroll that we previously saw the social media stock ticker on, that we have been viewing a felt replica of a

bright rural Ugandan landscape on. She turns the scroll so that we see the same landscape in grey and black colors.)*

Then, Bukenya tells me his story. He uses words like "Domestic Violence" but doesn't go into a lot of detail, only that his mother was killed by his stepfather when Bukenya was very young.

He sold used clothes and Matoke to put himself through school. In school, he studied journalism and was sent to interview people in the camps during the war. He says what he saw at the camps brought back bad memories. He created VAC-NET so that women wouldn't have to suffer like his mother.

Later they partnered with an American NGO. The one I got here through, the one I paid the $2000 participation fee to be here through. Very little of which, Bukenya tells me, actually trickled down to them in Northern Uganda.

(KRISTINA scrolls back and forth between colorful landscape and gray dead landscape during this story.)

Bukenya says he must constantly share this story with potential funders. And each time he says, it takes a little out of him.

But his story makes good click bait. It hits the right emotions in the Western donor. It has kept VAC-NET running.

At what point does the trauma a charity attempts to alleviate become its best commodity? At what point does telling a very personal story become a show that has to be told over and over again to keep our donations coming in?

(KRISTINA peels apart the fish prop to reveal its skeleton and places that skeleton back in the river of the colorful tapestry landscape.)

Scene 17: MUSIC STUDIO, LATE IN THE DAY

(Video: KRISTINA, Nerio and MC Kash rehearsing music in the studio. KRISTINA indicates to the video.)

And now, I'm down to my last hours in Northern Uganda.

I'm laying down the last tracks of my five song rap album, Mzungu Price. That's MC

Kash who manages the other rappers. That's Nerio on the side. Insider trading secret: "Nerio"? Not his real name. His real name is Mugufu Henry. Even in Uganda where men are named Hillary and women are named Kevin, Nerio knew that "Henry" would cement the death of his hip hop street cred. So he took his rapper name from a disc burning software called "NERO" – added an "i" and he works for this studio under the producer name Nerio Badman, not "BadBoy" but BadMAN.

Three weeks ago, I came here with the intent of empowering women, restoring justice in post conflict zones, and developing long range poverty reduction solutions.

Instead, I cried in front of a bunch of women, and solidified my role as the Northern Ugandan version of Iggy Azalea…. Not really the legacy I had hoped to leave, and now it's time to say goodbye to Nerio.

(Sound cue: Nerio's voice)

"You are my first mzungu friend. I will be missing you"

I will miss you too, Nerio. You will always be my #1 – and only – music producer.

(Sound cue: Nerio's voice)

"When you go back to America next week, can you sponsor for me my own music studio?"

Sponsor a studio? Nerio. I can't just be a Mzungu who gives people things. What's wrong with working for this studio?

(Sound cue: Nerio's voice)

"For you, is not too expensive to make a music studio."

Nerio, in America, I do live theater shows for small audiences, I don't have the power that you think I have.

(Sound cue: Nerio's voice)

"If you sponsor for me a studio, I will call it WONG RECORDS."

(Sound: Whispers of "Wong Records" akin to the earlier echoes of "White Privilege." KRISTINA is drunk with joy.)

Kristina Wong may not be a big brand like Facebook, Apple, or Jesus Christ.

But this is Kristina's Wong's moment to speak in third person and leave a legacy beyond hashtags, Twitter followers and Youtube views.

Capitol Records!

(Slide of Capitol Records in Hollywood.)

Sony Music!

(Slide of Sony Music building.)

Wong Records!

(Slide of Wong Records -a hand painted sign over a shack.)

Will LITERALLY give Northern Ugandan music artists a venue to proliferate their voices under Nerio, Uganda's #1 music producer! And under me, Wong Records! This will be the legacy I will leave when I die!

(Sound: Festo Wine's "MUNU MUNU" (Munu is Acholi for "White Person") plays as KRISTINA "returns" to America. LYRICS: "Mzungu I will follow you. Twitter Page will follow you. Facebook page I will be with you. Always I stay in touch with you.")

OK, Nerio. I'm going to America. But when I come back here, I will bring you Wong Records—I promise! I'll message you every day on Facebook! Good-bye.

(KRISTINA rolls scroll backwards through all the scenic landscapes to the social media tickers we saw at the top of the show.)

Scene 18: INT. KRISTINA's home, Los Angeles

America I'm back. TV! Macbook. iPhone! iPad! Toilet!

(Sound: Flush)

Aaaah! Freedom!

Oh, comfort. I'm back in the armchair full time and I'm dealing with American problems!

#StopPoliceBrutality   #StopTransphobia and this old chestnut #StopRacism. It's ok America, we still have what it take to fix the rest of the world's problems!

Rappers from all over northern Uganda are messaging me every other day on Facebook

"Heard your songs on the radio Wong! When are you going to come back and record the next album?" Working on that legacy as we speak, boys!

(Graphic: GRANT APPLICATION, each "Grant Buzz word" flashes as KRISTINA reads it.)

Wanna see all the buzz words I wrote in my grant application for Wong Records Uganda?

"Capacity Building."

"In conversation with."

"Innovative."

"The field."

Who the fuck knows what all those grant buzzwords mean? They have to give me this money!

(Graphic/Sound: "REJECTED" stamped large over GRANT APPLICATION)

Uh-oh. Ok - well there's always crowd-funding! i.e., cyberbegging.

(KRISTINA in Sally Struthers' "Save the Children Commercial" voice.)

"Friends… For the cost of twenty cups of coffee per day, you could help insure that an Asian American performance artist leaves her legacy as the Dr. Dre of Northern Uganda."
And my friends ask…
"Oh, my god a music studio, Kristina? What's the business plan exactly?"
"Oh, my god a music studio, Kristina? What happens if the equipment gets stolen? Or lost?"
"Oh my god, a music studio, Kristina? How much more are you going to ask us for Kristina Wong in addition to all the other shit you make us give you money for you for every month?"
Uh Oh.
Then, a message from LMG Silver.

(Slide: LMG's message on Facebook.)

"Festo Wine says you give presents to Nerio but not to us."
And then a message from Nerio.

(Slide: Nerio message.)

"When will you return with Wong Records? My boss heard a rumor that you were bringing me a studio and was not happy with me."
There's so many details that still aren't clear. Will Wong Records put other music studios out of business? Will I have to become an NGO to keep the money coming in? Will I have to fundraise for my "fundraising costs"?
This is the nightmare of every Western NGO. In our best intentions for helping a poor country "develop," just our presence creates such a big ripple in the local economy, that - when we leave, everything has the potential to collapse in our wake.
And then! Urgent Facebook Message from Nerio!

(Slide: Nerio message.)

Because of these rumors that I'm showing up with a competing studio? He's been fired from his job. Now Nerio is without income or a studio to make music.
In aspiring to be a savior, I've ruined Uganda.

(Sound: Whispers of WHITE PRIVILEGE SOUNDS and Video: Fireball image from White Privilege video earlier in the play)

Is this the legacy that I will leave? The seeds of jealousy, panic, violence? The Mzungu who came bearing false promises only to leave a trail of destruction in my wake?
Am I fighting the man? Am I becoming the man? Or have I always been the man?

(Turns to beat up the armchair.)

Noo no nooo nooo! You should have never left the armchair. NO!
Then I get a message from Nerio.

(Slide: Nerio message.)

What now? Are you messaging me from the deathbed I have singlehandedly put your entire continent in?
Turns out that since Nerio was without a job, and I had no resources to give him a studio, he went to the capital city to borrow money from his father. He combined it with his savings, and bought some used recording equipment.
And now he just needs some money to rent a small space to start a recording studio.
"Can you send me proceeds of our album in America so I can rent a studio?"
Yes! I can!

(Slide: Album cover for "Mzungu Price.")

Hey America! Your purchase of our album Mzungu Price will help Nerio get his music studio.
The internet responds in masse to my call and in three weeks, our album sales total… $72. As it turns out being an international rap sensation isn't as lucrative as I thought. So I force people to put money in the hat at my shows. And I send Nerio $400. Enough for 3 months rent in a 3 room studio with a flushing toilet.

(Slide: Image of Nerio's studio.)

Ladies, Gentlemen, and nongender conforming people, put your hands together for Nerio Badman's legacy on the world... Empire Records Uganda!

(Image: Empire Records, Nerio's song plays.)

He sends me his first song. Apparently I'm shouted out in it. Even though I can't hear my name in this song. Where's my name... Where's my name?

I so badly wanted to leave a bigger legacy. I am a woman of modest goals. I just wanted to liberate all of Africa. I wanted my ghost to come to Uganda years after my death and watch everyone gather an annual festivals, chanting "Wong Wong Wong Wong! Our great liberator!"

I wanted to leave an anti-colonial legacy in the most colonial way possible.

(KRISTINA goes to sewing machine, turns it on and sews for a moment in silence.)

(Slide of sewing studio in Gulu.)

In Gulu, I visited a NGO where women who had once been abducted were sewing hipster style purses and making bead necklaces that would later be sold to the West. Black and white photos of them smiling hung in the walls around them. Each of these items includes a tag with the name and brief biography of the woman who sewed it. I wonder if the women who sew imagine Americans buying their purses, reading their bios, and patting ourselves on the back for redeeming their lives with the almighty dollar. I wonder if they think about that when they imagine that redemption plays out this way, or if sewing is just a job. I wish I spoke enough Acholi, that I could ask them.

I mean my grandfather didn't necessarily want to do people's laundry for a living. He escaped by boat in 1938, on a boat from Toisan, China, running from Japanese imperialism. He took one of the few jobs available to Chinese immigrants in San Francisco at the time—working in a laundry. Eventually, he saved enough to start his own family-run laundry business under his house where they did laundry and alterations.

For me, sewing is a hobby. I sew to sit inside the slowness of time. To feel my personal energy in the present moment move into the thing in front of me.

All these threads are archival transcripts of hundreds of hours of snipping, stitching, jamming up this machine. In anticipation of this moment where you'd take in all the handcrafted details, and be wowed by how I frayed the fabric of capitalism.

How do we stand in solidarity with those rising up against the odds of globalization, when the resources we have are a result of globalization?

What do we want to make? I don't know! What I do know is this...

The larger you tattoo a name across the top of your ass, the closer you are to God.

(KRISTINA pulls down her pants enough to reveal a tramp stamp in crude ink reading "Empire Records Uganda.")

Thank you Uganda!

(LIGHTS OUT)

Larissa FastHorse

Biography

Larissa FastHorse is an award winning playwright, director, and choreographer based in Santa Monica. She was awarded the NEA Distinguished New Play Development Grant, Joe Dowling Annaghmakerrig Fellowship, AATE Distinguished Play Award, Inge Residency, Sundance/Ford Foundation Fellowship, Aurand Harris Fellowship, and numerous Ford and NEA Grants. Larissa's produced plays include: *Urban Rez, Landless, Average Family, Teaching Disco Square-dancing to Our Elders: a Class Presentation,* and *Cherokee Family Reunion.* She has written commissions for  Cornerstone Theatre Company, Children's Theatre Company of Minneapolis, AlterTheater, Kennedy Center TYA, Native Voices at the Autry, Artist's Rep, and The Eagle Project and Mountainside Theatre. She developed plays with Kansas City Rep, Artist's Rep in Portland, Arizona Theater Company, the Center Theatre Group Writer's Workshop, and Berkeley Rep's Ground Floor. She is a current member of the Playwright's Union, Director's Lab West 2015, Theatre Communications Group board of directors, Playwright's Center Core Writers and is an enrolled member of the Rosebud Sioux Tribe, Lakota Nation. www.hoganhorsestudio.com

Artistic statement

Up to now as a writer, I've been consciously writing on a human scale. I ask audience to take crazy journeys with me who also have social justice ideas in them. I chose to take the audience on that journey psychologically instead of theatrically. My plays are intentionally naturalistic to the point of being deceptively simple because my personal belief is that if I can get inside people's heads and hearts, the "message" will stick longer.

This is especially the case with *What Would Crazy Horse Do?*, which is easily my most read and taught play, but has taken three years to get a theater to commit to the first production. The premise of the play is the collision of two seemingly improbably worlds, the modern Ku Klux Klan and the last two surviving members of a Native American tribe. However, both of those worlds are very real and written from a great deal of truth.

I was originally inspired to write this story after coming across a flyer in the State Museum of South Dakota. I grew up going to that museum hundreds of times but never saw this flyer until three years ago. It is an advertisement for a Klan gathering in 1926 on the South Dakota/Iowa border to welcome Dr. Hiram Wesley Evans, the nationally famous leader of the Klan. The day's festivities would include a parade, picnic, car classic and for the big finale, a pow wow with original American Indians dancing. My mind was blown. The Klan sponsored a pow wow? I couldn't find anyone who would admit to participating in that event, so I moved my play into the near present with fictional descendants of that day. I started writing with the final image in mind (very unusual for me) so my task was to get the audience to accept this world and take the roller coaster ride to the end. It took a lot of drafts to smooth out the turns and keep everyone in the car, but this draft has been read a few times now and the tension is enough to keep everyone together to the end. At this time, I am months away from the world premiere, so I look forward to seeing what more will change by then.

In this play, I give the audience glimpses of lives that are beyond difficult and possibly unsolvable. I introduce them to the new Klan that is based on personal contact and far more frightening than the old Klan hiding behind hoods. I use a lot of humor and laughter that sometimes makes the audience cringe with discomfort. I ask many questions in this play, really hard questions that I do not answer because I want the audience to be challenged to think for themselves and talk it out. If I do my job, the audience leaves the theater seeing the world around them a little differently than when they entered. That is why I write.

Production history

The world premier by Kansas City Rep is slated for April 28, 2017.

What Would Crazy Horse Do? was developed with Center Theater Group Writer's Workshop (2013) William Inge Residence Workshop (2013), Berkeley Rep's Ground Floor (2013), The Lilly Award/Kilroy's List Readings (2015), Santa Clara University Workshop Production (2016), KCRep Origin KC Festival (2016), and the Mixed Blood WD40 Reading Series (2016). The script made the Kilroy List Top 46 in 2014.

21 *What Would Crazy Horse Do?*
Larissa FastHorse

Scene 1

Most of the stage is the main room of the Walter Good Eagle house. It belonged to an old man of extremely limited means. Old mismatched furniture, piles of things that are no longer useful but can't be parted with line the walls. Strewn here and there are feathers, leather medicine bags, dried plants, tobacco, rocks, bits of beading; a collection of gifts to an elder. The front door of the home opens onto a small porch. Several steps are visible and lead into the yard and off stage. More things are piled outside. JOURNEY storms onto stage in traditional regalia of a Plains style. CALVIN chases after her in regalia as well. Their faces and hands are covered in white paint or makeup. JOURNEY frantically wipes at her face and hands, trying to get the white off. She bursts inside the house and spots a water bottle. She grabs for it. CALVIN follows, closing the door behind them. JOURNEY drops the bottle.

JOURNEY FUCK!

CALVIN Journey, calm down. I'll get it for you.

(She scrambles for the water and knocks it further. She violently runs her sleeve across her face.)

JOURNEY Get it off! Get it off!!

(CALVIN gets the bottle and unscrews the cap. He carefully extends it to her. JOURNEY pours the water over her face and drags her sleeves across hard enough to peel skin.)

CALVIN You'll hurt yourself.

(CALVIN grabs for her arms.)

JOURNEY Get it the fuck off!

(They struggle. CALVIN keeps coming at her, steady and calm.)

JOURNEY Please Calvin. Get it off of me.

CALVIN I will. I'll take care of you. I promised.

(JOURNEY relaxes, CALVIN rips his shirts off, including an undershirt. He uses the undershirt to clean the white from her face.)

CALVIN You got it all over your eyes. Hold still one sec.

(He grabs the water bottle. A little left. He positions her head and pours it into her eyes.)

JOURNEY Ow!

CALVIN Sorry.

JOURNEY Making it run into my eyes is so much better.

(She grabs the shirt from him.)

CALVIN Fine do it yourself.

JOURNEY I am.

CALVIN I see that.

JOURNEY You gonna pout now?

CALVIN I don't pout.

JOURNEY My dear brother, you are the King of Pout. You have the certificate to prove it.

CALVIN You making me a crazy certificate does not make it true.

JOURNEY It has an official seal.

CALVIN A lip imprint from your sister is creepy, not official.

JOURNEY Admit it, you want me to get more shit in my eyes so you can save me, don't you?

CALVIN No.

JOURNEY Just a little bit, right?

(They smile.)

CALVIN Stop it. I want you to feel better. You know that.

JOURNEY I know.

(She finishes wiping the white off and gives his shirt back. He cleans his own face.)

CALVIN Even though you're a nut job.

JOURNEY I should make myself a certificate.

CALVIN Don't. You feel better?

JOURNEY Yeah. I felt like it was suffocating me.

CALVIN A Native American feeling suffocated by whiteness. So. Many. Jokes.

JOURNEY Don't joke about traditions. At least not funeral ones.

CALVIN I don't know what to tell you. We've worn this paint a hundred times before.

JOURNEY More.

CALVIN Yeah.

JOURNEY Maybe we did it wrong? We haven't made it alone before.

CALVIN It's just chalk and bark and oils. I watched Grandpa do it every time.

JOURNEY Doesn't matter. We never have to wear funeral paint again.

CALVIN Maybe.

JOURNEY We promised. Today is the last time.

CALVIN I know.

JOURNEY We won't leave each other. Ever.

CALVIN I'm stuck with you Journey, womb to tomb.

JOURNEY Womb to tomb.

Scene 2

Day. Everything is cleaned up. CALVIN works on his laptop at the desk. JOURNEY studies a chess board across from him. She makes a move. CALVIN looks up and makes a quick move.

JOURNEY Shit.

CALVIN You trying for a long slow death?

JOURNEY You know I like quick and clean.

CALVIN Figure out who you're gonna sacrifice.

(She goes back to studying the pieces. Outside, EVAN and REBEL enter. EVAN is solid as a rock, REBEL is uncomfortable. They knock.)

JOURNEY *(yelling.)* We don't want any more funeral food!

CALVIN They're giving it out of respect for Grandpa. Be gracious.

JOURNEY Screw that. It's death food and I don't want it in our house!

CALVIN *(Calls out.)* One sec. *(to JOURNEY)* Seriously, leave the room if you can't control yourself. Someone will have you committed and I'm left alone. I'm serious.

(CALVIN pulls himself together and opens the door. JOURNEY studies the board.)

CALVIN Oh, hello?

EVAN Evan Atwood. And this is my associate Rebel Shaw. We are looking for Walter Good Eagle.

JOURNEY Too late.

EVAN We came a long way for this meeting. When he didn't show at the restaurant I was concerned, but if you're saying he has skipped out on us and–

JOURNEY He's gone.

REBEL We have an agreement.

CALVIN He passed away last week.

(EVAN and REBEL make significant eye contact.)

EVAN Oh. I am so sorry.

CALVIN What kind of agreement?

EVAN Were you related to him?

CALVIN He was our grandfather. You knew him?

EVAN We've only been in contact recently. Walter knew my grandfather. Could we come in and explain? I think you may be able to help us.

JOURNEY We're busy.

CALVIN Stop it. *(to REBEL and EVAN)* Come in. I'm Calvin and this is my sister, Journey.

JOURNEY Twin sister.

(CALVIN glares at her.)

JOURNEY It makes us exotic.

(They enter. CALVIN motions for a seat. He and EVAN sit. REBEL hovers on alert. Annoyed, JOURNEY joins him.)

EVAN Again, I am so sorry to hear of your loss. My own grandfather passed away before I was born, but I owe my life's work to his legacy.

CALVIN Our grandfather raised us.

EVAN That's wonderful.

JOURNEY Because our parents died.

EVAN I'm sorry.

JOURNEY Why did you kill them?

EVAN Not that I am aware of. But you never know do you?

JOURNEY Fair enough. What do you want?

(EVAN pulls a folder out of her bag and hands a photo to CALVIN.)

EVAN This is your grandfather, correct?

CALVIN That's his dance regalia, so it must be, but I've never seen a picture of him this young.

(CALVIN studies the picture.)

JOURNEY Where did you get this?

EVAN That man with Walter is my grandfather.

CALVIN I've never seen so many Marahotah dancers in one place. Where was this taken?

EVAN At an event in honor of my grandfather in 1926.

JOURNEY "In honor" of your grandfather? You saying our people were a bunch of dancing monkeys for your white grandfather?

CALVIN Journey.

EVAN I misspoke. The event was in celebration of your people and mine. My grandfather was at the head of the organization that sponsored this Marahotah pow wow so he was a special guest.

JOURNEY Who are your people? White people? *(Looking to REBEL.)* Redneck people?

CALVIN I'm sorry. She's-

JOURNEY Don't be sorry for me brother.

REBEL I don't need your sorry's either son.

CALVIN Ms. Atwood I'd like to know more about this photo. I am...well...I'm now the leading expert on our tribe and I've never heard of a pow wow of this many Marahotah.

EVAN There was a unique connection between our grandfathers. Do you recognize this?

(EVAN pulls a beaded medallion out of her bag. CALVIN and JOURNEY are visibly struck. CALVIN goes to a closet and pulls out his regalia from the opening scene. We see a matching medallion in the center of his shirt.)

CALVIN My grandfather gave this to me when I became a man.

EVAN As you can see, there are two of them on his regalia. He gave you one, but after he had given my grandfather the other.

(JOURNEY and CALVIN take it all in.)

CALVIN Who was your grandfather?

EVAN His name was Doctor Evans. He was on the cover of Life Magazine once.

CALVIN An academic? Did he study our people? *(Indicating medallion.)* Are there other pieces like this we don't know about?

(EVAN and REBEL decide something. EVAN pulls a piece of paper out of the folder. REBEL gently moves behind JOURNEY.)

EVAN Have you ever seen this?

(CALVIN and JOURNEY read. Both stiffen. JOURNEY turns on REBEL.)

JOURNEY Stay where I can see you redneck.

(He eases back in front of her.)

CALVIN I don't understand.

EVAN It's very clear. That is Walter Good Eagle posing on a flyer for a pow wow sponsored by the Ku Klux Klan.

CALVIN Your grandfather is this Hiram Wesley Evans?

EVAN Yes. Walter gave his medallion to the Imperial Wizard of the Klan.

JOURNEY You said your grandfather gave you your life's work.

EVAN Yes.

CALVIN You're affiliated with a man who led the Klan?

REBEL We are the Klan.

(Silence. Then CALVIN and JOURNEY laugh.)

REBEL *(to EVAN)* This never happened when we wore the robes.

CALVIN OK, you had us going. But really, this isn't funny. Our grandfather died only a week ago and he was a jokester, but this is crossing the line. Who-

EVAN I regret the unfortunate timing, but this is not a joke. The medallion-

JOURNEY What he's saying is get the hell out of our house.

EVAN I understand your confusion, but I assure you everything we've said is true.

CALVIN There's no KKK anymore.

EVAN Not publicly, but we do exist like you've never imagined.

(EVAN extends a business card.)

CALVIN Anyone can make a fake card.

EVAN Seriously, who makes a fake Ku Klux Klan business card? I've got hundreds of them.

(She pulls out a card holder. CALVIN has to wonder.)

CALVIN What the hell are you doing here?

EVAN This pow wow was a watershed moment for my grandfather that caused him to radically change the doctrine of the Klan and grow it to the largest public numbers in the organization's history before it was taken over by hate-filled radicals. Today Rebel and I are poised to bring the Klan into the light again, and your grandfather agreed to help us.

CALVIN I don't know how you got this medallion and the photo, but you are obviously lying. You need to leave.

EVAN We are holding a commemorative pow wow event to launch the Klan into the public once again as the "Free Americans." But we are only as free as our brothers, the first Americans. We plan to honor your grandfather and his influence that put us on this new path.

CALVIN Seriously, go.

(CALVIN ushers EVAN and REBEL toward the door.)

EVAN I understand you need time, but we have a signed contract. As an act of good will we paid your grandfather in advance. We have poured an incredible amount of money and marketing into this event.

CALVIN If this is true, you can have your money back. How much was it?

REBEL Twenty thousand dollars.

JOURNEY You're a fucking liar. This is my grandfather's house. He doesn't have that kind of money.

EVAN Walter received the check.

CALVIN We'll get to the bottom of it, but he's gone so he won't be able to fulfill the contract. If there is one.

EVAN A Marahotah will be part of this event. Are there others we should talk to instead?

CALVIN Good luck with that.

EVAN Fine. Keep this copy of the contract for your records. We'll be back.

CALVIN You're serious.

EVAN Absolutely. This is going to be an event of historic proportions.

JOURNEY Get the fuck out!

(She rushes toward them. REBEL jumps in front of EVAN, ready to take JOURNEY on.)

REBEL Show some respect girl.

EVAN Rebel, stand down. We're going. But we'll be back. Look into the information. It's all true.

(They go.)

JOURNEY What the hell was that?

CALVIN Bullshit. Total bullshit… right?

(He studies the contract.)

JOURNEY Of course. This is our grandfather. He taught us everything about the Marahotah ways. He didn't make some deal with the wannabe KKK to buy a boat.

CALVIN A boat? In the middle of the prairie?

JOURNEY I don't know. Something that costs a lot of money.

CALVIN This is his signature. I'd know it anywhere. It says he got paid twenty k when he signed in exchange for showing up at this pow wow thing.

JOURNEY It's a lie. All of it.

CALVIN What if it's not?

JOURNEY It is.

CALVIN Of course.

JOURNEY What about the twin pact?

CALVIN There's no such thing as a "twin" pact. You made that up.

JOURNEY Whatever you call it, we have a plan. Maybe this is a sign we should do it now.

CALVIN When we leave this world it is going to mean something. Make a statement.

JOURNEY Our tribe going extinct via double suicide is a pretty strong message.

CALVIN Not if no one hears it.

JOURNEY Are you changing your mind about this?

CALVIN I promised on Grandpa's grave, we'll never be alone. Just give me some time to make a plan.

JOURNEY Suicide is pretty simple, brother.

CALVIN Yes, but making a statement takes planning.

JOURNEY You better not chicken out on me. Like when we were ten on that cliff and-

CALVIN We were just kidding around.

JOURNEY I wasn't.

CALVIN Then why didn't you jump?

JOURNEY You wish I did?

CALVIN Don't say that.

(JOURNEY makes chicken noises.)

CALVIN I was ten and heights aren't my thing.

JOURNEY It's gonna hurt you know.

CALVIN It doesn't have to. If we do it right.

JOURNEY Trust me brother, death's not pretty.

CALVIN Stop it. I'm in. Womb to tomb.

JOURNEY OK.

CALVIN But we can't leave these Klan idiots to smear Grandpa's name. I'll prove this shit is shit first.

JOURNEY Fine. But don't wait until it's too late brother.

CALVIN Thanks to us, the Marahotah will finally mean something to the world.

(JOURNEY holds the medallion. CALVIN gets on his computer. She looks at the chess board and makes her next move.)

Scene 3

A week later, mid-day. JOURNEY comes in with the mail. She's in a really good mood.

JOURNEY There's something from the bank. And my package!

(CALVIN, sullen, takes and rips open an envelope as JOURNEY excitedly opens a package.)

CALVIN Finally. Can't just give me the account information. Have to verify his death and mail it. The death certificate wasn't enough?

(He digs into a box of papers, adding the letter to a paper clipped bunch.)

JOURNEY You're such a whiner. What does it say? Is it Grandpa's secret account? Does it have millions in it?

CALVIN Nope and that's the last account I could track down on him. Unless he buried the money in the yard, there isn't any.

JOURNEY Bummer.

CALVIN That's good news.

JOURNEY No, this is… ta-da!

(She unfurls a banner that reads "What Would Crazy Horse Do?")

CALVIN What's that for?

JOURNEY I ordered it online to cheer you up. You've been so mopey.

(She gets on a chair to hang it from one side of the room.)

JOURNEY Help me.

CALVIN Why?

(JOURNEY waits. He gives in and takes the other end and tacks it up. JOURNEY is pleased.)

JOURNEY Catchy, isn't it?

CALVIN But what's the point?

JOURNEY It makes us happy. Come on, admit it, you wanna smile.

CALVIN Because you're a nut.

JOURNEY You've spent two years doing that paper thingy on Crazy Horse. You love him. You'd be gay for him.

CALVIN My dissertation is a serious comparison of celebrity and leadership today against the nearly invisible, reluctant leadership style of Crazy Horse. In this age of social media and the NSA–

JOURNEY "What Would Crazy Horse Do?" is perfect. WWCHD leather bracelets will become a worldwide meme for social justice and non-compliance with the invaders. A meme for saying screw you and doing whatever is necessary to rise up and fight back and survive!

CALVIN Or die.

JOURNEY Fuck them either way. But when they find our bodies, they'll see this and be all "What the hell?" They'll totally put it in the paper and people will Google it and order lots of bracelets. Crazy Horse everywhere.

CALVIN Bracelets from whom? We'll be gone.

JOURNEY I can set something up. The point is, Crazy Horse will live on because of us. And all the stuff he did.

CALVIN He's Lakota not Marahotah.

JOURNEY The Lakota took us in like three generations ago. We live on their reservation. We may as well be Lakota.

CALVIN But we're not.

JOURNEY The banner is a bonus message for your Lakota idol. I thought it would make you happy.

(CALVIN goes back to sorting papers in the box. She looks at the chess board.)

JOURNEY It's still your move.

CALVIN I'm a little busy organizing ten years of Grandpa's mail while you're designing banners on my computer that you didn't ask to use. Thanks for the help.

JOURNEY Oh my God. For months you complain that I'm not doing anything, now I do shit and you still complain.

(CALVIN opens mail as JOURNEY moves one of his chess pieces.)

CALVIN Hands off!

JOURNEY It's hardly news to you that I cheat. I knew your time at Yale would change you, but I didn't think we'd never be us again.

CALVIN We nearly have the same DNA. We can't be more us.

JOURNEY Maybe Crazy Horse was right to stay away from the white people. They can steal your soul.

CALVIN Yale did not steal my soul. Crushed it a little, but that was bound to happen eventually.

JOURNEY It's more than that.

CALVIN You seriously want to go down this road? You were a basket case last year.

JOURNEY Don't be dramatic.

CALVIN Grandpa and I thought we were going to lose you.

JOURNEY You didn't.

CALVIN And just when I think I can start work on my paper again, Grandpa dies and you… do what you did.

JOURNEY It was a natural reaction.

CALVIN It wasn't.

JOURNEY I'm fine now.

CALVIN Yeah, right. Just don't accuse me of being the one who changed.

(JOURNEY turns and admires her banner.)

JOURNEY I like it. But I guess it should be a Marahotah leader instead of Crazy Horse. In case it gets in the paper.

CALVIN It's OK to admire Crazy Horse, they killed Custer for all of us.

(CALVIN reads a letter.)

CALVIN Shit. From the State History Museum of South Dakota, a copy of the original Klan flyer and there's Grandpa.

(He holds up a photocopy of EVAN's KKK flyer.)

JOURNEY Maybe they stole his picture and photoshopped him in?

CALVIN In 1926? Besides why did he sign a contract three months ago?

JOURNEY I don't know.

CALVIN If they didn't pay him on signing, this contract is breached and we're done with that part of the bullshit. But I don't want that woman using the flyer to smear Grandpa's memory.

JOURNEY We'll think of something. They'll be here any moment.

CALVIN Damn it. We've been on the losing side for four hundred years. Just once I want to feel what it's like to win.

JOURNEY You won the lottery, brother. You got out of this hell hole.

CALVIN Yet here I am.

JOURNEY We could shoot both of them when they walk in. Problem solved.

CALVIN Ha ha. You know I don't believe in violence.

JOURNEY That's awesome, brother. You may not believe in violence, but it sure as hell believes in you. Tell me the truth, in our situation with Klan lady, what would Crazy Horse do?

CALVIN Probably the shooting thing.

JOURNEY There you go.

CALVIN Don't joke.

JOURNEY I'm not.

CALVIN I won't let the Marahotah be remembered as criminals. There's a better way.

(EVAN and REBEL enter outside. CALVIN reluctantly joins JOURNEY at the chess board. He makes a realization and takes one of her pieces. He smiles. She nods appreciatively.)

REBEL You know we gotta get this done, now.

EVAN I'm not letting a couple Indians stand between us and our future.

REBEL Neither will I.

EVAN Take it easy. The brother went to Yale. He's reasonable, but he has to be handled with restraint and decorum.

REBEL I can be decorous. Which is a word.

EVAN Trust me to handle it my way.

REBEL Let's just get this done and get off this ass backward reservation. Gawd, my people may be a bunch of hicks, but these Indians look like they're living in a war zone.

EVAN Maybe they are.

(They knock. EVAN smiles. CALVIN opens the door.)

EVAN Remember me?

JOURNEY Nope.

CALVIN Come in.

(CALVIN extends his hand. EVAN hesitates then extends hers. CALVIN suddenly doesn't want to take it. They both drop their hands. EVAN spots the flyer.)

EVAN You did your research. So you believe we are telling the truth?

CALVIN I believe you did not make up this flyer. Beyond that, I'm not sure what to believe.

EVAN We are sincere. The Ku Klux Klan is holding a pow wow and we need you to be in it.

(JOURNEY grabs the flyer.)

JOURNEY You know you can't just put a "K" in front of things and turn it Klan. I mean look at this thing. "The South Dakota Klavern invites you to a Kar" K-A-R "Klassic." K-L-A. "PopKorn will be served." They put a fucking K in the middle of popcorn.

EVAN It was a big event. They may have over done it a bit.

JOURNEY And topping it all off, a Klan Pow Wow. "With original American Indians for your entertainment."

EVAN This commemorative event will celebrate the coming together of our people in a new era of understanding. The way Dr. Evans envisioned before our organization was corrupted by hate.

CALVIN Technically, you are a hate group.

EVAN Our group is about racial pride, in the exact same way you take pride in your culture.

CALVIN You're proud of the culture of whiteness?

EVAN Basically.

JOURNEY What exactly does cultural whiteness look like?

EVAN George Washington, Thomas Edison, Bill Gates.

JOURNEY Hitler.

EVAN Funny. But the truth is, we do not hate anyone.

JOURNEY I hate lots of people.

EVAN I am sorry to hear that because there is another way to live.

JOURNEY Bullshit.

EVAN Our organization does not condone profanity, drink alcohol to excess, or use drugs.

JOURNEY I think she just called me a foul mouthed, drunk Indian.

EVAN I am pointing out that there are positives to our organization we can all agree on. There is a reason Dr. Evans grew us to four million open members and countless more in the 1920s.

CALVIN I've looked into this contract—

EVAN Come on Calvin, our people and your people have never had seriously strained relations.

JOURNEY Your people killed millions of our people.

EVAN I mean the Klan specifically. And according to this history, we had good relations at one point. We want to honor and explore that history.

JOURNEY By making us their token Indians.

EVAN By giving you a platform. Think about it, few groups have a stronger romanticized image than the Ku Klux Klan and Native Americans. Put us together for one day, and the whole world will tune in to watch. Our marketing machine is prepared to get every social media outlet, news network and Indian loving German tuned into this event.

CALVIN You can do that? That kind of coverage?

JOURNEY Coverage of the Klan parading behind us in a bunch of hoods.

EVAN We are no longer an invisible organization. The Free Americans stand proud, without hoods. And we are offering you full autonomy in the press. We bring them to you and you say whatever you want, alone.

CALVIN Wait. You mean that? You'd let us say anything we want?

EVAN Absolutely. My organization has survived by going underground and getting distance from the Nazi groups and hate speech that Dr. Evans did not teach. We simply want a chance to demonstrate that with this event.

CALVIN Are you really going to do this? As big as you say?

EVAN Our followers are mobilizing from every state and ten countries around the world.

Our message will sweep across this nation and beyond.

CALVIN Huh. If we did this—

JOURNEY That's enough. (*to EVAN*) Get out!

(*She puts herself between CALVIN and EVAN.*)

CALVIN What my sister means to say is that we have to discuss this privately.

JOURNEY No, we don't.

EVAN We'll wait outside.

JOURNEY Don't wait.

(*EVAN and REBEL duck out.*)

JOURNEY I better hear your car starting!

CALVIN Calm down.

JOURNEY You calm down. You aren't considering this, are you?

CALVIN Look, I'm committed to the twin suicide pact thing, but if we want it to send a message for our people—

JOURNEY The memory of our people.

CALVIN Whatever, I don't think that's something we can pull off by ourselves.

JOURNEY You want to partner with the Klan?

CALVIN Think about it, if we don't join them, we've made a bad enemy. If we join them, we're hated traitors at best, nut jobs at worst. But, if we say what we want to and kill ourselves right in the middle of their pow wow, with all that news coverage, we're martyrs. Better yet, we're Native American Indians who took on the Klan martyrs. If we're killing ourselves anyway, it doesn't get bigger than that.

JOURNEY The Klan will hijack our story and the Marahotah won't be remembered at all. We agreed to make our deaths do something. Action, not exploitation.

CALVIN We'll mess up the Klan on national TV. I'll be on national TV. Maybe international. This is so much better than Crazy Horse bracelets.

JOURNEY Why do you trust these guys? If they find out what you're planning we'll be back to nothing, maybe worse. I want us to be in control of our lives. Not them.

CALVIN Crazy Horse single handedly terrorized the miners in the Black Hills. Everyone thought it was too difficult to stop the mining, but he saw a way that one man, a solitary man, could move among them and make the United States think twice about panning for gold in Indian land. I believe I can be that man with these guys before I'm done.

JOURNEY "I'M done"?

CALVIN We're done. I think we can spin this thing.

JOURNEY Crazy Horse failed. All the gold's gone.

CALVIN He never lived among them so he didn't understand them like I do. I want to do this.

(JOURNEY studies her brother.)

JOURNEY I can see that. Get her back inside.

(CALVIN goes to get EVAN. JOURNEY goes to the desk and opens a drawer.)

JOURNEY Crazy Horse killed his people's horses rather than let them surrender to the reservations. This is what Crazy Horse would do.

(As soon as EVAN enters JOURNEY turns and aims a gun at her.)

CALVIN No!

(CALVIN jumps in front of JOURNEY. EVAN ducks for cover. JOURNEY fires. EVAN's and CALVIN's shoulders jerk back, dropping them both to the floor.)

JOURNEY Calvin!

(She rushes to him. He sits up.)

JOURNEY Are you OK?

CALVIN It grazed me. I'm fine.

JOURNEY Oh my God! I'm so sorry!

CALVIN You can't keep doing shit like this!

(EVAN groans. JOURNEY lifts the gun again. CALVIN grabs it from her. EVAN sits up, holding her shoulder. A red stain spreads through her clothes.)

CALVIN Oh my God.

(He rushes to help EVAN. She pulls away.)

EVAN Don't touch me.

CALVIN I won't hurt you. You have to understand this isn't her fault. My sister isn't right in her head. She's been through tragedy and–

EVAN I'm fine.

CALVIN You know you've been shot.

EVAN Not the first time.

(REBEL crashes through the door, gun drawn. CALVINN instinctively pulls JOURNEY'S gun. REBEL swings toward him. JOURNEY throws herself on CALVIN.)

EVAN Stop! Put the gun down Rebel.

(REBEL focuses on EVAN, he's visibly upset. He rushes to her, gun still in his hand.)

REBEL I go for one smoke– Shit. I'll quit the things tonight. Shit.

EVAN It's just a shoulder, no cause for profanity.

(REBEL rips right into her clothes, triage style.)

CALVIN *(to JOURNEY)* What if he had shot you? You would have left me alone.

JOURNEY I'm sorry. I felt like she was taking you away from me.

CALVIN We're together in this. Do you hear me?

JOURNEY Yes.

REBEL I need some towels, something to disinfect the wound and my bag from the car.

CALVIN You're not going to call the police?

EVAN Don't be stupid. Gunshot wounds are reported. My organization is not coming into the light unless it is in the way we have orchestrated.

CALVIN OK. Good.

REBEL The supplies, now! I'm not leaving her alone with you igits.

CALVIN Journey, get a towel.

JOURNEY Fuck that.

CALVIN Really? You shoot someone in our house, she's not calling the police and you're gonna be a shit about it?

(JOURNEY goes. REBEL tosses keys to CALVIN. He goes.)

REBEL I'll get you stabilized then we're out of here.

EVAN They know too much.

REBEL We can take care of that.

EVAN I sold this Indian transformation story to our people. We have to make it true. If the wolves in our organization smell blood, it is all they will need to rise up, scare the sheep and we're out.

REBEL It doesn't have to be the Klan. We could start another organization, without the wolves always coming after us.

EVAN You know that by the year 2042, white men and women will be the minority in America. Thanks to our ten long years of work, the KKK is the only organization prepared to fight back.

REBEL Does it have to be the pow wow, with this crazy squaw?

EVAN This Klan sponsored pow wow is part of our history. This new event with these Indians will not only bring us press, but GOOD press. And that's something the Klan has not been able to buy for over eighty years.

REBEL Where I come from, you see a rabid dog, you put it down. Not that I would. Just saying.

EVAN I underestimated her before, but I can handle her now.

(JOURNEY and CALVIN return and give REBEL the supplies. REBEL tends to her wound and keeps the gun handy. EVAN stays solid.)

EVAN You won't need the gun. Journey is going to be fine. Since we're all here now, we should discuss the event.

JOURNEY You're kidding.

EVAN We came with a job to do, and we're going to do it.

CALVIN I don't think–

EVAN But I do. Especially now. You are appearing at that pow wow. Think it out Calvin.

CALVIN If we don't, you call the police on Journey.

JOURNEY I don't care.

CALVIN Do you want us to be separated?

JOURNEY I won't dance for these people.

EVAN We haven't had a chance to discuss the money issue yet.

JOURNEY There wasn't any. We checked.

EVAN Wrong.

(REBEL pulls out a sheet of paper and gives it to CALVIN.)

CALVIN He signed the check over to my student loans? That's not possible. I would have known.

EVAN It didn't go through. He didn't have your loan information right. But we corrected that. You'll see it credited on your next statement. So, that's our end of the contract fulfilled.

REBEL Thought you guys went to school for free.

JOURNEY Yeah, Yale comes with our fantastic free health care.

REBEL I know a lot of folks who would kill for some free government health care.

JOURNEY Have you ever been to an Indian Health Services clinic?

REBEL Gotta be better than nothing.

JOURNEY Yeah, because there's nothing more reliable than a government-run agency. Nothing more safe. Shit, the same good liberals who believe the US government conspired to bomb the Twin Towers want to hand their lives over to that government in the form of socialized health care. People are idiots.

EVAN Calvin, you decide which way you want to go with this. We either take you to court for the money plus substantial damages and charge Journey with attempted murder, or we do this event and everyone wins.

CALVIN You don't have to threaten us. We're in.

EVAN Great. Let's talk about the pow wow. We want to be sure we treat your beliefs with the utmost respect and propriety. How would you like to be addressed, Native American or American Indian?

REBEL Oh my Gawd.

JOURNEY You're fucking kidding me.

CALVIN Journey and I are members of the Marahotah Tribe. That's our word for ourselves.

EVAN Thank you.

JOURNEY *(to REBEL)* How about you? What you like to be called? Nazi? Skin head? Redneck?

REBEL My title is Grand Giant.

(JOURNEY bursts out laughing.)

JOURNEY Seriously?

REBEL Shut up squaw.

JOURNEY Dick.

REBEL Pussy.

JOURNEY Cock sucker.

EVAN Rebel, language.

REBEL What? I'm talking about cats and bread.

CALVIN *(to EVAN)* What are you called?

EVAN My title is Imperial Dragon.

CALVIN Isn't that the president of the Klan?

EVAN More like vice president.

REBEL For now.

JOURNEY So if I was a better shot, I would have done the world a big favor?

CALVIN Be quiet and let me handle this.

JOURNEY Right, because we're best buds with the Ku Klux Klan now. And the whole world's gonna see it.

CALVIN Stop it.

JOURNEY Fuck that. I say we stick to the pact and be done with it before things get any worse.

(JOURNEY takes the gun and caresses it. REBEL pulls his gun, just in case.)

CALVIN Give it back Journey.

JOURNEY I see how people get hooked on shooting these things. It feels so good.

REBEL Girl, I'm not giving you another chance to shoot at us.

JOURNEY I'm not interested in either of you.

CALVIN Stop.

JOURNEY We're doing it anyway Calvin and like dragon lady said, we're screwed. I'm sick of fighting. You're sick of losing. Let's be done.

CALVIN Don't you dare go crazy on me again.

JOURNEY It's not crazy. It was a promise.

CALVIN Not like this. No one will remember like this. Don't let it be like Willow. Or Marianna. Or Vincent.

JOURNEY Or Martin.

CALVIN Joseph.

JOURNEY Neil.

CALVIN No one remembers them.

JOURNEY No one but us.

CALVIN Do it like this and no one will remember the Marahotah at all.

JOURNEY Or any of them.

EVAN Who were those people?

CALVIN Friends who have committed suicide. The most recent ones.

EVAN That many?

JOURNEY The last four count as one. Four kids took one gun and drew cards. Low card won and got to shoot himself first. The highest card went last.

REBEL Shit.

JOURNEY Neil watched three of his friends blow their brains out then still had the courage to pull the trigger, all alone. Can you imagine that? I try to all the time.

(JOURNEY pictures it. CALVIN gets scared.)

CALVIN Journey. Come back to me.

JOURNEY No one would have known if he didn't do it, but he made a promise and he fucking followed through.

CALVIN What about the twin pact? If we go, we go together.

JOURNEY My sweet brother. You know the chances are that we won't go exactly together. One heart will beat a moment longer. One breath more.

CALVIN You don't know that. If we plan it right… we came into this world together, we can leave it the same. Womb to tomb.

JOURNEY Womb to tomb.

(JOURNEY sets the gun down.)

EVAN You'd think we'd hear about four suicides on the news.

JOURNEY Turns out colonization is a perfect system. When they stopped killing us, they got us to do it ourselves.

EVAN You have to believe me, we're not here to ruin your life.

JOURNEY I really don't have to believe anything you say.

EVAN What is your ideal world Journey? How about one free of the white race? A world where your people live together and have children together and learn your culture completely free and clear of everyone else?

JOURNEY We had that once.

EVAN That is the dream of our organization. We do not want to abolish races, we simply want them to be allowed to live separately, as God intended. Whites with whites, Indians with Indians. Each race becoming clean and pure as they were meant to be. Imagine, a few generations from now, an entire race of full-blooded Marahotah, like it was before everything went bad.

JOURNEY That's not going to happen no matter how long you wait.

EVAN It's biology.

JOURNEY Calvin and I are the last Marahotah on the face of the earth. Nearly extinct with no warning. Shit, the world rallies to save frogs, but a race of people disappears and no one knows. We didn't, until a couple years ago.

REBEL There's gotta be others somewhere.

CALVIN The only ones that may be left are so mixed they wouldn't even call themselves Cherokee.

REBEL Then shouldn't you be in a museum or something?

JOURNEY Become Ishi? Become Crazy Horse? They turned themselves over to a white institution and it killed them both.

REBEL Not to live there. Jeez, that'd kill anybody. But so they record your culture and stuff.

JOURNEY For who? A bunch of white people running around speaking our language in a feather headdress. It's over. The Marahotah are done. Shouldn't you be happy about this?

REBEL No. If we let people screw around any way they please, one day we'll be one big brown family across the globe. But is that really what people want? No more white and black and Mexican and Marahotah? No more differences? But you try to point that out and you're called a racist.

JOURNEY So what are you saying we should do?

REBEL If there's one thing you people have taught us, it's that extinction is a real and present danger. Think of how many tribes were wiped out in the ten years after Columbus landed.

EVAN Your story is at the core of what Rebel and I have been trying to build for the last decade. That future I spoke about can save us all. People don't believe in racial extinction, but you are living proof. Tell your story. Save another tribe before it's too late.

(JOURNEY and CALVIN take it in for a moment. JOURNEY shakes herself out of it.)

JOURNEY You're good, lady. You nearly sucked both of us in in one night. White wash your "organization" all you want but it's still the Klan.

EVAN Much like the Native Americans, we've been portrayed inaccurately for hundreds of years.

CALVIN What about the lynching and terrorizing people for the color of their skin?

EVAN Fringe lunatics.

JOURNEY It's not polite to talk about Rebel right in front of him.

REBEL Don't speak for me girl.

EVAN Rebel has proven himself above the stereotypes of his Southern roots. He's quite decorous when you get to know him.

CALVIN It's easy to say that now, but there seemed to be a lot of people in hoods standing around those lunatics.

EVAN As easy as it is to dismiss the Natives that attacked and burned wagon trains of women and children?

JOURNEY That was self-defense.

EVAN Speaking of shooting defenseless women, another towel please.

(JOURNEY leaves the room.)

EVAN I'm worried about her, Calvin. She's obviously not stable.

CALVIN Grandpa's death… opened something in her. But I've gotten her through stuff before.

EVAN Stuff like shooting people?

CALVIN Not guns…

REBEL But violence right?

CALVIN I know how to take care of her.

REBEL Has she been diagnosed?

CALVIN For what?

REBEL Classic PTSD. We can help you son.

CALVIN That's crazy.

EVAN Is it? All the death she has seen, it makes sense.

CALVIN She's fine.

EVAN She could have killed either of us.

CALVIN But she didn't.

REBEL Yet.

(JOURNEY returns and tosses a towel at REBEL. CALVIN studies her. REBEL inspects the wound.)

REBEL I think the bleeding's stopped enough to stitch it.

EVAN I'm ready.

(REBEL stitches EVAN'S wound through the following. EVAN cringes but keeps herself together. CALVIN looks away. JOURNEY watches, impressed.)

CALVIN You want an… asprin or something?

REBEL I'll have a painkiller and antibiotics called in to the local pharmacy.

CALVIN We only have IHS here.

(REBEL glares at him.)

JOURNEY Don't you listen? The fantastic Indian Health Services. They don't treat white people.

REBEL You only help your own and you call us racist?

JOURNEY YOUR government only subjects Indians to their shitty care.

EVAN Calvin, do you have any doctor friends at IHS that would help us? Discretely.

CALVIN There's a nurse I know who may slip us a sample or two. Of antibiotics anyway.

JOURNEY Who?

CALVIN She's new.

REBEL Go get 'em.

CALVIN We're not leaving you two here, in our home.

JOURNEY Do I know her?

CALVIN No.

REBEL If anyone sees Evan's wound, they'll call the cops.

CALVIN We can put a jacket on her.

REBEL I don't want to move her until she has antibiotics. Risking an infection.

CALVIN Again, we're not leaving you here.

REBEL Then one of you go alone.

CALVIN Journey and I stay together.

JOURNEY How do you know this nurse?

CALVIN I used to go out, see other people besides you.

REBEL You some kind of creepy siblings?

JOURNEY If we were, we would have a baby and keep the tribe going.

CALVIN Why do you say stuff like that?

JOURNEY It's a joke.

REBEL Calvin has to go. He knows the nurse.

JOURNEY Pretty well apparently.

CALVIN Drop it. I'm not leaving you alone with them.

EVAN Rebel and Calvin go, I'll stay with Journey.

REBEL Hell no. Calvin goes alone.

CALVIN I told you, I'm not leaving Journey alone with-

REBEL I'm not leaving Evan alone with either of-

JOURNEY Oh my fucking God! Fine.

(She grabs the gun. REBEL jumps up. JOURNEY hands it to EVAN.)

JOURNEY Now she can shoot me if she wants. Go get her the medication before she gets infected and we're stuck with this bitch.

EVAN Go Rebel.

CALVIN *(to JOURNEY)* Don't you care that Rebel has a gun and I don't?

JOURNEY Say hi to your nurse friend for me.

CALVIN Seriously, will you be OK?

JOURNEY If we're sticking around, we're gonna have to be apart sometime. Rebel will keep you safe.

(Both REBEL and CALVIN look surprised.)

JOURNEY They need us. *(to REBEL)* If anything happens to him, I'll rip her throat out.

REBEL We'll be right back.

(She and CALVIN hug fiercely.)

CALVIN It's just a trip to town.

JOURNEY Yup. Done a million of them.

(She finally lets go.)

CALVIN I don't think you're ready for this.

JOURNEY It's been two weeks since the accident. We can't stay attached forever.

CALVIN But if anything happens to you...

JOURNEY Nothing can happen to me without you. We made a pact. Don't forget it.

CALVIN Not just any pact, a twin pact.

EVAN We'll be fine.

(CALVIN and REBEL go. JOURNEY is clearly upset.)

EVAN I've heard twins are close, but you two really are.

JOURNEY We always were, but there's something about being the last two on the planet.

(She looks out the window.)

EVAN Rebel has an array of military and defense training.

JOURNEY Some of the drunk drivers on that road have thirty years under their belt.

EVAN Oh, that's right. That's how Walter died, isn't it?

JOURNEY On that same road. Driving to town.

EVAN Tell me about your grandfather.

JOURNEY He raised us since we were ten. Which is why... I thought I knew him.

EVAN I thought I knew my grandfather too. I was born into the Klan. It was more

underground then, but I still grew up in the KKK Kiddies and the Triple K Teen Klub. When I found these pictures it seemed to go against everything we stood for. Then I went back and re-read every speech my grandfather gave. It was all there, plain as day. I was Klan before, but after that it was different. It became a passion. A true vision. I used my name and worked my way up to the highest ranking woman in the history of the organization. In the past ten years we've done- We've accomplished a lot, behind the scenes.

JOURNEY Like what?

EVAN Just things to pave the way.

JOURNEY For a pow wow?

EVAN For the glorious reemergence of the public Klan, free of the hate speech and violence lovers of the past.

JOURNEY Free of violence? You calling Rebel harmless?

EVAN No, he's willing to do what has to be done, but only if it has to be done. Not for love of it, trust me. I wouldn't call you harmless either.

JOURNEY Lately I've been thinking about the difference between dangerous and effective. I can sit here in the middle of nowhere, ready to pull the trigger, but if no one walks by I may as well be holding a marshmallow shooter.

EVAN Lucky you, people walked right into your line of fire.

JOURNEY Yeah. This isn't what I imagined, but everything's been bizarre lately.

EVAN This is actually not the strangest night of my life.

JOURNEY I don't know who's crazier right now, you or me.

EVAN I think we're both trying to find our way in unbelievably difficult situations.

JOURNEY But you actually think this will work. You'll have your pow wow with your press conference and we'll be a cautionary tale and everyone will love the Klan.

EVAN When you put it that way, it does sound crazy.

JOURNEY That's the way it is Evan.

EVAN People are scared. This world of virtual connectedness makes people feel more isolated than they've ever been. They need to be part of something that tells them they are amazing and perfect just as God made them. They want to know there is a path to true peace on this earth.

JOURNEY Peace through racial separation?

EVAN "Each nation has its own God-given qualities, but each can do its own work only if the racial and group qualities are preserved relatively pure. If any nation is mongrelized, that nation will lose its distinctive quality and its power to contribute to civilization." Dr. Evans wrote that the week after he met Walter. Can you honestly tell me Walter didn't think your people were special? That he didn't believe your blood should be preserved in order to enrich mankind?

JOURNEY Of course he did.

EVAN That's why Walter agreed to help us after all these years. We're fighting for the same thing. Other races have realized that. The Klan has had African American chapters since the beginning.

JOURNEY Really? *(Shakes herself out of it.)* Stop fucking with my mind.

EVAN It's just facts, Journey. Honest facts.

JOURNEY You aren't what I expected.

EVAN Then the mind f-word is working.

JOURNEY F-word? Seriously?

EVAN The Klan discourages swearing.

JOURNEY Come on. It's not swearing, it's a vulgarism. Try it.

EVAN No thank you.

JOURNEY If you're gonna fuck my mind, you at least gotta say it.

EVAN I'd rather not.

JOURNEY I think you rather would. Come on. It feels good.

EVAN You have been mind-fucked.

JOURNEY Nice.

EVAN Don't tell Rebel I said that.

JOURNEY Feels good through, right?

EVAN Lots of things feel good, but that doesn't make them right.

JOURNEY Lots of things feel pretty fucked up and we do them too.

EVAN Are you and Calvin really planning to kill yourselves?

JOURNEY Um…yeah. Some day.

EVAN It's such a waste.

JOURNEY We first talked about it when we were ten and lost our parents, but over the years, the idea always comes back. Long ago our people dispersed to various reservations and white cities and started intermarrying. One day we woke up and everyone was gone but the three of us. Then there were two. And those two are fucked by inevitability.

My brother and I live on a knife edge cutting through us slowly, draining Marahotah blood from the planet day by day. Any moment that knife could come up and slice us in half. But we won't let that happen. There won't be any last of the Marahotahs. At Grandpa's funeral ceremony we promised we'd go out together. Not one sad, lonely Indian, but a tribe for eternity.

EVAN With that story, you could change the world.

JOURNEY You can tell it when we're dead.

EVAN And when will that be?

(REBEL rushes in, carrying a Super Big Gulp.)

JOURNEY That was fast.

REBEL Calvin got arrested.

JOURNEY What the hell did you do?

REBEL I was sitting in the dam- darn car outside the clinic, which is shit by the way, and all these people are led out in handcuffs. Doctors, Indians, everything.

JOURNEY The tribal police know Calvin. They wouldn't-

REBEL It was the feds. I'd recognize their suits anywhere. *(to EVAN)* We gotta get out of here.

JOURNEY Feds? Are you sure? Where'd they take him?

REBEL How the heck do I know?

EVAN Let me make a call. We have informants in the government.

REBEL We're not using our connections for this. We've gotta get gone.

EVAN If they were looking for us they would be here by now.

(EVAN dials her phone. She speaks quietly.)

JOURNEY I knew we shouldn't separate.

REBEL They'll be looking to question us as soon as Calvin tells them to.

JOURNEY He's not a rat.

REBEL I could break him in two minutes.

JOURNEY Shit. I need Calvin back. Everything gets… wrong when he leaves me.

(EVAN hangs up.)

EVAN It's a federal raid on the clinic. The nurse was dealing prescription drugs. Too bad you didn't get there sooner, I'd be feeling great.

REBEL Still, we should go.

EVAN Perhaps.

JOURNEY No.

(*JOURNEY dives for EVAN and grabs the gun. She holds it on her as REBEL draws on JOURNEY.*)

REBEL Drop it.

JOURNEY No one leaves. No one does anything until Calvin gets back.

EVAN Journey, Calvin may not be back for a long time.

JOURNEY So? You try to leave and I'll shoot you. And this time Calvin won't be in the way.

REBEL I'm shooting on three. One–

JOURNEY I'll shoot on two. Then where the fuck will your organization be?

EVAN Look. It's the three of us now so we need to lower the guns and work this out.

JOURNEY Fuck that. I'm done with your pow wow, press conference bullshit. We wait until Calvin comes back.

EVAN OK, but I'm more likely to keep Rebel awake to shoot you than the other way around. Come on Journey, I know it's hard when Calvin leaves you. Let's talk about it.

JOURNEY I'm not saying shit until Calvin gets here.

REBEL Screw this. Let me shoot her.

JOURNEY Just try it.

EVAN Journey, truth is, Rebel can shoot you through your brainstem and have you on the ground before your finger can react. But that's not what we want here. Lower your gun and we'll talk.

(*REBEL smiles. JOURNEY is coming apart.*)

JOURNEY No. You'll go and I'll be alone. Shit. I need Calvin.

EVAN Calvin isn't coming back.

JOURNEY Why not?

EVAN He said he knew that nurse. They're going to lock him up and throw away the key. He'll be in a federal prison so far, far away that you'll never see him again.

JOURNEY No more mind fuck talking. Shut your mouth!

(*REBEL sights JOURNEY's head.*)

REBEL Bang. You're dead.

JOURNEY Shut up! Shut up! SHUT UP!!

(*JOURNEY clicks music on a computer. pow wow music blares. The drum beats annoy REBEL but soothe JOURNEY. EVAN, JOURNEY, and REBEL settle in, guns pointed and wait. REBEL takes a long drink from his cup.*)

Scene 4

Later, sunset colors the light. The music pounds on. Everyone is tired, but JOURNEY has calmed.

REBEL I can't take any more of this jungle music! Let me shoot her.

EVAN His job is to protect my life. Eventually he will kill you and there's nothing I can do.

JOURNEY I said no talking!

(*She cranks the music louder.*)

REBEL (*Singing at the top of his lungs.*) Rocky top, you'll always be, home sweet home to me! Good old Rocky Top, Rocky Top Tennessee! Rocky Top Tennessee-ee-eee-eee!

JOURNEY OK. OK.

(*JOURNEY stops the music.*)

REBEL Worse than Guantanamo.

JOURNEY Shut up or the music comes back.

(*REBEL sucks on his drink, empty. He sinks into a sulky silence. JOURNEY does the same.*)

EVAN You know what I've always wondered?

(*JOURNEY glares at her.*)

EVAN What made Walter agree to dance in the original pow wow in the first place? Let's be honest, the usual reaction to a request from the Klan is… yours. Do you have any idea why he did it?

JOURNEY No.

EVAN You knew him best. Why would a man like Walter agree to share his dances and songs with my grandfather? Then give him that medallion? It must have a meaning.

JOURNEY Well, the old Marahotah ways taught that if someone asks for the dances they are being led by a spirit because they need healing. Grandpa was traditional like that. So when Dr. Evans asked him for dances, Grandpa could not refuse. Nor would he want to.

EVAN Interesting. Awhile before the pow wow, my grandfather was part of a group of men who kidnapped a black man, beat him and carved three K's onto his forehead with acid before they let him go. Poor man had to see that every time he looked in the mirror.

JOURNEY Were they arrested?

EVAN The very next year Life Magazine put my grandfather on the cover. But he never committed a violent act again. I'm sure he regretted it the rest of his life.

JOURNEY So you're saying that Dr. Evans needed healing?

EVAN He did.

JOURNEY Which means that need led him to Walter.

EVAN Yes, that makes sense.

JOURNEY And now you're following in his footsteps, asking for the same dances. You need healing too. You could have done this all without Walter, but you had to come. You were led to him.

EVAN Whatever Walter said to Dr. Evans could be the key for all of our people.

JOURNEY It's more than that. Shit, that's why Grandpa signed the contract, because the spirits brought you here.

EVAN I did feel like that picture was a sign.

JOURNEY Yes. We should have seen that. Maybe Yale did steal Calvin's soul.

EVAN Whatever the impetus, I need this event to go as planned.

JOURNEY The Marahotah dances, the songs, they mean more than just words you know.

EVAN Not to you.

JOURNEY Of course they do.

EVAN When I asked you to be in the pow wow, you refused. If you believed in all of this you could not have refused me.

JOURNEY That was a mistake. I see that now.

EVAN So if I ask you again, you won't refuse?

JOURNEY I can't. It's bigger than me. It's about our people.

EVAN And mine. All those people will hear the songs. Be healed.

JOURNEY That's what Grandpa taught us. Maybe that's why Calvin wanted to do this, not because of the pact.

EVAN What?

REBEL That's it. I can't hold it anymore.

JOURNEY The bathroom is in the back.

(She focuses her gun on EVAN.)

REBEL I'm not going anywhere.

(He's in pain.)

JOURNEY I love it. The Grand Giant is taken down by a Super Big Gulp.

REBEL I'm not going down.

JOURNEY Gosh I think I hear rain. Or is that a flowing fountain? Water in a river-

(He winces.)

REBEL I'm pissing on the floor.

(He opens his fly clumsily while keeping his gun on JOURNEY.)

JOURNEY Don't pee on my floor. That's sick.

REBEL Can't hold it.

(REBEL faces the wall and a stream of piss comes out. Both women wince.)

JOURNEY What the hell?!?

EVAN Rebel Shaw!

JOURNEY Fine! Pee truce. Just stop!

REBEL Too late. Can't stop.

(JOURNEY lowers her gun.)

JOURNEY Forget it. Shoot me.

(She grabs a water bottle and comes at REBEL. She sprays him and his pee stain with water. REBEL jumps back.)

REBEL Hey! Watch it.

JOURNEY Are you kidding me? You just pissed on my wall! You're a fucking animal.

REBEL You're a fucking idiot.

(REBEL grabs her gun and holds both on JOURNEY.)

JOURNEY I don't care. Just zip first. I'm not having that be my last sight on this earth.

EVAN Agreed.

(He zips.)

REBEL Sit there, where I can keep an eye on you.

JOURNEY I'm not sitting by the pee.

REBEL Fine, sit over there.

(JOURNEY sits across from them.)

REBEL Seriously, why we haven't wiped you people off the face of the earth-

EVAN That's not our goal.

REBEL But natural selection should have run its course by now. We should get going.

EVAN I need to check with our contact first.

(She texts on her phone while REBEL and JOURNEY stare at each other. REBEL looks at the chess set.)

REBEL White's gonna lose big time.

JOURNEY Yeah.

REBEL You know that?

JOURNEY White's Calvin.

REBEL Thought he was the Yale genius.

JOURNEY It takes me weeks to throw a game with him. He's the worst player I've ever seen.

REBEL Why throw the game?

JOURNEY He needs a win.

(REBEL clicks on the computer.)

REBEL I need another song in my head. Oh my Gawd. How much of this drum music you got?

JOURNEY That music is sacred.

REBEL There's a song here called "Pow Wow Mighty Mouse." You pray to Mighty Mouse?

JOURNEY That's a kid's song. It's humor.

REBEL Crazy Horse bullshit, bullshit.

JOURNEY Get the fuck off Calvin's computer.

REBEL Most of the files are locked. Oh my gawd.

JOURNEY What?

REBEL You will not believe how many racist, domestic terrorist chat rooms he's in.

EVAN Please tell me you are kidding.

REBEL All the usual suspects; Hutaree, ALF, Stormfront, Advanced White Society, Sovereign Citizens.

EVAN Can you fix it?

JOURNEY There's nothing to fix. That's research for his dissertation. It's about Crazy Horse taking on the US government. Calvin's comparing leadership styles which included domestic terrorism and racial shit.

EVAN This is a problem. These are bad, hate-filled people, Journey.

JOURNEY Says the head of the KKK.

REBEL Crazy nigger lynching idiots like this are exactly the kind of people we're trying to get away from, not be tied to.

JOURNEY Sorry we're not the Klan poster children you were hoping for.

EVAN You're not understanding what's going on here. The government has him in custody. In case you haven't heard, the NSA tracks this information. Calvin could be going away for a long time. And the rest of us are implicated simply by being together in this room.

REBEL I need the password to the rest of these files. God only knows what else is on here.

JOURNEY He hasn't done anything.

REBEL The password.

(She grabs CALVIN's lap top.)

REBEL Give that back.

JOURNEY No.

REBEL I'm not playing girl. We need to know what we're dealing with.

EVAN We have been more than patient with you, Journey.

JOURNEY Thanks ever so much.

EVAN I am done. Rebel.

(REBEL grabs a picture frame and smashes it on the edge of the desk. He pulls the picture out and

starts ripping. JOURNEY freaks and runs toward him.)

JOURNEY That's our mother!

(REBEL goes for the closet and gets CALVIN's regalia. He rips the medallion off. He grabs his knife and takes it to the medallion.)

JOURNEY What the hell? Calvin will flip!

(JOURNEY goes for him, REBEL grabs her wrist and pulls her with him back to the desk as he pulls the computer out of her hands.)

REBEL I'm just starting. I will rip apart everything you care about, burn this house to the ground if you don't start being a little more cooperative.

(JOURNEY wrenches herself away.)

JOURNEY OK! You don't have to be an asshole.

EVAN I'm asking once. What is his password?

JOURNEY WWCHD.

EVAN Thank you.

JOURNEY There's nothing there. Calvin's just really touchy about people using his computer. Well, about me using his computer.

(REBEL and EVAN read CALVIN's computer.)

REBEL This is getting worse and worse. He's building a case for domestic terrorism. We should get rid of them both. Clean house.

JOURNEY Wait, what?

EVAN I don't know.

JOURNEY Hey. Are you guys serious?

EVAN He's inciting a civil war against the government.

JOURNEY It's a decolonized point of view.

EVAN Being in contact with those groups is already illegal. If the feds find all of this…

JOURNEY But you could help him. Right? You could use your connections before the feds find this stuff?

REBEL This is bad.

JOURNEY Look, I'll do whatever you want if you get Calvin home. Put me in front of a camera now.

EVAN I don't think there's anything we can do.

JOURNEY There has to be something.

EVAN I'm sorry Journey.

JOURNEY This is bullshit. You claim you have all this power. Laying groundwork. I think it's a lie. You're just a couple deluded skin heads who can't do shit.

EVAN This has been a long day. Everyone is tired. We should order some food before we decide anything. That always helps.

JOURNEY Screw you and this caring bullshit. You're just some scrawny white bitch–

(REBEL looks at her sharply.)

REBEL She's about to be the first female Imperial Wizard of the Ku Klux Klan. A leader of thousands. And she has your life in her hands. Show some fucking respect.

EVAN Even though things have become complicated, we should not lower ourselves to indecorous language.

REBEL This bitch is asking for some fucking language.

EVAN Perhaps. Journey, you know that everything I've told you is true. Think about it. I'm going to the restroom. This way?

(JOURNEY nods. EVAN gets up and cringes as she goes.)

REBEL You know, in another time and place, you'd be strung up in a tree with your boobs cut off by now.

JOURNEY You wish.

REBEL No. I don't. I really fucking don't. That only proves how stupid and inferior you Indians are. You can't even comprehend the evolution of thoughts that has gone on in the Klan. You can't ever understand that making it about killing each other off is us lowering ourselves to the level of animals. Evan Atwood has transformed my mind and the minds of thousands. I don't want you dead Journey Good fucking Eagle. I want you to live your pathetic pagan, dirt tent lives as free and pure as the day God put your ungrateful souls on this earth. I just want you to do it as far from me and my organization as possible. If that doesn't prove who's superior, then nothing fucking will.

(JOURNEY studies REBEL.)

JOURNEY You really believe that.

REBEL I do.

JOURNEY Know what I can't stand?

REBEL I really don't.

JOURNEY People who don't have the balls to follow through on what they believe in. Especially when it gets hard.

REBEL Look girl, I got balls.

JOURNEY I thought you did.

REBEL What's that mean?

JOURNEY If you're gonna get rid of me, just do it. Don't be a pussy about it.

REBEL God, do I have to spell out every fucking concept for you? Listen girl, I was the

bad ass redneck. I grew up in the worst of the Southern Klan, such as it was. Went into the special fucking forces to stay out of prison. Sent straight to Afghanistan. That's when I found out what fucked up monsters people really are. Women…children. All that shit I saw…screwed me up good. When I got back, I heard Evan speak. I didn't know what the hell she was going on about, but I knew I didn't want no more of good ol' boys playing at something they don't understand. I talked to Evan that night, and she helped me see another path. A peaceful path. She showed me it wasn't the rag heads' fault they did the shit they did. She made me see them, and you, as God's creatures, fucked up just the way he wanted them. She taught me to forgive and for the first time in my life, hate fell away and I could see things clearly.

JOURNEY I like my hate. It's the only thing keeping me going. Without my hate I'd be dead by now.

REBEL I used to believe that, but think about it, if no one mixed with no one in the Middle East or in Germany or Japan we wouldn't have fought any of these fucking wars. All those people wouldn't be dead if everyone just kept to their own. The vision of Evan Atwood let me see that. It brought hope to my life. Hope for peace.

JOURNEY I'm so fucking happy for you.

REBEL Look girl, I'm trying to share something with you. Watch your tone.

JOURNEY Or what? You rip up another picture? Tell me another story about your hope and enlightenment? Quote your fancy white cunt all you want but we both know you're just another piece of trailer trash, redneck dick that she wouldn't ever fuck.

(Fast as a snake, REBEL grabs JOURNEY's throat.)

REBEL Shut your mouth.

JOURNEY There he is. The true animal. White superiority my ass.

REBEL I'm warning you girl.

JOURNEY There's nothing you can do to hurt me.

REBEL You have no idea what I've done.

JOURNEY You ever blacked out after screwing a guy then woke up and found him and his three best friends dead on the floor? Slipped on their blood, crawled through their piss and shit and brains to get to the guy you just had inside of you. Find him holding a gun in one hand and a lousy eight of clubs in the other. *(She laughs.)* How fucked is that? Totally screwed over a lousy eight?

REBEL Shit.

JOURNEY I replay it in my head all the time. Even when I sleep. Especially when I sleep.

REBEL You shouldn't do that.

JOURNEY Neil watched his buddies shoot themselves one by one. He saw and smelled what I did, then still had the balls to pull the trigger all alone. I couldn't let it go. At first... Calvin came home to take care of me. But lately I feel like seeing that, imagining what they did, makes me stronger. When I saw Grandpa's body in that car and the drunk sleeping it off, I thought, "I can be as strong as Neil." So I hit that asshole over and over again as hard as I could. I felt his bones moving...

REBEL Blood spraying everywhere...

JOURNEY It felt so...

REBEL Good.

JOURNEY I would have killed him if Calvin hadn't come along.

REBEL You know that's fucked up right?

JOURNEY No shit.

REBEL You really never been diagnosed?

JOURNEY What the hell are you talking about?

REBEL Don't you read the news?

JOURNEY No.

REBEL God help us. Post Traumatic Stress Disorder. You've got all the signs. Shit, screwed up as you are, you should be dead by now.

JOURNEY I've got Calvin.

REBEL But that hate you got, it's all out of whack cause of your PTSD.

JOURNEY You don't know shit about me.

REBEL I know you don't have control over how you feel. You do shit you don't understand and it's escalating. You're gonna cause some real pain soon, and the collateral damage is probably gonna be Calvin.

JOURNEY I'd never hurt him.

REBEL You're making the guy kill himself.

JOURNEY He wants to too.

REBEL Really? 'Cause the only person I've seen with a gun in their hand tonight is you.

(JOURNEY is confused.)

REBEL Look, you've got plenty to be pissed about, but I'm telling you, there's help out there to get you back in control. That's what you want right?

JOURNEY I don't know.

REBEL Evan saved my life. She can save yours too.

JOURNEY None of her Klan shit pertains to me.

REBEL You haven't been listening girl. It's all about you. You and Calvin ARE the poster kids for racial separation. Think about it, killing yourselves or some other crazy shit, what's that really gonna do? Be honest, no one will fucking care. But Evan? Girl, she's national. She's got resources and funding you can't imagine. And once we announce, we'll be hounded by the press. And all that power and attention can be yours.

JOURNEY For what?

REBEL To mess up those that messed up your people. But legitimate like.

JOURNEY You guys would help us do that?

REBEL We've got no love for this government. Your lives can mean more than your deaths.

JOURNEY How?

(EVAN comes around the corner.)

EVAN Arizona.

JOURNEY What the hell does that mean?

EVAN Home of the nation's toughest anti-immigration laws.

JOURNEY You're gonna claim credit for that?

EVAN Do you know that in Arizona it is now a crime to harbor an illegal immigrant? Voila, automatic non-violent separation of races.

JOURNEY The Klan isn't going around passing anti-immigration laws in the middle of the desert.

EVAN Free Americans is. It was a test case of our political lobby structure. Just a beginning, but a pretty effective start. While staying completely underground, we have influence over an entire state. Once we unveil our full potential... its power you've never imagined. That power can be yours. Who do you blame?

JOURNEY The government.

REBEL That's right.

EVAN We're already working on the inside, dismantling it from within. Which agency pisses you off the most?

JOURNEY Indian Health Services. People die every day from shit no one else in this country does.

EVAN Let's expose them for exactly what they are. Then institute new policy to get better health care on reservations.

JOURNEY It's not that easy.

EVAN Has anyone tried? Except Indians, whom the government obviously doesn't care about.

JOURNEY I don't think so.

EVAN So let's do it. We start with this clinic right here. What do they need? Equipment? Staff? I can have things sent over next week.

JOURNEY You're not serious.

EVAN One call and I'll get you something they need. Not everything, but a good faith start.

JOURNEY They need… there's no one to go to for… depression and stuff.

REBEL Maybe someone who does PTSD, like Dr. Rainey? Half this reservation probably has it.

EVAN Good idea. Dr. Rainey could set up the program then rotate his residents through, under his guidance. I believe they get grants for working on a reservation, right?

JOURNEY There's a loan repayment thing doctors get for doing time here. But it just means we get a revolving door of shit young doctors counting their days.

EVAN But with Dr. Rainey at the helm and under my watch, we'll make it a model program. I'll send him an email now, letting him know we need to talk.

(EVAN types.)

EVAN Done.

REBEL He's good, Journey. Helped me with stuff.

JOURNEY An email doesn't mean you will make it happen.

EVAN I've worked ten years to cut the cancer out of this organization. Once we launch, the Klan transformation is complete. I will have their total support to do whatever I want.

REBEL But taking over a clinic is big. Gonna need someone to run it.

EVAN True. And someone who already knows the clinic, the Lakota people, the system would make a huge difference in changing it.

JOURNEY I don't know how to do anything like that.

EVAN Calvin does. It would keep him home, close to you.

JOURNEY You said he's not coming home.

EVAN I'm already working on it.

JOURNEY You can do that?

(EVAN looks at her phone and smiles.)

EVAN Speak of the devil. Calvin's been released. Our resources came through again.

JOURNEY Then they don't know about the terrorist research?

EVAN Not yet. Or they want to watch him. Use him.

JOURNEY No.

REBEL We can fix this.

EVAN Keep him safe.

JOURNEY Calvin won't want to work with you.

(REBEL hands JOURNEY a black chess piece.)

REBEL You know you can convince him, Journey.

EVAN Everything has to go perfectly for me to be made Imperial Wizard. I get one chance at this. I have to make the most of it or none of this happens for the clinic. It's too late to save the Marahotah, but you can save other tribes, like the Lakota. You can see the doctor too. Get help.

JOURNEY Why do you care?

EVAN I'm fighting for your life because it matters. Because what happened to your people should never happen again. Because Walter did heal my grandfather, and you were right. I want that healing too. But so do thousands of others. You and Calvin can give them all that healing.

JOURNEY What do I have to do?

EVAN Help us. Help me. I am asking you for the traditional dances. The traditional songs. It's what your grandfather wanted.

JOURNEY I guess.

EVAN Will you refuse me?

JOURNEY You know I can't.

EVAN But I need you to want to do it.

JOURNEY I don't know.

REBEL You know you want to feel better. Make your own decisions.

EVAN Isn't it the Marahotah way?

JOURNEY It is.

EVAN You and Calvin will give us a way to reach other races, to save lives. He'll be good at that, won't he?

JOURNEY He will.

REBEL But first we can help you erase all ties to this bullshit on his computer. I'll need your router, boosters, external drives, everything.

JOURNEY You can do that? Make it so Calvin is safe?

EVAN A fresh start. For all of us.

JOURNEY You'll really send the doctor?

EVAN I will.

REBEL Calvin will be home any minute. Help us help him.

JOURNEY The router and stuff are in the back bedroom.

REBEL Bring it here and we'll make this all go away.

(JOURNEY leaves the room.)

EVAN Good work Rebel. The pow wow will happen, just as we planned.

REBEL I think so.

EVAN Now that we've got Journey under control, Calvin will be easy. You can't really erase his online history, can you?

REBEL No. Once you click on it, it's done.

(CALVIN bursts in, smiling. He looks for JOURNEY.)

CALVIN Journey, I've got great news! Where is my sister?

EVAN She's fine. She's in the other room.

CALVIN Journey!

JOURNEY *(O.S.)* Calvin! Wait there. I'll be right out!

CALVIN What?

(He crosses toward her.)

REBEL She said wait.

(REBEL pulls a monitor out of his bag and sweeps it over CALVIN.)

REBEL Did they take your clothes, shoes, jewelry? Give you anything as simple as a pen?

CALVIN No. What the hell are you doing?

REBEL Sweeping for bugs. You're clean.

CALVIN Of course I am.

(He moves forward. REBEL gets in his way.)

REBEL Did they ask about anything else? About your research or-

CALVIN Why would I answer to you?

REBEL I'm trying to find out if this was truly random or-

CALVIN This is none of your business. I want to see my sister.

REBEL She'll be back.

(CALVIN pushes at REBEL, who stands firm.)

EVAN Calvin, she's fine. Relax.

CALVIN Journey!

(He pushes at REBEL again. It's like a wall.)

REBEL I don't want to do this Calvin.

CALVIN Get the hell out of my way!

(It turns into a scuffle. REBEL quickly flips CALVIN and has him on the floor.)

REBEL Settle down now, boy.

CALVIN Journey!

(JOURNEY runs in with a duffel bag.)

JOURNEY Calvin! I'm fine. It's OK.

CALVIN *(to REBEL)* Get off me.

JOURNEY Rebel's trying to help.

CALVIN What has happened here?

JOURNEY It's gonna be OK. We have a plan now. Just like you wanted.

REBEL You OK, son?

CALVIN Let me go.

(REBEL lets up cautiously. CALVIN gets up, grabs JOURNEY and pulls her away from EVAN and REBEL.)

CALVIN I want you out of our house. I don't give a shit about the contract or Journey shooting you or whatever. Get out!

JOURNEY Calvin wait. You trust me, right?

(CALVIN hesitates a little too long, torn.)

JOURNEY You don't trust me? Me? I'm your twin.

CALVIN I trust you with my life. I just… lately… you know.

JOURNEY They know about the drunk driver… everything.

CALVIN What the hell is wrong with you? Now they could have you put away for attempted murder twice. So, no. I don't trust you. But I know how to help you. Both of us.

REBEL We're gonna get her the help she needs.

CALVIN WE?

EVAN Calvin, we're going to start a mental health program at your IHS clinic.

CALVIN What?

EVAN To show our good faith and support of you and Journey. We'd like you to oversee the program. You can work right here on the reservation.

CALVIN You expect me to believe that in the last few hours the KKK has taken an interest in mental health on this reservation? To be nice and give me a job? I'm not an idiot. What the hell is going on?

JOURNEY Calvin, it's hard to explain, but this is what Grandpa wanted, a way to help others through the Marahotah ways. This is the sign we've been looking for.

CALVIN It's not a sign.

JOURNEY Just listen to them.

REBEL I know what she's going through. We can help her-

CALVIN She's going through your brainwash bullshit. If you won't leave, we will.

(CALVIN grabs JOURNEY and pulls her toward the door. JOURNEY resists. They struggle.)

JOURNEY No. We can't go. They're helping you! Let me go! *(Etc.)*

CALVIN I'm trying to save you! Stop fighting me! *(Etc.)*

(It turns bad, desperate. JOURNEY freaks and lashes out at CALVIN. He fights to control her.)

JOURNEY You're hurting me!

(REBEL steps in and breaks JOURNEY free from CALVIN. She stays with REBEL, shaken. The three face off against CALVIN.)

REBEL I don't care if she's your sister, don't lay a hand on her again.

CALVIN Are you fucking kidding me? Journey. Journey?

JOURNEY You hurt me!

CALVIN I'm sorry I scared you.

JOURNEY The Marahotah will mean something to the world. We can save people. Evan can help us all.

CALVIN They attacked me.

JOURNEY They're trying to protect us.

CALVIN What about the twin pact?

JOURNEY We don't need it anymore.

CALVIN They've taken you away from me.

JOURNEY You left me first brother.

CALVIN You told me to.

JOURNEY Not tonight. Years ago. You left me all alone.

CALVIN I thought I had too. It was Yale.

JOURNEY When we were ten you promised you would never leave me.

CALVIN We were kids. And I came back.

JOURNEY You hate me for it.

CALVIN No.

JOURNEY Yes you do. I've felt it every day since you got back.

CALVIN I gave up everything to take care of you.

JOURNEY Exactly. You thought I was screwed up all this time just for Neil?

CALVIN I'm sorry. Maybe I did blame you. But tonight I finally figured it out.

(CALVIN rushes for REBEL and knocks the chess pieces everywhere. He grabs JOURNEY's

gun. REBEL has his own gun on CALVIN instantly.)*

JOURNEY No! Trust me Rebel. Put the gun away.

(REBEL does it. CALVIN holds his hand out to JOURNEY. She takes it.)

CALVIN Tonight when the agents were taking us out of the clinic, all I could think of was you and your stupid meme. So I yell, "This is what Crazy Horse would do!" and I fight. The Indians all cheered and I felt fucking great as they wrestled me into the car. Then this huge fed looks me straight in the eye and says, "Who the fuck is Crazy Horse?" It was like he grabbed my heart with his fist. Then the guy leans in and says, "Is Crazy Horse the ring leader?" I said, "He's the greatest Lakota war chief in history. He defeated Custer. They're carving the world's largest monument in his honor." He says, "Too bad, could have cut yourself a deal." I rode alone in the back of that car and shit got simple. Everything in my life has been focused on meaning something to the world and I thought you screwed it up by going crazy. But in that car I realized we've been fighting all our lives against an enemy that doesn't even know we exist. We've already been mowed down and forgotten. We're mulch. We lost before we were even born. I swore if I ever got back to you, I'd never let you go again. We do it tonight. On our terms, together forever.

(They cling to each other fiercely. CALVIN holds their heads together.)

JOURNEY I love you, Calvin.

CALVIN I love you so much.

(CALVIN moves the gun to her head. Holding her head in line with his.)

JOURNEY But I was wrong. Our lives can make a difference.

CALVIN No one cares.

JOURNEY We have a plan to make them care.

CALVIN I can't join her.

JOURNEY In the end, even Crazy Horse went to the fort.

CALVIN And his own people killed him.

JOURNEY Hoka hey sweet brother.

(JOURNEY pulls away. CALVIN sees the truth and his heart breaks.)

(GUNSHOT. Blackout.)

Scene 5

The pow wow. We hear drums warming up. A spot light comes up on JOURNEY dressed in her regalia. EVAN and REBEL enter in suits.

EVAN There is an unbelievable amount of press out there.

JOURNEY The more the better.

REBEL They aren't necessarily friendly. But the followers are solid as a rock and standing proud. It's just like you said it would be.

EVAN "Then I saw a new heaven and a new earth, for the old earth had passed away." Today, we start this world over, the way God meant it to be.

(JOURNEY reaches for her dance shawl. REBEL takes it to help her.)

REBEL You know a lot of folks won't understand this right away. They're gonna be hard on you.

JOURNEY Crazy Horse's real power came from him being a thunder dreamer, a heyoka. Because of his sacred vision, he lived his life differently from others, often against their ways. Crazy Horse's people did not understand him in his youth. Many feared him. So, I welcome misunderstanding. I welcome fear. Because I have seen how I can heal the Native people of this world. It's my vision and I will see it come true.

(REBEL unfurls the shawl behind JOURNEY. EVAN takes the opposite side, as JOURNEY faces upstage. On the shawl is a Native American circle of the four directions. In the center is the KKK logo. Words are written around the logo, "Free American Indian Klavern - Strength in Purity". They place the shawl over her shoulders. The drums get louder.)

REBEL Welcome sister.

(They embrace. JOURNEY opens the shawl to its glory as REBEL opens an upstage curtain. Blinding cameras flash. Drums pound. JOURNEY and EVAN step into the light together. The shawl whirls as JOURNEY spins into a Native dance. She seems to float above the earth, timeless and free.)
(Black out.)

Kathryn Haddad

Biography

Kathryn Haddad is a writer, teacher, and community organizer. Her work explores contemporary Arab American experiences and reflects on the political reality of life for Arab and Muslim Americans.

Kathryn founded Mizna – one of the few Arab American Arts and literary organizations in the United States where she served as its Artistic and Executive Director for twelve years. Kathryn is a 2004–2005 recipient of an Archibald Bush Leadership Fellowship for her work with the Arab American community. As a writer, she received three Playwright's Center Many Voices Fellowships as well as awards from the Jerome Foundation, the Minnesota State Arts Board, and Intermedia Arts in Minneapolis. She currently serves as the co-founder and Artistic/Executive Director of New Arab American Theater Works in Minneapolis, Minnesota.

Past productions of work include *The Arab's In My Head* (Theater Mu 1996*)*, *With Love from Gaza* (staged performance Intermedia Arts 1995), *With Love from Ramallah,* co-written with Juliana Pegues (Mizna 2004; excerpts Arab American Comedy Festival, New York 2004), *Zafira the Olive Oil Warrior* (Pangea World Theater 2011; excerpts Golden Thread Theater, San Francisco 2013), *Safari* (staged performance RAWI National Writers Conference 2014), and *Road to the City of Apples* (New Arab American Theater Works 2015).

Artistic statement

The play *Zafira the Olive Oil Warrior* is one that addresses the current political climate that exists for Arab and Muslim Americans, which includes anti-Arab and Muslim bias in schools and the community. It tackles a post 9-11 environment where allegiances and Americanisms are questioned. In this piece, it imagines what would happen if a large terrorist attack would take place in the United States and if internment of Arab and Muslim Americans were to occur, as some have proposed. It explores the complex dynamics between different generations of Arab and Muslim

Americans as well as the hysteria that has occurred in the U.S. post 9-11-01. The play tackles such issues as freedom of religion and expression, and the U.S. role in international politics which is interconnected with domestic issues and attitudes toward Arab and Muslim Americans. Based on historical facts of Japanese Internment, this story is a chilling look at what could happen as the result of mass hysteria and Arab and Muslim bias in the United States.

The play gives a rich opportunity for discussion of these issues, but also gives an opportunity for Arab actors and artists to participate in theater as an art form and to experience a means of creative expression around Arab and Muslim issues.

Production history

The full production of *Zafira the Olive Oil Warrior* directed by Dipankar Mukherjee ran from September 11 to October 5, 2011 at the Pangea World Theater in Minneapolis, Minnesota.

A staged reading of the play was held at Alternate Visions Festival, Pangea World Theater in April 2011, Minneapolis, also directed by Dipankar Mukherjee. Excerpts were read during *What do the Women Say?* at the Golden Thread Theater in San Francisco, California in March 2013.

22 *Zafira the Olive Oil Warrior*
Kathryn Haddad

Characters

VICKI KHOURY/ ZAFIR   A Lebanese American woman, varies in age from 40s to 60s

MARGE   Homeless, white woman, late 60s

MARCUS JENKINS   High school student (any race)

JAMIE NORDGREN   High school student, white girl

MARISSA   High school student, any race

PRINCIPAL MONROE   Middle aged woman of color

SECRETARY DEB   Middle aged white woman

JOYCE HANSON   Teacher at school, white woman

GUARD   #1 White male, age late 20s

GUARD   #2 (HOWARD JACKSON) African American male, age late 20s

SHAHNAZ KHAN   Pakistani immigrant, age 30s, pregnant, South Asian accent

MAGDA KHALED   Egyptian American, teenage girl

REEMA KHAMIS   Palestinian immigrant woman, age 60s (only speaks Arabic)

HUDA ASFOUR   Young Arab American woman, bi-lingual

ACT I

Scene 1

The time is somewhere in the not too distant future after the United States has recovered from an internal war. Things are more run down then they used to be. There is the calm that exists after war when everyone wants to forget what has happened. VICKI is a former school teacher, and an Arab American. She is also a survivor of the internment camps that were the unfortunate reality of the internal war. She is now living under a bridge where she has made a makeshift home with another woman her age in a similar unlucky condition.

MARGE is white and is also a native to Minnesota. The scene is sparse. There are a few personal items, but not many. The time is late fall. VICKI has transformed herself into her alter-ego, the Arab American Superhero ZAFIRA. She wears a makeshift cape with the letter Z on it and wears a waist band of dancing coins like belly dancers wear. Her most important possession is a small bottle of olive oil which she carries with her and occasionally sprinkles when she speaks.

ZAFIRA ZAP! ZAP! ZAP! ZAP! ZAP!

I, Zafira, mysterious school marm of Minneapolis, debke demon of Dearborn, your falafel fantasy from Fresno, Baklawa babe of Biloxi, have super natural powers of reality warping and molecular manipulation! I right wrongs, expose lies, bring about understanding and just generally give you a zap into reality of what life is really like for someone else somewhere else.

Honed by the Arab and Muslim internment camps, sharpened by the blades of a collective ignorance and arrogance, my specialty is empathy manipulation. I use my skills of mental projection to zap experiences into an astral plane, make them hover and come down to inhabit the bodies of unsuspecting citizens of this great nation.

It will not be your exotic, erotic fantasy of the Middle East. It is not liberation through belly dance appropriation! It is not feminist power gained by capitalizing on brown women's pain.

Terrorist, you say? Freedom fighter I say. My secret weapon is in this jar. Beware! ZAFIRA. That's me! It means victory.

MARGE Vicki! Whatchu mumbling about? I can't think with you jawin' on and on.

VICKI I got some work to do, Marge. Arab American superhero style.

(She takes a pose.)

And it's not Vicki, I keep telling you. It's ZAFIRA!

MARGE Come over here, ZAFIRA. I have a sandwich we can share.

VICKI Is it meat? I don't eat meat.

MARGE What do ya mean, you don't eat meat? Yesterday we shared that double cheeseburger. Come on now!

VICKI I don't eat meat. It smells like death.

(She takes the sandwich, smells it and eats.)

MARGE Okay, okay. Now sit down here with me. Where is that bottle of Super Soda you stole from the Super America?

(She digs in VICKI's pocket to retrieve the can.)

Here it is.

(Taking out two Styrofoam cups from her bag, opening the coke and pouring, handing it to VICKI.)

Drink.

VICKI *(VICKI drinks the coke)* I didn't steal that.

MARGE Okay.

VICKI I hear that sound again. Do you hear it?

(They listen. There is a faint sound of a siren. A police siren.)

MARGE *(bored)* I don't hear nothing.

VICKI Sirens! I hear sirens!

(VICKI is frantic. She hears the sirens that will come back later in the final scene when REEMA is attacked. MARGE offers her a bottle of whiskey.)

MARGE That's the cops in the distance. They're not after you. You're not in the camps. You're here. Under the highway? I keep telling ya, it's not then, it's now. Have some of this. It'll make you feel better.

VICKI You know I don't drink that stuff.

(Grabs bottle and takes a swig. Hands it back.)

MARGE Umm hmmm.

(She turns over to sleep.)

VICKI Hide, Marge. They are coming! Hide.

(She looks around as if she is trying to quickly grab her belongings.)

MARGE *(Goading her on a bit.)* "The kids... Where are the kids?"

VICKI Cats, not kids.

MARGE You say kids. Whenever you start freaking out, you wonder where the kids are. What goddamn kids are you talking about?

VICKI I never say kids. I didn't have any kids. It's the cats. Where are the cats? The cats are gone! I couldn't find them! Here kitty! Here kitty! Kitty? Where are you? Wait, officer! Wait! I need to find the kitties! I can't find them! They'll starve if we leave without them! They need water. I can leave food, but what about water? Please, let me find my cats! Please!

(She hyperventilates.)

MARGE The goddamn cats are okay, Vicki. They can eat mice or rabbits or something.

VICKI And I never saw them again. Never saw kitties again...

MARGE There's lots of goddamn cats around here. They scream at night. You hear them!

VICKI In the camps, we weren't allowed animals. The guards wouldn't let us take them. Don't they know that the kitties were my babies? I never had kids.

MARGE I did. Three of them. A damn lot of good that ever did me. Where the hell are they now? Who knows? One in California, I think. The boy in St. Paul. Five miles away and he wouldn't spit in my face if he saw me. The youngest. She was my cutie. County took them all. What damn good are any of them? *(Pause)* Ever see that movie, Vicki?

VICKI Which one? *Black Hawk Down*?

(With disgust) Yes, I saw that movie.

MARGE No. *Sophie's Choice*. Ever see that one? Where she has to choose one of her kids to save. One will be killed. I couldn't make that choice. No way. So, I let the county have all of them.

VICKI I haven't seen any films in years. I never go watch those propaganda pictures! Boycott the cinema!

MARGE I know. You refused to go to the theater after they released you from the camps. But that was an old film. From the old days.

(VICKI sings part of the song "Walking Tall" by Marcel Khalife)

MARGE I'm going to sleep now.

(She burps.)

Come on, Vicki. Go to sleep.

VICKI Sleep? You think so? Not me. I got work to do. Superhero work. If only I had my powers back then when I was a teacher. What I could have done with superhero strength, or see through vision! Maybe I could have prevented it all from happening in the first place.

(Music of Marcel Khalife is played "Walking Tall" while it transitions to the school scene.)

Scene 2

Old VICKI walks out of the homeless scene under the bridge, does a brief change of clothes and becomes her younger self when she was a public school teacher and more sane. It is years earlier, and before the internment experience. VICKI is in her classroom. It's a suburban high school class and the subject is literature. Most of the students are white. They are lower middle class. The school is fairly run down, and the students are an average class – not an Honors class, and not a remedial class. They have been politicized by the internal war that is raging in the country. The garden metaphors abound.

VICKI Okay, students, tonight I want you to read the poem on page 27 in your Modern World Literature textbook. It's called "Your Logic Frightens Me, Mandela." Then answer the questions after. This is due tomorrow.

MARCUS But can't we just read it in class or something and discuss it? Can't you postpone this assignment?

VICKI No, we need to move ahead. We have a lot to cover before break, and we have already lost time.

JAMIE Why are we reading "World Literature" anyway? What about AMERICAN literature? I want to learn about America.

VICKI Last year was American literature. And every year before that. This is the year we study World Literature. We've gone over this. There are so many fantastic…

JAMIE I don't want to read about the world. I want to read about America.

MARCUS Mr. Johnson's class is reading *Old Man and the Sea*.

JAMIE Yeah, why can't we read that? I heard it was a really good book. And it's American.

MARCUS Ms. Khoury, I don't have time. Tonight I'm working at the war rally handing out flags.

VICKI Can't you do this before or after the rally? It's important to keep up with your school work.

JAMIE This poem about some foreigner is more important than the student war rally?

VICKI War rally? Why are students all going to a war rally anyway?

MARCUS Why are we going to a war rally? Because we are AT WAR. That's why!

(To the others) I can't believe she just said that.

VICKI Okay, since you brought it up. What is the purpose of all this rallying? Does everyone have to comply? What are the examples in literature where people have resisted? Doesn't each person have the right to their own beliefs and their own way of expressing them? This is what we have been talking about in this class. Some are uncomfortable with the way…

JAMIE *(to the others)* But it's the internal war. Operation Weed and Compost!

VICKI There are some people who are not comfortable with this bloodletting spirit, is all I am trying to say. Remember when we read…

MARCUS Bloodletting? What does that mean?

VICKI Some people have been attacked on the streets, innocent people. People live in fear now.

JAMIE Terrorists! Are you sticking up for the terrorists?

MARISSA Now what exactly is happening after school?

JAMIE You don't know? Where've you been — making some peace beads or singing kumbaya or something?

(MARCUS laughs at this. MARISSA gives them the finger. JAMIE scowls at her.)

MARCUS *(to MARISSA)* The whole school is meeting in the auditorium for the rally at seven. They're sending the first group of patriotic students off to the training for camp guards. You knew that.

JAMIE We are supposed to be making signs, but she wants us to read some poem about some old dead foreigner instead!

VICKI Nelson Mandela was not just "some old dead foreigner," Jamie. He was a very important...

JAMIE Are you coming to the rally, Ms. Khoury? *(to MARCUS)* Why won't she answer me?

VICKI No, Jamie, I am not.

JAMIE *(suspiciously)* Why aren't you coming?

VICKI There are things I need to do at home.

JAMIE If you don't mind me asking, Ms. Khoury, what kind of things?

MARCUS I don't understand why you're giving us work when the other kids are busy making "Hoe them out and compost them" signs...

MARISSA *(sarcastically to JAMIE)* And handing out "let's put weed killer on the old lady next door" stickers?

JAMIE Funny.

MARCUS None of the other teachers are giving homework anymore. Mrs. Knutson says that our duty to our country is more important. You're the only one making us do stupid stuff like this. We need to practice the "We'll Hoe and Root them out" song for the troops with everyone else. My mom's making the costumes.

(JAMIE and MARCUS impromptu a few bars from this song to the tune of "My Country 'Tis of Thee.")

JAMIE and MARCUS We'll hoe and root them out
Then we'll all scream and shout
(shouted) This country's free!
Make sure our land's secure
For future boys and girls

VICKI Okay! Enough! Look, this is a literature class, and I want you to be able to...

MARCUS Mr. Johnson is giving his students extra credit for every day they wear red white and blue to school!

JAMIE She said she's not coming to the rally!

MARISSA So what?

JAMIE Shut up! I bet you're not coming either!

MARISSA You shut up.

JAMIE Ms. Khoury, I just noticed something. There's no solidarity flag in this room.

MARCUS Yeah, why don't we have a solidarity flag in here? Weren't all the teachers given a flag to hang in their rooms?

VICKI Yes, we have a flag. I took it down because it was blocking the clock and I couldn't see what time it was.

JAMIE Where is it?

VICKI It's in the closet.

JAMIE In the closet! The flag is in the closet. Did you hear that?

(Students snicker.)

JAMIE Put up the flag!

(She motions to MARCUS to join in.)

JAMIE and MARCUS *(together)* Put up the flag! Put up the flag!

(MARISSA puts her head down. VICKI opens the closet door, gets the flag, and puts it up.)

VICKI *(tired)* Okay. There's the flag. Satisfied now?

JAMIE Ms. Khoury, can I ask you another question? What religion are you?

MARISSA Come on! Leave her alone you guys!

JAMIE Shut up, granola chick.

MARISSA Granola chick? Why should she answer you? Who cares what religion she is?

JAMIE You worship rocks, what do you care.

MARISSA Worship rocks?

MARCUS She's the teacher. She needs to set a good example for the students!

MARISSA You two are disgusting. How does her religion matter to you?

MARCUS What do you mean?

JAMIE Of course it matters! Isn't she some kind of Islamic? What religion ARE you, Ms. Khoury?

VICKI I really don't think my religion...

JAMIE *(to MARISSA)* She's one of the towel heads. One of them that was behind attacking our country!

VICKI You need to watch your language!

MARISSA *(disgusted)* Towel heads?

VICKI Let's have some order in this class!

MARCUS You think so, Jamie?

VICKI QUIET! Now let's think about what is going on here.

(Pause)

JAMIE *(to MARCUS)* Let's go to the office and talk to Principal Monroe about this. I'm not sitting in this class any more with a teacher who's against the war. I need a pass to the office Ms. Khoury. Let's get out of here. Come on, Marcus.

MARCUS Okay.

JAMIE *(JAMIE and MARCUS get up from their seats and walk to the door and leave class.)*

And if the rest of you are smart, you'll come too.

(*MARCUS walks over to VICKI to get a hall pass. He walks to the door to join JAMIE.*

MARCUS (*to Jamie*) I'm gonna tell my mom about this and she's gonna be SO mad!

(*They walk out humming the tune.*)

VICKI (*visibly shaken*) Okay class, let's open our literature books to page 34 and read some background information on Nelson Mandela.

MARISSA I'm interested in reading about Nelson Mandela, Ms. Khoury.

VICKI Thank you, Marissa.

(*MARISSA opens her book and begins to read the following and trails off as the lights switch to the next scene.*)

MARISSA Nelson Rolihlahla Mandela was the first South African president to be democratically elected. Before his presidency, Mandela was an anti-apartheid activist, and the leader of the armed wing of the African National Congress...

Scene 3

During each one of the following voiceovers, we see overt examples of attacks on Arabs and Muslim shopkeepers and individuals. A woman with a hijab is taunted, a business is vandalized, children are brutalized on a playground, Arabs and Muslims are stopped in the street and searched, people are fearful. The roundup begins during the last voice over, and people are pulled out of their businesses and places of worship and taken into custody. The voices are spoken by those in authority – newscasters, politicians, business leaders, etc...Note: These are actual quotes taken from media outlets during WWII and spoken about the Japanese Americans. "Japanese" has been replaced with "Arab" and "Muslim."

VOICEOVER "I don't want any of them here. They are a dangerous element. There is no way to determine their loyalty... It makes no difference whether he is an American citizen, he is still an Arab and/or Muslim. American citizenship does not necessarily determine loyalty... But we must worry about the Arabs and Muslims all the time until they are wiped off the map."

VOICEOVER "I am for the immediate removal of every Arab and Muslim on the East Coast to a point deep in the interior. I don't mean a nice part of the interior either. Herd 'em up,

pack 'em off and give 'em the inside room in the badlands... Personally, I hate the Arabs and Muslims. And that goes for all of them."

VOICEOVER "A viper is nonetheless a viper wherever the egg is hatched... So, a child born of Arab and or Muslim parents, nurtured upon their traditions, living in a transplanted atmosphere... notwithstanding his nominal brand of accidental citizenship almost inevitably and with the rarest exceptions grows up to be an alien, and not an American... Thus, while it might cause injustice to a few to treat them all as potential enemies, I cannot escape the conclusion... that such treatment... should be accorded to each and all of them while we are at war with these people."

Scene 4

It is an open room and the women are lining up with their suitcases for inspection before they get their room assignments. It is a bleak place with cold cement tables and scanning machines. There is a big table in the center. Women are waiting on folding chairs for their names to be called.

VOICE Okay, this way. Everyone step this way. Over here. If your last name is A-G you are in line over at the Grand Stand. H-N at the Dairy Building. O-Z you go to the Agriculture Building. All women with children proceed to the Arts and Crafts building. Keep the children quiet.

(*Crowds are dispersing, children crying, weary people holding papers and small bags. VICKI looks around. She is nervous and defiant. Two guards are standing near her. They are both in their late 20s. GUARD 1 is white, and GUARD 2 is black. GUARD 1 laughs as REEMA trips and falls. VICKI sees this. Disgusted, she spits toward him. He pulls her from the line roughly and brings her over to the side, shakes her. She gasps.*)

GUARD 1 Dirty Arab. You got a problem? Go back to where you came from.

VICKI I am as American as you are. What's happened to humanity? Laughing at an old woman? One day you'll be sorry.

GUARD 1 Is that a threat? Huh?!

(*VICKI spits again. The guard gets violent with her and slaps her across the face.*)

I'll show you what happens to those who spit! You want more of that? You think you can just spit at me? Things are different here.

(GUARD 2 walks over to the first guard to help out and see what's going on)

GUARD 2 (HOWARD JACKSON) What's going on here?

GUARD 1 This hajji spit. She says we'll be sorry!

GUARD 2 (HOWARD JACKSON) A live one! Hah! We'll be sorry?

(Walking right up to her and looking at her. Backs up in recognition and looks again. He turns around and steps back. Calling out to the other guard.)

Hey man, come here for a minute.

GUARD 1 What?

GUARD 2 (HOWARD JACKSON) Who is this woman?

GUARD 1 I don't know. She was in line with the others and she spit. Dirty people.

GUARD 2 (HOWARD JACKSON) I think I know her.

GUARD 1 What?

GUARD 2 (HOWARD JACKSON) I think I know this one.

GUARD 1 How?

GUARD 2 (HOWARD JACKSON) I think she was my teacher.

GUARD 1 What?

GUARD 2 (HOWARD JACKSON) Yeah, in high school. That looks like my English teacher. Ms. Khoury. Eleventh grade English class.

GUARD 1 *(laughing and teasing)* Pfft. Shit.

GUARD 2 (HOWARD JACKSON) Yeah. I think that was her.

(GUARD 1 walks over to VICKI.)

GUARD 1 Let me see your I.D. papers.

(She pulls out a packet of papers she is carrying. GUARD 1 takes them over to GUARD 2 (HOWARD JACKSON) and shows them to him.)

GUARD 2 (HOWARD JACKSON) *(reading)* Vicki Khoury, Place of birth: Minneapolis. Ethnicity: Lebanese. Religion: Christian. Age: 40. Marital Status: Single. Occupation: School Teacher. See! I told you. That is her.

GUARD 1 Hm. Your English teacher! Well, it's a reunion now, isn't it? I wonder how many she brainwashed or tried to convert to her terrorist religion.

GUARD 2 (HOWARD JACKSON) I don't really remember knowing her religion or her talking about... It says here that she is Christian.

GUARD 1 They're all a bunch of liars. I am sure these papers is made up. Teachers. They are on the Recycle list.

GUARD 2 (HOWARD JACKSON) *(Looking through papers)* Recycle List. Teachers, community "activists", scientists, religious leaders.

GUARD 1 Hey teacher lady! This here's one of your students! Ha! What do you think of that? One of your students here is now your boss. Bet you didn't think that when you was in your brainwashing job, did you?

VICKI Students?

GUARD 2 (HOWARD JACKSON) *(sheepishly)* Ms. Khoury, it's Howard Jackson. I was in your eleventh grade English class at Eagleton. Graduated ten years ago.

VICKI *(tired)* Really?

GUARD 2 (HOWARD JACKSON) Yeah. I was on the wrestling team. We went to state that year.

GUARD 1 *(to GUARD 2 (HOWARD JACKSON))* Come on. The reunion's over.

GUARD 2 (HOWARD JACKSON) *(quietly – almost under his breath)* I remember you.

VICKI Howard, where are they taking us?

GUARD 1 *(to VICKI – more urgently)* COME ON! Let's go!

VICKI Howard! Yes! I remember you! You were a nice kid! Howard?

(VICKI is dragged off to the roundup. HOWARD looks back one last time. The round up continues with guards checking in prisoners. People being hauled off in different lines. VICKI is taken away to the Recycle group where the women sit nervously waiting for their turn. During this scene, the guard goes through each one and removes items. Nail clippers, hair pins, belt buckles...)

GUARD 1 Wait until you are called. Magda Khaled. Step this way.

(Reading from her documents)

Magda Khaled. Let me verify this information. Age?

MAGDA Seventeen.

GUARD 1 Place of residence?

MAGDA Richfield.

GUARD 1 Richfield?

MAGDA Yeah.

GUARD 1 Richfield what?

(She looks at him blankly.)

State! Which state do you live in?

MAGDA Minnesota!

GUARD 1 I expect complete answers.

(She steps up to the table with her bag and the guard proceeds to scan her, and look through her suitcase, pulling out various items, holding them

up, scanning them, and throwing them back in the bag. The metal detector beeps and he stops. He waves it over one spot, feels the lining and rips it out. He pulls out a small music player and earphones)

GUARD 1 What's this?

MAGDA It's my Terabyte Wimax Music Lover.

GUARD 1 Your Terabyte Wimax Music Lover? It is hidden in the lining of the bag. Did you think you would get away with sneaking in this device?

MAGDA I wasn't sneaking it in.

GUARD 1 Wasn't sneaking it in? How did it get in this part of the bag?

MAGDA It must have fallen there.

GUARD 1 Fallen? Do you think we are stupid? Do you think we don't know the sneaky tricks of you people? No electronic devices allowed! It was clearly stated in the evacuation directions. No electronic devices, no metals! What else do you have in here?

MAGDA Nothing!

GUARD 1 An attitude? You think this is some school house scene and I'm the principal? This is real. Step aside. You will go into that room, remove your clothes and a female guard will search you.

MAGDA Remove my clothes? Are you kidding me?

GUARD 1 You heard me! Move!

MAGDA I'm not taking off my clothes.

GUARD 1 *(Going for his radio)* You will either go willingly, or unwillingly. Which will it be?

(She is silent)

Which?

(Calling on his radio)

I need back up.

(She is hauled off stage in protest. To the others)

Anyone else?

VICKI *(Standing)* Where are you taking her?

GUARD 1 *(Ignoring her)* You again! Are you related to her?

VICKI No, I don't know her, but I just am wondering where…

GUARD 1 QUIET! Sit down. It is none of your business. Shahnaz Khan. Step over here. I'm going to ask you some questions like the other girl. Let's hope it goes better for you. How old are you?

SHAHNAZ I'm thirty-two years old.

GUARD 1 Place of residence?

SHAHNAZ St. Paul, Minnesota.

(Timidly, she approaches the table.)

GUARD 1 When's your baby due?

SHAHNAZ In a few months.

GUARD 1 Where's your husband or boyfriend?

(He looks through her bag, lifts out underwear, photos, etc.)

SHAHNAZ My husband, sir.

GUARD 1 Where is he?

SHAHNAZ I don't know, sir. I haven't seen him in months.

GUARD 1 He took off on you, huh? And you pregnant?

(Shaking head)

SHAHNAZ No sir. He did not take off on me. He was arrested in the night by the secret police. They took him and I haven't heard from him since.

GUARD 1 *(Places a red sticker on her luggage and file, notes to himself.)* Husband arrested for terrorist activities.

SHAHNAZ Please, sir. He did not engage in terrorist activities. He was an accountant. He worked in a law firm.

GUARD 1 Mmm hmm.

SHAHNAZ May I ask why you put this picture of a lawn mower on my file, sir?

GUARD 1 You like to ask a lot of questions, don't you? I think it would be better if you kept your thoughts to yourself.

SHAHNAZ So sorry. I didn't mean anything by it.

GUARD 1 Let's hope not. Now, let's see what else you have here.

(He searches more thoroughly through her things, pulls out a photo of him.)

Was this the guy?

SHAHNAZ *(Holding back tears)* Yes. That is my husband.

GUARD 1 *(Hands her her blankets…)* Okay. Here are pillows and blankets and sheets for your beds. You are responsible for washing your own bedding. Bring this into your room and wait for further orders.

SHAHNAZ Thank you. Thank you very much, sir.

GUARD 1 *(SHAHNAZ leaves.)* Khoury. Vicki Khoury.

(She steps forward.)

VICKI Here I am.

GUARD 1 You again, huh? You're the teacher lady. Howard's English teacher?

VICKI Yes.

GUARD 1 You spit earlier.

VICKI I may have.

GUARD 1 You may have. Well spitting ain't nice, teacher lady. Don't they teach that in school? Or is it different for the Ayrabs? They spit, don't they?

VICKI Sometimes.

GUARD 1 Like camels?

VICKI Please just ask me your questions and look through my bags.

GUARD 1 I'll take my time.

(He takes VICKI's bag and looks through it, pulls out books and pages through them)

So you're how old?

VICKI I'm forty.

GUARD 1 And it says here you live in Minneapolis.

VICKI Yes.

GUARD 1 What kind of things are you reading?

VICKI I don't see how that matters.

GUARD 1 Everything matters. You think because you are a teacher, you can take that attitude with me?

(GUARD 1 takes two books, glances through them, and keeps them.)

We like to know what you are reading and thinking. Letting in this type of material is strictly not allowed.

VICKI But, that's poetry. Arabic poetry. What's wrong with poetry?

GUARD 1 Look. I don't make the rules, I just enforce them. No Arabic books allowed.

VICKI But it isn't in Arabic, it's English. Not that that should matter…

GUARD 1 No Arabic books! Are you deaf or just stupid?

(He writes something in her file. VICKI transforms herself into ZAFIRA and delivers the next monologue.)

ZAFIRA One of my super human powers is the ability to spit. I spit my image into a panoramic view that will hover above the horizon and sear itself into your vision so that whenever you look up, you will see me. My special powered megapixel saliva will become a painting of twenty-three members of my extended family sitting at a table eating dinner. It will be so detailed that you will be able to see the seed of the lemon that my mother wasn't able to strain when she made the baba ghanoush. You will see my saliva rise up in to the image of the beautiful woman that I am grasping you by the neck and hurling you across the Atlantic, across the Mediterranean and into Baalbeck in the center of Lebanon where eighteen members of my extended family are waiting for your arrival. You wrong me, and I will spit so powerfully that it will shape itself into a mark that will appear on the foreheads of the next three generations of your family. Because I am Zafira. Don't. Make. Me. Spit!

GUARD 1 What did you say?

VICKI Nothing.

GUARD 1 Anyone can be a teacher now days, can't they? Wait for instructions from us. Here are your pillows and bedding. Get out of here.

(VICKI leaves but watches from the sidelines.)

Reema Khamis. Step forward. Reema Khamis? Reema Khamis.

(Timidly, she steps forward.)

Alright, you saw the drill. Give me your age and place of residence.

REEMA Shu?

GUARD 1 AGE AND PLACE OF RESIDENCE. Don't you know English?

REEMA My English. Not good.

GUARD 1 Shit. Arabic? Anyone around here speak Arabic?

(He looks around, but grows impatient. Slowly.)

How old are you?

REEMA Sixty. I am sixty. I live Wisconsin. Wisconsin. I have husband. Two sons. My son, he.

GUARD 1 ENOUGH! I don't need your life story. Quiet.

(He looks through her suitcase, and pulls out some silver worry beads)

What are these?

(Louder)

What are these?

REEMA Mesbaha.

GUARD 1 English! In English.

REEMA Ma barrif Ingleesi. I don't know English good.

HUDA I speak Arabic.

GUARD 1 Who are you?

HUDA My name is Huda, sir.

GUARD 1 Let me see your papers.

(She hands over some papers and he looks at them.)

Born in Michigan. Okay. Stand by we might need your help. What did she say these things were?

HUDA They are prayer beads. Misbaha.

(The guard takes them and puts them in a basket to confiscate. HUDA stands to the side and watches. The guard inspects the metal worry beads carefully and puts them in a box. He looks through her suitcase again and pulls out a Palestinian flag.)

GUARD 1 What's this?

REEMA Filistene. Beladi.

GUARD 1 What flag is this?

REEMA My country. Palestine.

GUARD 1 Your country, huh? Your country?

(He writes something down in his notebook.)

If that is your country, what is this? What is this land you're in?

(She looks in confusion and tries to muster a smile.)

HUDA *(in Arabic)* He wants to know what country you are in.

REEMA Amreeka!

(He takes the flag and steps on it.)

GUARD 1 This is what we think of your country.

(He gives her the blankets, pillows, etc...)

Terrorist.

(He motions REEMA and HUDA to leave. They exit together. HUDA with her arm around REEMA's shoulder. The guard continues on with his job in pantomime. Lights come up on VICKI, who has changed to ZAFIRA.)

Scene 5

Back in the principal's office of Eagleton High School

PRINCIPAL MONROE *(Coming out of her office)* You can come in now, Vicki. Take a seat. How are you doing today?

VICKI Thank you, fine. Is there a problem?

PRINCIPAL MONROE Well, I will get straight to it. I called you here because some complaints have come in...

VICKI Complaints? About what?

PRINCIPAL MONROE Your World Literature class.

(VICKI knows that she is in a vulnerable position. She is not combative, but polite and restrained in her communications with her boss. There is an undertone of fear, and a resignation that this moment has come.)

VICKI World Literature?

PRINCIPAL MONROE Have there been some problems in class, Vicki?

VICKI No... not at all.

PRINCIPAL MONROE I've had several phone calls from concerned parents regarding some of the materials that you have been presenting to the students, and some of the discussions in class. What is your take on this?

VICKI Well, I guess I'm not sure what you mean.

PRINCIPAL MONROE The parents are concerned about conversations in your class about our current political situation. Now we are an educational institution which prides itself in the pursuit of knowledge, of course, but there is a line that we can cross as educators between intellectual inquiry and promoting our own beliefs.

VICKI Promoting our own beliefs...? What do you mean? Which students complained? What did they say?

PRINCIPAL MONROE That information is confidential. I cannot tell you who made any complaints against you or which parents are involved, but I want to hear from you what is going on in your classes. Have there been discussions about the current political situation in the country?

VICKI Well, it has come up once or twice. It can't be helped...

PRINCIPAL MONROE Come up once or twice? What do you mean? Can you expand on that?

VICKI Well, people are being rounded up... There is a war... Students talk... We have a literature class, so we discuss issues...

PRINCIPAL MONROE Is it true that you have defended the terrorists in your classes?

VICKI Defended the terrorists?

PRINCIPAL MONROE One of the parents is saying that you are in support of the prisoners. I know students sometimes may exaggerate a bit, but these are very serious allegations. This is troublesome to hear.

VICKI I think I should have my union representative here at this meeting, Mrs. Monroe.

PRINCIPAL MONROE That is not needed, Vicki. We are only having a casual discussion. There is no action being taken. I am just inquiring about your classroom. So, Vicki. Out of curiosity... have you made sympathetic statements about the people detained?

VICKI Mrs. Monroe, we discuss literature in my classes. We have read authors who have gone against the grain of society…

PRINCIPAL MONROE Authors that have gone against the grain of society?

VICKI And there may have been some comparisons to examples in literature and history…

PRINCIPAL MONROE What does this mean, Vicki? At this time in our nation, we can only praise our leaders and condemn anyone who fights against them. Several students are saying that you did not want them to attend the flag rally at the school that was designed to send off the young people to training for the internal camps.

VICKI I assigned homework that evening, that was all. I didn't discourage anyone from attending.

PRINCIPAL MONROE But did you question its purpose?

VICKI I may have discussed the purpose of the rally in class.

PRINCIPAL MONROE Is this an item for "discussion," Vicki? This rally to send off the young people was organized here and was a school sponsored activity. Let me ask you something – how long have you been in this community?

VICKI I grew up here, Mrs. Monroe.

PRINCIPAL MONROE In this community things are probably different from where you come from…

VICKI I was born here. I grew up here. I graduated from high school only 15 miles from here…

PRINCIPAL MONROE And discussions about religion. One parent has said that she fears you have been trying to convert the students to your Moslem religion.

VICKI What? Convert students?

PRINCIPAL MONROE They have said that you speak favorably about the Islamics.

VICKI I teach World Religions, Mrs. Monroe, as a part of the curriculum. I speak about many religions – Buddhism, Hinduism, Judaism…

PRINCIPAL MONROE And Christianity?

VICKI Of course.

PRINCIPAL MONROE Most of the students in this school are from Christian families. Of course we welcome diversity in our population. That is what makes America great. That is why we hired you. But, you cannot be presenting your way as the only way, so when you talk about your religion, although

you may be very enthusiastic about your beliefs, that is not appropriate in school.

VICKI Mrs. Monroe, if you must know, I am Christian.

PRINCIPAL MONROE What?

VICKI Yes, I was raised Christian. Lebanese Christian.

PRINCIPAL MONROE Do the students know that?

VICKI Well, yes, I have mentioned it.

PRINCIPAL MONROE If I were you, Vicki, I would not talk about being Lebanese in the classroom. Why not try to just avoid any discussions of your background? The parents allege that you spend a lot of time teaching the Middle Eastern literatures above and beyond the other subjects.

VICKI We spent one week on it! Out of the semester, we only spend one week. We spend time on Africa, Latin America, India, East Asia, it is a broad survey of World Literature.

PRINCIPAL MONROE And Europe?

VICKI Of course. If you don't mind me saying, Mrs. Monroe, this is all xenophobic. It is unfair…

PRINCIPAL MONROE Xenophobic? That's a bit harsh, Vicki. I am on your side, but the parents are quite concerned about what is going on. I would like to have you back next year, really I would…

VICKI I have only had positive reviews. You know that. No complaints. I've spent hours working on the school plays, coaching the speech team…

PRINCIPAL MONROE Yes, of course.

VICKI Would you like me to submit to you a detailed description of what we do in my class? Will that help?

PRINCIPAL MONROE No, no, Vicki. You are a professional, and we respect that.

VICKI Well, what do you recommend that I do now?

PRINCIPAL MONROE I would just say that you should go back to your class, don't talk about yourself, your views, your background, or any issues of the day. Just teach literature.

VICKI *(with resignation and the sarcastic realization that this is impossible. But, she will not make her understand.)* All right. Is that all?

PRINCIPAL MONROE You can go now, Vicki.

VICKI Thank you, Mrs. Monroe.

(She leaves the room.)

PRINCIPAL MONROE *(Speaking into an electronic device to the secretary)* Deb. Make a note to Technology Central to put a trace on Vicki Khoury's computer. I want to see everything she's reading and all she discusses. Every time her finger has hit a key on that keyboard from today back to the day she was hired, I want to know which one. These kind of dangerous elements must be watched and nipped in the bud. And please place the order for the "Weed 'Em Out and Pull 'Em Up" flags for all the students. In times like these we all must stand together.

Scene 6

The scene is in the lunchroom at school. A round table is in the center and a few teachers are seated eating their lunch. VICKI walks over to it and sits with DEB, the secretary, and JOYCE who is a teacher at the school.

VICKI May I join you?

SECRETARY DEB Of course. Sit down, Vicki. I don't see you in here very often.

VICKI No, I usually eat in my room and spend the 20 minutes preparing for class, but I forgot my lunch today, so I thought I would eat down here. I see it is Green Spaghetti Day.

SECRETARY DEB Yes. The school wartime special and student favorite. See what you're missing in your room?

(VICKI laughs at this.)

VICKI Yes, I guess I should eat here more often.

SECRETARY DEB *(to JOYCE)* What are you going to be doing for Spring Break this year, Joyce?

JOYCE Oh, Chris and I will just spend it around town. Not going anywhere special. How about you?

SECRETARY DEB We may go for the weekend to Little Falls to visit Jim's family.

JOYCE That's always fun.

SECRETARY DEB Yeah. Little Falls. The home of Charles Lindbergh.

JOYCE An American hero! Kids don't know enough about our own history. I bet my students don't even know Charles Lindbergh.

VICKI Charles Lindbergh? Well, you know he was actually kind of a racist.

SECRETARY DEB What?

JOYCE He was an American hero!

VICKI Well, he did support Germany in World War Two.

JOYCE Charles Lindbergh was a very important man in our country's history, Vicki, and a Minnesotan to look up to!

SECRETARY DEB *(Ignoring VICKI)* The kids like going there. They can ride their ATVs, harass their cousins. You know. But this year, they will have to be a little more careful.

JOYCE Why's that?

SECRETARY DEB Well, you know that Jim's parents live close to Fort Ripley, and they've just started to bring in the first round of terrorists to the new Camp Sprout. Jim's mother said she saw the trucks hauling them in last week. Amazing, isn't it? Right here in the Midwest, a camp for terrorists!

JOYCE Oh, Jeez.

SECRETARY DEB Yeah, Jim's mom is scared one of them might escape and make their way over toward town.

JOYCE They must have some good guards?

SECRETARY DEB Of course. She is always paranoid. I tell her. It's shoot first, ask questions later. She has nothing to be worried about.

JOYCE Well, at least they got them, that's all I can say.

SECRETARY DEB It's spooky, really. Those people here. When I was growing up we didn't have to worry about these things. I wish they'd just get it over with. Why waste our tax dollars on housing them, feeding them.

VICKI Get it over with? What do you mean?

SECRETARY DEB A bullet would do it, that's all I'm saying. Right between the eyes! And I know plenty in Little Falls that would be more than happy to finish 'em off!

(SECRETARY DEB laughs.)

Isn't that right!

VICKI A bullet?

(In disgust) What about due process? Innocent until proven guilty? Did you know it was just a general round up? They took anyone who was even remotely suspicious, whatever that means. If you had a falafel sandwich you were hauled in practically.

SECRETARY DEB *(with confusion)* Falafel sandwich?

JOYCE Our country was attacked. And we are going to be the next ones. Those people don't know anything about process. They only listen to violence. We're too nice to them as it is. Back in their country, they'd have their heads cut off. Coming over here and jealous of our freedoms. Making our lives hell. What are they doing here anyway in our country?

VICKI Just trying to live like everyone else.

JOYCE Well, in my grandparents' day, when you came to this country you learned English and you blended in. These people don't want to be one of us. And then they attack us after we give them freedoms they couldn't have in their country!

VICKI But the attacks were not by these people. These are just ordinary immigrants, shopkeepers, workers…

JOYCE Taking jobs from Americans!

SECRETARY DEB Send them all back, is what I say! Speaking their own languages and not speaking English, taking over our country. Oppressing their women. Making them wear those scarves on their heads. Not you, of course.

JOYCE Say, aren't you somehow connected to that part of the world? Where is it that you are from?

VICKI I'm Lebanese. American. Lebanese American. My parents are from Lebanon.

SECRETARY DEB So, what are your thoughts on what is going on now?

JOYCE That rally the other day for our young people going to training for the internal war was great, wasn't it? I never saw the kids so committed to something! Did you see it, Vicki?

VICKI No, I couldn't make it to that.

JOYCE I guess you do have a lot of papers to grade…

VICKI Yes, I do have a lot of papers. If you'll excuse me, I need to get back to class now.

(Lights change and she transforms into ZAFIRA and delivers the following monologue to the two women who are at lunch. They do not hear or see this, but continue with their silent conversation.)

ZAFIRA I have powers of transmutation teleportation. I will zap you to Gaza. In the middle of the night in an air raid to live the life of a refugee, no water, no work, house key in a pocket for a house stolen one hundred years ago. I will zap you to live with a family in Rafah.

Their name is Mohamed. Ahmed Mohamed and his wife Fatima and their five kids. Bassam, Basaam, Basil, Badr, and Lulu. They range in age from eight to one years old.

You have just left Eden Prairie, your SUV, your job downtown in the accounting firm, your softball league, your weekly trips to Boston Market for chicken for the family, your weekend up north, the internet where you post those inane, condescending and racist comments against Arabs, the backbone of which led you to lock me in a camp. You are zapped there. Now, sir, and madam, you are in Gaza.

Welcome! Or should we say, "Ahlan." "Marhaba!" Would you like some lentils? It is Mjaddarah. How about a glass of water? It tastes a bit funny? Where did it come from? What was put in that water and by whom? Which Israeli soldier took a bath in your water tank last night?

Here I am, I, Zafira, olive oil warrior, to introduce you, Mr. and Mrs. Middle America, to Ahmed and Fatima, Mr. and Mrs. Middle East. Sit down, please.

The kids stare at you. They have never seen someone in such tight shorts who is over four years old. Here, have a seat. Belly dancers are NOT appearing.

(She transforms back into VICKI and cafeteria din resumes.)

JOYCE Have a nice day.

VICKI Thanks. You, too.

(She gets up and leaves the table, brings her tray to the counter and leaves. The two women remaining flash knowing looks at one another.)

Scene 7: Cheese Scene

MARGE Huh?

VICKI Do you like spaghetti?

MARGE Spaghetti? Yeah, I like it.

VICKI The school made the most horrible spaghetti.

MARGE *(uninterested)* Really?

VICKI Yeah, you know what they would do? They used some kind of special green noodles, cooked the sauce and mixed it all together in one big pot. Then they'd scoop it out with an ice cream scoop! The spaghetti and the sauce would stick together in one big, round clump. Blech. That's really bad when you can't even make spaghetti. In the camps we had spaghetti all the time. And cheese.

MARGE Green noodles? Ugh. But, there's nothing wrong with cheese. I could eat cheese for every meal.

VICKI I HATE cheese! I told you that a hundred times! I don't want any cheese! Do NOT give me cheese. You hear me? *(screaming)* NO CHEESE!

MARGE Okay, okay. Quiet down. We don't want to bring people over here to bother us. I don't want to get kicked out of this place like we were last time. Don't worry about it. We won't have cheese.

VICKI Good. Promise?

MARGE Sure. Whatever. Just give me your cheese. I don't mind.

VICKI Marge, do you ever think about dying?

MARGE Dying?

VICKI Look at the cars drive by and people rushing to their important places. I mean, does it ever occur to you that all of these people we see walking by, all of the drivers of the cars, the people working in banks, the police, the crowds at football games and in movie theaters, the thousands at the state fair, the millions all over the world right now that are doing whatever they are doing – the people in India, in Brazil – all will be dead. Everyone. Not a trace left.

MARGE No. I don't think about that.

VICKI It is amazing really, isn't it? That there will not be one person who is breathing now still breathing in a not so long time from now.

MARGE It's better that way, I suppose. Peace.

VICKI Maybe that tree will be here. The river. Some of this concrete. But everything else will be gone and no one to tell about what is happening now. Everything that is so important now, will mean nothing. The things we see as tragedies, the funny stuff. Meaningless.

MARGE Who cares at that point? And why do you think of those things?

VICKI How can you not think of them? Sitting here under this bridge that collapsed all those years ago. Remember that?

MARGE Of course. Who doesn't?

VICKI People just driving down the road in their cars, air conditioners on, listening to music, fighting kids, then bang. Down into the water. Silence. For a minute. Then panic. Or peace.

MARGE Yeah. They built this bridge. It's supposed to be stronger now.

VICKI In one hundred years, everyone will forget all what happened here. They'll forget the bridge crash, the internment camps. I wonder if there will be two other women here then.

MARGE Hopefully the one like me won't have to listen to the one like you!

VICKI Ah, come on! You like it. You like my stories.

MARGE You drive me crazy, you know.

VICKI Funny how at the end, we have each other here! After all that's happened in life. Under the bridge with nothing. But you.

MARGE Except for the cold, it's not so bad.

VICKI Why don't we go to Arizona? It's warm there. Why do we stay here and suffer this weather?

MARGE How we going to get to Arizona? Walk?

VICKI We could find a ride somehow. Hitchhike like they did in the olden days.

MARGE And who would pick us up? Two homeless old ladies. One crazy camp survivor and one drunken fool. No, I want to be close to my children.

VICKI Your children? You haven't seen them in years.

MARGE I know. But, maybe we might get back to one another. It might happen.

VICKI Yeah. Maybe. Marge, where were you then? Where were you when they sent me to the camps? To Fort Ripley. For two years I was in those woods of Northern Minnesota.

MARGE You are still in Fort Ripley. In your head.

VICKI And did you know that they used the old Japanese internment camps? Jerome, Arkansas, the one in Nevada. In the desert, on the Indian reservations. Camps all over the United States were filled with Arabs, Muslims, and sympathizers. They took us all. First came for the men. Then for our stuff. Then the women. I remember going to the Minnesota State fairgrounds.

MARGE The fairgrounds? And you ate Sweet Martha's cookies, right?

VICKI Why are you making jokes with me? They sent me to the fairgrounds with all the Muslims, Arabs, and other women to check in before boarding the bus to the northern Minnesota woods. I went to the women's camp. I'm tired of explaining this over and over again to you, Marge.

MARGE Come on, Vicki. Lighten up. The war, the camps, all of that is the past. Enjoy our beautiful view of the highway, and the delicious smell of oil and gasoline. And get some sleep! The government. You can't trust them anyway. Did you ever think you could trust them?

VICKI Well, I guess I did think so at one time.

MARGE *(Laughs)* Not me, Vicki. Never. Anyway…good night. Gonna sleep now.

VICKI Good night. Thanks for being my friend, Marge.

MARGE You're a pain in the ass. Good night.

Scene 8

Flashback to the internment camps. It is the first day in the women's barracks.

GUARD 1 Khaled, Khan, Khamis, Khoury. This way follow me. You will all be sharing this room. Your personals go inside. Take your things and put them away and wait for the call for information over the loudspeaker.

(The four women walk into the small room. SHAHNAZ KHAN is pregnant and wears a hijab, REEMA KHAMIS does not speak English, MAGDA KHALED is a teenager. There are two sets of bunk beds in the room. They all stand for a minute, looking.)

VICKI Well, I guess this is home and we are all roommates now. Hopefully, this will be a short stay, huh? I'm Vicki.

SHAHNAZ I'm Shahnaz. Nice to meet you.

(She shakes everyone's hand.)

REEMA Reema. Ta Sharrafna. Allah y Khaleeky.

(She goes to kiss the women.)

VICKI *(to MAGDA)* And what's your name?

MAGDA Magda, but call me Maggie.

(Immediately MAGDA goes for the top bunk. She is snapping gum.)

VICKI Are you the one with the Wimax from earlier?

MAGDA Yeah.

SHAHNAZ What happened in there?

MAGDA Nothing. They searched me. I don't want to talk about it.
(Going for the top bunk) I want the top bunk. Hope you guys don't mind.

VICKI That's fine with me. I guess we might as well decide on beds.

SHAHNAZ Well, since I am pregnant, I will need the bottom bunk.

VICKI *(to REEMA)* What about you? Which bunk do you want – the top or the bottom?

(They all look at REEMA. She smiles.)

REEMA Arabi? B'Tehki Arabi?[1]

VICKI Oh. Okay. You don't speak English? La. Schwei bus.[2]
(to the others) Do either of you speak Arabic?

SHAHNAZ I speak Urdu.

MAGDA No. I don't speak Arabic. I was born here. I'm American. I don't know why I'm in this place.

(They all look at her helplessly. VICKI shrugs as she puts her hands up.)

VICKI Sorry. How do you say sorry in Arabic? I forgot. Min fudlak. No wait. That means please, I think. Dammit. Where is that woman from line who spoke Arabic? I hope she's close by.

(She shrugs and motions to both beds trying to ascertain which REEMA wants.)

REEMA *(in very broken English)* No broblem. I sleep here.

(She puts her things on the other bottom bunk.)

VICKI I guess that means I get the other top bunk.
(to MAGDA) Are you Egyptian?

MAGDA My dad is Egyptian. I'm American. I've never been to Egypt. How did you know?

VICKI Just a guess – your name actually. Magda.
(to REEMA) Min wein, Reema?

REEMA Ana min Filistene.

VICKI *(to the others)* She said she's Palestinian.

MAGDA *(with mild disgust)* I understood that.

SHAHNAZ So you do speak Arabic.

MAGDA Maybe a little.

SHAHNAZ How old are you?

MAGDA Seventeen.

VICKI Where's your family?

MAGDA I don't know.

SHAHNAZ You don't know?

MAGDA My dad was sent to Jerome Camp in Arkansas. My mom is American. She left to be with her second husband.

VICKI No brothers or sisters?

MAGDA I have two half-sisters – my mom's kids by her second marriage. When they took my dad, I've been living alone until they came and got me.

VICKI Why didn't you go live with your mom?

MAGDA I haven't seen her since I was twelve. I'm old enough to live alone anyway. I'm seventeen.

VICKI *(to SHAHNAZ)* When's your baby due?

SHAHNAZ In two months.

VICKI Your first?

SHAHNAZ Yes. It will be. My husband was taken six months ago. I don't know where he is. They were talking about sending him back to Pakistan. He doesn't even know about this baby.

MAGDA That sucks.

SHAHNAZ *(to VICKI)* Do you have kids?

VICKI No.

SHAHNAZ A husband?

VICKI No.
SHAHNAZ No husband, no kids?
VICKI No. I have cats…
SHAHNAZ Why …?
VICKI *(Ignoring her. To REEMA)* Bint? Fi Binet?
REEMA Aiowa. Endi.[3]

(She brings out a photo and shows the others and starts to cry.)

Hada Hassan ou hada Mohammed. Il Jaysh akhadoon. Ya dhillee…[4]

VICKI I'm so sorry. She said something about the army taking her kids, I think. Not sure if she means the American army or the Israeli army… Guess it doesn't really matter.

(She hugs her.)

VOICE OVER LOUDSPEAKER Everyone report to the mess hall for information. No jewelry. No attitudes. It's a good day at Camp Ripley!

(Tune of "My Country 'Tis of Thee" is played over loudspeaker. VICKI leaves the scene and transforms into her ZAFIRA costume and stands during the song as if saluting the flag. MARGE walks into the scene and watches her. Into the air, she walks over and ZAPS the audience. MARGE pulls her back into the scene.)

Scene 9

Back under the bridge with VICKI and MARGE.

VICKI ZAP! ZAP! ZAP! ZAP! ZAP!
MARGE Come on, Zafira.

VICKI Zap.
MARGE We need to find something to eat. Let's go.
VICKI No. I'm staying here to plan.
MARGE But it's chicken and gravy tonight at the shelter! And it's going to be a cold one.
VICKI That's okay. I've got this to protect me.

(Holds up the jar of olive oil)

MARGE Well, I prefer blankets and a cot. You know, one day, I'm going to get out of this life and get me a nice little house in the suburbs. With flowers and a little dog. Maybe you can live in the extra bedroom, Vicki.
VICKI The extra bedroom? The extra bedroom? Oh, no. No! They deserve it. For what they did to me. They deserve this. I am going to finish it all. You know they took my house? They took my job? They took my dignity. Like an animal. The fight has not ended. I have breath in me. You have no idea what I've been through, Marge.
MARGE I'm leaving, Vicki.
VICKI Go ahead. Go. I don't need you. Go.
MARGE I'm going to the shelter tonight. I'm going to have that chicken and gravy!
VICKI *(sarcastically)* Sukhtein.
MARGE What did you say?
VICKI I said, "Sukhtein."
MARGE Don't insult me. I'm out of here, Vicki. Or should I say "Zafira."

(She leaves.)

VICKI *(to herself)* It means "To your health. Two times." It's not an insult. Whatever.

★

Act II

Scene 1

It is a meeting after school of the Eagleton Revolutionary Guards — a newly formed patriotic group to help support the at home war effort. In attendance are several students including MARCUS, JAMIE, and their advisor, JOYCE.

JOYCE Okay students, you can have some pizza. Take a napkin, please, and only one piece per person! Make sure there is enough to go around!
JAMIE Thanks for the pizza, Mrs. Hanson!
JOYCE Oh, no problem. Actually, there was a little extra money in the slush fund, so we decided to spring for it!

MARCUS Yum! Is there anything to drink?
JOYCE Oh, I almost forgot!

(Reaching into a bag and pulling out a bottle of juice and some cups.)

Here you go. I bought some apple juice.

(Students come over and take some juice.)

Pick up a flier before you sit down! This explains what we will be doing in this newly formed club and also has a permission slip for your parents to sign.

(She makes sure students take the fliers on the table.)

Once you have your pizza and drinks, please sit down so we can get started.

(Students find their seats.)

Okay. Let's start by introducing yourself. Tell a little something about yourself and what it is you would like to get out of this Eagleton Eagle Guard group! Let's start with you.

(Points to MARCUS.)

MARCUS My name is Marcus Jenkins and I am a senior. I am on the basketball team. I would like to just support my country. My brother is serving as a guard at the detention camps, and I would like to do that, too.

JOYCE Great, Marcus! Where is your brother serving now?

MARCUS In Arkansas. In the Red Camps – the high security prisoners – you know. The noxious weeds?

JOYCE I bet he has some stories he can tell you!

MARCUS Oh, yeah! He is in charge of the work area of the camp. He makes sure that everyone does what they're supposed to. He says they are lazy mostly, and they want to speak in their language, so he is responsible for making sure they speak English.

JOYCE Interesting! I'm sure we'll hear more about that later. Thanks for sharing, Marcus. Okay, next…

JAMIE I'm Jamie Nordgren, and I am also a senior. Marcus and I are in some classes together. Like English class with Ms. Khoury. I just wanted to join this group because I don't think it is right that we have teachers and adults in our school who support the terrorists and I want to help make sure that we only have patriotic people working here. So, I hope this group can do that. And I want to be a guard, too.

JOYCE Well, Jamie, we can't really be checking up on people in school as our mission, but naturally if you see anything that is troublesome, you should always report it to a trusted authority, you know.

JAMIE Yeah, kids can really be brainwashed by their teachers!

JOYCE Teachers do have power. But, for the most part, they want only what is best for you.

JAMIE That is not what my dad says. And *some* teachers obviously have other motives for teaching.

MARCUS You can say that again.

JOYCE Well, I hope we can look to you two as leaders in this school to make sure that we do have a very supportive student body who takes time to appreciate what our country has done for us, and also is vigilant if there is any problem.

JAMIE Yes.

JOYCE You know Principal Monroe really supports what you do, so never feel afraid!

JAMIE So, what kind of things do we do in this group?

MARCUS Maybe we should have a barbecue so people know what we're doing!

JAMIE Yeah, we could have music or something and then get students involved in our group – pass out flags and stuff!

JOYCE That's a great idea! Let's write the ideas down. I think the school would support such an activity.

JAMIE Can we take a field trip to one of the recycling camps to see what it's like?

JOYCE I don't know about that. It is kind of dangerous.

MARCUS But, my brother said there is lots and lots of security!

JOYCE Well, let me think about that. Our secretary, Deb's in-laws live by Camp Sprout. That is not such a bad idea. Maybe we could arrange something!

JAMIE Cool! I think that would be a great idea, Mrs. Hanson. I'll help organize it.

MARCUS I know I'd like to go, and I'm sure other kids would too.

JOYCE Okay, kids, you know, I like that idea. I think this group has some real possibility.

JAMIE Let's make a visit to Camp Sprout one of our first activities! Kind of like an initiation into the group.

JOYCE I'll talk to Principal Monroe and see what she says about that. I bet she'll like that idea.

Scene 2

VICKI is alone on stage and has brought out a makeshift cape. She has transformed herself into ZAFIRA.

ZAFIRA I am Zafira! As philosophical as Kahlil Gibran, as steadfast as Helen Thomas, as avant garde as Frank Zappa, as beautiful as Selma Hayek, and as wise as Edward Said. I am able to zap the greedy and arrogant and entitled into the bodies of those they despise in order to make them experience empathy.

With a sprinkle of olive oil, I can transport you from your world of plenty to a world where you are not the master of the West, but its servant. This is a world where your story is told through someone else's eyes, and you cannot protest enough to change it. Where you look at the movies, the television, open your school books, listen in on inane conversations in coffee shops, read the on-line comments in articles about you written by someone who hates you, and you can do nothing.

This amazing Arab American battles to turn a population of apathetic ignoramuses into caring and intelligent citizens. Zafira uses her superhuman saliva, strength, vision, and mental projections to transform this citizenry that has gone astray into an astral plane of empathy. She is forcing the world to care. Zap!

(She steps out of her ZAFIRA gear and back into the internment camps as VICKI.)

Scene 3

In the internment camps again. REEMA and VICKI are trying to wash some clothes together in a bin in the room. SHAHNAZ is laying on the bed, very pregnant and uncomfortable. MAGDA is not in the room.

VICKI Zap! Just like that! Got the stain out, Reema.

(She shows her the cloth.)

REEMA Shukran, habibti! Shukran!

(She goes to kiss her.)

VICKI How are you feeling, Shahnaz?

SHAHNAZ Not too well. It will be soon, I think.

VICKI Is there anything we can get you to make you more comfortable?

SHAHNAZ Maybe a ticket out of this place?

VICKI I hear you. Wish I could get one out for all of us.

SHAHNAZ I wonder what my husband is doing now.

VICKI *(In an attempt to cheer SHAHNAZ)* I'm sure he's dreaming of you, Shahnaz.

(She goes to hug her.)

Come now. Let's think of something else. Something good. Food!

SHAHNAZ That always cheers me up!

(They laugh.)

VICKI Me too. Okay, if you could have anything to eat right now, what would you have?

SHAHNAZ Um. I don't know. You go first.

VICKI Okay. That's easy! Dinner at the Beirut Deli.

SHAHNAZ Tell me what you like there!

VICKI Well, everything there was fabulous, and made fresh every day. My favorite was – Daily Special number one. A nice bowl of fresh tabbouli – lemony with juicy tomatoes and just the perfect amount of burghul! Served with Arabic bread in these little cheap red plastic baskets. And kibbee... Do you know what kibbee is?

SHAHNAZ We don't eat kibbee. I've heard of it. Isn't it lamb?

REEMA *(Perking up and coming over with a recognizable word.)* Kibbee?!

VICKI *(laughing)* Kibbee Kwayyis, kteer, ya Reema!

REEMA Ah! Kibbee!
(In Arabic) Eshtaat al kibbee. Il Libnaneeya bimooto bil kibbee u nahna kamaan. Enti Libnaneeya. She yom inshallah manaykool kibbee sawa. Isa a la rod. In sha allah.[5]

(She tweaks VICKI's cheek.)

VICKI Nom. Ana Libnani, Reema!
(Back to SHAHNAZ) And then the best cabbage rolls you ever had – garlicky and full of rice and meat.
(to REEMA) Malfouf? Tarif Malfouf, Reema. Hubee malfouf?[6]

REEMA Malfouf! Bi Hubi Malfouf! Zaki! Kint amaloo la jouzee u walaydee. Kin Yachu killen nahar. Riz Allah a ayam zamaan.[7]

VICKI I don't know how they can roll them so perfectly. Mine never turn out like that. And my favorite – stuffed grape leaves. Umm... let's see... how do you say that in Arabic... Oh, I know!
(to REEMA) Waraa' Anib!

REEMA Ah! Waraa diwali! Aiowa. Um il shawanee, habibti.[8]

(She sits down and smiles bittersweet.)

SHAHNAZ Sounds heavenly!

VICKI I hope it's still there. The last I heard, a lot of the Arabic restaurants closed or went underground. Or changed to serve Italian food. Okay. Your turn, Shahnaz. What would you have?

SHAHNAZ Kofta Ka Salan.

VICKI Tell me about it!

SHAHNAZ Well, it's got two stages of cooking and it would take me all day to prepare. In fact, Mohammed's friends would request it because it was my specialty! You make a big thick sauce of onion and tomatoes and mix in the spices letting it simmer slowly, slowly on the stove.

VICKI What spices do you use?

SHAHNAZ Oh, ginger and garlic, cayenne, turmeric, garam masala, coriander seed, and salt and pepper. You put all the spices in the meat as well and cook it for about two hours. A lot of people put spinach in the sauce as well about one half hour before it's done. Actually, come to think of it, the farmers are the ones that do that. We don't use spinach. It's served with rice or bread, of course. You can smell this delicious food from the street! Mohammed used to tease me about it and say that he could tell it was kofta wa salan once he turned the corner to our house — even in winter with all the windows rolled up on the car and the heater on inside.

VICKI Mmm. When we get out of here, let's make some together, okay? You'll teach me?

SHAHNAZ Yes, of course, Vicki. We will. We'll have dinner together and laugh about this time here.

(Pause)

VICKI Will things ever return to normal?

(REEMA goes over to get a deck of cards, and comes back to sit by the two women. She holds it up. They think she wants to play cards.)

VICKI La. Shukran. I don't really know any card games. Ma barrif – hayda.

(She nods "no." REEMA proceeds to sit next to them on the bed. She mixes the cards, and motions for SHAHNAZ to cut the deck. SHAHNAZ hesitates, but comes over and divides them. REEMA takes the cards from SHAHNAZ and looks at them, makes a startled face.)

REEMA Ma lesh. Ma lesh.[9]

(REEMA shuffles them again and once more asks SHAHNAZ to cut the deck – repeating the motions again.)

Shufi! Hada Mneeh. Hada Hiloo. Inshallah Ibnik haikoon owi. Good. Strong. Baby.

(SHAHNAZ moves away from this fortune telling exercise, and politely motions a "no, thank you" to REEMA for her further attempts at fortune telling. REEMA then motions to VICKI to come over, and goes through the process again of telling her fortune. Again, a bad card has been chosen by VICKI – we are to imagine a much worse card, in fact, has been drawn. REEMA makes a face, puts it back again, and quickly folds the card game.)

Ma lesh. La'abee sakheefee. Ma byani shi. Allah Yustoor![10]

(Looking around)

Wayn Magda?[11]

VICKI *(Looking around also)* Ma barrif.[12]

(to REEMA) Have you seen Magda lately?

SHAHNAZ No, I haven't seen her since this morning. She left the room early and hasn't returned since.

VICKI I wonder where she went.

SHAHNAZ Who knows? That girl is wild.

VICKI I've seen kids like her before. She'll be okay.

SHAHNAZ But growing up with no mother! A girl needs her mother. What happens in this country, I don't know. I'm afraid for my child. Back in Pakistan, a girl would never behave the way she does. Those low cut blouses… Shameful.

VICKI She wants to be American more than anything. She was born here.

SHAHNAZ You were born here, too. How did you turn out so different?

VICKI When I was her age, I am sure that I was rebellious, too.

SHAHNAZ I saw her talking with that blond guard yesterday – the one who gave her the music? It's dangerous! For all of us. Who knows what kind of trouble she could be getting in to.

VICKI I'll try to talk to her when she returns.

(Just then MAGDA reenters the room.)

Maggie! We were just talking about you! Where have you been? We were worried.

MAGDA I've just been out a while walking around, and sitting in the sun, looking at the woods and stuff.

SHAHNAZ Well, you've been gone all day!

MAGDA So? I don't want to sit in here.

SHAHNAZ What were you doing?

MAGDA I told you I was walking around looking at plants and stuff.

SHAHNAZ All day? Walking all day? Alone?

MAGDA So?

SHAHNAZ So? This place is not a place to be walking aimlessly around! You never know what could happen.

MAGDA What could happen? We're fenced in! Besides that little spot beyond the mess hall that has some woods, there are only rows of cabins like ours.

SHAHNAZ Well, please next time, if you are going to be gone all day, at least inform one of us.

MAGDA Inform you? At home I don't have to tell anyone where I'm going, why should I have to tell you here?

SHAHNAZ (*under her breath*) Such attitude. Where did you get those flowers?

(*MAGDA lays on the bed ignoring the question.*)

I asked you a question, Magda.

MAGDA I told you my name is Maggie!

SHAHNAZ What kind of flowers are those?

MAGDA Daisies. Don't you know daisies?

SHAHNAZ Did your boyfriend give those to you?

MAGDA Who says he's my boyfriend?

SHAHNAZ Shameful! You are putting us in danger!

MAGDA How am I putting us in danger. Leave me alone!

VICKI Where did you get that? We aren't supposed to have any electronic devices!

(*MAGDA shrugs*)

Really, Magda, tell me. Where did you get it?

MAGDA Why?

VICKI Because we should know! You have something we are not supposed to have and we could all get in trouble! How did you get that?

MAGDA Don't worry. We won't get in trouble. I got it from Mark.

VICKI Who? Who's Mark?

MAGDA Mark! The blonde prison guard in the mess hall.

SHAHNAZ (*Sitting up*) A guard gave you a gift?

MAGDA So. What about it?

SHAHNAZ Magda, I'm not your mother or any relative of yours, but you must know that you should stay as far away as possible from the guards. It's dangerous. And accepting gifts! That's a promise.

MAGDA How so?

VICKI She's right. They have a lot of power. They are guards. They don't have our interests in mind. And he might now expect something from you.

MAGDA What? We just like the same kind of music, that's all. And he felt sorry for me.

SHAHNAZ How do you know him?

MAGDA We talked after lunch a few times.

SHAHNAZ What did you talk about?

MAGDA He told me where he grew up. Did you know he played on the basketball team in high school? We talked about stuff like that. So what?

VICKI Magda! Really! I agree with Shahnaz. This could be a problem.

MAGDA I don't see a problem. Maybe for you because you didn't get one of these. You're just jealous.

VICKI Believe me, I am not jealous. But having a relationship with a prison guard is not a good idea!

MAGDA Who says I'm having a relationship. We just talked a few times. There's no one else here my age that I like. And besides, He's kind of cute.

SHAHNAZ What would your father say?

MAGDA My father is not here.

SHAHNAZ See. This is why I said it is easier to have boys. Okay, let me be blunt with you, Magda. Men want certain things from women. You are a prisoner with no power. He has a gun. And now he's giving you gifts. The next thing you know, he will be taking you out at night and...

(*MAGDA laughs.*)

MAGDA This is not the Middle East! These guys are nice. Just like the ones at school.

SHAHNAZ You are so naïve! They are not like the boys at your school. We are at war with them. We have nothing here. They think of us like animals.

MAGDA Animals? Mark likes me. You're just paranoid! And I'm American like him! MYOB, okay?

(*She turns around to the window and turns up her music. SHAHNAZ comes over and takes it out of her ears.*)

SHAHNAZ Listen to me. You are jeopardizing us with a relationship with a prison guard. You don't know what could happen! And you are not American like he is. You need to give that back to him!

MAGDA Stay away from me! How dare you! You have no idea. You just happen to live here because your last name starts with a "KH" like mine, okay? KH! KH!

(She exaggerates the Arabic KH sound.)

Not American? Who's American? Why do you wear that stupid thing on your head anyway?

(MAGDA puts her headphones back on and SHAHNAZ comes over and rips them out of her ears. In response, MAGDA grabs SHAHNAZ's hijab and pulls it off. REEMA clutches in chest in pain. Commotion between SHAHNAZ and MAGDA stops as all eyes are on REEMA who is suffering in pain loudly.)

REEMA *(in Arabic)* Ya Allah! My heart! An old woman is not fit to be here. Not fit to be in this condition. Why is it that we must always suffer? What is it that we have done wrong in our lives that the Arabs must always suffer?

(REEMA sits and hyperventilates.)

VICKI Ash bikay, Reema? Oh, God. Magda! Run and get some help!

MAGDA There's no doctors here today. It's Tuesday.

VICKI Well, try to find that young woman who speaks Arabic next door. Huda. Bring her in! Please get a translator at least so we can see what she needs.

SHAHNAZ Hurry!

(Magda runs out of the door. Vicki helps Reema to sit down and covers her with a blanket. Reema rocks back and forth, her head in her hands.)

VICKI Don't worry, Reema. We are getting someone to come and help you. What's wrong?

(REEMA points to her medicine bag and holds her chest. SHAHNAZ goes over to look in the bag.)

SHAHNAZ This, Reema? Is this what you want?

REEMA Mai. Mai.

VICKI Water. Get her some water. Don't worry, Reema. It will be okay. Everything will be okay.

REEMA Ma lesh. Ma lesh.

(She grips her head.)

SHAHNAZ Her color does not look good, Vicki. Reema. Stick out your tongue. Like this.

(She pantomimes sticking out her tongue.)

Here's the water. What's wrong with her, Vicki?

VICKI I don't know.

SHAHNAZ She seems to have some condition. She has medicine.

(She goes to hug REEMA.)

VICKI I don't really know much about her or why she is taking the medicine.

SHAHNAZ The medicine is called hydrochloro-thiazide. What does that mean?

VICKI I don't know.

SHAHNAZ *(impatiently)* Where's Magda anyway?

(VICKI pantomimes with the bottle and holding her chest trying to ask her what is wrong. REEMA understands and clutches her heart. Just then MAGDA returns with HUDA from next door.)

SHAHNAZ Finally you return!

MAGDA It was only a minute!

VICKI Thank you for coming, Huda. She is sick and we don't know what is wrong. Could you help and tell us what she is saying?

HUDA Of course.

(She is rushing over to REEMA to check on her.)

(In Arabic) Shu bikay, khalti?[13]

REEMA Albi! Albi![14]

VICKI Her heart?

HUDA *(in Arabic)* Shu biki albi?[15]

REEMA *(in Arabic)* I have a heart condition. I have this medicine to take to prevent a heart attack. My heart is weak!

HUDA She says that she has a heart condition and is taking medicine to prevent heart attack. *(In Arabic)* Where did you get this medicine, Reema?

REEMA *(in Arabic)* The doctor gave it to me.

HUDA *(in Arabic)* Which doctor? Here in the states or back in Palestine?

REEMA *(in Arabic)* The doctor in Palestine gave me the medicine and then the doctor in the states also gave me some medicine.

SHAHNAZ What is she saying?

HUDA She says she got the medicine from doctors here and also back in her country.

MAGDA Is she having a heart attack?

HUDA *(in Arabic)* Aunty, what are your symptoms? What is happening?

REEMA *(At this point in the play something surreal happens – REEMA speaks in English so the audience can understand what she is saying. The others in the camp do not know what she is saying, for them she is still speaking in Arabic. The contrast between what she says in English and what the translator reports is great. This is done for effect. No one onstage knows that the translations are wrong – only the audience sees it.)* My heart burns for Palestine. My heart burns in America. My heart is burning.

HUDA She says that she has some chest pain.

REEMA My heart burns for the land and the people. My heart burns for my sons. My heart burns seeing the evils that the people commit on each other. My heart is burning for justice and my heart is burning having seen cruelty. When I close my eyes at night and see God my heart is burning with questions of why we are in such a condition. My heart is burning for revenge. It's collaborators! Collaborators got us here and collaborators are around us. I can feel it!

HUDA She says that she is sad and her heart has a burning in it.

MAGDA Is that all she said? She spoke for a long time!

HUDA Well, that's about all she said. You know, Arabic is more flowery than English. I am just giving you the substance of it.

SHAHNAZ Her heart has a burning? What does that mean? Did she eat something that upset her?

MAGDA Probably the food from the cafeteria. It would make anyone sick.

SHAHNAZ Well, that is easy to solve. For heartburn, we used to mix lime with some sugar.

VICKI There is no lime here.

MAGDA And not much sugar either.

REEMA As an old woman in Palestine I was kept from the hospital when my heart had pain. The ambulance could not take me past the check points. The Israelis would not allow it. My son brought me here to America to have a better life. *(Laughs sarcastically at the irony.)* Oh how I wish I could talk to you all in English. The things I could tell you would make your blood begin to boil.

HUDA She says that her son brought her here to see doctors because we have much better medical care in the United States and she wishes she could speak English.

REEMA *(Grabbing MAGDA and clutching her. Looking into her eyes.)* Young girl, striving for being a woman. It is hard being a woman here and everywhere. We women are powerful though. Don't forget that! You have so much power, young girl! Use it wisely. Don't let them persuade you to join them!

MAGDA What?

HUDA She said that gender roles are very strictly defined, especially in Palestine and that you have many opportunities in the United States as a woman.

REEMA There are people all around us who mean us harm, who will try to convince us to do bad things. In the end, if we agree, it will destroy us. We must stand together, child! Think of yourself as a woman, but a strong woman. In the yard, although the rooster crows, the hen lays the eggs.

VICKI I heard something about chicken and eggs! Is she hungry?

HUDA No, she didn't say she is hungry, but I can ask her. *(in Arabic)* Are you hungry, Aunty?

(REEMA shakes her head no.)

She's not hungry.

REEMA At night when I am sleeping, I secretly hope that I can leave this world, but when I do, I would like to be buried back in Palestine. Back in my home. They want us to have forgiveness in our hearts? Why forgiveness? I will not forgive. I still have power in me. Forgiveness will not get us our freedom. Believe me, I know.

HUDA She is a very stubborn woman. She is saying that she has no peace in her heart and no forgiveness.

REEMA Do you know what happened in Algeria? The women were the heroes in Algeria! They dressed like the French and they were able to free their people. No one suspected those Algerian women. I have always admired them!

VICKI Niswan Aljazayriat? She is talking about Algerian women, no? I understood that.

SHAHNAZ What about Algerian women? She is Palestinian.

VICKI Maybe she is talking about the women in the Algerian revolution? I thought I understood something about war. I don't know. Huda, what is she saying? Did she mention the Algerian revolution against the French?

HUDA Yes, she did mention that. Very good. You understand.

VICKI *(Feeling good about her understanding)* Yes!

SHAHNAZ What about it?

VICKI She is saying that the women were in that war, right? Isn't that what she is saying?

HUDA Yes, very good, Vicki. You seem to know more Arabic than I thought you did.

VICKI Thanks! Did you see that movie, *Battle of Algiers*? The women who dressed like the French and took down the French army with little handbaskets and short haircuts? I love that movie.

MAGDA Hand baskets?

VICKI Yeah, the women were able to infiltrate the markets undetected and they carried these little baskets.

HUDA *(to VICKI)* And why does this interest you?

VICKI It is kind of interesting, you know.

(She looks at SHAHNAZ and makes a face.)

REEMA You think that I am a poor, stupid woman who only likes to play cards and make food and tell fortunes? You think I don't remember what happened in 1967? In 1948? You think I don't feel pain for what I see happening now? And you, young Magda especially, the fire in your eyes and your heart. Make it a good fire that burns bright and takes down this camp and frees our people. Think of Layla Khaled, Magda!

MAGDA Why does she keep talking to me?

(MAGDA, disgusted, makes a face and leaves.)

HUDA Layla Khaled? I think I should go now. She is just ranting and not making much sense. She seems to be comfortable. Good bye.

VICKI Thank you, Huda. I appreciate your help.

HUDA Anytime, girls. I'm just next door. Wait up, Magda! I want to talk to you!

REEMA The future will be better than the past! *(to VICKI, in English first and then Arabic)* Bring me some olive oil and let us plan together. Wain Huda?

VICKI She's gone, Reema.

REEMA *(in Arabic)* Vicki. I am an old woman, but you are still young. Habibti. Move those Arabs to action in America! Where is the American Intifada?

ZAFIRA *(While saying this, VICKI transforms into ZAFIRA. REEMA sings Marcel Khalife's "Walking Tall" under the words of the following monologue.)* Arab Americans where are you? Shisha smoking shopkeepers, henna painted beauty queens, engineering students at the University of Michigan, Professors of Comparative Literature, Poets, Musicians? Lawyers? Doctors? Teachers? Mothers? Fathers? Turn off the cooking oil, step out of your crowns, tear up your thesis, delete your poems, stop the romantic music, retire the stethoscope, put down the dry erase markers. None of that will help us now.

Those worshipping in mosques, shopping at Walmart, smashing garlic, smoking in hookah bars, third generation women trying to find their identity, hummous eating, hijab wearing friends of friends of roommates in college. Where are you, my people?

Make a debke line and one two three STOMP let's take it to the streets. Get out of your suburban souk, your academic induced cloud, the twirl of the shawarma machine and join me in an Arab American revolution. Let's make a nakba in Nashville, do the debke in Dallas, turn Minneapolis into a maklouba, and together with one strong fist break through all that is holding us back and grab our freedom together.

(At this, the women of the camp – SHAHNAZ, VICKI, REEMA, and MAGDA – do the debke together. HUDA joins in last. She enters the line, takes MAGDA aside, and whispers to her. They leave together.)

Scene 5: Inspection – Visit

Sirens go off. The women are in their cabin. It is the continuation of the previous scene. MAGDA is not there. REEMA is looking at her cards, the other two are in conversation.

ANNOUNCEMENT Attention! It is 4pm and time for the daily check. Report to your cabins. Stand at attention and wait for further instructions.

(The women drop their things, and move to the outer cabin.)

SHAHNAZ Where's Magda? It's the Inspection!

ANNOUNCEMENT There are observers here today. Students from several area high schools are on a tour of the area. They will be looking through your cabins and observing the camp.

VICKI Shit. High schools?

(GUARD 1 walks into the women's cabin and briefly inspects each one – looking them up and down. He briefly lifts up a few pillows, etc. ... checking for anything suspicious. The women remain at attention.)

GUARD 1 Remain in line until the entire camp has been inspected.

SHAHNAZ *(to GUARD)* Please sir, it is hard for me to stand. Can I sit down?

GUARD 1 Quiet! No talking during inspection.

VICKI She's pregnant!

GUARD 1 Did you hear me? Shut up!

VICKI Shut up? Have you no heart?

REEMA Vicki! Khallas!

(GUARD 1 glares at REEMA and walks over to VICKI.)

GUARD 1 Look, lady. You're about this close to being sent to the Greenhouse.

VICKI Greenhouse? Your euphemisms. Why not call it what it is?

(He walks up to her – ready for a confrontation. Just then the visiting student group comes through for a tour with Howard as their tour guide.)

GUARD 2 (HOWARD JACKSON) As you can see, this is the area where the people live. Four to a cabin. There is a sink and wash area, beds, and all the comforts of apartment living!

JAMIE Our tax dollars pay for this luxury! They have it so much nicer than I thought.

(JOYCE is holding her purse close to her body and looking around nervously. MARCUS is lagging behind and looking at something outside the group.)

JOYCE Kids, you know that Howard here used to be a student at Eagleton! I remember him in the old days. You remember us, don't you, Howard?

GUARD 2 (HOWARD JACKSON) Of course, Mrs. Hanson. That is why they had me show you all around.

JOYCE That's so nice! Almost like home. You were such a nice boy!

MARCUS Where's the torture chamber?!

GUARD 2 (HOWARD JACKSON) We don't have a torture chamber – just a greenhouse area for those prisoners who are dangerous to the others. It's not much worse than the quiet room at Eagleton!

JAMIE Really?

MARCUS But, my brother says that there is an area where he can hear screams coming out day and night. He's a guard at the Jerome Camp.

GUARD 2 (HOWARD JACKSON) Well, the Jerome Camp. The Jerome Camp is the highest security camp – for the noxious weeds – it mostly has foreign nationals, those deemed dangerous to the state in the highest level. That's a red camp – level one. Here in the north woods at Camp Sprout, we have the crabgrass detainees – those deemed a security risk to the state, but it is a blue area.

JAMIE You know that, Marcus! This is a blue camp for the crabgrass detainees!

MARCUS We never get anything exciting in Minnesota.

GUARD 2 (HOWARD JACKSON) Right this way.

(He leads them past the four women. VICKI recognizes the group and looks down immediately. They do not recognize her and go on.)

JOYCE Come on, students. Keep moving!

MARCUS When are we going to have dinner?

JOYCE It's only four o'clock. Are you hungry already?

MARCUS Yeah. I only had some chips for lunch on the bus.

JOYCE After this, we'll stop at McDonald's.

JAMIE Yay!

(The students move out of the scene and on to another area of camp.)

ANNOUNCEMENT The visitors have left the camp. You may resume your normal activities until the dinner bell rings at six p.m. It's a good day at Camp Sprout!

(The women relax and go back to the cabin and lie on their beds.)

Scene 6

It is later at night and the three women are lounging on their beds. Guard knocks and enters the room.

GUARD 2 (HOWARD JACKSON) I've been sent here to get the things that were Magda Khaled's.

VICKI What?

GUARD 2 (HOWARD JACKSON) Here's a bag. Please gather her things for me.

SHAHNAZ Where is she going?

GUARD 2 (HOWARD JACKSON) No questions. Just do as I say. Get Magda Khaled's belongings, put them in this bag and do it fast.

VICKI *(Sitting up)* What do you mean get her things? Is she okay? Has she been transferred to another location? Don't you have any information at all?

GUARD 2 (HOWARD JACKSON) No. No information.

SHAHNAZ Where are you taking her things?

VICKI Howard?

GUARD 2 (HOWARD JACKSON) If you must know, we are taking her things to the Pruning Room here in camp. Which things are hers?

SHAHNAZ Here, I can help you. What happens at the Pruning Room?

GUARD 2 HOWARD JACKSON) It is the growth headquarters. She has been with us since the morning.

VICKI Growth Headquarters?

GUARD 2 (HOWARD JACKSON) Yes, she is in the office.

SHAHNAZ In a cell?

GUARD 2 (HOWARD JACKSON) No. Not in a cell. She is taking the oath.

VICKI The oath? What oath?

GUARD 2 (HOWARD JACKSON) The military oath. For soldiers. She has joined the army.

SHAHNAZ What! The army?

GUARD 2 (HOWARD JACKSON) Yes. Magda isn't staying here anymore in your cabin. She will move to another location to get trained after the swearing in ceremony. Now I need to get her things.

(He goes to the closet and looks in.)

You're getting a new bunkmate. Huda Asfour.

(Gathering up MAGDA's belongings in a bag. He leaves the room.)

VICKI *(Looking after him)* My god. Imagine that. She joined the army.

SHAHNAZ What does that mean for us?

VICKI I don't know.

REEMA Shu? Shu? Shu sar? Wayn Magda? Wayn be akdoo a ghrada?[16]

VICKI Jaysh. Magda… Jaysh.

REEMA A'jaysh akhad Magda?[17] Yah, Allah! Yah Allah!

VICKI *(Pantomiming someone taking an oath and holding a gun.)* Magda – bil Jaysh.

(HUDA walks in during this point.)

REEMA Magda dukhalat al jaysh?[18]

HUDA Hi girls. I guess I'm in here now! Aiowa! Magda dukhalat al jaysh, Reema![19]

(HOWARD leaves and the women look at each other.)

REEMA Allah yustoor.

Scene 7

MARGE Vicki, I brought you some buns from the shelter. You're not supposed to take them out, but I snuck em in my pocket. Here!

VICKI Zafira, the Olive Oil Warrior. I am Zafira. Get it right, Marge.

MARGE Okay, Zafira.

VICKI *(Taking the food and eating)* There's been an uprising at Camp Sprout!

MARGE I got you something else, too. A surprise treat…

VICKI Reema! Huda! I can't believe this…

MARGE Come over here. I want to show you what I got Vicki. I mean Zafira…

VICKI I gotta find Howard. There's something going on and… There he is!

(Scene shifts back to internment camp and older VICKI wanders into the memory and becomes younger VICKI.)

YOUNGER VICKI Howard, come here. Can I talk to you privately?

GUARD 2 (HOWARD JACKSON) *(Looking over his shoulder)* What, Ms. Khoury?

YOUNGER VICKI I am asking for your help. People are disappearing all around here, and no one knows what's happening! First Magda, then the women in block seven. Now Huda's in our cabin… we're nervous. The mood seems to be changing around here. Can you get me some information?

GUARD 2 (HOWARD JACKSON) I don't know anything about all that, Ms. Khoury. I'm just an enlisted man.

VICKI Please. I know you have access to computers. Can you please look around, ask some questions, somehow find out what's going on?

GUARD 2 (HOWARD JACKSON) Look at the computer? No.

VICKI Please, Howard, I am begging you. Please. It won't take much.

GUARD 2 (HOWARD JACKSON) I would get in trouble.

VICKI Well, surely you must be able to be in the office alone at night. You could look then and no one would know?

GUARD 2 (HOWARD JACKSON) Look, Ms. K. It's best to just stay quiet here. Let me tell you that. You'll survive that way.

VICKI Survive?

GUARD 2 (HOWARD JACKSON) I have a son, you know. I need this job. I can't risk being kicked out or worse.

VICKI Please, I need to know some information. Anything. Remember when you came to me in school and how I helped you out when you weren't going to pass English?

GUARD 2 (HOWARD JACKSON) Yes, ma'am. I did appreciate it.

VICKI And when the kids were picking on you because you couldn't read so well?

GUARD 2 (HOWARD JACKSON) *(embarrassed)* Yeah.

VICKI Please, Howard, I hate to bring these things up, but I am only asking for information, that's all.

GUARD 2 (HOWARD JACKSON) Look, you gotta understand the situation for me.

VICKI I know. But, we're scared. I'm only asking for you to do a quick search for notes. Just a little search is all. I won't tell anyone. No one will even know you did it. There is something going on and... we're very scared, Howard. Please. For your old teacher?

GUARD 2 (HOWARD JACKSON) Well, if I am in the office and no one's around, maybe I could look a little.

VICKI Thank you, Howard. Thank you. God bless you.

GUARD 2 (HOWARD JACKSON)'S RADIO 10-4 to Howard Jackson. You copy?

GUARD 2 (HOWARD JACKSON) I have to go now. I'm being called.

(He starts to leave, and another officer walks up to him while he is still standing with VICKI.)

GUARD 1 What are you doing here, Howard? Fraternizing with the detainees?

GUARD 2 (HOWARD JACKSON) No, sir. Just correcting one. The latrines are a mess!

(He looks at VICKI – pleading.)

VICKI Yes, sir. I will see to it that I clean the bathrooms better next time.

(She hums to herself, then breaks into "Walking Tall" as she walks back to her cabin.)

GUARD 2 (HOWARD JACKSON) *(For the benefit of the other soldier)* English only!

VICKI It's a song. A love song.

GUARD 1 You know the rules. English only.

VICKI Yes, sir.

(VICKI walks back into the scene under the bridge – she becomes old VICKI again.)

Yes, sir.

MARGE You've told me this story a million times, Vicki... Try to forget it!

OLD VICKI It was later that week. We were having lunch in the commons area. It was cheese day and we were having those awful cheese sandwiches again. You know what I mean? That cheap yellow government cheese and dry bread? They fed that to us in the camps almost every day. I saw Howard at the door.

GUARD 2 (HOWARD JACKSON) *(from the past)* I found out some info, Ms. K. Meet me

outside behind the cafeteria and I'll hand it to you. I'm going there now. Quick!

(VICKI leaves the bustling cafeteria area and meets HOWARD.)

VICKI Thank you so much, Howard. You don't know what this means.

GUARD 2 (HOWARD JACKSON) Here's a report I printed out for you about your cell block. Don't let anyone know I did this and please destroy it immediately. It's very serious. I have to go. They'll be looking for me!

(Old VICKI takes the paper and walks over to the corner. The voice of HUDA reports.)

HUDA Operation Mloukhia
Report on Block one: Cabin 3.
Magda Khaled – Alert level 1. Little allegiance to community. Easily can be made an internal spy.
Shahnaz Khan – Alert level 4. Must remain under watch. Possible seizure of infant after birth. Reevaluate at that time.
Vicki Khoury – Alert level 8. Reports from workplace indicate extreme radical position of influence. Continue to watch. Recommendation forthcoming.
Reema Khamis – Alert level 10. Little allegiance to United States, no desire or ability to integrate. Problematic past political activity and views. Statements made in support of uprisings. Extremely dangerous element. Recommendation: Fumigation.
All work should look accidental as not to arouse suspicion or stimulate upheaval in camp. Look for moments of chaos and move quickly. Report filed by Huda Asfour.

VICKI My god. Huda! I knew it. Fumigation? I need to find Reema.

(She looks around, but HOWARD is not there. At this VICKI runs to the cafeteria where it appears some sort of chaos has already happened. VICKI tries to reach REEMA to talk to her.)

GUARD 1 What do you have there?

REEMA Zeit Zaytoon!

GUARD 1 What is in that container? Answer me!
(Into his radio) I need back up in the cafeteria!
(to REEMA) Drop it!

REEMA Hayda Zeit Zaytoon!

(REEMA is clutching the bottle of olive oil in her hand identical to the one that ZAFIRA has had with her throughout the play. The guard lunges at her to take it away and she resists. They wrestle her to the ground. Guards come and drag REEMA

away. She ends in a crumpled heap in the floor. She drops the bottle of olive oil and VICKI picks it up. She walks slowly out and back to the bridge.)

VICKI *(Reading from an old newspaper)* "Sixty year old Reema Khamis died of a heart attack in Camp Sprout today. She will be buried in the military camp grave yard. She has no survivors."

(Dramatic pause. VICKI weeps.)

MARGE Come on Vicki. Sleep now. It'll be better in the morning. It's over now. The war is over. You're here.

VICKI They beat Reema! An old woman! I didn't have time to warn her, Marge. And I couldn't speak to her. I couldn't speak. All I could say was "La" and "Ta'i!"

MARGE I know. Here. Sit down.

VICKI And I was silent and afraid after that point. If they could kill an old woman, what would they do to me? I did nothing to liberate us, Marge. Nothing. Just protected myself.

MARGE Anyone would have done the same! You would have been next.

VICKI Poor Reema. They didn't care about her. Didn't ever really "see" her as the beautiful Arab woman she was.

MARGE I know, Vicki. That's how it is. They don't see any of us.

VICKI And I did nothing, Marge. And that poor woman died. Shahnaz's baby was taken later that month. And the war ended and the world went on.

MARGE The world always goes on, Vicki. With all your schooling and talking, don't you know that?

(Pause)

VICKI Of course I know, but does that mean I have to like it? Does that mean I have to accept it?

(Pause)

You know, there is one good thing that came out of all of it. This.

(Sobering and turning back as ZAFIRA. She holds up the bottle of olive oil that REEMA had in her hand.)

I got this. Do you know what is in this bottle? Her weapon! My weapon!

MARGE Yeah, I've heard this story before, but go ahead. Tell me again.

VICKI/ZAFIRA *(Gaining speed and energy with the lines)* It is Zayt Zaytoon! The oil of the olive!

It has been the magic weapon of all the prophets from the beginning of time. Zeus sent it down as the most important gift to man, Christians believe that Christ will return to earth through its groves, Isis was buried with it, the prophet Mohammed instructed people to use it and respect it. Babies are bathed in it at birth, it can rejuvenate old people's feeble minds, cure cancer, soften your skin, and it tastes very good on bread. It gives power to queens and priestesses and me!

The olive oil in Reema's tiny jar was powerful. I have it now. Watch how I will use it Marge! Olive oil is my weapon.

MARGE *(pause)* Yeah, it's good stuff. Tasty, too! Look. Here's the surprise for you, Vicki. I bet you won't guess what I got? It's humis!

VICKI /ZAFIRA *(mumbling quietly)* Hummous, Marge. It's pronounced HUMMMMMM MMMMMMMMMOUS! And it's Zafira now. Not Vicki. ZAFIRA THE OLIVE OIL WARRIOR!

MARGE Okay, Zafira. Let's eat hummmmmmmmmmous.

VICKI Zafira. It means victory! With only a drop of olive oil, Marge. I am powerful! Put a little of this olive oil on that hummous, Marge, and we are dangerous! Zayt Zaytoon on our skin and now we are sublime. It is from heaven. A little piece of heaven. Here, have some! I share it with you.

(She puts some olive oil on her own and then MARGE's hands and they rub it on their skin.)

MARGE Thanks. Wow. This is the first time I have gotten some of Zafira's secret weapon.

VICKI You are powerful, too, Marge.

MARGE Thanks Zafira.

VICKI Together we will change the world!

(Pause)

MARGE So, olive oil's the weapon of the gods?

VICKI Yep. And us.

MARGE Hmm. That easy?

VICKI That easy. Let's do some superhero work together, Marge.

MARGE An empathy revolution, Zafira!

VICKI An empathy revolution, Marge!

MARGE We can start in the morning!

VICKI In the morning? Let's start now. Why are we waiting? Watch out world. Here we come! Zayt Zaytoon!

(Lights dim as they continue to plan…)

★

Notes

1. Arabic? Do you speak Arabic?
2. No, a little only.
3. Yes. I do have.
4. This is Hassan and this is Mohammed. The army took them. Oh my…
5. I miss kibbee! Lebanese people love kibbee! We do, too. You are Lebanese! One day we will eat kibbee together, habibti. God willing.
6. Cabbage rolls? You know cabbage rolls, Reema. Do you like them?
7. Cabbage rolls! I love cabbage rolls! They are delicious! I would always make it for my husband and sons! It took all day, but every minute was worth it. Those were good days.
8. Ah! Grape leaves. Yes. You are making me sad, habibti.
9. It doesn't matter.
10. It doesn't matter! These cards mean nothing. It's just a silly game. May God protect you!
11. Where's Magda?
12. I don't know
13. What's wrong, aunty?
14. My heart! My heart!
15. What is the problem with your heart?
16. What is going on? Where is Magda? Where are they taking her things?
17. Magda got taken by the army?
18. Magda joined the army?
19. Yes! Magda joined the army, Reema!

———————————

Appendix

Published plays by American women of color: selected works after 1940

African American

Anderson, Christina. BlackTop Sky. *Contemporary Plays by African American Women: Ten Complete Works*. Ed. Sandra Adell. Champaign: University of Illinois Press, 2015.

_____. Good Goods. *The Methuen Drama Book of Post-Black Plays*. Eds. Harry J. Elam, Jr. and Douglas A. Jones, Jr. London: Methuen Publishing, 2012.

Barfield, Tanya. *Blue Door: A Play Of Original Songs*. New York: Dramatists Play Service, Inc., 2007.

_____. Without Skin or Breathless. *O Solo Homo: The New Queer Performance*. Eds. Holly Hughes and David Roman. New York: Grove Press, 1998.

Brooks, J. Nicole. *Black Diamond*. New York: Bloomsbury Drama, 2013.

_____. Fedra. *Contemporary Plays by African American Women: Ten Complete Works*. Ed. Sandra Adell. Champaign: University of Illinois Press, 2015.

_____. Shotgun Harriet. *The Midnight Sky and the Silent Starts: Five New Plays by Women*. NoPassport Press, 2011.

Brown-Guillory, Elizabeth. Mam Phyllis. *Wines in the Wilderness: Plays by African American Women from the Harlem Renaissance to the Present*. Ed. Elizabeth Brown-Guillory. New York: Greenwood Press, 1990.

Carlos, Laurie. White Chocolate for My Father. *Moon Marked and Touched by the Sun: Plays by African-American Women*. Ed. Sydne Mahone. New York: Theatre Communications Group, 1994.

Childress, Alice. Florence. *Wines in the Wilderness: Plays by African American Women from the Harlem Renaissance to the Present*. Ed. Elizabeth Brown-Guillory. New York: Greenwood Press, 1990.

Cleage, Pearl. *A Song for Coretta*. New York: Dramatists Play Service, Inc., 2008.

_____. *Blues for an Alabama Sky*. New York: Dramatists Play Service, Inc., 1999.

_____. *Bourbon at the Border*. New York: Dramatists Play Service, Inc., 2006.

_____. *The Nacirema Society Requests the Honor of Your Presence at a Celebration of Their First One Hundred Years*. New York: Dramatists Play Service, Inc., 2013.

Clunie, Gloria Bond. North Star. *Seven Black Plays: The Theodore Ward Prize for African American Playwriting*. Ed. Chuck Smith. Evanston: Northwestern University Press, 2004.

Corthron, Kia. Cage Rhythm. *Moon Marked and Touched by the Sun: Plays by African-American Women*. Ed. Sydne Mahone. New York: Theatre Communications Group, 1994.

_____. Come Down Burning. *Colored Contradictions: An Anthology of Contemporary African-American Plays*. Eds. Robert Alexander and Harry Elam, Jr. New York: Plume, 1996.

Davis, Eisa. Bulrusher. *The Methuen Drama Book of Post-Black Plays*. Eds. Harry J. Elam, Jr. and Douglas A. Jones, Jr. London: Methuen Publishing, 2012.

Davis, Thulani. X. *Moon Marked and Touched by the Sun: Plays by African-American Women*. Ed. Sydne Mahone. New York: Theatre Communications Group, 1994.

Diamond, Lydia R. *The Gift Horse: A Play*. Woodstock: Dramatic Publishing, 2007.

_____. *Harriet Jacobs: A Play*. Evanston: Northwestern University Press, 2011.

_____. *Smart People: A Play*. Evanston: Northwestern University Press, 2016.

_____. *Stage Black: A Play*. Woodstock: Dramatic Publishing, 2008.

_____. *Stick Fly: A Play*. Evanston: Northwestern University Press, 2008.

_____. Voyeurs de Venus. *Contemporary Plays by African American Women: Ten Complete Works*. Ed. Sandra Adell. Champaign: University of Illinois Press, 2015.

Dove, Rita. *The Darker Face of the Earth: Completely Revised Second Edition*. Pasadena: Story Line Press, 1996.

Forbes, Kamilah and Hip Hop Theatre Junction. A Rhyme Deferred. *The Fire This Time: African American Plays for the 21st Century*. Eds. Robert Alexander and Harry Elam, Jr. New York: Theatre Communications Group, 2002.

Garrett, Keli. Uppa Creek: A Modern Anachronistic Parody in the Minstrel Tradition. *Contemporary Plays by African American Women: Ten Complete Works*. Ed. Sandra Adell. Champaign: University of Illinois Press, 2015.

Gurira, Danai. *Eclipsed*. New York: Dramatists Play Service, Inc., 2010.

Gurira, Danai and Nikkole Salter. In the Continuum. *The Methuen Drama Book of Post-Black Plays*. Eds. Harry J. Elam, Jr. and Douglas A. Jones, Jr. London: Methuen Publishing, 2012.

Hall, Katori. *Hoodoo Love*. New York: Dramatists Play Service, Inc., 2009.

_____. Hurt Village. *Plays 1*. London: Methuen Publishing, 2011.

_____. The Mountaintop. *Plays 1*. London: Methuen Publishing, 2011.

_____. Saturday Night/Sunday Morning. *Plays 1*. London: Methuen Publishing, 2011.

Hansberry, Lorraine. The Drinking Gourd. *Les Blancs: The Collected Last Plays*. New York: Vintage Books, 1994.

_____. Les Blancs. *Les Blancs: The Collected Last Plays*. New York: Vintage Books, 1994.

_____. What Use Are Flowers? *Les Blancs: The Collected Last Plays*. New York: Vintage Books, 1994.

Jackson, Judith Alexa. WOMBmanWARs. *Moon Marked and Touched by the Sun: Plays by African-American Women*. Ed. Sydne Mahone. New York: Theatre Communications Group, 1994.

Jackson, Marsha A. Sisters. *The National Black Drama Anthology: Eleven Plays from America's Leading African-American Theaters*. Ed. Woodie King, Jr. New York: Applause Theatre & Cinema Books, 2000.

Jones-Meadows, Karen. Henrietta. *The National Black Drama Anthology: Eleven Plays from America's Leading African-American Theaters*. Ed. Woodie King, Jr. New York: Applause Theatre & Cinema Books, 2000.

Jones, Rhodessa. Big Butt Girls, Hard-Headed Women. *Colored Contradictions: An Anthology of Contemporary African-American Plays*. Eds. Robert Alexander and Harry Elam, Jr. New York: Plume, 1996.

Kai, Nubia. Harvest the Frost. *The National Black Drama Anthology: Eleven Plays from America's Leading African-American Theaters*. Ed. Woodie King, Jr. New York: Applause Theatre & Cinema Books, 2000.

Kein, Sybil. Get Together. *Wines in the Wilderness: Plays by African American Women from the Harlem Renaissance to the Present*. Ed. Elizabeth Brown-Guillory. New York: Greenwood Press, 1990.

Kennedy, Adrienne. The Dramatic Circle. *Moon Marked and Touched by the Sun: Plays by African-American Women*. Ed. Sydne Mahone. New York: Theatre Communications Group, 1994.

_____. *Funnyhouse of a Negro*. New York: Samuel French, Inc., 2011.

_____. *Sleep Deprivation Chamber*. New York: Dramatists Play Service, Inc., 2001.

Lampley, Oni Faidi. The Dark Kalamazoo. *The Fire This Time: African American Plays for the 21st Century*. Eds. Robert Alexander and Harry Elam, Jr. New York: Theatre Communications Group, 2002.

McCauley, Robbie. *Sally's Rape*. New York: Free Press, 1996.

Morisseau, Dominique. *Detroit '67*. New York: Samuel French, Inc., 2014.

_____. *Sunset Baby*. London: Oberon Books, 2013.

Nicholas, Denise. Buses. *The National Black Drama Anthology: Eleven Plays from America's Leading African-American Theaters*. Ed. Woodie King, Jr. New York: Applause Theatre & Cinema Books, 2000.

Nottage, Lynn. *By the Way, Meet Vera Stark*. New York: Dramatists Play Service, Inc., 2013.

_____. *Crumbs from the Table of Joy*. New York: Dramatists Play Service, Inc., 1998.

_____. *Fabulation or, The Re-Education of Undine*. New York: Dramatists Play Service, Inc., 2005.

_____. *Intimate Apparel*. New York: Dramatists Play Service, Inc., 2005.

_____. *Las Meninas*. New York: Dramatists Play Service, Inc., 2003.

_____. *Mud, River, Stone*. New York: Dramatists Play Service, Inc., 1998.

_____. Poof. *Crumbs from the Table of Joy and Other Plays*. New York: Theatre Communications Group, 2003.

_____. Por'Knockers. *Crumbs from the Table of Joy and Other Plays*. New York: Theatre Communications Group, 2003.

_____. *Ruined*. New York: Theatre Communications Group, 2009.

Orlandersmith, Dael. Beauty's Daughter. *Beauty's Daughter, Monster, The Gimmick: Three Plays*. New York: Vintage Books, 2000.

_____. Black N Blue Boys/Broken Men. *Black N Blue Boys/Broken Men*. Berkeley: Soft Skull Press, 2013.

_____. The Gimmick. *Beauty's Daughter, Monster, The Gimmick: Three Plays*. New York: Vintage Books, 2000.

_____. *Horsedreams*. New York: Dramatists Play Service, Inc., 2012.

_____. Monster. *Beauty's Daughter, Monster, The Gimmick: Three Plays*. New York: Vintage Books, 2000.

_____. My Red Hand, My Black Hand. *Yellowman*. New York: Vintage Books, 2002.

_____. Yellowman. *Yellowman*. New York: Vintage Books, 2002.

Parks, Suzan-Lori. *The Book of Grace*. New York: Theatre Communications Group, 2016.

_____. The Death of the Last Black Man in the Whole Entire World. *Moon Marked and Touched by the Sun: Plays by African-American Women*. Ed. Sydne Mahone. New York: Theatre Communications Group, 1994.

_____. *Father Comes Home from the Wars (Parts 1, 2, & 3)*. New York: Theatre Communications Group, 2015.

_____. *Fucking A*. New York: Theatre Communications Group, 2001.

_____. *In the Blood*. New York: Dramatists Play Service, Inc., 2000.

_____. *Topdog/Underdog*. New York: Theatre Communications Group, 2001.

_____. *Venus*. New York: Theatre Communications Group, 1997.

Perry, Shauneille. In Dahomey. *The National Black Drama Anthology: Eleven Plays from America's Leading African-American Theaters*. Ed. Woodie King, Jr. New York: Applause Theatre & Cinema Books, 2000.

Rahman, Aishah. The Mojo and the Sayso. *Moon Marked and Touched by the Sun: Plays by African-American Women*. Ed. Sydne Mahone. New York: Theatre Communications Group, 1994.

Salter, Nikkole. *Carnaval*. Raleigh: Lulu, 2014.

Sanchez, Sonia. Sister Son/ji. *Wines in the Wilderness: Plays by African American Women from the Harlem Renaissance to the Present*. Ed. Elizabeth Brown-Guillory. New York: Greenwood Press, 1990.

Shepard-Massat, S. M. Levee James. *Contemporary Plays by African American Women: Ten Complete Works*. Ed. Sandra Adell. Champaign: University of Illinois Press, 2015.

Smith, Anna Deavere. *Fires in the Mirror: Crown Heights, Brooklyn, and Other Identities*. New York: Dramatists Play Service, Inc., 1997.

_____. *House Arrest: A Search for American Character in and around the White House, Past and Present*. New York: Dramatists Play Service, Inc., 2002.

Thompson, Lisa B. *Single Black Female*. New York: Samuel French, Inc., 2012.

Vance, Danitra. Live and in Color! *Moon Marked and Touched by the Sun: Plays by African-American Women*. Ed. Sydne Mahone. New York: Theatre Communications Group, 1994.

West, Cheryl. Before It Hits Home. *Colored Contradictions: An Anthology of Contemporary African-American Plays*. Eds. Robert Alexander and Harry Elam, Jr. New York: Plume, 1996.

Asian American

Akemi Saito, Dawn. *Ha*. Dawn Akemi Saito, 1996.

Barroga, Jeannie. Talk Story. *But Still, Like Air, I'll Rise: New Asian American Plays*. Philadelphia: Temple University Press, 1997.

Chanse, Samantha. *Lydia's Funeral Video*. California: Kaya Press, 2015.

Cho, Julia. *99 Histories*. New York: Dramatists Play Service, 2005.

_____. *BFE*. New York: Dramatists Play Service, 2006.

_____. *The Architecture of Loss*. New York: Dramatists Play Service, 2005.

_____. *How to Be a Good Son: A Drama in One Act*. New York: Playscripts, 2003.

_____. *Durango*. New York: Dramatists Play Service, 2007.

_____. *The Piano Teacher*. New York: Dramatists Play Service, 2007.

_____. *The Language Archive*. New York: Dramatists Play Service, 2012.

Cho, Julia and Florence Yoo. *Bay and the Spectacles of Doom: A Short Comedy for Young Audiences*. New York: Playscripts, 2007.

Chomet, Sun Mee. Asiamnesia. *Other Spaces of Asia America: Plays for a New Generation*. Philadelphia: Temple University Press, 2011.

Dever-Smith, Ana. *Twilight: Los Angeles*. New York: Dramatists Play Service, 1992.

_____. *Fires in the Mirrors: Crown Heights, Brooklyn and Other Identities*. New York: Dramatists Play Service, 1997.

Faigao-Hall, Linda. Woman from the Other Side of the World. *Savage Stage: Plays by Ma-Yi Theatre Company*. New York: Ma-Yi Theatre Company, 2007.

Hagedorn, Jessica. *Dogeaters*. New York: Theatre Communications Group, 2002.

_____. Tenement Lover: No Palm Trees/in New York City. *Between Worlds: Contemporary Asian-American Plays*. Ed. Misha Berson. New York: Theatre Communications Group, 1990.

Hill, Amy. Tokyo Bound. *Asian American Drama: 9 Plays from the Multiethnic Landscape*. Ed. Brian Nelson. New York: Applause Theatre and Cinema Books, Hal Leonard Books, 1997.

Huie, Karen. Yasuko and the Young S-S-Samurai. *Multicultural Theatre II: Contemporary Hispanic, Asian, and African-American Plays*. Ed. Roger Ellis. Englewood, CO: Meriwether Publishing, 1998.

Hasu-Houston, Velina. As Sometimes in a Dead Man's Face. *Asian American Drama: 9 Plays from the Multiethnic Landscape*. Ed. Brian Nelson. New York: Applause Theatre and Cinema Books, Hal Leonard Books, 1997.

_____. Kokoro (True Heart). *But Still, Like Air, I'll Rise: New Asian American Plays*. Philadelphia: Temple University Press, 1997.

Iiuka, Naomi. *Anon(ymous): A Drama*. New York: Playscripts, 2007.

Khoo, Aurorae. Happy Valley. *Other Spaces of Asia America: Plays for a New Generation*. Philadelphia: Temple University Press, 2011.

Lee-Yang, May. Sia(b). *Other Spaces of Asia America: Plays for a New Generation*. Philadelphia: Temple University Press, 2011.

Lee, Young-Jean. The Appeal. *New Downtown Now: An Anthology of New Theatre of Downtown New York*. Minneapolis: University of Minnesota Press, 2006.

_____. *Straight White Men*. New York: Theatre Communications Group, 2016.

_____. *We're Gonna Die*. New York: Theatre Communications Group, 2015.

_____. *The Shipment*. New York: Theatre Communications Group, 2010.

_____. *Lear*. New York: Theatre Communications Group, 2010.

_____. Church. *Songs of the Dragons Flying to Heaven and Other Plays*. New York: Theatre Communications Group, 2009.

_____. Songs of the Dragons Flying to Heaven. *Songs of the Dragons Flying to Heaven and Other Plays*. New York: Theatre Communications Group, 2009.

_____. Pullman, WA. *Songs of the Dragons Flying to Heaven and Other Plays*. New York: Theatre Communications Group, 2009.

_____. The Appeal. *Songs of the Dragons Flying to Heaven and Other Plays*. New York: Theatre Communications Group, 2009.

_____. Groundwork of the Metaphysic of Morals. *Songs of the Dragons Flying to Heaven and Other Plays*. New York: Theatre Communications Group, 2009.

_____. Yaggoo. *Songs of the Dragons Flying to Heaven and Other Plays*. New York: Theatre Communications Group, 2009.

Roberts, Dmae. Breaking Glass. *But Still, Like Air, I'll Rise: New Asian American Plays*. Philadelphia: Temple University Press, 1997.

Son, Diana. BOY. *Version 3.0: Contemporary Asian American Plays*. New York: Theatre Communications Group, 2011.

_____. *Stop Kiss*. New York: Dramatists Play Service, 2000.

_____. *Satellites*. New York: Dramatists Play Service, 2008.

Tuan, Alice. *Coastline*. New York: Alexander Press, 2004.

_____. *F.E.T.C.H.* Hanover, NH: Smith and Kraus Publishers, 2001.

_____. Ajax (por nobody). *New Downtown Now: An Anthology of New Theatre of Downtown New York*. Minneapolis: University of Minnesota Press, 2006.

_____. The Last of the Suns. *Version 3.0: Contemporary Asian American Plays*. New York: Theatre Communications Group, 2011.

Wang, Lucy. Junk Bonds. *But Still, Like Air, I'll Rise: New Asian American Plays*. Philadelphia: Temple University Press, 1997.

Wong, Elizabeth. Letters to a Student Revolutionary. *Multicultural Theatre II: Contemporary Hispanic, Asian, and African-American Plays*. Ed. Roger Ellis. Englewood, CO: Meriwether Publishing, 1998.

_____. Kimchee and Chitlins. *But Still, Like Air, I'll Rise: New Asian American Plays*. Philadelphia: Temple University Press, 1997.

Yamauchi, Wakako. The Music Lessons. *Songs my Mother Taught Me: Stories, Plays, and Memoir*. New York: Feminist P, 1994.

_____. And the Soul Shall Dance. *Between Worlds: Contemporary Asian-American Plays*. Ed. Misha Berson. New York: Theatre Communications Group, 1990.

Yee, Lauren. *A Mother's Touch: A Dramatic Monologue*. New York: Brooklyn Publishers, 2003.

_____. Ching Chong Chinaman. *Other Spaces of Asia America: Plays for a New Generation*. Philadelphia: Temple University Press, 2011.

*Uyehara, Denise. Hiro. *Asian American Drama: 9 Plays from the Multiethnic Landscape*. Ed. Brian Nelson. New York: Applause Theatre and Cinema Books, Hal Leonard Books, 1997.

_____. *Hello (Sex) Kitty: Mad Asian Bitch on Wheels*. New York: Grove Press, 1998.

_____. Big Head. *The Methuen Drama Anthology of Testimonial Plays: Bystander 9/11, Big Head, the Fence, Come out Eli, the Travels, On the Record, Seven, Pajarito Nuevo La Lleva: The Sounds of the Coup*. Ed. Alison Forsyth. Northhampton: Smith College, 1993.

Latina

Alvarez, Lynne. Esperanza Rising. *Plays by Lynne Alvarez: Later Plays & Selected Poems*. New York: Broadway Play Publishing Inc., 2008.

_____. Snow Queen. *Plays by Lynne Alvarez: Later Plays & Selected Poems*. New York: Broadway Play Publishing Inc., 2008.

_____. Eddie Mundo Edmundo. *Lynne Alvarez: Collected Plays, Vol. 1*. Lyme, NH: Smith & Kraus, 1998.

_____. The Argonomist. *Lynne Alvarez: Collected Plays, Vol. 1*. Lyme, NH: Smith & Kraus, 1998.

_____. Thin Air: Tales from a Revolution. *Lynne Alvarez: Collected Plays, Vol. 1*. Lyme, NH: Smith & Kraus, 1998.

_____. On Sundays. *Lynne Alvarez: Collected Plays, Vol. 1*. Lyme, NH: Smith & Kraus, 1998.

_____. The Reincarnation of Jaime Brown. *Lynne Alvarez: Collected Plays, Vol. 1*. Lyme, NH: Smith & Kraus, 1998.

_____. The Wonderful Tower of Humbert Lavignet. *Lynne Alvarez: Collected Plays, Vol. 1*. Lyme, NH: Smith & Kraus, 1998.

_____. Analiese. *New Plays from ACT's Young Conservatory Vol. III*. Lyme: Smith & Kraus, 1999.

_____. Deux Mariages: Romola and Nijinsky. *Women Playwrights: The Best Plays of 2001*. Lyme: Smith & Kraus, 2002.

Arizmendi, Yareli. Who Buys Your Shoes? *La Voz Latina: Contemporary Plays and Performance Pieces by Latinas*. Eds. Elizabeth C. Ramirez and Catherine Casiano. Champaign: University of Illinois Press, 2011.

Baez, Josefina. Dominicanish. *La Voz Latina: Contemporary Plays and Performance Pieces by Latinas*. Eds. Elizabeth C. Ramirez and Catherine Casiano. Champaign: University of Illinois Press, 2011.

Blecher, Hilary and Cruz, Migdalia. Frida: The Story of Frida Kahlo. *Puro Teatro: A Latina Anthology*. Eds. Alberto Sandoval-Sanchez & Nancy Saporta Sternbach. Tucson: The University of Arizona Press, 2000.

Coppel, Fernanda. *Chimichanga and Zoloft*. New York: Samuel French, Inc., 2014.

Cram, Cusi. *Dusty and the Big Bad World*. New York: Samuel French, Inc., 2010.

_____. *Fuente*. New York: Samuel French, Inc., 2009.

_____. *A Lifetime Burning*. New York: Samuel French, Inc., 2011.

_____. *Lucy and the Conquest*. New York: Samuel French, Inc., 2009.

_____. West of Stupid. *The Best American Short Plays: 2000-2001*. Ed. Mark Glubke. New York: Applause Theatre & Cinema Books, 2002.

_____. A Moment Defined. *HB Playwrights Short Play Festival: 2003 The Subway Plays*. Eds. William Carden and Pamela Berlin. Lyme: Smith & Kraus, 2004.

_____. Landlocked. *Women Playwrights: The Best Plays of 2000*. Ed. D. L. Lepidus. Lyme: Smith & Kraus, 2002.

_____. Trepidation Nation. *Humana Festival 2003: The Complete Plays*. Eds. Tanya Palmer and Adrien-Alice Hansel. Lyme: Smith & Kraus, 2005.

Cruz, Migdalia. Fur. *Out of the Fringe: Contemporary Latina/o Theatre and Performance*. Eds. Maria Teresa Marrero and Caridad Svich. New York: TCG, 2000.

_____. Another Part of the House. *La Voz Latina: Contemporary Plays and Performance Pieces by Latinas*. Eds. Elizabeth C. Ramirez and Catherine Casiano. Champaign: University of Illinois Press, 2011.

_____. El Grito Del Bronx. *El Grito Del Bronx & Other Plays*. Eds. Randy Gener, Jorge Huerta, Otis Ramsey-Zoe, Stephen Squibb, Caridad Svich. South Gate: No Passport Press, 2010.

_____. Salt. *El Grito Del Bronx & Other Plays*. Eds. Randy Gener, Jorge Huerta, Otis Ramsey-Zoe, Stephen Squibb, Caridad Svich. South Gate: No Passport Press, 2010.

_____. Yellow Eyes. *El Grito Del Bronx & Other Plays*. Eds. Randy Gener, Jorge Huerta, Otis Ramsey-Zoe, Stephen Squibb, Caridad Svich. South Gate: No Passport Press, 2010.

_____. Cigarettes & Moby-Dick. *Envisioning the Americas: Latina/o Theatre & Performance*. Eds. Migdalia Cruz, John Jesurun, Oliver Mayer, Alejandro Morales, and Anne Garcia-Romero. South Gate: No Passport Press, 2011.

_____. Lucy Loves Me. *Latinas on Stage: Criticism & Pratice*. Eds. Alicia Arrizon and Lillian Manzor Coats. Berkeley: Third Woman Press, 2000.

_____. So...& Mariluz's Thanksgiving. *Positive/Negative: Women of Color and HIV/AIDS*. Eds. Imani Harrington & Cheryl Bellamy. San Francisco: Aunt Lute Books, 2002.

Del Valle, Janis Astor. I'll Be Home Para La Navidad. *Amazon All-Stars: Thirteen Lesbian Plays: with Essays and Commentary*. Ed. Rosemary Keefe Curb. New York: Applause Theater & Cinema Books, 2000.

_____. Fuschia. *Puro Teatro: A Latina Anthology*. Eds. Alberto Sandoval-Sanchez & Nancy Saporta Sternbach. Tucson: The University of Arizona Press, 2000.

Duarte, Stella Pope. Joe Arpaio Meets La Virgen de Guadalupe. *Latina/o Heritage on Stage: Dramatizing Heroes and Legends*. Ed. Daniel Enrique Perez. Phoenix: The Lion and the Seagoat LLC., 2015.

Fernandez, Evelina. *A Mexican Trilogy*. New York: Samuel French, Inc., 2015.

—————. Luminarias. *La Voz Latina: Contemporary Plays and Performance Pieces by Latinas*. Eds. Elizabeth C. Ramirez and Catherine Casiano. Champaign: University of Illinois Press, 2011.

Fornes, Maria Irene. Mud. *Plays: Maria Irene Fornes*. New York: PAJ Publications, 2001.

—————. Sarita. *Plays: Maria Irene Fornes*. New York: PAJ Publications, 2001.

—————. The Danube. *Plays: Maria Irene Fornes*. New York: PAJ Publications, 2001.

—————. The Conduct of Life. *Plays: Maria Irene Fornes*. New York: PAJ Publications, 2001.

—————. *Fefu and Her Friends*. New York: PAJ Publications, 2001.

—————. *Letters from Cuba*. *Letters from Cuba and Other Plays*. New York: PAJ Publications, 2007.

—————. *Terra Incognita*. *Letters from Cuba and Other Plays*. New York: PAJ Publications, 2007.

—————. Desperate Crossing. *Letters from Cuba and Other Plays*. New York: PAJ Publications, 2007.

—————. Promenade. *Promenade and Other Plays*. New York: PAJ Publications, 2007.

—————. The Successful Life of 3. *Promenade and Other Plays*. New York: PAJ Publications, 2007.

—————. Tango Palace. *Promenade and Other Plays*. New York: PAJ Publications, 2007.

—————. Dr. Kheal. *Promenade and Other Plays*. New York: PAJ Publications, 2007.

—————. A Vietnamese Wedding. *Promenade and Other Plays*. New York: PAJ Publications, 2007.

—————. Molly's Dream. *Promenade and Other Plays*. New York: PAJ Publications, 2007.

—————. Abingdon Square. *What of the Night? Selected Plays*. New York: PAJ Publications, 2008.

—————. What of the Night? *What of the Night? Selected Plays*. New York: PAJ Publications, 2008.

—————. The Summer in Gossensass. *What of the Night? Selected Plays*. New York: PAJ Publications, 2008.

—————. Enter the Night. *What of the Night? Selected Plays*. New York: PAJ Publications, 2008.

Garcia-Crow, Amparo. Cocks Have Claws and Wings to Fly. *Amparo Garcia-Crow: The South Texas Plays (Between Misery and the Sun)*. South Gate: No Passport Press, 2009.

—————. Under a Western Sky. *Amparo Garcia-Crow: The South Texas Plays (Between Misery and the Sun)*. South Gate: No Passport Press, 2009.

—————. The Faraway Nearby. *Amparo Garcia-Crow: The South Texas Plays (Between Misery and the Sun)*. South Gate: No Passport Press, 2009.

—————. Esmeralda Blue. *Amparo Garcia-Crow: The South Texas Plays (Between Misery and the Sun)*. South Gate: No Passport Press, 2009.

García-Romero, Anne. *Earthquake Chica*. New York: Broadway Play Publishing Inc., 2007.

—————. *Juanita's Statue*. New York: Broadway Play Publishing Inc., 2013.

—————. Land of Benjamin Franklin. *Envisioning the Americas: Latina/o Theatre & Performance*. Eds. Migdalia Cruz, John Jesurun, Oliver Mayer, Alejandro Morales, and Anne Garcia-Romero. South Gate: No Passport Press, 2011.

—————. Paloma. *New Playwrights: The Best Plays of 2013*. Lyme: Smith & Kraus, 2013.

—————. *Mary Peabody in Cuba*. New York: Broadway Play Publishing Inc., 2007.

—————. Santa Concepcion. *Anne Garcia-Romero: Collected Plays*. South Gate: No Passport Press, 2008.

Gonzalez, Silvia S. *Waiting Women*. Woodstock: Dramatic Publishing, 1998.

—————. *Alicia in Wonder Tierra (Or I Can't Eat Goat Head)*. Woodstock: Dramatic Publishing, 1996.

—————. *The Migrant Farmworker's Son*. Woodstock: Dramatic Publishing, 1996.

—————. *La Llorona Llora*. Woodstock: Dramatic Publishing, 1996.

Grise, Virginia. *blu*. New Haven: Yale University Press, 2011.

Hudes, Quiara Alegría. *Elliot, A Soldier's Fuge*. New York: TCG, 2012.

—————. *The Happiest Song Plays Last*. New York: TCG, 2014.

—————. *Water by the Spoonful*. New York: TCG, 2012.

—————. *26 Miles*. New York: Dramatists Play Service Inc., 2010.

—————. *Yemaya's Belly*. New York: Dramatists Play Service Inc., 2007.

Lopez, Josefina. Detained in the Desert. *Detained in the Desert & Other Plays*. Dillon: WPR Publishing, 2011.

_____. Lola Does Roma. *Detained in the Desert & Other Plays*. Dillon: WPR Publishing, 2011.

_____. Trio Los Machos. *Detained in the Desert & Other Plays*. Dillon: WPR Publishing, 2011.

_____. Boyle Heights. *Detained in the Desert & Other Plays*. Dillon: WPR Publishing, 2011.

_____. When Nature Calls. *Detained in the Desert & Other Plays*. Dillon: WPR Publishing, 2011.

_____. *Food for the Dead and La Pinta*. Woodstock: Dramatic Publishing, 1996.

Lopez, Melinda. *Sonia Flew*. New York: Dramatists Play Service Inc., 2009.

_____. The Lesson. *Boston Theatre Marathon Anthology*. Quincy: Baker's Play, 2000.

_____. What the Marker Will Bear. *Boston Theatre Marathon Anthology*. Quincy: Baker's Play, 2001.

Mena, Alicia. Las Nuevas Tamaleras. *Puro Teatro: A Latina Anthology*. Eds. Alberto Sandoval-Sanchez & Nancy Saporta Sternbach. Tucson: The University of Arizona Press, 2000.

Moraga, Cherrie. Waiting For Da God. *La Voz Latina: Contemporary Plays and Performance Pieces by Latinas*. Eds. Elizabeth C. Ramirez and Catherine Casiano. Champaign: University of Illinois Press, 2011.

_____. The Hungry Woman: A Mexican Medea. *Out of the Fringe: Contemporary Latina/o Theatre and Performance*. Eds. Maria Teresa Marrero and Caridad Svich. New York: TCG, 2000.

_____. Circle In The Dirt: El Pueblo De East Palo Alto. *Watsonville/Circle In The Dirt*. Albuquerque: West End Press, 2002.

_____. Watsonville: Some Place Not Here. *Watsonville/Circle In The Dirt*. Albuquerque: West End Press, 2002.

_____. Heart of the Earth: A Popul Vuh Story. *The Hungry Woman*. Albuquerque: West End Press, 2001.

Palacios, Monica. Greetings from a Queer Señorita. *Out Of The Fringe: Contemporary Latina/o Theatre and Performance*. Eds. Maria Teresa Marrero and Caridad Svich. New York: TCG, 2000.

_____. Tomboy. *Living Chicana Theory*. Ed. Carla Trujillo. Berkeley: Third Woman Press, 1997.

_____. Latin Lezbo Comic. *Latinas on Stage*. Eds. Alicia Arrizon & Lilian Manzor. Berkeley: Third Woman Press, 1997.

Parnes, Uzi and Tropicana, Carmelita. Memorias De La Revolucion. *Puro Teatro: A Latina Anthology*. Eds. Alberto Sandoval-Sanchez & Nancy Saporta Sternbach. Tucson: The University of Arizona Press, 2000.

Pedrero, Paloma. Una Estrella. *Hijas Olvidadas: Two Contemporary Plays by Hispanic Women Writers*. Eds. Karen Brunschwig and Maria Montoya. Lanham: University Press of America, 2008.

Pelaez, Carmen. El Postre de Estrada Palma. *La Voz Latina: Contemporary Plays and Performance Pieces by Latinas*. Eds. Elizabeth C. Ramirez and Catherine Casiano. Champaign: University of Illinois Press, 2011.

_____. My Cuba. *La Voz Latina: Contemporary Plays and Performance Pieces by Latinas*. Eds. Elizabeth C. Ramirez and Catherine Casiano. Champaign: University of Illinois Press, 2011.

Prida, Dolores. Botanica. *Puro Teatro: A Latina Anthology*. Eds. Alberto Sandoval-Sanchez & Nancy Saporta Sternbach. Tucson: The University of Arizona Press, 2000.

Rivera, Carmen. *La Gringa*. New York: Samuel French, Inc., 2009.

_____. Delia's Race. *Positive/Negative: Women of Color and HIV/AIDS*. Eds. Imani Harrington & Cheryl Bellamy. San Francisco: Aunt Lute Books, 2002.

_____. Julia De Burgos: Child of Water. *Julia De Burgos: Child of Water*. New York: Red Sugar Cane Press, 2014.

_____. Betty's Garage. *The Women's Project and Productions: Rowing to America And 16 Other Short Plays*. Lyme: Smith & Kraus, 2002.

Rodriguez, Delia Herrera. Cositas Quebradas: Performance Codex. *La Voz Latina: Contemporary Plays and Performance Pieces by Latinas*. Eds. Elizabeth C. Ramirez and Catherine Casiano. Champaign: University of Illinois Press, 2011.

Rodriguez, Diana. The Path to Divadom, or How to Make Fat-free Tamales in G Minor. *La Voz Latina: Contemporary Plays and Performance Pieces by Latinas*. Eds. Elizabeth C. Ramirez and Catherine Casiano. Champaign: University of Illinois Press, 2011.

Rodriguez, Nora. paula.doc. *Hijas Olvidadas: Two Contemporary Plays by Hispanic Women Writers.* Eds. Karen Brunschwig and Maria Montoya. Lanham: University Press of America, 2008.

Romero, Elaine. *Barrio Hollywood.* New York: Samuel French, Inc., 2008.

————. ¡Curanderas! Serpents of the Clouds. *Women Playwrights: The Best Plays of 2000.* Ed. D.L. Lepidus. Lyme: Smith & Kraus, 2002.

————. The Fat-Free Chicana and the Snow Cap Queen. *Puro Teatro: A Latina Anthology.* Eds. Alberto Sandoval-Sanchez & Nancy Saporta Sternbach. Tucson: The University of Arizona Press, 2000.

————. If Susan Smith Could Talk. *Ten Minute Plays from Actors Theatre of Louisville, Vol 4.* Eds. Michael Bigelow Dixon and Michele Volansky. New York: Samuel French, Inc., 1998.

————. Rain of Ruin. *2007: The Best Ten-Minute Plays for Three or More Actors.* Ed. Lawrence Harbinson. Lyme: Smith & Kraus, 2008.

————. Day of Our Dead. *Ten Minute Plays from Actors Theatre of Louisville, Vol. 6.* Eds. Tanya Palmer, Steve Moulds, and Adrien-Alice Hansel. New York: Samuel French, Inc., 2005.

————. A Simple Snow. *2007: The Best Ten-Minute Plays for 2 Actors.* Ed. D.L. Lepidus. Lyme: Smith & Kraus, 2007.

————. The Sniper. *Take Ten II" More Ten-Minute Plays.* Eds. Eric Land and Nina Shengold. New York: Vintage, 2003.

Sanchez-Scott, Milcha. Roosters. *La Voz Latina: Contemporary Plays and Performance Pieces by Latinas.* Eds. Elizabeth C. Ramirez and Catherine Casiano. Champaign: University of Illinois Press, 2011.

Saracho, Tanya et al. Oh, Gastronomy! *Humana Festival 2012: The Complete Plays.* Eds. Amy Wegener and Sarah Lunnie. New York: Playscripts, 2012.

Svich, Caridad. Alchemy of Desire/Dead-Man's Blues. *Out of the Fringe: Contemporary Latina/o Theatre and Performance.* Eds. Maria Teresa Marrero and Caridad Svich. New York: TCG, 2000.

————. Antigone Arkhe. *Antigone Project: A Play in Five Parts.* South Gate: No Passport Press, 2009.

————. Lucinda Caval. *Blasted Heavens: Five Contemporary Plays Inspired by the Greeks.* Roskilde: EyeCorner Press, 2012.

————. Steal Back Light from the Virtual. *Blasted Heavens: Five Contemporary Plays Inspired by the Greeks.* Roskilde: EyeCorner Press, 2012.

————. The Archaeology of Dreams. *The Archaeology of Dreams and Other Plays.* South Gate: Santa Catalina Editions/No Passport Press, 2015.

————. The Spell of Eden. *The Archaeology of Dreams and Other Plays.* South Gate: Santa Catalina Editions/No Passport Press, 2015.

————. Relish My Tears. *The Archaeology of Dreams and Other Plays.* South Gate: Santa Catalina Editions/No Passport Press, 2015.

————. Calculating Genesis. *The Archaeology of Dreams and Other Plays.* South Gate: Santa Catalina Editions/No Passport Press, 2015.

————. A Little Story. *A Little Story and Other Plays.* South Gate: No Passport Press, 2016.

————. 40 Ounces of Sand. *A Little Story and Other Plays.* South Gate: No Passport Press, 2016.

————. Nobody's Children. *A Little Story and Other Plays.* South Gate: Santa Catalina Editions/No Passport Press, 2016.

————. *Hide Sky.* South Gate: Santa Catalina Editions/No Passport Press, 2016.

————. *Spark.* South Gate: Santa Catalina Editions/No Passport Press, 2016.

————. *Guapa.* South Gate: Santa Catalina Editions/No Passport Press, 2013.

————. Fugitive Pieces. *The Land and Country Plays: Fugitive Pieces, Thrush, and Rift.* South Gate: Santa Catalina Editions/No Passport Press, 2012.

————. Thrush. *The Land and Country Plays: Fugitive Pieces, Thrush, and Rift.* South Gate: Santa Catalina Editions/No Passport Press, 2012.

————. Scar. *Early Plays: Volume One: Scar, Torch, Nightwood, Carnival.* South Gate: Santa Catalina Editions/No Passport Press, 2012.

————. Torch. *Early Plays: Volume One: Scar, Torch, Nightwood, Carnival.* South Gate: Santa Catalina Editions/No Passport Press, 2012.

_____. Nightwood. *Early Plays: Volume One: Scar, Torch, Nightwood, Carnival*. South Gate: Santa Catalina Editions/No Passport Press, 2012.

_____. Carnival. *Early Plays: Volume One: Scar, Torch, Nightwood, Carnival*. South Gate: Santa Catalina Editions/No Passport Press, 2012.

_____. Prodigal Kiss. *Prodigal Kiss and Perdita Gracia: Two Plays*. South Gate: Lizard Run Press/No Passport Press, 2011.

_____. Perdita Gracia. *Prodigal Kiss and Perdita Gracia: Two Plays*. South Gate: Lizard Run Press/No Passport Press, 2011.

_____. *Rift*. South Gate: No Passport Press, 2010.

_____. *Something Simple, Plain-Spoken*. South Gate: No Passport Press, 2007.

_____. *The Tropic of X*. South Gate: No Passport Press, 2011.

_____. *Wreckage*. South Gate: No Passport Press, 2013.

_____. *12 Ophelias (a play with broken songs)*. South Gate: No Passport Press, 2008.

_____. JARMAN (all this maddening beauty). *JARMAN (all this maddening beauty) and Other Plays*. Chicago: University of Chicago Press/Intellect Ltd, 2016.

_____. Carthage/Cartagena. *JARMAN (all this maddening beauty) and Other Plays*. Chicago: University of Chicago Press/Intellect Ltd, 2016.

_____. The Orphan Sea. *JARMAN (all this maddening beauty) and Other Plays*. Chicago: University of Chicago Press/Intellect Ltd, 2016.

_____. *Iphigenia Crash Land Falls on the Neon Shell That Was Once Her Heart*. New York: Broadway Play Publishing Inc., 2012.

Tropicana, Carmelita. *Milk of Amnesia, Leche De Amnesia (A Play)*. New York: Grove Press, 1998.

Wood, Silviana. *And Where Was Pancho Willa When You Really Needed Him? Puro Teatro: A Latina Anthology*. Eds. Alberto Sandoval-Sanchez & Nancy Saporta Sternbach. Tucson: The University of Arizona Press, 2000.

_____. *Una Vez, En Un Barrio de Suenos. Barrio Dreams: Selected Plays*. Eds. Norma Elia Cantu and Rita E. Urquijo-Ruiz. Tucson: The University of Arizona Press, 2016.

_____. *Amor de Hija. Barrio Dreams: Selected Plays*. Eds. Norma Elia Cantu and Rita E. Urquijo-Ruiz. Tucson: The University of Arizona Press, 2016.

_____. *A Drunkard's Tale of Melted Wings and Memories. Barrio Dreams: Selected Plays*. Eds. Norma Elia Cantu and Rita E. Urquijo-Ruiz. Tucson: The University of Arizona Press, 2016.

_____. *Yo, Casimiro Flores. Barrio Dreams: Selected Plays*. Eds. Norma Elia Cantu and Rita E. Urquijo-Ruiz. Tucson: The University of Arizona Press, 2016.

_____. Anhelos Por Oaxaca. *Barrio Dreams: Selected Plays*. Eds. Norma Elia Cantu and Rita E. Urquijo-Ruiz. Tucson: The University of Arizona Press, 2016.

Zacarias, Karen. The Sins of Sor Juana. *Latina/o Heritage on Stage: Dramatizing Heroes and Legends*. Ed. Daniel Enrique Perez. Phoenix: The Lion and the Seagoat LLC., 2015.

LGBTIQ

*Barfield, Tanya. *Without Skin or Breathlessness*. New York: Grove Press, 1998.

_____. *Blue Door: A Play with Original Songs*. New York Dramatist Play Service Inc., 2007.

_____. *The Call*. Dramatist Play Service Inc., 2014.

*Hagedorn, Jessica. *Dogeaters*. New York: Theatre Communications Group, 2002.

_____. Tenement Lover: No Palm Trees/in New York City. *Between Worlds: Contemporary Asian-American Plays*. Ed. Misha Berson. New York: Theatre Communications Group, 1990.

*Uyehara, Denise. *Hello (Sex) Kitty: Mad Asian Bitch on Wheels*. New York: Grove Press, 1998.

_____. Hiro. *Asian American Drama: 9 Plays from the Multiethnic Landscape*. Ed. Brian Nelson. New York: Applause Theatre and Cinema Books, Hal Leonard Books, 1997.

_____. Big Head. *The Methuen Drama Anthology of Testimonial Plays: Bystander 9/11, Big Head, the Fence, Come out Eli, the Travels, on the Record, Seven, Pajarito Nuevo La Lleva: The Sounds of the Coup*. Ed. Alison Forsyth. Northhampton: Smith College, 1993.

Native/Indigenous (Native American & Native Hawaiian)

Arekeketa, Annette. Hokti. *Stories of Our Way: An Anthology of American Indian Plays*. California: UCLA American Indian Studies Center, 1999.

_____. Ghost Dance. *Keepers of the Morning Star: An Anthology of Native Women's Theater*. Eds. Jaye T. Darby and Stephanie J. Fitzgerald. Los Angeles, CA: UCLA American Indian Studies Center, 2003.

Baker, Tammy Haili'ōpua. Kupua. Hawaii: Kumu Kahua (Theatre Group), 2001.

Borse, Murielle. More than Feathers and Beads. *Staging Coyote's Dream: An Anthology of First Nations Drama in English*. Toronto: Playwrights Canada Press, 2003.

Cataluna, Lee. Da Mayah. *New Voice: Hawaiian Playwrights*. Hawaii: Bamboo Ridge Press, 2003.

De Montano, Martha Kreipe and Jennifer Fell Hayes. Harvest Ceremony: Beyond the Thanksgiving Myth. *Footpaths and Bridges: Voices from the Native American Women Playwright Archive*. Eds. Huston-Findley and Howard. Ann Arbor: University of Michigan Press, 2011.

FastHorse, Larissa. *Teaching Disco Square Dancing to Our Elders: A Class Presentation*. Illinois: Dramatic Publishing Company, 2011.

Glancy, Diane. Holy Cow! *War Cries: A Collection of Plays*. Duluth, Minnesota Press, 1995.

_____. Woman Who Was a Read Deer Dressed for the Red Dance. *Seventh Generation: An Anthology of American Plays*. Ed. M. Gisolfi D'Aponte. New York: Theatre Communications Group, 1999.

_____. American Gypsy. *Six Native American Plays*. Norman: University of Oklahoma Press, 2002.

_____. *Cargo*. Virginia: Alexander Street Press, 2006.

_____. *The Collector of a Three-Cornered Stamp*. Virginia: Alexander Street Press, 2006.

_____. *The Conversion of Inversion*. Virginia: Alexander Street Press, 2006.

_____. *The Distant Cry of Betelgeuse*. Virginia: Alexander Street Press, 2006.

_____. *Man Red*. Virginia: Alexander Street Press, 2006.

_____. *The Words of My Roaring*. Virginia: Alexander Street Press, 2006.

Gomez, Terry. Inter-Tribal. *Contemporary Plays by Women of Color: An Anthology*. Eds. Kathy A. Perkins and Roberta Uno. London: Routledge, 1996.

_____. Reunion. *Gathering Our Own: A Collection of IaIa Student Playwrights*. Eds. Dana Dickerson, Brian Lusk, Ti Stalnaker. Santa Fe: Institute of American Indian Arts, 1996.

Howe, Leanne and Roxy Gordon. Indian Radio Days: An Evolving Bingo Experience. *Seventh Generation: An Anthology of Native American Plays*. Ed. Mimi G. D'Aponte. Theatre Communications Group, 1999.

Keams, Geraldine. The Flight of the Army Worm. *The Remembered Earth: An Anthology of Contemporary Native American Literature*. Ed. Geary Hobson. Albuquerque: University of New Mexico Press, 1981.

Kneubuhl, Victoria Nalani. *Ola Nā Iwi*. Hawaii: Kumu Kahua (Theatre Group), 1994.

_____. *Ka Wai Ola*. New Voice: Hawaiian Playwrights. Hawaii: Bamboo Ridge Press, 2003.

_____. The Story of Susanna. *Seventh Generation: An Anthology of Native American Plays*. Ed. Mimi G. D'Aponte. Theatre Communications Group, 1999.

_____. The Conversation of Ka'ahumanu. *But Still, Like Air, I'll Rise: New Asian American Plays*. Philadelphia: Temple University Press, 1997.

Manuel, Vera. Strength of Indian Women. *Footpaths and Bridges: Voices from the Native American Women Playwright Archive*. Eds. Huston-Findley and Howard. Ann Arbor: University of Michigan Press, 2011.

Mojica, Monique. *Princess Pocahontas and the Blue Spots*. Toronto: Women's Press, 1991.

Olivia, Judylee. Te Ata. *Footpaths and Bridges: Voices from the Native American Women Playwright Archive*. Eds. Huston-Findley and Howard. Ann Arbor: University of Michigan Press, 2011.

_____. Mark of the Feather. *Introducing Theatre*. Eds. Joy H. Reilly & M. Scott Phillips. Thompson Learning, 2002.

Spiderwoman. Winnetou's Snake Oil Show from Wigwam City. *Footpaths and Bridges: Voices from the Native American Women Playwright Archive*. Eds. Huston-Findley and Howard. Ann Arbor: University of Michigan Press, 2011.

—————. *Sun, Moon, Feather*. New York: American Indian Community House, 1997.

—————. Power Pipes. *Seventh Generation: An Anthology of Native American Plays*. Ed. Mimi G. D'Aponte. Theatre Communications Group, 1999.

Middle Eastern/Arab American

Ayvazian, Leslie. *Motherhood Out Loud*. New York: Dramatists Play Service, 2012.

Buck, Leila. ISite. *Four Arab American Plays*. Ed. Michael Malek Najjar. Jefferson, NC: MacFarland, 2013.

Filloux, Catherine. Silence of God. *Silence of God and Other Plays*. Chicago: Seagull Books Publisher, 2009.

—————. White Trash: A Ten Minute Play. *Thirty-Five Ten Minute Plays*. New York: Playscripts, 2007.

—————. Eyes of the Heart. *Silence of God and Other Plays*. Chicago: Seagull Books Publisher, 2009.

—————. The Beauty Inside. *Silence of God and Other Plays*. Chicago: Seagull Books Publisher, 2009.

—————. Mary and Myra. *Silence of God and Other Plays*. Chicago: Seagull Books Publisher, 2009.

—————. Lemkin's House. *Silence of God and Other Plays*. Chicago: Seagull Books Publisher, 2009.

Handal, Nathalie. Between Our Lips. *Salaam. Peace: An Anthology of Middle Eastern-American Drama*. New York: Theatre Communications Group, 2010.

Issaq, Lameece. *Motherhood out Loud*. New York: Dramatists Play Service, 2012.

Issaq, Lameece and Jacob Kader. Food and Fadwa. *Four Arab American Plays*. Ed. Michael Malek Najjar. Jefferson, NC: MacFarland, 2013.

Khalil, Hannah. *Scenes from 68* Years*. London: Bloomsbury, 2016.

—————. Plan D. *Inside/Outside. Six Plays from Palestine and Diaspora*. New York: Theatre Communication Group. 2015.

—————. Bitterenders. *Skyes-Picot the Legacy: Five Modern Plays by Hannah Khalil, Hassan Abdulrazzak and Joshua Hinds*. Kent, UK: Kenneth Pickering, 2015.

—————. The Worst Cook in the West Bank. *Skyes-Picot: The Legacy, Five Modern Plays by Hannah Khalil, Hassan Abdulrazzak and Joshua Hinds*. Kent, UK: Kenneth Pickering, 2015.

Raffo, Heather. Nine Parts of Desire. *Salaam. Peace: An Anthology of Middle Eastern-American Drama*. New York: Theatre Communications Group, 2010.

Shamieh, Betty. The Black Eyed. *The Black Eyed & Architecture*. New York: Broadway Play Publishing, 2009.

—————. Inside/Outside. *Six Plays from Palestine and Diaspora*. Territories. New York: Theatre Communication Group. 2015.

Taha, Dalia. Keffiyeh/Made in China. *Inside/Outside: Six Plays from Palestine and Diaspora*. New York: Theatre Communication Group. 2015.

Yeghiazarian, Torange. Call Me Mehdi. *Salaam. Peace: An Anthology of Middle Eastern-American Drama*. New York: Theatre Communications Group, 2010.